THE CULINARY CHRONICLE

http://www.culinaryworld.com

Copyright © 2000 Opt Art Lizenz AG
Bahnhofstrasse 59b
CH - 3401 Burgdorf/Switzerland

Photography copyright © Bruno Hausch
Except the photographs, wine lists, menu cards and other documents
reproduced with the kind permission of the hotels and restaurants.
p. 26, p. 27 © Francesc Guillamet
p. 144, p. 145 © Pedro J. Moreno
p. 166 © Jose Luis Galiana

Overall production by: Metzger Druck GmbH, Germany

ISBN 3-7750-0603-6 Walter Hädecke Verlag

English recipes feature both metric and American measures.
Inevitable rounding off may lead to slight deviations from the
original. We cannot take any responsibility for consequences
that may arise from this fact.

Photography, Paintings and Design

Bruno Hausch

Text

Chris Meier

Editorial director and recipe editor

Christine Messer Hausch

Translation from the German

Claudia Spinner

HÄDECKE

OptArt

CONTENTS · INHALT

EDITORIAL

Two Worlds – Two Fascinating Experiences

Dear Reader,

for the fourth volume of the Culinary Chronicle, we were traveling in two very different cooking cultures. Our first trip was to South East Asia, where we encountered both strictly traditional Asian cuisine – like on the paradisiacal island Pangkor Laut – as well as new, innovative culinary concepts such as at the Marriott in Kuala Lumpur. There, guests are able to order original Japanese, Chinese or Malay specialties from the different sections of an open show kitchen, topping it all off with a first-rate espresso on the palm-lined boulevard. On our trip, we came to appreciate the immense variety and wealth of spices that characterize Asian cooking and indulged in many a stroll through the fascinating, colorful markets. Unfortunately, at the time the multitude of impressions was only for the eyes and ears, since we shared the common fate of many a traveler unable to prepare any meals himself – a state that may be instantaneously rectified with this book.

Leaving behind this spicy diversity, we then traveled to Spain, where we were extraordinarily impressed by the creativity of the country´s three-star-chefs: The capricious genius of Ferran Adrià (El Bulli) ushering his guests along his menus with a great sense of drama, the supposed classic chef Juan-Mari Arzak, whose cuisine turned out to be highly creative and playful, and the down-to-earth Santi Santamaria acting out his dream of cooking for friends only in his elegant countryside restaurant. All of them, and their colleagues who are featured in this volume, have radically changed any existing preconceived notions about Spain´s top notch gastronomy.

Behind every cuisine, there are committed chefs who know how to delight their guests with a sense of tradition and an innovative spirit. It is these personalities we present here, accompanied by beautiful photographs, carefully worked out recipes and instructive articles. Naturally, we will be able to make books like this one only as long as there are such chefs truly dedicated to their trade. To them, the protagonists of our books, we are deeply indebted, and we would like to extend our heartfelt thanks and praise to them here.

And now you may judge for yourself as to whether we have been singing their praises too loudly. We wish you an enjoyable time browsing through the fourth volume of the Culinary Chronicle, hoping to be able to provide you with many an inspiration.

EDITORIAL

Zwei Welten – Zwei Faszinationen

Liebe Leserin, lieber Leser,

für diese vierte Ausgabe des Culinary Chronicle waren wir in zwei sehr unterschiedlichen Koch-Kulturen unterwegs. Unsere erste Reise führte nach Südost-Asien, wo wir, wie auf der paradiesischen Insel Pangkor Laut, streng-traditionelle asiatische Küche kennen lernten. Es begegneten uns aber auch, beispielsweise im Marriott in Kuala Lumpur, neuartige, moderne Küchen-konzepte, wo man von original-japanischen, -chinesischen oder -malaiischen Sektionen einer Showküche sein Essen bestellen kann. Anschließend genehmigt man sich auf der Palmen-gesäumten Promenade einen wohlschmeckenden Espresso. Wir haben die Vielfalt und Würze asiatischer Gerichte schätzen gelernt, und haben, so oft es uns möglich war, die faszinierenden, bunten Märkte durchstreift. Leider konnten wir die vielen Eindrücke nur mit Augen und Ohren geniessen, da es dem Reisenden nicht vergönnt ist, einzukaufen und auch einmal selbst zu kochen.

Im Gegensatz zur Gewürzvielfalt der asiatischen Küche beeindruckte uns in Spanien die kreative Kunst der Drei-Sterne-Köche. Die geniale Verrücktheit von Ferran Adria (El Bulli), der seine Gäste mit ausgeklügelter Dramaturgie durch das Menü führt, der vermeintliche Klassiker Juan-Mari Arzak, dessen Küche sich als hochkreativ und unerwartet spielerisch herausstellte, und der bodenständige Santi Santamaria, der seinen Traum, für Freunde zu kochen, in seinem elegant-rustikalen Restaurant auslebt. Sie und ihre Kollegen, die wir Ihnen im vor-liegenden Band vorstellen, haben unsere Vorstellung von Spaniens gehobener Küchenlandschaft von Grund auf verändert.

Hinter jeder Küche stehen engagierte Köche, die ihre Gäste mit Traditions-bewusstsein, Kreativität und Innovationsfreude zu verwöhnen wissen. Wir stellen diese Persönlichkeiten vor – natürlich bemühen wir uns, dies mit schönen Fotos, sorgfältig ausgearbeiteten Rezepten und informativen Reportagen angemessen zu realisieren. Doch nur solange es diese engagierten Köche gibt, können wir Bücher wie das vor Ihnen liegende produzieren. Ihnen allen, den Protagonisten unserer Bücher, gebührt deshalb an dieser Stelle unser Lob und Dank.

Aber nun sehen Sie selbst, ob unser Lob zu hoch gegriffen ist. Wir hoffen Ihnen mit diesem Buch einige Anregungen liefern zu können und wünschen Ihnen beim Lesen viel Spass und Genuss.

El Paseo de La Concha - 1914

LA BODEGA DEL BODEGÓN
TINTO RESERVA CAMPILLO 2 6 25
" CRIANZA CAMPILLO 1 5 50
" MARQUES DE GRIÑON 1 8 75
ROSADO CHIVITE 1 1 50
" CAMPILLO 1 1 50
" FERRET (Aguja) 1 0 25
BLANCO CHIVITE 1 3 25
" CAMPILLO 0 75
" SUMARROCA 9 00
ALBARIÑO TERRAS GAUDAS 1 8
CAVA FERRET BRUT 1 1 2 5
" CLAVEROL 10 25
PRUEBE NUESTRO LICOR DE
MELOCOTÓN VALENCIANO

S
P
A
I
N

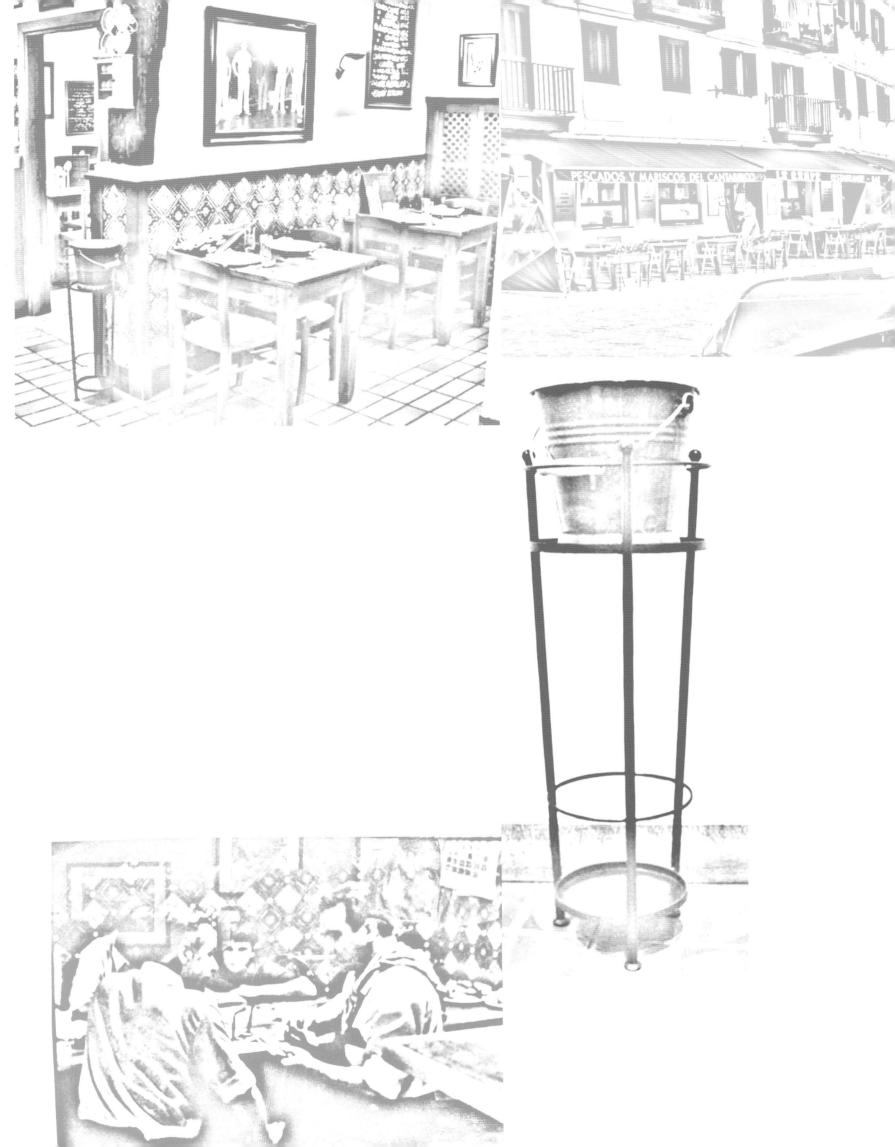

There always remains something to be discovered. If you travel through Spain the next time, don´t just head for the beach, which might be crowded anyway, but add a few restaurant visits to your map, to experience things you may not have tried before. The blue sky not only spans the world of bathers but also a culinary landscape which until recently has been unknown even to those of us who are otherwise used to looking for culinary delicacies all over the world – every-

cooking, however, known only to insiders and some gastronomical guides, does not yet seem to have found its way into the minds of a broader fan club. Quite unjustifiably. A hideous gap in culinary knowledge as a matter of fact. The gastronomical pulse of Europe is beating in the southwest of the continent, and quite vigorously. Just a little bit south of the Pyrenées, a small elite of culinary artists lives and works in incredible proximity, and the results can only be insufficiently

where but Spain. Nothing against the very popular paella, fried fish at the coast or Barcelona´s hearty country fare, which even the hero of Montalban´s criminal stories, Pepe Carvalho, enjoys quite regularly and with great dedication. All this has its place, but culinary highlights are not to be found there. The yardstick is out, wielding stars or comparable criteria, and it now sends culinary travelers across the ocean to the States, well beyond France, the mother country of grande cuisine, or Italy´s voluptuously sparkling fare. Spain´s art of

explained by the closeness to France. Towards the south, the air is getting thinner, and comparable sites in this category are rarely sighted. In the north of Spain, by contrast, people speak self-confidently of a revolution, especially the revolutionaries themselves, who liberated the cuisine from the simple stewing pot country fare and lead it to new horizons. This happened twenty years ago, quite unnoticed at first. Ocean, mountains, and fields, all close together, provide any flavor and ingredient needed for such an art. Wines of this provenance have made

Ferran Adrià

Santi Santamaria

Juan-Mari Arzak

Jokin de Aguirre

Martín Berasetegui

Pedro Subijana

Hilario Arbelaitz

their entry into our cellars quite some time ago, and now, renowned advocates of this "Nueva Cocina" have opened their kitchens and recipe books for us, talked about their work, their ideas, at the same time enchanting our palates.

Most of them have one thing in common: a love for the local cooking traditions, la cocina de la madre – mother's cooking. And all of them have made their experiences with gastronomical traditions outside of Spain. They have found the fine balance between the two poles, neither subscribing dutifully to a modern international mix nor neglecting the valuable roots of their own tradition. All of them have found their very own, idiosyncratic way. That is what makes the culinary excursion an adventure, a horn of plenty, a fascinating experience. Some of them do their thing at Catalonia's Costa Brava, others on the Northern coast, in the Basque country. The Gulf of Biscay, especially, surprises with an amazing number of top restaurants. Food is the primary topic there, before soccer and politics – on the streets and at home – and already many gene-

rations ago, so-called sociedades gastronomicas, male-only clubs, banded together for the purpose of cooking. It´s a unique phenomenon within Europe, and may be an explanation for the culinary enthusiasm found in this region.

At the moment, the stoves are still occupied by the founding generation. The masters of the new Spanish cuisine, between almost-forty and their middle-fifties, still hold the spoons firmly in their grip. Yet, a new generation of young men and women is waiting in the wings, ready to take their turn. Their teachers eliminated superfluous ballast, paving the way. They will have the chance to set their own marks in already fortified terrain, and bring Spanish cuisine even further. Today, our culinary compass points to Spain. Far away from tourist fare, hidden stars await discovery. Just drive there, or hop on a plane and enjoy. Or in the words of Santi Santamaria: "Without time, there is no enjoyment, no fun, no life – nothing. It´s the knowledge of life that counts. And cooking helps. We help the people to learn how to live."

gibt immer noch etwas zu entdecken. Wenn Sie das nächste Mal nach Spanien reisen, steuern Sie nicht gleich auf den Strand zu, der vielleicht eh schon überfüllt ist, sondern merken Sie sich auf Ihrer Karte ein paar Visiten vor, die dort möglicherweise noch nicht verzeichnet sind. Der blaue Himmel wölbt sich auf der Iberischen Halbinsel nicht nur über die Badelustigen, sondern auch über einer kulinarischen Landschaft, die noch vielen jener verwöhnten Zeitgenossen unbekannt ist, die es sonst gewohnt sind, überall in der Welt nach delikaten Gaumengenüssen zu suchen. Das soll nicht sprechen gegen die allseits beliebte Paella, gebratenen Fisch an der Küste oder die eher derbe Hausmannskost Barcelonas, der auch Montalbans Krimiheld Pepe Carvalho regelmäßig und mit großem Eifer huldigt.

All dieses hat seinen berechtigten Platz, doch kulinarische Höhen erreicht man damit nicht. Die Messlatte liegt an, bei den Sternen oder vergleichbaren Kriterien, die den reisenden Feinschmecker über das französische Mutterland der Großen Küche oder Italiens lustvoll spritzige Kost hinaus mittlerweile in die Staaten, nach Übersee reisen lässt. Doch Spaniens Kochkunst, wiewohl schon entdeckt von Insidern und Gastroführern, scheint noch nicht so recht ins Bewusstsein einer breiteren Fangemeinde gerückt zu sein. Ganz zu unrecht. Eine sträfliche Bildungslücke. Der gastronomische Puls Europas schlägt im Südwesten des Kontinents mit fröhlicher Lebhaftigkeit. Nur wenig südlich des Pyrenäenzugs tummelt sich in erstaunlicher Dichte eine kleine Elite kulinarischer Künstler, für deren Schaffen die Nähe zu Frankreich nur unzureichend Erklärung sein kann.

Weiter gen Süden wird die Luft leider dünner, und vergleichbare Stätten dieser Kategorie werden immer seltener gesichtet. Im Norden Spaniens spricht man dagegen sogar recht selbstbewusst von einer Revolution (vor allem die Revolutionäre selbst), welche vor immerhin schon über zwanzig Jahren, von vielen zunächst unbemerkt, die Küche aus den dampfenden Töpfen schlichter Hausmannskost zu neuer Klasse erlöst hat. Meer, Berge und Felder auf engstem Raum beieinander stellen hier alles an köstlichen Zutaten bereit, was solche Kunst benötigt. Die Weine dieser Provenienz haben ja schon seit geraumer Zeit ihren geschätzten Platz in unserem Keller gefunden. Die namhaftesten Protagonisten dieser „Nueva Cocina" haben uns ihre Küchen und Rezeptbücher geöffnet, uns von ihrer Arbeit, ihren Ideen erzählt und unseren Gaumen verzaubert.

Eines ist fast allen gemeinsam, die Liebe zur heimischen Tradition der Küche. La cocina de la madre – Mutters Küche. Und alle kennen sich aus in der gastronomischen Kultur außerhalb Spaniens Grenzen. Zwischen beiden Polen haben sie den schmalen Grat des Mittelwegs gefunden, auf dem sie weder anbiedernd einem modisch internationalen Mix huldigen, noch die wertvollen Wurzeln ihrer Tradition vernachlässigen. Und jeder ist seinen eigenen teils sehr unterschiedlichen Weg gegangen. Das macht die kulinarische Reise spannend, abwechslungsreich und zu einem faszinierenden Erlebnis. Die einen kochen in Katalonien an der Costa Brava, die anderen an der Nordküste, im Baskenland. Gerade an der Biskaya registriert man verwundert eine erstaunliche Häufung hochklassiger Restaurants. Das Thema Essen rangiert hier vor Politik und Fußball – auf den Straßen der Stadt wie daheim –, und schon vor vielen Generationen haben sich in Tausenden sogenannter Sociedades gastronomicas reine Männerclubs zum Kochen zusammengefunden. Ein wohl einmaliges Phänomen in Europa und Erklärung für den kulinarischen Enthusiasmus dieser Gegend.

NOCH

steht die Gründergeneration am Herd. Die Meister der neuen spanischen Küche, nun zwischen Fast-Vierzig und

Mitte-Fünfzig, halten den Kochlöffel noch fest in der Hand. Schließlich ist das ja kein Alter für einen Koch.

PANCETA ASADA CON LENTEJAS FRITAS Y CI CALI

Aber es wächst sichtbar eine neue Generation junger Männer und Frauen heran, die darauf drängt, ins Geschehen einzugreifen. Sie haben die Chance, auf dem von anderen eroberten Terrain ihre eigenen Marken zu setzen und die spanische Küche noch weiter zu bringen.

VIEIRAS Y CALAMARES EN GELEE DE POMELO

Ihre Lehrer haben den Ballast beiseite geräumt und ihnen den Weg geebnet. Der kulinarische Kompass weist heute nach Spanien. Fernab touristischer Banalkost liegen hier gastronomische Sterne versteckt, die der Entdeckung harren. Fahren, fliegen Sie einfach hin und genießen Sie in Muße. Oder mit den Worten von Santi Santamaria: „Ohne Zeit gibt es keinen Genuss, keinen Spaß, kein Leben – nichts. Es geht um das Wissen zu leben. Und Küche hilft dabei. Wir helfen den Leuten, zu lernen, wie man leben kann."

RAVIOLIS DE SEPIA Y COCO
A LA SOJA

1 SEPIA
GRANDE

60 gr de BROTES DE SOJA

1/2 L DE GIRASOL

1DL DE ACEITE

60g de hojas de menta

el bulli

The sun has gone down, the Costa Brava is slowly sinking into a mist. Nothing indicates the culinary events awaiting us at a small bay just south of the border to France. In a little while, we will be the guests of Ferran Adrià, at the restaurant "El Bulli". Leaving aside the chronology of our visit, here is a key experience, to be made with your eyes shut tightly. Eyes closed, mouth open that is. Here come "tagliatelle carbonara". The noodles, wrapped around a fork, reach the tongue and the tastebuds register the unmistakable flavor combination of the Italian classic. Soft, creamy egg yolk with cream, a little Parmesan, the smoky flavor of bacon on noodles. But something starts puzzling our tongues, something is not quite right. The consistency of the tagliatelle is mysterious, they taste unusually spicy. We open our eyes: a glance onto the plate solves the mystery, reveals the noodles as thin strips of gelatin made from glistening golden consommé. Adrià is a "provocateur culinaire". Not enough that the Spaniard is loose in the domain of Italian cuisine, a phenomenon usually frowned upon among the Mediterranean competition, he also has the nerve to play around with the archetype of Latin pasta and to transform the flour-born noodle into a transparent, jiggly something. What a cheek! "I have invented warm gelatin", the superchef self-confidently explains and inspects the work of two of his employees who are cutting strips of "noodles" with the pastry wheel from a baking sheet lined with the gelatin mixture. Adrià does not care about tradition. For him, tradition is an obligation to be done away with by means of merciless intellect, and with a robber´s pleasure for misappropriation, he strips its components down to individual atoms. Six months of the year, he is busy with the development of new recipes at the "Taller", his think tank in Barcelona. The restaurant? He just closes it down. He will and can afford that, since he finances its operation from Barcelona with consulting and catering services etc. "I only sell creativity", Ferran Adrià declares, "but it keeps my back free and I can do whatever I like at the "El Bulli". And every time more radically", he says with a grin. From October to March, the brain pool consisting of Adrià, his brother and alter ego Alberto as well as chef de cuisine Oriol then shut themselves off to work at the "Taller". Alberto and Oriol first fly around the world for two or three weeks, testing and searching for new products. Then the study, research and designing part begins. They look for the surprising, the unusual. New techniques are developed to present old favorites in a new form.

Alberto Adrià

Julio Soler

Ferran Adrià

"we don't make a better cuisine than any other very good restaurant", Adrià says, "we just feature a different kind of cooking." Eighty new culinary creations are produced here per year and subsequently offered to the impatiently waiting clients of the "El Bulli" in the summer months. Not surprisingly, the rustic finca is usually booked out a few months in advance. Gourmets from all over the world and gastronomical competition alike have been flocking to the small hidden bay near Roses for a number of years now. Since grand master Robuchon visited the "El Bulli" and declared it the world-wide best restaurant, the entire culinary community would like to be part of the birth of the second "New Cuisine" – after the so-called nouvelle cuisine in the sixties –, wanting to see and taste for itself what the chef provocateur has come up with this time. The avant-garde of cooking definitely lies near Roses, and any imitator will have a hard time to match the original. It was a grey, overcast day when our car made its way along the small windy road out of Roses, seven kilometers to the neighboring bay. Rocks, meager meadows and

wind-blown, stunted bushes. A little disconcerted, we more than once ask ourselves: Are we still on the right track? Why, for goodness sake, must anyone hide himself like that? Finally, the street did lead down to the bay of Montjoy, where, at the edge of a gravelly beach, Ferran Adrià´s field of action appeared. The "El Bulli" existed forty-five years before his time, and under previous owners, the "bull dog" was a simple bar.

In 1990, Ferran Adrià and his partner Julio Soler took over the restaurant, working in the kitchen with nine cooks. A little later they remodeled it into a jewel of interior design whose elegant, clear furnishings would rather suit a London loft than the bourgeois context of country-style finca. Black granite columns structure the room, black granite covers the floor, the back wall to the mountain is fully glassed in, and the pass made from natural wood is crowned by a massive bull´s head. Here, Adrià checks every dish which is carried out of the kitchen. Minimalist art. The smallest details are executed with studied precision. Several chefs work

on one plate, decorating it gingerly with baby flowers or arranging jelly cubes. Today, thirty-five chefs work for forty-five guests seated in the dining room. At the "El Bulli", the adventure begins with a series of mini appetizers which are remotely reminiscent of tapas. That is where the closeness to tradition ends, however, since eyes and palate alike at once experience consecutive shock waves. The combination and use of ingredients is surprising, but always highly delicate. Every plate brings new, contrasting sensations for the tastebuds, and unusual forms and colors for the eyes. Gelatin is Adrià's pet peeve. Let's take an unsorted look at the kaleidoscope of his creations: crisply roasted quinoa kernels are sucked from a cellophane casing, butter pieces are coated with jelly. Trout caviar is served in a coat of tempura, with a melting scoop of frozen olive oil. The couscous, a vegetarian highlight, is accompanied by seasoned black breadcrumbs, lavender flowers, herb leaves and jellied cubes of Campari. Yet, it has never seen a wheat kernel, it consists of cauliflower. The palate discovers it only while tasting it, since the crumby consistency, firm to the bite,

looks deceptively like couscous. What looks like wild rice turns out to be shaved sepia-colored soy bean sprouts. The squid ravioli are white, stuffed cushions of sepia tubes cut paper-thin. They arrive with drops of mint vinegar, ginger oil, soy and a warning. "Careful, don't cut them", the waitress advises, "put them into your mouth and bite them open!" There, ginger-scented coconut milk escapes from the casing, an aromatic explosion for the tastebuds. This is not fusion, not a willy-nilly mix, this is a sophisticated training course in flavors. Adrià does not make dishes, he works aromatic miracles. The traditional menu system has been revolutionized. While the appetizer course has always been the ramp for cooks to set off their culinary fireworks, he has raised it to a principle. A pearly string of small courses (the menu includes fourteen!) does not allow for boredom, you are in permanent suspense of the next surprise. The point, of course, is not to fill up, the dishes are too small for that, but at the end of the marathon you are nevertheless full – and happy.

Die Sonne hat sich verabschiedet, die Costa Brava versinkt im Nebel. Nichts deutet auf die kommenden kulinarischen Erlebnisse hin, die in einer kleinen Bucht südlich der Grenze zu Frankreich unser harren. Wir sind zu Gast bei Ferran Adrià, im Restaurant „El Bulli".
Die Chronologie des Tages außer acht lassend, ein Schlüsselerlebnis vorneweg, das man mit verbundenen Augen wagen sollte. Also erstmal Augen zu, Mund auf! Hier kommen „Tagliatelle a la carbonara". Die gabelgewickelte Nudelfracht erreicht die Zunge, und deren Geschmacksknospen registrieren die unverwechselbare Geschmackskombination des Italo-Klassikers. Sanftcremiges Eigelb mit Sahne, etwas Parmesankäse, die rauchige Würze von Speck. Doch diese Nudeln stiften Verwirrung, etwas stimmt nicht. Die Konsistenz der Tagliatelle ist rätselhaft, ihr Eigengeschmack ungewöhnlich würzig.

ugen wieder auf! Ein Blick auf den Teller enthüllt das Geheimnis, entlarvt die Nudeln als dünne Gelatinestreifen aus goldglänzender Consommé. Adrià ist ein 'provocateur culinaire'. Nicht genug damit, dass dieser Spanier im Revier italienischer Küche wildert, ein Phänomen, das sich der mediterranen Konkurrenz im Normalfall verbietet, er besitzt zudem noch die Unverfrorenheit, am Archetypus lateinischer Pasta herumzuspielen und mit frecher Nonchalance die mehlgeborene Teignudel in ein glasig-glibberiges Etwas zu transformieren. „Ich habe die warme Gelatine erfunden," erklärt der Superkoch selbstbewusst und begutachtet die Arbeit zweier Mitarbeiter, die mit Schneidrädchen streifenweise „Nudeln" vom Blech heben, das mit Gelatine ausgegossen ist.

Adrià schert sich einen Teufel um Überliefertes. Tradition ist für ihn eine Verpflichtung, der er sich mit gnadenlosem Intellekt entledigt, und deren Versatzstücke er mit räuberischer Lust zur Verfremdung in geschmackliche Atome zerlegt. Sechs Monate widmet er sich jedes Jahr im „Taller", seiner Denk-Werkstatt in Barcelona, der Entwicklung neuer Rezepte. Das Restaurant? – macht er einfach dicht. Das kann und will er sich leisten, da er dessen Betrieb in Barcelona, mit Consulting, Catering etc. mitfinanziert. „Ich verkaufe da nur Kreativität," erklärt Ferran Adrià selbstbewusst. „Aber damit habe ich den Rücken frei und kann im „El Bulli" tun und lassen, was ich will. Und jedes Mal radikaler," schmunzelt er. Von Oktober bis März geht dann der Brainpool, bestehend aus Adrià, seinem Bruder und Alter Ego Alberto sowie Küchenchef Oriol im „Taller" in Klausur und ans Werk. Alberto und Oriol fliegen noch zwei, drei Wochen in der Weltgeschichte herum, testen und forschen nach Produkten. Dann wird studiert, recherchiert und entworfen. Gesucht ist das Überraschende, das Ungewöhnliche. Vor allem neue Techniken werden entwickelt, um altbekannte Produkte in neuartiger Form zu präsentieren. „Wir machen keine bessere Küche als andere sehr gute Restaurants," meint Adrià, „wir produzieren nur das Andersartige." Achtzig kulinarische Neu-Schöpfungen werden alljährlich hier kreiert und in den sechs Sommermonaten dem schon wieder ungeduldig wartenden Publikum im „El Bulli" kredenzt. Die rustikale Finca ist in der Regel auch schon Monate im voraus ausgebucht. Zur versteckten Bucht bei Roses pilgert seit ein paar Jahren das Feinschmeckervolk und die gastronomische Konkurrenz gleichermaßen.

Seit Altmeister Robuchon „El Bulli" besucht und zum weltweit besten Restaurant deklariert hatte, will die kulinarische Gemeinde teilhaben an der Geburt einer zweiten „Neuen Küche" nach der Nouvelle Cuisine der Sechziger Jahre, will selbst sehen und schmecken, was dieser Provokateur sich wieder Neues hat einfallen lassen. Die Avantgarde der Küche liegt bei Roses. Doch jeder Nachahmer wird sich schwer tun, dem Original gleichzukommen. Der Tag war grau, als unser Auto seinen Weg über das kleine gewundene Sträßlein aus Roses hinaus die sieben Kilometer zur benachbarten Bucht suchte. Felsen, magere Wiesen und knorzige windzerzauste Büsche. Völlig verunsichert fragten wir uns nicht nur einmal, ist das noch der richtige Weg? Wie, um Himmels Willen, kann man es wagen, sich so zu verstecken? Schließlich wies der Weg doch noch nach unten in die Bucht von Montjoy, wo am Rande des kiesigen Strandes endlich Ferran Adriàs Wirkungsstätte auftauchte. Das „El Bulli" gab es schon fünfundvierzig Jahre vor seiner Zeit, die Vorbesitzer führten damals

„Die Bulldogge" als einfache Bar. 1990 übernahm Ferran Adrià zusammen mit Partner Julio Soler das Restaurant und kochte mit neun Köchen in der Küche. Diese modelte er wenig später zum architektonischen Schmuckstück um, dessen elegantes, klares Design man eher in einem Londoner Loft als im biederen Kontext einer ländlichen Finca erwarten würde. Schwarze Granitsäulen gliedern den Raum, schwarzer Granit bedeckt den Boden, die Rückwand zum Felsenhang ist voll verglast, und den Pass aus Naturholz krönt ein bulliger Stierschädel. Hier überwacht Adrià jedes Gericht, das aus der Küche herausgetragen wird. Minimalistische Kleinkunst. Die winzigsten Details werden mit einstudierter Präzision exerziert. Gleich mehrere Köche beugen sich über einen Teller, setzen mit Fingerspitzen Miniblütchen auf, platzieren kleine Geleewürfelchen. Für die fünfundvierzig Plätze im Saal arbeiten heute fünfunddreißig Köche.
Im El Bulli beginnt das Abenteuer mit einer Serie von Mini-Häppchen, die entfernt an Tapas erinnern. Doch die Nähe zur Tradition endet hier, denn sofort sind Augen und Gaumen

Zeugen von aufeinanderfolgenden Schockerlebnissen. Die Kombination wie die Verwendung der Zutaten ist äußerst verwirrend aber immer hochdelikat. Jeder Teller verblüfft mit neuen kontrastierenden Geschmackserlebnissen sowie Formen und Farben in der Präsentation. Und mit Gelatine spielt er leidenschaftlich gern.

Werfen wir einen unsortierten Blick ins Kaleidoskop Adrianscher Kreationen: knusprig geröstete Quinoakörner saugt man aus einer Zellophanhülle, Butterstücke sind geleeumhüllt. Forellenkaviar kommt in Tempurahülle, Olivenöl als zartschmelzende Nocke. Das Couscous ist ein vegetarisches Highlight und wird begleitet von Gewürzbrotbröseln, Lavendelblüten, Kräuterblättchen und gelierten Campariwürfelchen. Doch Weizengrieß hat es nie gesehen, es besteht aus Blumenkohl. Erst der Gaumen entdeckt's am Geschmack, denn die krümelig-bissige Konsistenz ist täuschend Couscous-echt. Wildreis entpuppt sich als sepiagefärbte Sojasprossenschnipsel. Die Tintenfischravioli sind

weiße gefüllte Kissen aus hauchdünn geschnittenen Sepiatuben. Sie kommen mit Tropfen von Minzessig, Ingweröl, Soja und einer Warnung zum Tisch: „Vorsicht, nicht schneiden," mahnt die Kellnerin, „erst im Mund darauf beißen!" Dort platzt ingwerparfümierte Kokosmilch aus der Hülle, und eine geschmackliche Explosion ergießt sich in den Gaumen.

Das ist nicht Fusion, kein beliebiger Mix, das ist die raffinierte Tour eines Aromen-Lehrgangs. Adrià kocht keine Gerichte, er zaubert Geschmacks-Sensationen. Das überlieferte System der Speisenfolge ist aufgehoben. Schon immer ist die Etappe der Vorspeisen die Rampe, auf der Köche ihr kulinarisches Feuerwerk abfeuern können. Hier ist dies zum Prinzip erhoben. Eine Juwelenkette kleiner Gänge (das Menü umfasst vierzehn davon!) lässt keinen Augenblick der Langeweile entstehen, und man ist ständig in hochgespannter Erwartung der nächsten Überraschung. Sättigung ist nicht Sinn und Zweck der einzelnen Gänge, dafür sind sie zu klein, doch am Ende des Marathons ist man satt – und glücklich.

LA COCINA DE FERRAN ADRIÀ

Menestra en texturas

3800

Espárragos verdes con envoltini de ceps

3900

Mousse de maíz con jugo de trufas y foie gras

3800

Paquetitos de habitas tiernas y panceta a la menta

3900

Raviolis de coco y sepia a la soja y jengibre

4250

Chop suey de almejas frío - caliente

4600

Sopa de horchata con buey de mar

3900

Pan, y *petit fours* 450   Surtido de quesos   1300

PRIMAVERA 2000

Fardos de "espardenyes" en agridulce

5900

Salmonetes con raviolis de remolacha y aceite de pistacho

4400

Rape con pimientos del piquillo y plátano

4600

Lenguado a las aromáticos

4900

Sesos al aceite de carbón

3900

Canetón con vieiras vegetales y algas

4300

Lomo de cordero a las hierbas aromáticas

4600

Postres a la carta 1800   Los precios no incluyen el 7 % de IVA

LIVER OF ANGLER FISH WITH A SOY MOUSSE AND BLOOD ORANGE JELLY

SEETEUFELLEBER MIT SOJAMOUSSE UND BLUTORANGENGELEE

Serves 4

For the angler fish liver cream: 120 g/4 oz fresh liver of angler fish, 200 ml/³/₄ cup sake, 140 ml/²/₃ cup water, a pinch of salt, 2.5 g/¹/₄ tsp sugar, 0.6 g/a small pinch of powdered agar-agar

For the soy mousse: 100 ml/¹/₃ cup light soy sauce, 100 ml/¹/₃ cup water, 1¹/₂ sheets of gelatin

For the caramel: 50 g/2 oz sugar, 25 g/1 oz glucose, 1 tbsp water

For the blood orange jelly: 125 ml/¹/₂ cup blood orange juice, 0.6 g/a small pinch of agar-agar

For the ginger oil: 50 g/2 oz ginger, peeled and finely diced, 100 ml/¹/₃ cup sunflower oil

Garnish: 12 coriander leaves, 12 ice plant leaves, 16 bean sprouts, 8 ripe tomatoes

Für 4 Personen:

Für die Seeteufelleber-Creme: 120 g frische Seeteufelleber, 200 ml Sake, 140 ml Wasser, 1 Prise Salz, 2,5 g Zucker, 0,6 g Agar-Agar in Pulverform

Für die Sojamousse: 100 ml helle Sojasauce, 100 ml Wasser, 1¹/₂ Gelatineblätter

Für den Karamell: 50 g Zucker, 25 g Glukose, 1 EL Wasser

Für das Blutorangengelee: 125 ml Blutorangensaft, 0,6 g Agar-Agar

Für das Ingweröl: 50 g Ingwer, geschält und fein gehackt, 100 ml Sonnenblumenöl

Garnitur: 8 reife Tomaten, 12 Korianderblättchen, 12 Eiskrautblätter, 16 Sojasprossen

Carefully remove all veins from the angler fish liver and soak in ice water for 24 hours. Drain and place into a small bowl, add sake and allow to marinate for 1¹/₂ hours. Remove liver from marinade, drip off excess marinade and purée in a blender with half of water, salt and sugar. Mix agar-agar with remaining water and bring mixture to a boil in a small saucepan. Add agar-agar mixture in the blender with the liver and mix well. Spread mixture into a flat dish. It should come up to about 1 cm/¹/₃ inch. Allow to cool. Cut out 5 cm/2 inch circles with a cookie cutter. Set aside in a cool place.
For the soy mousse: Combine soy sauce and water. Place soaked gelatin in a small saucepan with a quarter of the soy-water mixture. Heat and stir to dissolve. Place remaining soy water in a deep freezer. In a bowl, beat gelatin-soy water mixture with a hand mixer until cold. When mixture starts to fluff up, gradually add ice cold soy water from the freezer. Keep beating vigorously. The mixture ought to thicken and gain four times in its original volume. Pour into a flat dish to come up about 1.5 cm/¹/₂ inch and allow to chill in the refrigerator. Cut out 5 cm/2 inch circles. Refrigerate.
For the caramel: Heat water, sugar and glucose in a small saucepan until all sugar crystals are dissolved. The caramel ought to remain white. Pour thin 5 cm/2 inch circles onto a non-stick baking sheet, making them as round as you can. Allow to cool.
For the blood orange jelly: Combine blood orange juice and agar-agar in a small pot and bring to a boil. Pour liquid into a flat dish to come up 1 cm/1¹/₃ inch. Allow to cool and cut the jelly into 1 cm/1¹/₃ inch cubes. Keep refrigerated.
For the ginger oil: Combine ginger and oil in a small pot. Allow to get warm on low heat, then allow to steep in the oil at about 40° C/100° F for one hour. Strain through a fine sieve and reserve.
Serving: Top each liver cream circle with a circle of soy mousse, then scoop out a small piece with a spoon to make a crescent shape. Insert a slice of caramel in between the two shapes and place stacks onto plates. Halve tomatoes and scrape out the seeds. Place a spoonful of tomato seeds on both sides of the mousse and arrange a blood orange jelly cube in between. Garnish with coriander leaves, ice plant leaves and bean sprouts and drizzle with a little ginger oil.

Die Seeteufelleber sorgfältig von Adern befreien, in Eiswasser 24 Stunden wässern. Abtropfen lassen, mit Küchenpapier trocken tupfen, mit Sake vermischt 1¹/₂ Stunden marinieren. Herausnehmen, abtropfen lassen und mit der Hälfte des Wassers, Salz und Zucker im Mixer pürieren. Agar-Agar mit dem restlichen Wasser verrühren und in einem kleinen Topf zum Kochen bringen. Zu der Leber in den Mixer geben, gut vermischen. Die Masse in eine 1 cm hohe flache Form einfüllen, erkalten lassen. Mit einer Ausstechform 5 cm große Kreise ausstechen, kühl stellen.
Für die Sojamousse: Sojasauce und Wasser verrühren. Eingeweichte Gelatine in einem Viertel des Sojawassers auflösen. Restliches Sojawasser in den Gefrierschrank stellen. Das Gelatine-Sojawasser in einer Schüssel mit dem Rührgerät oder einem Schneebesen kalt schlagen. Wenn die Mischung schaumig wird, unter kräftigem Schlagen nach und nach das eisgekühlte Sojawasser zugeben, die Masse soll ihr Volumen etwa vervierfachen und dick werden. In eine flache Form ca. 1,5 cm hoch einfüllen, in den Kühlschrank stellen. Mit der Ausstechform 5 cm große Kreise ausstechen. Kühl stellen. Für den Karamell: Zucker und Glukose mit Wasser in einem Topf unter Rühren erhitzen, bis sich alle Kristalle aufgelöst haben, der Zucker soll dabei weiß bleiben. Auf ein beschichtetes Blech runde, dünne Kreise von 5 cm Durchmesser gießen. Erkalten lassen. Für das Blutorangengelee: Blutorangensaft mit Agar-Agar in einem kleinen Topf vermischen und zum Kochen bringen. In eine flache Form 1 cm hoch gießen und erkalten lassen. In 1 cm große Würfel schneiden. Kühl stellen.
Für das Ingweröl: Fein gehackten Ingwer mit Öl in einem kleinen Topf vermischen. Auf dem Herd leicht erwärmen und eine Stunde bei 40° C ziehen lassen. Danach durch ein feines Sieb passieren.
Zum Servieren: Lebercremescheiben mit je einer Scheibe Sojamousse bedecken. Mit einem Löffel ein Stück abstechen, so dass eine Halbmondform entsteht. Je eine Karamellscheibe dazwischen schieben, die Mousse auf Teller legen. Tomaten halbieren die Kerne auskratzen. Je einen Löffel Tomatenkerne auf zwei Seiten der Mousse setzen, dazwischen je einen Blutorangenwürfel platzieren. Mit Koriander, Eiskraut und Sojasprossen garnieren, mit Ingweröl beträufeln.

CAULIFLOWER COUSCOUS
BLUMENKOHL-COUSCOUS

Serves 4

For the couscous:
1 small cauliflower, 120 ml/^{1}/$_2$ cup reduced lamb stock

For the spice bread:
80 g/3 oz honey gingerbread, 3 tbsp olive oil, ^{1}/$_4$ tsp five-spice powder

For the Campari jelly:
50 ml/^{1}/$_4$ cup Campari, 0.7 g/a pinch of powdered agar-agar

For the vinegar reduction:
100 ml/^{1}/$_3$ cup mild wine vinegar,
preferably made from Cabernet Sauvignon grapes,
5 g/^{1}/$_2$ tsp sugar, 2 g/^{1}/$_4$ tsp glucose

For the garnish:
10 g/^{1}/$_3$ oz fresh ginger, peeled, ^{1}/$_2$ Granny Smith apple, ^{1}/$_2$ pear,
lemon juice, 10 g/^{1}/$_3$ oz coarse sugar,
12 saffron threads, slightly toasted in a pan, 4 juniper berries, minced,
4 small sprigs fresh fennel, 4 small mint leaves,
12 chervil leaves, 12 small basil leaves,
4 rosemary flowers, 4 almonds, blanched and peeled,
the zest of one orange and one lemon

Remove hard cauliflower stalks. With a sharp knife, cut off about 5 mm/ ^{1}/$_5$ inch of the outer layer of the flowerets and blend the pieces in the blender with a few short turns of the blade, until the cauliflower looks like couscous. Place blended cauliflower into a sieve and immerse the sieve into boiling salted water for a few seconds. Remove sieve from boiling water and immediately dip it into ice water. Drain well and allow the cauliflower to drain on paper towels.

For the spice bread: Finely chop the bread or crush it into crumbs with a mortar. Spread the crumbs out on a small baking sheet and dry them in a 150° C/300° F oven for 10 - 15 minutes. Allow to cool, then mix with them olive oil. Season with a pinch of five-spice-powder and set aside.

For the Campari jelly: Heat Campari in a small saucepan and mix in agar-agar. Bring the mixture to a boil and pour it into a flat dish to come up about 2 mm/^{1}/$_{10}$ inch. Refrigerate and allow to cool. When the jelly has solidified, cut it into 2 mm/^{1}/$_{10}$ inch cubes.

For the vinegar reduction: Reduce vinegar, sugar and glucose in a pot until you have a caramel consistency. Set aside.

For the garnish: Chop the ginger into 2 mm/^{1}/$_{10}$ inch cubes. Peel apple and pear and cut each into 16 even cubes of about 5 mm/^{1}/$_5$ inch. Dip the cubes into water acidulated with lemon juice. Allow to drain well.

Serving: Sprinkle a thin circle of spice bread mixture onto each plate. Place garnish ingredients onto the circle to make an attractive plate with alternating colors. Heat up the lamb stock. Heat the olive oil in a pan and fry the cauliflower couscous for a few seconds. Do not allow it to brown. Place small heaps of couscous onto the plates and drizzle the outer rim of the plates with lamb stock. Serve immediately.

Für 4 Personen:

Für das Couscous:
1 kleiner Blumenkohl, 120 ml reduzierter Lammfond

Für das Gewürzbrot:
80 g Honig-Gewürzbrot, 3 EL Olivenöl, ^{1}/$_4$ TL Spekulatiusgewürz

Für das Camparigelee:
50 ml Campari, 0,7 g Agar-Agar in Pulverform

Für die Essigreduktion:
100 ml milder Weinessig,
möglichst aus Cabernet Sauvignon Trauben,
5 g Zucker, 2 g Glukose

Für die Garnitur:
10 g frischer Ingwer, geschält, ^{1}/$_2$ Granny Smith Apfel, ^{1}/$_2$ Birne,
Zitronensaft, 10 g Hagelzucker, 12 Safranfäden, leicht geröstet,
4 Wacholderbeeren, fein gehackt, 4 kleine Zweige Fenchelgrün,
4 kleine Minzeblätter, 12 Kerbelblättchen,
12 kleine Basilikumblätter, 4 Rosmarinblüten,
4 Mandeln, blanchiert und geschält,
je 1 TL sehr dünn abgeriebene Orangen- und Zitronenschale

Die Strünke vom Blumenkohl entfernen. Mit einem Messer die äußerste Schicht des Blumenkohls ca. 5 mm dick abschneiden und im Mixer mit einigen kurzen Anläufen zerkleinern, bis der Blumenkohl wie Couscous aussieht. In ein Sieb füllen, einige Sekunden in kochendes Salzwasser tauchen, dann das Sieb sofort in Eiswasser halten. Gut abtropfen lassen und den Blumenkohl auf Küchenpapier trocknen.

Für das Gewürzbrot: Das Gewürzbrot fein hacken oder im Mörser zu kleinen Bröseln zerdrücken. Auf einem kleinen Blech auslegen, im Ofen bei 150° C 10 - 15 Minuten trocknen. Erkalten lassen, dann mit dem Olivenöl vermischen. Mit einer Prise Spekulatiusgewürz würzen, beiseite stellen.

Für das Camparigelee: Den Campari erhitzen, das Agar-Agar unterrühren, zum Kochen bringen und in eine kleine flache Form ca. 2 mm hoch einfüllen. Erkalten lassen und in den Kühlschrank stellen. Wenn das Gelee fest geworden ist, in ca. 2 mm große Würfel schneiden.

Für die Essigreduktion: Essig mit Zucker und Glukose in einem Topf zu Karamell einkochen. Beiseite stellen.

Für die Garnitur: Den Ingwer in 2 mm große Würfel schneiden. Den Apfel und die Birne schälen, aus dem Fleisch je 16 ca. 5 mm große Würfel schneiden und in mit Zitronensaft gesäuertes Wasser tauchen. Gut abtropfen lassen.

Zum Servieren: Aus den Gewürzbrotbröseln einen dünnen großen Kreis in die Teller streuen. Die vorbereiteten Zutaten der Garnitur farblich abwechselnd auf die Brösel verteilen. Den Lammfond erhitzen. Das Blumenkohl-Couscous in einer Pfanne im Olivenöl kurz anbraten, ohne Farbe nehmen zu lassen. In der Form kleiner Berge auf Teller anrichten, den äußeren Rand mit Lammfond begießen. Sofort servieren.

SQUID RAVIOLI WITH COCONUT AND SOY

TINTENFISCHRAVIOLI MIT KOKOS UND SOJA

Serves 4

2 coconuts, 1 large squid

For the mint oil:
60 g/2 oz mint leaves,
100 ml/¹/₃ cup sunflower oil

For the ginger soy vinaigrette:
30 g/1 oz ginger, peeled and minced,
60 ml/¹/₄ cup sunflower oil,
100 ml/¹/₃ cup light soy sauce

60 g/2 oz bean sprouts, 2 tbsp olive oil

For the mint oil: Place the mint leaves into a sieve and dip them into boiling water for a few seconds. Refresh in ice water. Allow excess water to drip off, then purée the mint leaves with the oil in a blender.
For the ginger-soy vinaigrette: Mix finely the diced ginger and oil in a small saucepan. Heat on the stove top to about 40° C/100° F and allow to steep for one hour. Strain through a fine sieve. Brush a plate with the ginger oil mixture and set it aside. Combine remaining ginger oil with soy sauce.
For the ravioli: Break open the coconuts. Peel off flesh, taking care to remove all brown peel and run the coconut pieces through a juicer. Pour juice into an ice cube tray. You should have frozen coconut cubes that weigh about 12 g/¹/₂ oz. Freeze in a deep freezer. Remove cubes from the tray when frozen, put them in a bag and return them to the freezer.
Remove skin and innards from squid and carefully wash the tube, inside and outside. Cut the flesh into 8 x 7 cm/2³/₄ x 3 inch rectangles. Lay them out flat between two pieces of foil, weight them down with a flat object and place them into the deep freezer to freeze. When the rectangles are frozen, cut them into large, thin sheets, as thinly as possible, with the help of a lunchmeat cutter. Place the sheets between layers of wax paper and reserve. When you are ready to make the ravioli, wrap one coconut juice cube as tightly and accurately as you can with a squid rectangle. Trim off edges. Set the packages onto the plate brushed with ginger oil and place into the refrigerator to allow the coconut cubes to melt.
Serving: Place two ravioli onto each plate and allow to stand at room temperature for ten minutes. Meanwhile, sauté the bean sprouts in olive oil and arrange them on the plates with the ravioli. Place the plates under the broiler for a few seconds to allow the contents of the ravioli to melt completely. Drizzle with ginger-soy vinaigrette and mint oil and serve.

Für 4 Personen:

2 Kokosnüsse, 1 großer Tintenfisch

Für das Minzöl:
60 g Minzeblätter,
100 ml Sonnenblumenöl

Für die Ingwer-Sojavinaigrette:
30 g Ingwer, geschält und fein gehackt,
60 ml Sonnenblumenöl,
100 ml helle Sojasauce

60 g Sojasprossen, 2 EL Olivenöl

Für das Minzöl: Die Minzeblätter mit Hilfe eines Siebes einige Sekunden in sprudelnd kochendes Wasser tauchen, anschließend die Blätter in Eiswasser abschrecken. Abtropfen lassen, mit dem Öl im Mixer fein pürieren.
Für die Ingwer-Sojavinaigrette: Fein gehackten Ingwer mit Öl in einem kleinen Topf vermischen. Auf dem Herd leicht erwärmen, eine Stunde bei 40° C ziehen lassen. Danach durch ein feines Sieb passieren. Einen Teller damit auspinseln und beiseite stellen, Ölrest mit der Sojasauce verrühren.
Für die Ravioli: Die Kokosnüsse aufbrechen. Das Fleisch herauslösen, von allen braunen Häutchen befreien und im Entsafter entsaften. Den Saft in Eiswürfelbehälter füllen, so dass 12 g schwere Würfel enstehen. Im Gefrierschrank gefrieren lassen, die Würfel aus den Formen lösem und erneut in den Gefrierschrank geben.
Den Tintenfisch häuten, ausnehmen und den Körper gut waschen. In 8 x 7 cm große Rechtecke schneiden. Zwischen zwei Folien flach auslegen, mit einem Gewicht beschwert im Tiefkühler gefrieren lassen. Wenn die Rechtecke gefroren sind, mit Hilfe einer Aufschnittmaschine in möglichst dünne und große Scheiben schneiden. Zwischen beschichtetem Papier aufbewahren. Zur Herstellung der Ravioli nun je einen Kokosmilchwürfel dicht und akkurat mit Tintenfisch umwickeln. Überstehendes Tintenfischfleisch abschneiden. Bis zum Servieren in den mit Ingweröl bepinselten Teller in den Kühlschrank stellen und die Kokosmilch auftauen lassen.
Zum Servieren: Je zwei Ravioli in tiefe Teller legen und zehn Minuten bei Raumtemperatur erwärmen. Inzwischen die Sojasprossen im Olivenöl anbraten und in die Teller verteilen. Die Teller kurze Zeit unter den Grill halten, so dass der Inhalt der Ravioli vollständig aufgetaut ist. Mit Ingwer-Sojavinaigrette und Minzöl umgießen und servieren.

WARM LEMON JELLY IN A CLOUD OF PARMESAN SERVED WITH ASPARAGUS

WARMES ZITRONENGELEE MIT PARMESANWOLKE UND SPARGEL

Serves 4

For the lemon jelly:
180 ml/³/₄ cup water,
50 ml/¹/₄ cup freshly squeezed lemon juice,
strained through a sieve,
20 ml/1 ¹/₂ tbsp syrup (equal amounts of
water and sugar),
2.5 g/¹/₄ tsp powdered agar-agar

For the asparagus:
12 green asparagus spears,
1 small French baguette bread,
crust removed, frozen,
120 ml/¹/₂ cup olive oil, salt

For the truffle oil:
50 g/2 oz black truffles, 2 tbsp sunflower oil

150 g/5 oz young Parmigiano Reggiano,
1 tsp lemon zest

For the lemon jelly: Combine water, lemon juice, syrup and agar-agar in a small saucepan and bring the mixture to a boil. Pour the liquid into a flat dish to come up 1 cm/ ¹/₃ inch. When the jelly has solidified, cut it into 1¹/₂ cm/¹/₂ inch cubes.
For the asparagus: Cut the asparagus about 5 cm/2 inches down the tip and carefully peel the tip pieces. Cut the frozen baguette into twelve paper-thin slices with a bread cutter. Wrap the thicker ends of asparagus tips with the bread slices.
Heat the olive oil in a frying pan. Sauté the asparagus tips on low heat until the asparagus are soft and the bread has turned brown and crisp. Remove them from oil, drain on paper towels and sprinkle with a little salt. Keep warm.
For the truffle oil: Peel and chop truffles and purée them finely in a blender with the oil. Add a pinch of salt.
Serving: Place fried asparagus tips on prewarmed plates. Heat the lemon jelly under the grill or in a salamander. Scatter cubes loosely onto the plates and sprinkle them with a little lemon zest. Grate Parmigiano cheese very finely and arrange three loose cloud-like heaps around the asparagus. Drizzle the fried asparagus tips with a little truffle oil and serve at once.

Für 4 Personen:

Für das Zitronengelee:
180 ml Wasser,
50 ml frisch gepresster Zitronensaft,
durch ein Sieb passiert,
20 ml Sirup
(Wasser und Zucker 1:1),
2,5 g Agar-Agar in Pulverform

Für den Spargel:
12 grüne Spargelstangen,
1 kleines französisches Baguette, die Rinde
entfernt, tiefgekühlt,
120 ml Olivenöl, Salz

Für das Trüffelöl:
50 g schwarze Trüffel, 2 EL Sonnenblumenöl

150 g junger Parmigiano Reggiano,
1 TL sehr dünn abgeriebene Zitronenschale

Für das Zitronengelee: In einem Topf das Wasser, Zitronensaft, Sirup und Agar-Agar verrühren, zum Kochen bringen. In eine flache Form füllen, so dass die Mischung 1 cm hoch darin steht. Wenn das Gelee fest geworden ist, in 1¹/₂ cm große Quadrate schneiden.
Für den Spargel: Die Spitzen ca. 5 cm lang abschneiden, dünn schälen. Das tiefgekühlte Baguette auf der Maschine in 12 hauchdünne Scheiben schneiden. Das dickere Ende der Spargelspitzen mit dem Brot umwickeln. Olivenöl in einer Pfanne erhitzen. Die Spargelspitzen darin bei kleiner Hitze braten, bis der Spargel weich und das Brot goldbraun und knusprig ist. Aus dem Öl nehmen, auf Küchenpapier gut abtropfen lassen, mit etwas Salz würzen. Warm halten.
Für das Trüffelöl: Trüffel schälen, hacken und mit dem Öl im Mixer fein pürieren. Mit einer Prise Salz würzen.
Zum Servieren: Die gebratenen Spargelspitzen auf vorgewärmte Teller anrichten. Das Zitronengelee unter dem Grill oder Salamander erwärmen. Die Würfel in die Teller verteilen, mit geriebener Zitronenschale bestreuen. Parmigiano sehr fein reiben und je drei kleine lockere Wolken rund um den Spargel setzen. Die Spargelspitzen mit Trüffelöl beträufeln, sofort servieren.

"TAGLIATELLE"

ALLA CARBONARA

Serves 4

For the consommé:
¹/₂ chicken, chopped into pieces,
1 beef bone from the shank,
¹/₂ calf's foot,
1 small onion, 1 carrot,
1 small leek, 2 sprigs of parsley,
10 black peppercorns

For the bacon butter:
60 g/2 oz lean bacon, cut into thin slices,
100 g/3¹/₂ oz butter

5 g/¹/₂ tsp powdered agar-agar,
250 ml/1 cup cream,
salt, 4 egg yolks,
50 g/1¹/₂ oz Grana Padano, finely diced

Halve onion and toast it in a dry non-stick pan on the cut surface until dark brown. Combine the onion and all remaining consommé ingredients in a large pot and add water barely to cover. Bring to a boil gradually, then turn down the heat to keep the liquid just before the below the boiling point. Allow to steep for three hours, then strain the consommé through a sieve and afterwards through a fine-meshed cloth. Check for salt.

Measure out 500 ml/2 cups of consommé. Combine agar-agar and the two cups of consommé in a pot and bring the liquid to a boil. Pour the mixture onto a 60 x 40/ 20 x 13 inch baking sheet. Take care that the jelly will be of even thickness everywhere. Allow to cool in the refrigerator for two hours, then cut the jelly into 5 mm/ ¹/₅ inch strips.

For the bacon butter: Cut the bacon slices into small cubes. In a small pan, render half of the cubes in butter for ten minutes, than strain them through a fine sieve. Add the remaining bacon cubes to the butter and heat just until they start rendering. Remove from stove and strain again through a fine sieve. Reserve bacon bits and butter.

On low heat, reduce cream by two thirds. Season with a pinch of salt. Strain the egg yolks through a sieve.

Serving: Place a heap of consommé jelly strips onto plates to make them look like real noodles. Sprinkle bacon bits and Parmesan cubes around the strips, then top jelly with a spoonful of hot bacon butter. Drizzle hot reduced cream around. Heat egg yolks until just warm (take care not to let them solidify) and drizzle them onto the cream in a thin stream. Sprinkle with a few drops of truffle oil and serve immediately.

Für 4 Personen:

Für die Consommé:
¹/₂ Huhn, in Stücke gehackt,
1 Rinderknochen aus der Haxe,
¹/₂ Kalbsfuß, gespalten,
1 kleine Zwiebel, 1 Karotte,
1 kleine Lauchstange, 2 Petersilienzweige,
10 schwarze Pfefferkörner

Für die Speckbutter:
60 g geräucherter, magerer Speck, in dünne
Scheiben geschnitten, 100 g Butter

5 g Agar-Agar in Pulverform,
250 ml Sahne, Salz, 4 Eigelb,
50 g Grana Padano,
in kleine Würfel geschnitten

Zwiebel halbieren, in einer beschichteten Pfanne mit der Schnittfläche nach unten ohne Fett dunkelbraun anrösten. Mit den restlichen Zutaten in einen Topf geben und mit Wasser auffüllen, bis alles knapp bedeckt ist. Langsam zum Kochen bringen, dann die Hitze zurücknehmen, so dass die Flüssigkeit immer knapp vor dem Siedepunkt ist. Drei Stunden ziehen lassen. Die Consommé erst durch ein Sieb, anschließend durch ein feines Tuch passieren. Mit Salz würzen. Von der Consommé 500 ml abmessen. In einem Topf mit 5 g Agar-Agar vermischen und zum Kochen bringen. In ein 60 x 40 cm großes Blech gießen, darauf achten, dass das Gelee gleichmäßig flach ist. Im Kühlschrank 2 Stunden fest werden lassen. In 5 mm dicke Streifen schneiden.

Für die Speckbutter: Die Speckscheiben in kleine Würfel schneiden. Die Hälfte mit Butter in einem Topf erwärmen, bei kleiner Hitze 10 Minuten ziehen lassen, durch ein Sieb passieren. Restliche Speckwürfel in der Butter solange erhitzen, bis der Speck beginnt zu braten. Den Topf vom Herd ziehen, erneut in ein Sieb gießen, die Speckwürfel und die Butter aufheben.

Sahne bei kleiner Hitze in einem Topf um zwei Drittel einkochen. Mit Salz leicht würzen. Eigelb durch ein Sieb passieren.

Zum Servieren: Auf vorgewärmte Teller die Consommé-Geleestreifen locker aufhäufen, so dass sie wie echte Nudeln aussehen. Mit Speck- und Parmesanwürfeln umstreuen, dann je einen Löffel heiße Speckbutter über die Tagliatelle geben. Nun die reduzierte heiße Sahne rundum angießen. Das Eigelb leicht erwärmen, es soll nicht gerinnen. In einem dünnen Faden über die Sahne geben. Die Tagliatelle mit einigen Tropfen Trüffelöl beträufeln und sofort servieren.

RED BEET SOUP WITH A VINEGAR JELLY AND SCOOPS OF FROZEN OLIVE OIL

ROTE BETE-SUPPE MIT ESSIGGELEE UND GEFRORENEN OLIVENÖL-NOCKEN

Serves 4

For the soup:
300 g/11 oz red beet,
pepper

For the vinegar jelly:
20 ml/1 1/2 tbsp syrup
(equal amounts of water and sugar),
40 ml/1/8 cup water,
0.6 g/a small pinch of powdered agar-agar,
37 ml/1/8 cup balsamic vinegar

For the yoghurt powder ice cream:
250 g/1/2 lb natural yoghurt,
100 ml/1/3 cup water

Garnish:
250 ml/1 cup high quality, cold-pressed olive oil
2 tbsp spice breadcrumbs, toasted in the oven

For the soup: Peel red beets and cut them into quarters. Run pieces through the juicer and strain the resulting juice through a fine sieve. Pour juice into a saucepan and heat it to just below the boiling point (do not boil). Strain through a sieve again and allow to cool. Keep refrigerated.

For the vinegar jelly: Combine syrup, water and agar-agar in a small pot and bring the mixture to a boil. Cool down immediately and mix with the balsamic vinegar. Pour the mixture into a flat dish. The jelly should come up about 5 mm/1/5 inch. Allow to solidify in the refrigerator and cut the solid jelly into 5 mm/1/5 inch cubes.

For the yoghurt powder ice cream: Mix the yoghurt and water and freeze the mixture overnight in a flat dish. Unmold the block of ice cream and scrape thin layers of ice cream off the top of the block. Place each portion of powder back into the refrigerator at once, or make the powder only right before serving. (At the El Bulli, the ice cream is made in a Paco Jet device which makes for a very fine texture.)

Pour olive oil into a plastic dish and place it into the deep freezer for twenty-four hours. Remove from the freezer 2 - 3 hours before serving.

Serving: Arrange jelly cubes on one side of deep plates. Place a small heap of spice breadcrumbs on the other side and put a scoop of half-frozen olive oil on top. Check red beet soup for salt and pepper and carefully pour a ladle of soup into the plates. Place a spoonful of yoghurt powder ice cream onto the vinegar jelly cubes and serve immediately.

Für 4 Personen:

Für die Suppe:
300 g Rote Bete,
Pfeffer

Für das Essiggelee:
20 ml Sirup
(Wasser und Zucker 1:1),
40 ml Wasser,
0,6 g Agar-Agar in Pulverform,
37 ml Balsamessig

Für das Joghurt-Pulvereis:
250 g Naturjoghurt,
100 ml Wasser

Garnitur:
250 ml sehr gutes, kalt gepresstes Olivenöl,
2 EL Gewürzbrotbrösel, im Ofen geröstet

Für die Suppe: Rote Bete schälen und in Achtel schneiden. In den Entsafter geben, den Saft durch ein Sieb passieren. In einem Topf bis kurz vor den Siedepunkt bringen (nicht kochen). Erneut durch ein Sieb passieren, erkalten lassen, kühl stellen.

Für das Essiggelee: Sirup, Wasser und Agar-Agar in einem kleinen Topf verrühren und zum Kochen bringen. Sofort abkühlen, mit dem Balsamessig vermischen und in eine flache Form gießen, so dass die Flüssigkeit 5 mm hoch steht. Im Kühlschrank fest werden lassen, dann das Gelee in 5 mm große Würfel schneiden.

Für das Joghurt-Pulvereis: Joghurt mit Wasser verrühren, in einer flachen Form über Nacht gefrieren lassen. Den Eisblock aus der Form stürzen und mit einem Messerrücken das Eis dünn und pulverig abkratzen. Jede Portion Pulver sofort zurück in den Gefrierschrank geben oder erst beim Anrichten das Pulver herstellen und dann gleich servieren. (Im „El Bulli" wird das Eis-Pulver im Paco Jet-Gerät hergestellt, dadurch wird es feiner).

Das Olivenöl in einem Kunststoff-Behälter 24 Stunden in den Gefrierschrank stellen. Vor der Verwendung 2 - 3 Stunden im Kühlschrank antauen lassen.

Zum Servieren: In tiefe Teller die Geleewürfel auf einer Seite anrichten. Auf der anderen Tellerseite je ein Häufchen Brösel platzieren und eine Olivenölnocke darauf setzen. Die Rote Bete-Suppe mit Salz würzen und vorsichtig in die Teller schöpfen. Je einen Löffel Joghurt-Pulvereis über die Essigwürfel geben und sofort servieren.

CAMPARI CAKE AND VANILLA ICE CREAM

CAMPARI-KUCHEN UND VANILLEEIS

Serves 4

For the sponge cake:
4 eggs, 125 g/4 oz sugar, 125 g/4 oz flour

For soaking:
75 ml/¹/₃ cup Campari, 45 ml/¹/₄ cup syrup
(equal amounts of water and sugar)

For the vanilla ice cream:
375 ml/1²/₃ cup milk, 50 ml/¹/₄ cup cream,
8 g/¹/₄ oz skim milk powder,
15 g/1 tbsp dextrose (pharmacy or health food store),
50 g/2 oz glucose, 25 g/1 oz sugar, 3 vanilla beans, slit lengthwise

For the vinegar foam:
1 sheet gelatin, 50 g/2 oz syrup (equal amounts of water and sugar),
75 ml/¹/₃ cup balsamic vinegar

For the pepper caramel:
60 g/2 oz sugar, 30 g/1 oz glucose, 2 tbsp water,
60 ml/¹/₄ cup hot water, black pepper, freshly and very finely ground

For the candied orange:
1 untreated orange, 500 ml/2 cups freshly squeezed orange juice,
100 g/3¹/₂ oz sugar, 50 g/2 oz glucose, 1 g/a pinch of agar-agar

For the sponge cake: Preheat the oven to 220° C/430° F. Beat eggs and sugar with a mixer until light and fluffy. Gradually add sifted flour, incorporating each portion thoroughly before adding more. Pour batter onto a greased, flour-dusted baking sheet and bake in the hot oven for 4 - 6 minutes, until lightly brown.
For soaking: Mix Campari and syrup.
For the vanilla ice cream: Combine all ingredients in a saucepan and mix well. Remove pan from heat just before the mixture begins to boil. Place the mixture into the refrigerator for twelve hours. Discard vanilla beans. Freeze in an ice cream maker.
For the vinegar foam: Dissolve gelatin in the warmed syrup. Add balsamic vinegar and mix well. Place the mixture into the refrigerator to cool and pour it into a soda siphon when cool.
For the pepper caramel: Combine sugar, glucose and water in a large pot and stir over low heat until all sugar crystals are dissolved. Allow to caramelize to medium brown. Douse with hot water (careful of splattering!) and cook, stirring constantly, until caramel has turned liquid again. Season with pepper and allow to cool.
For the candied orange: Bring water to a rolling boil and blanch the orange three times for thirty seconds. Combine orange, orange juice, sugar and glucose in a pot and simmer on low heat. When the syrup begins to thicken, remove orange and allow it to cool. Measure out 250 ml/1 cup of the syrup, stir in agar-agar and bring the mixture to a boil. Remove pot from heat. Cut the orange into pieces as soon as it is cool enough to handle and toss the pieces with thickened juice. Place in the refrigerator for two hours.
Serving: Cut the biscuit into cubes and drizzle it with Campari syrup until soaked. Arrange cubes on plates. Add candied orange pieces with juice and spray a little vinegar foam onto the plate with the siphon. Surround with pepper caramel. Garnish with vanilla ice cream. Decoration on the photograph: drawn basil sugar.

Für 4 Personen:

Für den Biskuit:
4 Eier, 125 g Zucker, 125 g Mehl

Zum Tränken:
75 ml Campari,
45 ml Sirup (Zucker und Wasser 1:1)

Für das Vanilleeis:
375 ml Milch, 50 ml Sahne,
8 g entrahmtes Milchpulver,
15 g Dextrose (Apotheke oder Reformhaus), 50 g Glukose,
25 g Zucker, 3 Vanillestangen, der Länge nach aufgeschlitzt

Für den Essigschaum:
1 Gelatineblatt, 50 g Sirup, (Wasser und Zucker 1:1),
75 ml Balsamessig

Für den Pfefferkaramell:
60 g Zucker, 30 g Glukose, 2 EL Wasser,
60 ml heißes Wasser, schwarzer Pfeffer, frisch und fein gemahlen

Für die konfitierte Orange:
1 unbehandelte Orange, 500 ml frisch gepresster Orangensaft,
100 g Zucker, 50 g Glukose, 1 g Agar-Agar

Für den Biskuit: Ofen auf 220° C vorheizen. In einem Rührgerät Eier und Zucker schaumig rühren. Nach und nach das gesiebte Mehl zugeben und vermischen. Auf ein gefettetes, mit Mehl bestäubtes Blech geben, im Ofen 4 - 6 Minuten hellbraun backen.
Zum Tränken: Den Campari mit dem Sirup vermischen.
Für das Vanilleeis: Alle Zutaten in einem Topf verrühren und erhitzen. Kurz vor dem ersten Aufkochen vom Herd ziehen, erkalten lassen. 12 Stunden in den Kühlschrank stellen, dann die Vanillestangen entfernen, die Masse in der Eismaschine gefrieren.
Für den Essigschaum: Eingeweichte Gelatine im erwärmten Sirup schmelzen lassen. Den Balsamessig unterrühren, die Mischung im Kühlschrank auskühlen lassen und dann in einen Siphon füllen.
Für den Pfefferkaramell: Den Zucker und die Glukose mit dem Wasser in einem Topf unter Rühren langsam erhitzen, bis sich alle Kristalle aufgelöst haben und der Zucker beginnt, mittelbraun zu karamelisieren. Mit heißem Wasser ablöschen (Vorsicht, kann spritzen!) und kochen, bis sich der Karamell wieder aufgelöst hat. Mit frisch gemahlenem Pfeffer würzen, erkalten lassen.
Für die konfitierte Orange: Die Orange dreimal in sprudelnd kochendem Wasser 30 Sekunden blanchieren. Anschließend in einem Topf mit Orangensaft, Zucker und Glukose bei kleiner Hitze köcheln. Wenn der Sirup beginnt einzudicken, die Orange herausnehmen und abkühlen lassen. Von dem Sirup 250 ml abmessen, mit dem Agar-Agar verrühren und zum Kochen bringen. Den Topf vom Herd ziehen. Die Orange in Stücke schneiden und mit dem eingedickten Saft vermischen. Im Kühlschrank 2 Stunden kühlen.
Zum Servieren: Den Biskuit in Würfel schneiden und im Campari-Sirup tränken. Auf Teller verteilen. Orangenstücke mit ihrem Saft zugeben, etwas Essigschaum aus dem Siphon dazu spritzen und mit Pfefferkaramell umgießen. Mit Vanilleeis garnieren und servieren. Dekoration auf Foto: Gezogener Basilikum-Zucker.

PETIT FOURS

LEMON HORNS OF PLENTY WITH RASPBERRY SORBET (PETIT FOURS)

ZITRONENCORNETS MIT HIMBEERSORBET (PETIT FOURS)

4 small horns of plenty

1 round phyllo dough sheet, about 17 cm/6.5 inches in diameter, butter for brushing

For the raspberry sorbet (makes 500 ml/2 cups of sorbet):
500 g/2 cups raspberries,
100 g/3 1/2 oz sugar,
100 ml/1/3 cup water

For the lemon marmalade:
30 g/1 oz lemon flesh, diced, 30 g/1 oz sugar

Garnish: lemon zest

Preheat oven to 200° C/390° F. Cut the phyllo dough sheet into quarter wedges. Brush with melted butter and roll up into horns of plenty. Bake in the oven for ten minutes until golden brown.
For the raspberry sorbet: Combine raspberries, sugar and water in a pot and simmer on low heat until the raspberries start to disintegrate. Strain the mixture through a sieve twice and freeze the purée in an ice cream maker.
For the lemon marmalade: Mix the lemon cubes and the sugar in a small pot. Heat up gradually and simmer on low heat, stirring constantly, until you have a thick, syrupy consistency. Allow the marmalade to cool.
Serving: Spread some lemon marmalade into the horns of plenty. Spoon the raspberry sorbet into a pastry bag and pipe a portion of sorbet into the horns. Garnish with lemon zest.

Für 4 kleine Cornets:

1 rundes Philo-Teigblatt von 17 cm Durchmesser,
Butter zum Bepinseln

Für das Himbeersorbet (ergibt 500 ml Sorbet):
500 g Himbeeren,
100 g Zucker,
100 ml Wasser

Für die Zitronenmarmelade:
30 g Zitronenfleisch in kleine Würfel geschnitten, 30 g Zucker

Garnitur: Zitronenschalenraspel

Den Ofen auf 200° C vorheizen. Das Philo-Teigblatt in Viertel schneiden. Mit flüssiger Butter bepinseln und zu Cornets formen. Im Ofen zehn Minuten goldbraun backen.
Für das Himbeersorbet: Himbeeren mit Zucker und Wasser bei kleiner Hitze köcheln, bis die Himbeeren zusammenfallen. Zweimal durch ein Sieb streichen, anschließend das Püree in der Eismaschine gefrieren.
Für die Zitronenmarmelade: Die Zitronenwürfel mit dem Zucker in einem kleinen Topf vermischen. Langsam erhitzen, unter Rühren bei kleiner Hitze zu einer dicken Konsistenz köcheln. Die Marmelade erkalten lassen.
Zum Servieren: Die Zitronenmarmelade in die Cornets füllen. Das Himbeersorbet in eine Spritztüte geben und in die Cornets spritzen. Mit Zitronenraspel garnieren.

WHITE CHOCOLATE WITH BLACK OLIVES (PETIT FOURS)

WEISSE SCHOKOLADE MIT SCHWARZEN OLIVEN (PETIT FOURS)

Serves 4

60 g/2 oz black olives, pitted,
100 g/3 1/2 oz white couverture chocolate

Dry the olives on a baking sheet for about four hours in a 80° C/170° F oven. When dry, finely chop the olives.
Melt the white chocolate very carefully in a double boiler. Add olives, mix well and spread the mixture with a palette knife onto a piece of heavy plastic foil. Cover with a second piece of foil and place into the refrigerator to set. Bend the chocolate into the desired shapes while still pliable or cut the set sheet into pieces of your own design.

Für 4 Personen:

60 g schwarze Oliven, entkernt,
100 g weiße Kuvertüre

Oliven auf einem Blech im 80° C heißen Ofen vier Stunden trocknen. Anschließend die Oliven fein hacken oder mahlen.
Die weiße Schokolade im Wasserbad sehr langsam schmelzen. Mit den Oliven vermischen, mit einer Palette dünn auf Frischhaltefolie aufstreichen. Mit einem zweiten Stück Folie bedecken, im Kühlschrank fest werden lassen. Solange die Schokolade noch biegsam ist, in die gewünschte Form bringen oder nach Belieben zuschneiden.

MERINGUE SKEWER WITH PINEAPPLE (PETIT FOURS)

BAISERSPIESS MIT ANANAS (PETIT FOURS)

For 4 skewers

For the pineapple:
4 pineapple cubes of 2 x 2 cm/3/4 x 3/4 inch,
2 tbsp sugar

For the meringue:
50 g/1 1/3 oz egg white, whipped into stiff peaks,
60 g/2 oz sugar,
40 g/1 1/2 oz glucose,
2 tbsp water

For the pineapple: In a small saucepan, caramelize the sugar and a few drops of water until light brown. Add pineapple cubes and simmer for a few minutes on low heat, stirring occasionally. Allow to cool.
Mix sugar, water and glucose in a small pot and stir over low heat until all sugar crystals are dissolved. Remove pot from heat and allow the sugar to cool down. Incorporate syrup into the whipped egg white and beat vigorously with a wire whip until the mixture is cool and has increased significantly in volume.
Stick pineapple cubes onto skewers and dip them into the meringue mixture, making a round meringue lightly pointy towards the top. Place skewers upright into the refrigerator to dry for an hour. Bake in a 150° C/300° F oven for 15 - 20 minutes.

Für 4 Spieße:

Für die Ananas:
4 Würfel Ananas von 2 x 2 cm,
2 EL Zucker

Für die Baisermasse:
50 g Eiweiß, zu Schnee geschlagen,
60 g Zucker,
40 g Glukose,
2 EL Wasser

Für die Ananas: Zucker mit ein paar Tropfen Wasser in einem kleinen Topf hellbraun karamellisieren. Ananaswürfel zugeben, von Zeit zu Zeit umrühren, ein paar Minuten bei kleiner Hitze garen. Erkalten lassen.
Zucker und Glukose mit Wasser in einem kleinen Topf bei geringer Hitzezufuhr köcheln, bis sich alle Kristalle aufgelöst haben. Vom Herd ziehen und warten, bis der Zucker nicht mehr kocht. Nach und nach unter den Eischnee ziehen, mit dem Schneebesen schlagen, bis die Masse erkaltet ist und an Volumen gewinnt.
Die Ananaswürfel auf Spieße stecken. In die Meringenmasse tauchen, so dass ein möglichst rundes, nach oben spitzes Baiser auf dem Spieß steckt. Aufrecht stehend eine Stunde in den Kühlschrank stellen, anschließend im 150° C heißen Ofen 15 - 20 Minuten backen.

BANANA AND APPLE

oil

mint sun

mint LEAVES

RED

flowers

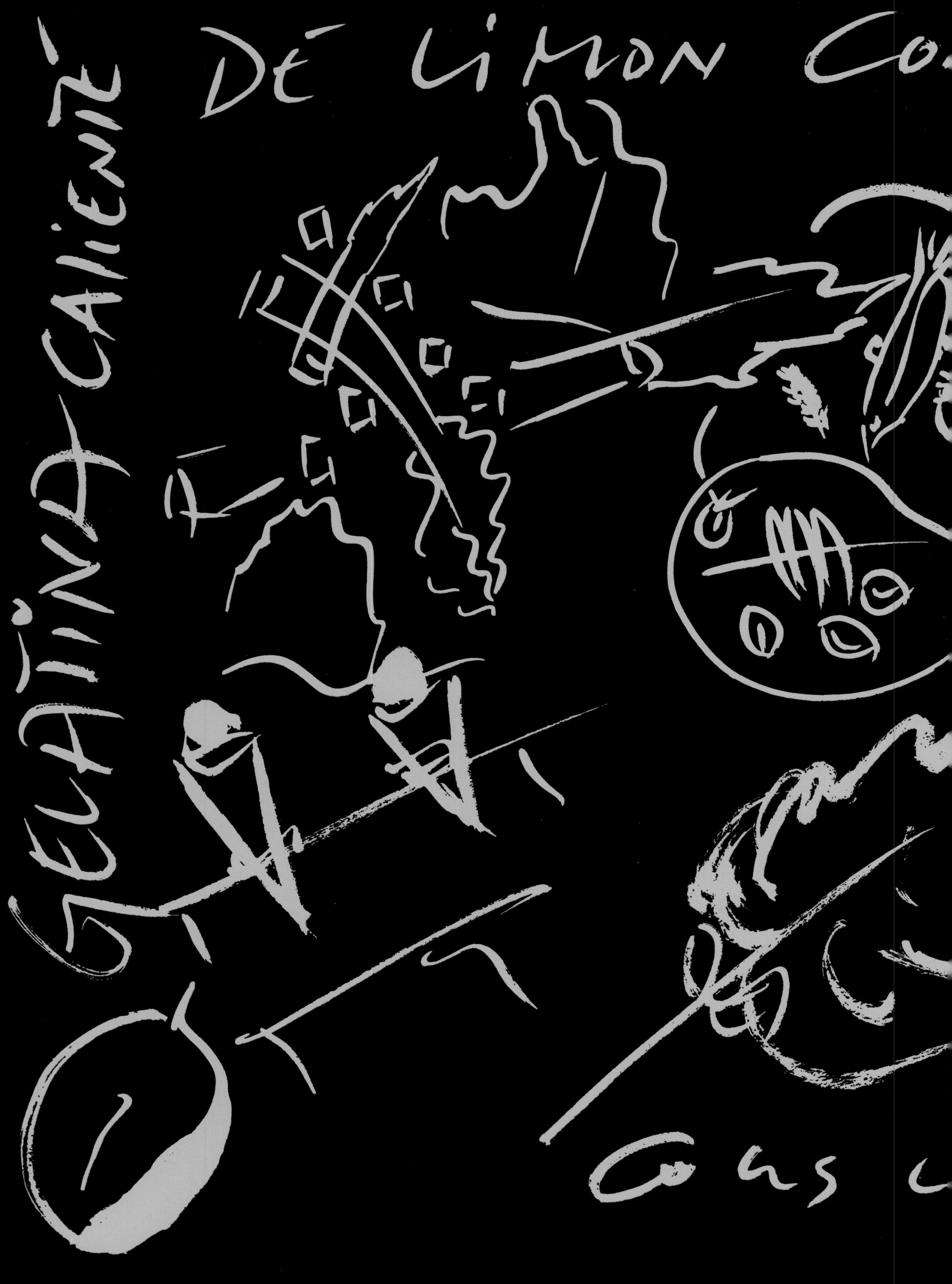
GELATINA CALIENTE
DE LIMON

NUBE DE

PARMESANO

CARBONARA

TAGARINES A LA

Y ESPARRAGOS

DE COLIFI

Racó de Can Fabes

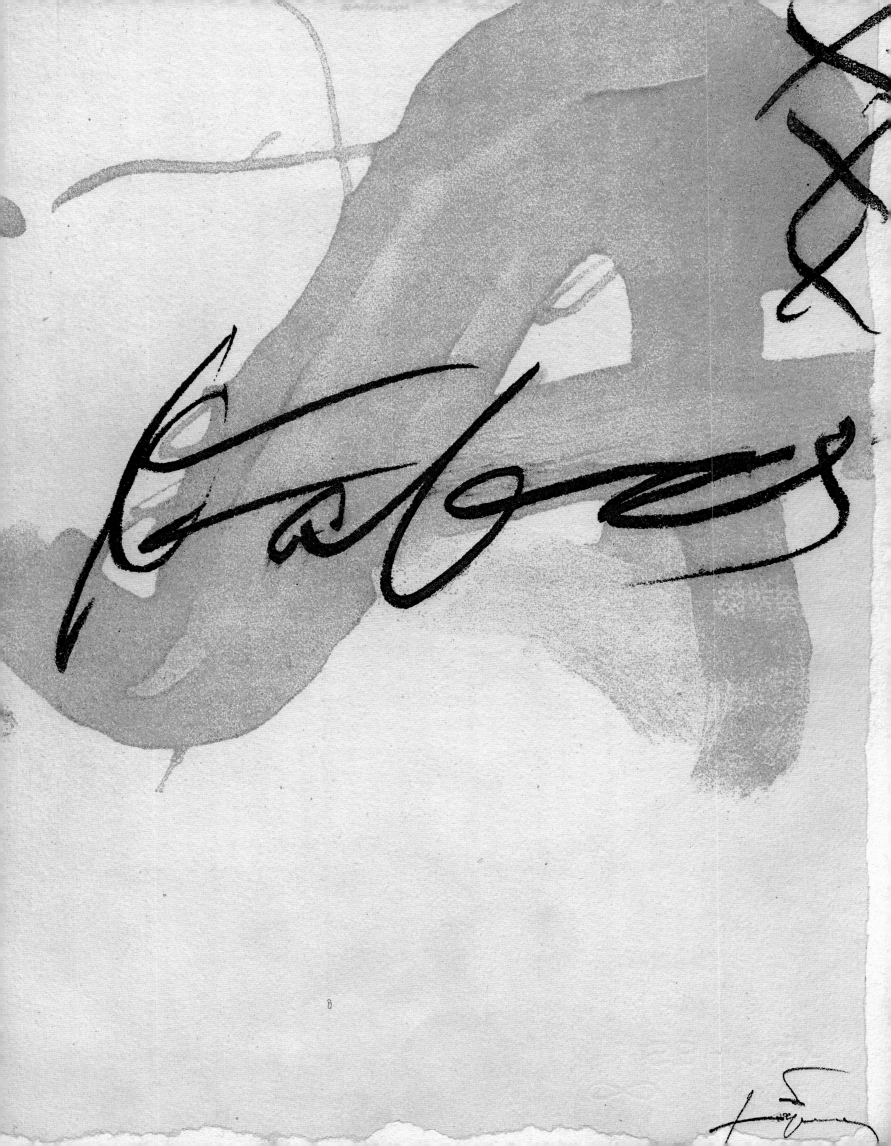

SPANISH CUISINE IS AS MULTI-FACETED AS ARE THE PERSONALTIES BEHIND IT.

Every chef tends to leave his own touch on the recipes of the cuisine he practices, his unmistakable hand-writing so-to-speak, reflecting dreams and images, concepts and philosophies. The Catalonian chef Santi Santamaria is one of those individualists who have left their mark on the culinary landscapes of Spain. People who forego heading straight for Barcelona and take the autopista exit to Sant Celoni about forty kilometers earlier instead are wont to meet a culinary maven who simply does not care to meet everyone´s taste. Santi Santamaria´s cooking comes from instinct.

HIS RESTAURANT "EL RACÓ DE CAN FABES" IS A PLACE FOR FRIENDS, HIS FRIENDS.

For friends who know how to enjoy food and who do not mistake a stay at a high-class restaurant with a visit to church or to a laboratory. The patron is quite sensitive about the topic. It actually seems to hurt him physically if he must watch even a well-meaning critic or would-be gourmet picking around on his plate looking for the components of taste – until nothing remains on the plate. "And where was the enjoyment of it all? He did not understand a thing", rants Santamaria. "It´s in the event, not in the analysis. I am against testing. Life is not a test and food should not come under the microscope."

The round head of the dyed-in-the-wool local patriot is graced by an eight millimeter crew cut and a three-day-old beard. A leftist without party card, a regionalist without blinders for the wide world, which nowadays is only a few hours away. This is the house where he was born and grew up thirty-four years ago. It is our luck that he was not born wealthy and has to make a living with his own hands. And this is exactly what he does, in his restaurant which belongs among the best in Spain. "I don´t need this for my self-confidence, though", he says, "I would rather cook only for my family and close friends. That would really be quite enough for me." In any

DE CAVIAR

ROYAL OCIÈTRE DE TOCINO DE LA PANTÉ DEL CUELLO

DE HUEVAS DE SALMON

TICINO CON CAVIAR

case, we are lucky to be able to enjoy his art, too, family atmosphere and all. This warm, personal touch is reinforced by his partner, friend and lover – as he lovingly calls her – his wife Àngels Serra. She is in charge of the figures in the computer and fills the role of the patronne in the dining-room. Her smile is easy and everywhere – for everyone. And yet, those looking for luxury at the Raco de Can Fabes will be in for a disappointment. The house has been squeezed into a corner of town, and the rooms are just as cramped, a fact that in no way diminishes the enjoyment, however. A wall of natural stone emphasizes the rustic charm of the place. In the adjacent, more recently built room, the tables are spaced more liberally, and the walls are kept in pastels. Santamaria and his kitchen crew of fifteen feed about forty-five guests at lunch and dinner. The large-format menu, designed by star artist friend Antoni Tàpies, provides a list of the delicious concoctions that may be enjoyed.

WHAT DOES SUCH A MASSIVE PERSON DO IN SUCH A SLEEPY LITTLE PLACE? WHERE DOES HE SPEND HIS ENERGY?

"I am a child of the country, and that's where I belong", Santamaria insists. "People who come through those restaurant doors come to me and my cuisine, not because a culinary guide has granted me stars or good grades, which, of course, is an honor." Gourmets, he thinks, are yesterday's breed, and dying out fast. Today's criteria are: I like it or I don't. In his restaurant, he is at liberty to do what he likes and put everything that is important to him into practice. One of these things is the work of the people from whom he and his profession indirectly benefit. Small farmers bring their fruits directly to his kitchen, ecologists provide the conditions for natural agriculture and the butcher slaughters animals whose meat stems form grazing on local pastures. "Strangers learn a lot about my cuisine, and beyond. My dishes tell of our country and of our culture." The former engineer is the very opposite of an analytical planner and constructionist of recipes. He works in unadorned simplicity with the raw materials of mountains and ocean. Wild vegetables such as wild asparagus, truffles and mushrooms, pigs raised in natural conditions as well as a grandiose range of fish and seafood are his favorites. "I am man of the Mediterranean. We have the very best products here. Without such great raw materials there can be no great cuisine." And yet, he does occasionally look beyond his own plate and knows very well what his colleagues are up to. But one thing he finds highly dubious: picking from different pots and the happy-go-lucky combination of products alien to each other. He calls that attention-getting. "These are cocktails, like a Martini Dry or a Negroni. My restaurant is no cocktail bar. That's not my world." Anybody according to his own taste, but he prefers wine. "Our culture is based on wine, and there is no good cuisine without wine. My way of cooking is a cuisine of transformation, of metamorphosis, where ingredients are cooked and not only mixed." His creations are results of a spontaneous process, not of a violent search for the innovative kick. There is no special force fiddling around in his gleaming kitchen looking for the culinary eye-teaser of the next season. His ingredients come from close by, but he does not hesitate to procure only the best if it is available in neighboring France, and he also resorts to a pinch of curry, if necessary. Yet, the mannered cuisine of many of his

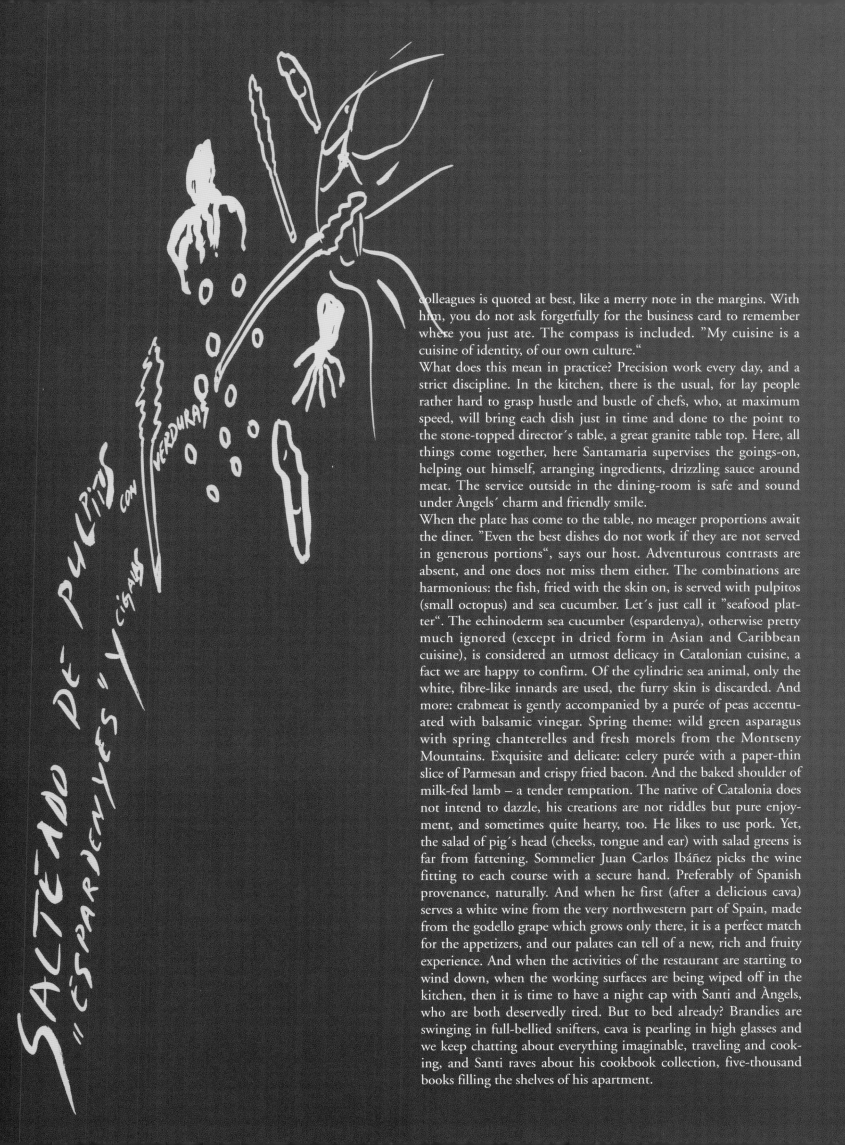

Salteado de Pulpitos "Espardenyes" y Cigalas con Verduras

colleagues is quoted at best, like a merry note in the margins. With him, you do not ask forgetfully for the business card to remember where you just ate. The compass is included. "My cuisine is a cuisine of identity, of our own culture."

What does this mean in practice? Precision work every day, and a strict discipline. In the kitchen, there is the usual, for lay people rather hard to grasp hustle and bustle of chefs, who, at maximum speed, will bring each dish just in time and done to the point to the stone-topped director's table, a great granite table top. Here, all things come together, here Santamaria supervises the goings-on, helping out himself, arranging ingredients, drizzling sauce around meat. The service outside in the dining-room is safe and sound under Àngels' charm and friendly smile.

When the plate has come to the table, no meager proportions await the diner. "Even the best dishes do not work if they are not served in generous portions", says our host. Adventurous contrasts are absent, and one does not miss them either. The combinations are harmonious: the fish, fried with the skin on, is served with pulpitos (small octopus) and sea cucumber. Let's just call it "seafood platter". The echinoderm sea cucumber (espardenya), otherwise pretty much ignored (except in dried form in Asian and Caribbean cuisine), is considered an utmost delicacy in Catalonian cuisine, a fact we are happy to confirm. Of the cylindric sea animal, only the white, fibre-like innards are used, the furry skin is discarded. And more: crabmeat is gently accompanied by a purée of peas accentuated with balsamic vinegar. Spring theme: wild green asparagus with spring chanterelles and fresh morels from the Montseny Mountains. Exquisite and delicate: celery purée with a paper-thin slice of Parmesan and crispy fried bacon. And the baked shoulder of milk-fed lamb – a tender temptation. The native of Catalonia does not intend to dazzle, his creations are not riddles but pure enjoyment, and sometimes quite hearty, too. He likes to use pork. Yet, the salad of pig's head (cheeks, tongue and ear) with salad greens is far from fattening. Sommelier Juan Carlos Ibáñez picks the wine fitting to each course with a secure hand. Preferably of Spanish provenance, naturally. And when he first (after a delicious cava) serves a white wine from the very northwestern part of Spain, made from the godello grape which grows only there, it is a perfect match for the appetizers, and our palates can tell of a new, rich and fruity experience. And when the activities of the restaurant are starting to wind down, when the working surfaces are being wiped off in the kitchen, then it is time to have a night cap with Santi and Àngels, who are both deservedly tired. But to bed already? Brandies are swinging in full-bellied snifters, cava is pearling in high glasses and we keep chatting about everything imaginable, traveling and cooking, and Santi raves about his cookbook collection, five-thousand books filling the shelves of his apartment.

REMO	En Tartar y huevos de salmón	4.950'
Cabeza de Cerdo	Ensalada de manzana y costrones de sobrasada	4.250'
GUISANTES	Y buey de mar, con una crema de las vainas	4.500'
SEPIA	Con mojama y patatas, aceite de tinta	4.600'
CIGALAS	Con sofrito de cebolla y tomate	5.500'
ENSALADA de pichón	Y foie-gras a la plancha con hierbas salvajes	4.500'
CAVIAR	Con tocino	7.500'
RANAS	Con patatas violeta al mortero con tuétano	5.200'
VERDURAS	De primavera en cocotte: habitas, guisantes...	4.250'
COLMENILLAS	Setas del tiempo con salsa de foie	5.250'
SETAS	De primavera salteadas: colmenillas, "rossinyols", "cama-secs", " moixernons"	5.250
BACALAO	Con emulsión de aceite de oliva e hinojo	4.950'
SALMONETES	Con flores de calabacín y setas de San Jorge	5.200'
"ESPARDENYES"	Salteadas con aceite de pimientos y alcachofas	5.200'
BOGAVANTE	Entero, a la americana moderna	7.950'
PULPITOS	De la costa con habitas	6.800'
VIEIRAS	A la piñonada con ciruelas	4.950'
CORDERO	Cabrero, de la Plana de Vic con su jugo	5.650'
FOIE-GRAS	Entero, hecho a la sal de hierbas mínimo dos personas, precio unitario	5.500'
CABRITO	Gigot caramelizado a la salvia	4.800'
PATO de sangre	Al horno lacado con miel y una "cocotte" de verduras y setas	5.500'
JARRETE	Ternera caramelizada con cebollitas mínimo dos personas, precio unitario	4.950'
ENTRECOT	De ternera con verduras primaverales	5.250'

Aperitivos, servicio de panera de pan de Can Moré y mantequilla de Echiré, 750' pts. IVA 7%

PRIMAVERA

La primavera es un estallido de frescor. Dentro de un guisante se puede descubrir todo un universo.

Santi Santamaria - Àngels Serra

Menú clássico

Tartar de remo con huevos de salmón
1997
Ravioli de gambas al aceite de ceps
1987
Setas de primavera
especialmente colmenillas, a la crema
1982
Pescado de mercado con tripitas de bacalao
1985
Cabrito lacado
o
Cordero cabrero de la Plana de Vic
con verduras de primavera
1999
***
Queso
***
Sorbete de chocolate
*
Timbal de fresones
***
Petits fours

precio menú 13.950' + 7 % IVA

Menú Tiempo

Sepia al aceite virgen con mojama
y patatas, aceite de tinta
*
Guisantes con buey de mar
crema de vainas
*
Espárragos y colmenillas
emulsión de gamonillo
*
Pescado de mercado
con puré de patatas al vino tinto
*
Costilla de ternera lechal
con verduritas de primavera
***
Queso
***
Sorbete de chocolate
*
Naranjas de Valencia al anís con fantasía
***
Petits fours

precio menú 12.950' + 7 % IVA

Gran Menú de Santi Santamaria 16.950' + 7% IVA

el precio de cada menú es por persona, mínimo mesa completa y el mismo menú para todos los comensales

QUESOS   Una selección preparada por nuestro Maître Cándido Tardío   1.950'

Postres calientes que deben pedirse con los demás platos

BUÑUELOS   De chocolate, con helado de coco

TARTALETA   De flores de primavera con miel

BLINIS   Con crema de manzana y jenjibre

D
ie Facetten des spanischen Küchenwunders sind zahlreich und so individuell
wie die Persönlichkeiten, die dahinterstecken. Jede Hand prägt die Rezepte der eigenen Küche mit der unverwechselbaren Schrift, in deren Zeichen sich Träume und
Bilder, Konzepte und Lebensphilosophien wiederspiegeln. Der Katalane Santi Santamaria gehört zu diesen Protagonisten, die der kulinarischen Landschaft Spaniens
ihren Stempel aufgedrückt haben. Wer, statt nach Barcelona durchzurauschen, auf
der Autopista knapp vierzig Kilometer früher die Ausfahrt nach Sant Celoni benützt,
hat nicht mehr weit zur Begegnung mit einem Urgestein, das sich wenig darum
schert, es allen recht zu tun. Santi Santamaria kocht mit dem Bauch.

Sein Restaurant „El Racó de Can Fabes" ist ein Platz für Freunde, seine Freunde. Für
Freunde, die zu genießen verstehen und den Besuch eines hochklassigen Restaurants
nicht mit der Kirche oder einem Labor verwechseln. Der Hausherr ist ausgesprochen
empfindlich, was das Thema anlangt. Es bereitet ihm förmlich körperliches Unbe-
hagen, mit zuzusehen, wenn auch noch der wohlmeinendste Kritiker oder Möchte-
gern-Feinschmecker auf seinem Teller herumpickt und nach Geschmackskomponen-
ten sucht – solange bis nichts mehr auf dem Teller liegt. „Und wo war der Genuss?
Nichts hat er kapiert," poltert Santamaria. „Es geht um das Erlebnis und nicht um
eine Analyse. Ich bin gegen Tests. Das Leben ist kein Test, und Essen gehört nicht
unters Mikroskop."

Acht Millimeter Haupthaar und ein Dreitage-Bart ziehen sich um den runden Schä-
del eines eingefleischten Lokalpatrioten. Ein Linker ohne Parteibuch, ein Regionalist
ohne Scheuklappen vor der großen Welt, die heute in wenigen Stunden zu erfahren
ist. Hier in diesem Haus ist er vor vierunddreißig Jahren geboren und aufgewachsen.
Man kann von Glück sagen, dass er nicht gerade mit Reichtümern gesegnet und somit darauf angewiesen ist, sein Geld mit eigenen Händen zu verdienen. Und das tut
er, recht erfolgreich, in seinem Restaurant, dessen Küche zu einer der besten Spaniens

zählt. „Aber zur Selbstbestätigung brauche ich das nicht," meint er, „viel lieber würde
ich nur für meine Familie und gute Freunde kochen. Das reicht mir eigentlich." Sind
wir froh, dass er seine Kunst auch uns zukommen lässt, die familiäre Atmosphäre
inklusive. Der persönliche und warmherzige Touch der gastlichen Stätte wird vervoll-
ständigt durch seine – wie er liebevoll sagt – Partnerin, Freundin und Geliebte, seine
Frau Àngels Serra. Ihr obliegen die Zahlen im Computer und die Rolle der Haus-
herrin im Speisesaal. Ihr Lächeln ist immer und überall – für jeden. Wer im Racó de
Can Fabes jedoch nach Luxus sucht, wird enttäuscht werden. So wie das Haus selbst
in eine Ecke des Städtchens gequetscht ist, so sitzt man eher dicht an dicht. Dem
Wohlbefinden tut's keinen Abbruch, eine Natursteinwand verstärkt den rustikalen
Charme des Lokals. Nur im geräumigen Nebenraum jüngeren Datums stehen die
Tische in lockerem Abstand, die Wände sind pastellfarben verputzt. Für etwa fünf-
undvierzig Gäste steht mittags und abends Santamaria mit fünfzehn Mitarbeitern
in der Küche, deren Angebot in einer großformatigen Speisekarte gelistet ist, von
Freund und Starkünstler Antoni Tàpies entworfen.

Was macht so eine wuchtige Person in diesem verschlafenen Nest? Wohin mit der
Energie? „Ich bin ein Kind vom Land, und da gehöre ich auch hin," erklärt Santamaria bestimmt. „Wer zu mir durch die Tür ins Restaurant tritt, der kommt wegen
mir und wegen meiner Küche hierher. Nicht nur weil ein Gourmetführer mir Sterne
oder gute Noten verliehen hat. Obwohl mich das ehrt." Gourmets, so findet er, sind
ein Kult von gestern. Im Aussterben begriffen. Heute lauten die Kriterien, es schmeckt
mir, es schmeckt mir nicht. In seinem Restaurant kann er gestalten und plastisch
demonstrieren, was ihm wichtig ist. Wichtig ist ihm dabei insbesondere die Arbeit
der Menschen, die mittelbar ihm und seiner Profession zugute kommt. Der kleine
Bauer bringt ihm Früchte in die Küche, Ökologen sorgen für artgerechte Land-
wirtschaft, und der Metzger kann Vieh schlachten, das in der Gegend auf grünen
Wiesen sich sein Fleisch angefressen hat. „Fremde können durch meine Küche und
über sie hinaus noch mehr erfahren. Meine Gerichte erzählen von Landschaft und
Kultur." Der Ex-Ingenieur ist das krasse Gegenstück des analytischen Planers und
Konstrukteurs von Rezepturen. In ungeschminkter Schlichtheit arbeitet er mit den
Rohstoffen der Landschaft zwischen Berg und Meer.

W ildwachsendes wie wilder Spargel, Trüffeln und Pilze, natürlich aufgezogene Schweine sowie die grandiose Palette an Fischen und Meeresfrüchten sind seine Favoriten. „Ich bin ein mediterraner Mann. Die besten Produkte stehen uns zur Verfügung. Ohne diese großartigen Lebensmittel kann es keine große Küche geben." Doch auch er blickt über den eigenen Tellerrand hinaus und weiß sehr wohl, was die Kollegen so treiben. Und eines erscheint ihm höchst suspekt: das Picken in verschiedenen Töpfen und bunte Zusammenwürfeln einander fremder Produkte. Aufmerksamkeit auf Teufel komm raus, nennt er das. „Das sind Cocktails, wie Martini Dry oder ein Negroni. Mein Restaurant ist keine Cocktailbar. Das ist nicht meine Welt." Das mag jeder halten wie er will, er aber zieht Wein vor. „Unsere Kultur ist eine Kultur des Weins, und es gibt keine gute Küche ohne Wein. Und meine Art zu Kochen ist eine Küche der Transformation, der Metamorphose, wo Zutaten auch gekocht und nicht nur gemischt sind." Seine Kreationen entstammen einem spontanen Prozess ohne gewaltsame Suche nach dem innovativen Kick. Keine Special Force tüftelt in seiner blitzenden Küche am kulinarischen Hit für die nächste Saison. Die Zutaten sucht er sich zuerst in nächster Nähe, ist sich aber nicht zu schade, nach dem Besten zu greifen, wenn es im Nachbarland Frankreich erhältlich ist und würzt auch mit einer Prise Curry, wenn erforderlich. Die artifizielle Küche seiner Kollegen wird aber allenfalls zitiert, wie eine fröhliche Randbemerkung. Bei ihm wird man nicht orientierungslos nach der Visitenkarte fragen, um sich zu erinnern, wo man gerade speist. Er liefert den Kompass mit. „Meine Küche ist eine Küche der Identität, der eigenen Kultur."

Die Praxis? Das heißt täglich exerzierte Präzisionsarbeit mit strenger Disziplin. In der Küche herrscht das übliche, für den Laien schwer durchschaubare scheinbare Durcheinander der Köche, die auch bei Hochgeschwindigkeit noch rechtzeitig und punktgenau jeden Teller zum steinernen Regietisch, einer großen Granitplatte, bringen. Hier läuft alles zusammen, von hier dirigiert Santamaria das Geschehen und legt selber Hand mit an, arrangiert Zutaten oder tröpfelt die Sauce ums Fleisch. Den Service draußen im Saal überwacht Àngels mit Charme und fröhlichem Lächeln.

Kommt das Gericht zu Tisch, erwarten uns keineswegs kleinlich bestückte Teller. „Auch die besten Speisen können nicht wirken," meint der Gastgeber, „werden sie nicht in generösen Portionen serviert." Mutwillige Kontraste fehlen, aber man vermisst sie auch nicht. Die Kombinationen ergeben sich harmonisch: der Fisch, auf der Haut gebraten, kommt mit Pulpitos (kleinen Kraken) und Seegurke daher. Sagen wir einfach „Meeresteller" dazu. Übrigens gilt der Stachelhäuter Seegurke (espardenya), sonst weitgehendst ignoriert (außer in getrockneter Form in Asien und der Karibik), in Kataloniens Küche als delikater Leckerbissen, was wir hiermit gerne bestätigen. Dabei werden nur die weißen strangförmigen Innereien des walzenförmigen Seetieres verwendet, die pelzige Hülle kommt in den Abfalleimer. Doch weiter: Krebsfleisch hat einen sanften Begleiter im Erbsenpüree, mit Balsamico vorsichtig akzentuiert. Frühlingsthema: wilder grüner Spargel wird begleitet von frischen Morcheln und Pfifferlingen vom Montseny Gebirge. Exquisit und delikat: das Selleriepüree mit je einer hauchdünnen Scheibe Parmesan und kross gebratenem Rauchspeck. Und die Milchlammschulter aus

dem Ofen – eine zarte Versuchung. Der Katalane will nicht blenden, seine Werke sind keine Rätselobjekte, sie sind schlicht Genussstücke. Zuweilen auch deftig, mit Schwein arbeitet er wirklich gern. Doch der Salat vom Schweinskopf (Bäckchen, Zunge und Ohr) mit Salatgrün ist alles andere als eine Kalorienbombe. Mit souveräner Sicherheit liefert Sommelier Juan Carlos Ibáñez den passenden Tropfen zu jedem Gang. Vorzugsweise von spanischer Provenienz. Und wenn er zum Auftakt (nach der köstlichen Cava) einen Weißwein aus dem äußersten Nordwestwinkel Spaniens kredenzt, von der nur dort heimischen Godello-Rebe, sind die Vorspeisen in bester Begleitung und unser Gaumen um eine fruchtige Erfahrung reicher. Als die Aktivitäten des Restaurants erkennbar nachlassen und in der Küche schon die Arbeitsplatten gewischt werden, ist es nicht mehr weit zum spätabendlichen Schlummertrunk mit Santi und Àngels, die beide rechtschaffen müde sind. Doch jetzt schon in die Federn? Der Brandy schwingt im bauchigen Glas, die Cava perlt, und man plaudert über Gott und die Welt, übers Reisen und Kochen, und Santi schwärmt von seiner Kochbuchsammlung, die mit fünftausend Exemplaren die Regale seiner Wohnung füllt.

TERRA BLANC
MONTSENY

MOSCADA SAL Y PIMIENTA

NUEZ

DE LECHE

DE TERNERA

CARRE DE TERNERA

CON SETAS DE

SQUID WITH DRIED TUNA FISH

TINTENFISCH MIT GETROCKNETEM THUNFISCH

Serves 4

For the squid:
250 g/¹/₂ lb fresh squid,
cold-pressed olive oil,
1 tbsp chives, minced very finely,
salt, freshly ground white pepper

150 g/5 oz frozen squid,
4 thin slices dried tuna fish

For the potato sails:
1 potato, peeled,
1 tbsp almonds, shaved,
1 tbsp garlic oil,
salt, freshly ground white pepper,
2 tbsp clarified butter

Clean and peel skin off the squid, catching the ink in a small dish. Mix ink with the same amount of olive oil and reserve. Wash the squid tubes under running cold water, shake off excess water and chop them finely with a knife. Blend finely diced squid in a blender until you have a fine purée. Mix the purée with two tablespoons of olive oil and minced chives and season the mixture to taste with salt and pepper. Spoon the purée into round dishes and refrigerate for one hour.

Cut the frozen squid into paper-thin slices. Roll up the dried tuna fish slices into small rolls.

For the potato sails: Preheat the oven to 80° C/ 170° F. Shave the potatoes into paper-thin, longish strips. Mix the strips with shaved almonds and garlic oil and season to taste with salt and pepper. Scatter strips loosely onto a baking sheet lined with baking paper. Brush the potatoes with clarified butter, cover with a second sheet of foil and weight down the whole with another baking sheet. Bake in the oven for twenty minutes. Remove from oven and allow the potato sails to cool on a wire rack.

Serving: Carefully press squid out of the molds onto plates. Cover with squid strips and stick a tuna fish roll upright into the squid. Drizzle a little squid ink oil around the edge of the plates. Lean two potato sails against the tuna fish rolls, one from each side, and serve.

Für 4 Personen:

Für den Tintenfisch:
250 g frische Tintenfische,
kalt gepresstes Olivenöl,
1 EL sehr klein geschnittene Schnittlauchröllchen,
Salz, weißer Pfeffer aus der Mühle

150 g tiefgekühlter Tintenfisch,
4 dünne Scheiben getrockneter Thunfisch

Für die Kartoffelsegel:
1 Kartoffel, geschält,
1 EL Mandelblättchen,
1 EL Knoblauchöl,
Salz, weißer Pfeffer aus der Mühle,
2 EL flüssige geklärte Butter

Die Tintenfische häuten, die Tinte in einem kleinen Gefäß auffangen und mit der gleichen Menge Olivenöl vermischen. Beiseite stellen. Das Tintenfischfleisch unter fließendem kaltem Wasser waschen, abtropfen lassen, mit dem Messer hacken, anschließend im Mixer fein pürieren. Mit 2 Esslöffeln Olivenöl und den Schnittlauchröllchen vermischen, mit Salz und Pfeffer würzen. In runde Formen füllen, eine Stunde in den Kühlschrank stellen.

Den tiefgekühlten Tintenfisch mit der Maschine in hauchdünne Streifen schneiden. Die getrockneten Thunfischscheiben zu Rollen aufwickeln.

Für die Kartoffelsegel: Ofen auf 80° C vorheizen. Die Kartoffeln in hauchdünne lange Streifen schneiden. Mit Mandelblättchen und Knoblauchöl vermischen, mit Salz und Pfeffer würzen, auf einem mit Backtrennpapier ausgelegten Blech locker und flach ausbreiten. Die Kartoffeln mit geklärter Butter bepinseln. Ein zweites Stück Papier darüberlegen, mit einem zweiten Blech beschweren. Im Ofen 20 Minuten backen. Auf einem Gitter auskühlen lassen.

Zum Servieren: Den Tintenfisch vorsichtig aus den Formen drücken und auf Teller verteilen. Mit Tintenfischstreifen belegen, je eine Thunfischrolle aufrecht stehend auf den Tintenfisch platzieren. Den Tellerrand mit etwas Tintenöl beträufeln. Je zwei Kartoffelstreifen wie Segel von zwei Seiten an den Tintenfisch lehnen und servieren.

SALAD OF PIG'S HEAD WITH MALLORQUIN SOBRASADA OIL

SCHWEINSKOPFSALAT MIT MALLORQUINISCHEM SOBRASADAÖL

Serves 4

For the pig's head:
50 g/1 ^{1}/$_2$ oz dry-cured Spanish ham (Jabugo), 50 g/1 ^{1}/$_2$ tongue,
30 g/1 oz pig's snout, 30 g/1 oz pig's ear, 2 pork jowls

For the stock:
1 onion, 1 carrot, ^{1}/$_2$ celeriac, ^{1}/$_2$ bunch parsley,
1 tsp black peppercorns, salt

For the sobrasada oil:
30 g/1 oz sobrasada (Mallorquin paprika-garlic sausage),
8 tbsp olive oil

For the apples:
2 apples (Royal Gala), 1 tbsp butter, 1 tbsp sunflower oil

For the toasted bread:
4 thin slices baguette, crust removed, 2 tbsp olive oil

For the salad:
2 handfuls of mixed green leaf lettuces such as oak leaf, head lettuce,
lamb's lettuce etc., mixed herbs such as chervil, parsley and chives,
60 ml/^{1}/$_4$ cup vinaigrette made from olive oil, sherry vinegar, salt
and black pepper

Für 4 Personen:

Für den Schweinskopf:
50 g spanischer Rohschinken (Jabugo), 50 g Zunge,
30 g Schweineschnauze, 30 g Schweineohr, 2 Schweinebacken

Für die Brühe:
1 Zwiebel, 1 Karotte, ^{1}/$_2$ Sellerieknolle, ^{1}/$_2$ Bund Petersilie,
1 TL schwarze Pfefferkörner, Salz

Für das Sobrasadaöl:
30 g Sobrasada (mallorquinische Paprika-Knoblauchwurst),
8 EL Olivenöl

Für die Äpfel:
2 Äpfel (Royal Gala), 1 EL Butter, 1 EL Sonnenblumenöl

Für das Röstbrot:
4 dünne Scheiben Baguette ohne Kruste, 2 EL Olivenöl

Für den Salat:
2 Hand voll grüne Blattsalate wie Eichblatt, Kopfsalat, Feldsalat etc.,
gemischte Kräuter wie Kerbel, Petersilie und Schnittlauch,
60 ml Vinaigrette aus Olivenöl, Sherryessig, Salz
und schwarzem Pfeffer

For the pig's head (best to be prepared one day ahead): Rinse the meats thoroughly under running cold water. Place meats and ingredients for the stock into large pot, add cold water to cover generously and bring to a boil. Add a little salt, turn down heat and simmer on low heat for 1 to 1^1/$_2$ hours. Occasionally skim off any foam that rises to the surface. When the meats are tender, remove pot from heat and allow them to cool in the stock. Drain and cut the meats into pieces. Finely dice the ham.

For the sobrasada oil: Remove peel from sausage and finely chop it. Purée sausage and oil in a blender. Scrape the purée into a small saucepan and heat it up slowly. Do not let it boil. Keep the mixture below the boiling point for an hour. Strain through a fine sieve and allow the oil to cool.

For the apples: Preheat the oven to 200° C/390° F. Peel apples and cut out four even slices, about 1 cm/^{1}/$_3$ inch thick. Core the slices. In a large pan, heat butter and oil. Fry apple slices on both sides until golden brown. Place apple rings on a piece of aluminum foil and bake them in the oven for another twenty minutes. Remove from oven and allow to cool.

For the toasted bread: Brush the slices of baguette with oil on both sides. Place on a non-stick baking sheet and toast in a 200° C/ 390° F oven until golden brown. Allow to cool on a wire rack.

Clean and wash lettuces and herbs and toss them with vinaigrette.

Serving: Place apple rings at the center of four plates. Top with pieces of meat and sprinkle with bacon cubes. Arrange a slice of toasted bread on top and cover with a small heap of dressed lettuce mixture. Surround the arrangement with sobrasada oil and serve.

Note: The dish is best when meats and apple slices are served still slightly warm.

Für den Schweinskopf (am besten am Vortag zubereiten): Das Fleisch unter fließendem kaltem Wasser gut waschen. Mit den Zutaten für die Brühe in einen Topf geben, mit kaltem Wasser aufgießen bis alles gut bedeckt ist und zum Kochen bringen. Etwas Salz hinzufügen, bei kleiner Hitze 1 bis 1^1/$_2$ Stunden köcheln, dabei von Zeit zu Zeit den Schaum entfernen. Wenn das Fleisch gar ist, in der Brühe erkalten lassen. Gut abtropfen lassen, in Stücke schneiden, den Schinken fein würfeln.

Für das Sobrasadaöl: Die Haut von der Wurst abziehen, dann die Wurst hacken. Mit dem Öl im Mixer weiter zerkleinern, dann in einen Topf umfüllen. Bei kleiner Hitze erhitzen, ohne kochen zu lassen. Die Mischung heiß halten, während einer Stunde ziehen lassen. Durch ein Sieb passieren, das Öl abkühlen lassen.

Für die Äpfel: Ofen auf 200° C vorheizen. Äpfel schälen und vier schöne, 1 cm dicke Scheiben herausschneiden. Das Kernhaus ausstechen. In einer Pfanne Butter und Öl erhitzen. Die Apfelscheiben von beiden Seiten goldbraun braten. Auf ein Stück Alufolie legen, im Ofen 20 Minuten fertig braten. Herausnehmen, erkalten lassen.

Für das Röstbrot: Die Baguettescheiben von beiden Seiten mit Öl bepinseln. Auf ein beschichtetes Blech legen und im 200° C heißen Ofen goldgelb rösten. Auf einem Gitter auskühlen lassen.

Salat putzen, mit den Kräutern und der Vinaigrette vermischen.

Zum Anrichten: Die Apfelscheiben auf vier Teller legen. Mit Fleisch aus dem Schweinskopf belegen, dann mit den Schinkenwürfeln bestreuen. Je eine Röstbrotscheibe darauf legen, den Blattsalat darüber türmen. Zum Schluß das Ganze mit Sobrasadaöl umgießen und servieren.

Anmerkung: Am besten schmeckt das Gericht, wenn das Fleisch und die Apfelscheiben lauwarm gereicht werden.

BACON WITH CAVIAR

SPECK MIT KAVIAR

Serves 4

1.2 kg/2²/₃ lb uncured bacon from the neck, rind on

For the marinade:
1 kg/2 lbs salt,
100 g/3¹/₂ oz paprika,
30 g/1 oz white pepper, ground,
3 garlic cloves, crushed, 1 bay leaf

For the stock:
2 garlic cloves, 1 carrot,
1 onion, 1 celery stalk,
1 tsp white peppercorns, salt

For the potato purée:
200 g/7 oz La Ratte potatoes,
30 g/1 oz butter, 2 tbsp milk, salt

For the butter sauce:
1 navet or white turnip,
1 small leek, 1 onion, 2 garlic cloves,
4 mushroom caps, 2 celery stalks,
4 black peppercorns, 1 small bunch parsley,
2 sprigs of chervil, 2 sprigs of thyme,
2 tbsp olive oil,
150 g/5 oz cold butter

120 g/4 oz caviar (Beluga)

For the bacon: Toss ingredients for the marinade without adding any liquid. Rub the bacon on all sides with the marinade, cover, and allow to sit for six hours. Rinse the bacon thoroughly under running cold water. Place bacon into a large pot together with the ingredients for the stock, add water to cover and bring to a boil. Turn heat down to low and simmer gently for five hours. Remove bacon from cooking liquid and allow to cool. Cut off rind and the lower part of the fat and cut the bacon into four even cubes.

For the potato purée: Peel potatoes and boil in salted water until tender. Drain in a sieve, allow steam to escape, then press them through a potato press. Heat milk and butter and incorporate into the potato purée. Check for salt and strain purée through a sieve.

For the butter sauce: Clean and trim the vegetables, chop them coarsely and sauté them in a large saucepan with some olive oil for four minutes. Add one liter/4 cups of water and bring it to a boil. Keep vegetables at a bare simmer for fifteen minutes, uncovered. Check for salt and strain vegetables through a cloth. Measure out 300 ml/1¹/₄ cups of the cooking liquid and bring it to a boil again in a small saucepan. Remove from heat and whisk in butter with a wire whip, one piece at a time. Right before serving, whip the sauce until frothy.

Serving: Spread the potato purée at the center of pre-warmed plates. Heat up bacon cubes in a steamer or in the cooking liquid and place them onto the potatoes. Drizzle bacon with foamy butter sauce. Top bacon cubes with a spoonful of caviar each and serve.

Für 4 Personen:

1,2 kg grüner Halsspeck mit Schwarte

Für die Marinade:
1 kg Salz,
100 g mildes Paprikapulver,
30 g gemahlener weißer Pfeffer,
3 Knoblauchzehen, zerquetscht, 1 Lorbeerblatt

Für den Sud:
2 Knoblauchzehen, 1 Karotte,
1 Zwiebel, 1 Zweig Schnittsellerie,
1 TL weiße Pfefferkörner, Salz

Für das Kartoffelpüree:
200 g La Ratte-Kartoffeln (oder Bamberger Hörnchen),
30 g Butter, 2 EL Milch, Salz

Für die Buttersauce:
1 Navette (Mairübchen), 1 kleine Lauchstange,
1 Zwiebel, 2 Knoblauchzehen,
4 Champignonköpfe, 2 Zweige Schnittsellerie,
4 schwarze Pfefferkörner, 1 kleiner Bund Petersilie,
2 Kerbelzweige, 2 Thymianzweige,
2 EL Olivenöl,
150 g kalte Butter

120 g Kaviar (Beluga)

Für den Speck: Die Zutaten für die Marinade vermischen, ohne Flüssigkeit zuzugeben. Den Speck mit der Marinade von allen Seiten bedeckt 6 Stunden ziehen lassen. Danach den Speck unter fließendem kaltem Wasser gut abspülen. Mit den Zutaten für den Sud in einen Topf geben, mit Wasser auffüllen, zum Kochen bringen. Hitze zurücknehmen, den Speck 5 Stunden sieden. Aus dem Sud nehmen und erkalten lassen. Schwarte und einen Teil der Fettschicht entfernen, den Speck in 4 gleichmäßige Würfel schneiden.

Für das Kartoffelpüree: Geschälte Kartoffeln in Salzwasser weich kochen. Durch ein Sieb abgießen, abdampfen lassen, durch die Kartoffelpresse drücken. Milch und Butter erwärmen, mit dem Püree vermischen, mit Salz abschmecken, durch ein Sieb streichen.

Für die Buttersauce: Gemüse putzen, grob schneiden und mit den Kräutern in einem Topf im Ölivenöl 4 Minuten anbraten. Mit einem Liter Wasser auffüllen, zum Kochen bringen, während 15 Minuten ohne Deckel köcheln. Mit Salz abschmecken, durch ein Tuch passieren. Von dem Sud 300 ml abmessen, in einem kleinen Topf zum Kochen bringen. Vom Herd nehmen, die Butter mit dem Schneebesen stückchenweise unterrühren, die Sauce vor dem Servieren zu Schaum aufschlagen.

Zum Servieren: Das Kartoffelpüree in der Mitte von vorgewärmten Tellern anrichten. Die über Dampf oder im Kochsud aufgewärmten Speckwürfel darauf setzen, mit der schaumig aufgeschlagenen Buttersauce übergießen. Je einen Esslöffel Kaviar auf den Speck geben und sofort servieren.

FRIED BABY SQUID, SEA CUCUMBERS AND ROCK LOBSTERS SERVED WITH VEGETABLES

GEBRATENE BABYTINTENFISCHE, SEEGURKEN UND KAISERGRANATEN MIT GEMÜSE

Serves 4

250 g/¹/₂ lb baby squid, ready-to-cook,
500 g/1 lb fresh sea cucumbers (holothuria tubulosa),
widely popular in Catalonia, if not available, increase
the amount of baby squid and rock lobsters accordingly),
12 rock lobsters

For the red pepper oil:
120 ml/¹/₂ cup olive oil,
¹/₂ red pepper, cored and diced

For the parsley sauce:
¹/₂ bunch parsley,
200 ml/³/₄ cup vegetable stock,
2 tbsp cold butter,
salt, freshly ground white pepper

200 g/7 oz young, tender fava beans,
8 green asparagus spears,
8 white asparagus spears,
24 wild asparagus spears,
120 ml/¹/₂ cup olive oil for frying,
salt

Remove insides of the baby squid if necessary (if they are very small you can leave them in). Thoroughly rinse them in cold water. Cut open sea cucumbers and remove inner white tubes. Discard the rest of the sea cucumbers. Carefully rinse inner white tubes under running cold water. Shell rock lobsters and set aside heads and tails separately.

For the red pepper oil: In a small pot, heat oil, red pepper dice and heads of the rock lobsters. Sauté on low heat for five minutes, then strain the oil through a fine sieve. Season to taste with salt and reserve.

For the parsley sauce: Pick parsley leaves from their stems. Blanch leaves in boiling salted water for a few seconds, then refresh them in ice water. Bring vegetable stock to a boil. Add blanched parsley leaves and purée the liquid in a blender, then strain it through a fine sieve. Add cold butter, a piece at a time, and season to taste with salt and white pepper.

Blanch fava beans in salted water for one minute. Strain through a sieve. (Remove tough outer skins if necessary.)

Snap off thick ends of all asparagus spears. Peel tips, if necessary, and boil the different kinds of asparagus separately in salted water until al dente.

Finish and serving: Sauté vegetables and seafood in two separate pans in olive oil over medium heat. Sprinkle with a little salt. Arrange vegetables and seafood on plates, drizzle with red pepper oil and parsley sauce and serve while still warm.

Für 4 Personen:

250 g Babytintenfische, küchenfertig,
500 g frische Seegurken, (Holothuria tubulosa), in Katalonien
verbreitet, außerhalb kaum zu bekommen, als Ersatz die Menge
der Tintenfische und Kaisergranaten erhöhen,
12 Kaisergranaten

Für das Paprikaöl:
120 ml Olivenöl,
¹/₂ rote Paprika, entkernt, in kleine Würfel geschnitten

Für die Petersiliensauce:
¹/₂ Bund Petersilie,
200 ml Gemüsebrühe,
2 EL kalte Butter,
Salz, weißer Pfeffer aus der Mühle

200 g junge, zarte Dicke Bohnen,
8 grüne Spargelstangen,
8 weiße Spargelstangen,
24 Stengel wilder Spargel,
120 ml Olivenöl zum Braten,
Salz

Das Innere der Babytintenfische wenn nötig entfernen (wenn sie sehr klein sind, ist das nicht nötig), die Tintenfische gut waschen. Die Seegurken aufschneiden und die innerern, weißen Stränge herausschneiden, den Rest der Seegurken entfernen. Das weiße Innere unter fließendem Wasser sorgfältig waschen. Die Kaisergranaten schälen, die Köpfe und das Schwanzfleisch getrennt beiseite legen.

Für das Paprikaöl: Das Öl in einem kleinen Topf mit den Kaisergranatköpfen und den Paprikawürfeln erhitzen. Bei kleiner Hitze 5 Minuten braten, dann das Öl durch ein feines Sieb passieren. Mit Salz abschmecken, beiseite stellen.

Für die Petersiliensauce: Die Petersilienblätter von den Stengeln zupfen. In Salzwasser einige Sekunden blanchieren, anschließend in Eiswasser abschrecken. Die Gemüsebrühe zum Kochen bringen. Die blanchierten Petersilienblätter zugeben, im Mixer pürieren, durch ein feines Sieb passieren. Die heiße Sauce mit der kalten Butter aufschlagen, mit Salz und weißem Pfeffer abschmecken.

Die Dicken Bohnen in Salzwasser 1 Minute blanchieren. Durch ein Sieb passieren, wenn nötig die Bohnenkerne enthäuten.

Von allen Spargelstangen die dickere Hälfte abschneiden. Die Spitzen wenn nötig schälen, in Salzwasser al dente kochen.

Fertigstellung und Servieren: Das Gemüse und die Meeresfrüchte getrennt in Olivenöl bei mittlerer Hitze braten, leicht mit Salz würzen. Auf Teller verteilen, mit Paprikaöl und Petersiliensauce beträufeln und lauwarm servieren.

STRIPED MULLET AND THEIR LIVERS IN A RED WINE SAUCE WITH WILD MUSHROOMS

ROTBARBEN UND IHRE LEBER AN ROTWEINSAUCE MIT WALDPILZEN

Serves 4

8 striped mullet, 250 g/ 1/2 lb each

For the sauce:
2 leeks, green part only,
2 shallots,
2 garlic cloves,
4 tbsp olive oil,
300 ml/ 1 1/4 cups red wine,
500 ml/2 cups vegetable stock,
2 tbsp cold butter,
salt, freshly ground white pepper

200 g/7 oz wild mushrooms,
2 tbsp olive oil,
salt, freshly ground black pepper,
1 tsp chives, finely minced,
4 slices of white bread, crust removed,
1 tbsp olive oil,
2 tbsp olive oil for frying the liver,
100 ml/ 1/3 cup peanut oil for frying the filets,
salt, freshly ground white pepper

Für 4 Personen:

8 Rotbarben à 250 g

Für die Sauce:
2 Lauchstangen, nur die grüne Hälfte,
2 Schalotten,
2 Knoblauchzehen,
4 EL Olivenöl,
300 ml Rotwein,
500 ml Gemüsebrühe,
2 EL kalte Butter,
Salz, weißer Pfeffer aus der Mühle

200 g Waldpilze,
2 EL Olivenöl,
Salz, schwarzer Pfeffer aus der Mühle,
1 TL sehr fein geschnittene Schnittlauchröllchen,
4 Weißbrotscheiben ohne Kruste,
1 EL Olivenöl,
2 EL Olivenöl zum Braten der Lebern,
100 ml Erdnussöl zum Braten der Filets,
Salz, weißer Pfeffer aus der Mühle

Scale the striped mullet and cut them into filets. Reserve bones for the sauce. Pick out the four nicest looking livers (take care to remove the gall bladder in one piece). Set fish and livers aside.

For the sauce: Heat up olive oil in a large saucepan. Sauté the fish bones and coarsely chopped vegetables until coated with oil on all sides. Douse with wine and allow the liquid to reduce. Add the vegetable stock, reduce by half again, then strain the stock through a sieve. Whisk in cold butter with a wire whip and season to taste with salt and pepper.

Carefully clean and trim the wild mushrooms, peeling the stems if necessary. Slice mushrooms and sauté them in olive oil until they take on color. Season with a little salt and pepper and mix in the minced chives.

Preheat the oven to 200° C/390° F. Brush the white bread slices with olive oil. Toast in the oven until golden brown.

Heat the olive oil in a pan and fry the striped mullet livers on all sides for a few seconds. Arrange livers on top of the toasted bread rounds.

Rub the striped mullet filets with salt and pepper. Heat peanut oil in a large pan and fry the filets on high heat until lightly brown on all sides.

Serving: Arrange striped mullet filets on pre-warmed plates and garnish the plates with liver-toast rounds and wild mushrooms. Add red wine sauce and serve.

Note: For the full flavor of this dish, it is very important to prepare the individual components à la minute, i.e. right before serving.

Rotbarben schuppen, die Filets herausschneiden, Gräten für die Sauce beiseite legen. Von den Lebern die vier schönsten aussuchen (Vorsicht, die Galle nicht verletzen und vollständig entfernen), ebenfalls auf die Seite legen.

Für die Sauce: Fischgräten mit dem grob zerkleinerten Gemüse in einem Topf im Öl von allen Seiten anbraten. Mit dem Wein ablöschen, die Flüssigkeit einkochen. Die Gemüsebrühe zugießen, auf die halbe Menge einkochen, dann den Fond durch ein feines Sieb passieren. Mit einem Schneebesen die kalte Butter unterrühren, mit Salz und Pfeffer abschmecken.

Die Waldpilze sorgfältig putzen, wenn nötig die Stiele schälen. In Scheiben schneiden, in Olivenöl braten, bis sie beginnen, Farbe anzunehmen. Mit Salz und Pfeffer leicht würzen, mit den Schnittlauchröllchen vermischen.

Ofen auf 200° C vorheizen. Weißbrotscheiben mit Olivenöl bepinseln, im Ofen goldbraun rösten. Lebern in heißem Öl von allen Seiten kurz anbraten und auf die gerösteten Brotscheiben legen.

Fischfilets mit Salz und Pfeffer würzen. In der Pfanne bei großer Hitze im heißen Erdnussöl von beiden Seiten leicht bräunen.

Zum Servieren: Rotbarbenfilets auf vorgewärmte Teller anrichten, mit Leber-Toastschnitten und Waldpilzen garnieren. Zum Schluss die Rotweinsauce zugießen und servieren.

Anmerkung: Damit der volle Geschmack dieses Gerichtes richtig zur Geltung kommt, ist es besonders wichtig, dass die einzelnen Bestandteile des Rezeptes à la minute zubereitet werden, d.h. direkt vor dem Auftragen.

DUCK FOIE GRAS IN A SALT CRUST
WITH BAKED APPLE

ENTENSTOPFLEBER IM SALZTEIG
MIT GESCHMORTEM APFEL

Serves 4

For the sauce:
120 ml/¹/₂ cup sherry,
120 ml/¹/₂ cup brown duck stock,
2 tbsp cold butter,
salt, freshly ground black pepper

4 apples

For the liver:
1 duck foie gras of about 500 g/1 lb,
1 kg/2 lbs coarse salt,
4 egg whites,
1 tbsp dried mixed herbs: thyme, rosemary,
sage and bay,
1 tbsp peppercorns, coarsely crushed

For the sauce: In a small pot, reduce sherry by half. Add duck stock, bring it to a boil, then whisk in cold butter, one piece at a time, with a wire whip. Season to taste with salt and pepper and strain the sauce through a fine sieve.
Preheat the oven to 220° C/430° F (convection heat if possible). Wrap the apples tightly in aluminum foil. Place them onto a rack and bake them in the hot oven for forty-five minutes.
For the liver: Mix coarse salt with herbs and pepper, then add egg whites and mix well with your hands. Take two thirds of the dough to make a bed for the liver on a baking sheet. Place liver on top and cover tightly with the remaining salt. Press down with your hands to make an even, intact crust. Bake in a 220° C/430° F oven for seventeen minutes.
Serving: Cut a lid off the hardened salt dough. Carefully lift out liver, scraping off any remaining salt with the back of a knife. Cut the liver into slices. Arrange slices on plates, add a baked apple to each plate and surround with sauce.

Für 4 Personen:

Für die Sauce:
120 ml Sherry,
120 ml brauner Entenfond,
2 EL kalte Butter,
Salz, schwarzer Pfeffer aus der Mühle

4 Äpfel

Für die Leber:
1 Entenstopfleber von 500 g,
1 kg grobes Salz,
1 EL getrocknete gemischte Kräuter: Thymian,
Rosmarin, Salbei und Lorbeer,
1 EL Pfefferkörner, grob zerdrückt,
4 Eiweiß

Für die Sauce: In einem Topf den Sherry auf die halbe Menge einkochen. Entenfond zugeben, zum Kochen bringen, die kalte Butter stückweise mit dem Schneebesen unterrühren. Mit Salz und Pfeffer abschmecken, Sauce durch ein feines Sieb passieren.
Den Heißluftofen auf 220° C vorheizen. Die Äpfel rundum dicht in Alufolie wickeln. Auf ein Gitter legen, im heißen Ofen 45 Minuten backen.
Für die Leber: Das grobe Salz mit Kräutern und Pfeffer vermischen, Eiweiß hinzufügen und mit den Händen gut vermengen. Aus gut zwei Dritteln des Teigs ein Bett für die Leber auf einem Blech formen. Die Leber hineinlegen, mit dem restlichen Salzteig bedecken. Den Teig gleichmäßig leicht festdrücken. Im 220° C heißen Ofen 17 Minuten garen.
Zum Servieren: Aus dem hart gebackenen Salzteig einen großen Deckel schneiden und abheben. Die Leber vorsichtig herausheben, Salzrückstände mit einem Messerrücken abstreifen, die Leber in Scheiben schneiden. Mit je einem geschmorten Apfel auf Teller anrichten, mit der Sauce umgießen.

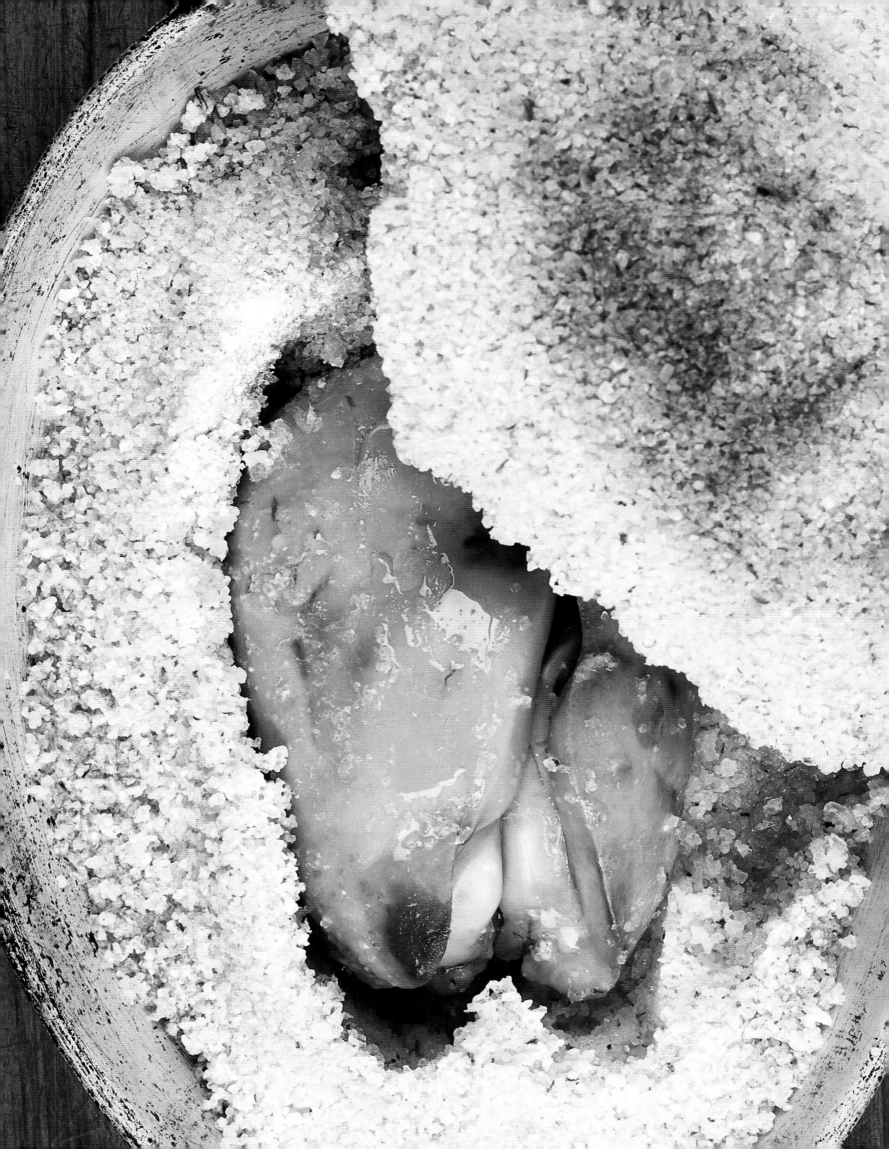

VEAL CHOP WITH SPRING MUSHROOMS

KALBSKOTELETT MIT FRÜHLINGSPILZEN

Serves 4

For the mushrooms:
120 g/4 oz baby morels,
120 g/4 oz baby chanterelles,
120 g/4 oz small porcini,
1 shallot, finely minced,
3 tbsp butter,
salt, freshly ground black pepper,
1 tsp chives, minced

4 thick veal chops, 250 g/¹/₂ lb each,
bones neatly trimmed,
salt, freshly ground black pepper,
a pinch of nutmeg,
4 tbsp olive oil,
2 tbsp butter

For the sauce:
250 ml/1 cup brown veal stock,
2 tbsp cold butter

For the mushrooms: Clean and trim the mushrooms carefully with a knife and cut them into even pieces. Melt butter in a small saucepan and sauté shallot until translucent. Add mushrooms and sauté on medium heat for five minutes, stirring constantly. Add salt and pepper to taste and stir in chives. Fill mushrooms into round molds or other molds according to taste, pressing them down slightly.
Preheat oven to 210° C/410° F. Tie veal chops into desired form. Rub on all sides with salt, pepper and a pinch of nutmeg. In a shallow, heavy-bottomed casserole, heat olive oil and butter until very hot. Sear veal chops on both sides, then place casserole into the oven for 10 - 15 minutes, depending on the thickness of the chops. Remove from casserole and allow chops to rest for ten minutes in a warm place.
Degrease the pan juices in the casserole. Add veal stock, scraping up brown bits from the bottom of the pan, and boil hard for five minutes. Season to taste with salt, pepper and nutmeg, then whisk in the cold butter one piece at a time and strain the sauce through a sieve.
Serving: Unmold mushrooms onto plates. Cut the veal chops open and arrange them next to the mushrooms. Surround with sauce and serve.

Für 4 Personen:

Für die Pilze:
120 g frische Morcheln,
120 g junge Pfifferlinge,
120 g kleine Steinpilze,
1 Schalotte, fein geschnitten,
3 EL Butter,
Salz, schwarzer Pfeffer aus der Mühle,
1 TL fein geschnittener Schnittlauch

4 dicke Kalbskoteletts à 250 g,
die Knochen sauber geputzt,
Salz, schwarzer Pfeffer aus der Mühle,
1 Prise Muskat,
4 EL Olivenöl,
2 EL Butter

Für die Sauce:
250 ml brauner Kalbsfond,
2 EL kalte Butter

Für die Pilze: Die Pilze mit dem Messer sorgfältig putzen und in gleichmäßige Stücke schneiden. In einem Topf die Schalotte in Butter glasig dünsten. Pilze zugeben, unter Rühren bei mittlerer Hitze fünf Minuten braten. Mit Salz und Pfeffer würzen, zum Schluss Schnittlauch unterrühren. Nach Belieben die Pilze in runde Formen füllen, etwas anpressen.
Ofen auf 210° C vorheizen. Die Kalbskoteletts nach Belieben in Form binden. Mit Salz, Pfeffer und einer Prise Muskat rundum würzen. In einem flachen Bräter das Olivenöl mit der Butter erhitzen. Die Koteletts von beiden Seiten heiß anbraten, anschließend den Bräter, je nach Dicke des Fleisches, 10 - 15 Minuten in den heißen Ofen schieben. Die Koteletts aus dem Bräter nehmen und 10 Minuten mit Folie bedeckt an der Wärme ruhen lassen.
Den Bräter entfetten. Bratsatz mit dem Kalbsfond lösen, 5 Minuten kochen lassen. Mit Salz, Pfeffer und Muskat abschmecken, mit einem Schneebesen die kalte Butter unterrühren und die Sauce durch ein Sieb passieren.
Zum Servieren: Die Pilze aus den Formen auf vorgewärmte Teller stürzen. Die Koteletts einmal aufschneiden und daneben legen. Mit Sauce umgießen und servieren.

VALENCIA ORANGES WITH ANISE

VALENCIA-ORANGEN MIT ANIS

Serves 4

4 large, fleshy oranges
(Valencia type, if possible),
1 tsp star anise,
8 tbsp sugar, 250 ml/1 cup water

For the Bavarian cream:
250 ml/1 cup freshly squeezed orange juice,
250 ml/1 cup cream, whipped into stiff peaks,
6 egg yolks, 90 g/3 oz sugar,
2 tsp star anise,
6 sheets gelatin

For the puff pastries:
100 g/3 1/2 oz puff pastry, 1 tbsp clarified butter

Garnish:
2 strawberries,
4 small sprigs of mint,
confectioners' sugar

Peel the oranges with a very sharp knife all the way down to the flesh. Remove segments from their compartments and place them into a bowl. Combine water, sugar and anise and bring the mixture to a boil in a small pot. Remove pot from heat, allow syrup to cool and strain it through a sieve onto the orange segments. Toss. Keep refrigerated.
For the Bavarian cream: Combine orange juice and star anise and heat to just below the boiling point. Allow to cool a little. Pre-soak gelatin in cold water, add it to the juice and stir until dissolved. Strain the juice through a sieve. Allow to cool completely. Beat egg yolks and sugar in a large bowl until fluffy. Mix in orange juice, then fold in soft-whipped cream. Pour cream into small round molds and place them in the refrigerator for about two hours, until set.
Cut the puff pastry into four equal pieces and roll out the pieces as thinly as possible. Brush with clarified butter and place them onto a baking sheet lined with baking paper. Cover puff pastries with another sheet of baking paper and weight it down with another baking sheet. Bake in a pre-heated hot oven for 10 - 12 minutes, until golden brown. Carefully remove baking paper from the pastries and set them on a rack to cool.
Serving: Arrange marinated orange filets onto plates in a fan shape. Unmold a Bavarian cream onto each plate (dip forms into hot water for a few seconds), and drizzle syrupy marinade onto the orange filets. Garnish with crisp puff pastries, strawberry halves and sprigs of mint dusted with confectioners' sugar.

Für 4 Personen:

4 große, fleischige Orangen
(nach Möglichkeit Sorte Valencia),
1 TL Sternanissamen,
8 EL Zucker, 250 ml Wasser

Für die Bavaroise:
250 ml frisch gepresster Orangensaft,
250 ml halbsteif geschlagene Sahne,
6 Eigelb, 90 g Zucker,
2 TL Sternanissamen,
6 Blatt Gelatine

Für die Teigblätter:
100 g Blätterteig, 1 EL geklärte Butter

Garnitur:
2 Erdbeeren,
4 kleine Minzezweige,
Puderzucker

Die Orangen mit dem Messer bis aufs Fleisch schälen, mit einem kleinen scharfen Messer die Filets herausschneiden und in eine Schüssel geben. Das Wasser mit Zucker und Anissamen in einem Topf zum Kochen bringen. Topf vom Herd ziehen, Sirup erkalten lassen, durch ein Sieb auf die Orangenfilets passieren. Kühl stellen.
Für die Bavaroise: Orangensaft mit Sternanissamen bis kurz vor den Siedepunkt erhitzen. Etwas abkühlen lassen, die zuvor in kaltem Wasser eingeweichte Gelatine darin auflösen und den Saft durch ein Sieb passieren. Auskühlen lassen. Eigelb in einer Schüssel mit dem Zucker schaumig rühren. Mit dem Orangensaft vermischen, zum Schluss die halbfest geschlagene Sahne unterziehen. Die Creme in runde Förmchen füllen, im Kühlschrank ca. 2 Stunden fest werden lassen.
Blätterteig in vier Stücke teilen und möglichst dünn ausrollen. Mit geklärter Butter bepinseln, auf ein mit Backtrennpapier ausgelegtes Blech legen. Ein zweites Stück Papier und ein Blech zum Beschweren darüber legen. Im vorgeheizten Ofen 10 - 12 Minuten goldbraun backen. Die Teigblätter vorsichtig vom Papier lösen, auf einem Gitter erkalten lassen.
Zum Servieren: Die marinierten Orangenfilets fächerförmig im Kreis auf Teller auslegen. Je eine Bavaroise darauf stürzen (zuvor die Formen kurz in heißes Wasser tauchen), die Orangenfilets mit Marinadensirup übergießen. Mit knusprig gebackenen Teigblättern, halbierten Erdbeeren und mit Puderzucker bestäubten Minzezweigen garnieren.

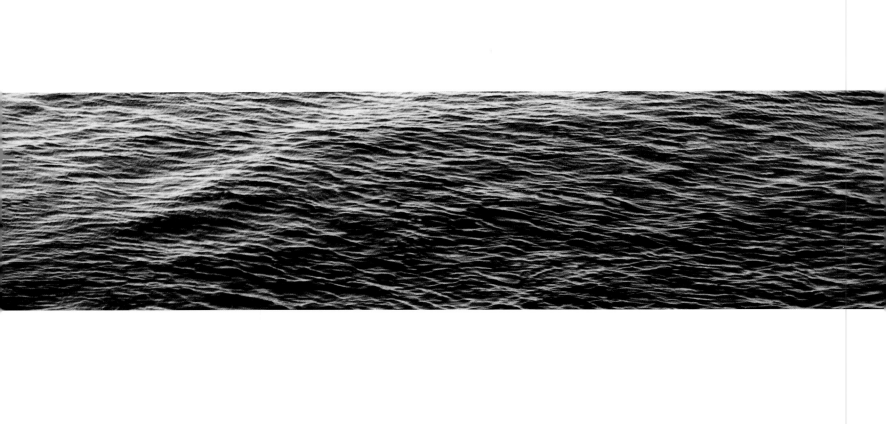

San Sebastián

Donostia

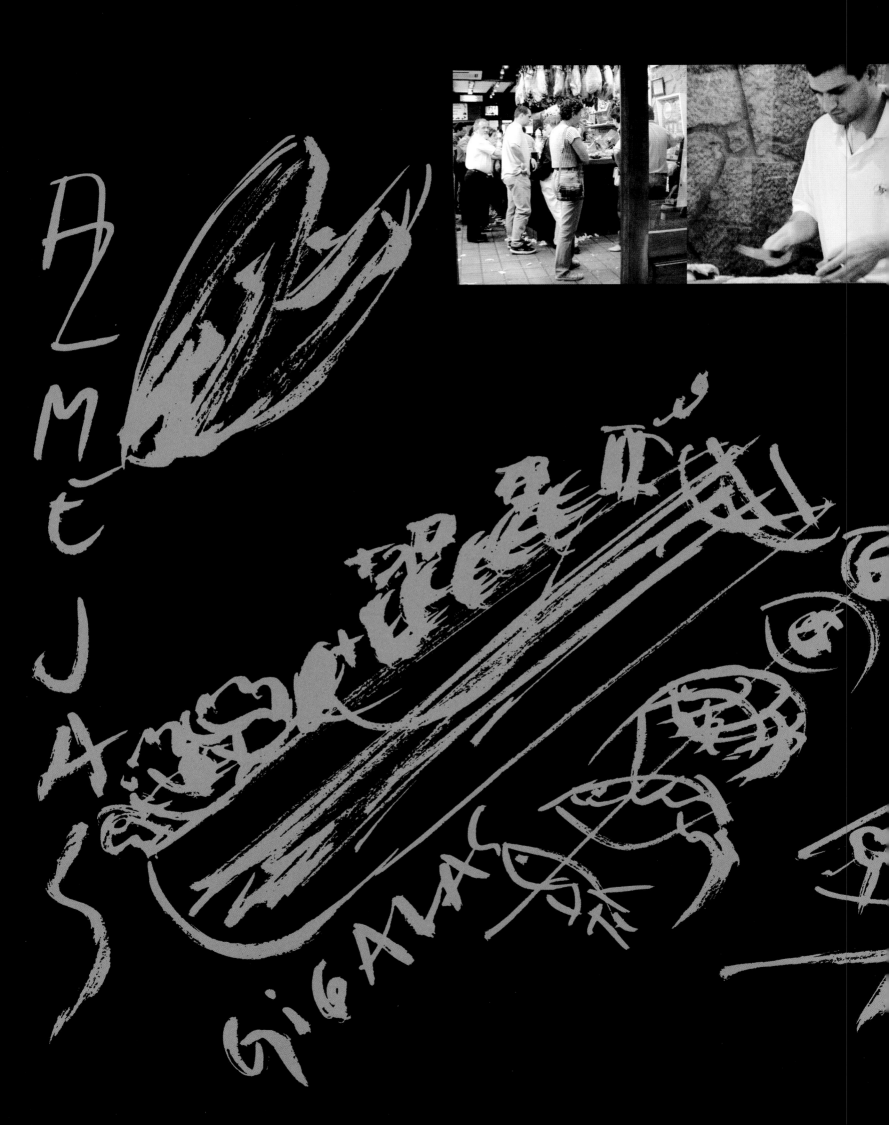

Juan-Mari Arzak

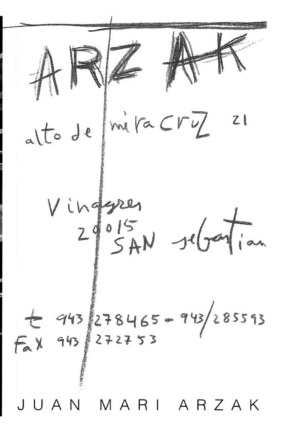

ARZAK

alto de mira cruz 21

Vinagres
2 0015
SAN sebastian

t 943 278465 - 943/285593
Fax 943 272753

JUAN MARI ARZAK

Here in Spain, the clocks tick differently. He who intends to take lunch will hardly ever do so before one thirty if he is a local, a real Spaniard, and those who have more staying power appear at three. If you happen to turn up at the restaurant's door at an earlier time you definitely have given yourself away as a foreigner, but fortunately, you are not turned away. Everything is ready. The kitchen is bustling, the telephone is ringing constantly. "A table for tonight? Sorry, we are all booked out. Tomorrow, if you like." The foyer of the "Arzak" is just as busy. Juan-Mari Arzak's cooking attract gourmets from near and far. Even cultural travelers are advised to complement their visit at the Bilbao Guggenheim by enjoying a menu at Arzak's in San Sebastián. A high bar counter made of solid wood holds several well-chilled bottles of cava in an ice cube-filled silver tray. First guests are arriving. Outside, the city of San Sebastián is visibly and audibly encroaching on the formerly sleepy little village of Alza, where Arzak's grandparents used to pour wine and serve good old country-style cooking at the very same place a hundred years ago. Traffic in the direction of France is roaring by the building. The red brick façade has withstood this permanent acoustic attack quite stoically, and the small door to the inside of the culinary oasis gives way only reluctantly. At the bar, you first take a deep breath, then your first apéritif. The dining room exudes peace and quiet. The room is bathed in a diffuse sunlight filtering through panes of milky glass and linen pelmets. The interior is kept in a subdued and traditional style, oil paintings adorn the walls. The background is dominated by an imposing buffet, a staircase leads up to the next floor, which holds the greater part of the seventy restaurant seats.

The matadors of the so-called "Nova Cocina Vasca" are no longer the youngest, but their culinary art is as lively and fresh as in the first days when the cuisine of the Iberian peninsula, not far from the Pyrenées, woke up from its beauty sleep. Juan-Mari Arzak was one of the princes who kissed awake Spanish, or shall we say Basque, cuisine more than twenty years ago. Since then, much water has run in and out of the bay of San Sebastián, and now a whole flock of young, ambitious chefs are following in his footsteps. Elena Arzak is one of them. Papa Juan-Mari is in Mexico City for a few days, advising some friends in their

Elena Arzak

restaurant. Meanwhile, Elena is shouldering the whole burden with ease and charm. Things are going well. The young chef with Swiss training has been in the kitchen with her father for more than ten years. To her, he has passed on the knowledge that catapulted him into the upper echelons of the cooking league, in reach of the much coveted three stars. Stations in the kitchen foremost of French star chefs (Troisgros, Gagnaire) have provided the finish and the tools which she can now wield quite independently. At the El Bulli of Ferran Adrià's, a friend of the family's, she has risked a glance into the avant-garde pots of Spanish cooking, but, if anything, her ideal is her father Juan-Mari. Father and daughter – invincible together. They don't compete, they work together like friends and colleagues. "My father has always granted me great liberties", recounts the thirty-one year old chef, "and when I told him I wanted to work in his kitchen he just said yes." Both are responsible for the day's business. With respect to the development of new recipes, however, they operate independently from each other, each with his own assistant. The result is then compared, modified, no longer pursued if that is the mutual decision, or approved of and put onto the menu. The third in the trio is the chef de cuisine Pello Aramburu, who, with unshakable calm and a gift for the grand overview holds the threads of the hustle and bustle of the many-cornered kitchen in his hands. In the early morning, the three can be seen at fish market booths composing their menu of the day, selecting what seems to be fit for their kitchen. For them, it's an almost daily routine in San Sebastián's old quarter Casco Viejo. Fish, crustaceans and vegetables are ordered. Many small farmers bring their carrots or pota-

Pello Aramburu

toes directly to the restaurant, mushroom gatherers present their baskets from the mountains. Thus, the menu is reconsidered every day, adjusted to respective purchases and – with the help of the computer – printed anew. Classicism, regional traditions or modernism? The "Arzak" succeeds in keeping a balance between all three. The dishes, in their unspoilt originality deeply rooted in traditional Basque cooking, are altered in the direction of a modern and light cuisine, inspired by optical presentation. Many dishes possess quite a bit of poetry and wit. A "spring image" (imagen de primavera) aligns obligatory items from the season: a strip of green peas, shaved asparagus and mushrooms each together with slices of green fava beans. In a dish called "chipirones cambiantes", black squid ink ravioli are doused with broth at the table, and the black outside miraculously disappears and leaves a yellow pumpkin package. Yet, the chef is not after cheap effects. At the "Arzak", the focus is on taste and flavors and natural products, freed from the superfluous ballast of old cooking traditions. New techniques are always in demand, and they may be foreign, too – if it helps the result. The Chinese wok, for example, may well find its uses, but lemongrass, well, we'd rather leave that out. Nobody would understand that in a Basque context.

Tradition is perpetuated with a light hand. Thus, elements of traditional recipes may change their usual state of appearance: garlic becomes garlic purée, parsley leaves turn into a highly concentrated essence drizzled loosely around the protagonist on the plate. Well-known flavors and tastes are not piously conserved, but pepped up with verve and served in new contexts. It is both for they eye and the palate – textures and forms start playing a new melody which holds us in its spell.

Ladies to the front. The service is ready, the apron strings of the twelve waitresses are tied, it is one o´clock in the afternoon. The first guests are arriving. In the narrow, crowded kitchen, everyone takes his place. Ingredients are placed within reach. Elena Arzak with her hearty laugh is omnipresent all of the time – in the kitchen as well as the dining-room, where she comes to the table herself to take orders. In her white chef´s outfit, she gives recommendations and explains the menu. The kitchen is starting to buzz, it is teamwork that counts now. More than one pair of hands work on one plate with sea perch, the plate is dotted with black drops of caramelized leek sauce, one chef is piping leek mousse onto the filet, and Elena provides a glistening lacquer with an oiled brush. Others divide paper-thin, crispy fried skin of squab into rectangles, one chef plucks off mint leaves with his fingertips. Everything is running smoothly – despite of the high speed level – quite unhurriedly and with the precision of a clock. The kitchen keeps busy (with less and less personnel) until almost evening, until the last table has paid its bill. There is little time to rest, around nine, when evening guests will start to arrive, the whole routine will start again. It will probably be foreigners. Spaniards are expected at the earliest at ten or half past ten.

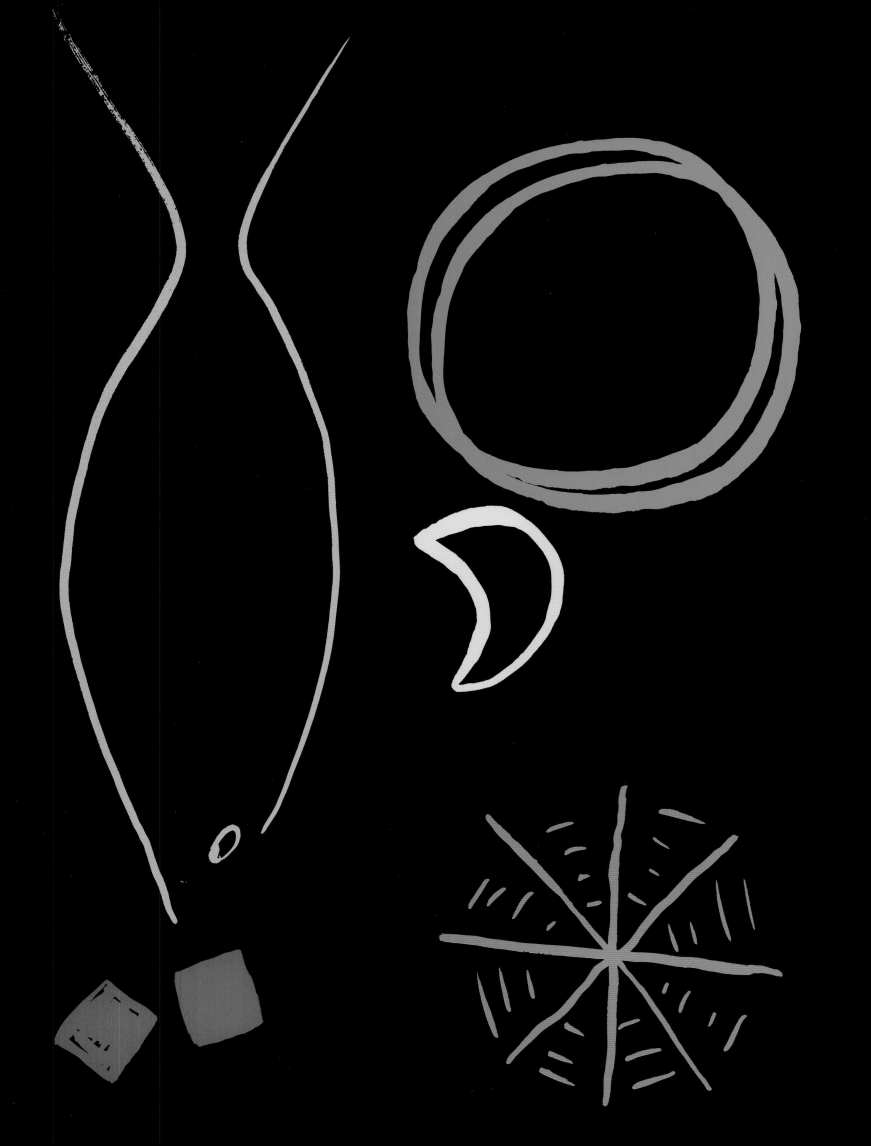

Hier gehen die Uhren anders. Wer zum mittäglichen Mahle strebt, wird als Einheimischer, als echter Spanier dies kaum vor ein Uhr dreißig mittags tun. Und wer es noch länger aushält, erscheint erst gegen drei. Begehrt man zu früherem Zeitpunkt im Lokal Einlass, ist man eindeutig als Ausländer entlarvt, wird jedoch gleichwohl nicht von der Tür gewiesen. Denn alles steht schon parat. Die Küche vibriert und das Telefon klingelt unaufhörlich. „Ein Tisch für heute Abend? Tut uns leid, schon alles ausgebucht. Aber morgen gern." Im Entreé des „Arzak" geht es rund. Zu Juan-Mari Arzaks Töpfen eilen Gourmets von nah und fern. Auch Kulturreisenden sei angeraten, ihren Besuch des Guggenheim Museums in Bilbao durch ein Menü bei Arzak in San Sebastián genussvoll zu ergänzen. Ein hoher Bartresen aus gediegenem Holz trägt in eiswürfelgefüllter Silberschale mehrere gut gekühlte Flaschen Cava. Zur Türe tröpfeln die ersten Gäste herein. Draußen hat unüberhörbar und unübersehbar die Stadt San Sebastián ihre Tentakel ausgestreckt und sich das ehemals kleine verschlafene Dorf Alza einverleibt, wo an gleichem Platze noch vor hundert Jahren Arzaks Großeltern Wein ausschenkten und rustikale Hausmannskost servierten. Dröhnend braust heute der Verkehr in Richtung Frankreich am Gebäude vorbei. Die rote Backsteinfassade trotzt stoisch diesem akustischen Dauerangriff und öffnet nur widerwillig die kleine Tür ins Innere der Feinschmecker-Oase. An der kleinen Bar atmet man erst mal durch und nimmt einen ersten Aperitif. Im Speisesaal herrscht beschauliche Ruhe. Der Raum dämmert im diffusen Sonnenlicht, das weich gefiltert durch Milchglas und Leinenschabracken ins Innere fließt. Die Einrichtung, gutbürgerlich und gediegen, Öl an den Wänden. Ein ausladender Büffetschrank dominiert den Hintergrund, eine Treppe schwingt sich hinauf zum nächsten Geschoss, wo sich der Großteil der siebzig Restaurantplätze befindet.

Die Matadore der „Nueva Cocina Vasca" sind auch nicht mehr die Jüngsten, doch ihre Kochkunst ist noch so lebendig und frisch wie in den ersten Tagen, als die Küche der Iberischen Halbinsel, unweit des Pyrenäenzugs, aus dem Dämmerschlaf erwachte. Juan-Mari Arzak ist einer der Prinzen, die damals Spaniens, oder genauer die baskische Küche wachgeküsst hatten. Das ist nun schon über zwanzig Jahre her. Seitdem ist viel Wasser in San Sebastiáns Bucht geschwappt, und eine ganze Schar junger ehrgeiziger Köche eifern ihm nach. Elena Arzak ist eine davon. Papa Juan-Mari weilt derzeit ein paar Tage in Mexiko City, wo er beratend dem Restaurant von Freunden zur Seite steht. Elena schultert allein die Bürde mit Charme und Leichtigkeit, und der Laden läuft. Schon bald zehn Jahre steht die in der Schweiz ausgebildete Köchin mit dem Vater in der Küche. Bei ihm hat sie sich die Kenntnisse erworben, die ihn in die Oberliga der kochenden Zunft, zu den begehrten drei Sternen befördert hatten. Gastspiele in den Küchen vor allem französischer Stars (Troisgros, Gagnaire) haben der energischen jungen Frau dann Feinschliff und das Rüstzeug verpasst, mit dem sie nun ganz eigenständig weit vorne mithalten kann. Beim befreundeten Ferran Adrià (El Bulli, Roses) riskiert sie einen Blick auf die Avantgarde spanischer Kochkunst, aber, wenn überhaupt, dann ist Juan-Mari ihr Vorbild. Vater und Tochter – ein unschlagbares Team. Konkurrenzen gibt es keine, man arbeitet kollegial und freundschaftlich zusammen. „Mein Vater hat mir schon immer große Freiheit gelassen," erzählt die Einunddreißigjährige, „und er sagte einfach ja, als ich zu ihm in die Küche kommen wollte." Beide sind zuständig für das Tagesgeschäft. Und für die Weiterentwicklung der Rezepte operieren sie unabhängig voneinander mit dem eigenen Assistenten. Das Ergebnis wird dann verglichen, modifiziert, in beiderseitigem Verständnis nicht weiterverfolgt oder für gut befunden – und schließlich auf die Speisekarte gesetzt. Der Dritte im Dreigestirn ist Küchenchef

Pello Aramburu, der recht unaufgeregt und mit großer Übersicht die Fäden im Trubel der verwinkelten Küche in der Hand behält. Frühmorgens streifen die Drei durch die Stände des Fischmarkts und stellen das Tagesmenü zusammen, lassen einpacken, was ihnen für die Küche tauglich erscheint. Das ist für sie fast tägliche Routine in San Sebastiáns altem Quartier Casco Viejo. Fische, Krustentiere, und Gemüse werden geordert. Ins Restaurant direkt aber liefern viele kleine Bauern, bringen ihre Möhren oder Kartoffeln, und Sammler kommen mit dem Pilzkörbchen aus den Bergen. Die Speisekarte wird folglich täglich neu gesichtet und – dem Computer sei Dank – den Einkäufen angepasst und neu ausgedruckt.

Klassik, regionale Tradition oder Moderne? Im „Arzak" gelingt der Balanceakt zwischen allen dreien. Die Gerichte, in ihrer urtümlichen Eigenart zutiefst der traditionellen baskischen Küche verpflichtet, erfahren hier eine Mutation, die auf dem Teller von einer modernen und leichten, wie auch von optischen Ideen bestimmten Konzeption erzählen. Die Gerichte besitzen auch Poesie und Witz. Ein „Frühlingsbild" (Imagen de Primavera) liiert Versatzstücke dieser Jahreszeit: je ein Streifen grüne Erbsen, Spargelspäne, Pilze sowie Scheibchen von Dicken Bohnen. Über die „Chipirones Cambiantes" wird erst am Tisch Brühe auf tintenfischschwarze Ravioli gegossen, und wundersamerweise verschwindet die schwarze Hülle und gibt ein gelbes Kürbispäckchen frei. Aber niemand will hier billige Effekthascherei betreiben. Im „Arzak" geht es vorwiegend um Geschmack und Aromen und um die Natürlichkeit der Produkte, vom überflüssigen Ballast alter Kochweisen befreit. Neue Techniken kommen da immer zupass, und die dürfen auch fremdartig sein – sofern es der Sache dienlich ist. So könnte möglicherweise der chinesische Wok zum Einsatz kommen, aber Zitronengras – das lassen wir lieber beiseite, das würde im baskischen Kontext wohl niemand verstehen. Die Tradition wird mit leichtem Kochlöffel hochgehalten. So verändern Elemente überlieferter Rezepte ihren herkömmlichen Aggregatzustand. Knoblauchwürze wird zum Püree, und Petersilienblätter zu hochkonzentrierter Essenz, die locker um den Hauptdarsteller herumgeträufelt wird. Die bekannten Aromen und Geschmacksnoten werden nicht andächtig konserviert sondern frech aufgepeppt und in neue Zusammenhänge gebracht. Es ist was für Auge und Gaumen, Texturen und Formen spielen eine neue Melodie – und schon wird's spannend.

Ladies an die Front. Der Service steht bereit, die Schürzen der zwölf Saaldamen sind gebunden, es ist ein Uhr mittags. Die ersten Gäste werden erwartet. In der gedrängten Enge der Küche begeben sich alle auf ihre Startplätze. Zutaten werden griffbereit platziert, mis en place. Elena Arzak, die gerne und herzlich lacht, ist ständig und überall präsent. In der Küche wie im Saal, wo sie selbst zum Tisch kommt, um die Bestellung aufzunehmen. Im weißen Koch-Outfit gibt sie ihre Empfehlungen und erläutert die Speisenfolge. In der Küche wird es nun lebhafter. Teamarbeit ist angesagt. Gleich mehrere Hände arbeiten gemeinsam an einem Teller mit Seebarsch, schwarze Tropfen von gebrannter Lauchsauce werden aufgesetzt, eine Köchin spritzt Lauchmus über das Filet, und Elena gibt mit eingeöltem Pinsel dem Ganzen das glänzende Finish. Wieder andere teilen hauchdünne, knusprig gegarte Taubenhaut in Rechtecke, ein Koch zupft mit spitzen Fingern Minzeblättchen zurecht. Aber alles läuft – trotz großer Geschwindigkeit – unaufgeregt und mit der Präzision eines Uhrwerks ab. Die Küche brummt noch (in abnehmender Besetzung) fast bis zum Abend, bis auch der letzte Tisch bezahlt hat. Wenig Zeit zum Verschnaufen, denn etwa ab neun geht der Tanz wieder los. Dann kommen die ersten Abendgäste – wahrscheinlich Zugereiste. Die Spanier werden erst ab zehn, halb elf erwartet.

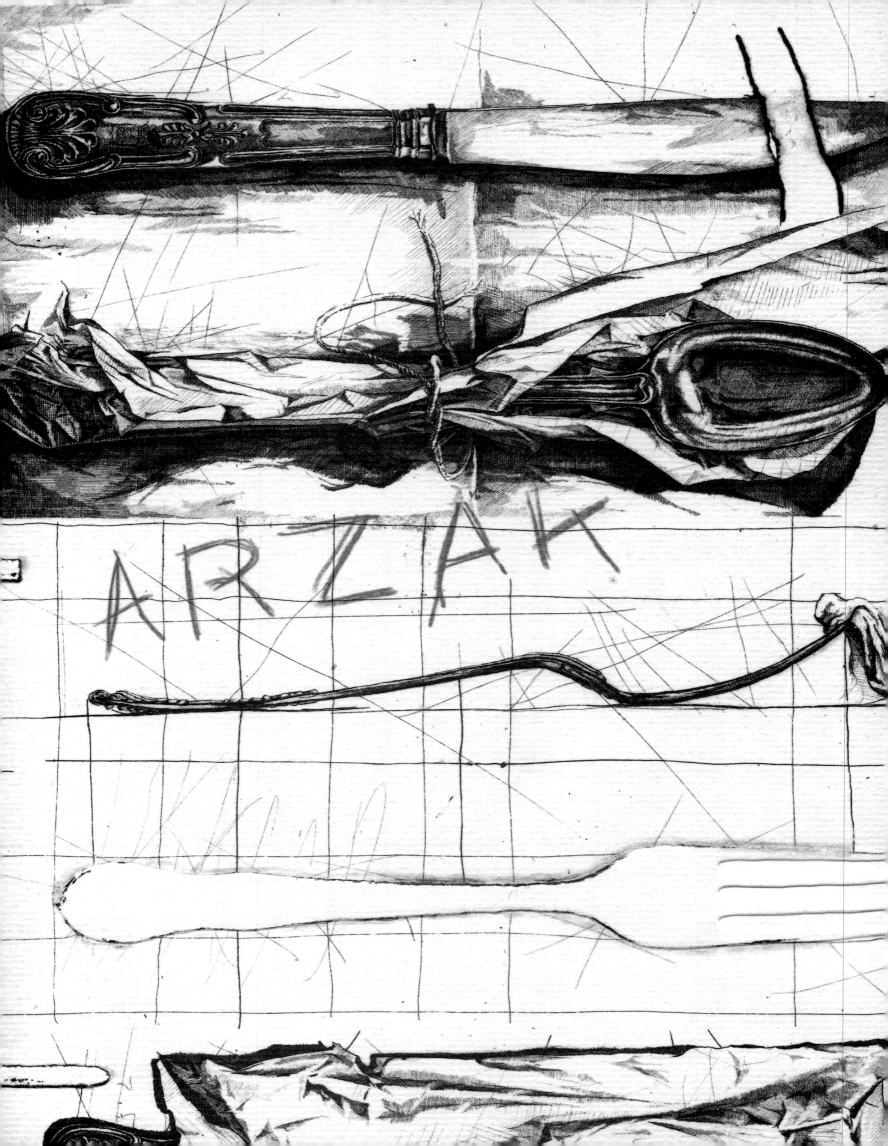

The amuse-gueules at Arzak are not only palate-pleasers in the most literal sense but also an unforgettable experience for the eyes – true culinary works of art.

Die, in der deutschen Sprache leider unzureichend und etwas lieblos „Appetithäppchen" genannten Amuse-Gueules, die bei Arzak das Menü einleiten, sind wahre Kunstwerke: fürs Auge schön anzuschauen, im Gaumen ein unvergessliches Geschmackserlebnis.

LEEKS STUFFED WITH BLOOD PUDDING IN A PEPPER SAUCE
LAUCH MIT BLUTWURSTFÜLLUNG UND PAPRIKASAUCE

COLD LEEK SOUP WITH CARPET CLAMS
KALTE LAUCHSUPPE MIT TEPPICHMUSCHELN

NETTED FISH ROLL IN A RED BEET VINAIGRETTE
FISCH-NETZWURST MIT ROTE BETE-VINAIGRETTE

TAPIOCA CRACKERS WITH POTATO TORTILLAS (PAGE 98)
TAPIOKA-KRÄCKER MIT KARTOFFEL-TORTILLAS (SEITE 98)

MARINATED SARDINE FILETS WITH A FISH MOUSSE (PAGE 99)
MARINIERTE SARDINENFILETS MIT FISCHMOUSSE (SEITE 99)

13 de mayo 2000

Caldo de txipirones cambiante 3.800

Foie con tallos de esparragos, yogur y orejones 3.950

Foie frío con uvas blancas y reducción de mosto 4.300

Cigalas rebozadas con maíz y piperrada 3.900

Ensalada de carabineros con hierbas silvestres y laminas de arroz 3.800

Buñuelos de frutos de mar con melaza y boniato 3.800

Flor de huevo y tartufo en grasa de oca con txistorra de dátiles 3.900

Los productos de temporada en cuatro lineas -

(esparragos, habas, guisantes, y xixas 3.950

Espárragos frescos, blancos y verdes con trigueros salteados 3.800

Guisantes, habas y patatitas del pais (plato tradicional) 3.800

Sopa ligera de alubias, sobre yema, jugo de trufa y berza seca 3.300

Pescado del día con ceniza de puerro 4.950

Lenguado en su jugo con pistachos verdes, infusiones y confitados 4.950

Rape con torreznos y espuma suave de especias 4.950

Kokotxas de merluza al pil - pil 5.600

Merluza con emulsión de algas,y hierbas de primavera 4.950

Lomo de merluza en salsa verde con almejas 4.950

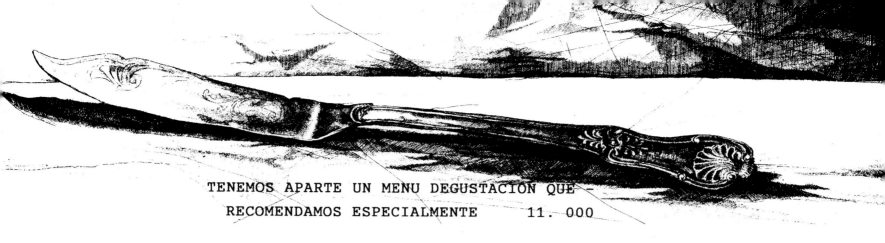

TENEMOS APARTE UN MENU DEGUSTACIÓN QUE -
RECOMENDAMOS ESPECIALMENTE   11. 000

Foie caliente con sal de orégano y bizcocho de frutas 5.500
Lacado de pichón 5.200
Cordero asado y untado con caña de azucar, mostaza y vermut 5.200
Guiso de ternera con porrusalda y patatas dulces 3.990
Chuleta de buey a la brasa (ración) 3.500
Chuleta troceada con garbanzos fritos y cristales de sal 4.850

- POSTRES QUE DEBEN SER ENCARGADOS AL PRINCIPIO DE LA COMIDA -

Sopa de chufas con pan de frutas 1.990
Arroz con leche inflado con sorbete de avellana y tamarindo 1.990
Burbujas rápidas de champán con leche quemada y un postre de siempre 1.990
Poso de cacao con badiana y pilé de limón 1.990
Chocolate ahumado envuelto en crema 1.990
Canutillos de membrillo y queso con helado de zanahoria y aceite de nuez 1.990
Crujiente de frambuesas y salsa de melocotón seco 1.990

- POSTRES QUE SE PUEDEN ENCARGAR AL MOMENTO -

Plato de quesos seleccionados 1.990
Helado de queso blanco sobre crema de grosella 1.990

IVA.7%

Salones privados almuerzos - cenas (4 - 60 personas)

EGG FLOWER WITH TRUFFLE OIL AND DUCK FAT SERVED WITH A DATE-CHORIZO CREAM

EIERBLUME MIT TRÜFFELÖL UND ENTENSCHMALZ UND DATTEL-CHORIZO-CREME

Serves 4

For the chorizo breadcrumbs:
20 g/³/₄ oz chorizo (Spanish paprika-garlic sausage), very finely diced,
16 g/¹/₂ oz lean bacon (dry-cured), very finely diced,
¹/₄ tsp garlic, minced,
100 g/3¹/₂ oz breadcrumbs, freshly grated,
3 tbsp truffle juice, 3 tbsp water

For the grape vinaigrette:
50 g/1¹/₂ oz white grapes, finely chopped,
30 g/1 oz blue grapes, finely chopped,
100 ml/¹/₃ cup olive oil,
30 ml/¹/₈ cup rice wine vinegar,
a pinch of parsley, finely chopped, a pinch of ground ginger,
1 tsp chives, very finely minced,
salt, freshly ground white pepper

For the date-chorizo cream:
120 g/4 oz dates, pitted,
150 g/5 oz chorizo (see above), peeled and chopped,
100 ml/¹/₃ cup water, a pinch of ground ginger

For the mushrooms:
100 g/3¹/₂ oz mushroom caps, 1 tbsp butter, salt

For the eggs:
4 eggs, truffle oil and liquid duck fat for drizzling,
salt, 1 egg yolk, 1 tsp olive oil, a pinch of salt

For the chorizo breadcrumbs: Fry chorizo, breadcrumbs and garlic in a small frying pan until golden brown, stirring constantly. Douse with truffle juice and water and allow to dry on low heat for about twenty minutes. Keep stirring. Set aside.
For the grape vinaigrette: Combine all ingredients in a small bowl and allow to marinade.
For the date-chorizo cream: Combine all ingredients in a blender and mix until you have a fine purée. Scrape mixture into a small saucepan. Reheat on low heat, stirring constantly, just before you are ready to serve.
For the mushroom caps: Finely chop caps. Melt butter in a small pan and sauté mushrooms on low heat until tender. Add a little salt.
For the eggs: Brush 4 large pieces of heat-proof foil with a little oil and line individual serving bowls with them. Crack eggs open separately and slide one egg into each lined bowl. Drizzle with 6 drops of truffle oil and 3 drops of duck fat and sprinkle with a little salt. Fold over edges of the foil and tie them into a knot. Place pouches into boiling water and boil for four and a half minutes.
Strain egg yolk through a sieve and mix with oil and a pinch of salt.
Serving: Cut open pouches and carefully unwrap the poached eggs. Place eggs on plates and drizzle with egg yolk mixture. Arrange the date-chorizo cream and breadcrumbs next to the eggs side by side and shape them into elongated forms with a spoon. Add a spoonful of sautéed mushroom caps and drizzle the egg with a little grape vinaigrette. Serve at once.

Für 4 Personen:

Für die Chorizo-Brotbrösel:
20 g Chorizo (spanische Paprika-Knoblauchwurst),
gehäutet und sehr fein gehackt,
16 g magerer Räucherspeck (roh), sehr fein gehackt
¹/₄ TL fein gehackter Knoblauch, 100 g frisch geriebene Semmelbrösel,
3 EL Trüffelsaft, 3 EL Wasser

Für die Trauben-Vinaigrette:
50 g weiße Trauben, fein geschnitten,
30 g blaue Trauben, fein geschnitten,
100 ml Olivenöl,
30 ml Reisweinessig,
1 Prise gehackte Petersilie, 1 Prise Ingwerpulver,
1 TL fein geschnittene Schnittlauchröllchen,
Salz, weißer Pfeffer aus der Mühle

Für die Dattel-Chorizo-Creme:
120 g Datteln, entkernt,
150 g Chorizo (siehe oben),
100 ml Wasser, 1 Msp. Ingwerpulver

Für die Champignons:
100 Champignonköpfe, 1 EL Butter, Salz

Für die Eier:
4 Eier, Trüffelöl und flüssiges Entenschmalz zum Beträufeln,
Salz, 1 Eigelb, 1 TL Olivenöl, 1 Prise Salz

Für die Chorizo-Brotbrösel: Chorizo, Speck, Brösel und Knoblauch in einer kleinen Pfanne unter Rühren goldbraun braten. Mit dem Trüffelsaft und Wasser benetzen, unter Rühren bei geringer Hitzezufuhr ca. 20 Minuten trocknen lassen. Beiseite stellen.
Für die Traubenvinaigrette: Alle Zutaten vermischen und in einer Schüssel ziehen lassen.
Für die Dattel-Chorizo-Creme: Alle Zutaten im Mixer fein pürieren und in einen kleinen Topf füllen. Erst kurz vor dem Servieren bei kleiner Hitze unter Rühren langsam erwärmen.
Für die Champignons: Die Pilzköpfe hacken, in einem kleinen Topf in der Butter bei kleiner Hitze weich garen. Mit Salz würzen.
Für die Eier: Vier große Stücke hitzefeste Plastikfolie mit etwas Öl bepinseln und dann in kleine Schalen legen. Die Eier einzeln aufschlagen, je eines in jede Folie gleiten lassen. Mit je 6 Tropfen Trüffelöl und 3 Tropfen Entenschmalz beträufeln, leicht salzen. Folienränder oben zusammenfassen und zu einem Beutel verknoten. Die Eier in kochendem Wasser schwimmend 4¹/₂ Minuten kochen.
Das Eigelb durch ein Sieb streichen, mit dem Öl und einer Prise Salz vermischen.
Zum Servieren: Die pochierten Eier vorsichtig aus den aufgeschnittenen Beuteln heben und auf Teller anrichten, das angerührte Eigelb über die Eier verteilen. Dattel-Chorizo-Creme und Brösel neben den Eiern mit einem Löffel nebeneinander in Längsrichtung auf die Teller geben. Einen Löffel voll Champignons dazulegen, zum Schluss mit etwas Trauben-Vinaigrette garnieren.

LIME BLOSSOM SOUP
WITH SQUID AND PUMPKIN

Serves 4
For the squid jelly: 1 small onion, chopped, ¹/₃ leek,
1 tsp garlic, minced, 2 tbsp olive oil, 100 g/3¹/₂ oz squid, chopped,
3 tbsp red wine, the ink of one medium-large squid,
350 ml/1¹/₂ cups water, 17 sheets gelatin

For the stock: 3 onions, 1 leek, 1 carrot, 1 garlic clove,
2 tbsp olive oil, 300 g/11 oz squid, coarsely chopped,
a pinch of ginger, salt, 3 g/¹/₄ tsp dried lime blossoms

For the packets:
80 g/3 oz coarsely chopped vegetables: onion, leek, carrot,
60 g/2 oz baby squid, coarsely chopped, 1 garlic clove, chopped,
1 tbsp olive oil, 1 tbsp chopped parsley, 16 paper-thin slices of
pumpkin, cut into rectangles of about 10 x 4 cm/4 x 1²/₃ inch

For the vinaigrette: 50 ml/¹/₄ cup olive oil, juice of half a lemon,
1 tbsp chopped parsley, 25 g/1 oz rhubarb, peeled

For the coconut caramel: 75 g/2¹/₂ oz sugar,
35 ml/2 tbsp water, 50 g/1¹/₂ oz coconut, cut into strips

Garnish: 30 g/1 oz squid flesh, cut into paper-thin strips,
¹/₂ tsp garlic, finely minced, 1 tbsp parsley,
1 tbsp olive oil, 10 g/1 tsp rhubarb, cut into thread-like strips,
1 tbsp finely minced chives and parsley for sprinkling

For the squid jelly: Sauté onions, leeks and garlic in olive oil, add squid and sauté for few seconds more. Douse with wine and add squid ink. Simmer for half an hour. Strain mixture through a fine sieve, measure out 200 ml/³/₄ cup of the stock and dissolve the pre-soaked gelatin in it. Pour mixture onto a baking sheet stretched tautly with foil and allow to set in the refrigerator.
For the stock: Coarsely chop vegetables, sauté in oil, add squid and sauté for a little longer. Add 1 liter/4 cups of water and bring to a boil. Allow to poach for 1¹/₂ hours just below the boiling point. Add lime blossoms and allow to steep for five minutes. Season with ginger and salt and strain it through a fine sieve.
For the packets: Cover the vegetables with water in a small pot and boil them for five minutes. Add the chopped squid and simmer on low heat for fifteen minutes. Strain through a sieve and chop vegetables and squid again with a knife. Place two pumpkin rectangles on top of each other to form a cross shape, place a heap of filling at the center and fold over the ends to make a packet.
For the vinaigrette: Purée all ingredients in a blender until you have a fine purée.
For the coconut caramel: Boil sugar and water until you have a light syrup. Add coconut strips and mix well. Allow to cool.
For the garnish: Sauté squid strips, garlic and parsley in oil. Remove pan from heat and mix with rhubarb threads.
Finish: Gently sauté the pumpkin packets in olive oil. Allow to cool until tepid, cover with a square sheet of squid jelly cut to size and place the stacks into pre-heated deep plates. Add garnish and caramelized coconut strips, sprinkle with minced herbs and drizzle a little vinaigrette on top. Serve and ladle on some hot stock directly in front of your guests. The black gelatin will dissolve and reveal orange pumpkin-squid packets.

LINDENBLÜTENSUPPE
MIT TINTENFISCH UND KÜRBIS

Für 4 Personen:
Für das Tintenfischgelee: 1 Zwiebel, gehackt, ¹/₃ Lauch, grob gehackt,
1 TL Knoblauch, gehackt, 2 EL Olivenöl, 100 g Tintenfischfleisch,
gehackt, 3 EL Rotwein, die Tinte von einem größeren Tintenfisch,
350 ml Wasser, 17 Gelatineblätter

Für die Brühe: 3 Zwiebeln, 1 Lauchstange, 1 Karotte,
1 Knoblauchzehe, 2 EL Olivenöl, 300 g Tintenfisch, grob geschnitten,
1 Msp. Ingwerpulver, Salz, 3 g getrocknete Lindenblüten

Für die Päckchen:
80 g grob geschnittenes gemischtes Gemüse: Zwiebel, Lauch, Karotte,
60 g Babytintenfische, grob gehackt, 1 Knoblauchzehe, gehackt,
1 EL Olivenöl, 1 EL gehackte Petersilie, 16 hauchdünne Scheiben
Kürbis, zu ca. 10 x 4 cm großen Rechtecken zugeschnitten

Für die Vinaigrette: 50 ml Olivenöl, Saft einer halben Zitrone,
1 EL gehackte Petersilie, 25 g Rhabarber, geschält

Für die Kokoseinlage:
75 g Zucker, 25 ml Wasser, 50 g Kokosnuss, in Streifen geschnitten

Garnitur: 30 g Tintenfischfleisch, in hauchdünne Streifen geschnitten,
¹/₂ TL fein gehackter Knoblauch, 1 EL gehackte Petersilie,
1 EL Olivenöl, 10 g Rhabarber, in fadendünne Streifen geschnitten,
1 EL fein geschnittener Schnittlauch und Petersilie zum Bestreuen

Für das Tintenfischgelee: Zwiebel, Lauch und Knoblauch im Olivenöl anschwitzen, den Tintenfisch kurz mitdünsten, mit Wein ablöschen, einkochen. Mit Wasser aufgiessen, Tinte unterrühren, bei kleiner Hitze eine halbe Stunde köcheln. Durch ein feines Sieb passieren, von der Brühe 200 ml abmessen, die eingeweichte Gelatine darin auflösen und die Mischung auf ein mit Folie bespanntes Blech giessen. Im Kühlschrank fest werden lassen.
Für die Brühe: Gemüse grob schneiden, im Öl anschwitzen, Tintenfisch mitdünsten. Mit 1 Liter Wasser auffüllen, langsam zum Kochen bringen, 1¹/₂ Stunden knapp unter dem Siedepunkt pochieren. Lindenblüten zugeben, 5 Minuten ziehen lassen, mit Ingwer und Salz würzen, die Brühe durch ein Tuch passieren.
Für die Päckchen: Das Gemüse in einem Topf mit Wasser bedeckt 5 Minuten kochen. Tintenfischfleisch zugeben, eine Viertelstunde köcheln. Durch ein Sieb giessen, die Füllung mit dem Messer nicht zu fein hacken. Je zwei Kürbisrechtecke über Kreuz auslegen, mit Füllung belegen, zu Päckchen zusammenschlagen.
Für die Vinaigrette: Alle Zutaten im Mixer fein pürieren.
Für die Kokoseinlage: Zucker mit Wasser zu hellem Karamel kochen. Kokosnussstreifen unterrühren, bis alles gut vermischt ist.
Garnitur: Tintenfischfleisch, Knoblauch, und Petersilie im Öl anbraten. Pfanne vom Herd ziehen, Inhalt mit Rhabarberfäden vermischen. Fertigstellung: Kürbispäckchen von beiden Seiten in Olivenöl anbraten. Lauwarm abkühlen lassen, mit je einem quadratisch zugeschnittenen Tintengeleeblatt belegen und in vorgewärmte Suppenteller verteilen. Garnitur und die karamellisierte Kokosstreifen zugeben, mit gehackten Kräutern bestreuen, mit Vinaigrette beträufeln. Die Kürbispäckchen vor dem Gast mit heisser Brühe übergiessen. Die schwarze Gelatine wird sich auflösen und die orangefarbenen Kürbis-Tintenfischpäckchen enthüllen.

MOSAIC OF SPRING VEGETABLES

Serves 4
For the peas: 100 g/3 1/2 oz tender, young peas, shelled, 1/2 onion,
1 tbsp olive oil, 1 tsp flour, 2 tbsp vegetable stock, salt,
250 ml/1 cup beer, reduced to 50 ml/1/4 cup,
50 ml/1/4 cup green tea, mixed with a few drops of lemon juice
For the fava beans:
100 g/3 1/2 oz tender, young fava beans, shelled, 1/2 onion,
1 tbsp olive oil, 1 tsp flour, 2 tbsp vegetable stock, salt,
2 tbsp grapefruit pulp, finely diced,
a small piece of grapefruit zest, finely diced
For the truffle vinaigrette:
1 tbsp lemon juice mixed with 3 tbsp truffle oil and a little salt
For the asparagus:
2 thick white asparagus, a pinch of ginger, 1/2 tsp sugar, salt
For the mushrooms:
100 g/3 1/2 oz portobello mushrooms, caps only, sliced,
80 g/3 oz portobello mushrooms, diced, 2 tbsp olive oil,
2 young garlic cloves, minced, 1 tbsp parsley,
1 tbsp toasted shaved almonds, salt,
50 g/1 1/2 oz beef marrow, 1 tbsp walnuts, chopped, salt,
100 g/3 1/2 oz bacon, 12 juniper berries, 1 sprig of wild fennel,
oil for deep-frying, 1 onion, finely diced, 2 tbsp olive oil
Garnish: grated coconut, grated cheese, chopped mint leaves, chives,
champignon-parsley oil (allow raw, diced mushrooms to steep in oil for
24 hours then strain oil and mix with same amount of parsley purée)

For the peas: Sauté onion in oil until translucent, add peas and sauté for a few more minutes, dust with flour. Add stock and season to taste with salt. Simmer for a minute or two. Add reduced beer and tea and simmer for another minute. Set aside.
For the fava beans: Blanch fava beans in salted water for a minute, then drain in a sieve. Remove skins and halve the beans. Sauté onion in oil until translucent, add beans, sauté for another minute, and dust with flour. Add stock, season with salt and simmer for another minute. Mix in grapefruit cubes and grapefruit zest. Set aside.
For the asparagus: Peel and cut asparagus into paper-thin slices lengthwise. Cut slices into 3 cm/1 1/2 inch pieces and place into a small pot. Add ginger, sugar, salt and a spoonful of truffle vinaigrette, simmer until asparagus is done and most of liquid is evaporated. For the mushrooms: Sauté mushroom slices and diced mushrooms separately on low heat with half the garlic each. Mix with parsley and shaved almonds and season to taste with salt.
Fry marrow in oil, mix with nuts and season to taste with salt. Place bacon into a small pot, cover with water, add juniper berries and simmer for 20 minutes. Drain and cut bacon into small dice. Deep-fry the wild fennel in hot oil until golden brown and cut it into pieces. Sauté onion in oil until tender.
Finish: Place 4 bottomless square molds onto plates. Arrange a line of chopped mushrooms in the upper quarter and top with a layer of mushroom slices. In the second quarter, place a layer of sautéed onions, cover it with fava beans and top with deep-fried fennel pieces. In the third quarter, line the bottom with bacon cubes, cover with asparagus and sprinkle with grated coconut and grated cheese. In the last quarter, place a layer of marrow-nut mixture on the bottom, cover with peas and sprinkle with chopped mint. Reheat arrangement in the oven for a minute, and remove molds. Drizzle asparagus with truffle vinaigrette and sprinkle chives over the whole vegetable mosaic. Dot with mushroom-parsley oil and serve.

MOSAIK VON FRÜHLINGSGEMÜSE

Für 4 Personen:
Für die Erbsen: 100 g zarte, junge Erbsen, ausgehülst, 1/2 Zwiebel,
1 EL Olivenöl, 1 TL Mehl, 2 EL Gemüsebrühe, Salz,
250 ml helles Bier, auf 50 ml eingekocht,
50 ml grüner Tee, mit einigen Tropfen Zitronensaft vermischt
Für die Dicken Bohnen:
100 g zarte, junge Dicke Bohnen, ausgehülst, 1/2 Zwiebel,
1 EL Olivenöl, 1 TL Mehl, 2 EL Gemüsebrühe, Salz,
2 EL Grapefruitfleisch, in kleine Würfel geschnitten,
1 kleines Stück Grapefruitschale, fein gewürfelt
Für die Trüffelvinaigrette:
1 EL Zitronensaft, mit 3 EL Trüffelöl und etwas Salz vermischt
Für den Spargel:
2 dicke weiße Spargelstangen, 1 Msp. Ingwer, 1/2 TL Zucker, Salz
Für die Pilze:
100 g Rosa Champignons, nur die Köpfe, in Scheiben geschnitten,
80 g gehackte Rosa Champignons, 2 EL Olivenöl,
2 junge Knoblauchzehen, gehackt, 1 EL Petersilie,
1 EL geröstete Mandelblättchen, Salz
50 g Rindermark, 1 EL gehackte Walnuss, Salz,
100 g Speck, 12 Wacholderbeeren, 1 Zweig wilder Fenchel,
Öl zum Frittieren, 1 Zwiebel, fein gewürfelt, 2 EL Olivenöl
Garnitur: Kokosraspel, Reibkäse, gehackte Minze, Schnittlauch,
Champignon-Petersilienöl (rohe gehackte Champignons 24 Stunden
in Öl marinieren, passieren, mit Petersilienpüree vermischt)

Erbsen: Zwiebel im Öl glasig dünsten, Erbsen kurz mitdünsten, mit Mehl überstäuben, Brühe unterrühren, mit Salz abschmecken, ca. 1 Minute köcheln. Mit eingekochtem Bier und Tee vermischen und erneut 1 Minute köcheln. Beiseite stellen. Dicke Bohnen: Bohnenkerne in Salzwasser 1 Minute blanchieren, durch ein Sieb abgießen, die Häutchen entfernen und die Bohnenkerne halbieren. Zwiebel im Öl glasig dünsten, Dicke Bohnen kurz mitdünsten, mit Mehl überstäuben und gut vermischen. Brühe unterrühren, mit Salz abschmecken, 1 Minute köcheln. Mit Grapefruitwürfeln und -schale vermischen, beiseite stellen. Spargel: Spargel schälen, der Länge nach in hauchdünne Streifen schneiden. Die Streifen in 3 cm lange Stücke schneiden, in einem kleinen Topf mit Ingwer, Zucker, Salz und 1 Löffel Trüffelvinaigrette köcheln, bis der Spargel weich und die meiste Flüssigkeit verdampft ist. Pilze: In Scheiben geschnittene Köpfe und gehackte Pilze getrennt mit der Hälfte des Knoblauchs in Öl dünsten, mit Petersilie und Mandelblättchen vermischen, mit Salz würzen. Das Mark im Öl anbraten, mit den Nüssen vermischen, mit Salz würzen. Speck mit Wacholderbeeren in Wasser 20 Minuten kochen. Abtropfen lassen, den Speck in kleine Würfel schneiden. Fenchelkraut in heißem Öl goldbraun frittieren und klein schneiden, die Zwiebel in Öl weich dünsten.
Fertigstellung: In vorgewärmte Teller 4 quadratische Formen legen. Im obersten Viertel in Linienform eine Lage gehackte Pilze einfüllen und flach mit Pilzscheiben belegen. Im zweiten Viertel die Zwiebel aufstreichen, mit Dicken Bohnen belegen, mit frittiertem Fenchel bedecken. Im dritten Viertel Speckwürfel auslegen, mit Spargel bedecken, mit Kokosraspel und Reibkäse bestreuen. Im letzten Viertel Mark-Nussmischung einfüllen, mit Erbsen belegen, mit gehackter Minze bestreuen. Das Ganze im Ofen kurz erhitzen, die Formen entfernen. Den Spargelteil mit Trüffelvinaigrette beträufeln, das Gemüse-Mosaik mit Schnittlauch bestreuen. Zum Schluss mit Champignon-Petersilienöl garnieren und servieren.

SEA PERCH IN A ROSE HIP SAUCE SERVED WITH SCALLOPS AND LEEK ASHES

WOLFSBARSCH MIT HAGEBUTTENSAUCE, JAKOBSMUSCHELN UND LAUCH-ASCHE

Serves 4

For the rose hip sauce:
1 shallot, minced, 3 rose hips, minced,
4 raspberries, 80 ml/¹/₄ cup olive oil,
a pinch of finely grated ginger,
a pinch of finely grated liquorice,
¹/₂ tsp confectioners' sugar, ¹/₂ tsp ground millet,
1 tbsp toasted almonds, ground, 1 tsp sherry vinegar

For the pistachio cream:
20 g/³/₄ oz pistachios, ground,
6 spinach leaves, blanched in salted water and finely chopped

For the leek ashes:
3 leeks, green part only,
100 ml/¹/₃ cup olive oil

For the scallops:
8 scallops, white part only,
¹/₂ clove garlic, minced,
2 tsp sesame oil, 2 tsp olive oil,
1 tsp hazelnuts, powdered,
¹/₂ tsp sweet paprika,
¹/₂ tsp chives, minced very finely,
¹/₂ tsp lemon verbena (verveine), finely chopped

For the fish:
4 filets of sea perch, 100 g/3¹/₂ oz each, 1 tbsp olive oil, salt

Garnish: chive tips

For the rose hip sauce: Sauté the shallot in half of the oil until translucent. Add remaining ingredients and cook the mixture on low heat until you have thick cream-like texture. Remove pan from heat and fold in remaining olive oil.

For the pistachio cream: Take three spoonfuls of the rose hip sauce and beat it together with the ground pistachios and spinach into a homogenous cream. Set aside remaining rose hip sauce.

For the leek ashes: Coarsely chop green leek. Toast in a hot, dry, preferably cast-iron pan on medium heat until it turns black. Purée black pieces in a blender with oil and strain through a sieve.

For the scallops: In a small pan, heat up sesame oil and olive oil with the garlic. Combine powdered hazelnuts, paprika and herbs and dust the scallops with the mixture on all sides. Fry the scallops on medium heat on both sides until golden brown. Remove from pan and keep warm.

For the fish: Preheat the oven to 180° C/350° F. Brush the sea perch filets with the remaining rose hip sauce and bake them in the oven for 6 - 8 minutes, depending on the thickness of the filets. Remove from oven and keep warm.

Serving: Dot one side of the plate with drops of leek ashes oil. Arrange the sea perch filets next to the drops and drizzle it with ribbons of pistachio cream. Place two fried scallops next to the filets and garnish the plate with chive tips according to taste.

Für 4 Personen:

Für die Hagebuttensauce:
1 Schalotte, fein gehackt, 3 Hagebutten, entkernt, fein gehackt,
4 Himbeeren, 80 ml Olivenöl,
1 Msp fein geriebener Ingwer,
1 Msp geriebenes Süßholz (Lakritz),
¹/₂ TL Puderzucker, ¹/₂ TL Hirsemehl,
1 EL geröstete Mandeln, fein gerieben, 1 TL Sherryessig

Für die Pistaziencreme:
20 g Pistazien, gemahlen,
6 Spinatblätter, in Salzwasser blanchiert, fein gehackt

Für die Lauch-Asche:
3 Lauchstangen, nur die grünen Blätter,
100 ml Olivenöl

Für die Jakobsmuscheln:
8 Jakobsmuscheln, nur das weiße Nüsschen,
¹/₂ Knoblauchzehe, gehackt,
2 TL Sesamöl, 2 TL Olivenöl,
1 TL Haselnüsse, zu Mehl gemahlen,
¹/₂ TL süßes Paprikapulver,
¹/₂ TL sehr fein geschnittener Schnittlauch,
¹/₂ TL fein gehacktes Eisenkraut (Verveine)

Für den Fisch:
4 Wolfsbarschfilets à 100 g, 1 EL Olivenöl, Salz

Garnitur: Schnittlauchspitzen

Für die Hagebuttensauce: Die Schalotte in der Hälfte des Öls glasig dünsten. Die restlichen Zutaten untermischen und bei kleiner Hitze garen, bis eine kompakte Creme entsteht. Den Topf vom Herd nehmen, das restliche Olivenöl unterziehen.

Für die Pistaziencreme: Von der Hagebuttensauce 3 Löffel wegnehmen und mit Pistazien und Spinat kräftig zu einer homogenen Creme verrühren. Die restliche Hagebuttensauce aufheben.

Für die Lauchasche: Das Lauchgrün grob schneiden. In einer Eisenpfanne ohne Öl bei mittlerer Hitze rösten, bis es schwarz ist. Im Mixer mit Öl pürieren, durch ein Tuch passieren.

Für die Jakobsmuscheln: Sesam- und Olivenöl zusammen mit dem Knoblauch in einer kleinen Pfanne erhitzen. Das Haselnussmehl mit Paprika und den Kräutern vermischen, die Jakobsmuscheln damit bestäuben und bei mittlerer Hitze von beiden Seiten im Öl goldbraun braten. Herausnehmen, warm halten.

Für den Fisch: Ofen auf 180° C vorheizen. Die Fischfilets mit der restlichen Hagebuttensauce bepinseln. Je nach Dicke der Filets 5 - 8 Minuten im Backofen braten. Herausnehmen, warm halten.

Zum Servieren: Von dem gebrannten Lauchöl auf der einen Seite der Teller kleine Tupfen nebeneinander setzen. Die Wolfsbarschfilets daneben legen und mit einem Band aus Pistaziencreme überziehen. Je zwei gebratene Jakobsmuscheln daneben platzieren, die Teller nach Belieben mit Schnittlauchspitzen garnieren.

SQUAB WITH LACQUERED SKIN SERVED WITH STEWED RHUBARB AND ASPARAGUS

TAUBE MIT LACKIERTER HAUT UND RHABARBER-SPARGELGEMÜSE

Serves 4

For the lacquered squab: 4 squab, 2 tbsp maltose, 1 tbsp glucose, 2 tbsp sherry vinegar, 1 tsp spice mixture made from ground black, pink and white pepper, star anise and salt
For the squab: salt, black pepper, 50 g/1 1/2 oz squab livers (or foie gras), chopped, 4 prunes, pitted and chopped, 5 dates, pitted and chopped, 2 tbsp grapefruit pulp, cut into small cubes, 4 large leaves of leek (white part only), 2 tbsp sunflower oil, 2 dates for the legs, chopped
For the sauce: 100 ml/1/3 cup vegetable stock, 2 sage leaves, 5 lemon mint leaves, 1 tbsp walnut oil
For the vegetables: 2 stalks rhubarb, peeled, halved lengthwise and cut into pieces, 4 tbsp sugar, 4 green asparagus spears, peeled, halved lengthwise and cut into pieces, 1/2 red pepper, peeled, cored and chopped (or a piece of red chili pepper, according to taste), 1 tsp grapefruit zest, cut into thin strips, 40 ml/1/4 cup olive oil, 4 raspberries, halved, salt
Garnish: sage or lemon mint leaves

For the lacquered skin (prepare six hours ahead): Place squab onto a rack over the sink. Douse with boiling water on all sides and carefully remove skin in one piece. Dry skin thoroughly with a kitchen towel. Combine maltose, glucose, sherry vinegar and spice mixture in a small pot and heat until all sugar crystals are dissolved (do not boil). Brush the squab skins with the syrup on both sides. Hang skins (or place them on a rack) to dry for six hours in a drafty, airy place (or place them in front of a ventilator).

Preheat the oven to 160° C/325° F. Place dried skins between two sheets of baking paper, weight them down with a heavy object and bake in the oven for thirty minutes until brown and crisp. Cut skins into the desired form with scissors.

For the squab: Cut breasts off the bone, cut off legs and remove and discard back. Rub meat all over with salt and pepper. Lay the breasts out flat. Combine livers with prunes, dates and grapefruit and cover breasts with the mixture. Wrap breasts tightly in leek leaves. Heat oil in a heavy, non-stick casserole. Fry leek packets on all sides, then finish baking in the oven for five minutes. Remove casserole from oven. Stuff thighs of the squab with the remaining dates. Fry thighs in the casserole for two minutes on all sides. Unwrap squab breasts and scrape off stuffing. Reserve.

For the sauce: Fry leek leaves and stuffing in the squab casserole. Douse with vegetable stock. Carefully scrape the brown bits off the bottom with a wooden spoon, then purée the sauce in a blender and strain it through a sieve. Mix in walnut oil and season to taste with salt and pepper. Thin the sauce with a little stock if necessary.

For the vegetables: Sprinkle rhubarb with sugar and allow to sit for half an hour. Rinse off remaining sugar. Heat oil in a large frying pan and fry rhubarb, asparagus, paprika and grapefruit zest on for 2 - 3 minutes, stirring frequently. Add raspberries and salt.

Serving: Drizzle a pattern of your own design onto four plates, using half the sauce. Arrange squab breasts, thighs and vegetables on the plates and lightly brown them under a grill or in a sala-mander. Drizzle with remaining sauce, then garnish the plates with the crispy skins and herbs and serve.

Für 4 Personen:

Für die lackierte Taubenhaut: 4 Tauben, 2 EL Maltose, 1 EL Glukose, 2 EL Sherryessig, 1 TL gemahlene Gewürzmischung aus schwarzem, rosa und weißem Pfeffer, sowie Sternanis und Salz
Für die Tauben: Salz, schwarzer Pfeffer, 50 g Taubenlebern (oder Stopfleber), gehackt, 4 Trockenpflaumen, entkernt, gehackt, 5 Datteln, entkernt, gehackt, 2 EL Grapefruitfleisch, in kleine Würfel geschnitten, 4 große Lauchblätter (nur das Weiße), 2 EL Sonnenblumenöl, 2 gehackte Datteln für die Keulen
Für die Sauce: 100 ml Gemüsebrühe, 2 Salbeiblätter, 5 Zitronenmelisseblätter, 1 EL Walnussöl
Für das Gemüse: 2 Stangen Rhabarber, geschält, der Länge nach halbiert und in Stücke geschnitten, 4 EL Zucker, 4 grüne Spargelstangen, geschält, der Länge nach halbiert und in Stücke geschnitten, 1/2 rote Paprika, enthäutet, entkernt und gehackt (oder nach Belieben 1 Stück rote Chilischote), 1 TL dünn abgeschnittene Grapefruitschale, in dünne Streifen geschnitten, 50 ml Olivenöl, 4 Himbeeren, halbiert, Salz
Garnitur: Salbei- oder Zitronenmelisseblättchen

Lackierte Haut (6 Stunden Trockenzeit): Tauben auf einem Gitter über dem Spülbecken mit kochendem Wasser übergießen, die Haut am Stück abziehen. Mit einem Tuch sorgfältig trockentupfen. Maltose, Glukose, Sherryessig und Gewürzmischung in einem Topf erhitzen, bis sich die Zuckersorten aufgelöst haben (nicht kochen). Taubenhautstücke von beiden Seiten damit bepinseln. Frei hängend oder auf einem Gitter liegend die Haut an einem luftigen, zugigen Ort (oder vor einem Ventilator) 6 Stunden trocknen lassen. Ofen auf 160° C vorheizen. Getrocknete Häute zwischen zwei Backtrennpapiere legen, mit einem Gewicht beschwert im Ofen 30 Minuten knusprig-braun backen. In die gewünschte Form schneiden.

Tauben: Taubenbrüste vom Knochen schneiden, Keulen abtrennen, den Mittelknochen entfernen. Das Fleisch mit Salz und Pfeffer rundum würzen. Brüste flach auslegen. Lebern mit Pflaumen, Datteln und Grapefruit vermischen, die Brüste mit dieser Mischung bedecken. In Lauchblätter wickeln. Öl in einem Bräter auf dem Herd erhitzen. Die Lauchrollen von allen Seiten anbraten, im Ofen 5 Minuten weiterbraten. Bräter herausnehmen. Keulen mit restlichen Datteln füllen, im Bräter auf dem Herd 2 Minuten von allen Seiten anbraten. Lauch und Füllung von den Brüsten entfernen, aufheben. Für die Sauce: Lauch und Brustfüllung im Bräter bei mittlerer Hitze anbraten. Mit Brühe ablöschen, Kräuter zugeben und einkochen, bis der Bratsatz zu bräunen beginnt. Bratsatz mit einem Holzlöffel herauskratzen, in einem Mixer pürieren, anschließend durch ein Sieb passieren. Mit Walnussöl vermischen, mit Salz und Pfeffer abschmecken. Wenn nötig, die Sauce mit etwas Brühe leicht verdünnen.

Gemüse: Rhabarber 30 Minuten mit Zucker bestreut Wasser ziehen lassen. Zucker abwaschen, Rhabarber mit Spargel, Paprika und Grapefruitschale in einer Pfanne im heißen Öl unter Wenden 2 - 3 Minuten braten. Himbeeren unterrühren, mit Salz würzen.

Zum Servieren: Von der Hälfte der Sauce auf Teller ein beliebiges Muster gießen. Taubenbrüste, -Keulen und Gemüse anrichten, unter dem Salamander oder dem Grill leicht bräunen. Mit restlicher Sauce beträufeln, mit der knusprigen Haut und Kräutern garnieren.

CREAM-COATED CHOCOLATE MOUSSE AND SESAME-HONEY ICE CREAM

SCHOKOLADENMOUSSE IM CREMEMANTEL UND SESAM-HONIGEIS

Serves 4

For the cream coating:
500 ml/2 cups milk, 4 egg yolks, 100 g/3 1/2 oz sugar,
40 g/1 1/2 oz cornstarch, 1 vanilla bean, 1/2 cinnamon stick,
40 g/1 1/2 oz passion fruit pulp, a pinch of ground liquorice,
a pinch of ground ginger, 6 sheets gelatin

300 g/11 oz dark chocolate mousse

For the reduction:
200 g/7 oz sugar, 150 ml/2/3 cup sweet sherry, the scraped out seeds
of a vanilla bean, 75 ml/1/4 cup Sauternes (or another dessert wine)

For the sesame-honey ice cream (makes 1.2 liters/5 1/2 cups):
1 liter/4 cups milk, 100 ml/1/3 cup cream,
15 ml/1 tbsp sesame oil, 15 ml/1 tbsp olive oil,
15 g/1 tbsp sesame seeds, 10 egg yolks,
200 g/7 oz sugar, 150 g/5 oz honey

Garnish:
1/2 red pepper, 100 g/3 1/2 oz sugar, 60 g/2 oz pine nuts,
60 g/2 oz walnuts, 100 g/3 1/2 oz pistachios, shelled, 6 mint leaves

For the cream coating: Combine milk, cinnamon and vanilla and bring to a boil. Remove from the heat and allow to steep for five minutes. Whip egg yolks and sugar until light and fluffy, gradually add cornstarch and mix well. Strain the hot milk through a sieve and mix with the egg yolk mixture, beating vigorously all the time. Pre-soak and squeeze out gelatin. Season the egg yolk mixture with ginger and liquorice, bring to a boil again, then mix with gelatin. Stir to dissolve. Add passion fruit pulp and spread the cream thinly onto a non-stick baking sheet. Allow to set in the refrigerator. When the cream coating has solidified, cut it into eight rectangles of about 4 x 6 cm/1 1/2 x 2 1/2 inches.

If possible, smoke chocolate mousse in a smoker for five minutes. If you do not have a smoker, use ordinary chocolate mousse.

For the reduction: Combine sugar, sherry and vanilla beans in a pot and cook, stirring constantly, until sugar has turned a medium caramel brown. Douse with Sauternes (careful of splattering!) and reduce to the desired consistency. Strain through a sieve.

For the sesame-honey ice cream: Bring cream, milk, sesame oil, olive oil and sesame seeds to a boil. Whip egg yolks, sugar and honey in a bowl until light and fluffy. Add hot milk, beating vigorously. Return mixture to the pot and heat to just below the boiling point. Allow cream to cool and freeze in an ice cream maker.

Cut red pepper into small dice. Simmer in a syrup made of 100 g/3 1/2 oz sugar and 200 ml/3/4 cup of water and drain them in a sieve. Finely mince pine nuts and break walnuts into quarters. Coarsely chop pistachios. Chop the mint leaves just before serving.

Serving: Place one square of cream coating onto each plate. Cover with mousse and top with another cream square. Scatter red pepper dice, chopped pine nuts and walnut pieces across the plate and surround with Sauternes reduction. Sprinkle with pistachios and mint. Add a scoop of sesame honey ice cream and serve.

Für 4 Personen:

Für den Crememantel:
500 ml Milch, 4 Eigelb, 100 g Zucker,
40 g Maisstärke, 1 Vanillestange, 1/2 Zimtstange,
40 g Passionsfruchtfleisch, 1 Prise Süßholzpulver (Lakritz),
1 Prise Ingwerpulver, 6 Blätter Gelatine

300 g dunkle Schokoladenmousse

Für die Reduktion:
200 g Zucker, 150 ml süßer Sherry, das ausgekratzte Mark einer
Vanillestange, 75 ml Sauternes (oder anderer weißer Süßwein)

Für das Sesam-Honigeis (ergibt 1,2 Liter):
1 Liter Milch, 100 ml Sahne,
15 ml Sesamöl, 15 ml Olivenöl,
15 g Sesamsamen, 10 Eigelb,
200 g Zucker, 150 g Honig

Garnitur:
1/2 rote Paprika, 100 g Zucker, 60 g Pinienkerne,
60 g Walnüsse, 100 g Pistazienkerne, 6 Minzeblättchen

Für den Crememantel: Milch mit Zimt und Vanille zum Kochen bringen. Vom Herd ziehen, 5 Minuten stehen lassen. Eigelb und Zucker schaumig rühren, Maisstärke nach und nach zugeben und unterrühren. Die heiße Milch durch ein Sieb passieren, unter kräftigem Rühren mit dem Eigelb vermischen. Mit Süßholz und Ingwer würzen, nochmals kurz aufkochen lassen, dann die eingeweichte und ausgedrückte Gelatine darin auflösen. Das Passionsfruchtfleisch unterrühren, die Creme auf ein beschichtetes Blech dünn aufstreichen. Im Kühlschrank fest werden lassen. Wenn die Cremehaut fest ist, 8 ca. 4 x 6 cm grosse Rechtecke ausschneiden.

Die Schokoladenmousse wenn möglich in einem Räucherofen fünf Minuten räuchern. Wenn kein Räucherofen vorhanden ist, normale Schokoladenmousse verwenden.

Für die Reduktion: Zucker mit Sherry und Vanillemark in einem Topf unter Rühren kochen, bis der Zucker mittelbraun karamellisiert. Mit Sauternes ablöschen (Vorsicht, spritzt), zur gewünschten Konsistenz einkochen. Durch ein Sieb passieren.

Für das Sesam-Honigeis: Milch mit Sahne, Sesam- und Olivenöl und Sesamsamen zum Kochen bringen. In einer Schüssel Eigelb mit Zucker und Honig schaumig rühren. Heiße Milch unter kräftigem Rühren zugießen. Im Topf bis kurz vor den Siedepunkt erhitzen. Die Creme erkalten lassen, in der Eismaschine gefrieren.

Paprika in kleine Würfel schneiden. In einem Sirup aus 100 g Zucker mit 200 ml Wasser 20 Minuten köcheln, in einem Sieb abtropfen lassen. Pinienkerne fein hacken, die Walnüsse in je vier Teile brechen. Pistazien grob hacken, die Minzeblättchen hacken.

Zum Servieren: Je ein Cremerechteck auf vier Teller legen. Mit Mousse bedecken, dann ein zweites Cremerechteck darüber legen. Mit Paprikawürfeln, gehackten Pinienkernen und Walnussstücken umstreuen, mit Reduktion umgießen. Gehackte Pistazien und Minze auf die Creme streuen. Mit Sesam-Honigeis als Beilage servieren.

PUMPKIN ICE CREAM IN A CHOCOLATE COATING

KÜRBISEIS IM SCHOKOMANTEL

Serves 4 - 6

For the pumpkin marmalade:
750 g/1 $^1/_2$ lbs pumpkin,
100 ml/$^1/_3$ cup orange juice,
350 g/12 $^1/_2$ oz sugar,
the thinly grated zest of one untreated orange

For the pumpkin ice cream:
500 ml/2 cups milk,
a pinch of ground star anise,
$^1/_2$ tsp cocoa

For the ice crystals:
100 ml/$^1/_3$ cup orange juice,
100 ml/$^1/_3$ cup water,
3 g/a pinch cola nut, finely grated

For the chocolate mousse:
30 g/1 oz dark couverture chocolate,
80 g/2 $^1/_2$ oz butter,
8 egg yolks,
8 egg whites, whipped into stiff peaks

For the pumpkin marmalade (to be made one day ahead): Cut the pumpkin flesh into small cubes. In a small pot, combine pumpkin, orange juice, sugar and grated orange zest and cook for an hour on low heat. Stir frequently. Allow the mixture to cool and measure out 300 g/11 oz for the pumpkin ice cream. Reserve the rest.

For the pumpkin ice cream: Mix pumpkin marmalade and the remaining ingredients until well blended and freeze the mixture in an ice cream maker.

For the ice crystals: Pour orange juice into a flat plastic container and freeze in a deep freezer. Heat water with a pinch of cola nut until just below the boiling point. Remove pot from heat, allow liquid to cool and strain it through a fine sieve. Freeze cola nut liquid in the deep freezer.

For the chocolate mousse: Slowly melt the couverture chocolate in a double boiler without letting it get too hot. Incorporate egg yolks and loosely fold in beaten egg whites.

Serving: Place a spoonful of pumpkin marmalade into heat-proof serving dishes. Top with a scoop of pumpkin ice cream and coat the ice cream with a $^1/_2$ cm/$^1/_5$ inch coating of chocolate mousse. Brown for a few seconds under the broiler or in a salamander. With a spoon, scrape crystals off the top of orange and cola nut juices (remove them from the freezer half an hour before serving). Garnish chocolate mousse with the crystals and serve immediately.

Für 4 - 6 Personen:

Für die Kürbismarmelade:
750 g Kürbisfleisch,
100 ml Orangensaft,
350 g Zucker,
die dünn abgeriebene Schale einer unbehandelten Orange

Für das Kürbiseis:
500 ml Milch,
1 Msp Sternanispulver,
$^1/_2$ TL Kakao

Für die Eiskristalle:
100 ml Orangensaft,
100 ml Wasser,
3 g getrocknete Kolanuss, fein gerieben

Für die Schokoladenmousse:
30 g dunkle Kuvertüre,
80 g Butter
8 Eigelb,
8 Eiweiß, zu Schnee geschlagen

Für die Kürbismarmelade (vorzugsweise am Vortag zubereiten): Das Kürbisfleisch in kleine Würfel schneiden. Mit Orangensaft, Zucker und der abgeriebenen Orangenschale in einem Topf bei kleiner Hitze mindestens eine Stunde köcheln, dabei immer wieder umrühren. Auskühlen lassen, für die Herstellung des Kürbiseises 300 g abmessen, den Rest beiseite stellen.

Für das Kürbiseis: Die Kürbismarmelade mit den restlichen Zutaten gut verrühren und in der Eismaschine gefrieren.

Für die Eiskristalle: Orangensaft in ein flaches Kunststoff-Gefäß füllen und im Gefrierschrank gefrieren lassen. Das Wasser mit dem Kolanusspulver in einem kleinen Topf bis kurz vor dem Siedepunkt erhitzen. Topf vom Herd ziehen, die Flüssigkeit erkalten lassen, durch ein feines Sieb passieren, ebenfalls gefrieren lassen.

Für die Schokoladenmousse: Kuvertüre mit Butter im Wasserbad langsam schmelzen, ohne stark zu erhitzen. Eigelb unterrühren, zum Schluß den Eischnee locker unterziehen.

Zum Servieren: In feuerfeste Schalen je einen großen Löffel Kürbismarmelade einfüllen. Mit jeweils einer kleinen Kugel Kürbiseis belegen, dieses mit Schokoladenmousse ca. $^1/_2$ cm hoch überziehen. Kurz unter dem sehr heißen Salamander oder Grill bräunen. Von dem leicht angetauten Orangen- und Kolanuss-Saft jeweils mit einem Löffel Kristalle abkratzen. Die Schokoladenmousse damit garnieren und sofort servieren.

SHORT GRAIN RICE CREAM AND DEEP-FRIED RICE WITH TAMARIND-HAZELNUT ICE CREAM

MILCHREISCREME UND FRITTIERTER REIS MIT TAMARINDEN-HASELNUSSEIS

Serves 6 - 8

For the short grain rice cream:
800 ml/3 cups milk, 400 ml/1 1/2 cups cream,
60 g/2 oz short grain rice,
1 cinnamon stick, 1 vanilla bean, 8 cloves,
a pinch of black and white pepper, ground ginger,
liquorice and salt each, zest of two lemons,
6 sheets gelatin, 65 g/2 oz passion fruit pulp,
600 ml/2 1/3 cups cream

For the tamarind-hazelnut ice cream:
1 liter/4 cups milk, 20 g/3/4 oz tamarind pulp,
70 g/2 1/2 oz hazelnut paste, 6 egg yolks, 160 g/6 oz sugar

For the deep-fried rice:
75 g/2 1/2 oz rice, 1/2 liter/2 cups water, salt, oil for deep-frying

For the spice sauce:
50 ml/1/4 cup lemon juice, 50 ml/1/4 cup water, 100 g/3 1/2 oz sugar,
a pinch of ground ginger, liquorice and finely minced parsley each

For the raspberry jelly:
300 ml/1 1/3 cup raspberry purée, strained through a fine sieve,
11 sheets of gelatin

For the short grain rice cream: Combine milk, cream, rice, spices and lemon zest in a pot and bring to a boil. Simmer on low heat until the liquid is reduced to 750 ml/3 cups. Stir frequently. Strain liquid through a sieve. Pre-soak and squeeze out gelatin and mix it into the liquid. Add passion fruit pulp and allow the mixture to cool. When the mixture is cool, whip the cream into soft peaks and gently fold into the mixture. Refrigerate for two hours.

For the tamarind-hazelnut ice cream: Combine milk, tamarind pulp and hazelnut paste and bring the mixture to a boil. Whip egg yolks and sugar in a bowl until light and fluffy. Add hot milk to the egg yolk mixture, beating vigorously all the time, mix well and return to the pot. Heat to just below the boiling point and strain through a sieve. Allow to cool, then freeze it in an ice cream maker.

For the deep-fried rice: Cook rice for thirty-five minutes in heavily salted water. Drain in a sieve, douse with plenty of cold water. Spread the rice out flat onto a baking sheet and dry in a 60° C/ 140° F oven for about twelve hours. Deep-fry dry rice in hot oil, drain well and sprinkle with salt. For the spice sauce: Combine lemon juice, water, ginger and liquorice in a pot and simmer until you have a thick syrup. Allow to cool and mix with parsley.

For the raspberry jelly: Pre-soak and squeeze out gelatin, mix it into the raspberry purée and heat to dissolve. Pour purée onto a non-stick baking sheet in a thin layer and allow to set in the refrigerator. Cut the solid sheet into 5 x 5 cm/2 x 2 inch squares.

Serving: Place two raspberry jelly squares onto each plate. Sprinkle with deep-fried rice and place a scoop of short grain rice cream on top. Sprinkle with more deep-fried rice and cover with another jelly square each. Surround with spice sauce and garnish with a scoop of tamarind-hazelnut ice cream. Serve.

Für 6 - 8 Personen:

Für die Milchreiscreme:
800 ml Milch, 400 ml Sahne,
60 g Milchreis (Rundkornreis),
1 Zimtstange, 1 Vanillestange, 8 Nelken,
je eine Prise schwarzer und weißer Pfeffer, Ingwerpulver,
Süßholzpulver (Lakritz) und Salz,
mit dem Messer dünn abgeschnittene Schale von 2 Zitronen,
6 Gelatineblätter, 65 g Passionsfruchtfleisch, 600 ml Sahne

Für das Tamarinden-Haselnusseis:
1 Liter Milch, 20 g Tamarindenpaste,
70 g Haselnusspaste, 6 Eigelb, 160 g Zucker

Für den frittierten Reis:
75 g Reis, 1/2 Liter Wasser, Salz, Öl zum Frittieren

Für die Gewürzsauce:
50 ml Zitronensaft, 50 ml Wasser, 100 g Zucker, je eine Prise
Ingwerpulver, Süßholzpulver (Lakritz) und fein gehackte Petersilie

Für das Himbeergelee:
300 ml Himbeerpüree, durch ein feines Sieb passiert,
11 Gelatineblätter

Für die Milchreiscreme: Milch, Sahne und Reis mit Gewürzen und Zitronenschalen zum Kochen bringen. Bei kleiner Hitze köcheln, bis die Flüssigkeit auf 750 ml eingekocht ist, dabei immer wieder umrühren. Durch ein Sieb passieren, mit der aufgeweichten und ausgedrückten Gelatine vermischen. Passionsfruchtfleisch unterrühren, erkalten lassen. Wenn die Creme kalt ist, halbsteif geschlagene Sahne unterziehen, im Kühlschrank 2 Stunden durchkühlen.

Für das Tamarinden-Haselnusseis: Milch mit Tamarinden- und Haselnusspaste verrühren und zum Kochen bringen. Eigelb mit Zucker in einer Schüssel schaumig rühren. Unter kräftigem Rühren die heiße Milch zugießen, vermischen und nochmals bis kurz vor den Siedepunkt erhitzen. Durch ein Sieb passieren, erkalten lassen, die Creme in der Eismaschine gefrieren.

Für den frittierten Reis: Reis in stark gesalzenem Wasser 35 Minuten kochen. Durch ein Sieb abgießen, mit kaltem Wasser gut abspülen, abtropfen lassen. Auf einem Blech flach ausstreichen, im Ofen bei 60° C ca. 12 Stunden trocknen. Den trockenen Reis in heißem Öl frittieren, abtropfen lassen, mit Salz würzen.

Für die Gewürzsauce: Zitronensaft mit Wasser, Zucker, Ingwer und Süßholz zu einem dicken Sirup kochen. Erkalten lassen, mit Petersilie vermischen. Für das Himbeergelee: Himbeerpüree erhitzen, die eingeweichte, ausgedrückte Gelatine darin auflösen, als dünne Schicht auf ein beschichtetes Blech gießen, im Kühlschrank fest werden lassen. In ca. 5 x 5 cm große Quadrate schneiden.

Zum Servieren: Auf die Teller je zwei Himbeergeleequadrate legen. Mit frittiertem Reis bestreuen, einen Löffel Milchreiscreme darüber geben, erneut mit frittiertem Reis bestreuen, dann mit einem zweiten Himbeergeleequadrat bedecken. Mit Gewürzsauce umgießen, mit je einer Kugel Tamarinden-Haselnusseis garniert servieren.

EARTH ALMOND SOUP WITH MANGO BREAD CUSHIONS AND SHORT GRAIN RICE- AND-GRAPEFRUIT ICE CREAM

ERDMANDELSUPPE MIT MANGO-BROTKISSEN UND MILCHREIS-GRAPEFRUIT-EIS

Serves 4

For the earth almond soup:
100 g/3¹/₂ oz earth almonds (chufa), peeled,
500 ml/2 cups milk, 100 ml/¹/₃ cup cream, 200 g/7 oz sugar

For the mango sauce:
500 g/2 cups fully ripe mango pulp, 100 g/3¹/₂ oz sugar

For short grain rice-and-grapefruit ice cream:
500 ml/2 cups milk, 325 g/12 oz sugar,
zest of one pink grapefruit, 90 g/3 oz butter,
45 g/1¹/₂ oz short grain rice,
juice of one pink grapefruit, juice of half a lemon

For the mango bread cushions:
100 g/3¹/₂ oz white bread, crust removed, cut into small cubes,
150 ml/²/₃ cup milk, 100 ml/¹/₃ cup cream,
50 g/1¹/₂ oz sugar, 1 vanilla bean,
1 mango, peeled, 50 g/1¹/₂ oz brown sugar,
30 g/1 oz pistachios, chopped

garnish:
mint leaves, chopped pistachios

For the earth almond soup: Finely purée all the ingredients in a blender and allow to sit in the refrigerator for twenty-four hours. Strain the soup through a sieve and set it aside.

For the mango sauce: Purée the mango pulp and sugar in a blender and strain the mixture through a fine sieve. Refrigerate.

For the short grain rice-and-grapefruit ice cream: Wash the rice under running cold water, shake off excess water and place rice into a heavy-bottomed saucepan. Add milk and grapefruit zest and cook for forty minutes on low heat, stirring constantly. Add sugar and cook for another forty minutes. Remove pot from the burner. Stir in cold butter, one piece at a time and add juices. Purée the mixture in a blender and strain the cream through a sieve. Allow to cool and freeze in an ice cream maker.

For the mango bread cushions: Combine milk, cream, sugar and slit vanilla bean in a saucepan and bring to a boil. Place white bread cubes into a large bowl and douse with hot milk mixture. Allow to cool and refrigerate for twenty-four hours. Remove vanilla bean. Cut eight slices out of the mango, making them as large and thin as possible, and place them flat onto a working surface. Cut out eight evenly sized cross shapes. Stuff cross shapes with soaked bread and fold the ends over the top. Turn cushions over and sprinkle them with sugar. Caramelize the surface with a blow torch and sprinkle the cushions with chopped pistachios.

Serving: Ladle the earth almond soup into deep plates. Place two caramelized mango bread cushions into the soup and add a scoop of short grain rice-and-grapefruit sorbet. Drizzle a little mango sauce into the soup and garnish the plate with mint leaves and chopped pistachios. Serve at once.

Für 4 Personen:

Für die Erdmandelsuppe:
100 g Erdmandeln (Chufa), geschält,
500 ml Milch, 100 ml Sahne, 200 g Zucker

Für die Mangosauce:
500 g vollreifes Mangofleisch, 100 g Zucker

Für das Milchreis-Grapefruit-Eis:
500 ml Milch, 325 g Zucker,
abgeriebene Schale einer rosa Grapefruit, 90 g Butter,
45 g Rundkornreis,
der Saft einer rosa Grapefruit, der Saft einer halben Zitrone

Für die Mango-Brotkissen:
100 g Weißbrot ohne Rinde, in kleine Würfel geschnitten,
150 ml Milch, 100 ml Sahne,
50 g Zucker, 1 Vanillestange,
1 Mango, geschält, 50 g brauner Zucker,
30 g Pistazien, gehackt

Garnitur:
Minzeblättchen, gehackte Pistazien

Für die Erdmandelsuppe: Alle Zutaten im Mixer fein pürieren, anschließend 24 Stunden im Kühlschrank ziehen lassen. Die Suppe durch ein Sieb passieren, beiseite stellen.

Für die Mangosauce: Das Mangofleisch mit dem Zucker im Mixer pürieren und durch ein Sieb streichen. Kalt stellen.

Für das Milchreis-Grapefruit-Eis: Reis unter fließendem kaltem Wasser waschen, abtropfen lassen und in einem Topf mit schwerem Boden mit der Milch und Grapefruitschalenraspel unter Rühren 40 Minuten bei kleiner Hitze köcheln. Zucker unterrühren, weitere 40 Minuten köcheln. Den Topf vom Herd ziehen. Die kalte Butter nach und nach unterrühren, zum Schluss mit den Säften vermischen. Im Mixer pürieren, die Creme durch ein Sieb streichen, erkalten lassen und in der Eismaschine gefrieren.

Für die Mango-Brotkissen: Die Milch mit der Sahne, dem Zucker und der aufgeschnittenen Vanillestange in einem Topf zum Kochen bringen. Die Weißbrotwürfel in eine Schüssel füllen und mit der heißen Flüssigkeit übergießen. Erkalten lassen, die Mischung im Kühlschrank 24 Stunden ziehen lassen. Vanillestange entfernen. Aus dem Mangofleisch 8 möglichst große, dünne Scheiben schneiden. Die Scheiben flach auslegen und gleichmäßige exakte Kreuze ausschneiden. Mit eingeweichtem Brot füllen, und die Enden des Kreuzes oben zusammenschlagen. Die Kissen umdrehen, mit Zucker bestreuen und mit einem Bunsenbrenner karamellisieren. Mit gehackten Pistazien bestreuen.

Zum Servieren: Erdmandelsuppe in tiefe Teller schöpfen. Je 2 karamellisierte Mango-Brotkissen hinein legen, daneben eine Kugel Milchreis-Grapefruiteis geben. Etwas Mangosauce in die Suppe träufeln, mit Minzeblättchen und gehackten Pistazien garnieren.

Hotel Maria Cristina

Grandeza española.

The Hotel Maria Cristina is undoubtedly one of the most splendid survivors of the Belle Epoque, when San Sebastián was a summer resort popular with European nobility. Royal majesties and Hollywood stars used to vacation in the house, and the Paris Haute Couture showed its collections there. In the rooms of the hotel, the nostalgic charm of times past may be felt even today, after extensive renovation. A generous amount of velvet, an abundance of carpet and heavy curtains adorn the light and airy rooms. You can almost picture how open horse carriages used to draw up the drive, and, after the ladies and gentlemen had descended, an army of servants would rush to carry innumerable bags and suitcases into the hotel. For today's visitors, the palace is still an ideal starting point for strolls through the city: situated on the banks of the Urumea river, it's only a few meters to the new congress hall, to the beach or to the old quarter with ist typical "pintxos" bars. An evening stroll through its narrow alleyways, a sip of wine here, a snack there at a noisy bar belongs to the classical ouverture before dinner. Then, you may return to the hotel and slide down deep into the soft easy chairs of the "Easo" Restaurante and have your dinner served. The name "Easo" for the Maria Cristina restaurant testifies to the Latin name for the city of San Sebastián. Yet, as everybody knows, the Basque people are very proud of their tradition, and thus they always call the city by their own name, "Donostia". Old cultural values have always been held up high here, and the menus of better restaurants soon turn into a crash course in the Basque language: one line features the Basque ("marraskilo"), the next High Spanish, Castellan that is ("caracoles"), and finally English ("snails") or French ("escargots").

The chef de cuisine at the "Easo" is a native Basque, too, Jokin de Aguirre. Almost forty years old, he has traveled the world, has cooked in Mexico and Morocco and stood behind the stoves of master Robuchon. He knows how to delight his international customers with his version of local cuisine, and does not hesitate to mix in a few elements and influences from foreign cultures, either. "Our guests come from everywhere, from abroad and all corners of Spain", he explains. "I would like to tell them about my homeland. But many of them are used to far away cuisines, thus their experience here should not be one-dimensional. And not everyone likes our kind of food here." Such customers have to be taken care of, too, since the restaurant is part of a big hotel with more than one hundred thirty rooms and suites.

Jokin de Aguirre

*A*part from the daily restaurant business, Aguirre and his seven chefs are also in charge of large banquets and small private events. And if there is a convention at the neighboring congress center, all hell breaks loose here. Then the personnel is doubled or tripled, according to demand. Garlic and parsley. The cornerstones of Basque cooking, which is sheer inconceivable without them. These two ingredients impart their flavor to almost every recipe and have survived the change from simple country-style cooking to the spheres of top gastronomy. "One of the best examples of our cuisine", says the Basque native, "is merluza a la vasca", hake in a garlic-parsley sauce. This dish is as popular and ubiquitous as veal shanks in Bavaria. The ingredients of the original include garlic, parsley, olive oil, hake, clams, a hard-boiled egg and asparagus. And Aguirre continues: "This is how the dish has traditionally been prepared, and in earlier times, the egg was thought of as a cheap addition to provide protein. So you leave it out today. Yet, the kokotxas from the hake, which are eaten nowhere else than in the Basque country, have endured over time. Earlier, these head pieces form the fish (hake does not have cheeks) were something quite inexpensive and not very high class. Today, they are a delicacy since they have become rare. In the old times, angler fish was often used to fertilize mountain fields. I think in twenty years even our cheap sardines will be luxury items." Naturally, the dish also appears on the menu of the Easo. Its master chef loves regional products like his colleagues, yet being part of the Westin Group together with other hotels he mostly has to rely on the central purchasing department. This is not always to his taste, and thus, every Thursday, he gets into his car and drives across the border to France to a farmer he trusts and buys his vegetables there. He picks out his artichokes by hand and selects the herbs that provide his dishes with aroma. There he knows what he gets. He just has to make time for that. Once a year, his cooking colleagues and the purchasers of the hotel chain meet in Madrid and choose their suppliers by means of blind tests. Those chosen will then provide the restaurants with everything needed in the year to come, from coffee to oil, to fish, meat or vegetables. With Jokin de Aguirre, many products undergo double heat treatment. He stews them and then quickly broils them again, for example. He himself says that his style has been much influenced by the protagonists of the new Basque cuisine, by Arzak and Pedro Subijana, with whom he has a friendly and collegial relationship. "Here, everyone knows everyone, and we often meet to exchange our thoughts", says the likeable master chef. "Martin Berasetegui just was here for dinner." San Sebastián is home free for good chefs. The immense interest of the local population in food is not reflected only in numerous sites of top gastronomy. Enjoying food is a street phenomenon. Sidrerias and tavernas also make an effort to keep up – and they are just around the corner from the Maria Cristina. The city on the Gulf of Biscay is well worth a culinary excursion.

Grandeza Española. Das Hotel Maria Cristina ist unzweifelhaft eine der prachtvollen Erinnerungen an die Belle Epoque, als San Sebastián eine beliebte Sommerfrische des europäischen Adels war. Königliche Majestäten und Hollywoods Größen machten das Haus zu ihrem Urlaubsdomizil, und die Pariser Haute Couture zeigte ihre Kollektionen. Der nostalgische Charme vergangener Zeiten weht auch heute noch, nach umfangreicher Renovierung, durch die Räumlichkeiten des Hotels. Viel Samt, viel Teppich und schwere Vorhänge dekorieren die hellen Räume. Man kann sich geradezu bildlich vorstellen, wie damals die offenen Landauer vorfuhren und, nachdem ihm die Damen und Herren entstiegen waren, ein Heer von dienstbaren Geistern mit viel Mühe die Unzahl von Taschen und Koffern ins Hotel wuchtete. Auch für den heutigen Besucher ist der Palast ideales Zentrum für Stadterkundungsgänge: am Ufer des Urumea Flusses gelegen, sind es nur wenige Meter zur neuen Kongresshalle, zum Strand oder dem alten Stadtviertel mit seinen typischen „pintxos" Bars. Ein abendlicher Bummel durch enge Gassen, ein Schluck Wein hier, ein Happen dort am lauten Tresen gilt als klassische Ouvertüre vor dem Abendessen. Dann kann man zurückkehren zum Hotel, und sich in den weichen Polstersesseln des „Easo" Restaurants zum Mahle niederlassen. Mit dem Namen Easo hat man sich im Maria Cristina noch der lateinischen Bezeichnung der Stadt San Sebastián bedient. Doch grundsätzlich sind Basken, wie man weiß, sehr sehr stolz auf ihre Tradition, und so nennen sie die Stadt in ihrer Sprache „Donostia". Das alte Kulturgut wird hier immer und überall hochgehalten, und die Speisekarten der besseren Etablissements werden zum Schnellkursus in baskischem Sprachgut: eine Zeile fürs Baskische (beispielsweise „marraskilo"), dann kommt es Hochspanisch, auf castellán („caracoles") und schließlich die erlösende Erläuterung auf Englisch („snails") oder Französisch („escargots").

Ein Baske durch und durch ist auch Easos Küchenchef, der hier gebürtige Jokin de Aguirre. Aber mit seinen fast vierzig Jahren hat er die Welt gesehen, kochte in Mexiko und Marokko und stand auch bei Großmeister Robuchon schon am Herd. So versteht er es, die internationale Klientel mit seiner Version heimischer Küche zu verwöhnen, die sich nicht scheut, hier und da auch Elemente und Einflüsse fremder Kulturen einzusetzen. „Unsere Gäste kommen von überall her, aus dem Ausland und von allen Ecken Spaniens," erklärt er. „Ihnen will ich von meiner Heimat erzählen. Aber viele von ihnen sind ferne Küchen gewöhnt, und sie sollen auch bei mir nicht nur eine eindimensionale Erfahrung machen. Und nicht allen behagt, was wir hier so essen." Auch dafür muss gesorgt sein, schließlich ist dieses Restaurant Teil eines großen Hotels mit über hundertdreißig Zimmern und Suiten. So obliegt Aguirre mit seinen sieben Köchen neben dem täglichen Restaurantbetrieb auch die Ausrichtung großer Bankette und kleiner Privatveranstaltungen. Und wenn Kongresse im benachbarten Kongresszentrum stattfinden, geht hier die Post ab. Dann wird das Personal bedarfsweise aufs Doppelte oder Dreifache aufgestockt.

KNOBLAUCH UND PETERSILIE -

die Eckpfeiler baskischer Küche, aus der sie nicht wegzudenken sind. Diese beiden Zutaten prägen fast jedes Rezept und haben auch unbeschadet den Wechsel von alter Hausmannskost in die Sphären der gehobenen Gastronomie überlebt. „Unsere Küche erkennt man am besten," erklärt der Baske, „am Beispiel ,merluza a la vasca'." Auf Deutsch: Seehecht in Knoblauch-Petersiliensauce. Dieses Gericht ist hier so beliebt und häufig anzutreffen, wie die Schweinshaxe in Bayern. Die Ingredienzen des Originals sind Knoblauch, Petersilie, Olivenöl, Seehecht, Venusmuscheln, ein hart gekochtes Ei und Spargel. Aguirre fährt fort: „So hat man das Gericht schon immer zubereitet, und das Ei war früher als billiges Lebensmittel dazu gedacht, den Magen zu füllen. Das lässt man heute weg. Aber die Kokotxas vom Seehecht, die man nirgendwo sonst außer im Baskenland isst, haben sich bis heute erhalten. Früher waren diese Fleischstücke aus der Kehle (der Seehecht besitzt keine Backen) preiswert und nicht besonders geschätzt. Heute sind sie zur Kostbarkeit geworden, weil sie selten sind. Seeteufel wurde damals häufig als Dünger auf die Bergfelder ausgebracht. Ich glaube, auch unsere billigen Sardinen werden in zwanzig Jahren als Luxusartikel gehandelt werden." Und selbstverständlich ist diese Speise auch auf der Speisekarte des Easo zu finden. Dessen Küchenchef liebt die Produkte der Umgebung, wie seine Kollegen, doch im Verbund mit den anderen Hotels der Westin Gruppe ist er weitgehendst auf deren Zentraleinkauf angewiesen. Das schmeckt ihm nicht immer, und so setzt er sich jeden Donnerstag ins Auto, fährt über die Grenze nach Frankreich und kauft dort bei einem Bauern, den er sehr schätzt, das Gemüse ein. Da sucht er sich selbst die Artischocken aus und findet auch die Kräuter, die seinen Gerichten das Aroma geben. Da weiß er, was er bekommt. Soviel Zeit muss sein. Einmal im Jahr treffen sich dann die kochenden Kollegen und die Einkäufer der Hotelkette in Madrid und wählen in Blindverkostungen die Lieferanten aus, die in den folgenden zwölf Monaten ihre Restaurants mit allem Erforderlichen, von Kaffee bis Öl, Fisch, Fleisch oder Gemüse beliefern dürfen. Viele Produkte erfahren bei Jokin de Aguirre gleich zweimalige Hitzezuwendung. So packt er sie mit Vorliebe in den Schmortopf, um sie anschließend kurz zu gratinieren. Sein Stil ist, wie er selbst sagt, stark von den Protagonisten neuer baskischer Küche geprägt, von Arzak und Pedro Subijana, mit denen er auch ein herzliches und kollegiales Verhältnis pflegt. „Hier kennt jeder den Anderen, und wir treffen uns häufig zum Gedankenaustausch," erzählt der sympathische Küchenchef. „Martín Berasategui war erst vor ein paar Tagen zum Essen hier." San Sebastián ist für gute Köche wie ihn ein Heimspiel. Das immense Interesse der einheimischen Bevölkerung an Essensdingen zeigt sich aber nicht nur in den edlen Stätten gehobener Koch-Kunst. Die Lust am Genuss ist ein Phänomen der Straße. Sidrerias und Tavernas sind gleichfalls bemüht mitzuhalten – und die liegen gleich um die Ecke vom Maria Cristina. Die Stadt an der Biskaya ist eine kulinarische Reise wert.

CRABMEAT SALAD WITH PINK GRAPEFRUIT ON A COLD PEA CREAM

KREBSFLEISCHSALAT MIT ROSA GRAPEFRUIT AUF KALTER ERBSENCREME

Serves 4

For the salad:
300 g/11 oz crabmeat,
60 g/2 oz zucchini,
60 g/2 oz green beans,
60 g/2 oz carrots,
2 tbsp balsamic vinegar,
5 tbsp olive oil,
salt

For the pea cream:
100 g/3 1/2 oz young, tender peas,
100 g/3 1/2 oz young, tender fava beans,
50 g/1 1/2 oz blanched spinach,
4 tsp mustard,
the egg yolks of 3 hard-boiled eggs,
3 tbsp mayonnaise

For the red beet vinaigrette:
100 ml/1/3 cup balsamic vinegar,
300 ml/1 1/4 cup cold-pressed olive oil,
30 g/1 oz cooked red beet,
salt, freshly ground white pepper

1 pink grapefruit,
a handful of curly endive, torn into pieces, chives

Put the crabmeat into a bowl. Boil the vegetables in salted water until just tender but still firm to the bite and cut them into small pieces. Toss vegetables with crabmeat, vinegar and oil and check for salt.
For the pea cream: Boil peas and fava beans in salted water for five minutes, then drain them in a sieve and purée them in a blender with the spinach. Beat in egg yolks, mustard and mayonnaise and strain the cream through a fine sieve.
For the vinaigrette: Finely purée the red beet with vinegar and oil in a blender, check it for salt and pepper and pass the vinaigrette through a fine sieve. Peel the grapefruit down to the flesh with a very sharp knife and remove the segments of flesh from their compartments.
Serving: Spread a circle of the pea cream onto each plate. Press the crabmeat salad into four round dishes and turn them onto the pea cream circles. Top crabmeat with a little heap of curly endive, garnish the plates with pink grapefruit filets and drizzle on a little red beet vinaigrette.

Für 4 Personen:

Für den Salat:
300 g Krebsfleisch,
60 g Zucchini,
60 g grüne Bohnen,
60 g Karotten,
2 EL Balsamessig,
5 EL Olivenöl,
Salz

Für die Erbsencreme:
100 g junge, zarte Erbsen,
100 g junge, zarte Dicke Bohnen,
50 g blanchierter Spinat,
4 TL Senf,
Eigelb von 3 hart gekochten Eiern,
3 EL Mayonnaise

Für die Rote Bete-Vinaigrette:
100 ml Balsamessig,
300 ml kalt gepresstes Olivenöl,
30 g gekochte Rote Bete,
Salz, weißer Pfeffer aus der Mühle

1 rosa Grapefruit,
1 Hand voll Friséesalat, zerpflückt, Schnittlauch

Krebsfleisch in eine Schüssel geben. Das Gemüse in Salzwasser knapp gar kochen, erkalten lassen und in kleine Würfel schneiden. Mit Krebsfleisch, Essig und Öl vermischen, mit Salz abschmecken.
Für die Erbsencreme: Erbsen und Dicke Bohnen in Salzwasser 5 Minuten kochen. Durch ein Sieb abgießen, mit dem Spinat im Mixer pürieren. Mit Eigelb, Senf und Mayonnaise verrühren, die Creme durch ein Sieb streichen.
Für die Vinaigrette: Den Essig mit dem Öl und der Roten Bete im Mixer fein pürieren, mit Salz und Pfeffer würzen, anschließend die Vinaigrette durch ein Sieb passieren.
Grapefruit mit dem Messer dick abschälen und die Filets herauslösen.
Zum Servieren: Mit Erbsencreme auf jeden Teller ein rundes Bett ausstreichen. Den Krebssalat in vier runde Formen pressen und darüber stürzen. Jeweils ein Häufchen zerpflückten Salat daraufsetzen, mit Grapefruitfilets und Schnittlauch garnieren. Das Ganze mit der Roten Bete-Vinaigrette beträufeln.

WARM DUCK FOIE GRAS WITH STEWED APPLES
IN A CURRANT AND PINE NUT SAUCE

LAUWARME ENTENSTOPFLEBER MIT APFELPÜREE
AN KORINTHEN- UND PINIENKERNSAUCE

Serves 4

500 g/1 lb duck foie gras,
salt, white pepper

4 slices fresh toast bread,
50 g/2 oz sugar,
2 sweet apples, peeled, cored and cut into pieces,
1 tsp lemon juice

For the sauce:
40 g/1 1/2 oz currants,
40 g/1 1/2 oz pine nuts,
120 ml/1/2 cup port,
200 ml/3/4 cup brown veal stock,
1 tsp cornstarch, mixed with 4 tbsp water

Cut the foie gras into 1 cm/1/3 inch slices. Take care to remove all veins and tendons.
Toast the bread in a toaster or in the oven until golden brown and cut out circles with a large round cookie cutter. In a small pot, allow the sugar to caramelize until medium brown. Add apple pieces and lemon juice (careful of splattering!) and cook on low heat until the apples are disintegrated and you have a thick purée. Allow the purée to cool, then spread evenly onto the toast circles. Place circles in an oven-proof baking dish.
For the sauce: Place currants in a small pot, add cold water to cover and bring to a boil. Boil for three minutes, then drain. Toast pine nuts on a baking sheet in a hot oven until golden brown. In a small saucepan, reduce the port by half. Add veal stock, currants and pine nuts, thicken lightly with the cornstarch mixture and allow to simmer for five minutes. Check for salt and pepper and keep warm.
Finish: Preheat the oven to 180° C/350° F. Rub the foie gras slices all over with a little salt and pepper. Heat a non-stick pan until very hot and sear the foie gras slices on both sides without adding additional fat. The foie gras ought to be lightly brown on the outside but still red in the middle. Drain the slices on paper towels and allow to cool. Place several layers of foie gras on the prepared toast circles and bake in the preheated oven for 6 - 8 minutes. Place the stacks on plates and allow them to cool a little. Douse with sauce right before you are ready to serve.

Für 4 Personen:

500 g Entenstopfleber,
Salz, weißer Pfeffer

4 Scheiben frisches Kastenweißbrot oder Toastbrot,
50 g Zucker,
2 süße Äpfel, geschält, entkernt und in Stücke
geschnitten, 1 TL Zitronensaft

Für die Sauce:
40 g Korinthen,
40 g Pinienkerne,
120 ml Portwein,
200 ml brauner Kalbsfond,
1 TL Maisstärke in 4 EL Wasser angerührt

Die Stopfleber in 1 cm dicke Scheiben schneiden, dabei sorgfältig alle Adern und Sehnen entfernen. Brotscheiben im Toaster oder im Ofen goldbraun rösten und rund ausstechen. Den Zucker in einem kleinen Topf mittelbraun karamellisieren. Die Apfelstücke und den Zitronensaft zugeben (Vorsicht, kann spritzen) und bei kleiner Hitze unter Rühren köcheln, bis die Äpfel zerfallen und ein dickes Püree entsteht. Erkalten lassen, die Toastscheiben damit bestreichen und in eine feuerfeste Form legen.
Für die Sauce: Die Korinthen in kaltem Wasser aufsetzen und zum Kochen bringen. Nach drei Minuten durch ein Sieb abgießen. Die Pinienkerne auf einem Blech im heißen Ofen goldgelb rösten. In einem kleinen Topf den Portwein auf ein Drittel einkochen. Kalbsfond, Korinthen und Pinienkerne zugeben, mit der angerührten Maisstärke leicht abbinden, die Sauce fünf Minuten köcheln. Mit Salz und Pfeffer abschmecken, warm halten.
Fertigstellung: Den Ofen auf 180° C vorheizen. Die Stopfleberscheiben von beiden Seiten leicht mit Salz und Pfeffer würzen. Eine beschichtete Pfanne stark erhitzen und die Leberscheiben ohne Fettzugabe von beiden Seiten heiß anbraten, so dass sie leicht bräunen, innen aber noch weitgehend roh sind. Auf Küchenpapier abtropfen und erkalten lassen. Die vorbereiteten Toastscheiben mit mehreren Lagen Leber belegen und im vorgeheizten Ofen 6 - 8 Minuten überbacken. Auf Teller anrichten, etwas abkühlen lassen, vor dem Servieren mit der Sauce übergießen.

HAKE BASQUE STYLE IN A PARSLEY SAUCE WITH MUSSELS

SEEHECHT BASKISCH IN PETERSILIENSAUCE MIT MUSCHELN

Serves 4

4 filets of hake, skin and bones removed,
about 150 - 180 g/5 - 6 oz each,
salt, freshly ground white pepper,
2 garlic cloves, very finely minced,
4 tbsp olive oil,
250 g/¹/₂ lb clams, in the shell,
¹/₂ tbsp flour, 150 ml/²/₃ cup water,
200 g/7 oz throat meat from hake (kokotxa),
if available,
2 tbsp parsley, finely chopped

Lightly rub the hake filets with salt and pepper on both sides.
In a heavy-bottomed casserole, sauté the garlic in olive oil on low heat until translucent. Place the fish filets into the pan, skin-side up, add mussels and keep sautéeing on medium heat for three minutes. Do not allow the filets to brown. Turn over fish and add flour. Add water, mix well and add kokotxa pieces. Simmer on low heat for five minutes. Right before serving, add finely chopped parsley and check the sauce for salt and pepper.

Note: Kokotxa, the throat meat of the hake, is considered an exquisite delicacy in the Basque country. There, the above recipe is often prepared with this part of the fish only and served with mussels and green sauce.
If kokotxa is not available, the dish also tastes very good with filets only.

Für 4 Personen:

4 Seehechtfilets ohne Gräten, je 150 - 180 g,
Salz, weißer Pfeffer aus der Mühle,
2 Knoblauchzehen, sehr fein gehackt,
4 EL Olivenöl,
250 g Venusmuscheln in der Schale,
¹/₂ EL Mehl,
150 ml Wasser,
200 g Fleisch aus der Kehle des Seehechts (Kokotxa),
falls erhältlich,
2 EL fein gehackte Petersilie

Seehechtfilets von beiden Seiten leicht salzen und mit Pfeffer würzen. In einer schweren Kasserolle den Knoblauch bei kleiner Hitze im Olivenöl glasig dünsten. Fischfilets mit der Hautseite nach oben einlegen, Muscheln zugeben, bei mittlerer Hitze drei Minuten braten, ohne Farbe nehmen zu lassen. Den Fisch umdrehen, das Mehl einrühren. Mit Wasser aufgießen, gut umrühren, die Kokotxas zugeben. Bei kleiner Hitze fünf Minuten köcheln. Vor dem Servieren die gehackte Petersilie unterrühren und die Sauce abschmecken.

Anmerkung: Die Kokotxas, das Fleisch aus der Kehle des Seehechtes, ist im Baskenland eine sehr beliebte Delikatesse. Das vorliegende Rezept wird dort gerne auch nur mit diesem Teil des Fisches, zusammen mit den Muscheln und der grünen Sauce zubereitet. Falls keine Kokotxas erhältlich sind, schmeckt das Rezept durchaus auch mit nur den Filets zubereitet.

TURBOT STEAKS IN AN OLIVE OIL-APPLE CIDER VINEGAR SAUCE
WITH ROASTED VEGETABLES

STEINBUTTSTEAKS AN OLIVENÖL-APFELESSIGSAUCE
MIT RÖSTGEMÜSE

Serves 4

2 kg/4 lbs turbot

For the sauce:
200 ml/³/₄ cup olive oil,
4 garlic cloves, crushed with the back of a knife,
50 ml/¹/₄ cup mild apple cider vinegar,
50 ml/¹/₄ cup water,
salt, white pepper

2 tomatoes, peeled, cored, cut into strips and
dried with a little oil in a 100° C/210° F oven
for two hours,
16 black olives, pitted and halved,
8 garlic cloves, roasted under the broiler
or in the oven,
8 artichoke bottoms, cut into eighths,
2 tbs olive oil,
chervil for garnish

Cut the turbot into eight steaks and set them aside. Coarsely chop the remainder of the fish. Preheat the oven to 200° C/390° F. Heat the oil in a heavy-bottomed casserole. Sauté fish parts and crushed garlic until opaque, then place casserole in the hot oven for another twenty minutes. Douse with vinegar and water, bring the liquid to a boil and allow to boil for a minute. Strain the sauce through a sieve and check for salt and pepper. Keep warm.
Preheat the oven to 230° C/450° F. Place the turbot steaks into an oven-proof dish. Add the tomatoes, olives, roasted and peeled garlic and artichokes. Drizzle with a little olive oil and bake the steaks for 5 - 7 minutes. Cover and allow to rest for another five minutes.
Serving: Divide turbot steaks and vegetables equally between four plates. Whisk the sauce with a wire whip until frothy and spoon it over the fish steaks. Garnish with sprigs of chervil.

Für 4 Personen:

2 kg Steinbutt

Für die Sauce:
200 ml Olivenöl,
4 Knoblauchzehen, mit dem Messerblatt zerdrückt,
50 ml milder Apfelweinessig
50 ml Wasser,
Salz, weißer Pfeffer

2 Tomaten, gehäutet, entkernt, Fruchtfleisch
in Streifen geschnitten und mit wenig Öl
im 100° C heißen Ofen 2 Stunden getrocknet,
16 schwarze Oliven, halbiert und entkernt,
8 Knoblauchzehen, in der Schale auf dem Grill
oder im Ofen geröstet,
8 Artischockenböden, in Achtel geschnitten,
2 EL Olivenöl,
Kerbel zum Garnieren

Aus dem Steinbutt 8 Steaks schneiden und beiseite legen, die Abschnitte grob hacken. Den Ofen auf 200° C vorheizen. In einem Bräter das Öl erhitzen. Die Fischabschnitte und den zerdrückten Knoblauch zugeben und anbraten, im Ofen 20 Minuten weiter braten. Mit Essig und Wasser ablöschen, zum Kochen bringen, unter Rühren eine Minute kochen und die Sauce durch ein Sieb passieren. Mit Salz und Pfeffer würzen, warm halten.
Den Ofen auf 230° C erhitzen. Die Fischsteaks in eine feuerfeste Form legen. Tomaten, Oliven, den gerösteten und geschälten Knoblauch und die Artischocken zugeben. Das Ganze mit Öl beträufeln und im Ofen 5 - 7 Minuten backen. Anschließend zugedeckt 5 Minuten ruhen lassen.
Zum Servieren: Steinbuttsteaks und Gemüse auf Teller verteilen. Die Sauce mit dem Schneebesen aufschlagen und die Fischsteaks damit überziehen. Mit Kerbelblättchen garnieren.

DUCK BREAST WITH SAVOY CABBAGE, POTATOES AND APPLE CIDER SAUCE

ENTENBRUST MIT WIRSING, KARTOFFELN UND APFELWEINSAUCE

Serves 4

2 duck breasts with a thin layer of fat left on, about 400 g/14 oz each,
salt, freshly ground black pepper,
20 small potatoes, peeled and cut into even pieces, 50 g/1 1/2 oz butter

For the Savoy cabbage:
1 onion, minced, 1 garlic clove, minced, 50 ml/1 1/4 cup sunflower oil,
400 ml/1 1/3 cups water, 1 sweet apple, peeled and cored, cut into pieces,
1 Savoy cabbage, hard core removed, cut into fine strips,
1 tbsp apple cider vinegar, salt, freshly ground black pepper

For the sauce:
2 tbsp sugar, 2 tbsp water, 3 tbsp apple cider,
100 ml/1/3 cup brown duck stock

For the Savoy cabbage: Sauté onion and garlic in oil until translucent. Add apple and Savoy cabbage. Douse with water, cover and simmer on low heat for about forty-five minutes until tender. Season with apple cider vinegar, salt and pepper and keep warm.

Preheat the oven to 200° C/390° F. Rub the duck breasts all over with salt and pepper and place them into a heavy-bottomed casserole, fat-side down. Bake duck breasts in the oven for 10 - 12 minutes. The meat should still be slightly pink in the middle. Remove from oven and allow to rest for ten minutes, covered.

Fry the potatoes in butter until golden brown on all sides. Sprinkle them with a little water, cover and place the pan in the oven for 10 - 15 minutes.

For the sauce: Make a caramel from the sugar and water. Douse with apple cider and duck stock and simmer, stirring constantly, until you have a saucy consistency. Check for salt and pepper.

Serving: Arrange Savoy cabbage on plates. Cut duck breasts into slices and place a fan of slices on top of cabbage. Arrange potatoes all around and drizzle some sauce onto the meat.

Für 4 Personen:

2 Entenbrüste mit dünnem Fettrand, je ca. 400 g, Salz, schwarzer Pfeffer aus der Mühle,
20 kleine Kartoffeln, geschält, gleichmäßig zugeschnitten, 50 g Butter

Für den Wirsing:
1 Zwiebel, fein gehackt, 1 Knoblauchzehe, fein gehackt, 50 ml Sonnenblumenöl,
400 g Wasser, 1 süßer Apfel, geschält (Kernhaus entfernt), in Stücke geschnitten,
1 Wirsing (Strunk entfernt), fein geschnitten, 1 EL Apfelweinessig,
Salz, schwarzer Pfeffer aus der Mühle

Für die Sauce:
2 EL Zucker, 2 EL Wasser, 3 EL Apfelwein, 100 ml brauner Entenfond

Für den Wirsing: In einem Topf die Zwiebel und den Knoblauch im Öl glasig dünsten. Den Wirsing und den Apfel zugeben, mit Wasser auffüllen und zugedeckt bei kleiner Hitze ca. 45 Minuten weich garen. Mit dem Apfelessig, Salz und Pfeffer würzen, warm halten.

Den Ofen auf 200° C vorheizen. Die Entenbrüste mit Salz und Pfeffer würzen, mit der Fettseite nach unten in einen Bräter legen und 10 - 12 Minuten im Ofen braten. Das Fleisch soll innen noch zartrosa sein. Herausnehmen, zugedeckt 10 Minuten ruhen lassen.

Die Kartoffeln in der Butter rundum goldgelb anbraten. Mit wenig Wasser ablöschen und die Kartoffeln zugedeckt im Ofen 10 - 15 Minuten weich braten.

Für die Sauce: Aus Zucker und Wasser ein Karamell herstellen. Mit Apfelwein und Entenfond ablöschen, unter Rühren zu einer Sauce kochen. Mit Salz und Pfeffer abschmecken.

Zum Servieren: Wirsinggemüse in Teller anrichten. Die Entenbrüste in Scheiben schneiden und fächerförmig über das Gemüse legen. Die Kartoffeln rundherum verteilen, das Fleisch mit der Sauce übergießen.

Serves 4

For the mousse:
100 ml/¹/₃ cup orange juice, 1 tbsp Cointreau,
2 sheets gelatin, soaked in water,
4 egg yolks, beaten with 50 g/1¹/₂ oz sugar until light and fluffy,
2 egg whites, beaten into stiff peaks with 50 g/1¹/₂ oz sugar,
150 ml/²/₃ cup cream, beaten into soft peaks with 1 tsp sugar

For the sauce:
100 g/3¹/₂ oz sugar, freshly squeezed juice of one lemon,
250 ml/1 cup freshly squeezed orange juice,
25 g/1 oz green peppercorns

Garnish:
cocoa for dusting,
100 g/3¹/₂ oz raspberry purée (raspberries puréed in a blender
with powdered sugar and strained through a sieve),
4 small sprigs of mint

For the mousse: Warm up orange juice and Cointreau and dissolve the soaked gelatin in the liquid. Allow the mixture to cool and fold in egg yolk mixture, egg whites and cream. Take care not to overmix. Place the mixture into round molds and deep-freeze.
For the sauce: Heat the sugar and the lemon juice in a small pot until the sugar turns a medium caramel brown. Douse with the orange juice (careful of splattering!) and add the peppercorns. Simmer, stirring constantly, until the sauce begins to thicken.
Serving: Unmold the mousses onto plates (dip the molds into hot water for a second if necessary) and dust them with cocoa. Surround them with peppercorn-orange sauce. Dot the sauce with dollops of raspberry purée according to your own designs, garnish with sprigs of mint and serve.

FROZEN ORANGE MOUSSE

IN A GREEN PEPPERCORN-

ORANGE SAUCE

GEFRORENE ORANGEN-

MOUSSE AN GRÜNER

PFEFFER-ORANGENSAUCE

Für 4 Personen:

Für die Mousse:
100 ml Orangensaft, 1 EL Cointreau, 2 Gelatineblätter, in Wasser eingeweicht,
4 Eigelb, mit 50 g Zucker zu hellem Schaum geschlagen,
2 Eiweiß, mit 50 g Zucker zu Schnee geschlagen,
150 ml Sahne, mit 1 TL Zucker halbsteif geschlagen

Für die Sauce:
100 g Zucker, frisch gepresster Saft einer Zitrone,
250 ml frisch gepresster Orangensaft, 25 grüne Pfefferkörner

Garnitur:
Kakao zum Bestäuben,
100 g Himbeerpüree (Himbeeren mit Puderzucker im Mixer püriert und durch ein Sieb passiert),
4 kleine Minzezweigchen

Für die Mousse: Den Orangensaft mit dem Cointreau erhitzen und die eingeweichte und ausgedrückte Gelatine darin auflösen. Erkalten lassen, mit dem Eischaum, Eischnee und der Sahne locker vermischen. Die Masse in runde Förmchen füllen und gefrieren.
Für die Sauce: Den Zucker mit dem Zitronensaft in einem kleinen Topf erhitzen, bis der Zucker mittelbraun karamellisiert. Mit Orangensaft ablöschen (Vorsicht, spritzt) und die Pfefferkörner hinzufügen. Unter Rühren kochen lassen, bis die Sauce leicht eingedickt ist.
Zum Servieren: Die Mousse aus den Formen lösen (wenn nötig, zuvor kurz in heißes Wasser tauchen), mit etwas Kakao bestäuben und auf Teller legen. Mit der Pfeffer-Orangensauce umgießen. Von dem Himbeerpüree ein Muster in die Sauce zeichnen, mit Minzezweigchen garnieren und servieren.

WARM PINEAPPLE WITH PINEAPPLE RUM SORBET

LAUWARME ANANAS MIT ANANAS-RUM-SORBET

Serves 4

For the sorbet (makes 1 liter/4 cups):
100 g/3 ^{1}/$_2$ oz sugar,
350 ml/1 ^{1}/$_2$ cups water,
100 g/3 ^{1}/$_2$ oz glucose,
^{1}/$_2$ liter/4 cups pineapple juice,
60 ml/^{1}/$_4$ cup rum

For the dried pineapple:
50 g/1 ^{1}/$_2$ oz sugar,
50 ml/^{1}/$_4$ cup water,
4 thin pineapple slices (1 mm/^{1}/$_{25}$ th inch)

For the caramelized pineapple:
4 slices fresh pineapple, 1 cm/^{1}/$_3$ inch thick,
100 g/3 ^{1}/$_2$ oz brown sugar,
500 ml/2 cups pineapple juice

For the sorbet: Bring sugar and water to a boil until all sugar crystals are dissolved. Add glucose, pineapple juice and rum. Freeze in an ice cream maker according to directions.

For the dried pineapple: Preheat the oven to 90° C/ 190° F. Boil the sugar and water until syrupy. Dip the pineapple slices into the syrup, allow the excess syrup to drip off and place the slices on a non-stick baking sheet. Allow to dry in the oven for an hour.

For the caramelized pineapple: In a saucepan, caramelize sugar with two spoonfuls of pineapple juice until medium brown. Add the pineapple slices and the remaining pineapple juice, turn down heat to low and simmer, uncovered, until the liquid has thickened and is beginning to caramelize again. Turn the pineapple slices every now and then. Add a little water to obtain a thick saucy consistency and set aside.

Serving: Arrange the pineapple slices and the sauce on plates. Add a scoop of sorbet to each plate and garnish with one dried pineapple slice each.

Für 4 Personen:

Für das Sorbet (ergibt 1 Liter Sorbet):
100 g Zucker,
350 ml Wasser,
100 g Glukose,
^{1}/$_2$ Liter Ananassaft,
60 ml Rum

Für die getrocknete Ananas:
50 g Zucker,
50 ml Wasser,
4 dünn aufgeschnittene Ananasscheiben (1 mm)

Für die karamellisierte Ananas:
4 Scheiben frische Ananas, 1 cm dick,
100 g brauner Zucker,
500 ml Ananassaft

Für das Sorbet: Zucker mit Wasser zum Kochen bringen, bis sich alle Kristalle aufgelöst haben. Die Glukose zugeben, zum Schluß den Ananassaft und den Rum unterrühren. In der Eismaschine gefrieren.

Für die getrocknete Ananas: Den Ofen auf 90° C vorheizen. Aus dem Zucker und dem Wasser einen Sirup kochen. Die Ananasscheiben hineintauchen, abtropfen lassen und auf ein beschichtetes Blech legen. Im Ofen eine Stunde trocknen lassen.

Für die karamellisierte Ananas: Zucker mit 2 Löffeln Ananassaft in einem Topf mittelbraun karamellisieren. Ananasscheiben zugeben, mit dem restlichen Saft aufgießen und bei kleiner Hitze ohne Deckel köcheln, bis der Saft eingedickt ist und erneut beginnt, zu karamellisieren. Dabei die Ananasscheiben hin und wieder wenden. Etwas Wasser hinzugießen, so dass die Sauce dickflüssig wird. Beiseite stellen.

Zum Servieren: Die karamellisierten Ananasscheiben mit der Sauce auf Teller verteilen. Je eine Kugel Sorbet dazugeben und mit getrockneten Ananasscheiben garnieren.

Martín Berasategui.

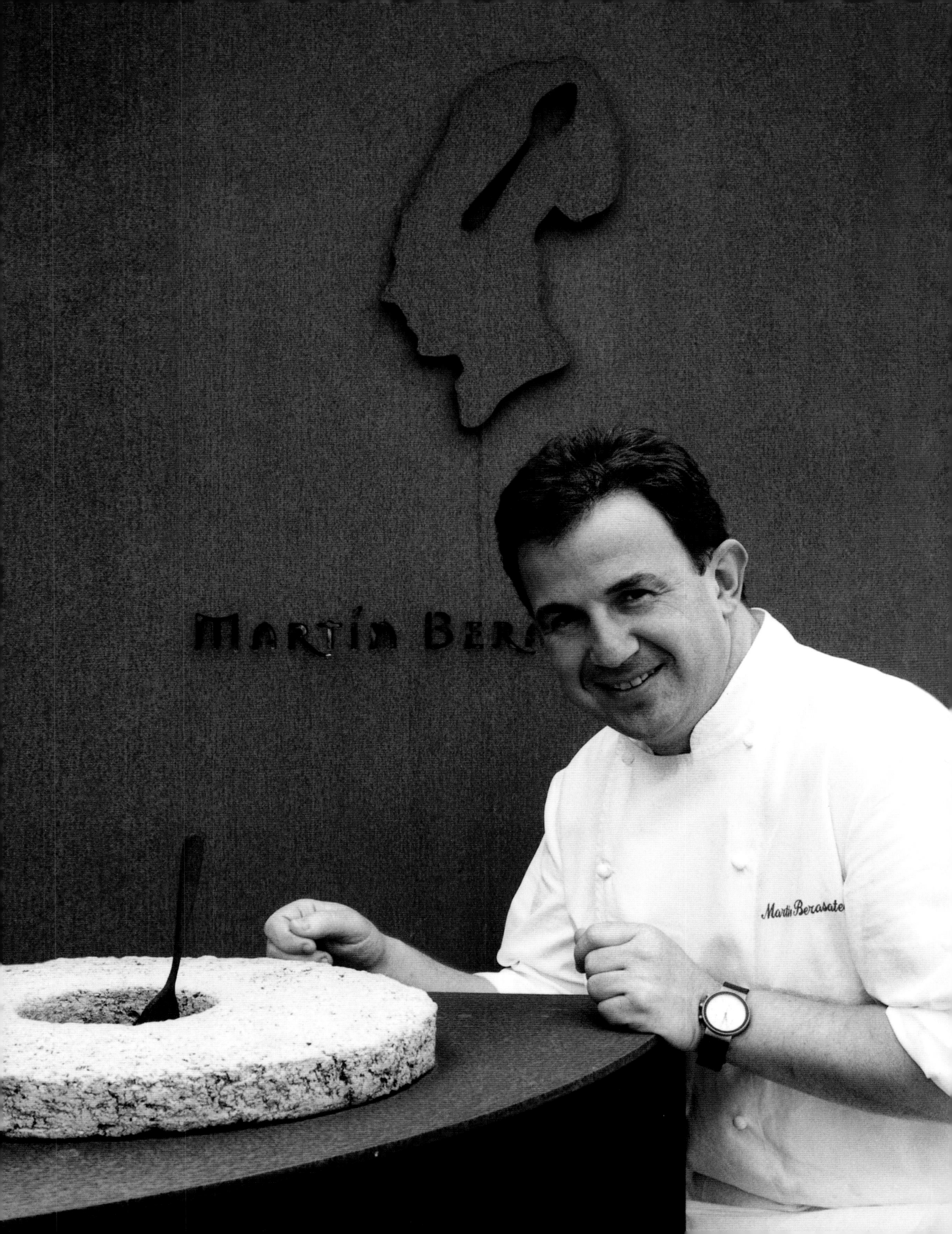
MARTÍN BERA
Martín Berasate

In San Sebastián in the Basque country, everyday life, thought and action are invariably dominated by three things: food, politics and soccer. Only thus it becomes plausibly why culinary appreciation (which is definitely taking first place) has led to such a massive accumulation of fine dining facilities in this area. San Sebastián, with its splendid architecture and Paris-style boulevard charm, is hiding a picturesque old town with a maze of small alleyways at its very core, between the fishing harbor at the bay and the newly built congress hall. Here, almost every second door opens up into one of the numerous tapas bars, whose counters feature platters heaped up high with layers of pintxos (small snacks) and bocadillos (sandwiches). There is hardly any room for the beaker of wine or beer, which, as a rule, is filled only a few centimeters high. You do not stay at one place forever, just for a chat with a few friends, to eat a few snacks, to pay by the piece and then hop on to the next bar. This way, you can spend your evening quite contentedly eating yourself through the entire selection of tapas. Who, then, would still be interested in sitting down rigidly at a table when eating, communication and strolling may be so delightfully combined?

Nevertheless, between the harbor and market hall, between fish and vegetables, we find the "Bodegón Alejandro", a small, very popular restaurant. Many years ago, mother and aunt used to serve Basque country-style cooking here, und Martín Berasetegui learned his trade from them. "It formed and influenced me", says he, forty years old by now, whose tables are sought even by gourmets from neighboring France. "I am a chef of the market (cocinero del mercado). Everything we use is fresh and from the surroundings. Fish, mushrooms, vegetables, milk and milk products. Just everything. Here are the roots of my cuisine." Yet, the chef now practices his art in the green surroundings of town, on the edge of the small, albeit not very charming suburb Lasarte. On the slope into which he built his restaurant "Martín Berasetegui" in 1992, countryside sounds and views may be enjoyed from the windows of the spacious restaurant. A dog and the lowing of cows from the pastures on the opposite slope can be heard in the kitchen. A rooster is crowing. Yes, we are in

the country, the surroundings which determine his kind of cooking. Basque cuisine rooted in the region, but without borders, he explains. "These are modern times, we live in a world without borders. All technologies, all products are available, but you never ought to forget where you were born and where you come from."

Below the restaurant's extensive terrace, he grows the seasonings for his cuisine himself in his own herb garden. "Our traditional kitchen has so much to offer, an inexhaustible wealth of dishes and products", the energetic Basque maintains. "And almost everything I can find close by here – on the country and in the ocean." It is spring, tomatoes and wild strawberries are just getting their best aroma. Chipirones (tiny squid) and tender anchoas (anchovies) are in season. "Collectors always bring me morels and farmers the freshest and most tender peas, which have not yet formed a hard shell. All my suppliers belong to my team, and my menus pay tribute to these people." Thus, the garden comes directly to his kitchen. But the seasons do not invariably determine the rhythm of his dishes, what he cooks is in his head. "My menu often changes during the year", he explains, "but not when new products become available, only when there is a new recipe forming in my head which is better than one on the menu. A separate section of the kitchen is always busy developing new recipes. The whole year, the whole week. An entire part of the kitchen devoted to thinking and testing. Two chefs and the master work on refining techniques and procedures, using the possibilities of modern kitchen technology. With respect to the ingredients, how-ever, they stick to what the region has to offer. There, he hardly makes any compromises.

Cooking and the knowledge of food has a long tradition here, and Berasetegui's fans are more often than not experienced connoisseurs of Basque cuisine. With him, they find the suspense, the kick with which he raises old favorites to new culinary heights. They are his best critics and admirers, and he enjoys serving them in the dining-hall, which features a touch of rural elegance. On one side, high panoramic windows are arranged in a quarter of a circle. The view is green and only green. Round tables are loosely placed in the

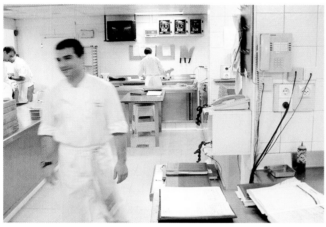

room, but more than forty-five to fifty guests are rather the exception. To keep his quality, he does not like to exceed that number. The floor is laid with yellow ceramic tiles, the tables have simple wooden chairs, the curtains and walls are kept in English green. An open fireplace, ferns and climbers here and there. There is room for dancing in the kitchen, too. Thirty white-hatted employees cut and chop at stainless steel tables, stirring their pots and juggling stacks of plates. Steam is rising, sizzling and bubbling is heard. The master is in the middle of it all, testing the degree of done-ness of the liver with his finger, wiping a little spot from the plate before he disappears in the direction of the dining-room. This is the domain of his wife, who supervises the service crew with a gentle, unobtrusive hand.

The name Martín Berasetegui is synonymous for the high art of cooking, a top restaurant, and it has become an idea, a trademark, a watermark of his philosophy. The name has risen above a growing number of so far six gastronomical enterprises which are no clones, no copies of his restaurant, however, but a group of satellites living their own existence remote from home, always somehow bearing the signature of the cuisine from which they originated. The "Grupo Martín Berasetegui" is a helpful background and start-up for the best chefs who have cooked in Berasetegui´s kitchens. His best friends who are now at the helm of their own, renowned restaurants, whether at Guggenheim museum in Bilbao, in the congress hall of San Sebastián or at the old "Bodegón Alejandro". The name Berasetegui has paved their way. He, who has been granted so much success wanted to let others take part in it. "We would like to demonstrate what the new generation of Basque chefs is capable of, but without help, only a few will get a chance to prove it. I don´t only think of myself. For me, the most important thing in life is the person, the human being", says Martín Berasetegui. "The professional comes afterwards. The chefs who learn from me and to whom I pass on my knowledge will improve on it. And therefore, the Basque cuisine of today will even be better in the future. That´s what I fight for. And yet", he adds, "my place is here, in my restaurant. I will always be in the kitchen."

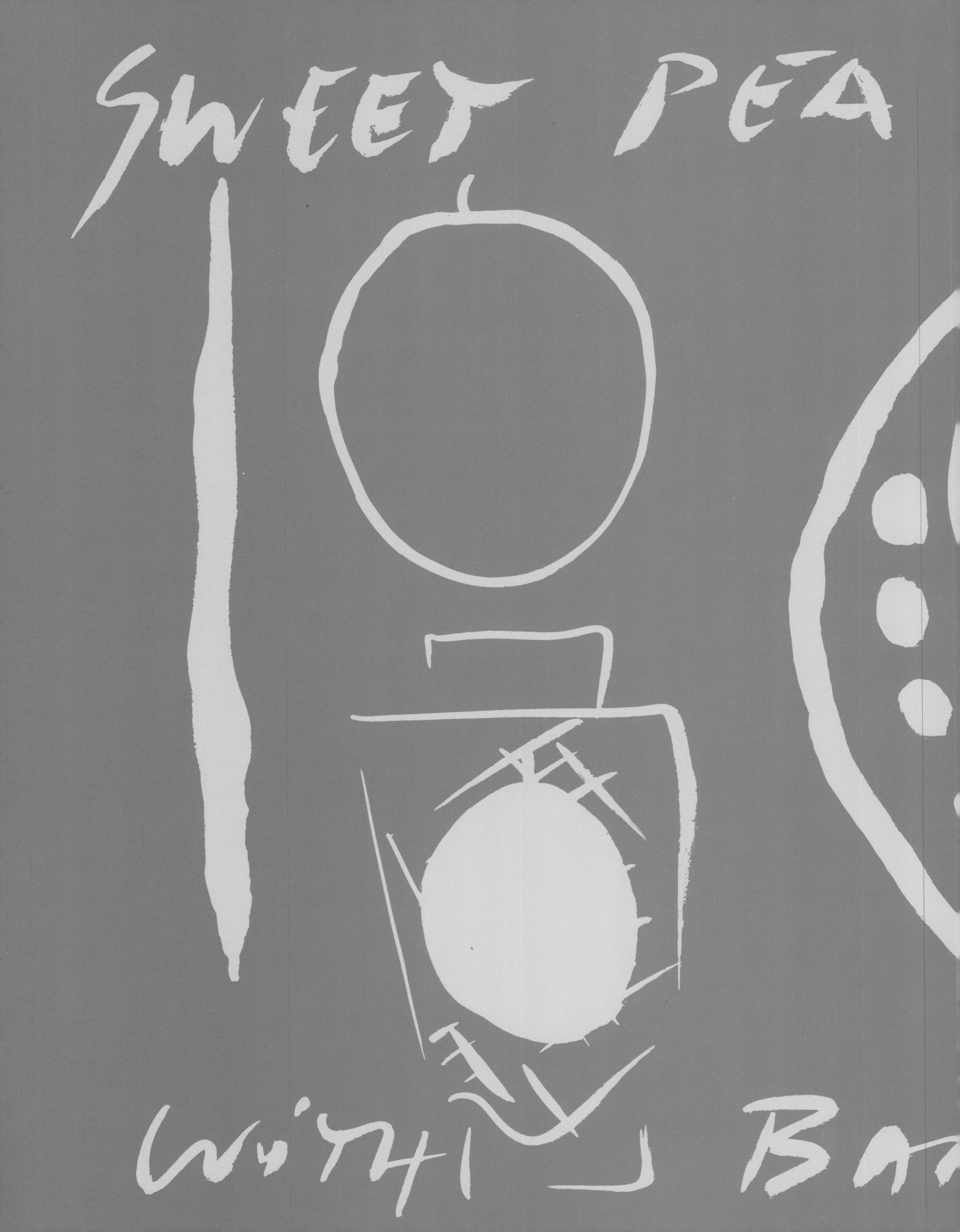
SWEET PEA
With

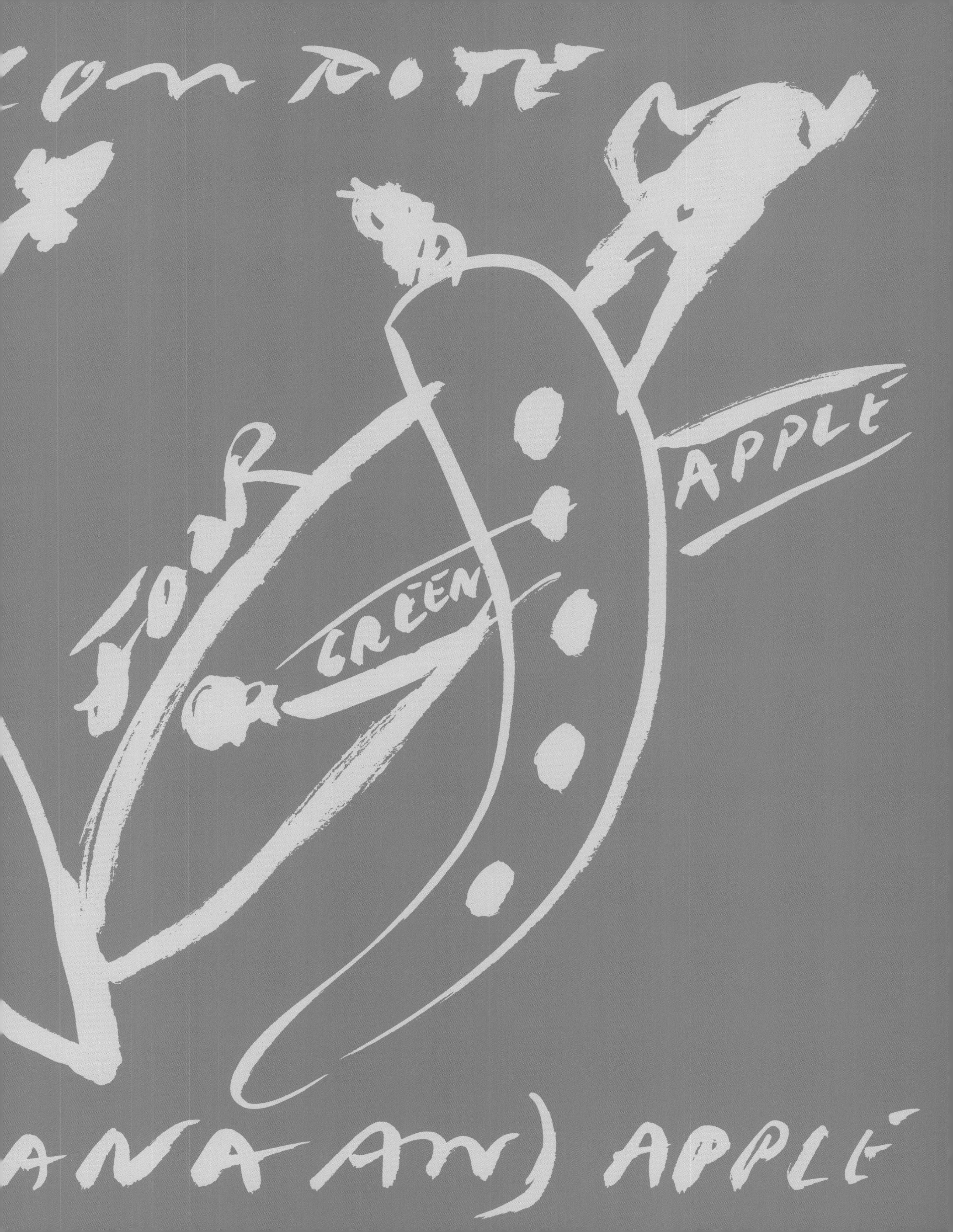
APPLE
GREEN
APPLE

Drei Dinge beherrschen im baskischen San Sebastián unübersehbar das tägliche Leben, Denken und Tun: Essen, Politik und Fußball. Nur so lässt sich plausibel erklären, weshalb hier die kulinarische Wertschätzung (die deutlich erkennbar an erster Stelle steht) ihren Niederschlag in solch massiver Anhäufung feiner Speiseplätze gefunden hat. San Sebastián, mit seiner prachtvollen Architektur und dem Pariser Charme seiner Straßenzüge, birgt im inneren Kern, zwischen Fischerhafen an der Bucht und der neu erbauten Kongresshalle, die kleinen Gässchen einer urgemütlichen Altstadt. Fast hinter jeder zweiten Tür öffnet sich eine der unzähligen Tapas-Bars, auf deren Tresen überbordend und Platten-weise pintxos (kleine Happen) und bocadillos (belegte Brötchen) ausgebreitet liegen. Da ist kaum Platz für das Becherglas Wein oder Bier, das in der Regel nur wenige Zentimeter hoch befüllt wird. Man will ja hier nicht auf ewig verweilen, sondern plaudert mit Freunden, nimmt ein paar Happen und bezahlt dann pro Stück, um das Lokal alsbald zu wechseln. Auf diese Weise kann man sich höchst genüsslich durch das Viertel futtern und den Abend verbringen. Wen interessiert noch das fest verankerte Sitzen an einem Tisch, wenn Essen, Kommunikation und Flanieren so abwechslungsreich miteinander verknüpft werden können.

Zwischen Fisch und Gemüse, zwischen Hafen und Markthalle lag und liegt das „Bodegón Alejandro", ein kleines, sehr populäres Restaurant. Hier kochten vor vielen Jahren Mutter und Tante baskische Hausmannskost, und der vierzehnjährige Martín Berasategui erlernte von ihnen sein Handwerk. „Das hat mich geprägt und beeinflusst," erklärt der heute Vierzigjährige, zu dessen Tischen selbst Franzosen aus dem Nachbarland streben. „Daher bin ich ein Koch des Marktes (cocinero del mercado). Alles konnten wir frisch und in nächster Umgebung einkaufen. Fisch, Pilze und Gemüse, Milch und Milchprodukte. Einfach alles. Hier sind die Wurzeln meiner Küche zu finden." Die exerziert der Kochkünstler aber mittlerweile im grünen Umland der Stadt, am Rande des kleinen, wenngleich wenig charmanten Vororts Lasarte. Aber am Hang, wo er 1992 sein „Martín Berasategui" hingebaut hat, dringt fast nur Ländliches hör- und sichtbar zu den Fenstern des weitläufigen Restaurants herein. Von der Wiese am Gegenhang sind Hundegebell und das Muhen der Kühe zu hören. Ein Hahn kräht. Wir sind auf dem Land. Die Umgebung, die seine Art von Kochen bestimmt. Regional verwurzelt. Baskische Küche, „jedoch ohne Grenzen," ergänzt er. „Wir leben in einer Zeit der Moderne, in einer Welt ohne Grenzen. Alle Techniken, jedes Produkt ist heute verfügbar, aber du darfst niemals vergessen, wo du geboren und wo du aufgewachsen bist."

Unterhalb der weitläufigen Terrasse zieht er im eigenen Kräutergarten Würzmittel für die Küche. „Unsere traditionelle Küche hat so viel zu bieten, einen unerschöpflichen Reichtum an Gerichten und Produkten," erläutert der energische Baske. „Und fast alles finde ich hier in der Umgebung – an Land und im Meer." Es ist Frühjahr, Tomaten und Walderdbeeren bekommen gerade ihr bestes Aroma. Chipirones (winzige Tintenfische) und zarte Anchoas (Sardellen) gibt es jetzt in dieser Saison. „Sammler bringen mir Morcheln und Bauern frischeste zarte Erbsen, die noch keine harte Schale haben. Alle meine Lieferanten gehören zum Team, und meine Speisekarte ist eine Hommage an diese Menschen."

So kommt der Garten direkt in seine Küche. Aber die Jahreszeiten bestimmen nicht zwingend den Rhythmus seiner Gerichte, sondern sein Kopf. „Meine Karte wechselt zwar häufig während des Jahres," erklärt er, „aber nicht nur, wenn es neue Produkte gibt, sondern erst wenn in meinem Kopf ein neues Gericht entsteht, das besser als das auf der Karte ist." Eine eigene Sektion der Küche ist nur damit beschäftigt, Rezepte zu entwickeln. Das ganze Jahr, die ganze Woche. Ein Teil der Küche, der nur denkt und ausprobiert. Zwei Köche feilen zusammen mit dem Meister an Techniken und Verfahren und bedienen sich dabei der Erkenntnisse, die die heutige Küchentechnologie zu bieten hat. Doch sie konzentrieren sich in den Zutaten auf das, was das regionale Umfeld zu bieten hat. Hier macht er kaum Kompromisse.

Kochen und das Wissen ums Essen hat hier lange Tradition, und Beraseteguis Fans sind nicht selten gewiefte Kenner der baskischen Küche. Bei ihm aber finden sie den spannenden Kick, mit dem er Altbewährtes zu neuen kulinarischen Höhen emporgekocht hat. Sie sind seine besten Kritiker und Bewunderer. Sie bewirtet er im ländlich-eleganten Saal des Restaurants. Hohe Panoramafenster spannen sich im Viertelbogen um die eine Seite. Der Blick geht nur ins Grün. Locker stehen runde Tische im großen Raum, doch mehr als fünfundvierzig bis fünfzig Plätze werden nie besetzt. Um seine Qualität zu halten, will er diese Zahl nicht überschreiten. Am Boden gelbe Keramikfliesen, die Tische mit schlichten Holzstühlen, Vorhänge und Wände in englischem Grün. Ein offener Kamin, Farne und Rankgewächse. Auch in der Küche ist Platz zum Tanzen. Dreißig weißbemützte Mitarbeiter schnippeln und hacken an Edelstahltischen, rühren in Töpfen und jonglieren mit Tellerstapeln. Es dampft, zischt und brodelt. Der Chef steht mittendrin und prüft mit dem Finger den Garzustand der Leber, wischt noch einen Fleck vom Teller, ehe der Richtung Speisesaal verschwindet. Hier ist seine Frau zuständig und lenkt mit unauffälliger Regie die Aktionen der Service-Crew.

Der Name Martín Berasetegui ist Synonym für exzellente Kochkunst, ein Restaurant der Spitzenklasse und er ist zu einem Begriff geworden, einem Markenzeichen. Ein Prägestempel seiner Philosophie. Dieser Name schwebt über einer wachsenden Gruppe von bisher sechs gastronomischen Unternehmen, die keine Klone, keine Kopien seines Restaurants darstellen, sondern eine Reihe von Satelliten, die einmal von zuhause losgelöst ihr eigenes Dasein leben, aber immer irgendwie die Handschrift der Küche tragen werden, aus der sie hervorgegangen sind. Die „Grupo Martín Berasetegui" ist stützender Hintergrund und Starthilfe für die besten Köche, die seine Küche durchlaufen haben. Es sind seine besten Freunde, die nun am Herd eigener, hoch geschätzter Restaurants stehen – ob im Guggenheim-Museum von Bilbao, in der Kongresshalle von San Sebastián oder im alten „Bodegón Alejandro". Ihnen hat der Name Beraseategui den Weg geebnet. Wem Lukullus so viel Erfolg beschieden hat, so dachte er, der sollte auch andere daran teilhaben lassen. „Wir wollen demonstrieren, zu was die neue Generation baskischer Köche fähig ist. Aber ohne Hilfe werden nur wenige die Chance bekommen, es auch zu beweisen. Ich denke einfach nicht nur ich, ich, ich. Für mich ist im Leben das wichtigste die Person, der Mensch," betont er. „Der Profi kommt erst danach. Die Köche, die ich ausbilde und denen ich mein Können beibringe, werden es noch verbessern. Und damit wird auch die baskische Küche von heute in der Zukunft noch besser sein. Dafür kämpfen wir. Doch," fügt er hinzu, „mein Platz ist hier, in meinem Restaurant. Ich werde immer in der Küche stehen."

Con la tradición de la cocina Vasca, los productos de esta tierra y siguiendo las estaciones, Martín Berasategui les ofrece...

Jamón de cerdo ibérico de gran bellota	3.100
Milhojas caramelizado de anguila ahumada, foie-gras, cebolleta y manzana verde	2.700
Verduras naturales con jamón ibérico	2.700
Infusión de tomate natural con bacalao, crema montada de patata y caviar de huevas de trucha	2.700
Helado de aceite de oliva con jamón ibérico, guisantes, cebolletas tiernas y cuajada líquida de pepino	3.100
Gelatina caliente de frutos de mar con sopa de anís y sorbete de hinojo	3.100
Sopa ligera de foie gras, hongos y flor de capuchina	3.100
Arroz cremoso con almejas, pulpo y tuétano	3.500
Ensalada de patata confitada con trufa, bacalao y vinagreta de mango	3.100

Lomos de merluza en salsa con almejas	3.600
Almejas a la marinera	3.600
Taco de bacalao a la vizcaina con caracoles	3.200
Kokotxas de merluza en salsa	4.750
Lenguado asado con alcachofas, hongos y ensalada de fideos de espárragos	3.600
Rape asado con panceta, tallarines de begi aundi y jugo yodado de mostaza	3.600

Callos a la manera tradicional	2.400
Chuletón de buey asado a la parrilla con terrina de patata y tocineta ibérica (mínimo 2 personas)	3.100 POR PERSONA
Foie-gras caliente con ragout, crema de calabaza asada y vinagreta de su jugo	2.900
Chuletas de cordero asadas con pastel de setas y foie, "melaza" de nueces y naranja	3.500
Manitas de cerdo ibérico rellenas, con tosta de hongos y queso Idiazábal	2.600
Pichón asado sobre ñoquis de queso, verduras y aceite de olivas negras	3.250
Mollejas de ternera de leche asadas con falso arroz de patata y salsa de lomo ibérico	3.250

DEBIDO A LA REPOSTERÍA NATURAL ARTESANA E INMEDIATA,
MARTÍN RECOMIENDA QUE LOS POSTRES SEAN PEDIDOS AL COMIENZO DE LA COMIDA.

Infusión de frutas rojas de nuestra huerta con helado de queso Idiazabal y remolacha seca	1.250
Sopa de mamia con higos confitados, su helado y cristal de pan de especies	1.250
Tarta fina de hojaldre con pera, vainilla y su jalea casera de reineta	1.250
Soufflé de chocolate con crema helada de caramelo y canela, gelatina de menta y jugo de cacao	1.250
El jugo de lágrima de guisante, plátano y naranja, sorbete de manzana y su crujiente de pistacho	1.250
Café con leche helado, sopas caramelizadas y ciruelas	1.250
El Yogur casero con mango, fruta de la pasión y su granizado de miel	1.250

MENÚ DEGUSTACIÓN
«ESPECIAL» 10.800

COMENZARÁ CON ESTOS CUATRO APERITIVOS:

Ensalada de pimientos, asados a la leña, con anchoa marinada.

El pastel de queso del País, asado al horno, con jamón.

Sorbete de apio.

Sopa cremosa de lentejas.

Con el milhojas caramelizado de anguila ahumada, foie gras,

cebolleta y manzana verde.

Y SEGUIRÁ EN PEQUEÑAS RACIONES CON:

Ensalada de patata confitada con trufa, bacalao y vinagreta de mango.

Arroz cremoso con almejas, pulpo y tuétano.

Gelatina caliente de frutos de mar con sopa de anís y sorbete de hinojo.

Helado de aceite de oliva con jamón ibérico, guisantes, cebolletas tiernas

y cuajada líquida de pepino.

Lenguado asado con alcachofas, hongos y ensalada de fideos de espárragos.

Pichón asado sobre ñoquis de queso, verduras y aceite de olivas negras.

El jugo de lágrima de guisante, plátano y naranja, sorbete de manzana y su crujiente de pistacho.

El Yogur casero con mango, fruta de la pasión y su granizado de miel.

CREAM OF SEA URCHINS WITH A FENNEL SAUCE AND FENNEL SORBET

SEEIGEL-CREME MIT FENCHELSAUCE UND SORBET

Serves 4

For the fennel sorbet:
1 liter/4 cups water 250 g/¹/₂ lb sugar, 200 g/7 oz glucose,
80 g/2¹/₂ oz saccharose, 800 g/1³/₄ lb fennel, freshly squeezed juice of
half a lemon, 3 sheets gelatin (only if a Pacojet device is available)

For the fennel sauce:
100 g/3¹/₂ oz fennel (the inner, tender core only), sliced thinly,
80 g/3 oz onion, sliced thinly, 40 g/1¹/₂ oz butter, salt,
500 ml/2 cups mussels stock, 300 g/11 oz double cream,
a pinch star anise, ground, ¹/₄ tsp fennel seed,
50 g/2 oz cold butter, freshly squeezed lemon juice

7 sea urchins, 40 ml/¹/₈ cup hearty, reduced lobster stock,
50 ml/¹/₄ cup milk, 2 eggs,
2 tbsp parsley juice (made from raw parsley run through a juicer),
¹/₂ tsp sugar, 1 tsp lobster coral, 4 scallops, white part only,
1 tbsp oil for frying, 2 young, thin stalks of leek, 1 tbsp butter

Für 4 Personen:

Für das Fenchelsorbet:
1 Liter Wasser, 250 g Zucker, 200 g Glukose, 80 g Invertzucker,
800 g Fenchel, frisch gepresster Saft einer halben Zitrone,
3 Gelatineblätter (nur nötig wenn ein Pacojet Gerät vorhanden ist)

Für die Fenchelsauce:
100 g Fenchel (den inneren, zarten Teil verwenden), in dünne
Scheiben geschnitten, 80 g Zwiebel, in dünne Scheiben geschnitten,
40 g Butter, Salz, 500 ml Muschelfond, 300 ml Doppelrahm,
1 Msp gemahlener Sternanis, ¹/₄ TL Fenchelsamen,
50 g kalte Butter, frisch gepresster Zitronensaft

7 Seeigel, 40 ml kräftiger, reduzierter Hummerfond,
50 ml Milch, 2 Eier, 2 EL Petersiliensaft (aus der rohen Petersilie im
Entsafter gewonnen), ¹/₂ TL Zucker, 1 TL Hummercorail,
4 Jakobsmuscheln, nur das weiße Nüsschen,
1 EL Öl zum Braten, 2 junge, dünne Lauchstangen, 1 EL Butter

For the fennel sorbet: Combine water and different kinds of sugar in a pot and bring to a boil. Chop fennel coarsely and cook in salted water to cover for 15 minutes, until tender. Run fennel pieces through a juicer. Measure out 500 ml (2 cups) of fennel juice and reserve remaining juice for later use. Combine the 2 cups of fennel juice, lemon juice and syrup. If a Pacojet device is available, fill 3 Pacojet molds with the liquid. Add one dissolved sheet of gelatin to each mold. Freeze. (Add a few spoonfuls of fennel juice to each mold before turning on the Pacojet. This will result in fewer crystals when mixing.) If you do not have a Pacojet device, freeze mixture without addition of gelatin in a standard ice cream freezer.

For the fennel sauce: Melt 40 g/1¹/₂ oz butter in a saucepan and sauté fennel and onion with a pinch of salt. Stir, cover and sauté for a few minutes on low heat. Add mussels stock and reduce to about half. Stir in double cream and season with star anise powder and fennel seed. Allow to simmer for 10 minutes. Check for salt and strain sauce through a fine sieve. Finally, whisk in cold butter, a small piece at a time. Adjust tartness with lemon juice.

Open sea urchins, catching juice in a bowl. Remove tongues and reserve for garnish. Measure out 80 ml/¹/₄ cup of juice and strain it through a fine sieve. Combine strained juice with lobster stock, milk, eggs, parsley juice, sugar and lobster coral and purée in a blender. Strain through a fine sieve three times. Divide sea urchin cream equally between four small deep dishes, cover with aluminum foil and steam in a 80° C/180° F steamer for 16 minutes.

For the garnish: Sear scallops in a very hot pan with a little bit of oil on all sides. Cut leeks into 7 cm/2³/₄ inch pieces. Blanch, allow to drain and sauté in butter on low heat until tender.

Finish: Remove aluminum foil covers from the sea urchin cream and place the dishes onto larger glass plates. Garnish plates with the sea urchin tongues, one scallop each and leek pieces. Pour the fennel sauce into four small pitchers, add a scoop of fennel sorbet and serve the arrangements immediately.

Note: Prepare this dish just before serving. The cream should be garnished and served as soon as it is done.

Für das Fenchelsorbet: Wasser mit den Zuckersorten in einem Topf zum Kochen bringen. Fenchel grob schneiden, in Salzwasser knapp bedeckt 15 Minuten kochen. In den Entsafter geben, von dem gewonnenen Saft 500 ml abmessen, den restlichen Saft aufheben. Die 500 ml Fenchelsaft mit Zitronensaft und dem Sirup vermischen. Wenn ein Pacojet Gerät vorhanden ist, drei Pacojet-Becher mit der Flüssigkeit füllen, je ein eingeweichtes Gelatineblatt darin auflösen. Gefrieren lassen, vor Gebrauch des Pacojets in jedes Gefäß ein paar Löffel Fenchelsaft zufügen, damit sich beim Mixen weniger Kristalle bilden. Wenn kein Pacojet vorhanden ist, die Masse ohne Gelatine normal in der Eismaschine gefrieren.

Für die Fenchelsauce: Fenchel mit der Zwiebel, 40 g Butter und einer Prise Salz in einem Topf erhitzen. Zugedeckt ein paar Minuten dünsten, ohne Farbe nehmen zu lassen. Muschelfond zugießen, ohne Deckel auf die Hälfte einkochen. Doppelrahm unterrühren, mit Sternanis und Fenchelsamen würzen, weitere 10 Minuten köcheln. Mit Salz abschmecken, durch ein Sieb streichen, die Butter stückchenweise unterrühren. Mit Zitronensaft abschmecken.

Seeigel öffnen, den Saft sammeln, Zungen herauslösen und für die Garnitur aufheben. Vom Saft 80 ml abmessen und durch ein feines Sieb passieren. Mit Hummerfond, Milch, Eiern, Petersiliensaft, Zucker und Corail im Mixer kurz pürieren, dann die Creme dreimal durch ein feines Sieb passieren. In kleine Schalen verteilen, mit Alufolie bedeckt im 80° C heißen Dampfofen 16 Minuten garen.

Für die Garnitur: Jakobsmuscheln in der sehr heißen Pfanne mit wenig Öl von allen Seiten kurz Farbe nehmen lassen. Lauchstangen waschen, in ca. 7 cm große Stücke schneiden, blanchieren, gut abtropfen lassen und in der Butter bei kleiner Hitze weichdünsten.

Fertigstellung: Die Alufolie von der Seeigelcreme entfernen, die Schalen auf große Glasteller stellen. Mit Seeigel-Zungen, je einer Jakobsmuschel und Lauchstücken garnieren. Die Fenchelsauce in kleine Kännchen füllen, je einen Löffel Fenchelsorbet dazugeben und sofort servieren. Anmerkung: Dieses Gericht erst kurz vor dem Servieren zubereiten, die Creme sollte sofort nach dem Garen garniert und aufgetragen werden.

MARINATED SCALLOPS WITH LIVER OF ANGLER FISH AND OLIVE OIL SORBET

MARINIERTE JAKOBSMUSCHELN MIT SEETEUFELLEBER UND OLIVENÖLSORBET

Serves 4

For the scallop carpaccio:
8 scallops,
15 g/1 tbsp ginger oil (50 g/1 1/2 oz ginger, peeled and diced, finely
puréed in a blender with 100 ml/1/3 cup olive oil),
40 ml/1/8 cup cold-pressed olive oil, 10 ml/a dash sherry vinegar,
1 tsp lime zest, finely diced, brought to a boil in cold water,
simmered until tender and drained,
1 tsp shallot, finely diced, 1 tsp onion, finely diced

For the olive oil sorbet:
250 ml/1 cup water, 150 g/5 oz sugar, 50 g/1 1/2 oz glucose, sifted,
180 ml/3/4 cup cold-pressed olive oil

For the truffled onion cream:
200 g/7 oz onion, peeled and cut into paper-thin slices,
250 ml/1 cup cold-pressed olive oil,
40 g/1 1/2 oz smoked ham, cut into 1 mm/1/25 inch slices,
100 g/3 1/2 oz black truffles, finely diced

1 liver of an angler fish, soaked in ice water for three hours

Garnish: freshly ground white pepper, salt, olive oil

Für 4 Personen:

Für das Jakobsmuschel-Carpaccio:
8 Jakobsmuscheln,
15 g Ingweröl (50 g Ingwer geschält und gehackt,
mit 100 ml Olivenöl im Mixer fein püriert),
40 ml kalt gepresstes Olivenöl, 10 ml Sherryessig,
1 TL dünn abgeschnittene Limettenschale, fein gewürfelt, in kaltem
Wasser aufgesetzt und weichgekocht, im Sieb abgetropft,
1 TL fein gewürfelte Schalotte, 1 TL fein gewürfelte Zwiebel

Für das Olivenölsorbet:
250 ml Wasser, 150 g Zucker, 50 g Glukose, gesiebt,
180 ml kalt gepresstes Olivenöl

Für die getrüffelte Zwiebelcreme:
200 g Zwiebel, geschält, in hauchdünne Scheiben geschnitten,
250 ml kalt gepresstes Olivenöl,
40 g geräucherter Speck, in 1 mm dünne Scheiben geschnitten,
100 g schwarze Trüffel, fein gehackt

1 Seeteufelleber, drei Stunden in Eiswasser gewässert

Garnitur: frisch gemahlener weißer Pfeffer, Salz, Olivenöl

Place the scallops in the freezer about two hours before you intend to use them. Combine prepared ginger oil, olive oil and vinegar and mix well. Combine lime zest, shallot and onion. Set both mixtures aside.
For the olive oil sorbet: Combine water, sugar and glucose in a large saucepan and bring to a boil. Keep at a rolling boil for one and a half minutes, then place the pot into a basin with ice water and allow to cool. Stir vigorously with a wire whip and drizzle in the olive oil in a small stream. When all the oil is incorporated, pour the suspension into an ice cream freezer and freeze.
For the truffled onion cream: Combine onion rings and olive oil in a pan. Cover and stew on low heat for about one hour, until the onions are tender. Do not allow to brown. Drain well in a sieve. Fry ham slices with a little oil until golden brown on both sides. Drain on paper towels and allow to cool. Crumble the bacon slices into small pieces, return bits to the pan and add drained onions. Add diced truffles and allow to simmer on low heat until most of the liquid is evaporated. Check for salt and pepper and keep warm.
Finish: Allow liver of angler fish to drain well, then dry the outside with paper towels. Cut the liver into four slices and fry the slices in a non-stick pan until golden brown on both sides.
Brush four plates with the ginger marinade and sprinkle them with a little lime zest-onion mixture. Remove scallops from the freezer und cut them into very thin slices. Arrange the slices on plates. Sprinkle the slices with the remaining lime zest-onion mixture and brush with ginger marinade. Add a spoonful of onion cream and top with a slice of fried liver. Garnish the plate with a small scoop of olive oil sorbet and sprinkle everything with freshly ground white pepper, salt and olive oil, according to taste. Serve at once.

Jakobsmuscheln zwei Stunden vor der Verwendung in den Gefrierschrank legen. Das Ingweröl mit dem Olivenöl und Essig gut verrühren, Limettenwürfel mit Schalotte und Zwiebel vermischen, alles beiseite legen.
Für das Olivenölsorbet: Das Wasser mit Zucker und Glukose in einem Topf zum Kochen bringen. Eineinhalb Minuten sprudelnd kochen, anschließend den Topf in Eiswasser stellen, Sirup erkalten lassen. Mit einem Schneebesen kräftig rühren und das Olivenöl in dünnem Faden zugeben. Wenn alles gut vermischt ist, die Flüssigkeit in der Eismaschine gefrieren.
Für die getrüffelte Zwiebelcreme: Zwiebelringe mit dem Öl in einem Topf zugedeckt bei kleiner Hitze ca. 1 Stunde garen, ohne Farbe nehmen zu lassen. In einem feinen Sieb gut abtropfen lassen. Speckscheiben mit wenig Öl in einer Pfanne von beiden Seiten goldbraun braten. Abtropfen und erkalten lassen, fein würfeln. Mit den abgetropften Zwiebeln und gehackten Trüffeln in der Pfanne bei kleiner Hitze köcheln, bis die meiste Flüssigkeit verdampft ist. Abschmecken, warm halten.
Fertigstellung: Seeteufelleber gut abtropfen lassen, mit Küchenpapier trocken tupfen, in vier Scheiben schneiden, in einer beschichteten Pfanne sehr heiß von beiden Seiten goldbraun braten.
Vier Teller mit Ingwer-Marinade auspinseln, mit Limettenschalen-Zwiebelgemisch bestreuen. Die halbgefrorenen Jakobsmuscheln in hauchdünne Scheiben schneiden und auf den Tellern auslegen. Mit den restlichen Limetten- und Zwiebelwürfelchen bestreuen, mit Ingwer-Marinade bepinseln. Je einen Löffel Zwiebelcreme darübergeben, mit gebratener Leber bedecken. Vom Olivenölsorbet ebenfalls einen kleinen Löffel voll dazugeben, nach Belieben mit weißem Pfeffer, Salz und Olivenöl garnieren. Sofort servieren.

RICE WITH BEEF MARROW, OCTOPUS AND CLAMS

REIS MIT RINDERMARK, OKTOPUS UND MUSCHELN

Serves 8 - 10

For the octopus:
1 kg/2 lbs octopus,
1 kg/2 lbs salt

For the clams:
1 tbsp garlic, minced,
75 ml/¼ cup olive oil,
2 kg/4 lbs clams or carpet clams,
3 liters/12 cups light fish stock

For the rice:
200 g/7 oz onion, diced,
40 g/1½ oz butter,
200 g/7 oz small squid, ready-to-use,
125 g/4 oz beef marrow,
500 g/1 lb short grain rice,
150 ml/⅔ cup white wine,
60 g/2 oz butter,
80 g/3 oz Parmesan, grated,
1 tbsp truffle oil

Für 8 - 10 Personen:

Für den Oktopus:
1 kg Oktopus,
1 kg Salz

Für die Muscheln:
1 EL gehackter Knoblauch,
75 ml Olivenöl,
2 kg Venus- oder Teppichmuscheln,
3 Liter leichter Fischfond

Für den Reis:
200 g Zwiebel, gehackt,
40 g Butter,
200 g kleine Tintenfische, küchenfertig,
125 g Rindermark,
500 g Rundkornreis,
150 ml Weißwein,
60 g Butter,
80 g geriebener Parmesan,
1 EL Trüffelöl

For the octopus: Place octopus into a large bowl, cover with salt and allow to marinate for forty-five minutes. Rinse octopus well in cold water. Bring a large pot of water to a rolling boil, drop in octopus and boil for two minutes. Drain, allow to cool and remove the tentacles. Freeze tentacles in a deep freezer for about two hours, then cut them into paper thin slices. Keep cool. Reserve remaining octopus meat for other uses.

For the clams: In a large pan, sauté the garlic in olive oil. Add the clams and sauté them, stirring constantly, until they start opening. Douse with fish stock, bring to a boil and cook until the clams are fully open. Remove clams with a slotted spoon. Discard any clams which are still closed and spread the opened ones out on a baking sheet. Allow to cool.

Remove clams from their shells and place the meat onto a rack covered with baking paper. Strain the clam stock through a sieve and set it aside for the rice.

For the rice: In a heavy-bottomed casserole, sauté onion in butter until translucent. Add squid and beef marrow and sauté for a few minutes. Do not allow to brown. Add rice and sauté until well-coated. Pour in white wine, and allow the liquid to evaporate. Add clam stock to cover. Allow to simmer on low heat for fifteen minutes, stirring frequently and adding a little more clam stock as it evaporates. Incorporate butter and Parmesan and ladle rice into deep soup plates. Drizzle each plate with a little truffle oil.

Finish: Steam clams until reheated (just a few seconds). Garnish the rice in plates with a layer of octopus slices and clams. Serve.

Für den Oktopus: Oktopus mit dem Salz bedeckt in einer Schüssel 45 Minuten ziehen lassen. Salz abspülen, in sprudelnd kochendem Wasser 2 Minuten kochen. Herausnehmen, erkalten lassen und die Tentakel abschneiden. Im Gefrierschrank ca. 2 Stunden anfrieren, anschließend in hauchdünne Scheiben schneiden. Kühl stellen. Restliches Oktopusfleisch für eine andere Verwendung weg stellen.

Für die Muscheln: Knoblauch in einem großen Topf im Olivenöl anbraten. Muscheln zugeben, unter Rühren braten, bis sie beginnen, sich zu öffnen. Mit Fischfond auffüllen, zum Kochen bringen, bis sich die Muscheln voll geöffnet haben. Mit einer Lochkelle herausheben, Muscheln, die sich nicht geöffnet haben entfernen, die anderen auf einem Blech ausgelegt abkühlen lassen. Muschelfleisch aus der Schale lösen und über einem mit Backtrennpapier belegten Gitter flach auslegen. Den Fond durch ein Sieb gießen, aufheben.

Für den Reis: In einem Topf mit schwerem Boden die Zwiebel in Butter glasig dünsten. Tintenfische und Rindermark zugeben und anbraten, ohne Farbe nehmen zu lassen. Reis zugeben und glasig dünsten. Mit Weißwein ablöschen und einkochen. Mit Muschelfond auffüllen, bis der Reis bedeckt ist. Während ca. 15 Minuten köcheln, bis der Reis gar ist, immer wieder umrühren und mit Muschelfond aufgießen. Zum Schluss Butter und Parmesan unterrühren, den Reis in tiefe Teller verteilen. Mit Trüffelöl beträufeln.

Fertigstellung: Die Muscheln über Dampf sehr kurz erhitzen (ein paar Sekunden nur). Den Reis mit einer Lage Oktopusscheiben und mit den Muscheln belegen, sofort servieren.

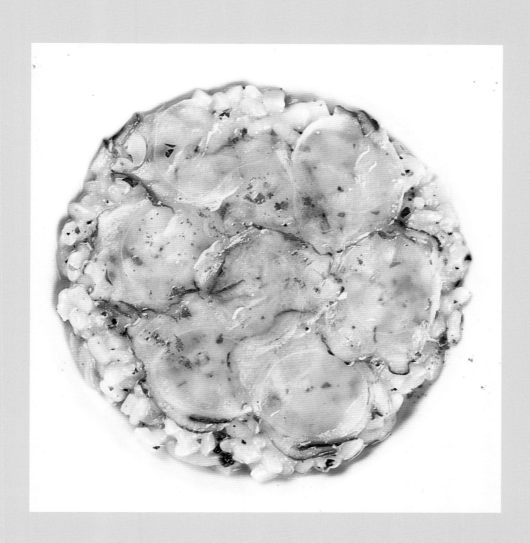

CARAMELIZED MILLEFEUILLE OF FOIE GRAS, SMOKED EEL, ONION AND APPLE

KARAMELLISIERTES MILLE-FEUILLE VON GÄNSESTOPFLEBER, GERÄUCHERTEM AAL, ZWIEBEL UND APFEL

Serves 16

1.1 kg/2¹/₂ lbs goose foie gras,
steamed until half done,
450 g/1 lb filet of smoked eel,
500 g/1 lb white onions, peeled,
cut into quarters,
500 g/1 lb butter,
3 - 4 Granny Smith apples,
sugar for caramelizing

Cut goose foie gras into 4 - 5 mm/¹/₅ inch slices.
Remove all bones from the smoked eel and cut the meat into thin slices lengthwise.
Cut or shave the quartered onions into very thin slices. Melt the butter in a small saucepan and sauté the onions on low heat until tender. Do not allow them to brown. Drain well in a sieve and place them onto a clean kitchen towel so that all excess liquid may be absorbed.
Just before you are ready to use the apples, shave them into 1 mm/¹/₂₅ inch pieces, right down to the core. Discard core.
Sprinkle a square dish of 28 x 28 x 3 cm (9 x 9 x 1 inch) with sugar. Layer the bottom with a apple slices. Cut the apple slices down to size if necessary so that there are no gaps in the layer. Top with a layer of stewed onions. Smooth out the top. Top with a neat layer of foie gras, then proceed with layers of apple slices, smoked eel, apple slices and foie gras. Finish with a layer of apple slices.
Cover the millefeuille with a lid and weight it down with a heavy object. Allow millefeuille to rest in the refrigerator for three hours.
Serving: Carefully unmold the millefeuille. Sprinkle with sugar and lightly caramelize the sugar with a blow torch. Cut the millefeuille into sixteen pieces with a sharp knife and serve.

Für 16 Personen:

1,1 kg Gänsestopfleber,
über Dampf halbdurch gegart,
450 g geräuchertes Aalfilet,
500 g Gemüsezwiebel, geschält,
in Viertel geschnitten,
500 g Butter,
3 - 4 Granny Smith Äpfel,
Zucker zum Karamellisieren

Gänsestopfleber in 4 - 5 mm dicke Scheiben schneiden, den geräucherten Aal sorgfältig entgräten, enthäuten und der Länge nach in dünne Scheiben schneiden.
Die Zwiebelviertel in hauchdünne Scheiben schneiden oder hobeln. Mit der Butter in einem Topf bei kleiner Hitze weich garen, ohne Farbe nehmen zu lassen. Im Sieb gut abtropfen lassen, anschließend auf einem sauberen Tuch auslegen, damit alle überflüssige Flüssigkeit absorbiert wird.
Äpfel kurz vor der Verwendung in 1 mm dicke Scheiben schneiden, bis das Kernhaus erscheint. Den mittleren Teil mit dem Kernhaus nicht verwenden.
Eine quadratische Form von 28 x 28 x 3 cm mit Zucker ausstreuen. Boden mit einer Lage Apfelscheiben auslegen, die Scheiben entsprechend zuschneiden, damit keine Lücken entstehen. Als nächstes eine dünne Lage pochierter Zwiebeln darüber streichen. Mit einer Schicht Stopfleber lückenlos bedecken, dann abwechselnd je eine Lage Apfel, Räucheraal, Apfel und Stopfleber einschichten, mit einer Lage Apfel abschließen. Mille-Feuille mit einem Deckel zudecken, mit einem Gewicht beschwert drei Stunden im Kühlschrank ruhen lassen.
Zum Servieren: Mille-Feuille vorsichtig aus der Form stürzen. Mit Zucker bestreuen, dann mit einem Bunsenbrenner leicht karamellisieren. Mit einem scharfen Messer in sechzehn Stücke schneiden und servieren.

DOVER SOLE WITH MUSHROOMS, ARTICHOKES, FOIE GRAS AND AN ASPARAGUS SALAD

SEEZUNGE MIT PILZEN, ARTISCHOCKEN, STOPFLEBER UND SPARGELSALAT

Serves 4

For the mushroom ragout:
500 g/1 lb mixed mushrooms, trimmed and cut into 4 x 4 mm/¹⁄₅ x ¹⁄₅ inch dice, 5 tbsp olive oil, 2 tsp young garlic, minced, 2 tbsp parsley, chopped, salt, freshly ground pepper

For the garlic sauce:
15 ml/1 tbsp mild apple cider vinegar, 90 ml/¹⁄₃ cup sunflower oil, 15 g/1 tbsp young garlic, ¹⁄₂ tsp salt

For the asparagus salad:
8 thick green asparagus spears, 1 tbsp freshly squeezed lemon juice, salt, white pepper, a few drops of truffle oil

For the herb vinaigrette:
15 g/1 tbsp parsley and chervil each, leaves only, 15 g/1 tbsp chives, salt, baking soda, 4 tbsp virgin olive oil, a dash of apple cider vinegar

For the garnish:
100 g/3¹⁄₂ oz artichoke hearts, diced, 100 g/3¹⁄₂ oz mixed mushrooms, trimmed and diced, 50 g/1¹⁄₂ oz fatback, finely diced, 60 g/2 oz white onion, minced, 40 ml/¹⁄₈ cup cold-pressed olive oil, 30 g/1 oz terrine of foie gras, diced, 1 tbsp butter, 1 tbsp parsley, minced, a few drops of truffle oil

4 filets of Dover sole, 150 g/5 oz each, skin on, oil for frying

For the mushroom ragout: Sauté mushrooms in olive oil until they start giving off water. Add garlic and cook for two minutes on low heat. Drain in a sieve and toss with parsley. Season with salt and pepper. For the garlic sauce: Purée ingredients in a blender, set aside. For the asparagus salad: Remove tips and lower third of asparagus spears and reserve for other purposes. Shave middle pieces of the spears into thin slices lengthwise, then cut into julienne strips. Dip in lemon water and sprinkle with salt, pepper and a little truffle oil. For the herb vinaigrette: In a small pot, bring water with salt and baking soda to a boil. When water has come to a rolling boil, add herbs and cook for a few second, then drain in a sieve, reserving the cooking liquid. Purée herbs with three tablespoons of cooking liquid in a blender. Strain the purée through a fine sieve. In a small bowl, combine purée, oil, vinegar and a little water if necessary and stir until you have a smooth sauce.

For the garnish: Sauté artichokes, mushrooms, fatback and onions separately in olive oil until tender. Drain well and allow to cool to room temperature. Right before serving, reheat all the vegetables and fatback in a small saucepan. Toss with foie gras, butter and parsley. Add a dash of water if necessary, check for seasonings and add a few drops of truffle oil. Fry sole filets in very hot oil, skin-side down, until crisp and brown. Flip filets over and fry on the other side for thirty seconds. Drain on paper towels, brush skin-side with a little garlic sauce and keep warm.

Serving: Arrange artichoke-mushroom garnish and mushroom ragout on plates and top with sole filets. Drizzle with herb vinaigrette. Cover the fish filets with asparagus salad and serve immediately.

Für 4 Personen:

Für das Pilzragout:
500 g gemischte Pilze, geputzt und in 4 x 4 mm große Würfel geschnitten, 5 EL Olivenöl, 2 TL fein gehackter junger Knoblauch, 2 EL gehackte Petersilie, Salz, Pfeffer aus der Mühle

Für die Knoblauchsauce:
15 ml milder Apfelweinessig, 90 ml Sonnenblumenöl, 15 g junger Knoblauch, ¹⁄₂ TL Salz

Für den Spargelsalat:
8 dicke grüne Spargelstangen, 1 EL frisch gepresster Zitronensaft, Salz, weißer Pfeffer, ein paar Tropfen Trüffelöl

Für die Kräutervinaigrette:
Je 15 g Petersilie und Kerbel, nur die Blättchen, 15 g Schnittlauch, Salz, Natron, 4 EL kalt gepresstes Olivenöl, ein Spritzer Apfelweinessig

Für die Garnitur:
100 g Artischockenherzen, in Würfel geschnitten, 100 g gemischte Pilze, geputzt, in Würfel geschnitten, 50 g fetter Speck, in kleine Würfel geschnitten 60 g Gemüsezwiebel, fein gehackt, 40 ml kalt gepresstes Olivenöl, 30 g Stopfleberterrine, in Würfel geschnitten, 1 EL Butter, 1 EL fein gehackte Petersilie, einige Tropfen Trüffelöl

4 Seezungenfilets à 150 g, mit Haut, Öl zum Braten

Für das Pilzragout: Die Pilze im Olivenöl anbraten, bis sie Wasser ziehen. Gehackten Knoblauch zugeben und bei kleiner Hitze zwei Minuten köcheln. In einem Sieb gut abtropfen lassen und mit der gehackten Petersilie vermischen. Mit Salz und Pfeffer würzen. Für die Knoblauchsauce: Alle Zutaten im Mixer fein pürieren. Für den Spargelsalat: Spitzen und unteres Drittel des Spargels entfernen, für eine andere Verwendung beiseite stellen. Mittelstücke der Länge nach in sehr dünne Streifen (Julienne) schneiden. Kurz in Zitronenwasser tauchen, mit Salz, Pfeffer und Trüffelöl würzen. Für die Kräutervinaigrette: In einem kleinen Topf Wasser mit Salz und Natron zum Kochen bringen. Kräuter einige Sekunden sprudelnd kochen, dann durch ein Sieb gießen, Kochwasser auffangen. Kräuter abtropfen lassen, mit 3 Löffeln Kochwasser im Mixer fein pürieren. Durch ein feines Sieb passieren, mit Öl, Essig und wenn nötig etwas Wasser zu einer homogenen Sauce verrühren.

Für die Garnitur: Artischocken, Pilze, Speck und Zwiebeln nacheinander im Olivenöl anbraten, weich dünsten, gut abtropfen und erkalten lassen. Garnitur kurz vor dem Auftragen in einem kleinen Topf erhitzen, mit der Stopfleber, Butter und Petersilie vermischen. Wenn nötig, mit einem Spritzer Wasser befeuchten, abschmecken, zum Schluss mit einigen Tropfen Trüffelöl würzen. Seezungenfilets mit Haut nach unten in sehr heißem Öl knusprig braten, umdrehen, die zweite Seite nur 30 Sekunden braten. Abtropfen lassen, mit etwas Knoblauchsauce bepinseln und warm halten.

Zum Servieren: Artischocken-Pilzgarnitur und Pilzragout nebeneinander auf Teller verteilen. Seezungenfilets darüberlegen, Kräutervinaigrette angießen. Fisch mit Spargelsalat bedecken, servieren.

FRIED SQUAB WITH POTATO GNOCCHI IN A TRUFFLE CREAM SERVED WITH SPRING VEGETABLES AND A PURÉE OF BLACK OLIVES

GEBRATENE TAUBE MIT KARTOFFELGNOCCHI AN TRÜFFELCREME UND FRÜHLINGSGEMÜSE MIT SCHWARZEM OLIVENPÜREE

<table>
<tr><td>

Serves 4

For the black olive purée:
150 g/5 oz black olives, pitted, 150 ml/²/₃ cup olive oil

For the gnocchi: 400 g/14 oz potatoes, 70 g/2 oz flour, sifted,
1 egg yolk, 1 tbsp cold-pressed olive oil,
70 g/2 oz Parmesan, finely grated, salt, nutmeg

For the spring vegetables:
4 young carrots, 4 spring onions, 2 stalks young leek,
100 g/3¹/₂ oz spring mushrooms, trimmed and coarsely chopped,
2 tbsp olive oil

4 squab, salt, 200 ml/³/₄ cup olive oil,
150 ml/²/₃ cup brown squab stock (or poultry stock),
3 spring onions, white part only, finely diced, 1 tbsp butter, salt,
15 g/1 tbsp truffles, finely diced,
500 ml/2 cups cream, reduced by half,
50 ml/¹/₄ cup double strength beef broth,
80 g/3 oz young Gruyère (Swiss cheese), finely grated

</td><td>

Für 4 Personen:

Für das schwarze Olivenpüree:
150 g schwarze Oliven, entsteint, 150 ml Olivenöl

Für die Gnocchi: 400 g Kartoffeln, 70 g Mehl, gesiebt,
1 Eigelb, 1 EL kalt gepresstes Olivenöl,
70 g fein geriebener Parmesan, Salz, Muskat

Für das Frühlingsgemüse:
4 junge Karotten, 4 Frühlingszwiebeln, 2 Stangen junger Lauch,
100 g Frühlingspilze, geputzt, grob geschnitten,
2 EL Olivenöl

4 Tauben, Salz, 200 ml Olivenöl,
150 ml brauner Taubenfond (oder Geflügelfond),
3 Frühlingszwiebeln, nur der weiße Teil, fein gehackt,
1 EL Butter, Salz, 15 g fein geschnittene Trüffel,
500 g Sahne, auf die Hälfte (250 ml) eingekocht,
50 ml doppelte Rinderkraftbrühe,
80 g junger Gruyère, fein gerieben

</td></tr>
</table>

For the black olive purée: Preheat oven to 100° C/210° F and dry olives on a baking sheet for about three hours. Purée them in a blender with the olive oil until you have a fine purée.

For the gnocchi: Boil potatoes in their jackets, peel while still hot and mash finely with a potato ricer or press through the potato press into a bowl. Measure out 350 g/12 ¹/₂ oz of the potato purée and mix with remaining ingredients. Season with a little salt and pepper. On a floured working surface, roll out mixture into rolls of a diameter of about 1 cm/¹/₃ inches. Cut into even 1 cm/¹/₃ inch pieces. Roll pieces around the tines of a fork to flatten them. In a large pot, simmer gnocchi in salted water until they rise to the surface. Remove them with a slotted spoon and refresh in ice water.

For the vegetables: Clean and trim vegetables, cut into 5 cm/2 inch pieces and blanch the pieces in salted water. Sauté mushrooms and blanched vegetable dice in a little olive oil until al dente.

Preheat oven to 200° C/390° F. Heat the oil in a heavy-bottomed casserole and fry squab on all sides until golden brown. Place casserole into the oven and bake for 15 minutes. Remove squab, allow to drain on a rack, cover and allow to rest for ten minutes. Degrease pan juices in the casserole, add stock and bring to a boil. Strain pan sauce through a sieve, check for salt and pepper.

Finish: Reserve a spoonful of chopped spring onions. Sauté the rest in a small saucepan in butter until tender. Add truffles and a little salt and keep sautéing for another minute. Stir in cream and stock, bring to a boil and simmer for two minutes. Check for salt and stir in remaining spring onions. Reheat well-drained gnocchi in a nonstick pan. Do not allow to brown. Sprinkle with cheese, add cream sauce and keep on the burner, stirring, until cheese has melted.

Serving: Remove meat from breasts and thighs of squab. Arrange gnocchi and vegetables on pre-warmed plates. Drizzle with a little squab pan sauce and place meat pieces on top, crispy skin-side up. Garnish with olive purée and the remaining pan sauce. Serve.

Für das schwarze Olivenpüree: Die Oliven auf einem Blech im 100° C heißen Ofen ca. drei Stunden trocknen. Anschließend mit dem Olivenöl im Mixer fein pürieren.

Für die Gnocchi: Kartoffeln in der Schale weich kochen, heiß schälen, fein zerstampfen oder durch die Kartoffelpresse in eine Schüssel drücken. Von dem Püree 350 g abmessen, mit restlichen Zutaten vermischen, mit Salz und Muskat leicht würzen. Die Masse auf der bemehlten Arbeitsfläche zu 1 cm dicken Würsten rollen, in 1 cm lange Stücke schneiden, jedes Stück mit einer Gabel halbflach drücken. Gnocchi in einem Topf in Salzwasser kochen, bis sie an der Oberfläche schwimmen. Herausnehmen, in Eiswasser abkühlen.

Für das Gemüse: Gemüse putzen, in 5 cm große Stücke schneiden und in Salzwasser blanchieren. Mit den Pilzen in wenig Olivenöl bei kleiner Hitze knapp gar dünsten.

Den Ofen auf 200° C vorheizen. Tauben in einem Bräter im heißen Öl von allen Seiten knusprig-braun anbraten. Bräter in den Ofen schieben, 15 Minuten weiterbraten. Tauben aus dem Ofen nehmen, auf einem Gitter abtropfen lassen, zugedeckt 10 Minuten ruhen lassen. Den Bräter entfetten, Fond zugießen und aufkochen lassen. Den Fond durch ein Sieb passieren und abschmecken.

Fertigstellung: Von den gehackten Frühlingszwiebeln ein Löffel voll beiseite legen, den Rest in einem Topf in Butter weich dünsten. Trüffel zugeben, leicht salzen eine Minute weiter dünsten. Sahne und Brühe zugießen, zum Kochen bringen, 2 Minuten köcheln. Mit Salz abschmecken, zum Schluss die rohen Frühlingszwiebeln unterrühren. Gnocchi gut abtropfen lassen, in einer beschichteten Pfanne erhitzen, ohne Farbe nehmen zu lassen. Gruyère und Sahnesauce zugeben, unter Rühren erhitzen, bis der Käse geschmolzen ist.

Zum Servieren: Brustfleisch und Schenkel der Tauben vom Knochen lösen. Gnocchi und Gemüse auf vorgewärmte Teller anrichten. Mit etwas Taubenfond begießen, das Fleisch darüber legen. Mit Olivenpüree und restlichem Taubenfond garnieren und servieren.

SWEET PEA COMPOTE WITH BANANA AND APPLE

SÜSSE ERBSENSPEISE MIT BANANE UND APFEL

Serves 4

For the green apple sorbet:
250 ml/1 cup water,
200 g/7 oz sugar, 25 g/1 oz dextrose,
60 g/2 oz confectioners´ sugar,
600 ml/2¹/₃ cup freshly made juice of peeled and cored
Granny Smith apples,
1 sheet gelatin, soaked (only if a Pacojet device is available)

For the compote:
50 ml/¹/₄ cup water,
120 g/4 oz sugar,
the freshly scraped seeds of one vanilla bean,
1 tbsp freshly squeezed lemon juice, 1 tsp lemon zest,
120 ml/¹/₂ cup freshly squeezed orange juice,
250 g/¹/₂ lb banana, cut into 3 x 3 mm/¹/₈ x ¹/₈ inch cubes,
150 g/5 oz young, tender peas

For the pea-vinegar cookies:
150 g/5 oz flour,
150 ml/²/₃ cup sherry vinegar,
80 g/3 oz confectioners´ sugar,
200 g/7 oz young, tender peas, blanched,
2 tbsp flour

Für 4 Personen:

Für das Grünapfelsorbet:
250 ml Wasser,
200 g Zucker, 25 g Dextrose, 60 g Puderzucker,
600 ml frisch gewonnener Saft von geschälten und entkernten
Granny Smith Äpfeln,
1 Gelatineblatt, eingeweicht (nur nötig, wenn ein Pacojet Gerät
vorhanden ist)

Für das Kompott:
50 ml Wasser, 120 g Zucker,
das ausgeschabte Mark einer Vanillestange,
1 EL frisch gepresster Zitronensaft,
1 TL fein abgeriebene Orangenschale,
120 ml frisch gepresster Orangensaft,
250 g Bananenwürfel (3 x 3 mm),
150 g junge, zarte Erbsen

Für das Erbsen-Essiggebäck:
150 g Mehl,
150 ml Sherryessig,
80 g Puderzucker,
200 g junge zarte Erbsen, blanchiert,
2 EL Mehl

For the green apple sorbet: In a large pot, combine water and the different kinds of sugar and boil until all sugar crystals are dissolved. Remove syrup from heat. (If you have a Pacojet device, stir gelatin into the syrup.) Strain mixture through a sieve and allow to cool. Mix with apple juice and place into a Pacojet (if available), alternatively freeze in an ice cream maker.

For the compote: Combine water, sugar, lemon juice and orange zest in a pot and bring to a boil. Remove pot from burner and strain the mixture through a sieve. Allow to cool to about 65° C/160° F. Mix with diced banana and orange juice and allow to cool completely. Add peas and refrigerate.

For the pea-vinegar cookies: Preheat the oven to 175° C/350° F. Combine flour with confectioners´ sugar and vinegar and strain mixture through a fine sieve. Spread the batter thinly and evenly onto non-stick baking sheet. Reserve two tablespoons of blanched peas. Purée remaining peas in a blender until you have a fine purée, add flour and strain mixture through a sieve. Mix reserved whole peas into pea batter and spread it onto vinegar batter on the baking sheet. Bake for 20 - 30 minutes. Allow to cool on the baking sheet, then cut the dough into 6 x 1 cm (2¹/₂ x ¹/₃ inch) sticks.

Serving: Place pea-banana compote into dessert bowls. Garnish with a scoop of apple sorbet and serve with pea-vinegar cookies.

Für das Grünapfelsorbet: In einem Topf das Wasser mit den verschiedenen Zuckersorten zum Kochen bringen, bis sich alle Kristalle aufgelöst haben. Den Sirup vom Herd ziehen, (für Pacojet-Gebrauch die Gelatine unterrühren), durch ein Sieb passieren und erkalten lassen. Mit Apfelsaft vermischen und (wenn vorhanden in den Pacojet füllen) in der Eismaschine gefrieren.

Für das Kompott: Wasser und Zucker mit Vanillemark, Zitronensaft und Orangenschale in einem Topf zum Kochen bringen. Vom Herd ziehen, durch ein Sieb passieren und auf ca. 65° C abkühlen lassen. Mit Orangensaft und Bananenwürfeln vermischen, vollends erkalten lassen. Zum Schluss die Erbsen zugeben, kühl stellen.

Für das Erbsen-Essiggebäck: Den Ofen auf 175° C vorheizen. Das Mehl mit dem Puderzucker und dem Essig vermischen und durch ein feines Sieb passieren. Auf ein beschichtetes Blech gleichmäßig und dünn ausstreichen. Von den blanchierten Erbsen 2 Löffel wegnehmen, den Rest im Mixer fein pürieren, mit Mehl vermischen und ebenfalls durch ein Sieb streichen. Den Erbsenteig mit den ganzen Erbsen vermischen und die Paste auf den Essigteig streichen. Im Ofen 20 - 30 Minuten backen, auf dem Blech auskühlen lassen und in 6 x 1 cm große Stangen schneiden.

Zum Servieren: Erbsen-Bananenkompott in Dessertteller verteilen, mit je einer Kugel Apfelsorbet und Essig-Erbsengebäck garnieren.

LANGOSTINOS

ALBA Y RABINDA

RESCOS CON SU CALDO

BACON WITH A CRISPY RIND

FRIENDS

LENTIS AND BACON FOAM

AKELAŔE

CLOUD 9 OF CULINARY DELIGHTS IS UNDOUBTEDLY FLOATING ABOUT THREE HUNDRED METERS ABOVE SEA LEVEL, ABOVE A HILLTOP.

The exclusive establishment with an ocean view is situated in the small village Igueldo, just a few kilometers west of the bay of San Sebastián. Mortals may enter, but the return back to earth is not easy. The octagonal flat building, behind whose broad window fronts far-traveled gourmets are spoilt at the "Akelare", protrudes from a gentle seaward slope like a command post. If the weather is good, the eye may roam endlessly along the coastline of the Cantabrian Sea, and all the way up to nearby France. If the weather is less favorably inclined, you may sit inside cloud nine, where the dimensions of space and time seem lost. That does not matter, however, since one thing you ought to have here is time, and reading the menu will soon remind you of your original purpose for coming here. One of them is undoubtedly the culinary arts of one of the most renowned artists of Spanish cuisine: Pedro Subijana.

The mustachioed chef recalls: "At home, everything always revolved around cooking and eating. There were huge feasts and many invitations with friends. My father worked at two pastry shops in San Sebastián, and even at home he was always baking. No wonder that I was infected." But who wanted to become a cook then, a profession without prestige, work without leisure, only work, not even free sundays. Pedro was well on his way to go to medical school. The family was happy since one had been hoping for a good career for the son. And a career he had, too – but in another field. Shortly before he began his studies he changed his mind and registered at the hotel school in Madrid. Good-bye medical studies. "I suddenly realized", he remembers with a laugh, "that cooking was a profession, too." And from this time on, he worked his way up the professional ladder that suited his true nature. Guests who come to the Akelare today are welcomed like friends, and if you are not the utterly quiet type, Subijana likes a little chat before guiding you to a table. He himself is driven by pure curiosity. He likes to travel and often does, and what he encounters will be tried out later. The first way is always to the local market. "In order to get to know the local products", he explains, "and the people. Like this, I can understand their cooking better." And only then he makes his way to the restaurant – to dine at the competition's. His uncontested communication skills and his way of approaching other people directly and without reserve are an additional benefit. In that, he is ahead of many of his colleagues, who prefer to hide in their kitchens and want to be left alone. For them, the short visit at the guests' table is a chore, for him, it is a joy. Not surprisingly, his face has been smiling from the screen in his highly popular cooking shows for years. And for the shooting of his daily show he leaves the kitchen twice to three times a week, hastening with flying apron strings to the TV studio.

It is the year 1975. Pedro Subijana, twenty-seven years old, stands for the first time behind the stove of the "Akelare" (the restaurant is five years old then, in 1980, it becomes his own). His chef colleague Juan-Mari Arzak (also San Sebastián, six years his senior), has already won himself a certain fame. At this time, however, members of the species gourmet are sighted rather rarely, and cooking is not yet a topic in the Spanish press. In Madrid, a "gastronomical round table" is established, and Subijana and Arzak take part. One of the speakers is Paul Bocuse propagating his "cuisine du marché": The Spaniards are fascinated, the brains start working. Subsequently, both chefs spend a few days with the master in Lyon, go to the market together, cook and probably empty many a glass of red wine discussing and talking shop, about the future in general and the one of the Basque country specifically. Back at the Gulf of Biscay, they call together the colleagues of the region and decide to start a revolution. All of them at once. The objective is to turn around Basque cooking without losing sight of its roots. That is the core of it. To renovate, renew and separate the authentic from dead-end developments – and to replace boredom with suspense. And, above all, using the advances of new kitchen technologies, they aim at replacing heaviness, butter and cream fat and the long stewing times with a new, fresh lightness. Pedro Subijana does not hesitate to admit that with respect to modern technology he especially approves of microwave and induction heat. "But you have to know how to use them", he emphasizes. And thus, this group of Basque chefs laid the cornerstone to the "Nueva Cocina Vasca", which represents a good part of the Spanish cooking miracle and which meanwhile has made its way into the upper echelons of top gastronomy by virtue of its strength and identity.

Pedro Subijana

It is a truism that good food promotes good health. Subijana, too, explicitly takes that into consideration (the would-be medical student coming through), but he also likes to spoil his guests and make eating a delightful experience beyond all health reformer´s sectarianism. Almost twenty persons assist him in a kitchen which has not been relegated to the cellar but is found at the same level as the restaurant and may also boast of an ocean view. This could be an explanation for the lightness and imagination that fill the plates. "If you yourself do not have fun cooking or eating, how can you succeed in selling enjoyment to your guests?", he asks and no one contradicts him. With the ocean close by, it is no wonder that the menu is dominated by fish and seafood. They swim right by the house, so-to-speak, and thus, quite understandably, are favorite objects of his cooking efforts. The Basque chef would not have such a reputation, however, if he hadn´t created his own, unmistakable style. In that, he provides classical ideas of the region with new and surprising, sometimes humorous touches, combining interesting flavors with unusual methods of preparation in order to attract the guest´s undivided attention with sometimes quite simple raw materials. Rather unpretentious: turbot with a garlic purée and a parsley risotto. A feast of flavors: parsley essence with a fresh oyster, served with oyster juice sorbet and deep-fried artichoke leaves. A hint of luxury: pure egg yolk beaten into a cream with a spatula, then lightly solidified and cut into fragile tagliatelle, topped with a dollop of beluga caviar – a play with contrasting aromas and textures.

The menu starts with three sardine rolls, crowned by a small scoop of black olive mousse. Suddenly, there are sparkles on your tongue, a crackle in the ear, the palate feels a slight tickle. You are irritated and keep looking a little disturbedly for the source of the crackle. The crackling keeps on, and Subijana laughs: "I always serve this appetizer first. The crackle comes from the olive mousse. You take a first bite and voilà, the food is the center of discussion.

¡QUE APROVECHE!"

WOLKE SIEBEN DER GAUMEN-FREUDEN SCHWEBT DREIHUNDERT METER ÜBER NORMAL NULL·

Auf Bergesrücken, im kleinen Weiler Igueldo, nur wenige Kilometer südwestlich der Bucht von San Sebastián, liegt dieser exklusive Essplatz mit Meerblick. Sterbliche haben Zutritt, doch die Rückkehr zur Erde fällt nicht leicht. Einer Kommandokanzel gleich ragt aus dem sanft zum Meer abfallenden Hang ein achteckiger Flachbau, hinter dessen breiten Fensterfronten das „Akelare" den zugereisten Feinschmecker verwöhnt. Schier endlos schweift der Blick an schönen Tagen über die Küstenlinie der Kantabrischen See bis hinauf zum nahen Frankreich. Will das Wetter aber nicht, so sitzt man nicht auf sondern in Wolke Sieben, und die Dimensionen von Raum und Zeit scheinen ausgelöscht. Macht auch nichts, denn Zeit sollte man sich hier nehmen, und die Lektüre der Speisekarte weist auf den eigentlichen Zweck des Aufenthaltes hin. Der gilt unzweifelhaft den Kochkünsten eines der profiliertesten Vertreter spanischer Kochzunft: Pedro Subijana. Der schnauzbärtige Koch erinnert sich: „Daheim gings immer ums Kochen und Essen. Es gab große Feste und viele Einladungen mit Freunden. Mein Vater arbeitete in zwei Konditoreien von San Sebastián und auch zuhause war er immer am Backen. Kein Wunder, dass ich da infiziert wurde." Aber wer wollte denn damals den Beruf des Kochs ergreifen, eine Profession ohne Prestige, eine Arbeit ohne Freizeit? Nur Schufterei, und sonntags nicht frei.

Pedro war auf dem besten Wege, Medizin zu studieren. Die Familie war glücklich, hatte man doch für den Sohn eine Karriere erhofft. Nun, die hat er wohl gemacht – allerdings auf anderem Wege. Kurz vor Studienbeginn wechselte er die Pferde und schrieb sich an der Hotelfachschule von Madrid ein. Medizin ade. „Mir ging plötzlich auf," lacht er, „Kochen ist auch ein Beruf." Und ab diesem Zeitpunkt wanderte er beharrlich vorwärts auf dem Lehr- und dann Berufsweg, der seinem eigentlichen Wesen entsprach. Der Gast, der heute zur Tür des „Akelare" hereinkommt, wird auch sofort wie ein Freund in Empfang genommen, und wer nicht gerade zu den Schweigsamen zählt, mit dem plaudert Subijana gern eine Weile, eher er ihn zum Tisch führt.

Seine Triebfeder ist ungezügelte Neugier. Er reist gern und oft, und was ihm da unterkommt, wird postwendend ausprobiert. Der erste Weg führt immer zuerst zum örtlichen Markt. „Um die einheimischen Produkte kennenzulernen," erklärt er, „und die Menschen. So kann ich die Küche besser verstehen." Erst dann geht's ins Restaurant – zum Essen bei der Konkurrenz. Sein anderes Kapital ist seine unbestrittene Kommunikationsfähigkeit und seine Art, direkt und ohne Scheu auf Menschen zuzugehen. Das hat er manchen Kollegen voraus, die sich am liebsten in der Küche verkriechen und in Ruhe gelassen werden wollen. Die kurze Tischvisite bei den Gästen ist ihnen ein Graus, ihm dagegen ein Vergnügen. Nicht ohne Grund flimmert seit vielen Jahren das schmunzelnde Gesicht über die Mattscheibe in seinen höchst beliebten Kochsendungen. Für die Aufnahmen zum täglichen Auftritt verlässt er zwei bis dreimal pro Woche, zwischen Mittag- und Abendservice, die Küche und entschwindet mit wehender Schürze zum Fernsehstudio. – Man schreibt das Jahr 1975. Pedro Subijana steht siebenundzwanzigjährig erstmals am Herd des

„Akelare" (das Lokal gibt es da unter diesem Namen schon seit fünf Jahren, 1980 wird es sein Eigentum). Kochkollege Juan-Mari Arzak (auch San Sebastián, sechs Jahre älter) hat sich schon ein gewisses Renommé erkocht. Die Spezies Gourmet wird aber zu dieser Zeit noch selten gesichtet, und Kochen ist noch kein Thema der spanischen Presse, als in Madrid eine „Gastronomische Tischrunde" veranstaltet wird. Subijana und Arzak nehmen teil. Auch Paul Bocuse ist anwesend und propagiert seine „Cuisine du Marché". Die Spanier sind fasziniert. Im Kopf beginnt es zu arbeiten. Anschließend verbrachten beide ein paar Tage beim Meister persönlich in Lyon, gingen gemeinsam zum Einkauf auf den Markt, kochten zusammen und leerten wohl manches Glas Rotwein beim Diskutieren und Fachsimpeln über die Zukunft der Küche im Allgemeinen und der baskischen im Speziellen. Wieder an die Biskaya zurückgekehrt, trommelte man die Kollegen der Region zusammen und beschloss:

„WIR STARTEN EINE REVOLUTION!"

Alle zusammen. Es galt die baskische Küche umzukrempeln, ohne die Wurzeln zu verlieren. Das war der Kernpunkt. Umbauen, erneuern und Authentisches von falschen Entwicklungen trennen – und Langeweile durch Spannung ersetzen. Und vor allem anderen wollte man mit den Möglichkeiten der modernen Küchentechnik das Schwere, Butter-und-Sahnefette und kaputt Geschmorte zu neuer Leichtigkeit führen. Pedro Subijana scheut sich nicht einmal zuzugeben, dass er an heutiger Technik beispielsweise Mikrowelle und Induktion besonders zu schätzen weiß. „Aber man sollte wissen, wie man sie anwendet," betont er. Und so legte diese Gruppe baskischer Köche damals den Grundstein zur „Nueva Cocina Vasca". Sie ist ein gut Teil des spanischen Küchenwunders, das nun auch allmählich aus eigener Kraft, mit eigener Identität in die Zirkel der gehobenen Gastronomie Einzug hielt.

Es ist eine Binsenweisheit, dass gute Ernährung körperlicher Gesundheit höchst förderlich ist. Auch Subijana nimmt darauf explizit Rücksicht (da blitzt der verhinderte Medizinstudent durch), doch jenseits gesundheitsfrömmelnder Erwägungen will er mit seinen Gerichten ergötzen und das Essen zum lustvollen Erlebnis gestalten. Fast zwanzig Personen assistieren ihm dabei in einer Küche, deren Arbeitsplätze nicht im Keller sondern auf Restaurantebene und gleichfalls in Sichtweite des Meeres liegen. Vielleicht ist das eine Erklärung für die Leichtigkeit und Fantasie, mit der die Teller bestückt sind. „Hast du selbst keinen Spass beim Essen und Kochen, wie soll es dir dann gelingen, deinen Gästen Genuss zu verkaufen?" fragt er – unwidersprochen. Das Meer in nächster Nähe, kein Wunder, auf der Karte dominieren Fische und Meeresfrüchte. Die schwimmen quasi draußen vorm Haus und sind leicht verständlich Lieblingsobjekte seiner Kochbemühungen. Der Baske besäße nicht seine Reputation, hätte er nicht einen eigenen, ganz unverwechselbaren Stil kreiert. Dafür kombiniert er die klassische Küche der Region mit neuen und überraschenden, bisweilen humorvollen Rezepturen, in denen er raffinierte Geschmacksrichtungen mit ungewöhnlichen Verarbeitungsmethoden austestet, um auch simplen Rohprodukten zu ungeteilter Aufmerksamkeit zu verhelfen. Ganz unprätentiös: Steinbutt mit Knoblauchpüree und Petersilienrisotto. Aromaknüller: Petersilienessenz an frischer Auster, dabei Austernwasser-Sorbet und frittierte Artischockenblättchen. Ein Hauch von Luxus: pures Eigelb mit dem Spachtel zur Creme verstrichen und leicht gestockt zu fragilen Tagliatelle geschnitten, von einem Klecks Beluga-Kaviar getoppt.

EIN SPIEL MIT KONTRASTEN VON AROMA UND TEXTUR IST DAS. DREI SARDINENRÖLLCHEN ERÖFFNEN DAS MENÜ, GEKRÖNT VON EINER SCHWARZEN NOCKE OLIVEN-MOUSSE. PLÖTZLICH BEGINNT ES AUF DER ZUNGE ZU PERLEN, ES KNISTERT DEUTLICH VERNEHMBAR IM GEHÖRGANG, DER GAUMEN PRICKELT. MAN IST IRRITIERT, SCHÜTTELT DEN KOPF, SUCHT VER-STÖRT NACH DER RÄTSELHAFTEN GERÄUSCHQUELLE. DAS KNISTERN BLEIBT, SUBIJANA LACHT: „DIESEN APERITIVO SERVIERE ICH MEINEN GÄSTEN IMMER ALS ERSTES. DAS KNISTERN KOMMT VON DER OLIVENMOUSSE. MAN NIMMT DEN ERSTEN BISSEN DAVON, UND SCHWUPPS, SCHON IST DAS ESSEN MITTELPUNKT DES GE-SPRÄCHS. ¡QUE APROVECHE!"

Raw marinated anchovy filets stuffed with cauliflower cream in lime-and-vanilla-scented olive oil. Served with a black olive sorbet, this amuse gueule is quite an extraordinary experience for the palate.

Roh marinierte Sardellenfilets mit Blumenkohlcreme gefüllt, an mit Vanille und Limette aromatisiertem Olivenöl. In Kombination mit einem Sorbet aus schwarzen Oliven ist dieses als Amuse-Gueule gereichte Gericht ein tolles Geschmackserlebnis.

Foie Frio al Natural, reducción de Sauternes   3.900 Ptas / 23,43 €

Huevo con caviar sobre puré de Coliflor y mantequilla de cebollino   4.100 Ptas / 24,6 €

Ostras con Alcachofas y jugo de Perejil   3.300 Ptas / 19,83 €

Ensalada de Bogavante al Vinagre de Sidra   4.900 Ptas / 29,44 €

Cintas de Pulpo, zanahoria y nabo con aceite de yerbas   3.300 Ptas / 19,83 €

Xangurro templado al horno con maíz frito y aceite de piparras   3.550 Ptas / 21,33 €

Cigala en Tempura de cortezas con Ortigas y yogur de Maní   3.450 Ptas / 20,73 €

Puntas de Espárragos frescos con Habitas y Granizado de tomate seco   3.300 Ptas / 19,83 €

Guisantitos del País con Mollejitas de cordero y gelatina de Jamón   3.450 Ptas / 20,73 €

Lonchita de Foie sobre royal y polvo de vino, ensalada loca con Flores y frutas fritas   3.400 Ptas / 20,43 €

Panceta asada con lentejas fritas y el caldo del potaje   3.300 Ptas / 19,83 €

Escarlata empanada en Harina de Alubias y Pistachos   3.250 Ptas / 19,53 €

Langostinos frescos con su caldo, Algas y Quinoa   3.450 Ptas / 20,73 €

Alubias rojas de Tolosa con todas sus guarniciones   2.900 Ptas / 17,42 €

Sopa de Pescados y Mariscos al estilo Donostiarra   2.550 Ptas / 15,32 €

La Zurrukutuna puesta al día   2.450 Ptas / 14,72 €

Rodaballo con caldo de puerros, Patata y aceite de oliva 4.400 Ptas / 26,44 €

Lomitos de rape con Pil Pil de habas a la menta, naranja y jamón   4.100 Ptas / 24,64 €

Filetes de Salmonetes con Risotto al ajo y perejil, ola de gamba   4.200 Ptas / 25,24 €

Merluza en salsa con Almejas   4.450 Ptas/26,74 €

Merluza escaldada, con Mejillones, jugo de Carabineros y aceituna negra   4.200 Ptas / 25,24 €

Bacalao en Potaje de garbanzos de Vigilia   4.200 Ptas / 25,24 €

Bogavante asado, con su agua cuajada, sus partes cremosas y hongos marinados   5.500 Ptas / 33,05 €

Buey asado a la parilla con sal de mar, pimienta negra, piquillos y jugo del asado   3.950 Ptas / 23,73 €

Foie sobre talo esponjoso, caramelo de Txakolí y Caviar de vinagre   4.600 Ptas / 27,64 €

Ternera de leche al Regaliz con Hongos y Patata   4.600 Ptas / 27,64 €

Corderito asado, servido sin huesos, con nube de patata frita y Ensalada gelatinoaldente   4.450 Ptas / 26,74 €

Manitas de Cerdo rellenas con Carrilleras, salsa y cuajado de Sidra   3.750 Ptas / 22,53 €

Rabo de Buey con Tuétano, ajo tierno y mayonesa de almendra   3.900 Ptas / 23,43 €

Pechuga de Pichón escalfado en su jugo y su muslo confitado 4.850 / 29,14 €

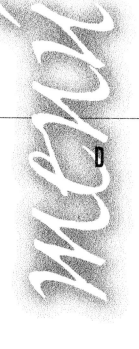

DEGUSTACION

Puntas de Espárragos frescos con Habitas y Granizado de tomate seco

Cigala en Tempura de cortezas con Ortigas y Yogur de Maní

Guisantitos del País con Mollejitas de cordero y gelatina de Jamón

Filetes de Salmonetes con risotto al ajo y perejil, ola de gamba

Ternera de leche al Regaliz con Hongos y Patata

Croquis de Arroz salvaje, con leche

Huevo en cocotte (Kumquat, leche de coco, Pomelo y haba de cacao)

El menú sólo se sirve por mesa completa. 10.500 Ptas / 61,3 €. por persona + 7% IVA.   No incluye bebidas.

Algunos de Nuestros Postres requieren tiempo, encárguelos al Principio

Bocado goloso de Chocolate y Ruibarbo con Fresas estofadas   1.800 Ptas / 10,81 €

Hojaldre de Cítricos con caramelo y Helado de Queso fresco   1.800 Ptas / 10,81 €

Pastel de Zanahoria y su Sorbete, a la salsa de Lima   1.800 Ptas / 10,81 €

Pastel de Frutas rojas, caliente   1.800 Ptas / 10,81 €

Cienhojas de Mango asado, con el helado de su escabeche   1.850 Ptas / 11,11 €

Croquis de Arroz salvaje, con leche   1.850 Ptas / 11,11 €

Helado de queso Idiazabal   1.800 Ptas / 10,81 €

Huevo en cocotte (Kumquat, leche de coco, Pomelo y haba de cacao)   1.850 Ptas / 11,11 €

Gin-Tonic helado   1.850 Ptas / 11,11 €

Biscuit helado de Fresas con infusión de Sésamo tostado 1.850/ 11,11 €

Pero también podrán pedir estos otros al final de la comida:

Mil Hojas con crema de Café y Chocolate   1.750 Ptas / 10,51 €

Helados o Sorbetes del día   1.300 Ptas / 7,81 €

Quesos   1.750 Ptas / 10,51 €

EGG YOLK SHEETS WITH CAVIAR ON A PURÉE OF CAULIFLOWER
SERVED WITH ALMOND SAUCE AND CHIVE BUTTER

EIGELBBLÄTTER MIT KAVIAR AUF BLUMENKOHLPÜREE
MIT MANDELSAUCE UND SCHNITTLAUCHBUTTER

Serves 4

For the egg yolk sheets: 2 egg yolks, salt, lemon juice

For the almond sauce:
100 g/3 1/2 oz peeled almonds, fresh ones if possible, chopped,
75 ml/1/3 cup water, 1/2 sheet gelatin

For the cauliflower purée:
100 g/3 1/2 oz cauliflower, flowerets only, 50 g/1 1/2 oz butter

For the chive butter:
80 g/3 oz butter, at room temperature,
10 g/1 tsp cocoa butter, heated until melted, 1 bunch chives

Garnish:
20 g/3/4 oz caviar (Beluga), 2 tsp foie gras fat (fat rendering
when steaming foie gras), 8 chive blades

Für 4 Personen:

Für die Eigelbblätter: 2 Eigelb, Salz, Zitronensaft

Für die Mandelsauce:
100 g geschälte, nach Möglichkeit frische Mandeln, gehackt,
75 ml Wasser, 1/2 Gelatineblatt

Für das Blumenkohlpüree:
100 g Blumenkohl, nur die Röschen, 50 g Butter

Für die Schnittlauchbutter:
80 g Butter, zimmerwarm, 10 g Kakaobutter, bis zu flüssiger
Konsistenz erwärmt, 1 Bund Schnittlauch

Garnitur:
20 g Kaviar (Beluga), 2 TL Stopfleberfett (austretendes Fett beim
Garen von Stopfleber über Dampf), 8 Schnittlauchhalme

For the almond sauce: Soak the chopped almonds in water over-night. On the following day, run the almonds through a juicer and strain the resulting juice through a cloth. Soak the gelatin in cold water, squeeze out excess water and heat in the almond juice until completely dissolved. Keep at room temperature.

For the cauliflower purée: Boil the cauliflower flowerets in salted water until tender, drain them a sieve and purée them in a blender with the butter until you have a fine purée. Strain cream through a sieve and allow to cool.

For the chive butter: Blanch chives in boiling water for a few seconds, remove from water and cool down quickly in ice water. Blend finely in a blender, strain purée through a sieve and measure out two tablespoons of the liquid. Mix butter and cocoa butter with chive liquid. Spread butter onto four 6 x 4 cm/ 2 1/2 x 1 2/3 inch strips of heavy-duty plastic foil and allow it to get semi-hard in the refrigerator. Cut strips lengthwise into 5 mm/1/5 inch strips with the back of a knife. Fold the foil strips over in a cushion shape, forming a hollow in the middle. Press down on both ends, removing the ends of the foil. Place in the refrigerator until solidified.

For the egg yolk sheets: Strain the egg yolks through a fine sieve into a small dish. Mix with a pinch of salt and a few drops of lemon juice. Line a flat dish with heat-proof foil. Spread egg yolk mixture very thinly onto the foil. Steam in a steamer at 120° C/ 250° F for about ten seconds, until set. Remove from the steamer and cut the sheet into four pieces. Roll up the pieces into the desired form, removing foil.

Serving: Divide the almond sauce equally between four deep plates and drizzle the plates with a little foie gras fat. Place a spoonful of cauliflower cream into the middle of each plate and top with an egg yolk sheet. Place a small spoonful of caviar and a chive butter cushion on top. Garnish with chive tips and serve.

Für die Mandelsauce: Gehackte Mandeln über Nacht in Wasser einweichen. Am nächsten Tag im Entsafter entsaften, den gewonnenen Saft durch ein Tuch passieren. Gelatine in kaltem Wasser einweichen, ausdrücken und mit dem Saft erwärmen, bis sie sich vollständig aufgelöst hat. Bei Zimmertemperatur aufbewahren.

Für das Blumenkohlpüree: Die Blumenkohlröschen in Salzwasser gar kochen, durch ein Sieb abgießen, mit der Butter im Mixer zu einem glatten Püree verarbeiten. Durch ein Sieb streichen, vollständig abkühlen lassen.

Für die Schnittlauchbutter: Schnittlauch in kochendem Wasser kurz blanchieren, herausnehmen und sofort in Eiswasser abkühlen. Im Mixer fein pürieren, durch ein Sieb passieren und von dem Saft 2 Löffel abmessen. Butter und Kakaobutter mit dem Schnittlauchsaft vermischen. Vier Streifen fester Folie von 6 x 4 cm mit der Butter bestreichen, im Kühlschrank halb fest werden lassen. Mit einem Messerrücken der Länge nach in 5 mm dicke Streifen teilen. Die Folie kissenförmig zusammenklappen, so dass die Butter in der Mitte ein Loch formt, an beiden Enden festdrücken, dabei die Folie ein Stück weit ablösen. Im Kühlschrank fest werden lassen.

Für die Eigelbblätter: Das Eigelb durch ein Sieb in eine kleine Schale streichen. Mit einer Prise Salz und ein paar Tropfen Zitronensaft verrühren. Eine flache Form mit hitzefester Folie ausschlagen. Das Eigelbgemisch hauchdünn ausstreichen. Im Dampfofen bei 120° C ca. 10 Sekunden fest werden lassen. Aus dem Ofen nehmen, in 4 Stücke teilen, abkühlen lassen. Die Eigelblamellen in die gewünschte Form biegen, dabei die Folie entfernen.

Zum Servieren: Die Mandelsauce in vier tiefe Teller verteilen und mit dem Stopfleberfett beträufeln. In die Mitte der Teller je einen Löffel Blumenkohlcreme geben und mit einem Eigelbblatt bedecken. Je einen Teelöffel Kaviar und ein Schnittlauchkissen darauf setzen. Mit Schnittlauchspitzen garniert servieren.

ASPARAGUS TIPS WITH FAVA BEANS AND GRANITA OF DRIED TOMATOES

SPARGELSPITZEN MIT DICKEN BOHNEN UND GRANITE VON GETROCKNETEN TOMATEN

Serves 4

For the asparagus:
16 white asparagus, 500 ml/2 cups water,
3 tsp salt, 2 tsp sugar, 2 tbsp butter,
oil for deep-frying, 2 tbsp olive oil, 200 ml/³/₄ cup cream

For the tomato granita:
200 g/7 oz ripe tomatoes, peeled and cored,
50 g/1 ¹/₂ oz dried tomatoes, 5 drops of tabasco

For the fava beans:
120 g/4 oz young, fresh fava beans,
1 tbsp olive oil, 1 pinch of salt

For the sabayon:
50 ml/¹/₄ cup apple cider, 2 egg yolks

Trim the nicest looking 12 asparagus tips to a length of about 6 cm/ 2¹/₂ inches. Boil the tips in salted and sugared water for about five minutes. Allow to drain and lightly brown them in hot butter on all sides. Reserve. Peel remaining asparagus. Shave the four thickest spears lengthwise into thin strips with a vegetable peeler. Select eight unblemished, broad strips and boil in salted water for five minutes. Refresh in cold water, drain and brush the strips with oil. Line the sides of four small spring forms with the oiled asparagus strips. Cut remaining asparagus strips into fine strips lengthwise. Blanch in salted water, allow excess water to drip off and deep-fry the strips in hot oil until golden brown. Drain on paper towels.

Cut the remaining asparagus into pieces. In a heavy-bottomed casserole, sauté the pieces in olive oil over low heat for about ten minutes. Add cream and simmer for another twenty minutes. Finely purée the mixture in a blender, strain it through a sieve and check for salt. Allow to cool and place into the refrigerator for twelve hours until well chilled.

For the tomato granita: Chop the fresh tomatoes and simmer them, uncovered, in a large pot for about five minutes, stirring constantly. Add finely diced dried tomatoes and tabasco. Continue to simmer on low heat for about five minutes. Strain the mixture through a sieve and pour it into a flat dish. Allow to cool and place it in a deep freezer.

For the fava beans: Blanch the fava beans in salted water for three minutes, then refresh in ice water. Remove outer skins if necessary. Allow beans to cool, mix with olive oil and sprinkle with salt.

For the sabayon: Beat egg yolks and apple cider in a double boiler until light and fluffy.

Serving: Beat asparagus cream with a wooden spoon until creamy. Ladle the cream into the asparagus-lined spring forms to come two-thirds of the way up, cover with sabayon and place the whole into deep plates. Carefully remove spring form. Insert three asparagus tips each into the cream. Scrape off top layers of tomato ice cream with a spoon and arrange alternate spoonfuls of the tomato granita and fava beans around the mousse. Garnish with deep-fried asparagus strips and serve.

Für 4 Personen:

Für den Spargel:
16 weiße Spargelstangen, 500 ml Wasser,
3 TL Salz, 2 TL Zucker, 2 EL Butter,
Öl zum Frittieren, 2 EL Olivenöl, 200 ml Sahne

Für das Tomaten-Granité:
200 g reife Tomaten, enthäutet und entkernt,
50 g getrocknete Tomaten, 5 Tropfen Tabascosauce

Für die Dicken Bohnen:
120 g frische, junge Dicke Bohnen,
1 EL Olivenöl, 1 Prise Salz

Für den Sabayon:
50 ml Apfelwein, 2 Eigelb

Von dem Spargel die schönsten zwölf Spitzen 6 cm lang abschneiden und im Wasser mit Salz und Zucker 5 Minuten kochen. Abtropfen lassen, dann in der Pfanne in der heißen Butter von allen Seiten leicht bräunen. Beiseite stellen.

Restlichen Spargel schälen. Die vier dicksten Stangen mit einem Gemüseschäler der Länge nach in dünne Streifen hobeln. Von den breitesten Streifen acht auswählen, in Salzwasser 5 Minuten kochen, abschrecken, mit Öl einpinseln und die Seiten von vier kleinen Springformen damit auskleiden. Restliche Streifen der Länge nach fein schneiden. In Salzwasser blanchieren, abtropfen lassen, im heißen Öl goldgelb ausbacken. Auf Küchenpapier abtropfen lassen. Den restlichen Spargel in Stücke schneiden. In einem Topf mit schwerem Boden in Olivenöl bei kleiner Hitze 10 Minuten dünsten. Sahne zugeben, weitere 20 Minuten köcheln. Im Mixer fein pürieren, durch ein Sieb streichen, die Spargelcreme mit Salz abschmecken. Erkalten lassen, im Kühlschrank zwölf Stunden durchkühlen.

Für das Tomaten-Granité: Die frischen Tomaten hacken, in einem Topf unter Rühren 5 Minuten bei großer Hitze kochen. Fein geschnittene getrocknete Tomaten und Tabasco unterrühren. Bei kleiner Hitze 5 Minuten köcheln. Die Masse durch ein Sieb streichen, in eine flache Form füllen, erkalten lassen und im Gefrierschrank gefrieren lassen.

Für die Dicken Bohnen: Bohnenkerne in Salzwasser 3 Minuten blanchieren, anschließend in Eiswasser abschrecken. Wenn nötig, die Häutchen abziehen. Erkalten lassen, mit Olivenöl vermischen und mit etwas Salz leicht würzen.

Für den Sabayon: Eigelb und Apfelwein über dem Wasserbad zu einem luftigen Schaum schlagen.

Zum Servieren: Die Spargel-Sahnecreme mit einem Holzlöffel aufschlagen. Zweidrittelhoch in die ausgekleideten Springformen füllen, mit Sabayon bedecken und das Ganze in tiefe Teller anrichten, die Formen entfernen. Je drei Spargelspitzen in die Creme stecken. Das Tomateneis mit dem Löffel abkratzen, mit Dicken Bohnen abwechselnd um die Spargelmousse arrangieren. Mit frittierten Spargelstreifen garnieren und servieren.

ROCK LOBSTERS IN THEIR JUICE WITH SEAWEED AND QUINOA

KAISERGRANATEN IN IHREM SAFT MIT ALGEN UND QUINOA

Serves 4

24 rock lobsters,
2 tbsp olive oil,
500 ml/2 cups water,
salt, white pepper

20 g/³/₄ oz quinoa (Inka rice),
oil for deep-frying,
40 g/1 ¹/₂ oz mustard seeds

40 g/1 ¹/₂ oz fresh seaweed (or dried, soaked in water),
1 bunch chives

For the mayonnaise:
1 egg yolk, 1 whole egg,
125 ml/¹/₂ cup olive oil,
125 ml/¹/₂ cup cold-pressed olive oil,
10 ml/1 tbsp vinegar, salt

Für 4 Personen:

24 Kaisergranaten,
2 EL Olivenöl,
500 ml Wasser,
Salz, weißer Pfeffer

20 g Quinoa (Peru-Spinat, Reismelde),
Öl zum Frittieren,
40 g Senfkörner

40 g frische Meeralgen, (oder getrocknete, in Wasser eingeweicht),
1 Bund Schnittlauch

Für die Mayonnaise:
1 Eigelb, 1 ganzes Ei,
125 ml Olivenöl,
125 ml kalt gepresstes Olivenöl,
10 ml Essig, Salz

Shell rock lobster tails, leaving the tail segment intact. Heat olive oil in a large sauce pan and fry the heads and shells of the rock lobsters until they take on color. Add water to cover and allow to steep on low heat for two hours. Keep temperature just below the boiling point. Strain the stock through a fine sieve and season to taste with salt and white pepper. Boil the quinoa kernels in salted water for thirty minutes. Strain in a sieve, rinse with running cold water and place the kernels into an oven-proof dish. Dry them in a 100° C/210° F degree oven for two hours, then deep-fry the kernels in a pan with hot olive oil. Drain well on paper towels.

Prepare half of the mustard seeds as described above for the quinoa. Mix quinoa, prepared mustard seeds and remaining mustard seeds. Pat seaweed dry with paper towels and deep-fry together with the chives in hot oil. Allow to drain on paper towels.

For the mayonnaise: Mix egg yolk and egg with a hand mixer at lowest speed. Add oil in a thin stream until mixture is beginning to thicken. Add remaining oil and vinegar and check for salt. Spoon mayonnaise into small round molds (about 3 cm/1 inch in diameter) and steam in a steamer at 120° C/250° F for about two minutes (alternatively, steam the molds in a double boiler). Unmold mayonnaise carefully onto serving dishes.

Finish: Broil rock lobster tails under the broiler or in a salamander for one minute per side. The flesh should still be juicy. Bring prepared stock to a boil and drizzle some of it onto the mayonnaise. Sprinkle quinoa-mustard seed mixture onto the mayonnaise and top with rock lobster tails. Garnish the plates with deep-fried seaweed and chive blades. Serve at once.

Kaisergranatschwänze aus der Schale lösen, das letzte Schwanzglied am Fleisch belassen. Köpfe und Schalen in einem Topf im Olivenöl anbraten, mit Wasser auffüllen und zwei Stunden bei kleiner Hitze vor dem Siedepunkt ziehen lassen. Den Fond durch ein feines Sieb passieren, mit Salz und weißem Pfeffer würzen.

Quinoa in Salzwasser 30 Minuten weich kochen. Durch ein Sieb abgießen, unter fließendem kaltem Wasser waschen und in eine feuerfeste Form geben. Im 100° C heißen Ofen zwei Stunden trocknen und weiter garen. Anschließend Quinoasamen in einer Pfanne im Olivenöl goldbraun frittieren. Gut abtropfen lassen. Die Hälfte der Senfkörner in der gleichen Weise zubereiten wie für das Quinoa beschrieben, anschließend mit Quinoa und restlichen Senfkörnern vermischen. Meeralgen mit Küchenpapier trocken tupfen, mit dem Schnittlauch ebenfalls im heißen Öl frittieren. Abtropfen lassen.

Für die Mayonnaise: Eigelb und das ganze Ei im Mixer bei kleinster Einstellung verrühren. Nach und nach das Öl zugeben, bis die Mischung beginnt zu binden. Restliches Öl und Essig zugeben, mit Salz würzen. Runde Förmchen von 3 cm Durchmesser mit Mayonnaise füllen, im Dampfofen bei 120° C (oder im Topf über Dampf) ca. 2 Minuten garen. Vorsichtig aus den Formen stürzen und in Servierschalen geben.

Fertigstellung: Kaisergranatschwänze unter dem Salamander oder Grill von beiden Seiten eine Minute rösten, so dass sie innen saftig bleiben. Vorbereiteten Fond erhitzen, zu der Mayonnaise in die Schalen gießen. Senfkorn-Quinoa-Gemisch über die Mayonnaise geben, dann die Kaisergranatschwänze darüber legen. Mit frittierten Algen und Schnittlauchhalmen garnieren und servieren.

OYSTERS WITH ARTICHOKE CREAM AND PARSLEY JUS

AUSTERN MIT ARTISCHOCKENCREME UND PETERSILIENJUS

Serves 4

24 oysters,
sea water for boiling (if not available, use water with
an appropriate amount of sea salt),
1 tsp very finely grated lime zest

For the foam:
50 ml/¹/₄ cup oyster water
(water caught when opening oysters),
50 ml/¹/₄ cup steamed clam juice,
50 ml/¹/₄ cup steamed lobster juice,
3 sheets gelatin

For the parsley jus:
1 bunch parsley,
1 sheet gelatin,
salt

16 artichokes,
120 ml/¹/₂ cup olive oil

In a large pot, bring sea water to a boil. Dip oysters into the water with a skimmer or a sieve and simmer for five minutes. Refresh in ice water. Work in batches until all oysters are done. Cool each batch in ice water. Open the oyster shells above a flat bowl to catch the juice. Measure out 50 ml/¹/₄ cup of the juice. Remove oysters from shells, place them in a shallow dish and keep refrigerated.

For the foam: Pre-soak the three gelatin sheets and squeeze out excess water. Heat the seafood juice and dissolve the gelatin sheets in it. Stir well, pass the liquid through a sieve and fill it into a soda siphon. Keep at room temperature.

For the parsley jus: Bring salted water to a rolling boil and blanch the parsley for three seconds. Refresh with ice water at once. Shake off excess water and purée in a blender for two minutes, then strain the purée through a cloth. Heat parsley juice just enough to dissolve the gelatin sheet. Mix, season with salt and set aside.

Carefully remove all leaves and chokes from the artichokes. Cut twelve of the artichoke hearts into quarters and boil them in salted water with a dash of olive oil for 4 - 6 minutes until al dente. Drain in a sieve. Heat a little bit of olive in a large pan and fry the artichoke quarters on low heat for 8 - 10 minutes, until soft. Finely purée artichoke quarters in a blender, check for seasonings and strain the purée through a sieve. Reserve.

Cut the remaining artichoke hearts into thin slices. Heat the remaining olive oil in a small pan and fry the artichoke slices on medium heat until golden brown. Remove from oil and drain on several layers of paper towels.

Finish: Spoon the artichoke purée onto plates. Place oysters on top. Sprinkle the oysters generously with lime zest. Glaze the whole with oyster foam from the siphon and drizzle a little parsley juice around the arrangement. Garnish with the deep-fried artichoke slices and serve.

Für 4 Personen:

24 Austern,
Meerwasser zum Kochen (wenn nicht möglich,
Wasser mit entsprechender Menge Meersalz würzen),
1 TL sehr fein geriebene Limettenschale

Für den Schaum:
50 ml Austernwasser
(beim Öffnen der Austern auffangen),
50 ml Saft von gedämpften Venusmuscheln,
50 ml Saft von gedämpftem Hummer,
3 Gelatineblätter

Für den Petersilienjus:
1 Bund Petersilie,
1 Gelatineblatt,
Salz

16 Artischocken,
120 ml Olivenöl

In einem großen Topf das Meerwasser zum Kochen bringen. Die Austern mit Hilfe einer Lochkelle fünf Minuten hineintauchen, anschließend in Eiswasser abkühlen. Nach und nach alle Austern so pochieren und abkühlen. Die Schalen öffnen, den austretenden Saft auffangen und 50 ml abmessen. Die Austern aus der Schale lösen, in eine flache Form legen und im Kühlschrank aufbewahren.

Für den Schaum: Die abgemessenen Säfte soweit erwärmen, daß sich die drei eingeweichten und ausgedrückten Gelatineblätter auflösen. Gut vermischen, durch ein Sieb passieren in ein Siphon (Rahmbläser) füllen und bei Zimmertemperatur aufbewahren.

Für den Petersilienjus: Die Petersilie drei Sekunden in sprudelnd kochendem Salzwasser blanchieren, sofort in Eiswasser abkühlen. Ausschütteln, im Mixer zwei Minuten pürieren und dann durch ein Tuch passieren. Den Saft soweit erwärmen, bis sich das eingeweichte und ausgedrückte Gelatineblatt auflöst. Gut umrühren, mit Salz abschmecken und beiseite stellen.

Blätter und Heu der Artischocken sorgfältig entfernen. Zwölf der Artischockenherzen in Viertel schneiden, in Salzwasser mit einem Schuss Olivenöl 4 - 6 Minuten al dente kochen. Durch ein Sieb abgießen. In einer Pfanne etwas Olivenöl erhitzen, Artischockenviertel 8 - 10 Minuten bei kleiner Hitze braten, bis sie weich sind. Im Mixer fein pürieren, abschmecken, durch ein Sieb streichen. Beiseite stellen. Restliche Artischockenherzen in dünne Scheiben schneiden. Das restliche Olivenöl in einer kleinen Pfanne erhitzen, die Artischockenscheiben bei mittlerer Hitze goldbraun braten. Aus dem Öl nehmen und auf Küchenpapier gut abtropfen lassen.

Fertigstellung: Das Artischockenpüree in Teller verteilen und mit Austern belegen. Die abgeriebene Limettenschale über die Austern streuen. Mit Austernschaum aus dem Siphon überziehen, den Petersilienjus rundherum gießen. Mit den frittierten Artischockenscheiben garniert servieren.

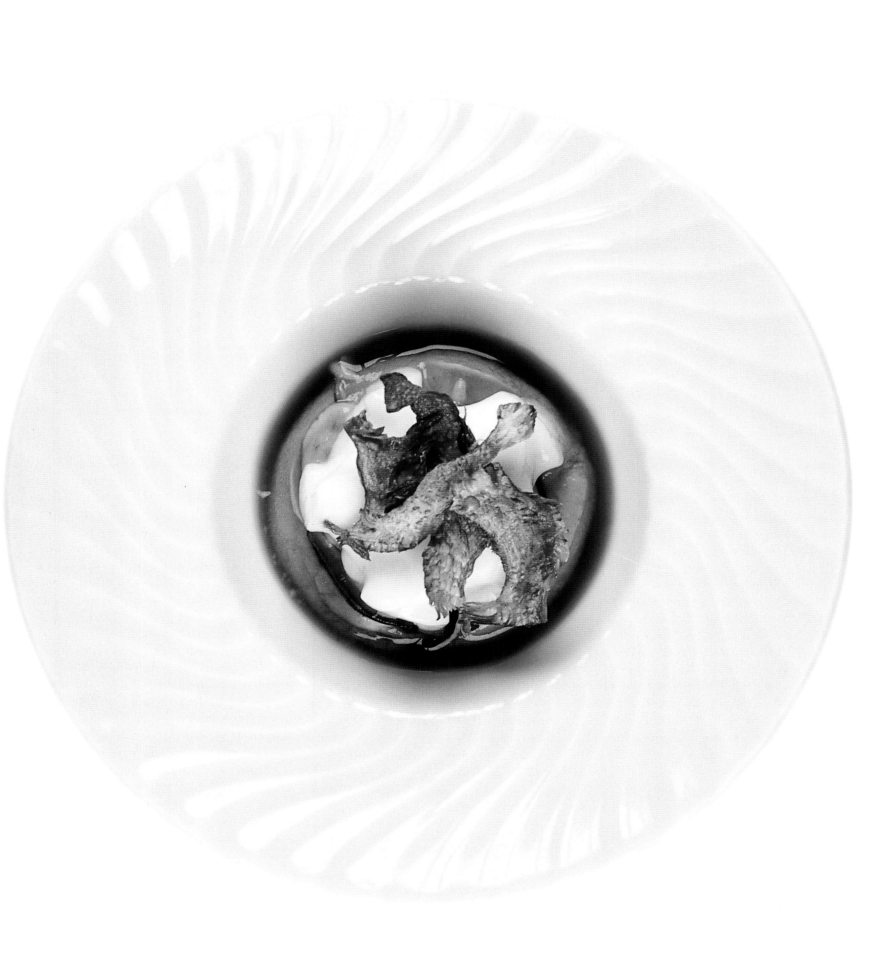

ROCK LOBSTERS IN CRACKED WHEAT TEMPURA
SERVED WITH A NETTLE SAUCE AND PEANUT YOGHURT

KAISERGRANATEN IN WEIZENSCHROTTEMPURA
MIT BRENNESSELSAUCE UND ERDNUSSJOGHURT

Serves 4

4 rock lobsters, shelled, 40 g/1 ¹/₂ oz cracked wheat, oil for deep-frying

For the yoghurt:
75 g/2 ¹/₂ oz peanuts, 1 egg white, 150 ml/²/₃ cup natural yoghurt

For the borage:
2 garlic cloves, 50 g/2 oz fatback, chopped,
100 ml/¹/₃ cup cold-pressed olive oil,
35 ml/¹/₈ cup sherry vinegar, 100 g/3 ¹/₂ oz borage stalks

For the peanut oil:
25 g/1 oz peanuts, 50 ml/¹/₄ cup olive oil

For the nettle sauce:
60 g/2 oz potatoes, 1 bunch stinging nettles, 2 tbsp olive oil,
60 ml/¹/₄ cup white wine, salt, freshly ground white pepper

For the yoghurt: Finely purée the peanuts, egg white and yoghurt in the blender. Strain the purée through a sieve, pour it into an oven-proof dish and steam the yoghurt cream at 100° C/210° F for ten minutes (or bake it in a steamer oven). Keep warm.

For the borage: Crush garlic and sauté it in olive oil with the fatback. Turn heat down to low and allow the fatback to render for twenty-five minutes. Strain through a cloth, allow to cool and mix in the sherry vinegar. Toss the uncooked borage stalks with the vinaigrette and place them into a flat dish. Broil or grill the stalks in a salamander for one to two minutes. The stalks should wilt but still be firm to the bite. Keep warm.

For the peanut oil: Finely purée peanuts and olive oil in a blender. Strain the oil through a fine sieve and reserve.

For the nettle sauce: Peel the potato and steam it until tender. Wash nettles, remove some small leaves and set them aside. In a small saucepan, sauté the remaining nettles in oil. Douse with white wine. Fine purée nettles and steamed potato in a blender, check for salt and pepper and reserve.

Blanch the reserved small nettle leaves in salted water, refresh them in ice water and allow to drain on paper towels. Deep-fry the leaves in hot oil until crispy and drain them on paper towels.

Finish: Grind cracked wheat coarsely in a cereal mill. Turn the rock lobsters in the wheat, pressing the crumbs into the meat with your fingers. Heat the oil in a pan and fry the rock lobsters on high heat until golden brown. The wheat ought to expand and get crispy, the rock lobsters should still be juicy on the inside.

Serving: Divide peanut oil equally between for deep plates. Place some nettle sauce and a spoonful of yoghurt at the center. Top with fried rock lobsters and garnish with borage stalks, its vinaigrette and a few deep-fried nettle leaves. Serve.

Für 4 Personen:

4 geschälte Kaisergranaten, 40 g Weizenschrot, Öl zum Frittieren

Für den Joghurt:
75 g Erdnüsse, 1 Eiweiß, 150 ml Naturjoghurt

Für den Borretsch:
2 Knoblauchzehen, 50 g fetter Speck, gehackt,
100 g kalt gepresstes Olivenöl,
35 ml Sherryessig, 100 g Borretschstengel

Für das Erdnussöl:
25 g Erdnüsse, 50 ml Olivenöl

Für die Brennesselsauce:
60 g Kartoffel, 1 Bund Brennesseln, 2 EL Olivenöl,
60 ml Weißwein, Salz, weißer Pfeffer aus der Mühle

Für den Joghurt: Die Erdnüsse mit dem Eiweiß und dem Joghurt im Mixer fein pürieren. Durch ein Sieb streichen, in eine ofenfeste Schale füllen und die Joghurtcreme über Dampf (oder im Dampfofen) bei 100° C zehn Minuten garen. Warm halten.

Für den Borretsch: Olivenöl mit dem zerquetschten Knoblauch und Speck in einem Topf erhitzen. Die Hitze zurückstellen und die Mischung vor dem Siedepunkt 25 Minuten ziehen lassen. Durch ein Tuch passieren, erkalten lassen, zum Schluss mit Sherryessig vermischen. Borretschstengel roh mit Vinaigrette vermischen, in einer flachen Form unter dem Salamander (oder Grill) 1 - 2 Minuten garen. Die Stengel sollen al dente bleiben. Warmhalten.

Für das Erdnussöl: Die Erdnüsse mit dem Olivenöl im Mixer fein pürieren. Durch ein Sieb passieren, beiseite stellen.

Für die Brennesselsauce: Kartoffel schälen und über Dampf weichkochen. Die Brennesseln waschen, die kleinen Blätter abzupfen und beiseite legen. Restliche Brennesseln in einem Topf im Öl anbraten. Mit Weißwein ablöschen, einkochen. Mit der gedämpften Kartoffel im Mixer fein pürieren, abschmecken, beiseite stellen.

Kleine Brennesselblätter in Salzwasser blanchieren, in Eiswasser abschrecken, auf Küchenpapier abtrocknen. In heißem Öl schwimmend knusprig backen, auf Küchenpapier abtropfen lassen.

Fertigstellung: Weizenschrot in einer Mühle nicht zu fein mahlen. Die Kaisergranaten damit rundum panieren, dabei das Schrot gut andrücken. In einer Pfanne im Öl schwimmend bei großer Hitze goldbraun ausbacken, das Schrot soll quellen und knusprig werden, der Kaisergranat im Innern nur knapp gegart sein.

Zum Servieren: Erdnussöl in vier tiefe Teller verteilen, da hinein die Brennesselsauce gießen und in die Mitte je einen Löffel Joghurt geben. Gebackene Kaisergranaten darüber legen, mit Borretsch, Vinaigrette und frittierten Brennesselblättern garnieren.

Serves 4

8 - 12 small filets of striped mullet, ready-to-cook,
4 tbsp olive oil, 1 tbsp mild apple cider vinegar
For the rice: 2 tbsp cold-pressed olive oil, 1 bunch parsley,
500 ml/2 cups water, 1 garlic clove,
3 tbsp olive oil, 100 g/3 1/2 oz short grain rice
For the garlic emulsion:
50 g/1 1/2 oz pickled garlic, 50 g/1 1/2 oz olive oil
For the shrimp chips: 80 g/3 oz small shrimp, 1 tbsp olive oil,
250 ml/1 cup water, 1 tsp cornstarch, oil for deep-frying
For the ajilis mojilis sauce (makes 160 ml/2/3 cup):
100 ml/1/3 cup olive oil, 50 ml/1/4 cup apple cider vinegar,
1 sprig of parsley, 1/2 sprig of thyme (leaves only),
2 garlic cloves, 6 black peppercorns, crushed in a mortar,
1/2 shallot, 1 tsp salt, a pinch of lemon zest
For the sauce: heads and bones of two striped mullet, 2 tbsp olive oil,
1 garlic clove, minced, 1 tbsp hot pepper, finely diced,
200 ml/3/4 cup water, 1 tbsp light roux (equal amounts of butter and
flour), 1 tbsp red pepper, diced as finely as possible, salt, white pepper

For the rice: Heat olive in a pan. Sauté parsley for a few seconds on all sides, then refresh it in ice water. Finely purée parsley and water in a blender and strain the mixture through a sieve. In a heavy-bottomed casserole, fry garlic in remaining oil until translucent. Strain garlic through a sieve and add parsley juice. Preheat the oven to 250° C/475° F. Sauté rice in the garlic oil in the casserole. Add parsley juice and place casserole into the oven for 10 minutes. Remove and finish cooking on the stove top until rice is soft and creamy. Set aside.

For the garlic emulsion: Purée pickled garlic and oil in a blender until you have a fine cream. Strain the cream through a sieve.

For the shrimp chips: Peel shrimp and dice the flesh very finely. Blanch the diced shrimp in salted water, drain in a sieve and allow to cool. In a small saucepan, sauté shrimp heads and shells in olive oil. Add water barely to cover. Bring the shells to a boil and allow to steep on low heat just below the boiling point for three hours. Strain through a sieve. Mix the cornstarch with a little cold water and thicken shrimp stock with the mixture. Simmer, uncovered, for five minutes until you have a thick sauce. Stir in shrimp dice and spread the mixture onto a non-stick baking sheet. Dry in a hot oven for two hours, then break the sheet into chip-size pieces. Heat the oil in a large frying pan and drop in shrimp chips. As soon as they puff up, remove them from the oil with a skimmer and allow them to drain on kitchen towels.

For the ajilis mojilis sauce: Combine all ingredients in a blender and blend into a fine purée. Allow to rest at room temperature for an hour, then strain the mixture through a fine sieve.

For the sauce: Coarsely chop heads and bones of striped mullet and sauté in oil in a heavy saucepan. Add garlic and hot pepper and four tablespoon of the prepared ajilis mojilis. Douse with water. Stir and allow to steep in the hot oven for 10 to 15 minutes. Strain sauce through a fine sieve, then thicken it lightly with roux if necessary. Blanch red pepper dice in salted water and fold it into the cream. Check for salt and pepper.

In a large frying pan, fry the striped mullet filets in hot oil, skin-side up. Brush with apple cider vinegar and keep warm.

Serving: Ladle sauce into deep plates. Spoon a portion of rice into the center of each plate, top with striped mullet filets and cover with shrimp chips. Drizzle a little garlic emulsion next to it. Serve.

Für 4 Personen:

8 - 12 kleine Rotbarbenfilets, küchenfertig,
4 EL Olivenöl, 1 EL milder Apfelweinessig
Für den Reis: 2 EL kalt gepresstes Olivenöl,
1 Bund Petersilie, 500 ml Wasser, 1 Knoblauchzehe,
3 EL Olivenöl, 100 g Rundkornreis
Für die Knoblauchemulsion:
50 g in Essig eingelegter Knoblauch, 50 g Olivenöl
Für die Garnelenchips: 80 g Garnelen, 1 EL Olivenöl,
250 ml Wasser, 1 TL Maisstärke, Öl zum Frittieren
Für die Ajilis-Mojilis-Sauce (ergibt 160 ml):
100 ml Olivenöl, 50 ml Apfelweinessig,
1 Zweig Petersilie, 1/2 Zweig Thymian (nur die Blättchen),
2 Knoblauchzehen, 6 schwarze Pfefferkörner, im Mörser zerstoßen,
1/2 Schalotte, 1 TL Salz, 1 Msp abgeriebene Zitronenschale
Für die Sauce: Köpfe und Gräten von 2 Rotbarben, 2 EL Olivenöl,
1 Knoblauchzehe, gehackt, 1 EL fein gehackte Chilischote,
200 ml Wasser, 1 TL helle Roux (Mehlschwitze 1:1),
1 EL rote Paprika, so fein wie möglich gehackt, Salz, weißer Pfeffer

Für den Reis: Olivenöl in einem Topf erhitzen. Petersilie kurz von allen Seiten darin schwenken, in Eiswasser abkühlen. Mit Wasser im Mixer fein pürieren, durch ein Sieb passieren. Knoblauch im restlichen Öl in einem Bräter weich dünsten, durch ein Sieb streichen, mit dem Petersilienwasser vermischen. Ofen auf 250° C vorheizen. Im Knoblauchöl im Bräter den Reis anschwitzen. Mit Petersilienwasser auffüllen, im Ofen 10 Minuten garen. Den Bräter auf den Herd stellen und den Reis bei kleiner Hitze unter Rühren weitergaren, bis er weich und cremig ist. Beiseite stellen.

Für die Knoblauchemulsion: Eingelegten Knoblauch mit Öl im Mixer zu einer feinen Creme pürieren, durch ein Sieb streichen.

Für die Garnelenchips: Die Garnelen schälen, das Fleisch sehr fein hacken, in Salzwasser blanchieren, in ein Sieb geben und erkalten lassen. Köpfe und Schalen in einer kleinen Pfanne im Olivenöl anschwitzen. Mit Wasser auffüllen, bis die Karkassen knapp bedeckt sind. Zum Kochen bringen, bei kleiner Hitze (vor dem Siedepunkt) 3 Stunden ziehen lassen. Durch ein Sieb passieren. Maisstärke mit wenig kaltem Wasser anrühren, den Garnelenfond damit binden, 5 Minuten ohne Deckel zu einer dicken Sauce kochen. Mit dem gehackten Garnelenfleisch vermischen, Masse auf einem beschichteten Blech dünn ausstreichen. Im Ofen 2 Stunden trocknen lassen, anschließend in Stücke brechen. Öl in einer Pfanne erhitzen, die Garnelenchips zugeben. Wenn sie beginnen aufzugehen, aus dem Öl fischen und auf Küchenpapier abtropfen lassen.

Für die Ajilis-Mojilis-Sauce: Alle Zutaten im Mixer pürieren, eine Stunde bei Raumtemperatur stehen lassen, durch ein Sieb streichen.

Für die Sauce: Rotbarbenköpfe und -gräten grob hacken, dann in einem kleinen Bräter im Öl anschwitzen. Knoblauch und Chilischote zugeben, mit 4 Löffeln von der vorbereiteten Ajilis-Mojilissauce und Wasser ablöschen. Gut vermischen, im Ofen 10 - 15 Minuten ziehen lassen. Sauce durch ein Sieb passieren, nach Bedarf mit Roux leicht binden. Gehackte Paprika in Salzwasser blanchieren und unter die Sauce ziehen. Mit Salz und Pfeffer abschmecken. Die Rotbarbenfilets mit der Hautseite nach oben in einer Pfanne im heißen Öl braten. Mit Apfelweinessig bepinseln, warmhalten.

Zum Servieren: Sauce auf vorgewärmte Teller schöpfen. Den Reis portionieren und in die Mitte setzen, mit Rotbarbenfilets belegen, mit Garnelenchips bedecken. Die Knoblauchemulsion daneben geben. Sofort servieren.

FILET OF STRIPED MULLET
IN A HOT SAUCE WITH PARSLEY
RISOTTO AND SHRIMP CHIPS

ROTBARBENFILETS IN SCHARFER
SAUCE MIT PETERSILIENRISOTTO
UND GARNELENCHIPS

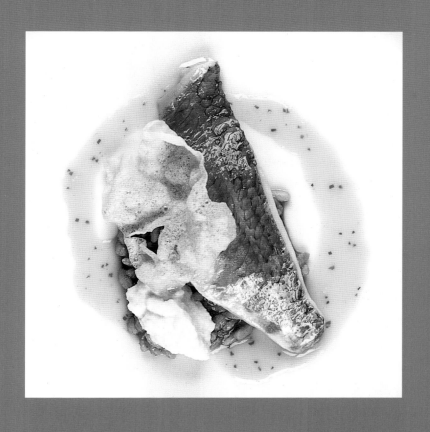

Serves 4

1 large potato, about 150 g/5 oz,
1 tbsp coarsely chopped herbs: parsley, tarragon and chervil,
2 tbsp cold-pressed olive oil, salt

300 g/11 oz leeks,
2 tbsp olive oil,
2 liters/8 cups water,
1 tbsp roux (flour and butter 1:1),
salt, 100 ml/^{1}/$_3$ cup olive oil

For the marinade (makes 160 ml/^{2}/$_3$ cup):
100 ml/^{1}/$_3$ cup olive oil,
50 ml/^{1}/$_4$ cup apple cider vinegar,
1 sprig of parsley,
^{1}/$_2$ sprig of thyme (leaves only),
2 garlic cloves,
6 black peppercorns, crushed in a mortar,
^{1}/$_2$ shallot,
1 tsp salt, a pinch of lemon zest

4 turbot steaks, with skin and bones, 200 g/7 oz each

20 g/^{3}/$_4$ oz sprouts,
1 tbsp vinaigrette (olive oil, apple cider vinegar, salt and pepper)

Preheat the oven to 150°C/300°F. Shave the potato into paper-thin slices and pick out eight nice slices. Set aside remaining slices. Line a baking sheet with baking paper and lay four of the potato slices flat onto the paper. Sprinkle with herbs. Top each slice with another one, place a second sheet of baking paper on top on bake in the oven for twenty minutes. Steam the remaining potato slices for about ten minutes at 120° C/250° F, until cooked through. Sprinkle with a little olive oil and salt and keep warm.

Cut the leeks into 3 cm/1^1/$_2$ inch pieces. Set aside outer green leaves. Halve the white parts lengthwise and rinse well. Sauté in olive oil, stirring constantly to keep them from browning, then add water to cover. Bring to a boil and simmer on low heat until the liquid is reduced by two thirds. Finely purée leeks in a blender and strain the purée through a fine sieve. Mix with roux, return to the pan and bring the mixture to a boil to let it thicken. Check for salt. Blanch the green leaves of the leeks in salted water, drain well and refresh in ice water. Allow excess water to drip off and purée the leaves in a blender with 100 ml/1/$_3$ cup olive oil. Strain through a fine sieve and reserve for later use.

For the marinade: Finely purée all ingredients in a blender. Allow to sit at room temperature for one hour, strain through a sieve.

Finish: In a large frying pan, sear the fish steaks on both sides in a little olive oil, then bake them in a hot oven for two more minutes. Remove from oven and carefully remove center bone. (Leave remaining bones in.) Brush the fish with marinade on all sides. Broil or grill the fish pieces in a salamander until the desired degree of doneness is reached, repeatedly brushing the surfaces with sauce.

Serving: Pour a thin circle of leek oil onto each plate. Spread the middle of the circle generously with leek sauce. Place a portion of steamed potato slices onto the leek purée and top with a fried turbot steak each. Mix sprouts with vinaigrette and place a small heap on top of the turbot steaks. Garnish the plates with the stuffed herb potato slices and serve.

Für 4 Personen:

1 dicke Kartoffel, ca. 150 g,
1 EL grob gehackte Kräuter: Petersilie, Estragon und Kerbel,
2 EL kalt gepresstes Olivenöl, Salz

300 g Lauch,
2 EL Olivenöl,
2 Liter Wasser,
1 EL Roux (Mehlschwitze 1:1),
Salz, 100 ml Olivenöl

Für die Marinade (ergibt 160 ml):
100 ml Olivenöl,
50 ml Apfelweinessig,
1 Zweig Petersilie,
^{1}/$_2$ Zweig Thymian (nur die Blättchen),
2 Knoblauchzehen,
6 schwarze Pfefferkörner, im Mörser zerdrückt,
^{1}/$_2$ Schalotte,
1 TL Salz, 1 Msp abgeriebene Zitronenschale

4 Steinbuttfilets mit Haut, Mittelgräte und Gräten, je 200 g

20 g Keimlinge,
1 EL Vinaigrette (Olivenöl, Apfelweinessig, Salz und Pfeffer)

Ofen auf 150° C vorheizen. Die geschälte Kartoffel in hauchdünne Scheiben hobeln, davon acht schöne Scheiben aussuchen, den Rest beiseite legen. Auf einem mit Backtrennpapier belegten Blech vier Scheiben auslegen und mit den Kräutern bestreuen. Je eine Kartoffelscheibe darüber legen, mit einer zweiten Lage Backtrennpapier bedeckt im Ofen 20 Minuten backen. Restliche Kartoffelscheiben über Dampf bei ca. 120° C 10 Minuten weich garen. Mit etwas Olivenöl und Salz würzen, warm halten.

Den Lauch in 3 cm lange Stücke schneiden, dabei die grünen Blätter beiseite legen. Die hellen Stücke der Länge nach halbieren und gut waschen. Im Olivenöl unter Rühren anschwitzen, dann mit dem Wasser aufgießen. Zum Kochen bringen und bei kleiner Hitze köcheln, bis zwei Drittel der Flüssigkeit verdampft sind. Lauch im Mixer fein pürieren und durch ein Sieb streichen. Mit der Roux vemischen, unter Rühren aufkochen lassen, bis die Sauce bindet, mit Salz abschmecken.

Das Lauchgrün 1 Minute in Salzwasser blanchieren, sofort abgießen, in Eiswasser abschrecken. Abtropfen lassen, dann im Mixer mit 100 ml Olivenöl fein pürieren. Durch ein Sieb passieren.

Für die Marinade: Alle Zutaten im Mixer fein pürieren, 1 Stunde bei Zimmertemperatur stehen lassen, durch ein Sieb streichen.

Fertigstellung: Fischstücke in Olivenöl in der Pfanne von beiden Seiten heiß anbraten, anschließend im Ofen 2 Minuten weiterbraten. Herausnehmen, vorsichtig die Mittelgräte abschneiden (die restlichen Gräten am Fleisch belassen), rundum mit Marinade bepinseln. Unter dem Salamander oder Grill im Ofen bis zum beliebigen Garpunkt weiterbraten, immer wieder mit Sauce bepinseln.

Zum Servieren: Auf vorgewärmte Teller aus dem Lauchöl einen dünne runden Kreis gießen. In die Mitte soviel Lauchsauce geben, bis der Kreis ausgefüllt ist. Die mit Olivenöl gewürzten Kartoffeln auf die Lauchsauce setzen, mit dem gebratenen Steinbuttfilet belegen. Die mit Vinaigrette vermischten Keimlinge darüber verteilen, zum Schluss mit den gefüllten Kartoffelscheiben garnieren.

TURBOT IN A LEEK CREAM

WITH OLIVE OIL POTATOES

STEINBUTT IN LAUCHSAUCE

MIT OLIVENÖLKARTOFFELN

FOIE GRAS WITH CAPERS AND VINEGAR CAVIAR PEARLS

STOPFLEBER MIT KAPERN UND ESSIGKAVIAR-PERLEN

Serves 4

8 slices foie gras, 50 g/2 oz each,
salt, freshly ground black pepper, 200 ml/³/₄ cup brown duck stock

For the capers:
12 large capers, 30 g/1 oz sugar, 30 ml/¹/₈ cup water

For the potato cakes:
2 potatoes, 1 tbsp butter

For the vinegar wafers:
25 g/1 oz flour, 25 ml/2 tbsp balsamic vinegar from Modena

For the vinegar caviar:
50 g/1 ¹/₂ oz small tapioca pearls, 100 ml/¹/₃ cup balsamic vinegar

For the Brussels sprouts:
150 g/5 oz Brussels sprouts, 1 garlic clove, minced,
1 thin slice of raw ham, finely diced, 1 tbsp butter

For the capers: Caramelize sugar with water until light brown. Add capers and stir well to coat them with caramel. Remove from pan and place them onto an oiled plate.

For the potato cake: Peel and grate potatoes. Melt the butter in a non-stick pan and fry potatoes on low heat until golden brown, turning them frequently. Cut out 4 circles of a diameter of 5 cm/ 2 inches and keep them warm.

For the vinegar wafers: Mix balsamic vinegar with flour and spread the batter thinly onto a non-stick baking sheet, then cut it into zig-zag strips with a knife. Bake in a medium oven for fifteen minutes. Carefully remove the strips to cool on a wire rack.

For the vinegar caviar: In a pot, bring salted water to a boil. Add tapioca pearls and allow to simmer for fifteen minutes. Drain in a sieve and allow to cool in cold water. Mix pearls with balsamic vinegar and keep them warm in a double boiler.

For the Brussels sprouts purée: Remove nice green leaves from Brussels sprouts and reserve. Chop remaining sprouts finely, blanch them in salted water for one minute and finely purée them in a blender. Strain the purée through a fine sieve and reserve. Dip the reserved green leaves into boiling salted water, refresh them immediately in ice water and allow excess water to drain off. Sauté garlic and ham in butter on low heat. Add Brussels sprouts leaves and sauté for another minute. Set aside.

Rub the foie gras slices with salt and pepper on all sides. Sear them in a non-stick pan on both sides. Bring duck stock to a boil and check the seasonings.

Finish: Place potato cakes on plates, top them with foie gras slices and garnish them with caviar pearls. Place spoonfuls of Brussels sprouts purée and Brussels sprouts leaves next to it and add a few caramelized capers and baked vinegar wafers. Surround with duck stock and serve.

Für 4 Personen:

8 Scheiben Entenstopfleber à 50 g,
Salz, schwarzer Pfeffer aus der Mühle, 200 ml brauner Entenfond

Für die Kapern:
12 große Kapern, 30 g Zucker, 30 ml Wasser

Für die Kartoffelkuchen:
2 Kartoffeln, 1 EL Butter

Für die Essigblätter:
25 g Mehl, 25 ml Balsamico-Essig aus Modena

Für den Essigkaviar:
50 g Perltapioka, 100 ml Balsamessig

Für den Rosenkohl:
150 g Rosenkohl, 1 Knoblauchzehe, fein gehackt,
1 dünne Scheibe Rohschinken, fein gehackt, 1 EL Butter

Für die Kapern: Zucker mit Wasser hellbraun karamellisieren. Die Kapern zugeben und rühren, bis sie von Karamell überzogen sind, auf einen geölen Teller legen.

Für die Kartoffelkuchen: Kartoffeln schälen und raspeln. In einer beschichteten Pfanne in der Butter bei kleiner Hitze von beiden Seiten goldbraun braten. Vier Scheiben von 5 cm Durchmesser ausstechen, warm halten.

Für die Essigblätter: Balsamessig mit Mehl vermischen. Die Masse dünn auf ein beschichtetes Blech streichen, mit einem Messer in zickzackförmige Streifen teilen. Im Ofen 15 Minuten backen, die Streifen vorsichtig auf ein Gitter legen und abkühlen lassen.

Für den Essigkaviar: In einem Topf Salzwasser zum Kochen bringen. Perltapioka einstreuen und 15 Minuten köcheln. Durch ein Sieb abgießen, in kaltem Wasser abkühlen. Mit Balsamessig vermischen und im Wasserbad warm halten.

Für das Rosenkohlpüree: Die schönen grünen Blätter vom Rosenkohl entfernen und aufheben. Den restlichen Kohl hacken, eine Minute in Salzwasser blanchieren und im Mixer fein pürieren. Durch ein Sieb streichen, beiseite stellen. Die Rosenkohlblätter in kochendes Salzwasser tauchen, sogleich in Eiswasser abschrecken und abtropfen lassen. Knoblauch und Schinken bei kleiner Hitze in der Butter dünsten. Die Blätter zugeben, unter Rühren eine Minute mitbraten, beiseite stellen.

Stopfleberscheiben mit Salz und Pfeffer würzen. In einer beschichteten Pfanne von beiden Seiten heiß anbraten.

Den Entenfond zum Kochen bringen und abschmecken.

Fertigstellung: Die Kartoffelkuchen auf Teller verteilen, mit den Leberscheiben bedecken und mit den Kaviarperlen garnieren. Das Rosenkohlpüree und die Rosenkohlblätter daneben geben, die karamelisierten Kapern und die gebackenen Essigblätter dazulegen. Mit Entenfond umgießen und servieren.

BACON WITH A CRISPY RIND, FRIED LENTILS AND BACON FOAM

SPECK MIT KNUSPRIGER SCHWARTE, GEBRATENEN LINSEN UND SPECKSCHAUM

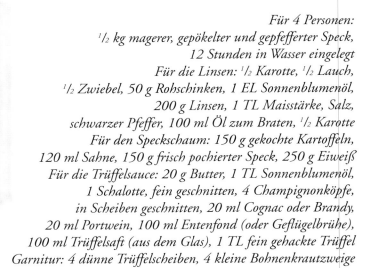

Serves 4
For the lentils: ¹/₂ kg/1 lb lean, salt-cured and
peppered bacon, watered for about twelve hours,
¹/₂ carrot, ¹/₂ stalk of leek, ¹/₂ onion, 50 g/1¹/₂ oz raw ham,
1 tbsp sunflower oil, 200 g/7 oz lentils, 1 tsp cornstarch,
salt, black pepper, 100 ml/¹/₃ cup oil for frying, ¹/₂ carrot
For the bacon foam: 150 g/5 oz boiled potatoes,
120 ml/¹/₂ cup cream, 150 g/5 oz freshly poached bacon,
250 g/¹/₂ lb egg white
For the truffle sauce: 20 g/³/₄ oz butter, 1 tsp sunflower oil,
1 shallot, minced, 4 mushroom caps, sliced,
20 ml/1¹/₂ tbsp Cognac or brandy,
20 ml/1¹/₂ tbsp port, 100 ml/¹/₃ cup duck stock (or poultry stock),
100 ml/¹/₃ cup truffle juice (jar), 1 tsp truffle, finely diced
Garnish: 4 thin slices of truffle, 4 small sprigs of summer savory

Für 4 Personen:
¹/₂ kg magerer, gepökelter und gepfefferter Speck,
12 Stunden in Wasser eingelegt
Für die Linsen: ¹/₂ Karotte, ¹/₂ Lauch,
¹/₂ Zwiebel, 50 g Rohschinken, 1 EL Sonnenblumenöl,
200 g Linsen, 1 TL Maisstärke, Salz,
schwarzer Pfeffer, 100 ml Öl zum Braten, ¹/₂ Karotte
Für den Speckschaum: 150 g gekochte Kartoffeln,
120 ml Sahne, 150 g frisch pochierter Speck, 250 g Eiweiß
Für die Trüffelsauce: 20 g Butter, 1 TL Sonnenblumenöl,
1 Schalotte, fein geschnitten, 4 Champignonköpfe,
in Scheiben geschnitten, 20 ml Cognac oder Brandy,
20 ml Portwein, 100 ml Entenfond (oder Geflügelbrühe),
100 ml Trüffelsaft (aus dem Glas), 1 TL fein gehackte Trüffel
Garnitur: 4 dünne Trüffelscheiben, 4 kleine Bohnenkrautzweige

Brush the rind of the bacon thoroughly. Place bacon into a large pot with water and bring it to a boil. Turn heat to low and keep at a bare simmer 4 to 5 hours. Allow bacon to cool in the cooking liquid, remove and cut it into 4 x 4 cm/1²/₃ x 1²/₃ inch cubes. Shave off rind thinly and fry it in a frying pan on both sides until crisp. Set aside. Return bacon cubes to the cooking liquid.

For the lentils: Fry carrot, leek, onion and raw ham in one piece in a little oil until lightly brown. Add lentils and cold water to cover twice. Bring water to a boil and simmer on low heat for 1¹/₂ to 2 hours, until tender. Remove lentils with a skimmer and spread out flat on a baking sheet. Reserve cooking liquid. Preheat the oven to 100° C/210° F. Dry a quarter of the lentils in the oven for forty minutes, then sauté them in a frying pan with hot oil. (Reserve remaining lentils for another use.) Strain cooking liquid through a sieve and measure out 200 ml/³/₄ cup. Mix with 100 ml/¹/₃ cup of cooking liquid from the bacon. Mix cornstarch with a little cold cooking liquid and lightly thicken the cooking liquid mixture. Check for salt and pepper and keep warm. Cut remaining carrot into paper-thin slices. Blanch in salted water, refresh them in ice water, allow to drain and spread the slices onto a baking sheet. Dry in a 100° C/210° F oven for about two hours.

For the bacon foam: Boil the potatoes in salted water until tender, drain off water, add cream and bring to a boil again. Purée the mixture with chopped bacon and egg white in a blender. Strain the purée through a sieve and season to taste with salt and pepper. Fill mixture into a siphon and keep warm in a double boiler.

For the truffle sauce: In a small saucepan, heat butter and oil. Sauté shallot until translucent, add mushrooms and sauté until they start giving off their juice. Season with salt and pepper. Douse with Cognac and port and allow the liquid to reduce. Add stock and allow to reduce again, then add truffle juice. Check the sauce for seasonings, strain it through a sieve and fold in chopped truffle.

Serving: Preheat oven to 250° C/475° F. Place bacon cubes and a little cooking liquid into a flat baking dish and heat in the oven for about five minutes. Pour lentil sauce into pre-warmed plates and sprinkle with fried lentils and dried carrot slices. Place a bacon cube into the sauce and spray a layer of bacon foam on top with the siphon. Top with a truffle slice each and spoon truffle sauce over it. Garnish with fried bacon rind and sprigs of summer savory.

Speck auf der Schwartenseite abbürsten. In einem Topf mit Wasser bedeckt zum Kochen bringen, Hitze zurückstellen, 4 bis 5 Stunden sieden. Anschließend den Speck im Kochsud erkalten lassen. Herausnehmen, in 4 x 4 cm große Würfel schneiden, die Schwarte dünn abschneiden, in einer Pfanne bei mittlerer Hitze von beiden Seiten knusprig braten. Speckwürfel im Kochsud aufbewahren.

Für die Linsen: Karotte, Lauch, Zwiebel und Rohschinken unzerteilt im Öl leicht Farbe nehmen lassen. Linsen zugeben, mit kaltem Wasser auffüllen, bis die Linsen doppelt hoch bedeckt sind. Zum Kochen bringen, 1¹/₂ bis 2 Stunden bei kleiner Hitze köcheln, bis sie gar sind. Mit einer Lochkelle herausnehmen, auf einem Blech flach ausbreiten, das Linsenkochwasser aufheben. Ofen auf 100° C vorheizen. Ein Viertel der Linsen (den Rest für eine andere Verwendung beiseite legen) im Ofen 40 Minuten trocknen, dann in einer Pfanne im heißen Öl braten. Auf Küchenpapier abtropfen lassen. Linsenkochwasser durch ein Sieb passieren, 200 ml abmessen. Mit 100 ml Speckkochsud vermischen. Maisstärke mit etwas kaltem Sud anrühren, das Linsen-Speckwasser damit leicht binden. Mit Salz und Pfeffer würzen, warm halten. Die halbe Karotte in hauchdünne Scheiben schneiden. In Salzwasser blanchieren, abtropfen lassen und auf einem Blech im 100° C heißen Ofen zwei Stunden trocknen lassen.

Für den Speckschaum: Kartoffeln in Salzwasser weich kochen, abgießen, mit der Sahne kurz aufkochen. Mit gehacktem Speck und Eiweiß im Mixer pürieren, durch ein Sieb streichen, mit Salz und Pfeffer abschmecken. In einen Siphon (Sodabehälter) füllen, im Wasserbad warm halten. Für die Trüffelsauce: In einem Topf Butter mit Öl erhitzen. Schalotte glasig dünsten, Champignons mitbraten, bis sie Wasser ziehen, mit Salz und Pfeffer würzen. Mit Cognac und Portwein besprenkeln, einkochen. Fond hinzufügen, erneut einkochen, dann den Trüffelsaft unterrühren. Sauce abschmecken, durch ein Sieb passieren, gehackte Trüffel unterziehen.

Zum Servieren: Ofen auf 250° C vorheizen. Speckwürfel mit etwas Kochsud in einer flachen Form im Ofen 5 Minuten erhitzen. Linsensauce in Teller verteilen, mit gebratenen Linsen und getrockneten Karottenscheiben bestreuen. Je einen Speckwürfel einlegen und mit einer Lage Speckschaum aus dem Siphon besprühen. Mit Trüffelscheiben bedecken, mit Trüffelsauce überziehen. Mit gebratenen Speckschwarten und Bohnenkraut garnieren und servieren.

FRIED MILK-FED LAMB IN A POTATO CLOUD

MILCHLAMM GEBRATEN MIT KARTOFFELWOLKE

Serves 4

$^1/_2$ milk-fed lamb (about 1.2 kg/2$^2/_3$ lb, bones in),
$^1/_2$ lemon,
salt,
80 g/2$^1/_2$ oz lard,
$^1/_2$ head of garlic, halved,
60 ml/$^1/_4$ cup white wine

For the spice powder:
2 garlic cloves, chopped,
2 tbsp olive oil,
1 dried bay leaf,
$^1/_2$ bunch dried thyme,
2 tbsp fine breadcrumbs

2 potatoes,
olive oil for frying

Preheat the oven to 150° C/300° F. Rub the lamb all over with lemon juice, salt and lard. Brown the lamb in a heavy-bottomed casserole on all sides. Add half a garlic head and 100 ml/$^1/_3$ cup of water. Bake in the oven for one hour, then turn up the temperature to 230° C/450° F. Turn the lamb over so that the meat side points upwards and add a little more water if necessary. Bake for another hour. Keep basting the meat with its pan juices for the first half an hour or so. The lamb should form a nice brown crust. Once the crust has formed, remove it very carefully and set it aside. Separate tender meat from all bones and veins and keep the meat warm. Degrease pan juices and add a little water, scraping up the brown bits at the bottom. Bring to a boil, check for salt and pepper and strain the jus through a sieve.

For the spice powder: Fry garlic in olive oil until golden brown and crispy. Remove from oil and allow to drain well on kitchen towels. Place garlic bits and spices into a mortar or spice grinder and grind everything into a fine powder. Strain powder through a sieve and mix it with breadcrumbs. Run the potatoes through a juicer. Bring potato juice to a boil in a small pot, allowing it to thicken slightly. Pour juice onto a non-stick baking sheet and bake it in a 150° C/ 300° F oven until solidified. Carefully remove potato juice from the sheet in thin pieces and deep-fry the chips in sufficient oil over moderate heat until golden brown.

Serving: Brush the lip of each plate with a little olive oil and sprinkle a little spice powder along the rim. Shake off excess powder. Divide meat equally between plates and drizzle a little jus over each portion. Cover with crispy fried rind and top with potato chips. Garnish with thyme and serve at once.

Für 4 Personen:

$^1/_2$ Milchlamm (ca. 1,2 kg, mit Knochen),
$^1/_2$ Zitrone,
Salz,
80 g Schweineschmalz,
$^1/_2$ Knoblauchknolle, quer halbiert,
60 ml Weißwein

Für das Gewürzpulver:
2 Knoblauchzehen, gehackt,
2 EL Olivenöl,
1 Lorbeerblatt,
$^1/_2$ Bund getrockneter Thymian,
2 EL fein geriebene Semmelbrösel

2 Kartoffeln,
Olivenöl zum Braten

Den Ofen auf 150° C vorheizen. Das Lamm mit Zitronensaft, Salz und Schweineschmalz rundum einreiben. In einem Bräter von allen Seiten anbraten. Die halbierte Knoblauchknolle zugeben, mit 100 ml Wasser aufgießen und eine Stunde im Ofen braten. Hitze auf 230° C erhöhen. Das Lamm umdrehen, so dass die Fleischseite nach oben zeigt, Weißwein und, wenn nötig, etwas mehr Wasser zugießen, eine weitere Stunde in den Ofen schieben, dabei die erste halbe Stunde immer wieder mit dem Bratsaft begießen. Die Oberseite des Lamms soll schön braun und knusprig werden. Knusprige Schicht vorsichtig entfernen und beiseite legen. Mit einem Löffel das weiche Fleisch von Knochen und Fett trennen und warm halten. Den Bräter entfetten, Bratsatz mit Wasser lösen, aufkochen, mit Salz und Pfeffer würzen, dann den Jus durch ein Sieb passieren.

Für das Gewürzpulver: Den gehackten Knoblauch im Olivenöl goldbraun braten. Aus dem Öl nehmen, auf Küchenpapier abtropfen lassen, mit den Kräutern in einer Gewürzmühle oder im Mörser zu feinem Pulver mahlen. Durch ein Sieb passieren, das Pulver mit den Semmelbröseln vermischen.

Kartoffeln im Entsafter entsaften. Den Saft in einem Topf kochen, bis er leicht bindet. Auf ein beschichtetes Blech gießen und in der Mitte des Ofens bei 150° C backen, bis er fest wird. Die hauchdünnen Blätter vorsichtig abheben und in einer Pfanne in genügend Öl bei nicht zu großer Hitze goldgelb ausbacken.

Zum Servieren: Auf jedem Tellerinnenrand etwas Olivenöl mit dem Pinsel ausstreichen und mit dem Gewürzpulver bestreuen, überflüssiges Pulver abschütteln. Das Fleisch anrichten, mit Jus begießen, die knusprigen Stücke und zum Schluss die Kartoffelblätter darüberlegen. Mit Thymian garniert servieren.

GIN TONIC JELLY WITH LEMON SORBET

GIN-TONIC-GELEE MIT ZITRONENSORBET

Serves 4

For the Gin Tonic jelly:
360 ml/1 ¹/₂ cups tonic water,
50 ml/¹/₄ cup gin,
5 sheets of gelatin

For the lemon sauce:
2 tbsp lemon zest, cut into very thin strips,
50 ml/¹/₄ cup water,
100 g/3 ¹/₂ oz sugar,
freshly squeezed juice of one lemon,
17 juniper berries, finely crushed in a mortar

For the wafers:
100 g/3 ¹/₂ oz confectioners' sugar,
50 g/2 oz flour,
50 ml/¹/₄ cup syrup (equal amounts of sugar and water, boiled),
50 g/2 oz glucose

For the lemon sorbet:
250 ml/1 cup freshly squeezed lemon juice,
500 ml/2 cups syrup made from 250 g/¹/₂ lb sugar
and 250 ml/1 cup water,
2 tbsp finely grated lemon zest,
2 egg whites

Für 4 Personen:

Für das Gin-Tonic-Gelee:
360 ml Tonicwasser,
50 ml Gin,
5 Gelatineblätter

Für die Zitronensauce:
2 EL dünn abgeschälte Zitronenschale,
in sehr feine Streifen geschnitten,
50 ml Wasser,
100 g Zucker,
frisch gepresster Saft einer Zitrone,
17 Wacholderbeeren, im Mörser fein zerstoßen

Für die Teigblätter.
100 g Puderzucker,
50 g Mehl,
50 ml Sirup (Zucker und Wasser 1:1 gekocht),
50 g Glukose

Für das Zitronensorbet:
250 ml frisch gepresster Zitronensaft,
500 ml Sirup, aus 250 g Zucker und 250 ml Wasser gekocht,
2 EL fein abgeriebene Zitronenschale,
2 Eiweiß

For the Gin Tonic jelly: Heat pre-soaked gelatin with half of the tonic water, stirring constantly until the gelatin is dissolved. Stir remaining tonic water in a large bowl until no longer fizzy. Add gin and carefully fold in the gelatin mixture. Be careful not to make bubbles while mixing. Pour the jelly gently into a flat dish, the liquid should come up about 1 cm/¹/₃ inch. Allow to set in the refrigerator.

For the lemon sauce: Boil strips of lemon zest with water and sugar until you have a thick syrup. Stir in the lemon juice and juniper berries, bring to a boil again and set aside.

For the wafers: Preheat the oven to 200° C/390° F. Combine all ingredients and mix well. Spread the batter thinly onto a non-stick sheet and bake in the oven for five minutes. Allow to cool and break or cut the dough into irregular pieces.

For the lemon sorbet: Combine lemon juice, syrup and lemon zest and lightly freeze in an ice cream maker. Whip the egg whites into stiff peaks and add them to the sorbet in the ice cream maker. Allow the sorbet to finish freezing.

Serving: Cut the Gin Tonic jelly into cubes and layer them with wafers. Place stacks onto plates. Add a scoop of lemon sorbet to each plate and drizzle with a little lemon-juniper sauce. Serve.

Für das Gin-Tonic-Gelee: Die eingeweichte Gelatine mit der Hälfte des Tonicwassers unter Rühren erhitzen, bis die Gelatine sich auflöst. In einer Schüssel die Kohlensäure aus dem restlichen Tonicwasser rühren. Den Gin zugeben, vorsichtig die aufgelöste Gelatine untermischen, so, dass sich keine Luftblasen bilden. In ein flaches Gefäß füllen, die Flüssigkeit soll ca. 1 cm hoch stehen. Im Kühlschrank fest werden lassen.

Für die Zitronensauce: Zitronenschalenstreifen mit Wasser und Zucker in einem Topf zu einem dicken Sirup kochen. Zitronensaft und Wacholder unterrühren, erneut aufkochen, beiseite stellen.

Für die Teigblätter: Den Ofen auf 200° C vorheizen. Alle Zutaten gut miteinander verrühren. Ein beschichtetes Blech mit der Masse dünn bestreichen, im Ofen 5 Minuten backen. Auskühlen lassen und in unregelmässige Stücke schneiden oder brechen.

Für das Zitronensorbet: Zitronensaft, Sirup und Zitronenschale gut verrühren und in der Eismaschine anfrieren lassen. Das Eiweiß zu Schnee schlagen, zugeben und das Sorbet fertig gefrieren lassen.

Zum Servieren: Das Gin-Tonic-Gelee in Würfel schneiden, mit den Teigblättern lageweise auf Teller schichten. Je eine Kugel Zitronensorbet dazugeben, die Zitronen-Wacholdersauce daneben gießen und servieren.

MANGO MILLEFEUILLES WITH MANGO SORBET

MANGO-MILLE-FEUILLES MIT MANGOSORBET

Serves 4

For the mango millefeuilles:
4 mangoes, 30 g/1 oz egg yolk, 25 g/³/₄ oz cream,
15 g/1 tbsp sugar; 2 tbsp brown sugar

For the sorbet:
100 ml/¹/₃ cup olive oil, 10 ml/1 tsp apple cider vinegar,
6 black peppercorns, 1 bay leaf, 1 sprig of thyme

For the mango wafers:
1 mango, 25 g/³/₄ oz soft butter, 50 g/1 ¹/₂ oz confectioners' sugar

For the wine dust:
250 ml/1 cup red wine, 100 g/3 ¹/₂ oz confectioners' sugar

For the garnish:
4 fresh bay leaves, 4 thyme flowers,
4 sprigs of lemon thyme, 1 tsp Szechuan peppercorns

Für 4 Personen:

Für die Mango-Mille-feuilles:
4 Mangos, 30 g Eigelb, 25 g Sahne,
15 g Zucker; 2 EL brauner Zucker

Für das Sorbet:
100 g Olivenöl, 10 ml Apfelweinessig,
5 schwarze Pfefferkörner, 1 Lorbeerblatt, 1 Zweig Thymian,

Für die Mangoblätter:
1 Mango, 25 g weiche Butter, 50 g Puderzucker

Für den Weinstaub:
250 ml Rotwein, 100 g Puderzucker

Für die Garnitur:
4 frische Lorbeerblätter, 4 Thymianblüten,
4 Zweige Zitronenthymian, 1 TL Szechuanpfefferkörner

For the millefeuilles: Preheat the oven to 160° C/325° F. Peel and halve the mangoes, remove pit and cut the flesh into very thin slices. Combine cream, egg yolk and sugar and mix well. Brush the nicest mango slices with the mixture. Reserve remaining mango slices and trimmings for the sorbet. Layer the brushed mango slices into four small spring forms, press them down gently and bake them in the oven for thirty minutes. Allow to cool in the form.

For the mango sorbet: In a small pot, heat olive oil and vinegar with pepper, bay leaf and thyme. Add sliced mango and reserved trimmings from the millefeuilles and simmer on low heat for twenty-five minutes. Purée pulp in a blender, strain through a fine sieve, allow mixture to cool and freeze it in an ice cream maker.

For the mango wafers: Peel the mango and cut it into fine strips. Combine with butter and sugar and cook in a microwave oven on medium heat for 4 minutes. If you do not have a microwave, place mixture into an oven-proof dish and bake it for 20 minutes in a 180° C/350° F oven, covered. Turn oven down to 150° C/300° F. Strain mango pulp in a sieve over a large bowl (reserve juice). Press down to squeeze out the juice, then spread the pulp thinly onto a baking sheet. Weight down with another sheet and bake in the oven for 7 minutes. Allow to cool and cut mango sheet into pieces.

For the wine dust: Reduce wine by half and allow to cool. Stir in confectioners' sugar and spread mixture onto a baking sheet. Dry slowly in a drying oven or in a convection oven at the lowest possible setting (it may take several days!). When mixture is very dry, grind it in a coffee grinder and then strain it through a sieve. Keep loosely in a dry place.

Serving: Unmold mango millefeuilles, halve them and sprinkle the cut surfaces with brown sugar. Lightly caramelize surfaces with a blow torch. Arrange on plates and add a scoop of mango sorbet each. Glaze with mango juice reserved from making the mango wafers. Insert a mango wafer into the sorbet and garnish with wine dust, herb bouquets and Szechuan peppercorns.

Für die Mille-feuilles: Ofen auf 160° C vorheizen. Mangos schälen und halbieren, Kern entfernen, Fleisch in dünne Scheiben schneiden. Sahne mit Eigelb und Zucker verrühren, die schönsten Mangoscheiben damit bepinseln, restliche Mangoabschnitte für das Sorbet aufheben. Lageweise in vier kleine Springformen schichten, festdrücken, im Ofen 30 Minuten backen. Auskühlen lassen.

Für das Mangosorbet: In einem kleinen Topf Olivenöl mit Essig, Pfeffer, Lorbeerblatt und Thymian erhitzen. Die Mangoscheiben und -Abschnitte zugeben und bei kleiner Hitze 25 Minuten leise köcheln. Im Mixer pürieren, durch ein Sieb streichen, dann die abgekühlte Creme in der Eismaschine gefrieren lassen.

Für die Mangoblätter: Mango schälen und in feine Streifen schneiden. Mit Butter und Zucker vermischen, in der Mikrowelle bei mittelstarker Einstellung 4 Minuten garen, oder im Backofen die Mango in einer feuerfesten Form zugedeckt bei 180° C im Ofen 20 Minuten backen. Dann den Ofen auf 150° C vorheizen. Die Mangomasse in einem Sieb ausdrücken (den Saft auffangen), dann die Masse auf einem beschichteten Blech flach ausstreichen. Mit einem zweiten Blech beschweren, im Ofen sieben Minuten backen. Erkalten lassen und in Stücke schneiden.

Für den Weinstaub: Wein auf die halbe Menge einkochen und erkalten lassen. Puderzucker unterrühren, die Mischung auf ein Blech streichen. Im Trockenofen oder Heißluftofen bei kleinster Hitzezufuhr langsam trocknen lassen (kann Tage dauern!). Wenn die Masse ganz trocken ist, in einer Kaffeemühle mahlen, durch ein Sieb streichen. Das Pulver luftig und trocken aufbewahren.

Zum Servieren: Mango-Mille-feuilles aus der Form drücken, halbieren, die Schnittflächen mit braunem Zucker bestreuen, dann mit einem Bunsenbrenner leicht bräunen. Auf Teller verteilen, je eine Kugel Mangosorbet dazugeben, mit Mangosaft von der Herstellung der Mangoblätter überziehen. Mangoblätter in das Sorbet stecken, mit Weinstaub, zu Sträußchen gebundenen Kräutern und Szechuanpfefferkörnern garniert servieren.

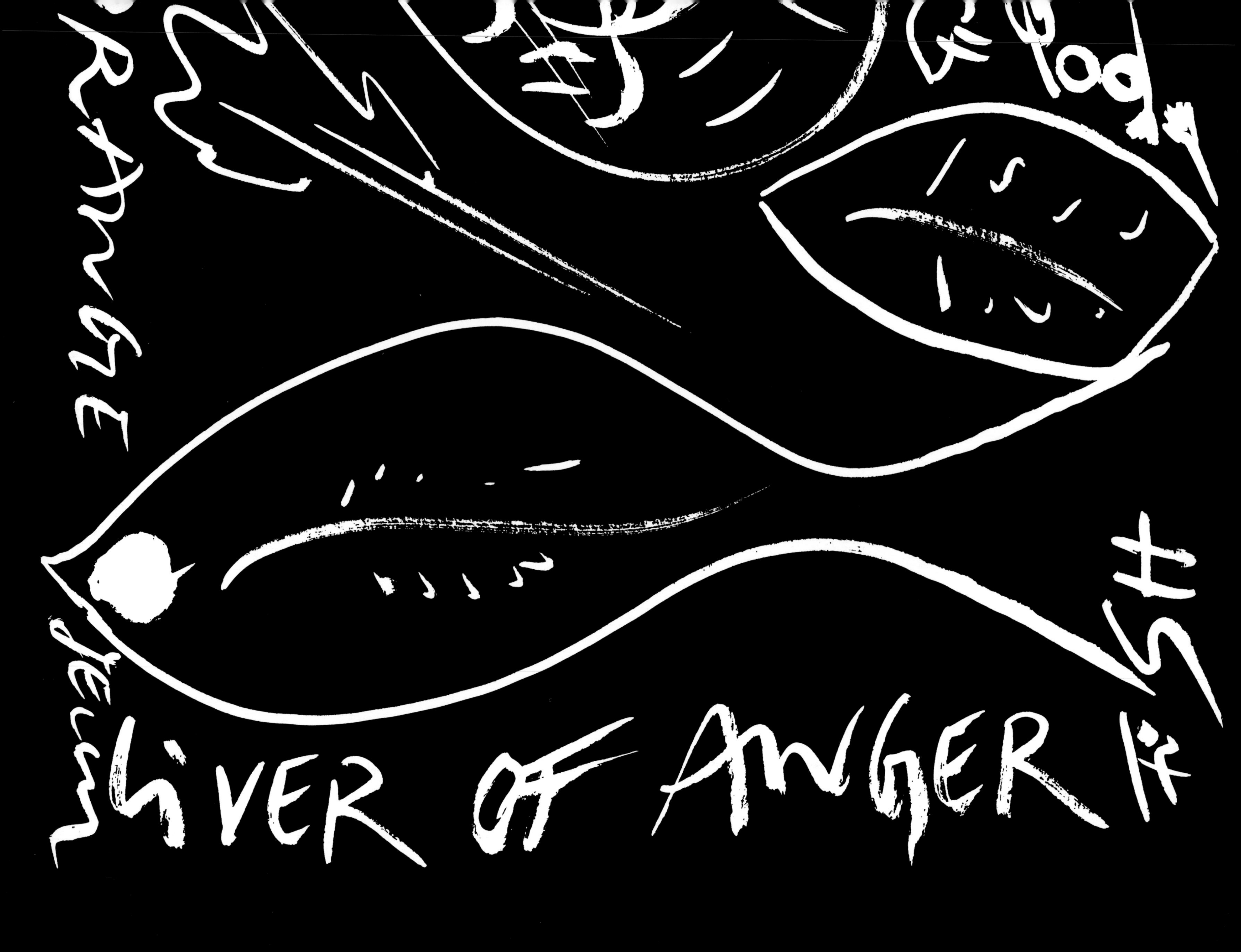
RIVER OF ANGER FISH

UBEROA
LARIO ARBELAITZ

SPANISH FIESTA.

The Basque are quite an individualistic and freedom-loving people, we all know that, and the newspapers are full of it. Naturally, we expected these people to be proud of their cooking traditions, something that was quickly confirmed by the fact that some cookbooks are published in the Basque language only. It did surprise us, however, that an important culinary guide showered the comparatively small area with an inordinate number of stars. Not without good reason as we found out. The fact that dining here was like living in a culinary dream will gladly be remembered, and probably for a long while. One of the reasons for all this may be found at Oiartzun.

Gastronomical tourists who descend on the region in the summer season usually visit the culinary quartet Berasetegui, Akelare, Arzak and Zuberoa, and the latter is also the destination of our visit today. In the borderlands between France and Spain, in a small hamlet called Oiartzun, cows are grazing on the pasture, dogs can be heard barking after cats. Pure countryside, that is. And there is this six-hundred-year-old farmhouse at a small but straight country road which seems to inspire some drivers to try to get the last out of their motors with respect to speed. Yet, the thick-set country house is no pit stop with standard fare but home of the rustic country restaurant "Zuberoa", even if its master chef does belong to the formula one elite of Spanish cooks. Nevertheless, no wind channel determines the perfection of the dishes here, but his well executed skills, and the audience does not come to see and be seen. No, Hilario Arbelaitz is visited by connoisseurs. Those who like to treat themselves to something good from the best will dine here – at home on the country-side, at the "Zuberoa".

Arbelaitz' cuisine is just as rooted to the soil as the land itself. He uses products which can be procured from Spanish and French sources close by. "My cuisine is my mother's cuisine", Arbelaitz himself says and recalls how, thirty years ago, he learned how to cook from his mother and aunt. Mother and aunt, that seems to be a well-tried training concept (not only with him) for future chefs. Berasetegui, too, went through this school. The family school, the range of familiar, well-tried recipes, and, above all, the tradition to have a certain standard of eating and cooking at home seems to be quite beneficial to a successful carreer in cooking. Originally, however, the forty-nine-year-old chef intended to become a priest. That did not come to pass. When his father died, the oldest of three sons was called home to the family. His parents operated an asador, a simple grill restaurant, in the house, and now the man was missing. For ten years, young Hilario cooked typical country fare with stews and rich sauces. "That was the main stay of Basque cooking", he explains. "The food was heavy and hearty, but always very tasty." From his mother, he learned that sauces were important. "When I talk about this topic, I always have to think about her sauces. They are still of central significance to me, are symbols of long stewing times and much patience. He still does them personally, but has liberated them from the heavy and the fatty, butter and cream that is, and replaced the gooey consistency with aromatic essence. He works only with vegetable, fish or meat stocks, reducing them mercilessly until their consistency is thick and their aroma concentrated enough to lend culinary support to the protagonist on the plate, to give it color. "It's always the taste of things that's important", he maintains. "And for that, I construct my sauce. And it is only for one product, everything else would lead to confusion. There is one primary taste, and all

other ingredients have to subject themselves to it. Nothing complicated. El sabor, the taste", he maintains, "for me is everything." Hilario Arbelaitz, honest and upright, may well have kept on fabricating stews and sauces like so many of his trade, and would probably still find thankful customers for them. We do not know why, but the decisive impulse to get rid of old hats and rethink the traditional for Arbelaitz came in a small village across the border, in the French part of the Basque country. He spent only a few days at Maurice Isebal's restaurant "Ithurria", and considers Isebal his mentor. This experienced broadened the horizon of the still young chef, and he returned with a wealth of ideas and many recipes which provided enough incentive to start reworking his native cuisine. He has never left his Basque roots, but is trying to tread new paths with the help of modern kitchen technology. For that, he took his younger brother aboard, and the family enterprise gradually worked its way up the gastronomical ladder. Meanwhile, the youngest of the three, a trained pâtissier, has left the nest and owns his own restaurant in San Sebastián, "Miramón". Yet, Jose Maria's dessert creations are still part of the "Zuberoa's" menu.

Hilario's brother Euxebio, three years his junior, has stayed with him and, with his wife Arantxa and nine other members of the service team, is in charge of the competent service. This means real work. On good days, most of the seventy-odd seats are booked, and eighteen cooks are busy filling the orders in time. Their working area is spacious, but there are many nooks and crannies which were added to the original old house at a later date. At every corner, there is someone carving, shaving, rinsing or spreading dough onto sheets. In chip baskets, scallops and head lettuces are awaiting their fate. The mostly young crew, men and women, is busy with preparations for lunch. Arantxa has already welcomed a few guests and accompanied them to the tables. The old country house is one of the rustic kind, stone and dark stained wood dominates. The windows are small, as it used to be the case. Light comes from spots and candle-shaped bulbs directed at the walls, providing the room with the necessary background lighting. Between the rafters, white plaster shimmers brightly and walls made from natural stone and painted in royal blue lend the dining room a rustic elegance. The whole building features highly polished marble floors in white, black and red. The doors are inlaid with stained glass. When it is warm, however, which is no rarity here, you should ask for a place on the roofed-in terrace, which may boast of some of the best seats. And when Euxebio pours cool Txakoli into your wine glass, pleasure is not far off. The green hedge towards the street does its utmost to keep the would-be race car drivers at an acoustic distance.

*S*panische Fiesta. Dass die Basken ein recht eigenwilliges und freiheitsliebendes Völkchen sind, ist uns bekannt. Die Zeitungen sind voll davon. Dass diese Menschen stolz auf ihre Küchentradition sind, setzten wir voraus. Und es hat sich bestätigt, einige Kochbücher erscheinen nur in baskischer Sprache. Dass ein wichtiger Gourmetführer viele Sterne auf diesen kleinen Fleck hat regnen lassen, hat uns erstaunt. Dass dieses nicht ohne Grund geschah, haben wir feststellen dürfen. Und dass wir hier wundervoll gespeist haben, wird uns genussvoll und sicherlich dauerhaft in Erinnerung bleiben. Einer der Gründe dafür liegt in Oiartzun.

Gastro-Touristen, die in die kleine Region einfallen, absolvieren in der Sommersaison mit schöner Regelmäßigkeit das kulinarische Quartett Berasategui, Akelare, Arzak und Zuberoa. Letzterem gilt heute unser Besuch. Im Grenzland zwischen Frankreich und Spanien, in einem kleinen Weiler namens Oiartzun, weiden Kühe auf den Wiesen und bellen Hunde Katzen hinterher. Wie es auf dem Land eben so ist. Und da steht auch dieses sechshundert Jahre alte Bauernhaus an kleiner aber pfeilgerader Landstraße, die manche Automobilisten geradezu anzuspornen scheint, auch noch die letzten PS ihrer Maschine zur Höchstgeschwindigkeit herauszukitzeln. Das gedrungene Landhaus aber ist kein Boxenstopp mit Standardkost, sondern beherbergt das ländlich-rustikale Restaurant „Zuberoa", dessen Küchenchef selbst zur Formel-Eins-Elite spanischer Köche zählt. Doch hier bestimmt kein Windkanal die Perfektion der Gerichte, sondern vorzüglich exerziertes Handwerk, und das Publikum reist nicht zu weihevoller Pilgerstätte an, um zu sehen und gesehen zu werden. Nein, zu Hilario Arbelaitz kommt der Genussmensch. Hier isst, wer sich etwas Gutes bei einem der Besten gönnen will. Zuhause auf dem Land, im „Zuberoa".

So bodenständig wie das Land, so ist auch seine Küche, die sich der Produkte bedient, die spanische wie französische Quellen in nächster Nähe bereitstellen können. „Meine Küche ist eine Küche meiner Mutter," sagt Arbelaitz selbst und erinnert sich, wie er vor dreißig Jahren bei Mutter und Tante das Kochen erlernt hatte. Mutter und Tante, das scheint ein relativ probates Ausbildungskonzept (nicht nur bei ihm) für angehende Köche zu sein. Auch Berasategui durchlief diese Schule. Die familiäre Klasse, der Fun-dus an heimischen erprobten Rezepten und überhaupt die Tradition, daheim anspruchsvoll zu essen und zu kochen, ist wohl einer erfolgreichen Kochkarriere äußerst förderlich. Doch ursprünglich hatte der heute Neunundvierzigjährige Priester werden wollen. Daraus wurde nichts. Als der Vater starb, hieß es für den ältesten dreier Söhne, du kommst nach Hause, wir brauchen dich. Die Eltern hatten schon vorher im Haus ein ‚Asador‘, ein einfaches Grilllokal geführt, und nun fehlte der Mann. Zehn Jahre kochte der junge Hilario typische Hausmannskost mit Schmorgerichten und üppigen Tunken. „Darin bestand im Wesentlichen die baskische Küche," erklärt Arbelaitz. „Das Essen war schwer und kräftig, hatte aber immer viel Geschmack." Von der Mutter hatte er gelernt, dass Saucen wichtig sind. „Wenn ich über dieses Thema rede, muss ich immer an ihre Saucen denken." Sie besitzen auch heute noch für ihn zentrale Bedeutung, sind Symbol für eine Küche langer Kochzeiten mit viel Geduld. Ihnen widmet er sich nach wie vor persönlich, nur hat er das Schwere und Fette, sprich Butter und Sahne, über Bord geworfen und die triefenden Tunken durch aromatische Essenzen ersetzt. Er arbeitet ausschließlich mit Fonds von Gemüse, Fisch oder Fleisch. Die reduziert er so gnadenlos ein, bis sie dick in Konsistenz und hoch konzentriert an Aroma sind, um den jeweiligen Hauptdarsteller seiner Gerichte geschmacklich zu stützen, ihm Farbe zu verleihen. „Es geht doch immer nur um den Geschmack der Dinge," betont er. „Und dafür baue ich meine Sauce. Und sie gilt nur einem Produkt, alles andere stiftet Verwirrung. Es gibt einen Hauptgeschmack, dem sich alle anderen Zutaten unterzuordnen haben. Das ist nichts kompliziertes. El sabor," betont er, „der Geschmack ist für mich das Wichtigste."

Wahrscheinlich würde Hilario Arbelaitz heute wie so viele seiner Zunft noch brav und bieder Eintöpfe und Saucen fabrizieren und sicherlich auch dafür eine dankbare Kundschaft finden. Wir wissen nicht warum, aber den entscheidenden Impuls, alte Klamotten auszumisten und Traditionelles auf den Prüfstand zu stellen, bekam Arbelaitz in einem kleinen Dorf über der Grenze, im französischen Teil des Baskenlandes. Nur wenige Tage verbrachte er bei Maurice Isebal im Restaurant „Ithurria", den er als seinen geistigen Vater bezeichnet. Diese Erfahrung erweiterte das Spektrum des damals noch jungen Kochs, und er kehrte zurück mit einer Fülle neuer Ideen und vielen Rezepten, die ihm Anlass genug waren, die heimische Küche umzukrempeln. Die baskischen Wurzeln hat er dabei nie verlassen, doch er suchte mit den Möglichkeiten moderner Küchentechnik von nun an neue Wege zu gehen. Dafür nahm er seine beiden jüngeren Brüder mit an Bord, und gemeinsam arbeitete sich das Familienunternehmen Arbelaitz Schritt für Schritt die gastronomische Stufenleiter empor.

Mittlerweile ist der jüngste der Drei, ein gelernter Patissier, ausgeflogen und betreibt in San Sebastián sein eigenes Restaurant „Miramón". Aber José Marias Dessertkreationen sind nach wie vor Bestandteil der Menükarte im „Zuberoa". Hilarios nur drei Jahre jüngerer Bruder Euxebio ist dabeigeblieben und betreut im versierten Doppelpass mit seiner Frau Arantxa und neun Servicekräften die Besucher des Restaurants. Das kann richtig Arbeit bedeuten. An guten Tagen sind die meisten der rund siebzig Plätze ausgebucht, und achtzehn Köche in der Küche haben alle Hände voll zu tun, den Orders rechtzeitig nachzukommen. Ihr Arbeitsbereich ist zwar geräumig, doch er erstreckt sich in viele Winkel und Räume, die teilweise als Anbau dem Grundriss des ursprünglichen Gebäudes hinzugefügt werden mussten. An jeder Ecke wird geschnitzt, gespült und gehobelt oder Teig auf Platten gestrichen. In Spankisten stehen Jakobsmuscheln und Kopfsalat bereit. Die überwiegend junge Crew, männlich wie weiblich, ist emsig mit den Vorbereitungen fürs Mittagessen beschäftigt. Arantxa hat auch schon einige Gäste in Empfang genommen und zum Tisch geleitet. Das alte Landhaus ist eines der urwüchsigen Sorte, wo Stein und dunkel gebeiztes Holz dominieren. Die Fenster sind klein, wie es damals halt so üblich war. Licht kommt folglich von Kerzenbirnen und Spots, die gegen die Wände gerichtet sind und dem Raum die erforderliche Grundhelligkeit verleihen. Zwischen den Balken weißer Putz, königsblau getünchte und naturstein-gemauerte Wände geben dem Speisesaal rustikale Eleganz. Spiegelblank polierte marmorne Bodenplatten ziehen sich in Weiß, Schwarz und Rot durch das ganze Gebäude, die Türen sind mit bunten Glasscheiben versehen. Ist es draußen aber warm, was hier keine Seltenheit ist, dann sollte man nach einem Platz auf der grossen überdachten Terrasse fragen. Hier sitzt es sich am schönsten. Und wenn Euxebio den kühlen Txakoli ins Weinglas gießt, kann der Genuss beginnen. Die grüne Hecke zur Straße tut dabei ihr Möglichstes, um die vorbeirasenden Rennfahrer auf akustische Distanz zu halten.

HASIERAKOAK

Izokin ketua, piper erreen krema mihilu berdeaz eta berberetxoak lurrinera, tarta txikian	3.000,-
Foie gras naturala, karamelua eta piku lehorrezko konfitura, ontzitxoan	3.500,-
Ostrak beren zukuaren gelatinan, limoi kremaz eta kabiarraz	3.600,-
Vieirak eta txipiroiak salteatuta, pomelo geleaz eta azalore kremaz	3.600,-
Azalore eta misera albahakaz eta bere koralaren binagretaz	4.000,-
Kuia krema eta curryarekiko foie gras flana, itsas fruituekin (zigala, ostra, berberetxo, txirla)	3.800,-
Bakailao, patata eta trufa entsalada oliboliaz	2.800,-
Zigala eta azazko rabiolia, basoilar eta trufen lurrunaz	4.200,-
Garaiko barazkiak menestran	2.500,-
Betiko arrain eta itsaski zopa	2.200,-
Risottoa, foie eta trufez egina, usakume errearen saltsaz	3.900,-
Foie grasa barbantzu saldaz, eta ogi frijituak	3.700,-

ARRAINAK

Misera erreta kanela olioz eta koral saltsaz	4.200,-
Misera bere maskorrean erreta	4.200,-
Sapoaren bizkarra labean erreta zitroi lurrinez	3.300,-
Lupia txipiroi eta oliba beltz salteatuaren gainean	3.900,-
Legatzaren bizkarra saltsa berdez, oliobolioz egindako purearen gainean	3.800,-
Legatzaren bizkarra piperradaren gainean eta txipiroien binagretarekin	3.800,-

HARAGIAK

Txekor muturrak beraiek egositako saltsaz	2.600,-
Txekor masaialdeak gisatuta eta barazkiekin plantxan braseatuta	3.000,-
Zerri hankak eta patata dominatxotan baba salteatuaren gainean eta beraiek egositako saltsaz	3.000,-
Osobuccozko rabioliak barazkiekin eta ardo beltz saltsaz	2.600,-
Solomiloa erreta entsaladarekin eta erre ondorengo bere saltsaz	3.200,-
Navazeko usakumea erreta, Calvadosez bustitako sagar konpotarekin	3.500,-
Ahate errea saltsa gezaminez	3.500,-
Risottoa arkume arandoiz eta gengibreaz karamelututako barazkiez	3.000,-

BUKAERAKOAK

Mozkorra, laranja gelearen eta amanda mikatz aparraren eta kokozko izozkiaren gainean	1.200,-
Amanda pastel beroa eta limoizko izozkia	1.200,-
Torrada karamelugustukoa Williams udarez egindako sorbetearekin	1.200,-
Arrozesne mila-orria, txokolatezko dadoak eta kanelazko izozkia	1.200,-
Sagar tarta fina berezko sorbetearekin	1.200,-
Fruitu lehorrezko kurruskaria, ezkai belarrezko izozkia eta txokolate kurruskaria	1.200,-
Txokolate zuri eta beltz kurruskaria mila-orri egina limoizko izozkiarekin	1.200,-
Txokolate urtu-bizkotxa, fruitu mazeratuak eta laranjazko izozkia	1.200,-
Ur eta txokolate-pastela, jogurrezko izozkia	1.200,-

Oharra: Bukaerakoak jaten hasi aurretik eskatuko dira.

BEZ-a (%7) ez dago sartuta.

ENTRADAS

Tartaleta de salmón ahumado y crema de pimientos
asados al hinojo verde y berberechos al vapor 3.000,–
Terrina de foie gras natural, caramelo y confitura de
higos secos 3.500,–
Ostras en gelatina de su jugo, crema de limón y caviar .. 3.600,–
Vieiras y salteado de chipirones, gelée de pomelo y
crema de coliflor 3.600,–
Crema de coliflor y bogavante a la albahaca y vinagreta
de su coral 4.000,–
Crema de calabaza y flan de foie gras al Curry con frutos
de mar (cigala frita, ostra, berberecho y almeja) 3.800,–
Ensalada de bacalao, patata y trufas al aceite de oliva .. 2.800,–
Raviolis de cigalas y col con aroma de faisán y trufas 4.200,–
Verduras de temporada en menestra 2.500,–
Sopa de pescado y mariscos al estilo tradicional 2.200,–
Risotto de foie y trufas con salsa de pichón asado 3.900,–
Foie gras en caldo de garbanzos y panes fritos 3.700,–

PESCADOS

Bogavante asado al aceite de canela y salsa de coral 4.200,–
Bogavante asado en su propio caparazón 4.200,–
Lomo de rape asado al horno y a los aromas de cítricos 3.300,–
Lubina sobre salteado de chipirones y aceitunas negras . 3.900,–
Lomo de merluza en salsa verde sobre puré de aceite
de oliva 3.800,–
Lomo de merluza sobre piperrada y vinagreta
de chipirones 3.800,–

CARNES

Morros de ternera en salsa de su propia cocción 2.600,–
Carrilleras de ternera guisadas y braseadas
con verduras a la plancha 3.000,–
Medallones de manitas de cerdo y patata sobre salteado
de habas y salsa de su cocción 3.000,–
Raviolis de ossobuco con verduritas y salsa de vino tinto 2.600,–
Solomillo asado con ensalada y salsa de asado 3.200,–
Pichón de Navaz asado con su compota de manzana
al Calvados 3.500,–
Pato asado con salsa agridulce 3.500,–
Risotto de mollejas de cordero y verduras caramelizadas
al gengibre 3.000,–

POSTRES

Borracho sobre gelée de naranja y espuma de almendra
amarga y helado de coco 1.200,–
Pastel de almendra caliente y helado de limón 1.200,–
Torrija caramelizada y sorbete de pera Williams 1.200,–
Milhojas de arroz con leche, dados de marquesa
de chocolate y helado de canela 1.200,–
Tarta fina de manzana con su propio sorbete 1.200,–
Crujiente de frutos secos, helado de tomillo limonero
y crocante de chocolate 1.200,–
Milhojas crujiente de chocolate blanco y negro con
helado de limón 1.200,–
Bizcocho de chocolate líquido, frutas maceradas
y helado de naranja 1.200,–
Pastel de avellana, chocolate y helado de yogur 1.200,–

Nota: Todos los postres se pedirán al comienzo de la comida.

El **IVA** no está incluído en los precios (7%)

SCALLOPS ON PARSLEY CREAM WITH SMOKED BACON SAUCE

JAKOBSMUSCHEL AUF PETERSILIENCREME MIT RÄUCHERSPECKSAUCE

Serves 4

4 large, fresh scallops, white part only,
coarse salt,
2 tbsp olive oil

For the smoked bacon sauce:
100 g/3 1/2 oz smoked bacon, diced,
50 ml/1/4 cup beef stock,
100 ml/1/3 cup cream

For the parsley cream:
1 bunch flat-leaf parsley,
500 g/1 lb potatoes, peeled, cut into small cubes,
500 ml/2 cups light fish stock,
200 ml/3/4 cup olive oil,
salt, freshly ground white pepper

Garnish:
4 thinly cut smoked bacon slices, cut into strips,
4 tbsp olive oil,
1 sprig flat-leaf parsley

Für 4 Personen:

4 große, frische Jakobsmuscheln,
nur das weiße Nüsschen,
grobes Salz, 2 EL Olivenöl

Für die Räucherspecksauce:
100 g geräucherter Speck, in Würfel geschnitten,
50 ml Rindfleischbrühe,
100 ml Sahne

Für die Petersiliencreme:
1 Bund glatte Petersilie,
500 g Kartoffeln, geschält, in kleine Stücke geschnitten,
500 ml leichter Fischfond,
200 ml Olivenöl,
Salz, weißer Pfeffer aus der Mühle

Garnitur:
4 dünn geschnittene Räucherspeckscheiben,
in Streifen geschnitten,
4 EL Olivenöl, 1 Zweig glatte Petersilie

For the smoked bacon sauce: Combine diced bacon, stock and cream in a small pot and allow to sit overnight. On the next day, simmer the bacon on low heat for twenty minutes. Finely purée the mixture in a blender, check for salt and pepper and strain it through a fine sieve.

For the parsley cream: Combine parsley, potatoes, stock and olive oil in a pot. Bring mixture to a boil and simmer on low heat for ten minutes. Purée mixture in a blender and strain it through a sieve into a fresh pot. Season to taste with salt and pepper, place the pot into ice water and stir until cool.

For the scallops: Turn the scallops in coarse salt and allow them to sit for ten minutes. Rinse scallops thoroughly under cold water and pat them dry with paper towels. Heat the olive oil in a pan. Fry the scallops on medium heat on both sides for one minute per side. Keep them in a warm place.

For the garnish: Fry the bacon strips in hot oil until crisp and allow to drain on paper towels.

Serving: Reheat parsley purée and bacon sauce in separate pots. Ladle parsley purée into deep plates. Place one scallop at the center of each plate. Whip bacon sauce until light and frothy and drizzle the scallops with it. Sprinkle scallops with crispy fried bacon strips and parsley leaves and serve.

Für Räucherspecksauce: Speckwürfel, Brühe und Sahne in einem kleinen Topf vermischen und über Nacht ziehen lassen. Am nächsten Tag bei kleiner Hitze 20 Minuten köcheln. Im Mixer pürieren, die Sauce abschmecken, durch ein Sieb passieren.

Für die Petersiliencreme: Petersilie mit Kartoffeln, Fond und Olivenöl in einem Topf zum Kochen bringen. Bei kleiner Hitze 10 Minuten köcheln, im Mixer pürieren, die Creme durch ein Sieb in einen sauberen Topf streichen. Mit Salz und Pfeffer würzen, den Topf in Eiswasser stellen, das Püree kalt rühren.

Für die Jakobsmuscheln: Die Jakobsmuscheln im Salz wenden und 10 Minuten ziehen lassen. Unter kaltem Wasser sorgfältig abspülen, dann mit Küchenpapier trocken tupfen. Das Olivenöl in einer Pfanne erhitzen. Die Jakobsmuscheln von beiden Seiten bei mittlerer Hitze je eine Minute braten. Warmhalten.

Für die Garnitur: Speckstreifen im heißen Öl knusprig braten, auf Küchenpapier abtropfen lassen.

Zum Servieren: Petersilienpüree und Specksauce unter Rühren getrennt erhitzen. Petersilienpüree in tiefe Teller schöpfen. Je eine gebratene Jakobsmuschel in die Mitte legen. Specksauce schaumig aufschlagen, über die Muscheln geben. Mit knusprig gebratenen Speckstreifen und Petersilie garniert servieren.

MARINATED SCALLOPS AND SQUID
WITH GRAPEFRUIT JELLY AND CAULIFLOWER CREAM

MARINIERTE JAKOBSMUSCHELN UND TINTENFISCH
MIT PAMPELMUSENGELEE UND BLUMENKOHLCREME

Serves 4

For the marinated scallops:
12 very fresh scallops, shelled, white part only,
120 ml/¹/₂ cup grapefruit juice, 120 ml/¹/₂ cup olive oil,
the zest of one untreated grapefruit, minced,
1 fennel bulb, cut into thin strips

For the squid: ¹/₂ kg/1 lb baby squid, 4 onions, finely diced,
¹/₂ green pepper, cored, finely diced, 1 garlic clove, minced,
150 ml/²/₃ cup olive oil, 200 ml/³/₄ cup white wine, salt

For the grapefruit jelly:
the very finely grated zest of four green grapefruits,
150 ml/²/₃ cup syrup (equal amounts of water and sugar),
150 ml/²/₃ cup freshly squeezed grapefruit juice, 3 sheets gelatin, salt

For the cauliflower cream:
500 g/1 lb cauliflower, hard stems removed,
50 g/1¹/₂ oz butter, 50 ml/¹/₄ cup cream, salt, white pepper

For the marinated scallops: Combine scallops and remaining ingredients in a large bowl and mix well. Allow to marinate in the refrigerator for twenty-four hours.
For the squid: Carefully wash the baby squid. Peel if necessary (depending on size). Cut flesh into small cubes and sauté in olive oil. Allow to drain. Sauté onion, pepper and garlic in the remaining oil, mix with sautéed squid, add wine and simmer on low heat until most liquid is evaporated. Season with salt.
For the grapefruit jelly: Cut the zest off the grapefruits very thinly. Blanch in boiling water, allow it to drain in a sieve and simmer in syrup for five more minutes. Purée the zest finely in a blender. Mix half of the purée with the grapefruit juice and strain it through a fine sieve. Pre-soak and squeeze out gelatin sheets, add them to the juice and heat until dissolved. Mix well, season to taste with salt and fill mixture into four round molds. Allow to set in the refrigerator. Reserve the remaining grapefruit zest purée for garnishing.
For the cauliflower cream: Cut the cauliflowerets into small pieces and boil them in salted water for two minutes. Strain the flowerets in a sieve, allow them to drain and combine cauliflower, butter and cream in a small pot. Check for salt and pepper and simmer on low heat until the cauliflower is tender. Finely purée mixture in a blender, allow to cool and set aside.
Serving: Remove scallops from the marinade and arrange three of them per person on plates. Top with squid-onion stew. Unmold jellies next to the scallops. Place a scoop of cauliflower cream on top of each jelly. Spread out a dollop of grapefruit zest purée on the plate with the back of a spoon and sprinkle the plate with a few chive tips, according to taste. Serve.

Für 4 Personen.

Für die marinierten Jakobsmuscheln:
12 sehr frische Jakobsmuscheln, ausgelöst, nur das weiße Nüsschen,
120 ml Pampelmusensaft, 120 ml Olivenöl,
die dünn abgeschnittene und gehackte Schale einer Pampelmuse,
1 Fenchelknolle, in dünne Streifen geschnitten

Für den Tintenfisch: ¹/₂ kg Babytintenfische,
4 Zwiebeln, fein gewürfelt, ¹/₂ grüne Paprika, entkernt, fein gewürfelt,
1 Knoblauchzehe, gehackt, 150 ml Olivenöl, 200 ml Weißwein, Salz

Für das Pampelmusengelee:
die sehr dünn abgeschnittene Schale von 4 grünen Pampelmusen,
150 ml Sirup (Wasser und Zucker 1:1),
150 ml frisch gepresster Pampelmusensaft, 3 Gelatineblätter, Salz

Für die Blumenkohlcreme:
500 g Blumenkohl, die dicken Strünke entfernt,
50 g Butter, 50 ml Sahne, Salz, weißer Pfeffer

Für die marinierten Jakobsmuscheln: Die Jakobsmuscheln mit den übrigen Zutaten in einer Schüssel gut vermischen. Im Kühlschrank 24 Stunden marinieren. Für den Tintenfisch: Babytintenfische sorgfältig waschen, wenn nötig (je nach Grösse) Haut abziehen. Fleisch in kleine Würfel schneiden, in etwas Olivenöl anbraten, abtropfen lassen. Zwiebel, Paprika und Knoblauch im restlichen Öl weich dünsten. Mit gebratenem Tintenfisch vermischen, Wein zugießen, bei kleiner Hitze köcheln, bis der Tintenfisch weich und die meiste Flüssigkeit verdampft ist. Mit Salz würzen.
Für das Pampelmusengelee: Pampelmusenschale mit einem Messer hauchdünn abschneiden. In kochendem Wasser blanchieren, abtropfen lassen, dann die Schalen im Sirup 5 Minuten kochen. Im Mixer fein pürieren, die Hälfte von dem Püree mit Pampelmusensaft vermischen und durch ein Sieb passieren. In einem Topf soweit erhitzen, daß sich die zuvor eingeweichte und ausgedrückte Gelatine auflöst. Gut vermischen, mit Salz abschmecken, in vier runde Förmchen einfüllen, im Kühlschrank fest werden lassen. Das restliche Pampelmusenschalenpüree für die Garnitur beiseite legen.
Für die Blumenkohlcreme: Blumenkohlröschen klein schneiden, in Salzwasser zwei Minuten kochen. Durch ein Sieb abgießen, gut abtropfen lassen, mit der Butter und der Sahne in einen Topf füllen. Mit Salz und Pfeffer würzen, bei kleiner Hitze köcheln, bis der Blumenkohl weich ist. Im Mixer fein pürieren, erkalten lassen.
Zum Servieren: Jakobsmuscheln aus der Marinade nehmen, auf Teller anrichten. Tintenfisch-Zwiebeleintopf darüber geben. Die Gelees aus den Formen stürzen, neben die Jakobmuscheln legen. Mit Blumenkohlcreme und Pampelmusenschalenpüree garnieren, zuletzt nach Belieben mit Schnittlauch bestreuen und servieren.

COLD CREAM OF FOIE GRAS WITH SWEET WINE JELLY AND CELERY CREAM

KALTE STOPFLEBERCREME MIT SÜSSWEINGELEE UND SELLERIECREME

Serves 6

600 g/1 1/3 lb duck foie gras,
200 ml/3/4 cup cream,
100 g/3 1/2 oz butter, room temperature,
salt, freshly ground black pepper

200 g/7 oz light, clarified poultry stock,
120 ml/1/2 cup Costa Dive (sweet Muscat wine from
Alicante, alternatively another sweet wine),
2 sheets gelatin

200 g/7 oz celeriac,
100 ml/1/3 cup cream,
120 ml/1/2 cup beef stock,
1 tsp flour, salt

Garnish:
4 small sprigs of chervil

Preheat the oven to 60° C/140° F. Remove all veins from the foie gras. Purée liver, cream and butter in a blender until you have a fine purée. Season with salt and pepper and pour the purée into a flat oven-proof dish. Bake in the preheated oven for two minutes. Strain the cream through a sieve and fill it into small, deep serving dishes. Smooth out the top, allow the mixture to cool and refrigerate.
Reduce the poultry stock by half. Mix in sweet wine and check for seasonings. Dissolve the pre-soaked gelatin in the liquid and allow it to cool. When the jelly is cold but still liquid, glaze the top of the foie gras cream with it. Place the molds in the refrigerator until almost set.
Cut the celeriac into cubes. Combine cubes, cream and stock in a small pot and simmer until the celeriac is tender. Mix flour with a little water, add the mixture to the celeriac and continue simmering for two minutes. Purée everything in a blender and strain it through a fine sieve. Check for salt. Allow cream to cool and fill it into a soda siphon.
Serving: Spray a pattern of celeriac purée from the siphon on top of the glazed foie gras cream. If you do not have a siphon, whip the celeriac cream until fluffy and place spoonfuls on top of the foie gras cream. Garnish with sprigs of chervil. Toasted bread rounds make an excellent accompaniment.

Für 6 Personen:

600 g Entenstopfleber,
200 ml Sahne,
100 g Butter, zimmerwarm,
Salz, schwarzer Pfeffer aus der Mühle

200 g geklärter heller Geflügelfond,
120 ml Costa Dive (süßer Muskatwein aus Alicante,
ersatzweise anderen Süßwein verwenden),
2 Gelatineblätter

200 g Knollensellerie,
100 ml Sahne,
120 ml Rinderbrühe,
1 TL Mehl, Salz

Garnitur:
4 kleine Kerbelzweige

Den Ofen auf 60° C vorheizen. Die Stopfleber von allen Adern befreien. Im Mixer mit der Sahne und der Butter fein pürieren, mit Salz und Pfeffer würzen und in eine flache feuerfeste Form füllen. Im vorgeheizten Ofen 2 Minuten garen. Die Creme durch ein Sieb streichen und in kleine, tiefe Servierschalen füllen. Glattstreichen, erkalten lassen und kühl stellen.
Den Geflügelfond auf die Hälfte einkochen. Mit dem Süßwein verrühren, abschmecken, dann die eingeweichte Gelatine darin auflösen. Erkalten lassen. Wenn das Gelee kalt, aber noch flüssig ist, die Stopflebercreme damit überziehen. Im Kühlschrank halb fest werden lassen.
Den Knollensellerie in Würfel schneiden. In einem Topf in der Sahne und der Brühe weich kochen. Das Mehl in wenig Wasser anrühren, zugeben und zwei Minuten mitkochen. Das Ganze im Mixer pürieren und durch ein Sieb streichen. Mit Salz abschmecken. Die Creme erkalten lassen und in einen Siphon füllen.
Zum Servieren: Das Selleriepüree aus dem Siphon auf die mit Gelee überzogene Stopflebercreme spritzen. Wenn kein Siphon vorhanden ist, die Creme locker aufschlagen und mit einem Löffel eine Nocke formen. Mit Kerbelzweigen garniert servieren. Als Beilage passt geröstetes Briochebrot.

STRIPED MULLET AND CRABMEAT WITH A FENNEL SAUCE

ROTBARBE UND KREBSFLEISCH AN FENCHELSAUCE

Serves 4

1 large crab of about 500 g/1 lb,
4 small striped mullets,
salt,
100 ml/¹/₃ cup olive oil

1 kg/2 lbs fresh fennel,
2 tbsp olive oil,
1 liter/4 cups fish stock,
2 pig's feet,
salt, freshly ground white pepper

4 potato slices, about ¹/₂ cm/¹/₅ inch thick,
salt,
4 tbsp olive oil

150 g/5 oz dark champignons, trimmed and cut into thin slices,
2 tsp shallots, finely diced,
2 tbsp olive oil,
salt, pepper,
1 tbsp chives, finely diced

Für 4 Personen:

1 Taschenkrebs von ca. 500 g,
4 kleine Rotbarben,
Salz,
100 ml Olivenöl

1 kg Fenchelgemüse,
2 EL Olivenöl,
1 Liter Fischfond,
2 Schweinsfüße,
Salz, weißer Pfeffer aus der Mühle

4 Kartoffelscheiben, ca. ¹/₂ cm dick,
Salz,
4 EL Olivenöl

150 g braune Champignons, geputzt, in dünne Scheiben geschnitten,
2 TL fein geschnittene Schalotten,
2 EL Olivenöl,
Salz, Pfeffer,
1 EL fein geschnittener Schnittlauch

Boil the crab in salted water, break open its shell and scrape out the meat into a small bowl. Cut the striped mullets into filets, set aside filets and bones separately.
Cut out the tender inner core of two fennel bulbs and cut them into thin slices. Sauté the slices in olive oil until tender. Reserve. Coarsely chop the remaining fennel. In a large pot, combine the fennel, fish stock, fish bones and pig's feet. Bring to a boil and simmer on low heat for fifty minutes. Strain the fennel through a fine sieve with a little cooking liquid and stir until you have a thick sauce. Check for salt and pepper.
Salt the potato slices and fry them in a small pan in olive oil. Do not let them brown.
Sauté the mushrooms and the shallots in olive oil. Keep sautéing, stirring constantly, until the juice given off by the mushrooms is evaporated. Season to taste with salt and pepper and mix in chives.
Preheat the oven to 220° C/430° F. Rub the striped mullet filets with salt and pepper and place them into a small oven-proof baking dish. Drizzle the filets with olive oil and bake them in the oven for 2 - 3 minutes.
Serving: Ladle the fennel sauce into deep plates. Top with one slice of potato per plate, cover the slice with crabmeat and top with a filet of striped mullet. Arrange sautéed mushrooms around the fish and garnish the plate with fennel slices. Serve.

Den Krebs in Salzwasser kochen, anschließend aufbrechen, Fleisch herauslösen und in eine Schüssel geben. Rotbarben filetieren, die Gräten und die Filets getrennt aufheben.
Von 2 Fenchelknollen die zarten Herzen im Innern herausschneiden und in dünne Scheiben schneiden. Im Olivenöl weich dünsten, beiseite stellen. Den restlichen Fenchel grob schneiden. Mit Fischfond, Fischgräten und Schweinsfüßen in einen Topf füllen. Zum Kochen bringen, bei kleiner Hitze 50 Minuten köcheln. Das Fenchelgemüse mit etwas Kochfond durch ein Sieb streichen und zu einer dicken Sauce rühren. Mit Salz und Pfeffer abschmecken.
Die Kartoffelscheiben mit Salz würzen. Im Olivenöl in einer Pfanne bei kleiner Hitze garen, ohne Farbe nehmen zu lassen.
Die Champignons und die Schalotten im Olivenöl anschwitzen. Unter Rühren weiterbraten, bis die ausgetretene Flüssigkeit verdampft ist. Mit Salz und Pfeffer würzen, zum Schluss mit dem Schnittlauch vermischen.
Den Ofen auf 220° C vorheizen. Die Rotbarbenfilets mit Salz würzen und in eine kleine feuerfeste Form legen. Mit Olivenöl übergiessen, im Ofen 2 - 3 Minuten garen.
Zum Servieren: Die Fenchelsauce in tiefe Teller anrichten. Eine Kartoffelscheibe in jeden Teller legen, mit Krebsfleisch bedecken, dann je ein Rotbarbenfilet darüber legen. Daneben die gedünsteten Pilze geben, mit den Fenchelscheiben bestreut servieren.

SALT COD STEWED IN OLIVE OIL WITH OYSTER SAUCE

KLIPPFISCH IM OLIVENÖL GEGART AN AUSTERNSAUCE

Serves 4

*4 cube-shaped pieces of salt cod (bacalao, salted and
dried cod), skin on,
olive oil for stewing*

*8 oysters,
100 g/3 1/2 oz butter,
120 ml/1/2 cup fish stock,
100 ml/1/3 cup cream,
salt, freshly ground white pepper*

*For the red beet sauce:
1 small red beet, peeled and cut into small cubes,
120 ml/1/2 cup beef stock,
2 tbsp olive oil,
a few drops of sherry vinegar*

*For the vegetable chips:
4 very thinly shaved slices of red beet,
4 leaves of leek, about 12 cm/5 inches long,
160 ml/2/3 cup syrup (equal amounts
of water and sugar)*

*Garnish:
2 thin leek stalks*

Für 4 Personen:

*4 würfelförmige Stücke Klippfisch (Bacalao, gesalzener
und getrockneter Kabeljau), mit Haut,
Olivenöl zum Schmoren*

*8 Austern, ausgelöst,
100 g Butter,
120 ml Fischfond,
100 ml Sahne,
Salz, weißer Pfeffer aus der Mühle*

*Für die Rote Bete-Sauce:
1 kleine Rote Bete, geschält und in Würfel geschnitten,
120 ml Rindfleischbrühe,
2 EL Olivenöl,
ein paar Tropfen Sherryessig*

*Für die Gemüse-Chips:
4 hauchdünn geschnittene Scheiben Rote Bete,
4 Lauchblätter, ca. 12 cm lang,
160 ml Sirup
(Wasser und Zucker 1:1)*

*Garnitur:
2 dünne Lauchstangen*

Water the fish in cold water for thirty-six hours, replacing water frequently. When you are ready to cook, dry salt cod pieces thoroughly and place them into a small pan. Cover with olive oil and heat up slowly. Stew fish on low heat for ten minutes, remove it from the oil and keep warm.

For the oyster sauce: In a small pot, combine the oysters and their juice, butter, fish stock and cream. Simmer, uncovered, on low heat for five minutes. Purée the mixture in a blender, strain it through a sieve and season to taste with salt and white pepper.

For the red beet sauce: Simmer the red beet in stock and olive oil until tender. Purée in a blender, strain through a sieve and season the sauce to taste with sherry vinegar.

For the vegetable chips: Simmer the red beet slices and leek leaves separately in syrup for five minutes. Allow excess syrup to drain off and place the vegetables on a rack. Dry in a 100° C/210° F oven for two hours.

For the garnish: Cut the leeks into 5 cm/2 inch pieces and boil the pieces in salted water until tender. Drain well.

Serving: Ladle oyster sauce into plates and surround it with red beet sauce. Place one salt cod cube in the middle of each plate and garnish the plate with the vegetable chips and boiled leek.

Den Fisch 36 Stunden in kaltes Wasser einlegen, dabei häufig das Wasser wechseln. Klippfischstücke gut abtrocknen, in einer kleinen Pfanne mit dem Olivenöl bedeckt erhitzen. Bei kleiner Hitze den Fisch zehn Minuten garen. Aus dem Öl nehmen, abtropfen lassen, warm halten.

Für die Austernsauce: In einem kleinen Topf die Austern mit ihrem Wasser, Butter, Fischfond und Sahne zum Kochen bringen. Bei kleiner Hitze ohne Deckel fünf Minuten köcheln. Im Mixer pürieren, durch ein Sieb passieren, abschmecken.

Für die Rote Bete-Sauce: Die Rote Bete in Brühe und Olivenöl weichkochen, im Mixer fein pürieren, durch ein Sieb passieren und mit Sherryessig abschmecken.

Für die Gemüse-Chips: Rote Bete-Scheiben und Lauchblätter getrennt im Sirup fünf Minuten köcheln, gut abtropfen lassen und auf einem Gitter im 100° C heißen Ofen 2 Stunden trocknen.

Für die Garnitur: Die Lauchstangen in 5 cm lange Stücke schneiden und in Salzwasser weichkochen. Gut abtropfen lassen.

Zum Servieren: Die Austernsauce in Teller schöpfen und mit der Rote Bete-Sauce umranden. Je einen Klippfischwürfel in die Mitte setzen, mit den Gemüse-Chips und dem gekochten Lauch garnieren und servieren.

PIG'S FEET WITH TRUFFLED FAVA BEANS

SCHWEINSFÜSSE MIT GETRÜFFELTEN DICKEN BOHNEN

Serves 4

8 pig's feet,
2 onions,
2 carrots,
1 small piece of celery,
1 clove garlic,
1 bay leaf, 6 peppercorns, 2 cloves,
5 whole allspice and 1 small sprig of rosemary
tied in a piece of cheese cloth,
500 ml/2 cups red wine,
250 ml/1 cup beef stock,
1 tbsp roux (equal amounts of butter and flour),
salt, freshly ground black pepper

500 g/2 cups young, tender fava beans,
2 tbsp cold-pressed olive oil,
2 tbsp truffles, finely chopped

Combine pig's feet, trimmed and coarsely chopped vegetables, spices, red wine and stock in a large pot. Bring to a boil and simmer for two hours. Occasionally skim off any foam that rises to the surface. Remove pig's feet from stock and pick meat from the bones. Fill meat into four small round molds, pressing the meat down firmly. Allow to cool in the molds and reserve.

Thicken the cooking liquid with a little roux until you have a thin sauce. Remove the spice packet and purée the thickened cooking liquid with the vegetables in a blender. Strain through a sieve and check for salt and pepper.

Blanch the fava beans in salted water for about two minutes, drain and mix with the olive oil and half of the chopped truffle.

Serving: Reheat pig's foot meat in the oven and unmold it onto pre-warmed plates. Arrange the fava beans loosely around the meat. Glaze meat with a little sauce and sprinkle with remaining truffles.

Für 4 Personen:

8 Schweinsfüße,
2 Zwiebeln,
2 Karotten,
1 kleines Stück Sellerie,
1 Knoblauchzehe,
Gewürzsäckchen mit 1 Lorbeerblatt,
6 Pfefferkörnern, 2 Nelken, 5 Pimentkörnern und
einem kleinen Zweig Rosmarin,
500 ml Rotwein,
250 ml Fleischbrühe,
1 EL Mehlschwitze (Roux, Butter und Mehl 1:1),
Salz, schwarzer Pfeffer aus der Mühle

500 g junge, zarte Dicke Bohnen,
2 EL kalt gepresstes Olivenöl,
2 EL fein gehackte Trüffel

Schweinsfüße und geputztes, grob geschnittenes Gemüse mit dem Gewürzsäckchen, Rotwein und Brühe in einen Topf füllen. Zum Kochen bringen, bei kleiner Hitze zwei Stunden köcheln. Von Zeit zu Zeit den Schaum abschöpfen. Schweinsfüße herausnehmen, das Fleisch vom Knochen lösen und in vier runde Förmchen schichten. Gut festdrücken, in der Form erkalten lassen, beiseite stellen. Kochfond mit etwas Mehlschwitze zu einer dünnen Sauce binden. Gewürzsäckchen entfernen, den gebundenen Kochfond mit dem Gemüse im Mixer pürieren, durch ein Sieb passieren. Mit Salz und Pfeffer abschmecken.

Die Dicken Bohnen in Salzwasser zwei Minuten kochen, abgießen, mit Olivenöl und der Häfte der gehackten Trüffel vermischen.

Zum Servieren: Das Fleisch von den Schweinsfüßen im Ofen erhitzen und auf vorgewärmte Teller stürzen. Die Dicken Bohnen um das Fleisch herum verteilen. Fleisch mit Sauce überziehen und die restlichen Trüffel darüber streuen.

South East Asia

THE CUISINES OF SOUTH EAST ASIA

South East Asian cooking in its immense variety can hardly be compared with any other cuisine in the world. It may best be described as a merry get-together of Asian regional cuisines, a happy co-existence in and outside of innumerable air-conditioned restaurants and simple eateries under the open sky. Unlike in Western countries, this diversity may boast of quite a long tradition, having had ample time to grow together into a harmonious simultaneity of Chinese, Indian, Malay, Thai and other culinary elements. People, for whatever reasons, have been crossing the borders to the neighboring states for a long time, taking their cooking traditions along. In the new surroundings, ongoing exchanges of (cooking) culture with the local population ensued in the generations to follow – a process that also resulted in outright blends as reflected in the Chinese-Malay „Nyonya" cuisine. „Nyonya" is a fusion cuisine, a successful union which does not seek to bridge continental contrasts with spectacular food acrobatics, but has its – related – roots in different areas of the Asiatic hemisphere. As a Malay chef puts it: "We often use similar techniques and the same raw products. The largest difference is our way of cooking and seasonings."

On the other hand, however, the eating habits of the local populations and their preference for their own can in certain ways be compared with what remains of local and regional cooking traditions within Europe. Mother´s cuisine is considered the epitome of culinary pleasures and everything foreign is viewed with a bit of suspicion. The large majority of people in South East Asia has at the utmost been to a neighboring country, world-wide travels are often beyond their means or simply not of general interest.

THUS, ATTEMPTS TO INTRODUCE SOMETHING NEW, SOMETHING FOREIGN, SOMETHING WESTERN THAT IS, USUALLY MEETS WITH SOME RESERVE.

Naturally, this is different in the large cities Singapore, Kuala Lumpur or Bangkok, where international business concerns have long resulted in foreign contacts. The financial possibilities and interests of the younger generation especially brings many a new customer to one or the other Western-inspired top restaurant. These are the people who are able to appreciate the careful attempts made by creative foreign chefs to combine East and West – a slow, but steady development.

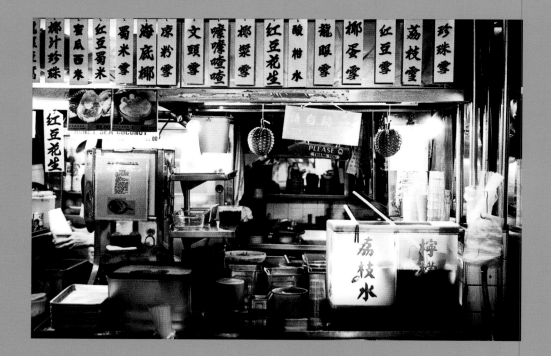

Die Küche Südostasiens ist in ihrer Vielfalt wohl mit keiner Küche der Welt zu vergleichen. Hier kommen jegliche Regionalküchen Asiens zusammen und finden sich in zahllosen klimatisierten Restaurants wie auch in schlichten Garküchen unter freiem Himmel in schönster Eintracht und Konkurrenzlosigkeit zusammen. Anders als in westlichen Ländern hat sich diese Verschiedenheit schon vor langer Zeit liiert zu einem harmonischen Nebeneinander von chinesischen, indischen, malaiischen, thailändischen und anderen Elementen. Menschen haben, warum auch immer, die Grenzen zum Nachbarland überquert – ihre Kochtradition im Gepäck. Und in der neuen Umgebung hat über Generationen hinweg ein Austausch der (Koch-)Kultur mit der ansässigen Bevölkerung stattgefunden. Bis hin zur völligen Verschmelzung, was sich am deutlichsten in der chinesisch-malaiischen „Nyonya-Küche" widerspiegelt. Eine harmonisch entstandene „Fusions-Küche", die nicht mit großem Spagat kontinentale Kontraste zu verklammern sucht, sondern im großen Raum der asiatischen Hemisphäre ihre (durchaus verwandten) Wurzeln hat. Wie es ein malaiischer Koch formuliert: „wir benutzen häufig ähnliche Kochtechniken und verwenden oft dieselben Rohprodukte. Der größte Unterschied liegt in der Art der Zubereitung und Würze."

Andererseits lassen sich die Essgewohnheiten der einheimischen Bevölkerung in ihrer Vorliebe fürs Eigene in gewisser Weise am anschaulichsten mit den Resten noch ländlich und regional verwurzelter Küchen Europas vergleichen. Da gilt Mutters Küche als Gipfel der Gaumengenüsse und alles Fremde wird argwöhnisch beäugt. Die große Mehrheit der Menschen in Südostasien hat im Höchstfall das Nachbarland besucht, weltweite Urlaubsreisen übersteigen oft die Möglichkeiten oder finden schlichtweg nicht das Interesse. Und so stoßen die Versuche, auch etwas Fremdes, sprich westliche Einflüsse einzubringen, erst zögerlich auf Zuspruch. Dies stellt sich ganz anders dar in den großen Städten Singapur, Kuala Lumpur oder Bangkok, wo internationales Business schon von selbst den Kontakt zum Ausland herstellt. Das finanzielle Potential und die Interessen, insbesondere auch der jüngeren Generation, spült in so manches der modern und westlich angehauchten Toprestaurants eine neue Klientel, die auch die vorsichtigen Versuche kreativer Ausländer, Ost mit West zu verbinden, zu schätzen lernt. Es ist eine Entwicklung, die langsam und Schritt für Schritt vonstatten geht.

THE SINGAPORE HAWKER CENTERS

Not far away from office highrises, the city is invaded by the picturesque compositions of a colorful food market teeming with people, and innumerable eateries tempt nose and palate as flavors carried along by smoke and steam are wafting through the air. The market caters to every taste and purse. The so-called Hawker Centers offer everything from fish and poultry to frogs and snakes (yes, those too!), everything locals seem to need for their pots or woks respectively. And suddenly, you sit right in the middle of it all at a simple table in front of a steaming bowl of noodle soup containing meat or fish, trying to eat it with chopsticks or a spoon. Malay, Chinese, Indian or Thai cooking – the selection is huge and the seasoning, depending on the cuisine, more often than not brings tears to the eyes of a Westerner. From the banker to the shoe seller, the tourist, taxi driver, monk – this simple, inexpensive yet incredibly varied fare is popular with everyone, regardless of the stratum of the population. Every booth offers something else, dishes from different regions, noodle soups or fried fish, vegetarian curries or crispy suckling pigs. Seating is not regulated, you simply compose your menu yourself from different cuisines. And you are bound to enjoy it.

Unweit hochaufragender Bürotürme zwängen sich in malerischer Buntheit wimmelnde Wochenmärkte ins Stadtbild, und unzählige Garküchen verströmen qualmend ihre Lockrufe für Nase und Gaumen. Hier wird jede Geschmacksrichtung und jeder Geldbeutel bedient. In den sogenannten „Hawker Centers" wird von Fisch und Geflügel über Gemüse bis zu Fröschen und Schlangen (ja auch diese) alles angeboten, was der Einheimische für den Kochtopf respektive Wok zu benötigen scheint. Und mittendrin sitzt man dann an einfachem Tisch vor einer großen Schüssel dampfender Nudelsuppe mit Fleisch- oder Fischeinlage, die man sich mittels Stäbchen und Löffel einzuverleiben versucht.

MALAIISCH, CHINESISCH, INDISCH ODER THAI – DIE AUSWAHL IST IMMENS UND DIE WÜRZE, JE NACH KÜCHE, BISWEILEN FÜR „WESTLER" ZU TRÄNEN RÜHREND SCHARF.

Vom Bankier bis zum Schuhverkäufer, vom Touristen, Taxifahrer bis zum Mönch – quer durch die Bevölkerung schätzt man die einfache, preiswerte und doch sehr abwechslungsreiche Speisemöglichkeit. Denn jeder Imbissstand hat anderes zu bieten, Kost anderer Regionen, Nudelsuppen oder gebratenen Fisch, vegetarische Curries oder kross gebratenes Spanferkel. Sitzordnung gibt es keine, und das Menü stellt man sich selbst an den verschiedenen Garküchen zusammen.

GOODWOOD PARK HOTEL S'PORE

GOODWOOD PARK HOTEL

The chinking, beeping and rattling of electronic cash registers hovers above Singapore like the mating call of some strange bird of commerce. In the shopping paradise of South East Asia, spend-happy tourists are beguiled with fantastic specials, design fashions and high-tech articles at (seemingly) low prices. The city state, kept inordinately clean by civil authorities – even the import of chewing gum is punishable by law – glitters and sparkles with gigantic shopping malls and department stores along the pulsating thoroughfares Orchard and Scotts Road. The sky is sometimes blue and sometimes cloudy, the humidity level always sweat-inducing. Not far away, picturesque Hindu temples and colorful Chinese markets nonchalantly invade the cityscape, and innumerable eateries produce a liberal amount of smoke sending off their enticing aromas for the nose and the palate. There is something to satisfy every culinary whim and every purse. And yet, Singapore, with its exotic contrasts, eludes every hapless attempt to describe its flair and atmosphere in a few words. Not far away from the noisy shopper's world of Orchard Road, a time-honored but quite sprightly old lady keeps court: The Goodwood Park Hotel, which now, at the turn of the millennium, may look back to one hundred years of history. It is the second oldest house in town, right after Singapore's classic hotel, the Raffles. Originally named "Teutonia Club", the Goodwood Park Hotel was built for the city's German colony in the style of a German Rhine castle. Various facelifts have helped to preserve the splendor of times past and to transfer its casual elegance to modern times – keeping the excitement of the noisy metropolis at a proper distance. The culinary flagship of the house, the "Chang Jiang Shanghai Restaurant", named after China's great river Yangtze ("Chang Jiang" in Chinese), is all subdued noblesse, with colors in brown, ivory and gold. In this establishment – nomen est omen – upscale Shanghai cuisine is being celebrated among green ferns, orchids on the table and a view through the window onto the large pool. And yet, the Chang Jiang Shanghai is only one of the many restaurants at the Goodwood, whose culinary activities are focused mainly on Chinese food – with some Italian and English cuisine. About 120 chefs, under the auspices of eight highly qualified master chefs, are busy chopping, stirring and frying in a variety of restaurants. This none-too-small armada of chefs is supported by a staff of 200 people, including everyone from kitchen help to waiter. Uninitiated palates will encounter a significantly more spicy version of Chinese cooking at the "Min Jiang Sichuan", where Szechuan-style hot-and-sour dishes, originally intended for a cold climate, are not only seasoned with garlic, vinegar and ginger but also with tear-jerking chili peppers. The "Garden Seafood Restaurant", on the other hand, serves lobster, crabs, shark fins and other seafood prepared in a Hong Kong-Cantonese style, even if the menu also includes wok-stirred frogs' legs and the old favorite Peking duck. All restaurants are managed individually, with their own kitchen, procuring their daily requirements from suppliers who have to import almost anything from near and far foreign countries since nothing grows in Singapore itself. Occasionally, the Chinese master chef may be spotted on a personal visit the local market, checking out turtles and other exotic ingredients. Even so, banquets for 500 people are calculated down to the last ginger root with incredible precision, with hardly any waste, whereas in Western kitchens a large amount of food is usually doomed for the trash can. And day after day, Mrs. Mavis Oei, whose family has owned the hotel since 1968, takes her dinner at one of the three Chinese restaurants. Any newly created dish must first pass her palate before being considered for a menu appearance. As executive chef Roger Seitz, Swiss-born but now a resident of Australia, explains: "The Chinese restaurants are our money-makers. Chinese cuisine dominates the scene here, after all, a large part of Singapore's population is Chinese." Foreigners may make good money here, but they prefer to take it home to their homelands – native gourmets, on the other hand, have plenty of money to spare.

At the "Gordon Grill", time has stopped altogether: It's a dinosaur from colonial times – time-honored traditions in the English style, dark wood and leather, subdued light and Western cuisine with an English-Scottish accent. Despite all efforts spent by the chefs on exquisite creations, the restaurant also has its regular customers – Asians and Westerners alike – who scorn oysters and smoked salmon, having been used to being served their prime rib steak here for more than thirty years. And they insist on it – complete with "peas and mashed potatoes, of course". It's the best steak in the city according to Roger Seitz. Not merely prime beef, but only premium cut is used, and Japanese Kobe beef (10 grams for $5.90) is also on the menu. "Our guests don't hesitate to pay 400 Singapore dollars for such an expensive piece," recounts Seitz. In the background, however, the young chef Paul Pereira is already working on more modern Euro-Asiatiac creations, which will be gradually introduced to the menu in order to attract a younger, more international clientele. The smart native of South Africa of Indian descent has already tried his hand in Michelin-starred restaurants in Paris and London. "I do not change the recipes as much as I do the ingredients, replacing heavy dishes with light ones and putting more emphasis on appearance. I use spices with deliberation, in order to counteract the effects of the hot climate, and I also indulge in some seasonal cooking when foreign ingredients such as asparagus or game is available."

T he light whir of large ventilator paddles moving through the tropically hot air high up on the ceiling generates a gentle, cool breeze. Sunlight falls through the slats of wooden blinds, drawing stripes onto the tables and marble floors of the roofed-in outdoor terrace. The open-air section of the "Coffee Lounge" has a certain magic charm. Its nostalgic atmosphere lures even heat-sensitive travelers to carry their plate – filled in the air-conditioned dining-room – to the outside in order to enjoy the delicacies of the extensive curry buffet there. Its Indian-Malay-Chinese selection of spicy dishes is probably the best introduction to the cuisines of South East Asia.

Garden Seafood Restaurant – Tudor Ballroom

Coffee Lounge

D

as Fiepsen, Zwitschern und Knattern elektronischer Einkaufskassen liegt wie eine Lockmelodie über Singapur. Mit Designer-Mode und High-tech-Ware betört das Einkaufsparadies Südostasiens einkaufslustige Touristen mit (scheinbar) günstigen Preisen und sagenhaften Schnäppchen. Der mit Gesetzeskraft peinlich sauber gehaltene Stadtstaat, der selbst die Einfuhr von Kaugummi unter Strafe stellt, glitzert und funkelt mit gigantischen Kaufhäusern und Shopping Centers entlang der pulsierenden Straßenfluchten von Orchard und Scotts Road. Der Himmel ist mal blau, mal verhangen, das schwülheiße Klima immer schweißtreibend. Nicht weit entfernt zwängen sich in malerischer Unbekümmertheit bunte Hindutempel und Chinesenmärkte ins Stadtbild, und die Düfte unzähliger Garküchen locken Nase und Gaumen. Hier wird jede Geschmacksrichtung und jeder Geldbeutel bedient und auf dem Teller findet sich, was der multinationale Mix dieser Stadt bedeutet. Doch Singapur entzieht sich mit seinen exotischen Gegensätzen jedem hilflosen Versuch, sein Flair und seine Atmosphäre in wenigen Worten einzufangen. Unweit der lärmenden Einkaufswelt von Orchard Road hält in grüner Parkland-schaft eine hochbetagte jedoch äußerst rüstige Dame Hof: das „Goodwood Park Hotel", das nun zur Jahrtausendwende auf einhundert Jahre Geschichte zurückblicken kann. Neben Singapurs Klassiker, dem „Raffles", ist es das zweitälteste Haus am Platze und war ursprünglich als „Teutonia Club" für die deutsche Kolonie im Stil deutscher Rhein-Burgen erbaut worden. Durch diverse Liftings hat es den Glanz vergangener Zeiten mit wohl-tuender Eleganz in die Moderne herübergerettet und konnte gleichzeitig die Aufgeregtheit der lärmenden Metropole auf schickliche Distanz halten.

In zurückhaltender Noblesse, in Braun, Elfenbein und Gold, präsentiert sich das kulinarische Flaggschiff des Hauses, das „Chang Jiang Shanghai Restaurant", benannt nach Chinas großem Jangtsekiang-Fluss (chinesisch: Chang Jiang). Inmitten grüner Farne, an Tischen mit Orchideen und mit Blick durchs Fenster zum Pool wird in diesem Etablissement – nomen est omen – edle Shanghai-Küche zelebriert. Doch das Chang Jiang Shanghai ist nur einer der vielen Speiseplätze im Goodwood, deren Schwerpunkt neben italienischer und englischer Küche vorwiegend auf der chinesischen liegt. Rund 120 Köche, über die acht hochqualifizierte Chefköche regieren, schneiden, rühren und braten in den verschiedenen Restaurants. Die stattliche Kocharmada wird durch weitere 200 Mitarbeiter ergänzt – von der Küchenhilfe bis zum Kellner. Ein deutlich schärferes Erlebnis widerfährt dem ungeübten Gaumen im „Min Jiang Sichuan", wo scharf-saure Gerichte nach Szechuan-Art, eigentlich für ein kaltes Klima gedacht, nicht nur mit Knoblauch, Essig und Ingwer sondern auch mit tränentreibendem Chili gewürzt werden. Hummer, Krebse, Haifischflossen und sonstiges Meeresgetier bietet schließlich das „Garden Seafood Restaurant" im Hongkong-Kanton-Stil. Doch auch wok-gerührte Froschschenkel oder die immer populäre Peking-Ente finden sich auf seiner Karte.

Alle Restaurants sind mit eigener Küche ausgestattet und ordern den Tagesbedarf bei Lieferanten, die fast alles aus dem nahen und fernen Ausland importieren müssen, da in Singapur nichts angebaut wird. Nur hin und wieder macht sich der chinesische Chefkoch höchstpersönlich auf den Weg zum örtlichen Markt, wo er Schildkröten oder andere exotische Zutaten zu finden weiß. Noch mit unglaublicher Präzision werden selbst 500-Personen-Bankette bis auf die letzte Ingwerknolle kalkuliert, sodass, wie in westlichen Küchen durchaus üblich, hier kaum ein Krümel übrig bleibt. Und tagtäglich pflegt Mrs. Mavis Oei, deren Familie das Hotel seit 1968 besitzt, in einem der drei China-Restaurants ihr Essen einzunehmen.

Wird ein neues Gericht kreiert, muss es erst auf ihrer Zunge bestehen, ehe es auf die Speisekarte kommt. Executive Chefkoch Roger Seitz, ein Schweizer mit Domizil in Australien, erläutert: „Die drei China-Restaurants sind unsere Money-Maker. Chinesische Küche dominiert hier die Szene, schließlich ist in Singapur der Großteil der Bevölkerung chinesisch."

Min Jiang Sichuan Restaurant

鸭、乳鸽类	鸭・鳩料理	DUCK & PIGEON	Small	Price ($) Medium	Large
北京填鸭	北京ダック（2種）	Roast Whole Peking Duck (2 Styles)	-	-	60
樟茶片鸭	鴨ささみ肉の薫製	Fillet of Smoked Duck	22	-	44
锅烧大鸭	骨なし鴨の唐揚げ	Deep Fried Boneless Duck	22	-	44
海参扒鸭	鴨とナマコの煮込み	Braised Duck with Sea Cucumber	22	-	44
荷叶全鸭	鴨、マッシュルーム、ハムの蓮の葉包み煮込み	Braised Duck with Mushroom & Ham in Lotus Leaf	22	-	44
烧烤乳鸽	鳩の丸焼き	Roast Whole Pigeon		§35 per no.	
鸡类	鶏肉料理	CHICKEN			
翡翠酥鸡	香ばしい骨なし鶏、塩漬け卵とエビそぼろ添え	Crispy Boneless Chicken with Salted Eggs & Minced Prawns	25	-	50
麻辣烧鸡	ローストチキンのゴマソース	Roast Chicken with Sesame Sauce	20	-	40
云腿玉兰鸡	蒸し鶏のハムとカイラン（野菜）添え	Steamed Chicken with Ham & Kai Lan	20	-	40
香柠酥鸡	香ばしい骨なし鶏のレモンソース	Crispy Boneless Chicken with Lemon Sauce	20	-	40
姜茸烧鸡	ローストチキンのジンジャーソース	Roast Chicken with Ginger Sauce	20	-	40
黑椒鸡柳	薄切り鶏の黒コショウ味	Sliced Chicken with Black Pepper	14	21	28
成都鸡柳	薄切り鶏の成都風	Sliced Chicken "Chengdu" Style	14	21	28
宫保鸡丁	鶏肉の干唐辛子炒め	Diced Chicken with Dried Red Chilli	14	21	28
腰果鸡丁	鶏肉とカシューナッツの炒め物	Diced Chicken with Cashew Nuts	14	21	28
酱爆鸡丁	鶏肉、タケノコ、椎茸の炒め物	Diced Chicken with Bamboo Shoots & Mushrooms	14	21	28
豆豉鸡丁	鶏肉のブラックビーンソース	Diced Chicken with Black Bean Sauce	14	21	28

Und während Ausländer in Singapur zwar gutes Geld verdienen, so tragen sie es lieber nach Hause in ihre Herkunftsländer – einheimischen Gourmets dagegen sitzt die Brieftasche unbedenklich locker. Im „Gordon Grill" ist die Zeit stehen geblieben – ein Ungetüm aus Kolonialzeiten. Ehrwürdige Tradition englischer Prägung, dunkles Holz und Leder, gedämpftes Licht und westliche Küche mit englisch-schottischem Zungenschlag. Trotz aller Bemühungen der Köche, nur das Feinste zu zaubern, hat der Grill ein angestammtes Publikum – asiatisch wie westlich – das schon seit 30 Jahren gewohnt ist, hier neben Austern und Räucherlachs sein Prime Rib Steak serviert zu bekommen. Und es besteht darauf – selbstverständlich mit „peas and mashed potatoes". Das wohl beste Steak der Stadt, meint Roger Seitz. Nicht prime beef, nur premium cut wird verwendet, und japanisches Kobe Beef (10 Gramm für 5,90 Dollar) darf ebenfalls nicht fehlen. „Die Gäste zucken mit keiner Wimper, für dieses teure Stück 400 Singapur-Dollar liegen zu lassen", erzählt Seitz. Doch hinter den Kulissen steht schon der junge Paul Pereira und bastelt an modernen Kreationen euro-asiatischer Küche, die nach und nach ihren Eingang in die Speisekarte finden sollen, um auch ein jüngeres, internationales Publikum anzulocken. Der smarte Südafrikaner indischer Herkunft hat zuvor bereits in Paris und London sein Können in Michelin-Sterne-Restaurants unter Beweis gestellt. „Ich verändere nicht so sehr die Rezepte als vielmehr die Zutaten, ersetze schwere Kost durch leichte und gebe der Optik mehr Finesse. Ich würze gezielt, als Ausgleich zu dem schwülheißen Klima, und koche natürlich auch jahreszeitlich orientiert, wenn es um ausländische Zutaten geht, wie Spargel oder Wild."

Mit leisem Surren schwingen hoch an der Decke die Flügel großer Ventilatoren durch tropisch-heiße Luft und spenden erholsame Kühlung. Sonnenlicht dringt durch die Lamellen von Holzjalousien und zeichnet Streifen über die Tische und den Marmorboden der überdachten Außenterrasse. Die Freiluftabteilung der „Coffee Lounge" übt magische Anziehungskraft aus. Ihr nostalgischer Charme verführt auch hitzeempfindliche Zeitgenossen, sich den im klimatisierten Speisesaal gefüllten Teller nach draußen zu tragen, um hier die Leckerbissen des reichhaltigen Curry-Büffets zu genießen. Dessen indisch-malaiisch-chinesischer Mix an würzigen Gerichten ist wohl die beste Einleitung zur Küche Südostasiens.

Chang Jiang Shanghai Restaurant

海鲜类	海鲜料理	SEAFOOD	Price ($) Regular	Medium
葱油元菜 (预订) (上海)	カメ、豚ひき肉、マッシュルームの蒸し物 (事前予約) (上海)	Steamed Turtle with Minced Pork & Mushrooms (Advance Order) (Shanghai)	$160 Per Order	
熏焗三文鱼	スモークサーモンのフルーツソース	Smoked Salmon with Fruity Sauce	Seasonal Price	
酱爆银杏带子 (杨州)	帆立とギンナンの中華味噌ソテー (揚州)	Sauteed Fresh Scallops with Gingko Nuts & Preserved Salted Beans (Yangzhou)	$30	$50
芦笋鲜带子	帆立とアスパラガスの炒め物	Stir Fried Fresh Scallops with Asparagus	$30	$50
虾子大乌参 (上海)	ナマコとエビの卵のブラウンソース煮込み (上海)	Braised Sea Cucumber with Shrimp Roe in Dark Brown Sauce (Shanghai)	$30	$50
糟溜鱼片 (上海)	切り身魚ときのこのワインソース炒め (上海)	Fried Sliced Fish with Black Fungus in Wine Sauce (Shanghai)	$24	$36
赛螃蟹 (上海)	カニ肉と緑色野菜の卵白あえ (上海)	Crabmeat with Green Vegetables & Egg White (Shanghai)	$22	$34
白汁鱼唇 (上海)	ナマコ、鶏、マッシュルーム、ハム、台湾野菜のホワイトソース煮込み (上海)	Braised Fish Slug with Sliced Chicken, Black Mushrooms, Jin Hua Ham & Taiwanese Greens in White Sauce (Shanghai)	$22	$34
泡椒鱼米 (带饼) (上海)	魚、唐辛子、ネギの炒め物 ゴマ袋包み (上海)	Pan Fried Aruwan Fish with Chilli & Spring Onions Served in Sesame Purse (Shanghai)	$20	$30
红烧鳝糊 (上海)	活ウナギのブラウンソースとガーリック煮込み (上海)	Braised "Live" Eel in Brown Sauce & Garlic (Shanghai)	$20	$30
银芽炒鳝丝 (上海)	細切りウナギ、モヤシ、ショウガ、ネギの炒め物 (上海)	Stir Fried Shredded Eel with Bean Sprouts, Ginger & Spring Onions (Shanghai)	$20	$30

BANANA LEAVES STUFFED WITH FISH PASTE

BANANENBLÄTTER MIT FISCHPASTE GEFÜLLT

Serves 4

300 g/11 oz Spanish mackerel, cut into filets

For the spice mixture:
2 tbsp dried chili pepper flakes,
1 stalk lemongrass,
4 macadamia nuts (original recipe: candlenuts),
3 tbsp ground galangal,
1 level tsp turmeric,
20 g/³/₄ oz shrimp paste,
5 shallots,
1 tbsp coriander seeds, toasted
and finely ground in a mortar

the grated pulp of one coconut,
3 tbsp vegetable oil,
5 kaffir lime leaves,
1 egg, beaten,
4 tbsp sugar,
1¹/₂ tsp salt

banana leaves (optional)

Purée the fish filets in the food processor, transfer purée in a bowl and refrigerate.

For the spice powder: Place chili pepper flakes into a small sieve and leave them to soak in a glass of water until soft. Drain well. Mince the lemongrass, then grind it finely in a mortar with the soaked chili pepper flakes, nuts, galangal, turmeric and shrimp paste. Finely dice the shallots and also grind them in a mortar. Combine the two other pastes and add ground coriander.

Mix the coconut pulp with a little water and place it into a cloth. Squeeze as much milk as possible into a bowl.

Heat the oil in a wok. Fry the spice paste over low heat for five minutes. Stir in coconut milk and heat to just below the boiling point. Remove from heat and gently whisk in the egg with a wire whip. Remove hard central vein from the kaffir lime leaves and cut the leaves into very thin slices. Incorporate fish purée and lime leaf strips into the spice paste. Check for sugar and salt.

To cook, either wrap the fish paste into banana leaves and broil or grill them until done, or bake the paste in an oven-proof dish set in a bain-marie in a 170° C/325° F degree oven for 20 - 25 minutes.

Für 4 Personen:

300 g Spanische oder Mittelmeer-Makrele, filetiert

Für die Gewürzmischung:
2 EL getrocknete Chiliflocken,
1 Zitronengrasstengel,
4 Macadamianüsse (Originalrezept: Candlenuts),
3 EL Galangapulver,
1 gestrichener TL Kurkuma,
20 g Garnelenpaste,
5 Schalotten,
1 EL Koriandersamen, geröstet und im Mörser
zu Pulver zerstossen

das geriebene Fleisch von 1 Kokosnuss,
3 EL pflanzliches Öl,
4 Kaffir-Limetten-Blätter,
1 Ei, verquirlt,
4 EL Zucker,
1¹/₂ TL Salz

Bananenblätter

Das Fischfilet im Mixer kurz pürieren, dann das Püree in eine Schüssel füllen und kalt stellen.

Für die Gewürzmischung: Die Chiliflocken in einem Sieb ins Wasser hängen und einweichen, anschließend gut abtropfen lassen. Das Zitronengras fein hacken, mit den Chiliflocken, Nüssen, Galanga, Kurkuma und der Garnelenpaste im Mörser zu einer Paste verstampfen. Schalotten fein hacken, ebenfalls im Mörser zerstampfen, zum Schluss das Korianderpulver einarbeiten.

Das Kokosnussfleisch mit etwas Wasser vermischen und in ein Tuch füllen. Den Saft auspressen, in einer Schüssel auffangen. Das Öl im Wok erhitzen. Bei kleiner Hitze die Gewürzpaste 5 Minuten rösten. Die Kokosmilch unterrühren, bis kurz vor den Siedepunkt erhitzen. Vom Herd nehmen, mit dem Schneebesen vorsichtig das Ei unterrühren. Von den Limettenblättern den inneren harten Teil herausschneiden, die Blätter in sehr feine Streifen schneiden. Mit dem gekühlten Fisch unter die Gewürzmasse rühren, mit Zucker und Salz würzen.

Die Fischpaste nun entweder in Bananenblätter wickeln und auf dem Grill garen, oder in eine feuerfeste Form füllen und im 170° C heißen Ofen im Wasserbad 20 - 25 Minuten backen.

FRIED STRING BEANS

WITH MINCED MEAT

GEBRATENE BOHNEN

MIT GEHACKTEM FLEISCH

Serves 4

600 g/1 1/3 lb string beans (original recipe: asparagus beans),
2 tbsp sunflower oil,
120 g/4 oz ground pork,
80 g/3 oz dried shrimp,
2 garlic cloves, minced,
2 tbsp ginger, freshly grated,
300 ml/1 1/4 cups hearty chicken stock,
made with some raw ham,
2 tbsp Chinese wine (Hua Tiao Chiew),
3 tbsp light soy sauce,
4 tsp Chinese black vinegar,
1 tsp MSG,
2 green onions, chopped,
2 tbsp sesame oil

Trim and string the beans if necessary. Heat the sunflower oil in the wok. Stir-fry the beans without browning them. Remove beans from wok and stir-fry minced meat, shrimp, garlic and ginger in the same oil. Douse with stock and allow the liquid to reduce by half. Return the beans to the wok and add the wine, soy sauce, vinegar and MSG. Simmer for five minutes on low heat, uncovered. Stir in chopped green onions and sesame oil. Remove from wok and divide equally into four portions. Arrange on pre-warmed plates. Serve at once.

Für 4 Personen:

600 g grüne Bohnen (Originalrezept: Spargelbohnen),
2 EL Sonnenblumenöl,
120 g gehacktes Schweinefleisch,
80 g getrocknete Garnelen,
2 Knoblauchzehen, fein gehackt,
2 EL frisch geriebener Ingwer,
300 ml kräftige Hühnerbrühe,
mit Rohschinken gekocht,
2 EL chinesischer Wein (Hua Tiao Chiew),
3 EL helle Sojasauce,
4 TL chinesischer schwarzer Essig,
1 TL Glutamat,
2 Frühlingszwiebeln, gehackt,
2 EL Sesamöl

Bohnen putzen, eventuelle Fäden entfernen. Das Sonnenblumenöl im Wok erhitzen. Die Bohnen bei mittlerer Hitze unter Rühren braten, ohne Farbe nehmen zu lassen. Aus dem Fett nehmen. Im gleichen Wok das Hackfleisch, die Garnelen, den Knoblauch und den Ingwer anbraten. Mit der Brühe ablöschen, auf die Hälfte einkochen, dann die Bohnen, den Wein, die Sojasauce, den Essig und das Glutamat zugeben und bei kleiner Hitze fünf Minuten ohne Deckel köcheln, dabei von Zeit zu Zeit umrühren. Zum Schluss die Frühlingszwiebeln und das Sesamöl unterrühren und die Bohnen auf vorgewärmte Teller anrichten.

Serves 4

800 g/1³/₄ lb Chinese cabbage,
60 ml/¹/₄ cup sunflower oil,
100 g/3¹/₂ oz jin hua ham (or another raw ham), sliced

150 ml/²/₃ cup chicken stock made with some raw ham,
1 tsp oyster sauce,
1 tsp Chinese rice wine,
1 tsp cornstarch,
¹/₂ tsp dark soy sauce,
¹/₂ tsp white pepper,
1 tsp light soy sauce,
¹/₂ tsp MSG,
¹/₂ tsp sugar

Sauté Chinese cabbage in hot oil until wilted. Remove cabbage from wok. Discard oil. Cut the cabbage into four pieces of equal size. Line four small oven-proof dishes with the raw ham slices. Cover the ham with cabbage. Steam the bowls with the cabbage mixture in a steamer oven or another steaming arrangement for twenty minutes. Heat the oil in the wok. Combine all remaining ingredients and mix well. Simmer in the wok until the sauce has slightly thickened.
Serving: Unmold the ham and cabbage onto plates and drizzle the plates with sauce.

BRAISED CABBAGE WITH HAM

GESCHMORTER KOHL MIT SCHINKEN

Für 4 Personen:

800 g Chinakohl,
60 ml Sonnenblumenöl,
100 g Jin Hua Schinken (oder anderer Rohschinken), in Scheiben geschnitten

150 ml Hühnerbrühe, mit Rohschinken gekocht,
1 TL Austernsauce,
1 TL chinesischer Reiswein,
1 TL Maisstärke,
¹/₂ TL dunkle Sojasauce,
¹/₂ TL weißer Pfeffer,
1 TL helle Sojasauce,
¹/₂ TL Glutamat,
¹/₂ TL Zucker

Den Chinakohl im heißen Öl braten, bis die Blätter zusammenfallen.
Aus dem Wok nehmen, das Öl abgießen. Den Kohl in vier gleich große Stücke teilen. Die Schinkenscheiben in vier hitzefesten Schüsselchen auslegen, den Chinakohl darüber legen.
Den Schüsselinhalt im Dampfofen (Steamer) oder in einem Topf über Dampf 20 Minuten garen. Den Wok erneut erhitzen. Die restlichen Zutaten verrühren, im Wok köcheln, bis die Sauce leicht eindickt.
Zum Servieren: Den Kohl mit dem Schinken auf Teller stürzen und mit der Sauce übergießen.

PRAWNS IN CHILI PEPPER SAUCE

GARNELEN MIT CHILISAUCE

Serves 4

400 g/14 oz medium shrimp, fresh,
60 ml/¹/₄ cup for frying

For the sauce:
2 tbsp sunflower oil,
1 finely diced green onion,
30 g/1 oz ginger, minced,
1 garlic clove, minced,
120 ml/¹/₂ cup chili sauce,
60 ml/¹/₄ cup tomato sauce,
1 egg white, beaten,
1 level tsp cornstarch,
mixed with a little water

Für 4 Personen:

400 g mittelgroße frische Garnelen,
60 ml Öl zum Braten

Für die Chilisauce:
2 EL Sonnenblumenöl,
1 fein gehackte Frühlingszwiebel,
30 g fein gehackter Ingwer,
1 fein gehackte Knoblauchzehe,
120 ml Chilisauce,
60 ml Tomatensauce,
1 Eiweiß, verquirlt,
1 gestrichener TL Maisstärke,
mit etwas Wasser angerührt

Shell and devein the prawns, rinse them under cold water and dry them well with paper towels. Heat the oil in a wok or a shallow frying pan. Sauté the prawns until they turn white, then remove them from the oil. Place them on a pre-warmed plate and keep them warm. Pour out oil.

Heat the sunflower oil in the wok and stir-fry the chopped green onion, ginger and garlic until wilted. Add chili sauce and tomato sauce.

Drizzle in egg white, stirring vigorously until the egg white solidifies. Thicken the sauce with a little cornstarch mixture. Pour the sauce into four small dishes for dipping. Arrange the fried prawns on four pre-warmed plates and decorate the plates with a little soy sauce and parsley, according to taste. Serve.

Garnelen schälen, Darm entfernen, waschen und auf Küchenpapier gut abtrocknen. Das Öl in einer Pfanne oder im Wok erhitzen. Garnelen braten, bis sie weiß sind, dann das Öl abgießen, die Garnelen auf einen Teller geben und warm halten.

Im Sonnenblumenöl die gehackte Frühlingszwiebel, den Ingwer und den Knoblauch unter Rühren gut anbraten. Mit Chili- und Tomatensauce auffüllen, dann unter kräftigem Rühren das verquirlte Eiweiß untermischen.

Die Sauce mit der angerührten Maisstärke leicht binden und zum Dippen der Garnelen in vier kleine Schälchen füllen. Die gebratenen Garnelen auf vier vorgewärmte Teller anrichten, nach Belieben mit etwas Sojasauce und Petersilie garnieren.

DEEP-FRIED GLUTINOUS RICE WITH SAUSAGE

SERVED IN A CRAB SHELL

Serves 4

4 crab shells, cleaned

*250 g/¹/₂ lb glutinous rice, 600 ml/1¹/₃ cups water, ¹/₂ tsp salt,
2 tbsp dried shrimp, soaked in water,
2 tbsp dried mushrooms, soaked in water, 2 tbsp sunflower oil,
80 g/3 oz dried Chinese sausage, finely diced, soy sauce, oyster sauce, salt*

*Side dishes: vegetables (e.g. asparagus, Chinese broccoli, carrots,
blanched and sautéed in a little oil until tender)*

Wash the rice in cold water until the water runs clear. Steam the rice in a rice steamer with water and salt for twenty minutes. Alternatively, place the rice in a heavy-bottomed casserole and add water to cover one finger deep. Cover and bring to a rolling boil. Turn off the heat and allow the rice to steam, covered and undisturbed, for another twenty minutes. Set aside.
Drain shrimp and mushrooms in a sieve. Squeeze out excess water. Heat the oil in a heavy-bottomed pan. Sauté shrimp, mushrooms and sausage, stirring constantly. Season with soy sauce and oyster sauce and keep sautéing for another minute. Check for salt.
Fill crab shells with mushroom mixture and rice, pressing it firmly into the shells.
Deep-fry the stuffed crab shells in hot oil until golden brown. Drain thoroughly on paper towels and serve with a vegetable combination of your choice.

FRITTIERTER KLEBREIS IN DER KREBSSCHALE

MIT WURST

Für 4 Personen:

4 Krebsschalen, geputzt

*250 g Klebreis, 600 ml Wasser, ¹/₂ TL Salz, 2 EL getrocknete Garnelen, in Wasser eingeweicht,
2 EL getrocknete Champignons, in Wasser eingeweicht,
2 EL Sonnenblumenöl, 80 g getrocknete chinesische Wurst, in kleine Würfel geschnitten,
Sojasauce, Austernsauce, Salz*

*Beilage: Gemüse (z.B. Spargel, chinesischer Broccoli, Karotten,
blanchiert und in etwas Öl fertig gebraten)*

Den Reis in kaltem Wasser waschen, bis das Wasser klar bleibt. Im Reiskocher mit dem Wasser und Salz 20 Minuten garen. Wenn kein Reiskocher vorhanden: Den Reis in einen Topf mit dickem Boden geben, mit Wasser aufgießen, bis er ein Fingerhoch bedeckt ist. Zugedeckt erhitzen, bis das Wasser sprudelnd kocht. Die Hitzezufuhr stoppen, den Reis, ohne den Deckel zu heben in dem entstandenen Dampf mit der Resthitze 20 Minuten garen. Die Garnelen und Champignons durch ein Sieb abgießen und gut ausdrücken. In einer Pfanne das Öl erhitzen. Die Garnelen und die Champignons mit den Wurstwürfeln anbraten. Mit Soja- und Austernsauce würzen, unter Rühren eine Minute weiterbraten. Mit Salz abschmecken. Die Masse in die Krebsschalen verteilen. Den Reis ebenfalls in die Schalen verteilen und in Krebsform andrücken.
Die gefüllten Krebsschalen im heißen Öl goldbraun frittieren. Gut abtropfen lassen, mit Gemüse nach Wahl garniert servieren.

SAUTÉED PRAWNS

WITH ASPARAGUS AND X.O. SAUCE

Serves 4

300 g/11 oz fresh prawns, shelled,
200 g/7 oz green asparagus, blanched,
1 carrot, cut into julienne strips, blanched, 2 tbsp sunflower oil,
1 tbsp Chinese rice wine (hua tiao chiew), $^1/_2$ tsp sugar, $^1/_2$ tsp salt

For the X.O. sauce:
2 tbsp dried shrimp, 2 tbsp raw ham (Hunan), finely diced,
2 tbsp red chili pepper, finely diced, 2 tbsp oil,
2 tbsp rice vinegar, 200 ml/$^3/_4$ cup chicken stock,
$^1/_2$ tsp MSG, $^1/_2$ tsp sugar, $^1/_2$ tsp salt

Blanch the prawns in salted water for one minute, drain in a colander and allow excess water to drip off. Cut the asparagus spears into 5 cm/2 inch pieces.
For the X.O. sauce: Sauté dried shrimp, raw ham and chili pepper in hot oil. Add the remaining ingredients to the mixture and allow to reduce to a thick sauce. Set aside for later use.
Wrap some prawns around four of the asparagus spears. Heat the oil in a wok. Sauté prawns, carrots and remaining asparagus on medium heat. Turn them carefully so that they cook evenly. Add half of the X.O. sauce and season with rice wine, sugar and salt.
Serving: Arrange fried prawns and asparagus on the plates and drizzle the plates with the remaining X.O. sauce.

GEBRATENE GARNELEN

MIT SPARGEL UND X.O. SAUCE

Für 4 Personen:

300 g frische Garnelen, geschält,
200 g grüner Spargel, blanchiert,
1 Karotte, in dünne Streifen geschnitten, blanchiert,
2 EL Sonnenblumenöl,
1 EL chinesischer Reiswein (Hua Tiao Chiew), $^1/_2$ TL Zucker, $^1/_2$ TL Salz

Für die X.O.Sauce:
2 EL getrocknete Garnelen,
2 EL fein gehackter Rohschinken (Hunan),
2 EL gehackte rote Chilischote, 2 EL Öl,
2 EL Reisessig, 200 ml Hühnerbrühe
$^1/_2$ TL Glutamat, $^1/_2$ TL Zucker, $^1/_2$ TL Salz

Die Garnelen in Salzwasser eine Minute kochen, durch ein Sieb abgießen und auf Küchenpapier abtropfen lassen. Spargelstangen in 5 cm lange Stücke schneiden.
Für die X.O. Sauce: Garnelen, Rohschinken und Chili im heißen Öl anbraten. Restliche Zutaten zugeben und zu einer dicken Sauce einkochen. Beiseite stellen.
Die Garnelen um je ein Spargelstück wickeln. Das Öl im Wok erhitzen. Die Garnelen, Karotten und den restlichen Spargel bei mittlerer Hitze braten, vorsichtig wenden. Die Hälfte der X.O. Sauce zugeben und mit Reiswein, Zucker und Salz würzen.
Zum Servieren: Die gebratenen Garnelen und den Spargel auf Teller anrichten, mit der restlichen X.O. Sauce garnieren.

DUMPLINGS WITH A TURNIP AND SHRIMP FILLING

TEIGTASCHEN MIT RÜBEN- UND GARNELEN-FÜLLUNG

Serves 4

For the filling:
3 tbsp lard,
1 tbsp crushed garlic,
1 tsp bean paste,
1 tsp sugar,
$^1/_2$ tsp MSG,
$^1/_2$ tsp salt,
60 g/2 oz small dried shrimp, soaked in water and drained,
450 g/1 lb navets or white turnips, cut into thin strips

For the dough:
300 g/11 oz rice flour,
570 ml/2$^1/_4$ cups water,
$^1/_2$ tsp salt,
70 g/2 oz sago flour,
55 ml/$^1/_4$ cup vegetable oil

Side dish: chili sauce for dipping

Für 4 Personen:

Für die Füllung:
3 EL Schweineschmalz,
1 EL zerdrückter Knoblauch,
1 TL Sojabohnenpaste,
1 TL Zucker,
$^1/_2$ TL Glutamat, $^1/_2$ TL Salz,
60 g kleine getrocknete Garnelen,
in Wasser eingeweicht und abgetropft,
450 g Mairüben (oder Navetten), in dünne Streifen geschnitten

Für den Teig:
300 g Reismehl,
570 ml Wasser,
$^1/_2$ TL Salz,
70 g Sagomehl,
55 ml Pflanzenöl

Beilage: Chilisauce zum Tunken

For the filling: Heat the lard in a large frying pan and sauté the garlic until it starts browning. Add bean paste, sugar, MSG and salt and mix well. Douse with 120 ml/$^1/_2$ cup water and stir in the drained shrimp. Bring everything to a boil and add the turnip strips. Keep stirring. Cook until the liquid is nearly evaporated and the vegetables are tender.

For the dough: Mix two spoonfuls of rice flour with a third of the water. Bring the remaining water and pheng say to a boil. Reduce heat and whisk in rice flour and water mixture, beating vigorously. Stir in remaining rice flour, beating with a wooden spoon, and work the mixture into a smooth dough. Remove pot from the burner and place the dough into a bowl. Add sago flour and oil and knead for five minutes.

Divide the dough into portions of the size of an egg. Flatten the dough pieces with your hand and place two spoonfuls of filling onto each circle. Fold dough over filling into crescent shapes and firmly press down on the edges to seal them.

Steam the dumplings on an oiled rack for 10 - 12 minutes. Serve with small dishes of chili sauce on the side for dipping.

Für die Füllung: Das Schmalz in einer Pfanne erhitzen. Knoblauch anschwitzen, bis er zu bräunen beginnt. Sojabohnenpaste, Zucker, Glutamat und Salz zugeben und gut vermischen. Mit 120 ml Wasser ablöschen, dann die abgetropften Garnelen unterrühren. Zum Kochen bringen, die Rübenstreifen zugeben, unter Rühren garen, bis die meiste Flüssigkeit verdampft und das Gemüse gar ist.

Für den Teig: Von dem Reismehl 2 Löffel mit einem Drittel des Wassers in einer Tasse anrühren. Das restliche Wasser mit Salz in einem Topf zum Kochen bringen. Hitze reduzieren, unter kräftigem Rühren mit dem Schneebesen das angerührte Reismehl zugeben. Nun mit einem Holzlöffel das restliche Reismehl unterrühren, zu einem glatten Teig verarbeiten. Vom Herd nehmen, in eine Schüssel umfüllen. Sagomehl und Öl zugeben, 5 Minuten kneten. Den Teig in knapp Ei-große Portionen teilen. Die Teigstücke flachdrücken und -ziehen, mit je 2 Löffeln Füllung belegen, und dann zu halbmondförmigen Päckchen verschließen, dabei die Ränder gut zusammendrücken. Die Teigtaschen auf einem geölten Gitter über Dampf 10 - 12 Minuten garen. Mit Chilisauce, zum Tunken in kleine Schälchen gefüllt, servieren.

CRISPY STRIPS OF BEEF WITH CARROT, CELERY AND CHILI PEPPER

KNUSPRIG GEBRATENE RINDFLEISCHSTREIFEN MIT KAROTTE, SELLERIE UND CHILI

Serves 4

400 g/14 oz beef, cut from the round,
1 carrot,
1 stalk celery,
2 green onions

100 ml/¹/₃ cup sunflower oil,
1 garlic clove, minced,
1 tbsp ginger, finely diced,
2 tbsp Chinese wine,
2 tbsp Chinese white vinegar,
salt, freshly ground white pepper,
1 level tsp MSG

1 tbsp red chili pepper, minced (according to taste)

Cut the beef, the carrot, the celery an the green onions evenly into matchstick strips.
Heat the sunflower oil in the wok. Stir-fry the beef strips until crispy. Remove meat from the wok and pour out excess oil. Stir-fry garlic and ginger. Return beef to the pan and add wine, vinegar, salt, pepper and MSG and stir until the liquid has evaporated. Add the carrot, celery and green onion strips and minced chili and continue to stir-fry for another minute. Arrange on pre-warmed plates and garnish according to taste. Serve.

Für 4 Personen:

400 g Rindfleisch (aus der Hüfte),
1 Karotte,
1 Selleriestange,
2 Frühlingszwiebeln

100 ml Sonnenblumenöl,
1 Knoblauchzehe, fein gehackt,
1 EL fein gehackter Ingwer,
2 EL chinesischer Wein,
1 EL chinesischer weißer Essig,
Salz, weißer Pfeffer aus der Mühle,
1 gestrichener TL Glutamat

1 EL gehackte rote Chili (oder Menge nach Belieben)

Das Rindfleisch, die Karotte, den Sellerie und die Frühlingszwiebeln in gleichmäßige streichholzgroße Streifen schneiden.
Das Sonnenblumenöl im Wok erhitzen. Die Rindfleischstreifen unter Rühren knusprig braten. Überschüssiges Öl abgießen, das Fleisch aus dem Wok nehmen, dann den Knoblauch und Ingwer anbraten. Das Rindfleisch mit dem Wein, Essig, Salz, Pfeffer und Glutamat zugeben und unter Rühren bei mittlerer Hitze braten, bis alle Flüssigkeit verdunstet ist. Die Karotten-, Sellerie- und Frühlingszwiebelstreifen und die gehackte Chili unterrühren und eine Minute mitbraten. Auf vorgewärmte Teller anrichten, nach Belieben garnieren.

Serves 4

1 duck, ready-to-cook

For the marinade:
120 ml/¹/₂ cup Chinese rosé wine (mei kuei lu chiew),
120 ml/¹/₂ cup Chinese yellow wine (shao hsing hua tiao chiew),
2 tbsp rice vinegar, 1 tbsp black peppercorns, crushed,
2 tsp salt, 2 star anise, crushed

3 tbsp maltose, 2 tsp Chinese jasmine tea leaves, 1 tsp rice, oil for deep-frying

For the marinade, combine all ingredients and mix well. Brush the duck, inside and outside. Place it in a shallow pan and pour the remaining marinade over it. Cover and allow to rest for 6 - 8 hours. Turn occasionally.
Combine maltose and the same amount of water in a small pot and cook for three minutes, until syrupy. Remove the duck from the marinade and brush it with the hot syrup. Then hang it up in a cool place to dry, about three hours. Pour the remaining marinade into a small saucepan and reduce it by half. Check for seasonings, pour it into a small jar and place in the refrigerator.
Heat the tea leaves and rice kernels in the dry wok on medium heat, until the tea leaves release their fragrance. Place the duck on a rack over the smoke, cover and smoke for five minutes. Turn duck and smoke for another five minutes. Remove wok from heat, discard tea rests and fill the wok with water to come up about 3 cm/1¹/₂ inches. Bring water to a boil. Place the duck back on the rack and steam, covered, for about one hour. Turn occasionally. Heat the deep-frying oil in the cleaned wok, and deep-fry the duck until brown and crispy.
Serving: Cut duck breast into slices and hack the remaining duck into serving pieces. Arrange on plates. Serve marinade in small bowls on the side for dipping.

CRISPY-FRIED
TEA-SMOKED DUCK

KNUSPRIG FRITTIERTE
TEE GERÄUCHERTE ENTE

Für 4 Personen:

1 Ente, küchenfertig

Für die Marinade:
120 ml chinesischer Rosé Reiswein (Mei Kuei Lu Chiew),
120 ml chinesischer gelber Reiswein (Shao Hsing Hua Tiao Chiew),
2 EL Reisessig, 1 EL schwarze Pfefferkörner, grob zerdrückt,
2 TL Salz, 2 Sternanis, zerdrückt

3 EL Maltose, 2 TL chinesische Jasmin-Teeblätter, 1 EL Reiskörner, Öl zum Frittieren

Alle Zutaten für die Marinade verrühren. Die Ente innen und außen damit bestreichen, in ein flaches Gefäß legen, mit der restlichen Marinade übergießen. Zugedeckt 6 - 8 Stunden marinieren, von Zeit zu Zeit wenden.
Die Maltose mit der gleichen Menge Wasser in einem kleinen Topf erhitzen und zwei Minuten zu Sirup kochen. Die Ente aus der Marinade nehmen, mit dem heißen Sirup bepinseln und an einem kühlen Ort während 3 Stunden zum Trocknen aufhängen. Die restliche Marinade in einem Topf erhitzen und um die Hälfte einkochen, abschmecken, im Kühlschrank aufbewahren.
Im Wok die Teeblätter mit dem Reis bei mittlerer Hitze erhitzen, bis der Tee zu duften anfängt. Die Ente auf ein Gitter über den Rauch legen und 5 Minuten bei aufgelegtem Deckel räuchern. Dann die Ente wenden und weitere 5 Minuten räuchern. Den Wok reinigen, ca. 3 cm hoch mit Wasser füllen und zum Kochen bringen. Die Ente wiederum auf das Gitter legen und eine Stunde über Dampf garen, von Zeit zu Zeit wenden. Zum Schluss das Frittieröl erhitzen und die Ente knusprig braun backen. Zum Servieren: Die knusprig gebackene Ente in Stücke teilen, die Brust in Scheiben schneiden und auf Teller anrichten. Die kalte Marinadensauce in einem separaten Schüsselchen dazu servieren.

STEAMED DUMPLINGS STUFFED WITH PORK

GEFÜLLTE DAMPF-KLÖSSE MIT SCHWEINEFLEISCH

Serves 4 - 6

For the dough:
600 g/1¹/₃ lb flour,
200 g/7 oz sugar,
¹/₂ tsp baking powder,
100 ml/¹/₃ cup vegetable oil,
200 ml/²/₃ cup water

For the filling:
500 g/1 lb roast pork, cut into small cubes,
2 tbsp oyster sauce,
20 g/³/₄ oz sugar,
20 g/³/₄ oz flour,
50 ml/¹/₄ cup water

For the dough: Combine the flour, sugar, baking powder, vegetable oil and water in a bowl and work the mixture into a smooth dough. Knead well, cover with a moist cloth and allow to rest for an hour.
For the filling: Combine all ingredients in a small bowl and allow to marinate for half an hour.
Shape the dough into little balls, pinch a hole into each ball and stuff it with a little filling. Close hole with dough. Steam the dumplings for ten to twelve minutes. Serve.

Für 4 - 6 Personen:

Für den Teig:
600 g Mehl,
200 Zucker,
¹/₂ TL Backpulver,
100 ml Pflanzenöl,
200 ml Wasser

Für die Füllung:
500 g fertig gebratener Schweinebraten,
in kleine Würfel geschnitten,
2 EL Austernsauce,
20 g Zucker, 20 g Mehl,
50 ml Wasser

Für den Teig: Das Mehl mit Zucker, Backpulver, Öl und Wasser in einer Schüssel zu einem Teig verarbeiten. Gut kneten, mit einem feuchten Tuch zugedeckt eine Stunde ruhen lassen.
Für die Füllung: Alle Zutaten in einer Schüssel vermischen, eine halbe Stunde durchziehen lassen.
Aus dem Teig kleine Kugeln formen, eine Vertiefung hineindrücken, mit Füllung belegen und den Teig oben verschließen. Die Klöße über Dampf zehn bis zwölf Minuten garen, heiß servieren.

GRILLED CODFISH

KABELJAU VOM GRILL

4 filets of cod, 150 g/5 oz each,
4 tbsp light soy sauce,
3 tbsp dark soy sauce,
1 tbsp honey

250 g/¹/₂ lb green beans, blanched,
250 g/¹/₂ lb Chinese broccoli, blanched,
2 tbsp butter

Heat the soy sauces and honey in a small pot until the honey is completely dissolved. Set aside to cool. Brush the fish pieces with the marinade and allow to rest in the refrigerator for half an hour. Sauté the vegetables in butter until tender. Keep warm.
Preheat the oven to 220° C/430° F. Broil the marinated fish filets for 6 - 8 minutes, depending on their thickness.
Serving: Arrange vegetables on pre-warmed plates. Place broiled cod filets on top and serve immediately.

Für 4 Personen:

4 Kabeljaufilets à 150 g,
4 EL helle Sojasauce,
3 EL dunkle Sojasauce,
1 EL Honig

250 g grüne Bohnen, blanchiert,
250 g chinesischer Broccoli, blanchiert,
2 EL Butter

Beide Sojasaucen mit dem Honig in einem kleinen Topf erwärmen, bis sich der Honig aufgelöst hat. Erkalten lassen. Die Fischstücke mit der Marinade bestreichen und im Kühlschrank zugedeckt eine halbe Stunde marinieren. Die beiden Gemüse in der Butter bei kleiner Hitze fertig braten, warm halten.
Den Ofen auf 220° C vorheizen. Die marinierten Fischfilets unter dem Grill 6 - 8 Minuten braten.
Zum Anrichten: Das Gemüse auf vorgewärmte Teller anrichten. Die gebratenen Kabeljaufilets darüber legen und servieren.

Serves 4

1 kg/2 lbs spareribs, cut into 10 cm/4 inch pieces,
100 ml/ ¹/₃ cup sunflower oil,
3 tbsp grated ginger,
2 green onions, chopped,
3 tbsp rice wine,
600 ml/2¹/₃ cups chicken stock,
8 dried red dates, 1 level tsp MSG,
3 tbsp light soy sauce, ¹/₂ tsp dark soy sauce,
¹/₂ tsp ground white pepper,
2 tbsp sugar, 3 star anise, 3 cloves,
a small piece of cinnamon stick,
a pinch of red food coloring,
4 small heads bok choy (Chinese cabbage)

SPARERIBS WUXI-STYLE

SPARERIBS NACH WUXI-ART

Deep-fry spareribs in hot oil for 3 - 4 minutes. Remove ribs with a skimmer and discard oil, leaving just a little to coat the pan. Stir-fry the ginger and green onions. Douse with rice wine and stock and stir in all remaining ingredients, including food coloring. Mix well and allow to simmer for 1¹/₂ hours on low heat. Blanch the bok choy in salted water for 3 minutes. Drain in a colander.
Serving: Arrange spareribs on plates. Correct seasonings of the sauce and pour it over the ribs. Garnish with bok choy and serve.

Für 4 Personen:

1 kg Spareribs (Schweinerippchen),
in ca. 10 cm lange Stücke geschnitten,
100 ml Sonnenblumenöl,
3 EL geriebener Ingwer,
2 Frühlingszwiebeln, gehackt, 3 EL Reiswein,
600 ml Hühnerbrühe,
8 getrocknete rote Datteln,
1 gestrichener TL Glutamat,
3 EL helle Sojasauce, ¹/₂ TL dunkle Sojasauce,
¹/₂ TL fein gemahlener weißer Pfeffer,
2 EL Zucker, 3 Sternanis, 3 Gewürznelken,
1 kleines Stück Zimtstange,
1 Msp rote Lebensmittelfarbe,
4 kleine Pak-Choi Köpfe (Chinesischer Senfkohl)

Die Spareribs im heißen Öl von allen Seiten etwa 3 - 4 Minuten braten. Herausnehmen, das Öl bis auf einen kleinen Rest abgießen. Ingwer und Frühlingszwiebeln im Restöl anbraten. Mit Reiswein und Brühe aufgießen, alle anderen Zutaten inklusive der roten Farbe unterrühren. Gut rühren, bei kleiner Hitze ohne Deckel ca. 1¹/₂ Stunden köcheln. Pak-Choi drei Minuten in Salzwasser kochen. Durch ein Sieb abgießen. Zum Servieren: Spareribs auf Teller anrichten. Die Sauce abschmecken und über das Fleisch gießen. Mit Pak-Choi garniert servieren.

PANCAKES WITH A COCONUT AND BANANA SAUCE
PFANNKUCHEN MIT KOKOS-BANANENSAUCE

Serves 4

For the coconut-banana sauce:
500 ml/2 cups coconut milk,
200 g/7 oz brown sugar, ¼ tsp salt,
2 pandan leaves (leaves of screwpine), finely diced,
wrapped into cheesecloth and firmly tied,
1 banana

For the pancakes:
250 g/½ lb rice flour,
150 g/5 oz grated coconut,
½ tsp salt,
600 ml/2⅓ cup coconut milk,
clarified butter

For the sauce: Simmer coconut milk, sugar, salt and the cheesecloth with pandan leaves, stirring constantly until the sauce has thickened. Peel and finely dice the banana and add it to the sauce. Simmer for another minute. Discard cheesecloth.

For the pancakes: Combine rice flour, grated coconut, salt and coconut milk and mix until you have a thick batter. Beat the batter with a wire whip for about ten minutes, until light and fluffy. Brush a non-stick pan with clarified butter and heat until the pan is very hot. Ladle in a portion of batter and fry until golden brown, then turn the pancake over and brown it on the other side. Repeat the procedure until all the batter is used up. Place pancakes in an oven-proof dish as they are done and keep them warm in the oven.

Serving: Arrange pancakes on plates, drizzle some sauce on top and around them and serve warm.

Note: In Asia, these pancakes are fried in especially designed, shallow woks which have flat depressions for the pancake batter and a tightly fitting lid so that the pancakes can brown on both sides at the same time.

Für 4 Personen:

Für die Kokos-Bananensauce:
500 ml Kokosmilch,
200 g brauner Zucker, ¼ TL Salz,
2 Pandanusblätter, fein gehackt, in ein Leinensäckchen
gebunden (Blätter vom Schraubenbaum, Screwpine),
1 Banane

Für die Pfannkuchen:
250 g Reismehl,
150 g geriebene Kokosnuss,
½ TL Salz,
600 ml Kokosmilch,
geklärte Butter

Für die Sauce: Die Kokosmilch mit dem Zucker, Salz und dem Säckchen unter ständigem Rühren zu dickflüssiger Konsistenz kochen. Die Banane schälen, fein würfeln und eine Minute mitkochen. Das Leinensäckchen entfernen.

Für die Pfannkuchen: Reismehl mit dem geriebenen Kokosfleisch, Salz und Kokosmilch zu einem dickflüssigen Teig verrühren. Mit einem Schneebesen ca. 10 Minuten schlagen, bis er weich ist und Blasen wirft. Eine beschichtete Pfanne mit etwas geklärter Butter auspinseln und stark erhitzen. Von dem Teig eine Portion eingießen, goldbraun braten, umdrehen, die zweite Seite ebenfalls leicht bräunen. Nach und nach alle Pfannkuchen backen, bis der ganze Teig verbraucht ist. Die fertigen Pfannkuchen in einer feuerfesten Form im Ofen warm halten. Zum Servieren: Die Pfannkuchen auf Teller verteilen, mit der Sauce um- und übergießen und warm servieren.

Anmerkung: In Asien wird für diese Pfannkuchen ein spezieller flacher Wok mit Vertiefungen verwendet, in die der Teig gefüllt wird. Der Deckel ist eine Art zweite Pfanne, so können die Pfannkuchen gleichzeitig von beiden Seiten gebacken werden.

STUFFED RICE FLOUR CAKES

Serves 4 - 6

For the filling:
300 g/11 oz mung beans, soaked overnight,
50 ml/ ¹/₄ cup water, 2 pandan leaves (leaves of screwpine),
cut into strips, 180 g/6 ¹/₂ oz sugar

300 g/11 oz glutinous rice flour, 90 g/3 oz sugar,
60 ml/ ¹/₄ cup corn oil, 180 ml/ ³/₄ cup boiling water,
a little red and yellow food coloring each

For the filling: Drain the beans in a sieve and steam for forty-five minutes. Mash with a potato ricer until you have a purée. Combine water, sugar and pandan leaves in a pot and simmer until syrupy. Add bean purée and mix well. Simmer, stirring constantly, until most of the liquid is evaporated and you have a dry paste. Allow to cool and remove pandan leaves.
Sieve the rice flour into a large bowl. Dust the insides of round half-sphere molds with a little rice flour. Combine sugar and flour, make a shallow depression in the middle and add the hot water, corn oil and food coloring. Work into smooth dough and knead until soft and shiny. Shape the dough into golf ball-sized spheres and place them into the flour-dusted molds. Pinch a small hole into the center of each ball and fill it with mung bean filling. Close the hole with dough. Carefully remove balls from the molds and place them onto an oiled banana leaf (or baking paper). Brush them with a little oil and steam them for twenty minutes. Allow to cool on a grid. Serve.

LAYER CAKE

Serves 8

100 g/3 ¹/₂ oz white flour, ¹/₂ tsp cinnamon, ¹/₂ tsp cumin, ground,
300 g/11 oz butter, at room temperature,
200 g/7 oz margarine, at room temperature,
3 tbsp sweetened condensed milk,
30 egg yolks, ¹/₂ tsp vanilla extract,
350 g/12 ¹/₂ oz confectioners' sugar,
butter for brushing, flour for dusting the baking dish

Sieve flour, cinnamon and cumin into a bowl. Combine butter, margarine and condensed milk in a bowl and whisk with a wire whip until smooth. Set aside.
Whisk egg yolks, vanilla extract and confectioners' sugar until light and fluffy. Incorporate butter mixture and mix well. Add flour, a little at a time, and mix well.
Line a 22 x 22 cm/8 x 8 inch baking dish with baking paper, brush the paper with butter and dust it with flour. Preheat the oven to 160° C/325° F, top heat only. Spoon three tablespoons of batter into the baking dish and spread them out as thinly and evenly as possible. Bake in the oven until golden brown. Remove baking dish from the oven and smooth out the surface of the cake with the back of a spoon, pressing down firmly. Spoon another layer of batter on top, bake and repeat the procedure until all the batter has been used up. Allow the cake to cool and carefully unmold it onto a board. Cut it into pieces and serve.

GEFÜLLTES REISMEHL-DAMPFGEBÄCK

Für 4 - 6 Personen:

Für die Füllung:
300 g Mungbohnen, über Nacht in Wasser eingeweicht,
50 ml Wasser, 2 Pandanusblätter, in Streifen geschnitten (Blätter des Schraubenbaumes, Screwpine), 180 g Zucker

300 g Klebreismehl, 90 g Zucker,
60 ml Maiskeimöl, 180 ml kochendes Wasser,
etwas rote und gelbe Lebensmittelfarbe

Für die Füllung: Bohnen in einem Sieb abgießen und über Dampf 45 Minuten garen. Mit dem Kartoffelstampfer in einer Schüssel zu Brei verstampfen. Wasser mit Zucker und Pandanusblättern in einem Topf zu Sirup kochen. Den Bohnenbrei zugeben, gut vermischen. Unter Rühren köcheln, bis die meiste Flüssigkeit verdampft und der Brei trocken ist. Erkalten lassen, die Pandanusblätter entfernen. Das Reismehl in eine Schüssel sieben. Die Innenseiten von runden Halbschalenformen mit etwas Reismehl bestäuben. Den Zucker zum Mehl geben, in die Mitte eine Vertiefung drücken, das Maiskeimöl, das heiße Wasser und die Lebensmittelfarbe hineingießen. Zu einem Teig verarbeiten und kneten, bis der Teig glatt und glänzend ist. Golfballgroße Portionen zu Kugeln formen, diese in die Formen legen, in der Mitte eine Vertiefung hineindrücken und mit Mungbohnenbrei füllen. Den Teig verschließen, vorsichtig aus den Formen lösen, auf ein geöltes Bananenblatt (oder Backpapier) legen, mit etwas Öl bepinseln, über Dampf 20 Minuten garen. Auf einem Gitter erkalten lassen.

SCHICHTKUCHEN

Für 8 Personen:

100 g Weißmehl, ¹/₂ TL Zimt, ¹/₂ TL Kreuzkümmelpulver,
300 g Butter, zimmerwarm,
200 g Margarine, zimmerwarm,
3 EL süße Kondensmilch,
30 Eigelb, 350 g Puderzucker,
¹/₂ TL Vanillezucker,
Butter zum Bepinseln, Mehl für die Form

Mehl und Gewürze in eine Schüssel sieben. Die Butter mit der Margarine und der Kondensmilch mit dem Schneebesen glattrühren, beiseite stellen.
Die Eigelb mit dem Puderzucker und Vanillezucker schaumig schlagen. Die Buttermischung unterrühren, gut vermischen. Nach und nach das Mehl zugeben und einrühren.
Eine Backform von 22 x 22 cm Backtrennpapier auslegen, dieses mit Butter bepinseln und mit Mehl bestäuben.
Den Ofen auf 160° C nur mit Oberhitze vorheizen. Von dem Teig drei Esslöffel voll in die Backform geben, dünn ausstreichen und im Ofen goldbraun backen. Die Backform aus dem Ofen nehmen, den Kuchen mit einem Löffelrücken plattdrücken. Nun eine weitere Lage Teig darüberstreichen, backen und diesen Vorgang wiederholen, bis der ganze Teig aufgebraucht ist. Den Kuchen auskühlen lassen. Vorsichtig auf ein Brett stürzen, in Stücke schneiden und servieren.

LAYERED SAGO PUDDING

Serves 4

50 g/1¹/₂ oz sago flour, 250 ml/1 cup coconut milk, 250 g/1 lb sugar

200 g/7 oz sago flour, 100 g/3¹/₂ oz rice flour,
¹/₂ tsp vanilla extract, ¹/₂ tsp salt, 550 ml/2 cups coconut milk

a little oil for the baking dish

Mix the sago flour with a little coconut milk. Bring the remaining coconut milk and sugar to a boil. Mix in the sago-coconut milk mixture and allow to cool.

Combine the 200 g/7 oz sago flour with the rice flour, vanilla extract and salt. Drizzle in the 550 ml/2 cups coconut milk and work into a smooth batter. Divide the batter into three equal parts and color one third with red, another third with green food coloring.

Preheat the oven to 180° C/350° F. Brush an oven-proof baking dish with oil. Pour in a thin 3 mm/¹/₁₀ inch layer of white batter and smooth out the top. Steam in a steamer oven for five minutes until set. (Alternatively, using a conventional oven, place a second dish with boiling water below the dish with the batter.) Repeat the procedure with alternate layers of differently colored batter. Bake each layer in the oven for five minutes. When all the batter is used up, finish baking the pudding in a 150° C/300° F oven for 15 - 25 minutes until firm. Remove from oven and allow to cool. Refrigerate pudding until cool before serving. Unmold onto a board and cut it into slices with a sharp knife. Serve.

GESCHICHTETER SAGOPUDDING

Für 4 Personen:

50 g Sagomehl, 250 ml Kokosmilch, 250 g Zucker

200 g Sagomehl, 100 g Reismehl,
¹/₂ TL Vanillezucker, ¹/₂ TL Salz, 550 ml Kokosmilch

etwas Öl für die Form

Das Sago mit etwas Kokosmilch anrühren. Die restliche Kokosmilch mit dem Zucker zum Kochen bringen, das angerührte Sago mit dem Schneebesen unterrühren, erkalten lassen.

Die 200 g Sagomehl mit dem Reismehl, Vanillezucker und Salz vermischen. Den gekochten Sagoteig unterrühren, gut vermischen. Nach und nach die 550 ml Kokosmilch unterrühren und zu einem glatten Teig verarbeiten. Den Teig in drei Teile teilen, ein Drittel mit roter, ein Drittel mit grüner Lebensmittelfarbe einfärben.

Den Backofen auf 180° C vorheizen. Eine feuerfeste Form mit Öl auspinseln. Vom weißen Teig eine 3 mm hohe Lage eingießen und glatt streichen. Im Ofen (möglichst Dampfofen, Steamer, ansonsten unterhalb der Puddingform eine zweite Form mit kochendem Wasser platzieren) 5 Minuten fest werden lassen. Nun die verschiedenfarbigen Teige abwechselnd nach und nach in der gleichen Weise zugeben und jeweils im Ofen 5 Minuten backen. Wenn aller Teig aufgebraucht ist, den Pudding bei 150° C 15 - 25 Minuten fertig backen. Aus dem Ofen nehmen, auskühlen lassen. Den Pudding vor dem Servieren im Kühlschraunk durchkühlen. Auf ein Brett stürzen, mit einem scharfen Messer in Schnitten schneiden.

THAI CUISINE

Rice plays the lead role in Thai cuisine. Rice, white and unseasoned (the dishes are spicy enough by themselves) is the basis, all other dishes are merely considered seasoning agents. Thus, the systematic menu plans of Western cuisines, featuring first and main courses and then dessert, a proscribed sequence of dishes, cannot be found in Thai cuisine. Everything is brought to the table at once, and everything ought to have been selected and balanced with great care by the guest, which involves choosing a little bit of the salty and savory, a bit of the spicy and bitter and of the sour and sweet. This may mean sauces or dips, curries or stir-fry dishes. The people sitting around the table may then help themselves to one thing or another, according to their pre- ference. The food is eaten with a fork (left) and spoon (right), without a knife, whose function is taken over by the fork. Thais like it hot, and an ample portion of rice ought to be on the table, or if the palate is burning, grated coconut to cool it down. Soups play an important role in the meal and are one of the most delicate parts of Thai cuisine. Tom-Yam soups with chicken or crab are hot (very hot) and sour and seasoned with lemongrass, lime leaves, chili pepper and tamarind. Thai chefs love to mix a good number of spices, dried and fresh, grinding the mixture into a paste with the help of a mortar - the basic seasoning for curries. As a rule, curries are cooked in coconut milk, with fresh turmeric imparting a yellow color. In the south, the food is very hot and spicy, with fish naturally being one of the mainstays. Northern dishes are a bit less liberally seasoned and a lot less hot. Here, far away from the coast, favorite ingre- dients are pork, beef and poultry and a great variety of vegetables.

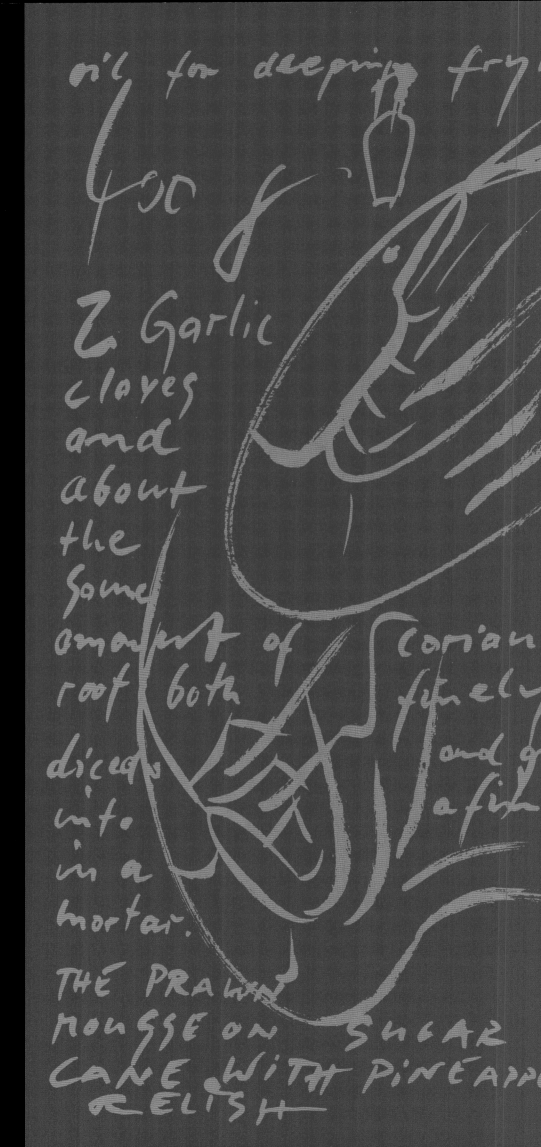

FOR THE PINEAPPLE RELISH
2 tbsp sugar 200g pineapple, cut
into 1/2 cm chilli peppers

24 Tiger Prawns, shelled

Point mint
Pieces of Sugar Cane
1 cup freshly grated breadcrumbs

EGG

...te

...sp salt

2 tsp Sugar

REIS

spielt die Hauptrolle in der Thai-
Küche. Reis, weiß und ungewürzt
(die Gerichte sind schon würzig
genug), ist die Basis. Alle anderen
Speisen sind geschmackliche
Zuträger. So ist auch die westlicher
Küche eigene Systematik von Vor-,
Haupt- und Nachspeisen, eine

geregelte Speisenfolge also, nicht
zu erkennen. Alles kommt zusammen auf den Tisch, und alles sollte
irgendwie ausgewogen und balan-
ciert zusammengestellt sein. Also
etwas vom Salzig-Würzigen, ein
wenig vom Scharfen und Bitteren,
vom Sauren und vom Süßen.
Saucen und Dips können dies sein,
Curries oder im Wok Gerührtes.
Die ganze Tischgesellschaft greift
in der Folge mal in dieses, mal
in jenes Töpfchen. Gegessen wird
mit Gabel (links) und Löffel (rechts).
Messer gibt es keines, dessen
Funktion übernimmt die Gabel.
Thais lieben es scharf, und so
sollte man ausreichend mit Reis
ergänzen, oder wenn der Gaumen
brennt, mit Kokosflocken lindern.
Suppen sind nicht wegzudenken,
und einer der delikatesten Bestandteile thailändischer Küche.

Tom-Yam-Suppen mit
Geflügel- oder Krabben-
einlage sind sauer-
scharf (sehr scharf)
abgeschmeckt mit Zitro-
nengras, Limettenblät-
tern, Chilischoten und
Tamarinde. Überhaupt
mischen Thais gern viele
Gewürze, frische wie
getrocknete, mörsern
die Mixtur und fertigen
eine Paste daraus – die
Würzbasis der Curries.
Diese werden in der
Regel mit Kokosmilch

gekocht, frische Kurku-
ma-Wurzel gibt ihnen
gelbe Farbe. Im Süden
Thailands kocht man
sehr scharf und kräftig
gewürzt. Fisch ist hier
der Hauptbestandteil
der Gerichte. Nördliche
Speisen nehmen sich
weitaus milder aus und
sind deutlich weniger
scharf. Fernab vom
Meer sind dann auch
die Favoriten Schwein,
Rindfleisch und Geflügel
– neben allerlei Gemüse.

arket women in straw hats in their
small sampans are poking their way through the
klongs of the floating market. About one hundred
kilometers southwest of Bangkok, the waters of
narrow channels bustle with life. Small vendors have
paddled in their goods. The floating market makes an
original and unspoilt impression despite a number of
tourists trying to ban such unusual happenings
(for them!) onto cameras or chips. Yet, these small
everyday transactions of local farmers and fishermen
offering and selling their goods to housewives and
urban suppliers have been a matter of course here
for generations: coconuts and green mangoes, freshly
cut banana stalks lie heavily and yellow in little boats.
Fruit, fish or meat – the selection is quite impressive.
A young Thai woman has fastened her boat to the
pier, working with flying hands, a cooking shovel
and a wok. About her, her boat is cluttered with
plastic containers and dishes from which she takes
what is needed for the dish in the making.
Whatever the customer´s fancy is stir-fried in just a
few minutes, sprinkled with a little bit of sauce and
shoved into a bag, which is then exchanged for a
few of the customer´s baht: fast food, Thai version.

The Floating Market of Damnoen Saduak - Thailand

The juice obtained from the large blossoms of the coconut palm is reduced to a syrup-like paste and used for sweetening dishes and desserts.

Der aus den Blüten der Kokospalme gewonnene Saft wird zu einer Karamell-ähnlichen Paste eingekocht, die zum Süssen von Gerichten und Süssspeisen dient.

Marktfrauen mit Strohhüten stochern in kleinen Sampans durch die Klongs des Schwimmenden Marktes. Rund einhundert Kilometer südwestlich von Bangkok herrscht reges Treiben auf dem Wasser enger Kanäle, auf denen die Kleinhändler ihre Ware herbeigepaddelt haben. Fast noch naturbelassen und original ist der Wassermarkt, wären da nicht auch die Touristen, die mit gezückter Kamera das ungewohnte Geschehen auf Film oder Chip bannen wollen. Doch im Wesentlichen spielt sich hier nach wie vor wie seit Generationen das alltägliche Handelsgeschäft umliegender Bauern und Fischer ab, die ihre Ware Hausfrauen und städtischen Einkäufern anbieten: Kokosnuss und grüne Mango, frisch geschlagene Bananenstauden liegen gelb und schwer im Kahn. Früchte, Fisch oder Fleisch – die Auswahl ist beeindruckend. Und am Steg hat eine junge Thai festgemacht, hantiert mit flinker Hand, Kochschaufel und Wok. Ringsum sie zwängen sich im Boot die Töpfchen und Plastikbehälter, aus denen sie fischt, was fürs gewünschte Gericht gerade vonnöten ist. In nur wenigen Minuten ist eine Mahlzeit fertiggerührt, ein Schuss Sauce darüber, und ab in den Beutel, der gegen nur wenige Baht vom Kunden in Empfang genommen wird. Fast Food auf Thai.

CHOCOLATE
xxxxxx LAKSI

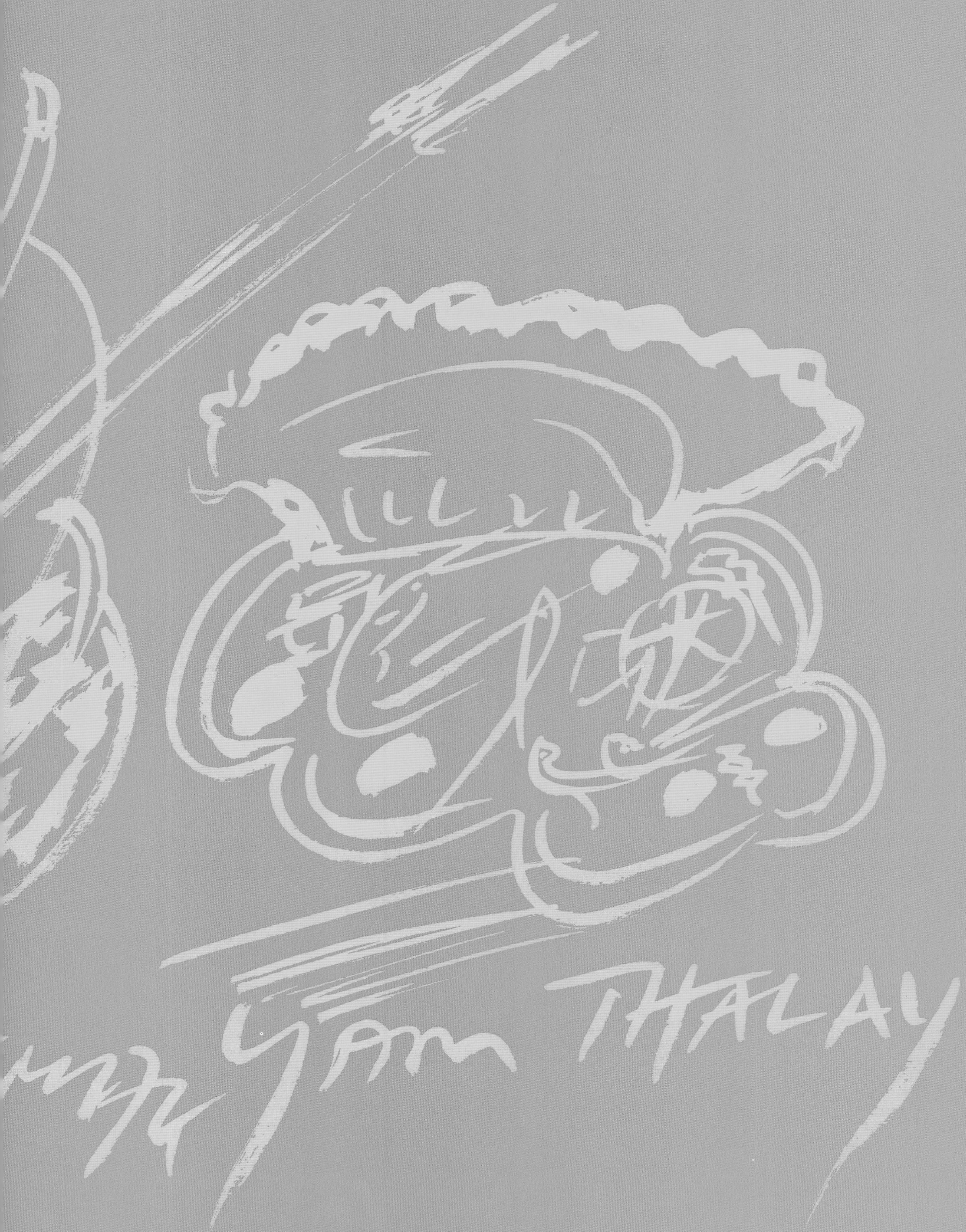
Yam THALAY

Human beings are curious by nature, a fact that has made for many a bad surprise in the history of mankind, but has also brought on some progress – even if it was not always in a very elegant way. Since homo culinarius may well be a modern mutation of homo sapiens, with his central controls seated on the palate rather than in the brain, his curiosity seems to be unbroken, too, and, in the truest sense of the word, insatiable when it comes to discovering new areas. And this is what has led him away from hearth and home into the world to discover new things, with his focus not so much on the contemplation of many an artfully carved temple frieze as on the contents of foreign pots and pans. A little bit of adventure and one or the other surprise are included.

Bangkok is exotic, baffling even, Bangkok is full of surprises. What are Swabian spätzle doing in a Chinese restaurant at a Thai hotel? Or even pizza baked in a wood-fired oven? We'll come back to that later. If it must be Bangkok, then it should first be local, i.e. Thai food, and thus we will leave Chinese or Japanese, fusion, East-meets-West food etc. aside and turn to the local cooking customs with unmitigated curiosity and not knowing what to expect. Below our feet, the waters of the Phrao Chayo make gurgling noises around the stilts which carry the wooden planks of a pavilion. Resembling a treasure chest made from teak, the "Salathip" with its pointy gables has pushed its way out of the garden of the Shangri-La hotel onto the river. The most popular seats in the Thai restaurant are doubtlessly among the storm lanterns on the spacious outdoor terrace, close to the edge near the water. The fork on the left, the

SHANGRI-LA HOTEL

spoon in the right hand – that's all of the instruments on the table. There are no chopsticks – they are only used for Chinese food. No knife, either. The fork has gladly taken over its tasks, dividing bigger pieces, which are generally stewed until tender, and pushing them onto the spoon, which will then happily transport them to the mouth. The menu only serves to contribute to the general confusion, since the English translations of the dishes listed, even if they do not appear in the foreign Thai curlicue script, do not impart much information in their cryptic unfamiliarity. Western guests are therefore apt to look rather confusedly at the menu, preferring to close it after a while only to utter any random number when ordering. Whatever will come to the table will be a surprise anyway. Glancing around helplessly, it does not take long for a helpful soul to appear.

Yet, ordering does provide some information after all. The systematics of Western cuisine – first course, main course and dessert that is –, a proscribed sequence of dishes, does not seem to apply here. It simply does not exist. Everything comes to the table at once, and everything ought to be chosen and composed with great care and a fine sense of balance. The meal ought to include something salty and savory, something sour and something sweet, with everyone at the table helping himself from one or the other, according to personal preference. As a rule, you are served your own soup – quite an integral part of Thai cuisine. Thus, in between sampling various dishes, you may always return to a sip of hot broth containing meat or fish, depending on your wishes. For the uninitiated, the soup may also constitute a bit of an anchor if, in careless greed, he has chanced on one of the hotter morsels. Heat, spice, that is, is fundamental to Thai cuisine. Thai people like it hot, and such heat may impressively blunt the taste buds beyond quick recovery. Shirt and forehead bathed in sweat indicate acute pain to one's fellow sufferers. In such a situation, never resort to your cold drink. Taking a draft of Singha beer may be quite alluring, of course, but is instantly punished. It only helps to spread the fiery sensations to the rest of your mouth and palate. For such cases of emergency, it is better to take white, unseasoned rice or grated coconut, both of which are always at the table. Having thus mastered the first obstacles, with the palate having recovered consciousness, you may proceed to further pleasures.

The "Salathip" is governed by a female hand – a lady chef. There are only four female chefs in a sous-chef position in Bangkok. Women in the kitchen or as entrepreneurs with small eateries are no rarity, but gradually and ever so slowly, women have also started conquering the male-dominated top positions in renowned restaurants in conservative Thailand (and Asia). The charming chef Gesinee Chakkrot cooked her way to the top with persistence and patience, and can now boast of quite a bit of expertise. She stood behind the stoves of different Shangri-La hotels all across Asia, and even tried to charm Japanese eaters in Tokyo with the high art of Thai cooking. Gesinee learned about good food on the mother's breast, so-to-speak. The family owned a restaurant and the ladies of the house, mother and grandmother, knew how to pique the little girl's interest in cooking quite early. Nevertheless, she first made her way through school and took her bachelor's degree in quite another subject, book-keeping that is. Her family finally emigrated to the States and opened two small and very popular Thai restaurants there. Gesinee stayed in her homeland, however, and, abandoning book-keeping altogether, returned to the stove in her own small restaurant. From then on, cooking was her great love, and her guests loved her for her delicious curries. With a twinkle in her eye, she then relates something private: love in the private sector was also a piece of luck – the new husband brought a highly brilliant mother-in-law into the marriage, with a profound knowledge of Thai cuisine in all its various facets, and the forty-two-year-old chef is now able to tap this rich source to offer her guests of the "Salathip" a sophisticated version of Thai cooking: Royal Thai Cuisine.

THIS CUISINE IS NEITHER BASED ON STREET EATERY COOKING (WHICH IS INCREASINGLY FASHIONABLE) NOR TRENDY WITH LOANS FROM WESTERN CUISINES: IT IS DEEPLY CLASSICAL.

And she loves playing with decorations, as is most stunningly revealed in the extravagant vegetable carvings that adorn almost every plate. The dishes on the "Salathip" menu also feature a selection of highlights from different regions of the country. According to the chef, cooking from the south is hot, very hot and heavily spiced. Most dishes include fish, with fresh turmeric root imparting its yellow color to almost all curries. Thais just love to mix a variety of spices together, fresh and dried ones, grind the mixture into a paste in a mortar – and there you have the basis for any curry. Gesinee always makes the paste herself instead of relying on pre-made versions. Northern dishes are a bit milder with fewer spices. Far away from the seaside, favorite ingredients are pork, beef and poultry next to all sorts of vegetables. The curries – stews made from meat, fish, poultry and vegetables – are generally cooked with coconut milk. Our chef herself likes to omit it, though, considering it too fatty, too rich and apt to cover up fine nuances of seasoning. Instead, she concentrates on vegetables and endeavors to highlight the fragrance of many a fine herb. Lemongrass and chili pepper are omnipresent, not least in the many (mostly hot) versions of Tom Yam soup, a culinary jewel of Thai cuisine. For the benefit of the numerous Western customers, the cuisine in the Shangri-La is a bit less hot than the cooking elsewhere, however. Yet, everything is relative, and some people are even tempted to sort out some of the hellishly hot chili pepper strips with the popular beef salad (Yam Nüa). Much more could be said, but a personal sampling is always better than any theory. Visitors are advised to add their own experiences to this rich repertoire and discover the treasures of this cuisine by themselves. At Gesinee Chakkrot's at the upscale "Salathip" or in the eateries on Bangkok's streets.

And yet, this is by no means all. Out here, by the river, you could almost forget that the Thai pavilion is only a station (even if it is a very picturesque one) among the gastronomical sites at the Shangri-La. Right next to the pier, where small junks glide up and down the river in their function as water taxis, the "Maenam terrace" attempts to recreate a street eatery atmosphere. Buffets and grilling stations offer seafood and international specialties from the grill, with dishes from the repertoire of Mongolian, Indian and Near East menues. A few meters off, the hotel-owned yacht "Horizon" takes off onto its dinner trip, gently rocking its guests, their cocktails and buffet morsels along the lights and temples of Bangkok, up and down the river. A top hotel of this class and size (no less than 850 rooms) is a tiny microcosm in itself, a small world of class. At the Shangri-La, the guest, whether he be a business traveler, tourist or native, is not offered the usual bland international fare, but pampered with a colorful variety of authentic delicacies – those of the Thai restaurant are only a part of it -, with more than four thousand dinners being served per day on average. The man in charge of this all is the thirty-year-old Australian-born Matthew Cropp, assisted by a German chef from Franconia. Of the 450 service and kitchen staff members, 156 are chefs. At the Japanese restaurant "Edogin", sushi bites and sashimi, tempura and sukiyaki are served. If the traveler happens to long for familiar European cooking – just for a change – Giuseppe Fornillo knows the cure. At the "Angeline" with its open show kitchen and Venetian furnishings, the breezy chic of fashionable Western-style restaurants glitters brightly. Featuring Mediterranean delicacies and pizza from the wood-fired oven, the smart Florentine chef made the place into the number one Italian restaurant in the city. Meanwhile, a fat golden buddha dominates the dining-room of the "Shang Palace", and behind its swinging doors, the sixty-two year old master chef Chanchai Arakvanich not only celebrates high Chinese cuisine, but also smuggles in a few alien elements every now and then. He seems to be especially fond of German cuisine and may occasionally be spotted making spätzle, something he does with genuine Swabian expertise, scraping them from the wooden board into the bubbling water. The youthful Chinaman grins broadly: "I know what my guests like. The French love small portions and several courses. Germans like plenty – a lot of sauce – and are always asking for salad." No question about it, homo culinarius is at home at the Shangri-La.

Der Mensch ist ein von Natur aus neugieriges Wesen. Dies hat ihm im Laufe seiner Entwicklung manch böse Überraschung beschert, stellenweise aber auch weitergebracht – wenn auch nicht immer elegant. Da der Homo culinarius möglicherweise eine neuzeitliche Mutation des Homo sapiens ist, dessen Zentralsteuerung weniger im Gehirn als im Magen angesiedelt ist, ist seine Neugier auch ungebrochen und (im wahrsten Sinne des Wortes) unersättlich, wenn es gilt, kulinarisches Neuland zu ergründen. Das hat ihn aus dem Dunstkreis des heimischen Herdes in die weite Welt geführt, wo er sich weniger der Betrachtung fein geschwungener Tempelfriese widmet als dem Inhalt fremder Kochtöpfe. Ein klein wenig Abenteuer ist immer dabei, und für Überraschungen ist gesorgt. Bangkok ist exotisch, Bangkok ist rätselhaft, und Bangkok ist immer für eine Überraschung gut. Was haben schwäbische Spätzle in einer chinesischen Küche in einem thailändischen Hotel zu suchen? Oder gar Holzofen-Pizza? Aber davon später. Wenn schon in Bangkok, dann bitte echt einheimisch, sprich thailändisch, und so wollen wir erst einmal chinesisch oder japanisch, fusion, east-meets-west etc. beiseite lassen und uns voller Neugier (und ziemlich ahnungslos) den hiesigen Ess-Gepflogenheiten hingeben. Unter den Füßen gurgeln die Wasser des Phrao Chaya um Stelzen, auf welchen die hölzernen Planken eines Pavillons ruhen. Einem Teakholz-Schmuckkästchen gleich schiebt sich das „Salathip" spitzgiebelig aus dem Garten des Shangri-La Hotels über den Fluss. Die begehrtesten Plätze im Thai-Restaurant befinden sich ohne Frage unter Windlichtern auf dessen großzügiger Freiluftterrasse, dicht an der Brüstung zum Wasser. Die Gabel links, der Löffel rechts. Am Platz liegt lediglich dieses Werkzeug. Essstäbchen gibt es keine, diese kommen nur bei chinesischer Speisung zum Einsatz. Der Neuling wundert sich. Also Essen auf Thai. Messer – Fehlanzeige. Dessen Funktion übernimmt die Gabel. Mit ihr werden größere Brocken, die meist weich geschmort sind, zerteilt und auf den Löffel geschoben, der sie dann mundwärts befördert. Die Speisekarte verbreitet weitere Ratlosigkeit, da die aufgelisteten Namen zwar nicht in thailändischer Schnörkelschrift erscheinen, doch in ihrer Fremdartigkeit selbst durch die englische Übersetzung nicht wesentlich verständlicher werden. So tastet man sich recht unbeholfen durch die Lektüre und würde viel lieber die Karte zuklappen, am Tische verharren und dann dem Kellner eine Nummer nennen. Was zu Tisch kommt, wird sowieso eine Überraschung sein. Hilfesuchend blickt man umher und seufzt dankbar, als ein dienstbarer Geist sich beratend zur Verfügung stellt.

Die Bestellung beschert dann doch einige Erkenntnisse. Die der westlichen Küche eigenen Systematik von Vor-, Haupt- und Nachspeisen, eine geregelte Speisenfolge also, ist nicht zu erkennen. Es gibt sie einfach nicht. Alles kommt zusammen auf den Tisch, und alles sollte ausgewogen und überlegt zusammengestellt sein. So bestelle man etwas vom Salzig-Würzigen, ein wenig vom Scharfen, vom Sauren und vom Süßen. Und die ganze Tischgesellschaft greift in der Folge mal in dieses, mal in jenes Töpfchen. Jedem ist in der Regel eine eigene Suppe beigeordnet, einer der wesentlichen Bestandteile thailändischer Küche. Zwischen einzelnen Happen nimmt man gern immer wieder einen Schluck der heißen Brühe, in der – je nach Gusto – mal Fisch, mal Fleisch enthalten ist. Für den Fremdling ist sie auch immer wieder ein Stück Erholung, wenn er in allzu sorgloser Gier einen der scharf gewürzten Bissen erwischt hat. Denn Schärfe ist ein untrügliches Kennzeichen dieser Kost. Thais lieben es scharf, und diese Schärfe kann dem Ungeübten mitunter auf eindrucksvolle Weise die Geschmacksknospen verstümmeln. Schweißperlen auf Hemd und Stirn künden den Anwesenden die aktuelle Pein. Greifen Sie in solcher Situation keinesfalls zum kalten Getränk. Der Griff zum Singha Beer mag zwar verlocken, wird aber umgehend bestraft. Denn die Schmerzen des Brandherdes verteilen sich dadurch lediglich im ganzen Mundraum. Zur Linderung solcher Notfälle greife man stattdessen zu weißem, ungewürztem Reis oder nehme sich von den Kokosflocken, die immer auf dem Tisch stehen. Sind so die ersten Klippen überwunden und Erfahrungen gewonnen, hat der Gaumen das Bewusstsein wiedererlangt, steht dem weiteren Genuss nichts mehr im Wege.

Im „Salathip" regiert eine weibliche Hand – eine Lady Chef. Nur vier weibliche Köche haben in Bangkok eine Position als Souschef inne. Frauen in der Küche oder als Unternehmerinnen kleiner Garküchen sind zwar keine Seltenheit, doch allmählich, wenn auch zögerlich, dringt im konservativen Thailand (und Asien) die Weiblichkeit selbst in die von Männern dominierten Spitzenpositionen namhafter Restaurants vor. Mit zäher Beharrlichkeit hat sich die charmante Gesinee Chakkrot ihren Weg nach oben gekocht und sich kann nun ein gerüttelt Maß an Erfahrung vorweisen. Quer durch Asien hat sie am Herd der verschiedenen Shangri-Las gestanden und in Tokio sogar versucht, Japanern die Hohe Schule der Thai-Küche näher zu bringen. Sie hat das Kochen sozusagen mit der Muttermilch eingesogen. Die Familie besaß ein eigenes Restaurant und die Damen des Hauses, Mutter und Großmutter, weckten bei der Kleinen schon früh die Lust am Kochen. Diese aber büffelte sich erst durch die Schule und machte ihren Bachelor auf einem ganz anderen Gebiet, in der Buchhaltung. Ihre Familie wanderte in die USA aus und eröffnete dort zwei kleine und sehr populäre Thai-Restaurants. Sie aber blieb in der Heimat, ließ Buchhaltung Buchhaltung sein und fand ihren Weg zurück in die Küche ihres eigenen kleinen Restaurants. Von da an war Kochen ihre große Liebe, und ihre Gäste liebten sie wegen ihrer delikaten Curries. Verschmitzt gibt sie etwas aus ihrem Privatleben preis: auch privat erwies sich die Liebe als Glücksfall – gleich zweifach. Der Neuangetraute brachte eine höchst patente Schwiegermutter mit in die Ehe, die über ein profundes Wissen der authentischen Thai-Küche in all ihren Facetten verfügt, und aus diesem Fundus schöpft die Zweiundvierzigjährige nun und bietet den Gästen des „Salathip" die Edelversion thailändischer Küche: Royal Thai Cuisine. Diese Küche ist weder den Garküchen der Straße entlehnt (was zunehmend in Mode kommt), noch trendy mit Anleihen westlicher Art, sondern zutiefst klassisch. Und sie liebt unübersehbar das Spiel mit der Dekoration. Ihr auffälligstes Merkmal ist wohl der aufwendige Einsatz kunstvoller Gemüseschnitzereien, die fast jeden Teller schmücken. Die Gerichte der Speisekarte des „Salathip" bieten außerdem einen Querschnitt durch die verschiedenen Regionen des Landes. Den Erläuterungen der Köchin zufolge kocht man im Süden scharf, sehr scharf, und kräftig gewürzt. Fisch ist hier der Hauptbestandteil der Gerichte, und frische Kurkuma-Wurzel verleiht ihre gelbe Farbe fast allen Curries. Überhaupt mischen Thais gern viele Gewürze, frische wie getrocknete, mörsern die Mixtur und fertigen eine Paste daraus – die Würzbasis der Curries. Gesinee stellt sie immer selber her, statt sich auf Fertigpasten zu verlassen. Nördliche Speisen nehmen sich weitaus milder aus und sind deutlich weniger scharf gewürzt. Fernab vom Meer sind die Favoriten Schwein, Rindfleisch und Geflügel – neben allerlei Gemüse. Die Curries – Schmorgerichte aus Fleisch, Fisch oder Geflügel und Grünem – werden in der Regel mit Kokosmilch gekocht. Sie selbst lässt diese lieber weg, weil sie ihr zu fett, zu mächtig ist, und feine Geschmacksnuancen allzu leicht überdeckt. Dafür arbeitet sie verstärkt mit Gemüsen und sucht deren Aroma mit Kräutern zu verfeinern. Zitronengras und Chili sind überall und allgegenwärtig. Nicht zuletzt in den vielen (meist scharfen) Variationen der Tom-Yam-Suppe, einem kulinarischen Höhepunkt der Thai-Küche. Der zahlreichen westlichen Klientel zuliebe wird im Shangri-La jedoch nicht ganz so scharf gegessen wie üblicherweise gekocht. Aber alles ist relativ, und auch beim beliebten Rindfleischsalat (Yam Nüa) ist mancher versucht, wenigstens einen Teil der höllisch scharfen Chili-Sprengsel auszusortieren. Doch ein praktischer Selbstversuch schlägt jede Theorie. Dem Neuling sei angeraten, seine eigenen Erlebnisse zu sammeln und nach und nach die Schätze dieser Kochkultur zu entdecken – bei Gesinee Chakkrot im edlen „Salathip" oder in den Garküchen auf Bangkoks Straßen.

Das ist aber längst nicht alles. Hier draußen am Fluss könnte man leicht vergessen, dass der Thai-Pavillon lediglich eine Station (wenn auch wahrscheinlich die malerischste) unter den gastronomischen Möglichkeiten des Shangri-Las darstellt. Dicht neben der Anlegestelle, wo kleine Dschunken als Wassertaxi über den Fluss hin und her pendeln, wird auf der „Maenam Terrace" eine Art Garküchen-Atmosphäre gezaubert. Büffets und Grillstände offerieren Seafood und internationale Grillspezialitäten, kochen quer durchs Brevier mongolischer, indischer und nahöstlicher Speisekarten. Allabendlich legt wenige Meter entfernt die hoteleigene Restaurant-Yacht „Horizon" zur Dinner-Fahrt ab und schaukelt ihre Gäste bei Cocktails und Büffetbissen den Fluss hinauf und wieder zurück, entlang der Lichter und Tempel Bangkoks. Ein Tophotel dieses Niveaus und dieser Größenordnung (mit immerhin 850 Zimmern) ist

Michael Gremer, Chanchai Arakvanich, Matthew Cropp, Gesinee Chakkrot

in sich ein kleiner Mikrokosmos. Eine kleine Welt mit Klasse. Im Shangri-La wird der Gast, ob Geschäftsreisender, Tourist oder Einheimischer, kulinarisch betrachtet nicht mit drögem internationalem Einheitsbrei abgespeist, sondern mit einer bunten Vielfalt authentischer Angebote gehätschelt. Das Thai-Restaurant ist da nur eines davon. Bis zu viertausend Essen gehen hier insgesamt Tag für Tag über den Tresen. Der Mann, der die Fäden in Händen hält, ist der dreißigjährige Australier Matthew Cropp, assistiert von einem deutschen Koch aus Franken. Von den 450 Personen Service- und Küchenpersonal sind allein 156 Köche. Sie schneiden im Japan-Restaurant „Edogin" Sushi-Häppchen und Sashimi-Bissen, servieren Tempura und Sukiyaki. Überfällt den Fremdling Sehnsucht nach vertrauter Kost, nur mal so zwischendurch, weiß Giuseppe Fornillo Abhilfe zu schaffen. Der fetzige Chic westlicher Fashion-Restaurants blitzt im „Angelini" mit offener Show-Küche und venezianischen Versatzstücken. Der flotte Florentiner Koch hat das Lokal mit Mittelmeer-Delikatessen und Holzofen-Pizza zum Nummer-Eins-Italiener der Stadt gekocht. Nicht weit weg dominiert ein dicker Goldbuddha den Speiseraum des „Shang Palace", hinter dessen Schwingtüren sich der zweiundsechzigjährige Chefkoch Chanchai Arakvanich nicht nur der hohen Kunst der Chinaküche widmet, sondern durchaus auch mit fremden Elementen spielt. An deutscher Küche hat er wohl einen Narren gefressen, und so kann man ihn hin und wieder beim Spätzleschaben beobachten – so richtig schwäbisch, vom Holzbrett ins sprudelnde Wasser. Der jugendlich wirkende Chinese verzieht breitgrinsend den Mund und meint schelmisch: „Ich weiß, was meine Gäste wollen. Franzosen lieben es in kleinen Portionen und mehreren Gängen. Die Deutschen mögen's eher üppig – mit viel Sauce – und verlangen ständig nach Salat." Keine Frage, im Shangri-La kommt Homo culinarius auf seine Kosten.

ประเภทซุป - ต้มยำ
CLEAR AND SPICY SOUPS
スープ料理

25. ต้มยำกุ้งก้ามกราม トム ヤム クン ガム グラム	TOM YAM GUNG GAM GRAM Spicy River Prawn Soup flavoured with Lemongrass, Lime Juice and Garden Chili トムヤムクン　スパイシーエビスープ	230.-
26. ต้มข่าไก่ トン カァー ガイ	TOM KHA GAI Spicy Chicken Soup with Coconut Milk flavoured with Thai Herbs チキンスープ　ココナッツ風味	180.-
27. แกงเลียงชาววัง カン リャン チャオ ワン	KAENG LIANG CHAO WANG Spicy Siamese Vegetable Soup with Shrimps and Thai Herbs エビ入り野菜のスパイシースープ	180.-
28. แกงจืดลูกรอก カン ジュウド ルック ロッグ	KAENG JUED LOOK ROG Chicken Consomme with Egg, Sausage and Vegetables ソーセージ、野菜入チキンコンソメスープ	170.-
29. ซุปเนื้อตุ๋น スープ ヌア トゥーン	SOUP NUA TOON Double Boiled Beef Shank Soup with Tomato and Thai Herbs トマトとタイハーブ入り　牛スネ肉のスープ	180.-
30. ต้มจิ๊วเนื้อหรือไก่ トム ジュウ ヌア ルゥア ガイ	TOM JEW NUA RUE GAI Clear Soup with Beef Shank or Chicken in Thai Herbs 牛のスネ肉またはチキンの澄ましスープ	180.-
31. ปลาช่อนต้ม ใบมะขามอ่อน プラ チョン トム バイ マーカム オーン	PLA CHON TOM BAI MA-KHAM OON Spicy River Fish Soup with Young Tamarind Leaves タマリンの葉入り　スパイシー川魚のスープ	170.-
32. แกงจืดนพเก้า ゲン ジョー ノッパガオ	KAENG JUED NOPPAGAO Clear Soup with Chicken, Shrimps and Vegetables 鶏肉・海老と野菜の澄ましスープ	190.-

Plus 10% Service Charge and Applicable Government Tax.

サービス料10%と消費税を別途いただきます。

ประเภทก๋วยเตี๋ยว ข้าว และ ผัก
NOODLES, RICE AND VEGETABLES
麺類、ライスと野菜料理

64. ผัดไทยกุ้งนาง
パッタイ クン ナン
PHAD THAI GUNG NANG
Fried Rice Noodles with River Lobster Thai Style
エビ入りタイ風ヌードル
210.-

65. หมี่กรอบไทย
ミー グロッブ タイ
MEE GROB THAI
Crispy Ayutthaya Rice Noodles with Baby Shrimps and Bean Curd
子エビと豆腐入りアユタヤヌードル
180.-

66. ก๋วยเตี๋ยวน้ำรวมมิตร
グァイ ティアオ ナム
ルゥアン ミット
GUAY TIEW NAM RUAM MITR
Noodle Soup with Shrimps, Squid and Fish Balls
海老・イカとつみれ入りヌードル
200.-

67. ก๋วยเตี๋ยวเนื้อตุ๋น
グァイ ティアオ
ヌア トーン
GUAY TIEW NUA TOON
Noodle Soup with Beef
牛肉入りヌードル
190.-

68. ก๋วยเตี๋ยวทะเลคั่ว
グァイ ティアオ
タレー クア
GUAY TIEW THALAY KUA
Fried Noodles with Seafood, Vegetables and Chili Sauce
海鮮と野菜のチリソースヌードル
200.-

69. ข้าวผัดรวมมิตร
カオ パッド ルオン
ミット
KHAO PHAD RUAM MITR
*Fried Rice with Pork, Prawns and Chicken
豚肉、エビとチキン入り炒飯
180.-

70. ข้าวอบสับปะรด
カオ オブ サッパッロ
KHAO OB SAB PAROS
*Baked Rice with Pineapple, Shrimps and Chicken Sausage served in a Pineapple Shell topped with Egg and Dried Pork
パイナッツプルの器入り五目炒飯
210.-

71. ข้าวคลุกน้ำพริก
カオ クルック ナム
プリック
KHAO KLUK NAM PRIK
*Stir-fried Rice with Shrimps and Chili Sauce served with Salted Egg and Vegetables
海老とチリの焼飯　塩漬け卵と野菜添え
210.-

72. ผัดผักรวมมิตร
パッド パック
ルアン ミット
PHAD PHAK RUAM MITR
Fried Mixed Vegetables with Oyster Sauce
ミックスベジタブル　オイスターソース添え
170.-

73. ผัดผักบุ้งไฟแดง
パッド パック ブン
ファイ プリック
PHAD PHAK BOONG FAI DAENG
Sauteed Morning Glory with Garlic, Soya Beans and Oyster Sauce
朝顔の種、にんにくとそら豆のソテー　オイスターソース添え
170.-

* This Item Contains Pork.
Plus 10% Service Charge and Applicable Government Tax.
＊こちらの料理は豚肉を使用しています。
サービス料10％と消費税を別途いただきます。

FRIED RICE NOODLES WITH SHRIMP, THAI-STYLE

GEBRATENE REISNUDELN MIT GARNELEN, THAILÄNDISCHE ART

Phad Thai

Serves 4

For the sauce:
150 g/5 oz palm sugar
(alternatively brown cane sugar),
150 ml/²/₃ cup tamarind juice,
150 ml/²/₃ cup Thai fish sauce (bottled),
250 ml/1 cup chicken stock,
60 ml/¹/₄ cup sunflower oil

2 shallots, finely diced,
100 g/3¹/₂ oz tofu, cubed,
200 g/7 oz large shrimp, shelled,
with final tail segment on,
2 tbsp dried shrimp,
350 g/12¹/₂ oz thin, flat rice noodles,
soaked in cold water,
200 g/7 oz bean sprouts,
1 green chili pepper, sliced
(according to taste),
60 g/2 oz roasted peanuts, chopped,
3 eggs,
1 tbsp ground chili pepper (according to taste)

For the sauce: Place all ingredients into a large pot and simmer for five minutes. Remove the pot from heat and allow to steep for one hour.

Heat oil in a wok and stir-fry shallots until wilted. Add tofu, both fresh and dried shrimp and the well-drained noodles. Fry, stirring vigorously, for three minutes. Add the sauce, bean sprouts, chili pepper and peanuts and bring to a boil again.

Beat the eggs in a small bowl and pour them over the mixture in the wok, stirring constantly until the egg has solidified. Season to taste with salt and ground chili peppers.

Arrange the noodles on lettuce leaves (photograph: banana buds) and decorate with red chili pepper strips and coriander leaves. Serve.

Für 4 Personen:

Für die Sauce:
150 g Palmzucker (ersatzweise
braunen Rohr-Rohzucker verwenden),
150 ml Tamarindensaft,
150 ml thailändische Fischsauce
(in Flaschen erhältlich),
250 ml Hühnerbrühe, 60 ml Sonnenblumenöl

2 Schalotten, fein gehackt,
60 ml Sonnenblumenöl,
100 g Tofu, in Würfel geschnitten,
200 g große Garnelenschwänze, geschält, den
hintersten Schwanzpanzer belassen,
2 EL getrocknete Garnelen,
350 g dünne, flache Reisnudeln,
in kaltem Wasser eingeweicht,
200 g Sojabohnensprossen,
1 grüne Chilischote (oder mehr nach Belieben),
entkernt, in Scheiben geschnitten,
60 g geröstete Erdnüsse, gehackt,
3 Eier, 1 EL (oder nach Belieben) Chilipulver

Für die Sauce: Alle Zutaten in einem Topf erhitzen und fünf Minuten kochen. Anschließend vom Herd nehmen und eine Stunde stehen lassen.

In einem Wok die Schalotten im Öl unter Rühren weich braten. Den Tofu, die frischen und die getrockneten Garnelen und die gut abgetropften Nudeln zugeben und unter Rühren drei Minuten braten. Die vorbereitete Sauce, die Sojabohnensprossen, die Chili und die Erdnüsse zugeben, zum Kochen bringen. Die Eier in einer kleinen Schüssel verquirlen und unterrühren. Mit Salz und Chilipulver abschmecken, kochen lassen, bis die Eier gestockt sind. Auf Salatblätter anrichten (Bild: Bananenblüten) und mit roten Chilistreifen und Korianderblättern dekoriert servieren.

ROCK LOBSTER SALAD WITH MANGOES

LANGUSTENSALAT MIT MANGO

Serves 2

2 pink rock lobsters, 500 g/1 lb each

For the mayonnaise:
1 egg,
1 tbsp powdered mustard,
$^1/_2$ tsp salt,
juice of half a lemon,
100 ml/$^1/_3$ cup sunflower oil,
60 ml/$^1/_4$ cup condensed milk

2 small ripe mangoes

In a large pot, bring plenty of salted water to a boil. Drop the rock lobsters into the water head first, cover the pot and boil them for eight minutes. Refresh the rock lobsters in ice water and allow them to drain. Remove the heads and flat tail segments and reserve them for garnish. Shell the tails and cut them into medallions.
For the mayonnaise: Beat the egg in a large bowl with a wire whip, adding powdered mustard, salt and a few drops of lemon juice. Slowly incorporate oil, a little at a time. Smooth out the mayonnaise with condensed milk and season to taste with lemon juice and salt.
Cut the mangoes in half lengthwise, remove the cores and scoop out the center of two halves. Peel the two remaining halves and cut the flesh into slices.
Serving: Place the two scooped-out mango halves onto oval serving platters. Fill them with alternate layers of rock lobster meat and mango slices. Spoon the mayonnaise into a pastry bag and pipe a pattern of your own design onto the salad. Garnish platters with lobster heads and tail segments. Serve.

Für 2 Personen:

2 rosa Langusten à 500 g

Für die Mayonnaise:
1 Ei,
1 EL Senfpulver,
$^1/_2$ TL Salz,
Saft einer halben Zitrone,
100 ml Sonnenblumenöl,
60 ml Kondensmilch

2 kleine, reife Mangos

In einem großen Topf Salzwasser zum Kochen bringen. Die Langusten kopfüber hineingeben und zugedeckt 8 Minuten kochen. In Eiswasser abkühlen, dann die Langusten abtropfen lassen. Den Kopf und das platte Schwanzglied abtrennen, für die Garnitur beiseite stellen. Das Fleisch auslösen und in Medaillons schneiden.
Für die Mayonnaise: Das Ei mit dem Senfpulver, Salz, und etwas Zitronensaft in einer Schüssel mit dem Schneebesen gut verrühren. Nach und nach das Öl einarbeiten, zum Schluss die Mayonnaise mit Kondensmilch glattrühren, mit Zitronensaft und Salz abschmecken.
Die Mangos der Länge nach halbieren, Kern entfernen und zwei der Hälften aushöhlen. Die restlichen zwei Mangohälften schälen, Fruchtfleisch in Scheiben schneiden.
Zum Servieren: Die zwei ausgehöhlten Mangohälften auf ovale Servierplatten legen. Das Langustenfleisch abwechselnd mit den Mangoscheiben einschichten. Mayonnaise in einen Spritzbeutel füllen, nach Belieben ein Muster über den Salat spritzen. Mit Langustenköpfen und -schwänzen garnieren.

FRIED TIGER PRAWNS IN A HOT CURRY SAUCE

GEBRATENE RIESENGARNELEN IN SCHARFER CURRYSAUCE

Choo Chee Kung

Serves 4	*Für 4 Personen:*
4 tiger prawns, *250 ml/1 cup coconut milk,* *4 kaffir lime leaves,* *30 g/1 oz red curry paste,* *2 tbsp Thai fish sauce,* *20 g/³/₄ oz sugar*	*4 Riesengarnelen,* *250 ml Kokosmilch,* *4 Kaffir-Limettenblätter,* *30 g rote Currypaste,* *2 EL thailändische Fischsauce,* *20 g Zucker*
Garnish: *4 kaffir lime leaves,* *cut into very thin strips*	*Garnitur:* *4 Kaffir-Limettenblätter,* *in sehr dünne Streifen geschnitten*

Remove shells from the prawns. Blanch heads and tail segments in salted water for a minute and set aside for decoration. Cut the prawns open lengthwise and devein them.

In a small pot, bring coconut milk and lime leaves to a boil and stir in curry paste. Simmer on low heat for five minutes. Season to taste with fish sauce and sugar. Heat a small amount of oil in a frying pan and sear the tiger prawns on all sides. Place them into the sauce and simmer on low heat for five minutes. Check seasonings.

Serving: Remove the lime leaves and arrange tiger prawns on pre-warmed plates. Drizzle a little sauce over them und sprinkle with thin lime leaf strips. Decorate with the reserved prawn heads and tail segments according to your own designs.

Die Garnelen schälen, den Kopf und das Schwanzglied kurz in Salzwasser blanchieren, für die Dekoration aufheben. Das Garnelenfleisch längs einschneiden, den Darm entfernen.

In einem kleinen Topf die Kokosmilch mit den Limettenblättern zum Kochen bringen und die Currypaste einrühren. Bei kleiner Hitze fünf Minuten köcheln, mit Fischsauce und Zucker würzen. Die Garnelen in einer Pfanne in wenig Öl von allen Seiten heiß anbraten. In die Sauce geben, fünf Minuten köcheln lassen. Abschmecken.

Zum Servieren: Limettenblätter aus der Sauce entfernen, die Garnelen auf vorgewärmte Teller anrichten. Mit der Sauce übergießen und mit Limettenblätterstreifen überstreuen. Nach Belieben mit Garnelenköpfen und -schwänzen garnieren.

PAPAYA SALAD WITH CASHEWS

PAPAYA-SALAT MIT CASHEWNÜSSEN

Som Tam

Serves 4

2 green papayas,
2 garlic cloves, diced,
1 small red chili pepper, seeded, finely diced,
4 tbsp Thai fish sauce (bottled),
4 tbsp lime juice, freshly squeezed,
3 tbsp palm sugar (alternatively brown cane sugar),
salt,
120 g/4 oz green beans (original recipe:
asparagus beans), cooked al dente,
120 g/4 oz cherry tomatoes, halved,
80 g/3 oz dried shrimp,
80 g/3 oz toasted cashews

Garnish:
mixed herbs,
4 red chili peppers, cut open
and shaped into "blossoms"

Halve the papayas lengthwise, core and seed them
and scoop out the flesh from the shells. Reserve
shells. Grind the garlic and chili pepper to a fine
paste in a mortar. Add the fish sauce, lime juice and
sugar. Check for salt. In a large bowl, combine the
papaya flesh, green bean pieces, cherry tomatoes,
dried shrimp and cashews. Mix until well blended.
Spoon the salad into the papaya shells and place the
shells on plates. Garnish with herbs and the chili
pepper blossoms. Serve.

Für 4 Personen:

2 grüne Papayas,
2 Knoblauchzehen, gehackt,
1 kleine rote Chilischote, entkernt, fein gehackt,
4 EL thailändische Fischsauce (in Flaschen erhältlich),
4 EL frisch gepresster Limettensaft,
3 EL Palmzucker (Ersatz: brauner Rohr-Rohzucker),
Salz,
120 g grüne Bohnen
(Originalrezept: Spargelbohnen), knapp gar gekocht,
120 g Kirschtomaten, halbiert,
80 g getrocknete Garnelen,
80 g geröstete Cashewnüsse

Garnitur:
gemischte Kräuter,
4 rote Chilischoten,
zu „Blüten" aufgeschnitten und geformt

Die Papayas der Länge nach halbieren, die Kerne
ausschaben und das Fleisch aus den Schalen lösen.
Den Knoblauch mit Chili im Mörser zu einer feinen Paste verreiben. Mit Fischsauce, Limettensaft
und Zucker würzen, mit Salz abschmecken. In einer
Schüssel das Papayafleisch, Bohnen, Kirschtomaten,
Garnelen und Cashewnüsse mit der Sauce gut vermischen. Den Salat in die Papayahälften füllen und
auf Teller verteilen. Mit Kräutern und zu Blüten ge-
formten Chilischoten garniert servieren.

HEARTY SHARK FIN SOUP
WITH WINTER MELON

KRÄFTIGE HAIFISCHFLOSSENSUPPE
MIT WINTERMELONE

Serves 4

*300 g/11 oz shark fin, superior quality,
soaked in cold water*

*1 liter/4 cups chicken stock, flavored with
raw ham (add a piece of bone or raw ham
trimmings to your stockpot),
1 tsp salt,
1 tsp instant chicken stock,
2 tbsp Chinese rice wine,
1 winter melon (or honeydew melon)*

In a large pot, bring chicken stock to a boil.
Stir in salt, instant stock and rice wine and
add shark fins. Simmer gently for twenty
minutes. Remove shark fins from the stock
with a skimmer and allow them to cool.
Carefully peel away all undesired parts from
the fine muscle fibers.
Cut off the top quarter of the winter melon
horizontally. Scoop out the flesh and chop
it coarsely.
Place shark fins, stock and melon pieces
into a pot. Seal tightly with heat-proof foil,
cover pot with a heavy lid and steam for
about two hours, ideally in a steamer. Or
heat the soup on top of the stove, tightly
covered, and keep it at a bare simmer for
two hours. Shake the pot occasionally,
taking care that the fish does not stick to
the bottom of the pot.
Check the seasonings and ladle the soup
into soup bowls or decorate the hollowed-
out melon shell with carvings and use it as
a tureen.

Für 4 Personen:

*300 g Haifischflosse „Superior-Qualität", in
kaltem Wasser eingeweicht*

*1 Liter Hühnerbrühe, mit Rohschinken
aromatisiert (ein Stück Knochen vom
Rohschinken oder Rohschinkenabschnitte
mitkochen lassen), 1 TL Salz,
1 TL gekörnte Hühnerbrühe,
2 EL chinesischer Reiswein,
1 Wintermelone (oder Honigmelone)*

Hühnerbrühe in einem Topf zum Kochen
bringen. Salz, gekörnte Brühe und Reiswein
einrühren, die Haifischflossen zugeben und
20 Minuten leise köcheln lassen. Die Haifischflossen mit der Schaumkelle herausnehmen und abkühlen lassen. Die feinen
Muskelfasern sorgfältig von allen Rück-
ständen befreien.
Von der Melone das obere Viertel horizon-
tal wegschneiden. Die Melone aushöhlen,
das Fleisch in grobe Stücke schneiden.
Die Haifischflossen mit der Brühe und den
Melonenstücken in einen Topf geben. Mit
hitzefester Folie verschließen, wenn möglich in einem Dampfofen (Steamer) zugedeckt ca. 2 Stunden dämpfen. Alternativ
die Suppe auf dem Herd bei kleinster Hitze
gut zugedeckt zwei Stunden ziehen lassen.
Dabei von Zeit zu Zeit umrühren und aufpassen, dass das Fischfleisch nicht anbrennt.
Die Suppe abschmecken und nach Belieben
in Suppentassen oder in der ausgehöhlten
Melone servieren.

STEWED ABALONE IN A BROWN SAUCE

GESCHMORTE MEERESSCHNECKEN IN BRAUNER SAUCE

Serves 4

4 dried abalone,
about 25 g/1 oz each

2 tbsp sunflower oil,
2 small garlic cloves, minced,
3 green onions, finely diced,
1 tbsp oyster sauce,
1 tsp dark soy sauce,
1 tsp sugar,
1 tsp instant chicken stock,
2 tbsp Chinese rice wine,
300 ml/1 1/3 cup meat stock,
200 g Chinese broccoli (kai-lan), cleaned,
1 tsp ground tapioca (or arrowroot powder),
1 tsp salt

Soak the abalone in cold water for twenty-four hours, changing the water several times. Place them into a small pot and cover them with salted water. Simmer at very low heat for forty-eight hours, occasionally replenishing the water in the pot. When the abalone are done, allow them to cool in the liquid. Drain and discard the liquid.

Heat the oil in the wok. Stir-fry the garlic and green onions until wilted. Season with oyster sauce, soy sauce, sugar, stock and rice wine. Douse with stock. Place abalone in the seasoned stock and simmer for another six hours. When you are ready to serve, add Chinese broccoli and simmer for about twelve minutes.

Finish: Remove abalone and broccoli from the wok and place them onto pre-warmed plates. Thicken cooking liquid with tapioca and check sauce for salt and pepper. Glaze the vegetables and the abalone with a little sauce and serve.

Für 4 Personen:

4 getrocknete Meeresschnecken (Abalone, Meerohren), à ca. 25 g

2 EL Sonnenblumenöl,
2 kleine Knoblauchzehen, fein gehackt,
3 Frühlingszwiebeln, fein gehackt,
1 EL Austernsauce,
1 TL dunkle Sojasauce,
1 TL Zucker,
1 TL gekörnte Hühnerbrühe,
2 EL chinesischer Reiswein,
300 ml Fleischbrühe,
200 g chinesischer Broccoli (Kai-Lan),
1 TL Tapiokamehl (oder Pfeilwurzmehl),
1 TL Salz

Die Abalone 24 Stunden in kaltes Wasser einlegen, von Zeit zu Zeit das Wasser wechseln. In einen kleinen Topf geben, mit Salzwasser bedecken und erhitzen. Bei kleinster Hitze 48 Stunden zugedeckt garen, dabei von Zeit zu Zeit Wasser nachfüllen. Wenn die Abalone gar sind, im Sud erkalten lassen. Den Kochsud abgießen.

Das Öl in einem Wok erhitzen. Knoblauch und Frühlingszwiebeln unter ständigem Rühren weichbraten. Mit der Austern- und Sojasauce, Zucker, gekörnten Brühe und Reiswein würzen, dann mit der Fleischbrühe aufgießen. Die Meereschnecken einlegen, bei kleiner Hitze 6 Stunden sieden lassen. Zum Schluss den chinesischen Broccoli zugeben und ca. 12 Minuten mitgaren.

Fertigstellung: Abalone und Broccoli aus dem Wok nehmen und auf vorgewärmte Teller anrichten. Den Kochsud mit dem Tapiokamehl andicken, die Sauce mit Salz abschmecken, das Gemüse und die Meeresschnecken damit überziehen.

STEAMED GROUPER IN A UNICORN SAUCE

ZACKENBARSCH IM DAMPF AN UNICORNSAUCE

Serves 6

1 grouper of about 1 kg/2 lbs,
6 fresh shiitake mushrooms, stems removed,
60 g/2 oz raw ham
(preferably Chinese Hunan ham),
sliced thinly,
30 g/1 oz ginger,
peeled and thinly sliced

400 g/14 oz Chinese broccoli (kai laan tsoi),
cut into 5 cm/2 in pieces,
1 tsp sugar, 1 tbsp Chinese rice wine,
1 tsp instant chicken stock,
2 tbsp oyster sauce,
2 tbsp soy sauce, salt,
2 tsp powdered tapioca

Filet the fish, reserving head and tail fin for garnish. Cut the filets into six pieces of equal size. On an oval, oven-proof platter, lay out two parallel rows composed of fish pieces alternating with mushroom caps and ham slices. Place the head and tail fin at the two ends. Scatter ginger slices on top and tightly cover the platter with aluminum foil. Steam in a professional steamer, or set in a bain-marie in a regular 220° C/425° F oven, for ten to fifteen minutes. Remove fish from the oven and allow to cool down slightly.

Meanwhile, boil the broccoli in the stock until just tender. Remove from the stock with a skimmer and keep warm.

Season the stock to taste with sugar, rice wine, instant stock, oyster and soy sauce and lightly thicken it with tapioca.

Remove the foil and the ginger slices from the platter with the steamed fish. Arrange broccoli on top and glaze everything with a little sauce. Serve immediately.

Für 6 Personen:

1 Zackenbarsch von ca. 1 kg,
6 frische Shiitakepilze, Stiele entfernt,
60 g Rohschinken (nach Möglichkeit
chinesischer Hunanschinken),
in dünne Scheiben geschnitten,
30 g Ingwer, geschält
und in dünne Scheiben geschnitten

400 g chinesischer Broccoli (Kai Laan Tsoi),
in ca. 5 cm große Stücke geschnitten,
250 ml Fleischbrühe, 1 TL Zucker,
1 EL chinesischer Reiswein,
1 TL gekörnte Hühnerbrühe,
2 EL Austernsauce, 2 EL Sojasauce,
Salz, 2 TL Tapiokamehl

Den Fisch sorgfältig filetieren, Kopf und die Schwanzflosse als Garnitur aufheben. Die Filets in 6 gleich große Stücke schneiden. Auf einer ovalen, feuerfesten Servierplatte die Fischstücke abwechselnd mit Pilzköpfen und Schinkenscheiben in zwei Reihen auslegen, den Kopf und die Schwanzflosse an die Enden setzen. Mit den Ingwerscheiben bestreuen, die Platte mit Alufolie gut zudecken. Im Dampfofen (Steamer) oder im normalen, vorgeheizten Ofen im Wasserbad bei 220° C 10 - 15 Minuten garen. Anschließend den Fisch aus dem Ofen nehmen und leicht abkühlen lassen.

Unterdessen den Broccoli in Brühe knapp gar kochen. Mit der Schaumkelle herausheben und warmstellen.

Die Brühe mit Zucker, Reiswein, gekörnter Brühe, Austern- und Sojasauce und Salz würzen, mit Tapiokamehl leicht binden.

Folie und Ingwerscheiben vom gedämpften Fisch entfernen. Das Gemüse darüberlegen und die Speise mit der Sauce überziehen.

CRISPY GLAZED SQUAB

KNUSPRIG GLASIERTE TAUBE

Serves 4

2 squabs, ready-to-cook

250 ml/1 cup chicken stock,
2 tbsp dark soy sauce,
1 tbsp light soy sauce,
1 tsp sugar,
1 tsp cinnamon,
2 tbsp ground white pepper

2 tbsp Chinese black vinegar,
2 tbsp glucose,
oil for deep-frying

1 potato, salt

Boil squab in salted water for five minutes, remove them from the water and allow the excess water to drip off.
Heat the stock in a wok and season it with soy sauces, sugar, cinnamon and pepper. Simmer for ten minutes, uncovered, then place the squab into the liquid and simmer for fifteen minutes more on low heat.
Remove squabs from the liquid and allow them to cool.
Combine black vinegar, glucose and a little hot water in a bowl and mix well. Brush the squab with the glaze on all sides and allow the glaze to dry a little. Repeat the procedure four times. Deep-fry the squab in hot oil until crisp and brown.
Peel the potato and cut it into very thin slices. Pat potato slices dry with a cloth and deep-fry them in the hot oil. Remove them from the oil with a skimmer and drain well on paper towels.
Serving: Cut the squab in half and place the halves on pre-warmed plates. Serve with the lightly salted, still warm potato chips.

Für 4 Peronen:

2 Tauben, küchenfertig

250 ml Hühnerbrühe,
2 EL dunkle Sojasauce,
1 EL helle Sojasauce,
1 TL Zucker,
1 TL Zimtpulver,
2 TL gemahlener weißer Pfeffer

2 EL chinesischer schwarzer Essig,
2 EL Glukose (Traubenzucker),
Öl zum Frittieren

1 Kartoffel, Salz

Die Tauben in Salzwasser fünf Minuten kochen, abgießen und gut abtropfen lassen.
Im Wok die Brühe mit Sojasaucen, Zucker, Zimt und Pfeffer verrühren und erhitzen. Ohne Deckel 10 Minuten kochen, dann die Tauben einlegen und bei kleiner Hitze 15 Minuten sieden. Aus der Brühe nehmen, gut abtropfen und erkalten lassen.
Den schwarzen Essig mit der Glukose und etwas heißem Wasser in einer kleinen Schale gut verrühren. Die Tauben von allen Seiten mit Glasur bepinseln, etwas antrocknen lassen, dann den Vorgang vier Mal wiederholen. Die Tauben im heißen Öl knusprigbraun ausbacken.
Die Kartoffel schälen und in hauchdünne Scheiben hobeln. Die Kartoffelscheiben auf einem Tuch trocken tupfen und im heißen Öl frittieren. Mit der Schaumkelle heraus heben, auf Küchenpapier abtropfen lassen.
Zum Servieren: Die Tauben halbieren und auf vorgewärmte Teller anrichten. Mit den noch warmen, leicht gesalzenen Kartoffelchips als Beilage servieren.

NORTHERN INDIAN DELICACIES

Selection of Indian Curries, To Be Served with Chutneys and Papadums

INDIAN LAMB CURRY (GOSCHT VINDALOO)

Serves 4

800 g/1³/₄ lb lamb, cut from the leg, cubed

*4 tbsp sunflower oil, 2 medium onions, chopped,
2 tsp black peppercorns, coarsely crushed,
1 tsp green cardamom pods, coarsely crushed,
1 tbsp green chili pepper, finely diced, 3 cloves,
2 tbsp ground red chili pepper (according to taste),
1 cm/¹/₃ inch cinnamon stick, coarsely crushed,
2 tsp cumin seeds, 2 tsp turmeric,
1 tsp coriander seeds,
2 garlic cloves, minced and ground into a fine paste in a mortar,
2 tbsp fresh ginger, minced and ground into a fine paste in a mortar*

*400 g/14 oz potatoes, 2 tbsp sunflower oil,
1 tbsp malt vinegar, salt, coriander leaves*

Heat the oil in a heavy-bottomed casserole. Add onions and sauté until golden brown, stirring constantly to prevent them from sticking. Stir in spices and spice pastes and sauté for another 2-3 minutes. Add lamb cubes and keep stirring, coating the meat evenly with spice mixture. Add water to cover and bring to a boil. Cover and simmer on low heat for 2-3 hours. Remove lid after an hour to allow the sauce to thicken. Stir occasionally to prevent the sauce from sticking to the bottom of the pan.
Peel the potatoes and cut them into 2 cm/³/₄ inch cubes. Heat oil in a pan and fry potatoes on low heat until golden brown. Mix potato cubes into the curry and continue to simmer until potatoes are tender. Correct seasonings, adding salt and a little malt vinegar. Transfer curry to a serving bowl and garnish with coriander leaves. Serve with steamed rice on the side.

INDIAN SAFFRON RICE

Serves 4

*400 g/14 oz basmati rice,
2 tbsp peanut oil, 1 tsp cumin seeds,
2 cloves, 2 bay leaves, salt,
a pinch saffron threads*

Heat the oil in a pot. Add cumin seeds and toast them on low heat until they start popping. Stir in rice and sauté for a few minutes. Add water to cover and bring to a boil. Stir in cloves, bay leaves and a pinch of salt, and turn heat to very low. Cover and allow to steam for ten minutes. Stir in saffron threads and allow to rest, covered, for another ten minutes. Serve.

INDIAN CHICKEN WITH TOMATOES AND FENUGREEK (KADHAI MURGH)

Serves 4

600 g/1 1/3 lb chicken breast,
1/2 garlic clove, 1 tsp fresh ginger, finely diced,
2 tbsp sunflower oil, 1/2 tsp coriander seeds,
600 g/1 1/3 lb tomatoes, coarsely chopped,
1 tsp green chili peppers, finely diced,
10 g/1/3 oz fresh ginger, sliced,
20 g/2/3 oz fresh coriander,
10 g/1 tbsp garam masala (see page 293), 1 tsp fenugreek,
200 g/7 oz onion, finely diced, salt

Cut the chicken meat into pieces of about 2 cm/3/4 inch. In a mortar, grind the garlic and diced ginger into a fine paste. Heat the oil in a heavy-bottomed pan, stir in paste and fry until lightly colored. Add coriander seeds and sauté for another minute, than add tomatoes and keep on a slow simmer for five minutes.

Add chicken pieces, diced chili pepper, ginger slices and fresh coriander and simmer for one to two hours on low heat, until the sauce has thickened considerably. Stir occasionally. Season with garam masala and fenugreek and a pinch of salt and simmer for another five minutes. Check for salt and serve.

INDIAN LENTIL STEW (DAL MAKHANT)

Serves 4

400 g/14 oz lentils (masoor dal), salt,
1 tbsp ground red chili pepper (according to taste),
2 tbsp spice paste,
made of equal amounts of garlic and ginger,
finely ground in a mortar,
150 g/5 oz crushed tomatoes,
100 g/3 1/2 oz butter,
100 ml/1/3 cup cream,
2 tbsp clarified butter

Carefully wash and sort through the lentils. Place them into a pot and add water to cover generously. Add a little salt and bring to a boil. Simmer, uncovered, until the lentils are tender to the bite and two thirds of the water has evaporated.

Lightly squash the lentils with a spoon. Add the spices, crushed tomatoes and butter. Simmer lentils on low heat for another thirty minutes. Keep stirring to prevent the lentils from burning. Add the cream and simmer for another ten minutes. Correct seasonings and ladle the dal into a serving bowl. Drizzle with clarified butter just before serving. Serve with chapati bread.

NORDINDISCHE KÖSTLICHKEITEN

Auswahl indischer Currygerichte, zu servieren mit Chutneys und Papadams

INDISCHER LINSENEINTOPF (DAL MAKHANT)

Für 4 Personen:

400 g Linsen (Masoor Dal), Salz,
1 EL rotes Chilipulver (oder Menge nach Belieben),
2 EL im Mörser zu Paste zerstoßener Knoblauch und Ingwer (50:50),
150 g Tomatenpüree, 100 g Butter,
100 ml Sahne, 2 EL flüssige Butter

Die Linsen sorgfältig waschen und verlesen. In einen Topf geben, mit Wasser auffüllen, bis sie gut bedeckt sind, leicht salzen und zum Kochen bringen. Ohne Deckel köcheln, bis die Linsen weich sind und zwei Drittel des Wassers verdunstet ist.

Mit einem Löffel die Linsen leicht zerdrücken, dann die Gewürze, Tomatenpüree und Butter unterrühren. Bei kleiner Hitze 30 Minuten köcheln, dabei immer wieder umrühren. Sahne unterrühren, weitere 10 Minuten köcheln. Abschmecken, in eine Servierschüssel füllen, kurz vor dem Servieren die flüssige Butter darüber gießen. Mit Chapati Brot servieren.

INDISCHES HUHN MIT TOMATEN UND BOCKSHORNKLEE (KADHAI MURGH)

Für 4 Personen:

600 g Hühnerbrust,
1/2 Knoblauchzehe,
1 TL fein gehackter Ingwer,
2 EL Sonnenblumenöl,
1/2 TL Koriandersamen,
600 g grob gehackte Tomaten,
1 TL fein gehackte grüne Chilischote,
10 g frischer Ingwer, in Scheiben geschnitten,
20 g frisches Koriandergrün,
10 g Garam Masala, (siehe unten),
1 TL Bockshornkleesamen (Fenugreek),
200 g Zwiebel, fein gehackt,
Salz

Das Hühnerfleisch in ca. 2 cm große Stücke schneiden. Knoblauch und Ingwer im Mörser zu einer feinen Paste zerstossen. In einem Schmortopf das Öl erhitzen, die Paste zugeben und leicht Farbe nehmen lassen. Koriandersamen zugeben, kurz anschwitzen, dann die Tomaten unterrühren und fünf Minuten köcheln lassen.
Die Hühnerbruststücke, die gehackte Chili, Ingwerscheiben und Koriandergrün zugeben, 1 - 2 Stunden bei kleiner Hitze köcheln, bis die Sauce gut eingedickt ist. Dabei regelmäßig umrühren. Garam Masala und Bockshornkleesamen unterrühren, leicht salzen und weitere 5 Minuten köcheln. Mit Salz abschmecken.

INDISCHER SAFRANREIS

Für 4 Personen:

400 g Basmati Reis,
2 EL Erdnussöl,
1 TL Kreuzkümmelsamen,
2 Gewürznelken,
2 Lorbeerblätter,
Salz,
1 Messerspitze Safranfäden

Das Öl in einem Topf erhitzen. Die Kreuzkümmelsamen zugeben und bei kleiner Hitze rösten, bis sie zu springen anfangen. Den Reis unterrühren und kurz andünsten. Mit Wasser auffüllen, bis der Reis bedeckt ist und zum Kochen bringen. Gewürznelken und Lorbeer zugeben, leicht salzen, zudecken, die Hitze auf die unterste Stufe zurückdrehen und den Reis zehn Minuten quellen lassen. Zum Schluss die Safranfäden unterrühren, weitere zehn Minuten zugedeckt ziehen lassen.

INDISCHES LAMMCURRY (GOSCHT VINDALOO)

Für 4 Personen:

800 g Lammfleisch aus der Keule, in Würfel geschnitten

4 EL Sonnenblumenöl,
2 mittelgroße Zwiebeln, fein geschnitten,
2 TL schwarze Pfefferkörner, grob zerstoßen,
1 TL grüne Kardamomsamen, grob zerstoßen,
1 EL fein gehackte grüne Chilischote,
3 Gewürznelken,
2 EL rotes Chilipulver (oder Menge nach Belieben),
1 cm Zimtstange, grob zerdrückt,
2 TL Kreuzkümmelsamen,
2 TL Kurkuma,
1 TL Koriandersamen,
2 Knoblauchzehen, fein gehackt und im Mörser
zu einer feinen Paste zerstoßen,
2 EL fein gehackter, frischer Ingwer, im Mörser
zu einer feinen Paste zerstoßen

400 g Kartoffeln,
2 EL Sonnenblumenöl,
1 EL Malzessig, Salz, Koriandergrün

Das Öl in einem schweren Schmortopf erhitzen. Die Zwiebeln zugeben und unter Rühren goldgelb anbraten. Die Gewürze und Gewürzpasten zugeben, unter Rühren 2 - 3 Minuten braten. Das Lammfleisch zugeben, gut vermischen, dann mit Wasser auffüllen, bis das Fleisch bedeckt ist. Zum Kochen bringen, bei kleiner Hitze zugedeckt 2 bis 3 Stunden schmoren. Nach 1 Stunde den Deckel abnehmen, die Sauce soll dick einkochen. Regelmäßig umrühren. Die Kartoffeln schälen und in ca. 2 cm große Würfel schneiden. In einer Pfanne im heißen Öl bei kleiner Hitze goldbraun braten. Unter das Curry mischen und weiter köcheln, bis die Kartoffeln gar sind. Mit Malzessig und Salz abschmecken, in eine Servierschüssel füllen und mit Koriandergrün garnieren. Mit gedämpftem Reis als Beilage servieren.

NOTE:
Garam masala is an Indian spice mixture made from cumin seeds, coriander seeds, black peppercorns, cardamom, cinnamon, cloves, star anise and nutmeg. All of the spices except the nutmeg are toasted separately in a dry pan and then ground into a fine powder in a mortar, spice grinder or blender.

ANMERKUNG:
Garam Masala ist eine indische Gewürzmischung aus Koriandersamen, Kreuzkümmel, schwarzem Pfeffer, Kardamom, Zimt, Gewürznelken, Sternanis und geriebener Muskatnuss. Die Gewürze (bis auf die Muskatnuss) werden separat in der Pfanne geröstet und dann im Mörser oder Mixer zu feinem Pulver verarbeitet.

JAPANESE FONDUE

JAPANISCHES FONDUE

Yosenabe

Serves 6

150 g/5 oz salmon filet,
150 g/5 oz mackerel filet,
150 g/5 oz chicken breast,
150 g/5 oz oysters,
150 g/5 oz shrimp,
150 g/5 oz scallops, shelled,
150 g/5 oz carpet clams

1 small Chinese cabbage,
150 g/5 oz white radish (daikon),
shaved into long thin strips,
250 g/1¹/₂ lb white cabbage, cut into strips,
200 g/7 oz shiitake mushrooms,
200 g/7 oz enoki mushrooms,
200 g/7 oz green onions, coarsely chopped,
200 g/7 oz leeks, coarsely chopped,
200 g/7 oz carrots, coarsely chopped

For the stock:
2 liters/8 cups fish stock made from
dried tuna flakes (bonito),
150 ml/²/₃ cup soy sauce,
150 ml/²/₃ cup mirin (Japanese
sweet rice wine),
salt

Preparation: Cut salmon, mackerel filets
and the chicken meat into 3 cm/1¹/₂ inch
cubes. Blanch the chicken cubes and the
fish pieces separately in boiling salted water
for one minute respectively. Allow to drain
in a colander and set aside.
Shuck oysters and wash them thoroughly
under running cold water. Keep the seafood
and chicken meat cool.
Bring salted water to a rolling boil and drop
in the Chinese cabbage whole. Boil for
three minutes. Remove the cabbage head
from the water and allow to cool. Wrap
tightly into a bamboo mat and squeeze out
as much excess water as possible. Cut the
cabbage into 2 cm/³/₄ inch slices.
For the stock: In an Oriental fondue pot,
bring fish stock, soy sauce and mirin to a
boil. Check for salt.
Serving: Arrange all ingredients for the fondue on a large platter and place the platter
directly onto the table. Set the fondue pot
onto a gas or petrol burner and put it next
to the platter.
Simmer ingredients in the stock one after
the other, or have the guests simmer their
own combination of ingredients in small
wire baskets, as you prefer.
Note: The original meaning of yosenabe is
„stew" made from all kinds of ingredients.
Thus, the ingredients used can vary according to season, taste and availability.

Für 6 Personen:

150 g Lachsfilet,
150 g Makrelenfilets,
150 g Hühnerbrust,
150 g Austern,
150 g Garnelen,
150 g ausgelöste Jakobsmuscheln,
150 g Teppichmuscheln

1 kleiner Chinakohl,
150 g weißer Rettich (Daikon),
in lange dünne Streifen gehobelt,
250 g Weißkohl, in Streifen geschnitten,
200g Shiitakepilze,
200 g Enokipilze,
200 g Frühlingszwiebeln,
in Stücke geschnitten,
200 g Lauch, in Stücke geschnitten,
200 g Karotten, in Stücke geschnitten

Für die Brühe:
2 Liter Fischbrühe, mit getrockneten
Thunfischflocken (Bonito) zubereitet,
150 ml Sojasauce,
150 ml Mirin (süßer, japanischer Reiswein),
Salz

Vorbereitung: Lachs- und Makrelenfilets
und Hühnerfleisch in ca. 3 cm große Würfel schneiden. Erst das Hühnerfleisch, anschließend die Fischstücke separat in kochendem Salzwasser 1 Minute blanchieren.
Im Sieb abtropfen lassen, beiseite stellen.
Die Austern aus der Schale lösen und unter
fließendem kaltem Wasser sorgfältig waschen. Alle Meeresfrüchte und das Hühnerfleisch kalt stellen.
Den Chinakohl im Ganzen in Salzwasser
3 Minuten sprudelnd kochen. Herausnehmen, erkalten lassen, in eine Bambusmatte
wickeln und gut ausdrücken. Den Kohl in
2 cm dicke Scheiben schneiden.
Für die Brühe: Fischbrühe mit Sojasauce
und Mirin in einem asiatischen Fonduetopf
zum Kochen bringen. Mit Salz würzen.
Zum Servieren: Alle Zutaten für den Eintopf auf einer große Platte anrichten und
auf den Tisch stellen. Den Fonduetopf auf
einen Gas- oder Petroleumrechaud ebenfalls auf den Tisch stellen. Nun nach Lust
und Laune die Zutaten nach und nach in
der Brühe garen und servieren oder jeder
Gast gart seine Auswahl mit einem Draht-
körbchen in der Brühe.
Anmerkung: Yosenabe ist der Bedeutung
nach ursprünglich ein Eintopf aus allen
möglichen Zutaten. Diese können je nach
Saison, Geschmack oder Erhältlichkeit beliebig zusammengestellt werden.

SASHIMI DELUXE

Tokujyo

Serves 4

100 g/3¹/₂ oz tuna fish, cut from the belly, very fresh,
100 g/3¹/₂ oz hamachi (yellowfin tuna fish), very fresh,
100 g/3¹/₂ oz salmon filet, very fresh,
1100 g/3¹/₂ oz octopus tentacles, cooked,
100 g/3¹/₂ oz Japanese ark shells,
100 g/3¹/₂ oz prawns, very fresh, blanched,
100 g/3¹/₂ oz surimi (crabmeat imitation), or fresh
crab claw meat, cooked,
1 white radish (daikon),
160 ml/²/₃ cup soy sauce,
60 g/2 oz wasabi (Japanese
green horseradish paste),
200 g/7 oz pickled ginger (jar)

Cut all ingredients into thin slices or pieces, according to taste. Peel the radish and shave it into julienne strips.

Spread the radish strips out on a serving platter and arrange prepared fish and seafood on top. Decorate with well-drained pieces of pickled ginger.

Spoon soy sauce and wasabi paste separately into four small bowls each. At dinner, guests may mix as much wasabi as desired into their soy sauce. The sauce then serves as a dip for the seafood.

Note: The most important thing with sashimi is the absolute freshness of the ingredients. The number, amount and selection of ingredients can vary, according to taste and availability.

Für 4 Personen:

100 g Thunfisch aus dem Bauchstück geschnitten,
sehr frisch,
100 g Hamachi (Yellowfin Tuna,
Gelbflossen-Thunfisch), sehr frisch,
100 g Lachsfilet, sehr frisch,
100 g Tentakel von der Krake, gekocht,
100 g japanische Archenmuscheln,
100 g große Garnelen, sehr frisch, blanchiert,
100 g Surimi (Krebsfleisch-Ersatzprodukt), oder
frisches, gekochtes Scherenfleisch von Krebsen,
1 weißer Rettich (Daikon), 160 ml Sojasauce,
60 g Wasabi (grüne japanische Meerrettichpaste),
200 g eingelegter Ingwer (im Glas erhältlich)

Alle Zutaten nach Belieben in dünne Scheiben oder Stücke schneiden. Den Rettich schälen und in dünne Streifen (Julienne) hobeln.

Die Rettichstreifen auf eine Servierplatte ausbreiten, die vorbereiteten Zutaten darauf arrangieren, mit abgetropftem Ingwer dekorieren.

Sojasauce und Wasabi in je vier kleine Schälchen verteilen. Zum Essen rührt sich jeder Gast mit Stäbchen soviel Wasabi in seine Sojasauce, wie er mag. Diese Sauce dient zum Dippen der Zutaten.

Anmerkung: Das Wichtigste bei Sashimi ist die absolute Frische der Fische und Meeresfürchte. Menge und Art der verwendeten Zutaten können frei nach Geschmack variieren.

Buri No Mitsuke

POACHED

YELLOWTAIL MACKEREL

POCHIERTE

GELBSCHWANZMAKRELE

Serves 4

800 g/1³/₄ lb yellowtail mackerel, ready-to-cook,
head and tail fin removed,
500 g/1 lb white radish (daikon), peeled,
150 g/5 oz ginger, peeled, sliced,
750 ml/3 cups water,
500 ml/2 cups sake (Japanese rice wine),
80 g/3 oz sugar,
150 ml/²/₃ cup soy sauce,
parsley for garnish

Cut the fish into 4 cm/1¹/₂ inch pieces. In a large pot, bring salted water to a boil. Drop in fish pieces and remove them after 10 - 20 seconds with a skimmer.
Cut the radish into thick slices. Boil the slices in salted water for fifteen minutes, drain thoroughly in a colander.
In a heavy-bottomed casserole, layer fish pieces with radish and ginger slices. Pour in water and sake. Bring to a boil, reduce heat and allow to steep for fifteen minutes (liquid should not boil). Remove any foam that is rising to the surface with a skimmer. Stir in sugar and poach for another hour, until the liquid is reduced by about half. Add soy sauce and allow to steep for another hour.
Serving: Carefully place radish and fish pieces into soup bowls, ladle soup on top and garnish the bowls with a generous amount of parsley. Serve.

Für 4 Personen:

800 g Gelbschwanzmakrele (Yellowtail), küchenfertig,
ohne Kopf und ohne Schwanzflosse,
500 g weißer Rettich (Daikon), geschält,
150 g Ingwer, geschält, in Scheiben geschnitten,
750 ml Wasser,
500 ml Sake (japanischer Reiswein), 80 g Zucker,
150 ml Sojasauce,
Petersilie (Garnitur)

Den Fisch in ca. 4 cm große Stücke schneiden. In einem Topf Salzwasser zum Kochen bringen. Die Fischstücke zugeben, nach 10 - 20 Sekunden mit der Lochkelle wieder herausheben.
Den Rettich in dicke Scheiben schneiden. In Salzwasser fünfzehn Minuten kochen, anschließend den Kochsud abgießen.
In einem Schmortopf die Fischstücke mit dem Rettich und dem Ingwer einschichten. Mit Wasser und Sake aufgießen. Zum Kochen bringen, dann 15 Minuten bei reduzierter Hitze pochieren (Flüssigkeit soll nicht kochen). Mit einer Lochkelle regelmäßig den Schaum abschöpfen. Den Zucker unterrühren und ca. eine Stunde pochieren, bis sich die Flüssigkeit um ca. die Hälfte reduziert hat. Dann die Sojasauce zugeben und eine weitere Stunde pochieren.
Zum Servieren: Die Fischstücke und den Rettich vorsichtig in Suppenschalen verteilen, mit Suppe aufgießen, mit Petersilie garnieren und servieren.

Serves 4

600 g/1¹/₃ lb U.S. beef sirloin,
2 onions,
300 g white radish,
1 tsp ground chili pepper, salt,
120 ml/¹/₂ cup Ponzu sauce (Japanese sauce made from soy
sauce, lemon juice, rice wine and seaweed),
lettuce leaves

Rub the beef with salt and sear it in a pan in hot oil until dark brown on all sides. Remove the meat from the pan, let it cool and cut it into evenly thin slices.

Cut the onion in half, slice the halves and pull the rings apart with your fingers. Blanch the onion pieces in boiling salted water for one minute, place them in a sieve and douse them with cold water to cool them down quickly. Allow to drain well.

Peel the radish and shave it into long thin slices. Grate the radish trimmings finely, add ground chili pepper and a little salt and knead the mixture into an orange paste.

Serving: Arrange circles of beef slices on plates. Place a leaf of lettuce in the middle of each plate, top with radish strips and finish with blanched onions. Shape the chili-radish paste into four small balls and place them on top of the onions. Spoon the sauce into small bowls. Place the bowls next to the plates for dipping. Serve.

Für 4 Personen:

600 g US Beef Sirloin (Roastbeef),
2 Zwiebeln,
300 g weißer Rettich (Daikon),
1 TL Chilipulver,
Salz,
120 ml Ponzu-Sauce (japanische Sauce aus Sojasauce,
Zitronensaft, Reiswein und Seealgen),
4 Salatblätter

Das Rindfleisch mit Salz bestreuen und in einer Pfanne im heißen Öl rundum dunkelbraun anbraten. Aus der Pfanne nehmen, erkalten lassen und das Fleisch in geichmäßig dünne Scheiben schneiden.

Die Zwiebeln halbieren, in Scheiben schneiden und mit den Fingern in einzelne Ringe teilen. In kochendem Salzwasser eine Minute blanchieren, dann die Zwiebeln in ein Sieb gießen, in kaltem Wasser rasch abkühlen und gut abtropfen lassen.

Den Rettich schälen und in lange dünne Streifen hobeln. Die Abschnitte vom Rettich fein reiben, mit Chilipulver und etwas Salz zu einer orangefarbenen Paste verarbeiten.

Zum Servieren: Die Rindfleischscheiben kreisförmig auf Teller auslegen. In die Mitte jeweils ein Salatblatt legen und die Rettichstreifen darüber häufen. Mit blanchierten Zwiebeln bedecken. Aus der Rettich-Chilipaste vier Kugeln formen und obenauf setzen. Die Sauce in kleine Schälchen füllen und zum Tunken neben die Teller legen.

BEEF
IN A PONZU SAUCE

RINDFLEISCH
MIT PONZU SAUCE

Gyniku No Tataki

JAPANESE MEAT FONDUE

JAPANISCHES FLEISCHFONDUE

Sukiyaki

Serves 4

600 g/1¹/₃ lb U.S. beef sirloin, cut into thin slices,
200 g/7 oz white cabbage,
300 g/11 oz Swiss chard,
200 g/7 oz carrots,
150 g/5 oz onions,
150 g/5 oz green onions,
100 g/3¹/₂ oz shiitake mushrooms,
100 g/3¹/₂ oz enoki mushrooms,
200 g/7 oz fresh tofu, cut into pieces,
200 g/7 oz Japanese wheat noodles (somen),
boiled, refreshed in cold water, well-drained

For the sauce:
180 ml/³/₄ cup soy sauce,
150 ml/²/₃ cup mirin (Japanese sweet rice wine),
150 ml/²/₃ cup sake (Japanese rice wine),
120 g/4 oz sugar

For the stock:
1.5 liters/6 cups vegetable stock,
2 tbsp beef tallow

Trim all vegetables and cut them into bite-sized, not too small pieces. Arrange them with the meat, tofu and noodles on a large serving platter.
For the sauce: Combine all ingredients in a pot and bring the mixture to a boil. Allow to cool.
For the stock: Combine vegetable stock and tallow, stirring until the fat is dissolved. Season the stock with the finished sauce, according to taste. Spoon remaining sauce into four small bowls for dipping.
Finish: Pour stock into a fondue pot and place the pot onto a burner on the table. Regulate the heat of the burner such that the temperature of the liquid remains just below the boiling point.
At dinner, place equal portions of meat, noodles, vegetables and tofu into the stock. Guests may take out what they please with their chopsticks, dipping the pieces into their sauce bowls according to taste. At the end, bring the stock to a boil again and ladle it into four soup bowls for drinking.

Für 4 Personen:

600 g US Beef Sirloin, in dünne Scheiben geschnitten,
200 g Weißkohl,
300 g Mangold,
200 g Karotte,
150 g Zwiebeln,
150 g Frühlingszwiebeln,
100 g Shiitakepilze,
100 g Enokipilze,
200 g frischer Tofu, in Stücke geschnitten,
200 g japanische Weizennudeln (Somen), gekocht,
kalt abgeschreckt, gut abgetropft

Für die Sauce:
180 ml Sojasauce,
150 ml Mirin (süßer japanischer Reiswein),
150 ml Sake (japanischer Reiswein),
120 g Zucker

Für die Brühe:
1,5 Liter Gemüsebrühe,
2 EL Rinderfett

Gemüse und Pilze putzen und in mundgerechte Stücke schneiden. Mit dem Fleisch, dem Tofu und den Nudeln auf eine große Servierplatte anrichten.
Für die Sauce: Alle Zutaten in einem Topf zum Kochen bringen, anschließend erkalten lassen.
Für die Brühe: Die Gemüsebrühe mit dem Fett zum Kochen bringen und rühren, bis sich das Fett aufgelöst hat. Die Brühe mit der vorbereiteten Sauce nach Geschmack würzen, die restliche Sauce zum Dippen in vier kleine Schälchen anrichten.
Fertigstellung: Die Brühe in einem Fonduetopf auf einem Rechaud auf den Tisch stellen und die Hitzezufuhr so regulieren, dass die Flüssigkeit stets vor dem Siedepunkt steht. Zum Essen je eine Portion Fleisch, Nudeln, Gemüse und Tofu in die Brühe geben. Jeder Gast fischt sich mit Stäbchen die gegarten Zutaten heraus und dippt sie nach Belieben in die Sauce. Zuletzt die Brühe zum Kochen bringen, zum Trinken in vier Suppenschalen verteilen.

HOT-AND-SOUR SOUP WITH COCONUT MILK AND NOODLES

SCHARF-SAURE SUPPE MIT KOSKOSMILCH UND NUDELN

Laksa Lemak

Serves 4

800 ml/3 cups coconut milk

For the spice paste:
40 g/1 ¹/₂ oz red chili pepper, finely diced,
40 g/1 ¹/₂ oz shallots, peeled, finely diced,
1 tbsp finely diced lemongrass
(use core only),
20 g/1 oz galangal root, peeled, finely diced
(alternatively ground galangal),
1 tsp finely diced fresh turmeric
(alternatively ground turmeric),
1 tsp shrimp paste,
3 tbsp sunflower oil

16 Vietnamese mint leaves (rau bac ha,
alternatively ordinary mint leaves),
200 g/7 oz fresh tofu, cubed,
500 g/1 lb yellow egg noodles, cooked,
200 g/7 oz bean sprouts,
12 medium prawns, blanched, cleaned and shelled,
1 red chili pepper (or according to taste), seeded, cut
into thin strips,
4 quail eggs, hard-boiled, peeled, halved

In a small pot, bring the coconut milk to a boil, uncovered, and allow to reduce by half.
For the spice paste: Finely purée all ingredients in a blender. Heat the oil in a small pot and sauté spice paste for ten minutes on low heat. Allow to cool.
Combine reduced coconut milk and spice paste and mix well. Add laksa leaves and bring to a boil once more.
Place noodles, bean sprouts, tofu cubes and shrimp into soup bowls. Ladle on some hot coconut soup and garnish the bowls with halved quail eggs and strips of red chili pepper. Serve.

Für 4 Personen:

800 ml Kokosmilch

Für die Würzpaste:
40 g rote Chili, entkernt, fein gehackt,
40 g Schalotten, geschält, fein gehackt,
1 EL fein gehacktes Zitronengras (nur den inneren,
weichen Teil verwenden),
20 g Galangawurzel, geschält, fein gehackt,
(ersatzweise Galangapulver verwenden),
1 TL fein gehackte frische Kurkumawurzel,
(Gelbwurzel, ersatzweise Kurkumapulver verwenden),
1 TL getrocknete Garnelenpaste,
3 EL Sonnenblumenöl

16 vietnamesische Minzblätter (Rau bac ha,
ersatzweise normale Minze verwenden),
200 g frischer Tofu, in Würfel geschnitten,
500 g gelbe Eiernudeln, gekocht,
200 g Sojabohnensprossen,
12 mittelgroße Garnelen, blanchiert, geputzt, geschält,
1 rote Chilischote (oder Menge nach Belieben),
entkernt, in dünne Streifen geschnitten,
4 Wachteleier, hart gekocht, geschält, halbiert

Die Kokosmilch in einem Topf ohne Deckel bei kleiner Hitze um die Hälfte einkochen.
Für die Würzpaste: Alle Zutaten im Mixer fein pürieren. Das Öl in einem kleinen Topf erhitzen, die Gewürze bei kleiner Hitze zehn Minuten braten. Erkalten lassen. Die eingekochte Kokosmilch mit der Würzpaste gut verrühren, die Minzeblätter zugeben, einmal aufkochen lassen.
Nudeln, Sojabohnensprossen, Tofuwürfel und Garnelenschwänze in Suppenschalen anrichten. Mit der heißen Kokossuppe übergießen, mit Wachteleierhälften und Chilistreifen garnieren.

THAI PRAWN MOUSSE ON A SUGAR CANE
WITH PINEAPPLE RELISH

THAILÄNDISCHE GARNELENMOUSSE AUF ZUCKERROHRSTÄNGEL
MIT ANANAS-RELISH

Serves 4

400 g/14 oz tiger prawns, shelled,
2 garlic cloves and about the same amount of
coriander root, both finely diced and ground
into a fine paste in a mortar,
1 egg,
1 tsp salt,
2 tsp sugar,
4 pieces of sugar cane,
1 cup freshly grated breadcrumbs,
oil for deep-frying

For the pineapple relish:
2 tbsp sugar,
200 g/7 oz pineapple, cut into $^1/_2$ cm/$^1/_5$ inch cubes,
2 tsp finely diced chili peppers,
salt,
60 ml/$^1/_4$ cup lime juice

Dice the tiger prawns very finely with a sharp knife. Combine the prawn pieces, coriander root paste, garlic, egg, salt and sugar in a bowl. Mix well. Shape the mixture into four cones, each around a piece of sugar cane.

Right before serving, turn the skewered cones in breadcrumbs und fry them in hot oil until golden brown. Drain well on paper towels.

For the pineapple relish: In a small pot, caramelize the sugar until medium brown. Add the pineapple cubes and the diced chili pepper (Be careful of splattering!). Stir until well blended. Add lime juice and simmer until the sauce has thickened. Season with salt and remove from heat. Allow to cool.

Serving: Arrange the fried prawn mousse skewers on plates and serve the relish on the side in separate small bowls for dipping.

Für 4 Personen:

400 g Riesengarnelen, geschält,
2 Knoblauchzehen und ca. die gleiche Menge
Korianderwurzel, beides fein gehackt und im Mörser
zu einer feinen Paste zerstoßen,
1 Ei,
1 TL Salz,
2 TL Zucker,
4 Zuckerrohrstangen,
1 Tasse frisch geriebene Semmelbrösel,
Öl zum Ausbacken

Für das Ananas-Relish:
2 EL Zucker,
200 g Ananas, in $^1/_2$ cm große Würfel geschnitten,
2 TL fein gehackte rote Chilischote,
Salz,
60 ml Limettensaft

Die Riesengarnelen mit einem großen Messer sehr fein hacken. In einer Schüssel mit der Korianderwurzel-Knoblauchpaste, Ei, Salz und Zucker gut vermischen. Aus der Masse vier Kegel formen und diese auf je einen Zuckerrohrstängel spießen. Kurz vor dem Servieren in Semmelbröseln wenden und im heißen Öl goldbraun ausbacken. Auf Küchenpapier abtropfen lassen.

Für das Ananas-Relish: In einem kleinen Topf den Zucker mittelbraun karamellisieren. Ananas- und Chiliwürfel vorsichtig zugeben (kann spritzen!) und unterrühren. Limettensaft zugießen und köcheln, bis die Sauce eingedickt ist. Mit Salz würzen, das Relish vom Herd nehmen und abkühlen lassen.

Zum Servieren: Die goldbraun frittierten Garnelenmousse-Spieße auf Teller anrichten, das Relish zum Dippen in einem separaten Schälchen servieren.

HOT SEAFOOD SALAD

SCHARFER MEERESFRÜCHTE-SALAT

Yam Thalay

Serves 4	*Für 4 Personen:*

150 g/5 oz squid, cut into strips,	*150 g Tintenfisch, in Streifen geschnitten,*
150 g/5 oz scallops, quartered,	*150 g Jakobsmuscheln, in Viertel geschnitten,*
150 g/5 oz red snapper filet, cut into strips,	*150 g Red Snapper-Filet, in Streifen geschnitten,*
150 g/5 oz shrimp, shelled	*150 g Garnelen, geschält (nach Belieben das*
(tail segment on if desired)	*Schwanzglied belassen)*

40 g/1¹/₂ oz dried curry paste (according to taste),	*40 g getrocknete Chilipaste (oder nach Belieben),*
70 ml/¹/₄ cup Thai fish sauce,	*70 ml thailändische Fischsauce,*
70 ml/¹/₄ cup lime juice, freshly squeezed,	*70 ml frisch gepresster Limettensaft,*
1 tbsp brown sugar,	*1 EL brauner Zucker,*
4 shallots, halved	*4 Schalotten, halbiert und in dünne*
and cut into fine slices,	*Scheiben geschnitten,*
2 stalks lemongrass, chopped into pieces,	*2 Zitronengrasstängel, in Stücke geschnitten,*
6 kaffir lime leaves,	*6 Kaffir-Limettenblätter,*
cut into very thin strips	*in sehr dünne Streifen geschnitten*

Garnish: lettuce leaves, peppermint leaves,	*Garnitur: Salatblätter, Pfefferminzblätter,*
1 red chili pepper, cut into fine strips	*1 rote Chilischote, in dünne Streifen geschnitten*

Bring salted water to a boil and cook the seafood on low heat for three minutes. Drain in a colander and rinse with cold water to cool down quickly. Allow excess water to drip off and keep cool.

In a bowl, combine the curry paste and fish sauce with lime juice and sugar. Mix well. Add shallots, lemongrass and lime leaves. Allow to rest for an hour, then toss the sauce with the seafood. Correct seasonings.

Serving: Line four plates with lettuce leaves. Arrange seafood salad on top and sprinkle with strips of chili pepper and peppermint leaves.

Photograph: pumpkin carved into a shell shape.

Die Meeresfrüchte in kochendem Salzwasser bei kleiner Hitze drei Minuten garen, durch ein Sieb abgießen, unter fließendem kaltem Wasser schnell abkühlen. Gut abtropfen lassen, kühl stellen.

Die Chilipaste in einer Schüssel mit der Fischsauce, Limettensaft und Zucker verrühren. Die Schalotten, Zitronengras und Limettenblätter zugeben. Eine Stunde stehen lassen, dann mit den Meeresfrüchten gut vermischen. Den Salat abschmecken.

Zum Servieren: Vier Teller mit Salatblättern auslegen. Den Meeresfrüchtesalat darauf verteilen, mit Chilistreifen und Pfefferminzblättern bestreuen.

Foto: muschelförmig geschnitzter Kürbis.

SESAME NOODLE SALAD WITH SOY CHICKEN

SESAM-NUDELSALAT MIT SOJA-HUHN

Serves 4

200 g/7 oz Thai baby eggplants ("green tiger"),
70 ml/¹/₄ cup olive oil,
200 g/7 oz chicken breast,
4 tbsp sweet soy sauce,
300 g/11 oz thin egg noodles, cooked,
refreshed in cold water and well-drained,
100 g/3¹/₂ oz snow peas, blanched,
cut into julienne strips,
120 g/4 oz baby carrots, blanched,
cut into julienne strips,
100 g/3¹/₂ oz red cabbage, cut into julienne strips,
1 tsp finely chopped parsley,
1 tsp toasted white sesame seeds,
1 tsp toasted black sesame seeds

For the dressing:
3 tbsp sweet soy sauce,
3 tbsp light soy sauce,
1 tbsp sesame oil,
2 tbsp sunflower oil,
3 tbsp rice wine vinegar,
white pepper

Garnish: lotus root, cut into thin slices
and fried in hot oil

Halve eggplants and roast them under the broiler on both sides. Brush them with a little olive oil and dressing made by combining the ingredients for dressing listed above.
In a small pot, braise chicken breast in soy sauce for about 15 minutes, turning the meat several times. Remove from the pot and allow to cool. Broil on both sides until lightly brown.
In a large bowl, mix noodles, vegetable julienne, parsley and sesame seeds. Toss with part of the dressing. Check for salt and pepper.
Serving: Arrange the noodle salad on plates. Surround with broiled eggplant halves. Cut the chicken breast into thin slices and place them on top of the salad. Garnish with lotus chips and drizzle some of the remaining dressing around it.

Für 4 Personen:

200 g thailändische Baby-Auberginen („Green Tiger"),
70 ml Olivenöl,
200 g Hühnerbrust,
4 EL süße Sojasauce,
300 g dünne Eiernudeln, gekocht, kalt abgeschreckt
und gut abgetropft,
100 g Zuckerschoten, blanchiert,
in dünne Streifen geschnitten,
120 g Minikarotten, blanchiert,
in dünne Streifen geschnitten,
100 g Rotkohl, in dünne Streifen geschnitten,
1 TL fein gehackte Petersilie,
1 TL helle, geröstete Sesamsamen,
1 TL schwarze, geröstete Sesamsamen

Für das Dressing:
3 EL süße Sojasauce,
3 EL helle Sojasauce,
1 EL Sesamöl,
2 EL Sonnenblumenöl,
3 EL Reisweinessig,
weißer Pfeffer

Garnitur: Lotoswurzel, in dünne Scheiben geschnitten
und in heißem Öl ausgebacken

Die Auberginen halbieren und auf dem Grill von beiden Seiten rösten. Mit Olivenöl und etwas angerührtem Dressing bepinseln und marinieren.
Die Hühnerbrust mit der Sojasauce in einem kleinen Topf unter mehrmaligem Wenden ca. eine Viertelstunde schmoren. Herausnehmen, erkalten lassen, unter dem Grill von beiden Seiten anrösten.
In einer Schüssel die Nudeln, die vorbereiteten Gemüsestreifen, Petersilie und die Sesamsamen mit etwas Dressing gut vermischen. Mit Salz und Pfeffer abschmecken.
Zum Servieren: Den Nudelsalat auf Teller anrichten. Mit den gegrillten Auberginenhälften umlegen. Die Hühnerbrust in dünne Scheiben schneiden und auf dem Salat verteilen. Mit Lotos-Chips garnieren, mit dem restlichen Dressing umgießen.

ASIAN GLAZED FILET OF RED SNAPPER

ASIATISCH GLASIERTES FILET VOM ROTEN SCHNAPPER

Serves 4

4 filets of red snapper, skin on, about 120 g/4 oz each,
¹/₂ tsp white pepper, freshly ground,
2 tbsp olive oil

For the glaze:
1 tsp onion, finely diced, ¹/₂ garlic clove, finely diced,
¹/₂ tsp ginger, finely diced, 1 tbsp sesame oil,
120 ml/¹/₂ cup hearty fish stock, 1 tbsp veal stock,
60 ml/¹/₄ cup sake (Japanese rice wine),
1 tbsp freshly squeezed lemon juice,
2 tbsp rice wine vinegar, 1 tsp turmeric

For the vinaigrette:
2 tbsp sesame oil, 2 tbsp rice wine vinegar,
1 tsp Shichimi togarashi (Japanese spice mixture
made from chili peppers, poppy-seeds, white sesame seeds,
tangerine peel, hemp,
dried shiso leaves and nori seaweed),
60 ml/¹/₄ cup Japanese soy sauce, 3 tbsp dry sherry,
1 tbsp freshly squeezed lemon juice, 2 tsp honey,
2 tbsp finely diced mixed peppers (red, yellow, green),
2 tsp finely diced red onion,
1 tbsp finely chopped parsley,
1 tbsp lightly toasted sesame seeds

200 g/7 oz fresh, tender spinach leaves, washed,
30 g/1 oz arugula leaves, washed,
1 tbsp olive oil, salt, freshly ground white pepper,
4 pumpkin slices of a diameter of about 12 cm/5 inches, cooked in
salted water until al dente)

Garnish:
4 lotus leaves (or 4 banana leaves trimmed into rounds),
4 edible blossoms,
¹/₂ tsp dried red chili pepper, coarsely crushed in a mortar

Rub fish filets with white pepper. Heat the oil in a pan. When oil is very hot, sear the filets on both sides, then place them on a baking sheet, skin-side up.
For the glaze: Sauté onion, garlic and ginger in sesame oil until translucent. Douse with fish stock, veal stock, sake, lemon juice and vinegar and stir in turmeric. Reduce the liquid by half and pass it through a fine sieve.
For the vinaigrette: Combine all ingredients and mix well.
Finish: Sauté spinach and arugula leaves in olive oil until wilted. Season with a little salt and pepper. Drop the pumpkin slices into hot salted water until heated through. Brush the fish filets with the glaze and cook under the broiler until done.
Serving: Line the plates with the lotus or banana leaves. Place a pumpkin slice on top and on it a little spinach-arugula mixture. Top with one piece of fish each. Drizzle on a little vinaigrette and garnish with edible blossoms and some crushed chili pepper. Serve.

Für 4 Personen:

4 Filets vom Roten Schnapper, mit Haut, je ca. 120 g,
¹/₂ TL weißer Pfeffer, frisch gemahlen,
2 EL Olivenöl

Für die Glasur:
1 TL fein gehackte Zwiebel, ¹/₂ Knoblauchzehe, fein gehackt,
¹/₂ TL fein gehackter Ingwer, 1 EL Sesamöl,
120 ml kräftiger Fischfond, 2 EL Kalbsfond,
60 ml Sake (japanischer Reiswein),
1 EL frisch gepresster Zitronensaft,
2 EL Reisweinessig, 1 TL Kurkumapulver

Für die Vinaigrette:
2 EL Sesamöl, 2 EL Reisweinessig,
1 TL Shichimi Togarashi (japanische Gewürzmischung
aus Chili, Mohnsamen, weißen Sesamsamen,
Mandarinenschale, Hanf, getrockneten Shisoblättern
und Nori-Algen),
60 ml japanische Sojasauce, 3 EL trockener Sherry,
1 EL frisch gepresster Zitronensaft, 2 TL Honig,
2 EL fein gewürfelte gemischte Paprika (rot, gelb und grün),
2 TL fein gewürfelte rote Zwiebel,
1 EL fein gehackte glatte Petersilie,
1 EL hell geröstete Sesamsamen

200 g frische, zarte Spinatblätter, gewaschen,
30 g Rucolablätter, gewaschen,
1 EL Olivenöl, Salz, weißer Pfeffer aus der Mühle,
4 Kürbisscheiben von ca. 12 cm Durchmesser,
in Salzwasser knapp gar gekocht

Garnitur:
4 Lotosblätter (oder 4 rund zugeschnittene Bananenblätter),
4 essbare Blüten,
¹/₂ TL getrocknete rote Chilischote, grob zermörsert

Fischfilets mit weißem Pfeffer würzen. Das Öl in einer Pfanne stark erhitzen. Die Filets von beiden Seiten kurz anbraten, dann mit der Hautseite nach oben auf ein Blech legen.
Für die Glasur: Zwiebel, Knoblauch und Ingwer im Sesamöl glasig dünsten. Mit Fischfond, Kalbsfond, Sake, Zitronensaft und Essig aufgießen, Kurkuma unterrühren, die Flüssigkeit auf die Hälfte einkochen. Durch ein Sieb passieren.
Für die Vinaigrette: Alle Zutaten in einer Schüssel gut verrühren.
Fertigstellung: Spinat und Rucolablätter in Olivenöl dünsten, bis die Blätter zusammenfallen. Mit Salz und weißem Pfeffer würzen. Die Kürbisscheiben in Salzwasser erhitzen. Die Fischfilets mit der Glasur bestreichen und unter dem Grill fertig garen.
Zum Servieren: Die Lotosblätter auf Teller auslegen. In die Mitte jeweils eine Kürbisscheibe legen, darüber etwas Spinat-Rucola-Gemüse häufen, mit je einem Fischfilet bedecken. Mit Vinaigrette beträufeln, mit Blüten garnieren, mit etwas Chilipulver bestreuen.

SPICY FRESHWATER SHRIMP SOUP WITH LEMONGRASS, LIMES AND CHILI PEPPER

WÜRZIGE SÜSSWASSERGARNELEN-SUPPE MIT ZITRONENGRAS, LIMETTEN UND CHILI

Tom Yam Kung

Serves 4

*600 g/1 1/3 lb freshwater shrimp
cleaned and shelled according to taste*

*1.5 liters/6 cups mixed chicken and crustaceans stocks,
2 stalks lemon grass, cut into pieces,
200 g/7 oz mushrooms (champignons, shiitake),
1 piece coriander root,
6 kaffir lime leaves,
100 ml/ 1/3 cup fish sauce,
60 ml/ 1/4 cup lime juice, freshly squeezed,
1 tsp finely diced strips of red chili pepper,
1 - 2 tbsp dry red curry paste,
1 bunch coriander, leaves only*

In a large pot, bring stock mixture to a boil. Add lemon-grass, mushrooms, coriander root and lime leaves. Simmer on low heat for ten minutes. Add shrimp and simmer for another five minutes. Season the soup to taste with fish sauce, lime juice, chili pepper strips and curry paste.
Serving: Ladle the soup into shallow bowls and sprinkle a generous amount of coriander leaves on top.

Für 4 Personen:

600 g Süßwassergarnelen, geputzt, nach Belieben geschält

*1,5 Liter Hühner- und Krustentierbrühe, gemischt,
2 Stängel Zitronengras, in Stücke geschnitten,
200 g Pilze (Champignons, Shiitake),
1 Stück Korianderwurzel,
6 Kaffir-Limetten-Blätter,
100 ml Fischsauce,
60 ml frisch gepresster Limettensaft,
1 TL fein geschnittene rote Chilistreifen,
1 - 2 EL getrocknete rote Chilipaste,
1 Bund Koriandergrün, nur die Blättchen*

Die Brühe in einem Topf zum Kochen bringen. Das Zitronengras, Pilze, Korianderwurzel und Limettenblätter zugeben, bei kleiner Hitze 10 Minuten sieden. Die Garnelen zugeben, weitere 5 Minuten köcheln. Die Suppe mit Fischsauce, Limettensaft, Chilistreifen und -paste würzen und abschmecken.
Zum Servieren: Die Suppe in Schalen füllen und großzügig mit Korianderblättchen überstreuen.

ROAST DUCK CURRY WITH COCONUT
AND THAI HERBS

CURRY VON GERÖSTETER ENTE MIT KOKOSNUSS
UND THAILÄNDISCHEN KRÄUTERN

Kaeng Phed Ped Yang

Serves 4

¹/₂ roasted, glazed duck,
1 liter/4 cups coconut milk,
2 tbsp red curry paste (according to taste),
80 g/3 oz water chestnuts (can),
200 g/7 oz small Thai eggplants
(the hazelnut-sized, green round variety),
100 g/7 oz cherry tomatoes,
1 red chili pepper, seeded, cut into strips,
100 ml/¹/₃ cup Thai fish sauce

Garnish:
8 kaffir lime leaves,
cut into very thin strips,
12 Thai basil leaves
(alternatively ordinary basil)

Bone the glazed duck and cut it into bite-sized pieces with the skin on. Set them aside.
Combine coconut milk and curry paste in a pot and heat slowly over low heat, stirring constantly. Add water chestnuts and duck meat and bring to a boil. Simmer on low heat, uncovered, for ten minutes. Add eggplants, cherry tomatoes and chili pepper strips and simmer for another three minutes. Stir in fish sauce and season to taste.
Serving: Ladle the duck curry into small bowls and sprinkle with thin lime leaf strips and basil leaves. Serve.

Für 4 Personen:

¹/₂ geröstete, glasierte Ente,
1 Liter Kokosmilch,
2 EL rote Currypaste (oder nach Belieben),
80 g Wasserkastanien, geschält (in Dosen erhältlich),
200 g kleine thailändische Auberginen,
(haselnussgroße, grüne Kugeln),
100 g Kirschtomaten,
1 rote Chili, entkernt, in Streifen geschnitten,
100 ml thailändische Fischsauce

Garnitur:
8 Kaffir-Limettenblätter,
in sehr dünne Streifen geschnitten,
12 thailändische Basilikumblätter
(ersatzweise normales Basilikum)

Die glasierte Ente entbeinen und mit der Haut in Stücke schneiden. Beiseite stellen.
In einem Topf die Kokosmilch mit der Currypaste verrühren, langsam erhitzen. Wasserkastanien und Entenfleisch zugeben, zum Kochen bringen, ohne Deckel bei kleiner Hitze 10 Minuten köcheln lassen. Auberginen, Kirschtomaten und Chilistreifen zugeben, weitere 3 Minuten köcheln. Mit der Fischsauce würzen und abschmecken.
Zum Servieren: Das Curry in Schüsselchen anrichten, mit Limettenblätterstreifen und Basilikumblättern überstreuen.

STEAMED CHICKEN BREASTS STUFFED WITH SHIITAKE MUSHROOMS IN A LEMONGRASS SAUCE

GEDÄMPFTE HÜHNERBRUST MIT SHIITAKE GEFÜLLT AN ZITRONENGRASSAUCE

Serves 4

500 g/ 1 lb chicken breast, boned, skin on,
1 tsp salt, freshly ground white pepper,
50 g/1¹/₂ oz cashews and 50 g/1¹/₂ oz flat-leaf parsley,
ground into a very fine paste in a mortar,
150 g/5 oz shiitake mushrooms, cleaned, stems removed, diced finely,
4 stalks lemongrass

For the rice cakes:
400 ml/1²/₃ cup chicken stock,
4 pandan leaves (leaves of screwpine, sweet and aromatic in flavor)
1 tbsp shallot, minced, 1 tbsp butter,
150 g/5 oz short grain rice, 80 ml/¹/₄ cup coconut milk,
1 tbsp grated ginger, 2 tbsp butter for frying

For the lemongrass sauce:
120 ml/¹/₂ cup lobster stock,
80 ml/¹/₄ cup coconut milk,
1 stalk lemongrass, chopped, 1 tsp ginger, minced, 2 tbsp cold butter

2 heads bok choy, halved, blanched,
200 g/7 oz baby carrots, peeled and blanched, 2 tbsp sunflower oil

Garnish:
1 beetroot, cut into very fine angel hair strands (mandolin) and fried
until crisp in hot oil, 1 tbsp chili pepper oil, 1 tbsp basil oil

Für 4 Personen:

500 g Hühnerbrust, mit Haut (ohne Knochen),
1 TL Salz, weißer Pfeffer aus der Mühle,
50 g Cashewnüsse und 50 g Koriandergrün,
im Mörser zu einer feinen Paste verarbeitet,
150 g Shiitakepilze, geputzt, Stiele entfernt,
in kleine Würfel geschnitten, 4 Zitronengrasstängel

Für die Reiskuchen:
400 g Hühnerbrühe, 4 Pandanusblätter (Screwpine Leaf, Blätter
vom asiatischen Schraubenbaum, würzig-süß im Aroma),
1 EL fein gehackte Schalotte, 1 EL Butter,
150 g Rundkornreis, 80 ml Kokosmilch,
1 EL geriebener Ingwer, 2 EL Butter zum Braten

Für die Zitronengrassauce:
120 ml Hummerfond, 80 ml Kokosmilch,
1 Zitronengrasstängel, gehackt,
1 TL gehackter Ingwer, 2 EL kalte Butter

2 Pak-Choi Stauden, halbiert, blanchiert,
200 g Minikarotten, geschält, blanchiert, 2 EL Sonnenblumenöl

Garnitur:
1 Rote Bete, in haarfeine Streifen geschnitten (Maschine) und in
heißem Öl knusprig frittiert, 1 EL Chiliöl, 1 EL Basilikumöl

Lay the chicken breast out flat in a heavy-duty plastic bag (e.g. a freezer bag) and pound into an even thickness. Remove it from the bag and insert the nut-parsley paste in between meat and skin. Spread the chicken breast out flat on the counter with the skin-side down. Sprinkle with salt and pepper and top with a layer of diced mushrooms. Roll the meat into a firm roll and wrap it tightly in aluminum foil. Steam the roll for 15 - 20 minutes and allow it to cool in the foil. Unwrap the roll and cut it into eight equal pieces, about 2 cm/³/₄ in thick. Skewer two slices at a time diagonally with a lemongrass stalk. Set skewers aside.

For the rice cakes: Simmer pandan leaves in chicken stock for fifteen minutes. Strain and discard leaves. In a heavy-bottomed casserole, sauté shallot in butter. Add rice and sauté until coated with butter. Add chicken stock, coconut milk and ginger and cook until you have a thick, risotto-style mixture. Allow to cool and shape the rice into flat cakes. Fry the cakes in butter on both sides until golden brown. Keep warm.

For the lemongrass sauce: Bring lobster stock and coconut milk to a boil with chopped lemongrass and ginger and reduce by a third. Pass the sauce through a fine sieve and whisk in cold butter, one piece at a time. Check for salt and pepper.

Finish: Sauté the vegetables in hot oil until just done and keep warm. Finish steaming chicken breast skewers carefully, until done.

Serving: Arrange vegetables on plates and place skewers on top. Sprinkle with red beet angel hair and decorate with colored oils.

Die Hühnerbrust in einen starken Plastikbeutel (z.B. Gefrierbeutel) legen und gleichmäßig flachklopfen. Aus dem Beutel nehmen, die Nuss-Korianderpaste unter die Haut streichen. Das Fleisch mit der Haut nach unten flach auslegen. Mit Salz und weißem Pfeffer bestreuen, mit gehackten Pilzen belegen. Zu einer festen Rolle aufwickeln und gut in Alufolie einpacken. Im Dampf 15 - 20 Minuten garen, in der Folie auskühlen lassen. Die Rollen auspacken, das Fleisch in acht ca. 2 cm dicke Scheiben schneiden. Je einen Zitronengrasstängel quer durch zwei Scheiben stecken, beiseite legen.

Für die Reiskuchen: Hühnerbrühe mit Pandanblättern 15 Minuten köcheln, anschließend die Blätter entfernen. In einem Topf mit schwerem Boden die Schalotte in der Butter anschwitzen. Reis zugeben und dünsten. Mit Hühnerbrühe und Kokosmilch auffüllen, den Ingwer zugeben und den Reis zu einem dicken Risotto kochen. Erkalten lassen, zu flachen Kuchen formen und diese in Butter von beiden Seiten goldbraun braten. Warmhalten.

Für die Zitronengrassauce: Hummerfond und Kokosmilch mit gehacktem Zitronengras und Ingwer um ein Drittel einkochen, durch ein Sieb passieren, dann mit einem Schneebesen die kalte Butter unterrühren. Abschmecken.

Fertigstellung: Gemüse im Öl knapp gar dünsten, warm halten. Die Hühnerscheiben im Dampf vorsichtig fertig garen.

Zum Servieren: Gemüse auf Teller anrichten, mit den Hühnerbrust-Spießen belegen. Die frittierten Rote-Bete-Streifen darüber streuen, mit aromatisierten Ölen farblich abwechselnd beträufeln.

STEAMING LEMONGRASS AND GINGER SHERBET

DAMPFENDES ZITRONENGRAS-INGWER-SORBET

Makes about 1 liter/4 cups of sherbet

For the sherbet:
3 fresh lemongrass stalks,
1 liter/4 cups syrup (500 g/1 lb sugar and
60 g/2 oz glucose heated with 450 ml/1²/₃ cups water
until the sugar crystals are dissolved),
75 g/2¹/₂ oz fresh ginger, peeled, finely grated,
zest of one lime,
1 egg white, beaten

Finely dice the heart (the inner core) of the lemongrass stalks and mix with the syrup, the finely grated ginger, the lime zest and the beaten egg white. Freeze the mixture in an ice cream maker.
Fill a Japanese teapot with dry ice and pour a little hot water over it. Scoop the sorbet into a suitable dish and place it on top of the dry ice smoking in the teapot. Decorate with blossoms, candied fruits and lemongrass, according to taste.

Ergibt ca. 1 Liter Sorbet:

Für das Sorbet:
3 frische Zitronengrasstängel,
1 Liter Sirup (500 g Zucker und 60 g Glukose
in 450 ml Wasser unter Rühren erhitzen,
bis sich der Zucker aufgelöst hat),
75 g frischer Ingwer, geschält, fein gerieben,
die dünn abgeriebene Schale einer Limette,
1 Eiweiß, zu Schnee geschlagen

Das Herz (den innersten, weichen Teil) der Zitronengrasstängel fein hacken und mit dem Sirup, dem geriebenen Ingwer, der Limettenschale und dem Eischnee gut vermischen. In der Sorbetiere gefrieren.
Einen japanischen Teekrug mit Trockeneis füllen und mit etwas heißem Wasser übergießen.
Das Sorbet in ein passendes Gefäß anrichten und über den kalt rauchenden Teekrug platzieren.
Nach Belieben mit Blüten, karamellisierten Früchten und Zitronengras dekorieren.

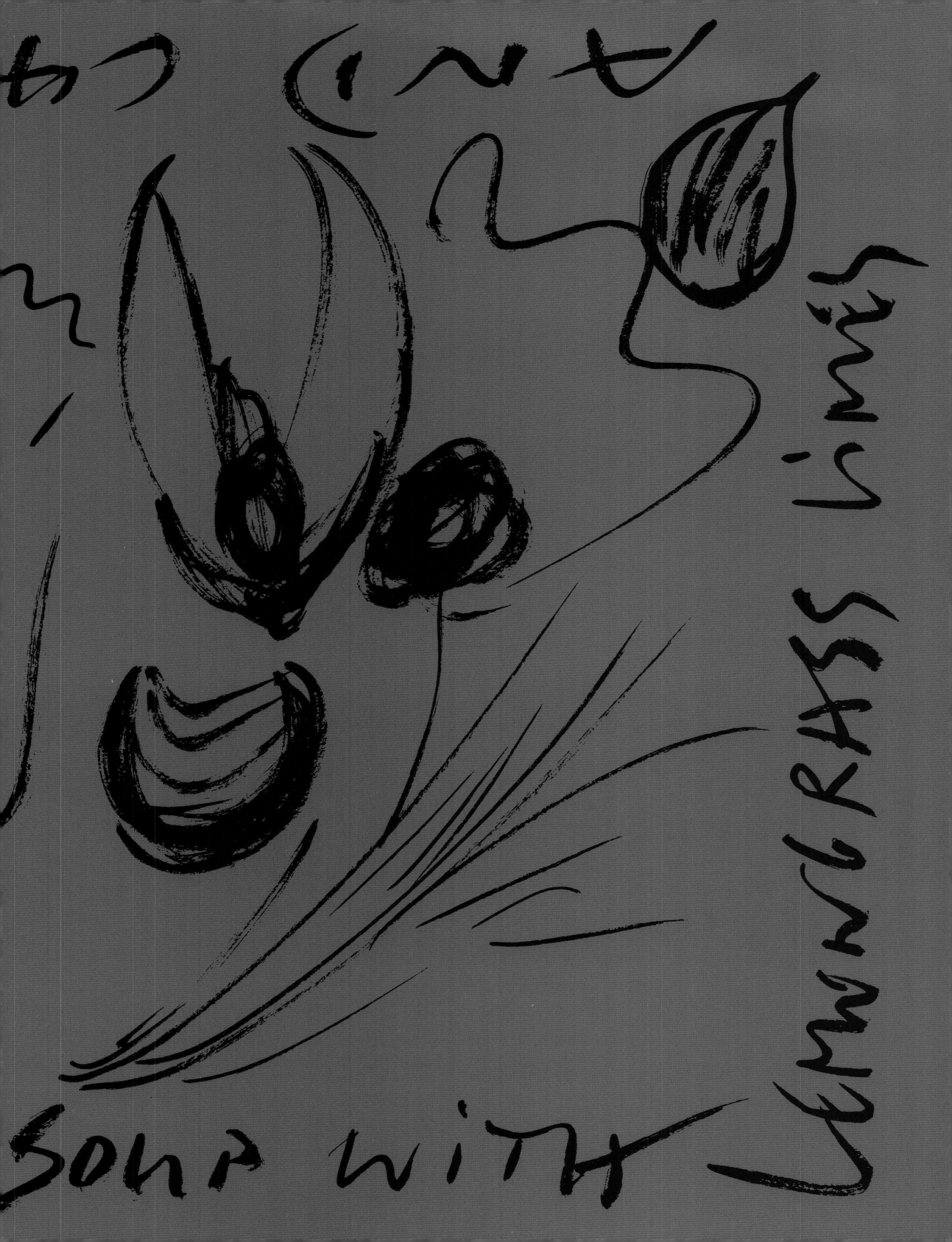
SOUP WITH
LEMONGRASS

THE PENINSULA

A good fairy must have meant well with us. Bangkok lies at our feet, the wide Chao Phraya River lazily flowing in the direction of the sea, and we are enjoying the pleasures of a beautiful room with a view onto Bangkok Peninsula. At home it is cold, but here, the effects of tropical heat are not limited to a sweaty forehead. The newest member in the circle of deluxe hotels stands like a lonely obelisk on the bank of the "mother of rivers". The lifeline of the city and its innumerable side channels named "klongs" run through the surrounding neighborhoods. Heavy barges, packed high with impressive teak logs, are taking on much water as they hang on the ropes of small tugboats towing their huge burdens like ants, and sleek longtail boats with tourists aboard chase each other up and down the river at incredible speeds.

The good fairy has fulfilled yet another one of our other wishes, having reserved seats at the "Jesters", the culinary showpiece of the Peninsula. Surprise sets in as one looks around after having pushed aside the heavy door plate. The cool interior seems to correspond more to an avant-garde idea of a luxury discotheque than a place to celebrate fine dining. The effect is not unintended. Colorful projections move across the wall plates and metallic arched ceilings. The side towards the river is fully glassed in, behind it Bangkok's skyline is basking in its nightly glitter. Cinemascope on the broadest screen. A platform is hovering above the room, resting on thin supports, carrying its burden and a live band without visible strain. There is music à la carte, according to the wishes of the audience, accompaniment to the menu so-to-speak. For many, this is quite an unexpected, for others even a slightly strange experience. Even so, the focus is not a fashionable bow to the fast lane, but culinary pleasures in the pleasingly fresh context of today. Here, you do not have to bow down low before the master's art, you can enjoy your food with a loosened necktie (which is quite unnecessary here anyway).

THE "JESTERS" IS A CLOWN

with a bag full of practical jokes, comic interludes and seemingly effortless tricks who makes you forget that in the background a culinary artist is working with a high degree of concentration. The American-born Dan Ivarie is the culinary soul of the establishment. "Jesters" was originally modeled on the "Felix" in Hong Kong. But Bangkok is not Hong Kong. Everything is different: the people, the food, the cuisine. And luckily, no dogma, no corporate identity was flogged to death here. Instead, a masthead, a chef, who was to give the restaurant his personal note, was to be found. Enter Dan Ivarie. "They told me", Ivarie relates still somewhat perplexed, "here is the restaurant, turn it into a success. That was it." Hats off. Not many enterprises treat themselves to that. But the concept works, and the harmonious interchange between hotel master chef Daniel Lichtensteiger (of Swiss origin, incidentally) and the American Ivarie won the still fledgling "Jesters" a high degree of acceptance among a demanding local audience and the hotel's European guests. With six employees only ("if one is missing that's a medium-sized catastrophe"), he practices "Pacific rim", or what is nowadays called trans-ethnic cuisine. This is what the globetrotting chef brought with him from Hawaii, his last station in several years of travel. There, the food includes a lot of fruit, is rather voluminous and more aggressive in its presentation. Here, a little more elegant, less daring, but quite modern will do. There is only one thing he tries to avoid – to imitate local, Asiatic cuisine.

"My food is definitively Western," he says. "I am a Westerner, not from China or Thailand. I can't cook like them. They would chew me up and spit me out." Yet, he knows how to observe the smallest detail, he is a master of it, that's what he has been trained in, at home, in all corners of the States. In foreign cuisines of foreign countries, whose chefs showed him their techniques. And as a training cook he even took some time off in order to really get to the base of things, working his way through five years of university as well as a wealth of cooking literature.

His very personal motto ever since has been "back to the roots". "If you study cooking you study cultural history," Ivarie explains and has come to the conclusion that even his homeland harbors treasures of regional cuisines whose elements were brought into the country by immigrants. For him, such basic research must be the foundation of every serious cuisine. Without the knowledge about where, how and why, things have a tendency to degenerate to a hapless and helpless stirring around in the pot of unlimited possibilities. Dan therefore does not think much of "fusion". "For me, that's too vague. Don't play with the food if you don't know the food!" That's his creed, and he knows even how to win the favor of local customers (who can be quite enthusiastic but are rather picky). His concept is as convincing as it is simple: With his cooking clearly and identifiably Western, he offers only best quality, introducing a few basic modifications in the recipe inspired by Asian cuisine. "I carefully add local aromas, the people here like that," he says.

"GIVE THEM SOMETHING FAMILIAR BUT MAKE SOME-THING NEW OF IT. THEY WILL PAY FOR IT AND RETURN."

We are following Dan Ivarie to the kitchen. He prefers local sea bass to imported fish. In Thailand, fish is as popular as spareribs are in the States. We just take the products available here and accentuate their taste," he explains at the chopping board, scoring the skin of the sea bass with short, well-practiced cuts, then rolling it up and placing it in a steamer basket. Off to the steamer. Five minutes will do. Thai people love white rice, but Ivary is busy mashing potatoes. He seasons the purée with wasabi, and it is an instant hit. The fish roll is placed on top of the purée and drizzled with a soy sauce flavored with lime leaves. Finished! His creations are far from complicated. When Ivarie likes a basic product, tongue and palate come into action in an effort to refine its flavor. He tries out herbs and spices that will enhance, fortify the effect. Then he designs the accompanying flavors, the side dishes, which must subject themselves to the main feature. Or he casually sets a daring counterpoint, a small stopper so-to-speak, waking up and amusing taste buds that have previously been lulled to sleep.

A change of scenery: We are leaving the vibrating "Jesters" to take a tour through the various other culinary sites within the hotel gastronomy. The "Mei Jiang" is an oasis of peace. In a luxurious atmosphere of subdued colors and fragile sliding panels Chinese cooking is celebrated. The menu lists dishes from fine Cantonese cuisine. One story below, the gigantic machinery of the hotel kitchen is buzzing under the auspices of master chef Lichtensteiger, from morning to night. A walk past the many stations allows for a small glimpse into the fascinating kitchen logistics of a luxury hotel, quite unfathomable for lay persons. A female Thai cook directs the work for the "Cilantro Restaurant" (buffet and à la carte), the room service for 370 rooms as well as for all private events and banquets. In another corner, Japanese cooks are shaking freshly made soy noodles and next door, a Thai cook immerses shark fins crammed in between large woven sieves into boiling water. Large cooler rooms are reserved for fish, meat or vegetables respectively, and steaming ovens eject brown, glistening Peking ducks and suckling pigs. There is quite a machinery in the background, its activities hidden to the eyes of the guests, who prefer taking a walk on the river front terrace between the delicacies of the buffet stationed there. The river is alive until late at night and full of traffic. Junks swing from one bank to the other, crossing the wake made by trains of barges. At the "Jesters", dessert is served.

Eine freundliche Fee hat es gut mit uns gemeint. Bangkok liegt zu unseren Füßen, der breite Chao Phraya River fließt träge zum Meer, und wir genießen die Annehmlichkeiten eines wunderschönen Zimmers mit Aussicht im The Peninsula Bangkok. Daheim ist es kalt, aber hier treibt einem die tropische Hitze den Schweiß nicht nur auf die Stirn.

Wie ein einsamer Obelisk steht das jüngste Mitglied im Reigen der De-Luxe-Herbergen am Ufer der „Mutter der Flüsse". Die Lebensader der Stadt durchzieht in unzähligen, Klong genannten Seitenarmen die angrenzenden Wohngebiete. Schwere, tief im Wasser liegende Frachtverbände, hochbepackt mit wuchtigen Teakholzstämmen, werden von kleinen Schleppern, die wie Ameisen aussehen, gezogen, und schnittige Longtail Boats jagen mit Touristen an Bord und rasanter Geschwindigkeit den Fluss hinauf und hinunter.

Die gute Fee hat uns einen weiteren Wunsch erfüllt und hat Plätze reserviert im „Jesters", dem kulinarischen Aushängeschild des Peninsula. Schiebt man die schwere Türplatte auf und betritt das Innere, so ist man erst einmal überrascht. Dessen kühles Interieur ähnelt eher den avantgardistischen Visionen einer Nobeldiskothek als dem weihevollen Hort großer Cuisine. Nicht ganz von ungefähr. Farbprojektionen wandern über Wandscheiben und metallisierte aufgewölbte Deckenflächen.

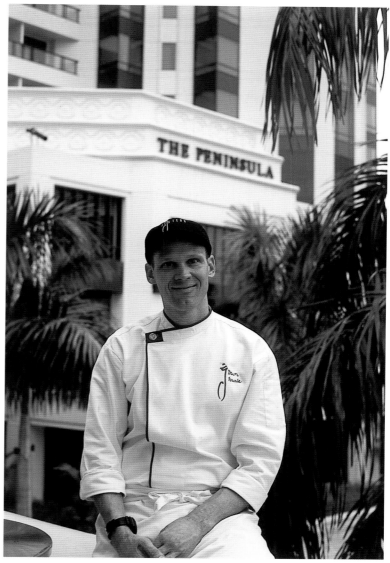

Dan Ivarie

DIE DEM FLUSS ZUGEWANDTE SEITE BESTEHT NUR AUS GLAS, DAHINTER AALT SICH BANGKOKS SKYLINE IM NÄCHTLICHEN LICHTERGEFUNKEL. CINEMASCOPE AUF BREITESTER LEINWAND.

Freischwebend schiebt sich eine Plattform in den Raum, nur von dünnen Stützen durchstochen, die ihre Last nebst einer Live-Band spielerisch zu tragen scheinen. Musik gibt's à la carte, nach Wunsch des Publikums, als Menü-Begleitung sozusagen. Dies ist für manchen ganz sicher ein unerwartetes, für andere sogar ein befremdliches Erlebnis. Und doch wird hier nicht modische Anbiederung an flüchtigen Lifestyle exerziert, sondern Speisegenuss im wohltuend frischen Kontext heutiger Zeit geboten. Man beugt hier nicht demütig den Kopf vor der Kunst des Meisters, sondern kann sich mit gelockertem Schlips (der hier übrigens absolut unnötig ist) den kulinarischen Genüssen der Küche widmen.

Das „Jesters" ist ein Clown, der mit lustigen Späßen, elegantem Klamauk und scheinbar mühelosen Tricks vergessen macht, dass hinter den Kulissen ein Küchenartist mit höchster Konzentration zu Werke geht. Der Amerikaner Dan Ivarie ist die kulinarische Seele des Etablissements. „Jesters" war ursprünglich nach dem Vorbild von „Felix" im Peninsula Hongkong entworfen worden. Aber Bangkok ist nicht Hongkong.

ALLES IST ANDERS: DIE MENSCHEN, DAS ESSEN, DIE KÜCHE. UND IN KLUGER WEISE WURDE HIER KEIN DOGMA, KEIN CORPORATE IDENTITY ZU TODE GERITTEN. MAN SUCHTE STATTDESSEN EINE PERSÖNLICHKEIT, EINEN KOCH, DESSEN EIGENE NOTE DAS RESTAURANT PRÄGEN SOLLTE, UND MAN FAND DAN IVARIE.

„Man sagte mir nur", berichtet er, noch immer völlig perplex, „hier ist das Restaurant, mach einen Erfolg daraus. Das war's." Alle Achtung. Nicht viele Unternehmen leisten sich das. Doch das Konzept geht auf, denn im reibungslosen Wechselspiel mit dem Schweizer Hotel-Chefkoch Daniel Lichtensteiger hat der Amerikaner das noch junge „Jesters" vor allem in die Gunst des anspruchsvollen einheimischen Publikums und der europäischen Hotelgäste hineingekocht. Mit nur sechs Mitarbeitern („wenn einer fehlt, ist das eine mittlere Katastrophe") praktiziert er „Pacific Rim", oder wie es neuerdings heißt, transethnische Küche. Die hat der kochende Globetrotter aus Hawaii mitgebracht, der letzten Station seiner Wanderjahre. Dort ist das Essen fruchtlastiger, ist voluminöser und aggressiver in der Präsentation. Hier darf es eine Spur eleganter, weniger frech, aber durchaus modern sein. Nur eines will er nicht: einheimische, asiatische Küche imitieren.
„Mein Essen ist eindeutig westlich", meint er. „Ich bin Westler, kein Chinese und kein Thai. Ich kann nicht wie sie kochen. Die würden mich abwatschen und ausspucken." Aber genau zuschauen und lernen, das beherrscht er, das hat er trainiert. Daheim, in allen Ecken der Staaten. In fremden Küchen fremder Länder, deren Köche ihn in ihre Technik einwiesen. Und als Kochstudent, der sich dann zwischendurch eine Auszeit nahm, um den Dingen einmal wirklich auf den Grund zu gehen, und sich durch fünf Jahre Universität sowie deren Schätze an Kochliteratur ackerte.
Sein ganz persönliches Fazit lautet seither „back to the roots". „Wenn du Kochkunst studierst, studierst du Kulturgeschichte", erklärt Ivarie und kam zur Erkenntnis, daß selbst sein Heimatland Schätze an regionaler Küche birgt, deren Elemente wiederum durch Einwanderer ins Land gebracht worden waren. Und solche Quellenforschung ist für ihn die Grundlage jeder seriösen Küche. Ohne das Wissen, woher, wie und warum, gerät vieles zum stil- und hilflosen Rühren im großen Topf der unbegrenzten Möglichkeiten. Von „Fusion" hält Dan folglich nichts. „Das ist mir zu schwammig. Don't play with food, if you don't know the food!" ist sein Credo. Und er weiß, wie er sich auch seine einheimische Klientel (die begeisterungsfähig aber höchst wählerisch ist) gewogen macht. Sein Konzept ist so einfach wie überzeugend: er kocht klar und eindeutig westlich, bietet beste Qualität, modifiziert aber die Grundrezeptur mit kleinen Schritten hin zum Asiatischen. "Ich füge vorsichtig hiesige Aromen hinzu, das schätzen die Leute hier," erzählt er. „Gib ihnen etwas Vertrautes, doch mach etwas Neues daraus. Sie werden dafür zahlen – und wiederkommen."
Wir folgen Dan Ivarie in die Küche. Heimischen Seabass zieht er Importfisch vor. Der Fisch ist in Thailand so beliebt wie Spare Ribs in den Staaten. „Wir nehmen einfach die hier gebräuchlichen Lebensmittel und akzentuieren ihren Geschmack," erklärt er am Arbeitsbrett und kerbt mit kurzen, routinierten Schnitten die Haut

des Seebarschfilets, dreht es zur Rolle, setzt es in ein Dampfkörbchen, und ab in den Steamer. Fünf Minuten im Dampf. Thais lieben weißen Reis, er aber stampft Kartoffeln. Doch er schmeckt das Püree mit Wasabi ab, und schon findet es Gnade unter ihren Augen. Fischrolle aufs Püree gesetzt, eine mit Lime Leaves aromatisierte Sojasauce darübergezogen. Fertig. Das geht zack-zack. Seine Kreationen sind alles andere als kompliziert. Wenn Ivarie Gefallen an einem Grundprodukt gefunden hat, dann arbeitet erst die Zunge und der Gaumen feilt am Geschmack. Er testet Kräutlein und Gewürze, die stützend und verstärkend wirken können. Dann gestaltet er die geschmackliche Umgebung, die Beilagen, die sich nun ihrerseits der Hauptfigur unterzuordnen haben. Oder aber er setzt mit lockerer Hand einen frechen Kontrapunkt, einen kleinen Stopper sozusagen, der die eingelullten Geschmacksknospen weckt und bei Laune hält.

Szenenwechsel: Wir verlassen das vibrierende „Jesters" und durchstreifen die weiteren Schauplätze der Hotelgastronomie. Das „Mei Jiang" ist eine Oase der Ruhe. Im edlen Ambiente gedämpfter Farben und fragiler Schiebewände wird Chinesisches zelebriert. Die Karte listet die Speisen feiner Canton-Küche. Ein Stockwerk tiefer aber brummt die gigantische Maschine der Hotelküche unter der Ägide von Chefkoch Lichtensteiger von morgens früh bis abends spät auf vollen Touren. Der Spaziergang durch die weitläufigen Stationen erlaubt einen kleinen Einblick in die faszinierende Küchenlogistik eines Luxushotels. Eine Thai-Köchin dirigiert die Arbeiten für das „Cilantro-Restaurant" (Büffet und à la carte), den Roomservice für 370 Zimmer sowie für alle Privatveranstaltungen und Bankette.

IN EINER NISCHE SCHÜTTELN JAPANISCHE KÖCHE FRISCH GESCHNITTENE SOJANUDELN AUF UND NEBENAN TAUCHT EIN THAI ZWISCHEN GROSSE FLECHTSIEBE GEPRESSTE HAIFISCHFLOSSEN INS SPRUDELNDE WASSER.

Große Kühlräume sind speziell für Fisch, Fleisch oder Gemüse reserviert, und aus dampfenden Öfen werden braun glänzende Pekingenten und Spanferkel gezogen. Eine Maschinerie im Hintergrund, deren Aktivitäten den Hotelgästen verborgen bleibt. Diese wandeln auf der Uferterrasse zwischen den Lustbarkeiten des dort aufgebauten Büffets umher. Der Fluss ist bis spät lebendig und noch voller Verkehr. Dschunken schaukeln von einem Ufer zum anderen, kreuzen das Kielwasser der Schleppverbände. Und im „Jesters" werden Desserts serviert.

DUCK WITH FRIED SESAME CHIPS AND CRISPY SALADS

ENTE MIT FRITTIERTEM SESAMGEBÄCK UND KNUSPERSALATEN

Serves 4

12 fresh wonton skins,
2 egg whites, beaten,
1 tsp black and white sesame seeds each,
oil for deep-frying

500 ml/2 cups hoisin sauce (Oriental sauce made from
soy beans, garlic and spices),
2 tbsp Thai sweet chili sauce,
400 g/14 oz roasted duck breast, sliced,
5 large shiitake mushrooms, stems removed, sliced

a handful of tatsoy leaves (or other lettuce leaves),
50 g/2 oz snow peas,
1 tbsp shredded carrot, cucumber and red pepper,
cut into very thin strips,
20 g/³/₄ oz enoki mushrooms,
2 kaffir lime leaves, cut into thin strips,
1 tbsp finely diced coriander leaves

For the vinaigrette:
1 tsp yellow mustard powder,
2 tbsp light soy sauce,
2 tbsp rice vinegar,
4 tbsp olive oil,
¹/₂ tsp finely diced ginger,
1 tbsp finely diced red pepper,
1 tbsp finely chopped parsley

Spread the wonton skins out on a flat surface. Brush them with egg white and sprinkle them evenly with sesame seeds.
Heat the oil for deep-frying to 175° C/350° F. Fry the wonton skins in batches until golden brown. Allow to drain well on paper towels. Place the crispy skins on a baking sheet.
Combine hoisin sauce and chili sauce, dip the duck breast slices and sliced mushrooms into the mixture and place them on top of the wonton skins. In a small bowl, combine lettuce leaves, snow peas, shredded vegetables, enoki mushrooms, lime leaf strips and coriander and mix well.
For the vinaigrette: In a small dish, mix mustard powder and soy sauce. Beat in the vinegar with a wire whisk, then gradually incorporate olive oil into the mixture. Add ginger, diced pepper and chopped parsley at the very last only.
Finish: Reheat the wonton skins with their topping in a 200° C/ 390° F oven until hot. Toss the salad-vegetable mixture with a little vinaigrette. Place a wonton skin on each plate, top with a handful of salad and cover the salad with another wonton skin. Place the remaining salad portions on top and finish with another wonton skin. Surround the stacks with the remaining vinaigrette and serve immediately.

Für 4 Personen:

12 frische Wontonblätter,
2 Eiweiß, verquirlt,
je 1 TL schwarze und weiße Sesamsamen,
Öl zum Frittieren

500 ml Hoisinsauce (asiatische Sauce aus Sojabohnen,
Knoblauch und Gewürzen),
2 EL süße thailändische Chilisauce,
400 g geröstete Entenbrust, in Scheiben geschnitten,
5 große Shiitakepilze, ohne Stiel, in Scheiben geschnitten

1 Hand voll Wasserspinatblätter (oder andere
kleine grüne Salatblätter), 50 g Zuckerschoten,
je ein EL in sehr feine Streifen geschnittene Karotte,
Gurke und rote Paprika,
20 g Enokipilze,
2 Kaffir-Limettenblätter, in dünne Streifen geschnitten,
1 EL fein gehacktes Koriandergrün

Für die Vinaigrette:
1 TL gelbes Senfpulver,
2 EL helle Sojasauce,
2 TL Reisessig,
4 EL Olivenöl,
¹/₂ TL fein gehackter Ingwer,
1 EL fein gehackte rote Paprika,
1 EL fein gehackte glatte Petersilie

Die Wontonblätter auf der Arbeitsfläche auslegen, mit Eiweiß bepinseln und mit den Sesamsamen gleichmäßig überstreuen. Das Frittieröl auf 175° C erhitzen. Wontonblätter nach und nach goldbraun ausbacken, auf Küchenpapier abtropfen lassen, auf einem Backblech auslegen.
Hoisinsauce mit Chilisauce verrühren. Entenbrust und in Scheiben geschnittene Pilze darin schwenken und auf den Wontonblättern verteilen. Spinatblätter mit Zuckerschoten, Gemüsestreifen, Enokipilzen, Limettenblattstreifen und Koriander in einem Schüsselchen vermischen.
Für die Vinaigrette: Das Senfpulver mit der Sojasauce anrühren. Mit einem Schneebesen den Essig untermischen, unter kräftigem Rühren nach und nach das Olivenöl einarbeiten. Zum Schluss den Ingwer, die Paprikawürfel und die gehackte Petersilie unterziehen.
Fertigstellung: Die belegten Wontonblätter im auf 200° C vorgeheizten Ofen heiß werden lassen. Die Salat-Gemüsemischung mit etwas Vinaigrette anmachen. Je ein Wontonblatt auf Teller legen, etwas Salat darübergeben, mit einem zweiten Wontonblatt bedecken, den restlichen Salat darüber verteilen und mit dem letzten Wontonblatt abschließen. Die restliche Vinaigrette über und um die Schichten gießen.

AVOCADO ROLLS WITH SMOKED TROUT, WASABI
AND TOBIKO CAVIAR

AVOCADOTÖRTCHEN MIT GERÄUCHERTER FORELLE,
WASABI UND TOBIKO-KAVIAR

Serves 4

2 ripe avocados,
juice of half a lemon

150 g/5 oz smoked trout filet, skin removed,
1 tsp wasabi powder,
2 tbsp mayonnaise,
2 heaping tbsp orange tobiko caviar

4 tbsp olive oil,
1 tbsp lemon juice,
1 tbsp orange tobiko caviar,
1 tsp chopped parsley,
1/4 tsp freshly ground black pepper,
1/2 carrot, cut into julienne strips,
1 small beetroot, cut into julienne strips,
a small handful of mixed baby greens

Garnish:
1 nori sheet, cut into small strips

Carefully peel and halve the avocados. Remove the cores and cut the meat into slices. Brush with a little lemon juice, then line the side walls of four rings with a diameter of about 7 cm/2³/₄ inch with the avocado slices. Refrigerate.
Cut the trout filet into small cubes. Mix wasabi powder with a little water and stir until you have a fine paste. Incorporate the mayonnaise and tobiko caviar. Toss diced trout cubes with the sauce.
For the dressing: Combine olive oil and lemon juice with tobiko caviar, parsley and pepper. Mix well. Toss lettuce leaves and vegetable strips with dressing.
Finish: Place the avocado rings onto plates and fill them with trout salad. Carefully open the metal rings and remove them. Scatter the salad loosely on top of the avocado-trout disks and garnish the plates with nori strips. Spoon the remaining vinaigrette around the arrangement. Serve.

Für 4 Personen:

2 reife Avocados,
Saft einer halben Zitrone

150 g geräuchertes Forellenfilet, ohne Haut,
1 TL Wasabipulver,
2 EL Mayonnaise,
2 gehäufte EL orangefarbener Tobiko-Kaviar

4 EL Olivenöl,
1 EL Zitronensaft,
1 EL orangefarbener Tobiko-Kaviar,
1 TL gehackte Petersilie,
1/4 TL schwarzer Pfeffer aus der Mühle,
1/2 Karotte, in lange dünne Streifen geschnitten,
1 kleine Rote Bete, in dünne Streifen geschnitten,
1 kleine Hand voll gemischte kleine Salatblätter

Garnitur:
1 Noriblatt, in kleine Streifen geschnitten

Die Avocados sorgfältig schälen, halbieren, Kerne entfernen und das Fleisch in Scheiben schneiden. Mit etwas Zitronensaft bepinseln, dann die Seitenwände von vier Ringformen mit ca. 7 cm Durchmesser mit den Avocadosscheiben auslegen. Kalt stellen.
Das Forellenfilet in Würfel schneiden. Wasabipulver mit etwas Wasser zu einer Paste anrühren, dann die Mayonnaise und den Tobiko-Kaviar unterziehen. Die Forellenwürfel mit dieser Sauce vermischen.
Für das Dressing: Das Olivenöl mit Zitronensaft, Tobiko-Kaviar, Petersilie und Pfeffer verrühren. Die Salatblätter und Gemüsestreifen damit mischen.
Fertigstellung: Die Avocadosringe auf Teller stellen und mit Forellensalat füllen. Die Metallringe vorsichtig öffnen und entfernen. Den Salat locker über die Rollen häufen, mit Noristreifen garnieren, mit der restlichen Vinaigrette umgießen.

SASHIMI OF SALMON
WITH PICKLED VEGETABLES
AND A HAWAIIAN VINAIGRETTE

LACHS-SASHIMI
MIT EINGELEGTEM GEMÜSE
UND HAWAIIANISCHER VINAIGRETTE

Serves 4

300 g/11 oz salmon filet, prime quality

5 g/a pinch of dried wakame (Japanese seaweed),
2 tbsp rice vinegar,
2 tbsp cucumber, cut into julienne strips,
1/2 red pepper, halved, seeded, cut into julienne strips,
2 spring onions, sliced,
1 tsp sugar, 1 tbsp diced pickled ginger,
4 large mussels, cooked, shelled and diced

For the vinaigrette:
4 tbsp light soy sauce, 2 tbsp sesame oil,
1 tbsp finely diced white onion,
1/2 garlic clove, minced,
1 tsp finely diced red chili,
1/2 tsp wasabi powder, mixed with a little water,
1/2 tsp grated ginger

Garnish:
a handful of mixed salad greens,
2 tbsp toasted macadamia nuts, coarsely crushed,
4 fried wonton skins, crumbled,
the green tips of spring onions

Slice the salmon as thinly as possible and arrange the slices on plastic foil, shaping them as perfectly as possible into four circles. Cover with foil, weight down slightly and refrigerate.
In a small bowl, soak the wakame in rice vinegar until softened. Toss with cucumber, pepper, spring onion, sugar, pickled ginger and diced mussels and mix well. Allow to rest in the refrigerator for at least one hour.
For the vinaigrette: In another bowl, combine the soy sauce and sesame oil, chopped onion, garlic, chili, wasabi paste and ginger. Mix well. Allow vinaigrette to rest for an hour in the refrigerator before proceeding.
Finish: Toss lettuce leaves with vinaigrette and divide them equally between four plates. Carefully remove salmon circles from the foil and lay them onto the salad, as evenly as possible. Top the salmon with marinated vegetables and sprinkle macadamia nut splinters and crushed wonton skins over everything. Drizzle the stacks with the remaining vinaigrette. Garnish with spring onion tips. Serve.

Für 4 Personen:

300 g frisches Lachsfilet, beste Qualität

5 g getrocknete Wakame (Meeresalgen mit langen schmalen Strähnen),
2 EL Reisessig,
2 EL dünn geschnittene Gurkenstreifen,
1/2 rote Paprika, halbiert, entkernt, in dünne Streifen geschnitten,
2 Frühlingszwiebeln, in Scheiben geschnitten,
1 TL Zucker, 1 EL eingelegter, gehackter Ingwer,
4 große Miesmuscheln, gekocht, aus der Schale gelöst, gehackt

Für die Vinaigrette:
4 EL helle Sojasauce, 2 EL Sesamöl,
1 EL fein gehackte Gemüsezwiebel,
1/2 Knoblauchzehe, fein gehackt,
1 TL fein gehackte rote Chili,
1/2 TL Wasabipulver, mit etwas Wasser zur Paste angerührt,
1/2 TL geriebener Ingwer

Garnitur:
1 Hand voll gemischte Salatblätter,
2 EL geröstete Macadamianüsse, grob zerdrückt,
4 frittierte Wontonblätter, grob zerbröselt,
grüne Spitzen von Frühlingszwiebeln

Das Lachsfilet so dünn wie möglich aufschneiden, daraus auf Frischhaltefolie vier möglichst runde Kreise auslegen und formen. Mit Folie bedecken, leicht beschweren und kühl stellen.
In einer Schüssel das Wakame in Reisessig einlegen, bis es aufgeweicht ist. Mit Gurke, Paprika, Frühlingszwiebel, Zucker, eingelegtem Ingwer und gehackten Muscheln gut vermischen, dann eine Stunde im Kühlschrank ziehen lassen.
Für die Vinaigrette: In einer anderen Schüssel die Sojasauce mit Sesamöl, gehackter Zwiebel, Knoblauch, Chili, Wasabipaste und Ingwer gut verrühren. Vor der Weiterverwendung eine Stunde im Kühlschrank ziehen lassen.
Fertigstellung: Salatblätter mit etwas Vinaigrette vermischen und auf vier Teller verteilen. Den Lachs vorsichtig aus der Folie lösen und möglichst flach auf den Salat legen. Die eingelegten Gemüse darüber häufen, mit Macadamianusssplittern und Wontonblatt-Bröseln bestreuen, die restliche Vinaigrette darübergießen. Mit Frühlingszwiebelgrün garnieren.

FRIED TOFU SOUFFLÉ

WITH GARLIC, A HINT OF CURRY

AND A SOY GLAZE

FRITTIERTES TOFU-SOUFFLÉ

MIT KNOBLAUCH, CURRYAROMEN

UND SOJAGLASUR

Serves 4

400 g/14 oz fresh tofu, well-drained,
16 egg whites, beaten into soft peaks,
8 whole eggs,
3 garlic cloves, minced,
1 tbsp red chili, diced, salt, white pepper,
4 tsp cornstarch, oil for deep-frying

For the sauce:
1 small white onion, finely diced,
1 tbsp sunflower oil,
1 small garlic clove, minced,
1 medium tomato, peeled, seeded and finely diced,
2 tsp finely diced hot pepper (according to taste),
100 ml/¹/₃ cup sweet soy sauce

2 tbsp sunflower oil, 80 g/3 oz snow peas,
the leaves of one head of bok choy (remove all thick rib pieces),
8 large shiitake mushrooms, stems removed, sliced,
30 g/1 oz enoki mushrooms,
1 red chili pepper, sliced

For the soufflé mixture: In a large bowl, combine tofu, soft beaten egg whites, whole eggs, garlic, chili and cornstarch. Mix well. Season with salt and pepper.
Place a high metal cylinder mold which is open on both sides into a deep-fryer so that it rests on the floor. The oil should come halfway up the cylinder. Heat the oil to 160° C/325° F. Fill the mold with about a quarter of the soufflé mixture (the mixture in the cylinder should come ²/₃ of the way up). Fry for a few minutes while you keep ladling hot oil on top. Unmold set batter from the cylinder and continue frying the soufflés until done. Repeat the procedure until all four soufflés are done and keep them warm in the oven.
For the sauce: Heat sunflower oil in a small frying-pan and sauté onion, garlic, diced tomato and chili until you have a thick sauce. If it gets too concentrated, thin it with a little water. Allow the sauce to cool to room temperature. Heat oil in a wok. Stir-fry snow peas, bok choy leaves, mushrooms and sliced chili over medium heat until just tender but still crisp to the bite.
Serving: Arrange the vegetables on four plates and top with a tofu soufflé each. Drizzle sauce around and over the soufflés. Serve hot.

Für 4 Personen:

400 g frische Tofumasse, gut abgetropft,
16 Eiweiß, zu halbfestem Schnee geschlagen,
8 ganze Eier,
3 Knoblauchzehen, fein gehackt,
1 EL gehackte rote Chili, Salz, weißer Pfeffer,
4 TL Maisstärke, Öl zum Frittieren

Für die Sauce:
1 kleine Gemüsezwiebel, fein gehackt,
1 EL Sonnenblumenöl,
1 kleine Knoblauchzehe, fein gehackt,
1 mittelgroße Tomate, enthäutet, entkernt und fein gewürfelt,
2 TL fein gehackte scharfe Chilischote (oder nach Belieben),
100 ml süße Sojasauce

2 EL Sonnenblumenöl, 80 g Zuckerschoten,
die Blätter von einer Staude Pak-Choi (alle dicken Rippen entfernt),
8 große Shiitakepilze, ohne Stiel, in Scheiben geschnitten,
30 g Enokipilze,
1 rote Chilischote, in Scheiben geschnitten

Für die Soufflés: Den Tofu in einer Schüssel mit dem halbfesten Eischnee, ganzen Eiern, Knoblauch, Chili und Maisstärke gut vermischen, mit Salz und Pfeffer würzen. Eine hohe zylinderförmige Metallröhre, die auf beiden Seiten offen ist, in die Fritteuse stellen, so dass sie auf dem Boden steht und das Frittieröl bis zur halben Höhe reicht. Das Öl auf 160° C erhitzen. Ein Viertel der Soufflémasse in die Röhre füllen (die Röhre sollte ca. ²/₃ voll sein), während einigen Minuten immer wieder mit der Kelle etwas heißes Öl darüber gießen. Die Röhre vorsichtig von der fest gewordenen Masse entfernen, das Soufflé fertig backen. Die Soufflés einzeln nach dieser Methode herstellen, anschließend im vorgeheizten Ofen warm halten.
Für die Sauce: In einem kleinen Topf die Zwiebel mit Sonnenblumenöl, Knoblauch, Tomatenwürfeln und Chili schmoren, bis alles gar ist. Wenn nötig, mit etwas Wasser verdünnen. Auf Raumtemperatur abkühlen lassen. In einem Wok das Öl erhitzen. Zuckerschoten mit den Pak-Choi-Blättern, Pilzen und Chilischeiben bei mittlerer Hitze unter Rühren braten, bis sie knapp gar sind.
Zum Servieren: Gemüse auf vier Teller anrichten und je ein Tofu-Soufflé darauf setzen. Die Sauce über und um die Soufflés gießen.

SEAFOOD SOUP WITH SALMON AND RICE WINE

SUPPE VON MEERESFRÜCHTEN MIT LACHS UND REISWEIN

Serves 4

400 g/14 oz salmon filet,
60 ml/¹/₄ cup olive oil,
salt,
1 tsp coarsely crushed black pepper

2 garlic cloves, sliced,
1 small leek, finely diced,
2 tbsp olive oil,
8 scallops, shelled,
12 mussels,
12 carpet clams,
8 sweet water shrimp,
200 g/7 oz potato balls cut with a melon baller,
boiled in salted water,
1 carrot, finely diced,
boiled in salted water,
60 ml/¹/₄ cup rice wine,
400 ml/14 oz fish stock, seasoned with saffron,
2 tbsp basil, cut into julienne strips,
salt, freshly ground white pepper

Cut the salmon into four pieces. Marinate the pieces for half an hour in olive oil, salt and pepper. Fry them in a large pan on both sides until just done. Remove them from the pan and keep warm.
In the same pan, sauté the garlic and leek over low heat until tender. Add a little more olive oil and sear the scallops on both sides, then add the remaining seafood, boiled potatoes and carrot. Sauté mixture for a minute, then douse with rice wine. Simmer for three minutes, then add the hot saffron fish stock. Allow to simmer for another three minutes. Finally add the basil strips and season to taste with salt and white pepper.
Serving: Divide the seafood equally between four soup bowls. Top each bowl with a fried salmon filet and ladle some hot broth over everything. Serve.

Für 4 Personen:

400 g Lachsfilet,
60 ml Olivenöl,
Salz,
1 TL grob zerstoßener schwarzer Pfeffer

2 Knoblauchzehen, in Scheiben geschnitten,
1 kleine Lauchstange, in kleine Würfel geschnitten,
2 EL Olivenöl,
8 Jakobsmuscheln, ohne Schale,
12 Miesmuscheln,
12 Teppichmuscheln,
8 Süßwassergarnelen,
200 g rund ausgestochene Kartoffelbällchen,
in Salzwasser knapp gegart,
1 Karotte, in kleine Würfel geschnitten,
in Salzwasser knapp gegart,
60 ml Reiswein,
400 ml Fischfond, mit Safran gewürzt,
2 EL Basilikumstreifen,
Salz, weißer Pfeffer aus der Mühle

Den Lachs in vier Stücke schneiden. Im Olivenöl, Salz und Pfeffer eine halbe Stunde marinieren. In einer Pfanne von beiden Seiten leicht bräunen. Aus der Pfanne nehmen, warm halten.
In der gleichen Pfanne bei kleiner Hitze den Knoblauch und Lauch weich dünsten. Etwas mehr Olivenöl hinzufügen, die Jakobsmuscheln anbraten, die restlichen Meeresfrüchte, pochierten Kartoffeln und Karotten zugeben, kurz anschwitzen, mit Reiswein ablöschen. Drei Minuten köcheln, dann mit dem heißen Safran-Fischfond aufgießen und weitere drei Minuten köcheln. Zum Schluss Basilikum unterziehen, mit Salz und weißem Pfeffer abschmecken.
Zum Servieren: Die Meeresfrüchte in vier Suppenschalen verteilen, mit je einem gebratenen Lachsfilet belegen, mit der Suppe aufgießen.

FOIE GRAS IN A CORNMEAL CRUST WITH PAPAYA PRESERVES

STOPFLEBER IN DER MAISKRUSTE MIT EINGEMACHTEN PAPAYA

Serves 4

8 slices foie gras, cleaned, about 1 cm/¹/₃ inch thick, 30 g/ 1 oz each,
2 tbsp cornmeal,
salt, white pepper,
2 tbsp olive oil

2 leaves iceberg lettuce, cut into thin strips,
a small handful of arugula leaves,
¹/₂ tsp confectioners´ sugar,
2 tsp finely diced shallots,
2 tbsp olive oil,
salt, white pepper

1 ripe but firm papaya,
100 ml/¹/₃ cup rice vinegar, 50 g/1 ¹/₂ oz sugar,
1 tbsp grated ginger,
2 star anise, 1 cinnamon stick,
100 ml/¹/₃ cup water

For the green papaya salad:
100 g/3¹/₂ oz flesh from a green (unripe) papaya,
shredded,
1 tsp seeds from a ripe papaya,
1 tsp lemon juice, 1 tbsp olive oil,
salt, freshly ground black pepper,
1 tsp flat-leaf parsley, chopped

For the sauce:
50 ml/¹/₄ cup reduced veal stock, 1 tsp grated ginger,
2 tbsp port, 4 kaffir lime leaves

Für 4 Personen:

8 Scheiben Stopfleber pariert, ca. 1 cm dick, à 30 g,
2 EL Maisgrieß,
Salz, weißer Pfeffer,
2 EL Olivenöl

2 Blätter Eisbergsalat, in dünne Streifen geschnitten,
eine kleine Hand voll Rucolablätter,
¹/₂ TL Puderzucker,
2 TL fein gehackte Schalotten,
2 EL Olivenöl,
Salz, weißer Pfeffer

1 reife, aber noch feste Papaya,
100 ml Reisessig, 50 g Zucker,
1 EL geriebener Ingwer,
2 Sternanis, 1 Zimtstange,
100 ml Wasser

Für den grünen Papayasalat:
100 g Fleisch von der grünen (unreifen) Papaya,
in Streifen geschnitten,
1 TL Kerne von der reifen Papaya,
1 TL Zitronensaft, 1 EL Olivenöl,
Salz, schwarzer Pfeffer aus der Mühle,
1 TL gehackte glatte Petersilie

Für die Sauce:
50 ml Kalbsglace, 1 TL geriebener Ingwer,
2 EL Portwein, 4 Kaffir-Limettenblätter

Prepare the papaya preserves one day in advance: In a small pot, combine rice vinegar, sugar, ginger, star anise, cinnamon and water and bring it to a boil. Core and peel papaya and cut it into quarters lengthwise. Place them into a low dish. Douse with hot marinade, cover with foil and allow to rest in the refrigerator overnight.

For the green papaya salad: Mix shredded papaya with seeds, lemon juice, olive oil, salt, pepper and parsley. Cover and set aside. Allow to marinate for at least one hour.

For the sauce: In a small pot, combine reduced veal stock, lime leaves, ginger and port and simmer for about fifteen minutes. Strain the liquid through a sieve and keep warm.

Finish: Arrange marinated papaya quarters on plates to form a circle. Dust the iceberg lettuce and arugula leaves with a little confectioners´ sugar and sauté them in olive oil until wilted. Add salt and pepper and arrange the vegetables on top of the papaya circles. Sprinkle the foie gras pieces with salt and pepper and turn them in cornmeal. Fry in hot olive oil on both sides until lightly brown. Drain well on paper towels and place them on top of the salad. Garnish the plates with marinated papaya salad and surround the whole with sauce. Serve at once.

Am Vortag die Papaya vorbereiten: In einem kleinen Topf Reisessig mit Zucker, Ingwer, Sternanis, Zimt und Wasser zum Kochen bringen. Papaya entkernen, schälen, der Länge nach in Viertel schneiden, in ein flaches Gefäß legen. Mit heißer Marinade übergießen, mit Folie bedeckt im Kühlschrank über Nacht ziehen lassen.

Für den grünen Papayasalat: Die Papayastreifen mit den Kernen, Zitronensaft, Olivenöl, Salz, Pfeffer und Petersilie gut vermischen. Zugedeckt beiseite stellen und eine Stunde ziehen lassen.

Für die Sauce: Die Kalbsglace mit den Limettenblättern, Ingwer und dem Portwein in einem kleinen Topf erhitzen, ca. 15 Minuten leise köcheln. Durch ein Sieb passieren, warm halten.

Fertigstellung: Die marinierten Papayastücke auf Tellern kreisförmig anrichten. Den Eisbergsalat und Rucola, mit Puderzucker überstäubt, in Olivenöl anbraten, bis der Salat zusammenfällt. Mit Salz und Pfeffer würzen, über die angerichteten Papaya häufen. Die Stopfleberscheiben mit Salz und Pfeffer würzen, mit Maisgrieß rundum panieren und in heißem Olivenöl von beiden Seiten hellbraun braten. Auf Küchenpapier abtropfen lassen, über dem Salatgemüse anrichten. Mit dem marinierten Papayasalat garnieren, mit Sauce umgießen und sofort servieren.

FRIED COD ON A BED OF GARLIC RISOTTO WITH WILTED LETTUCE

GEBRATENER KABELJAU AUF KNOBLAUCH-RISOTTOBETT MIT GEDÜNSTETEM SALAT

Serves 4

4 filets of cod, 150 g/5 oz each,
2 tbsp olive oil,
2 sprigs of thyme and rosemary each,
4 garlic cloves, crushed, salt, freshly ground black pepper

For the risotto:
200 g/7 oz short-grain rice, 50 g/1¹/₂ oz butter,
5 garlic cloves, sliced,
60 ml/¹/₄ cup white wine, 500 ml/2 cups chicken stock,
10 cherry tomatoes, halved,
10 black olives, pitted, cut into strips,
60 ml/¹/₄ cup cream, salt, freshly ground black pepper

For the sauce:
1 sprig rosemary, 1 garlic clove, diced,
1 tbsp sunflower oil,
100 ml/¹/₃ cup white wine, 4 tbsp cream,
150 g/5 oz cold butter, salt, freshly ground white pepper

1 large shallot, diced, 1 tbsp butter,
6 iceberg lettuce leaves, shredded,
a handful of arugula, a pinch of powdered sugar, salt

1 tbsp flat-leaf parsley, chopped

Marinate the cod filets in olive oil, thyme, rosemary, garlic, salt and pepper for an hour.
For the risotto: Melt the butter in a heavy-bottomed saucepan. Sauté the garlic until translucent, add the rice and sauté for two more minutes, stirring constantly. Take care that the rice does not brown. Douse with white wine and water and simmer on low heat for fifteen minutes, stirring constantly. Add a little more water if necessary.
Stir in the tomato halves and olive strips and simmer the rice for another five minutes. Finish by adding the cream. Check risotto for salt and pepper and keep warm.
For the sauce: In a small pot, sauté the rosemary and garlic in sunflower oil. Refresh with white wine and reduce by half. Add cream and reduce by half again. Whisk in cold butter, a piece at a time, with a wire whip. Correct seasonings and strain the sauce through a fine sieve.
In a small pan, sauté the shallot in butter until translucent. Add the lettuce leaves, dust them with powdered sugar and sauté until the leaves are wilted. Add a pinch of salt.
Finish: Preheat the oven to 180° C/350° F. Sear the marinated cod filets on both sides in a hot pan. Place filets in a baking pan and bake them in the oven for ten more minutes.
Arrange the risotto on pre-warmed plates. Cover with the wilted lettuce and top with one cod filet each. Spoon some sauce around the rice and sprinkle parsley over everything. Serve.

Für 4 Personen:

4 Kabeljaufilets à 150 g,
2 EL Olivenöl,
je 2 Zweige Thymian und Rosmarin,
4 Knoblauchzehen, zerdrückt, Salz, schwarzer Pfeffer aus der Mühle

Für den Risotto:
200 g Rundkornreis, 50 g Butter,
5 Knoblauchzehen, in Scheiben geschnitten,
60 ml Weißwein, 500 ml Hühnerbrühe,
10 Kirschtomaten, halbiert,
10 schwarze Oliven, entkernt, in Streifen geschnitten,
60 ml Sahne, Salz, schwarzer Pfeffer aus der Mühle

Für die Sauce:
1 Zweig Rosmarin, 1 Knoblauchzehe, gehackt,
1 EL Sonnenblumenöl,
100 ml Weißwein, 4 EL Sahne,
150 g kalte Butter, Salz, weißer Pfeffer aus der Mühle

1 große Schalotte, gehackt, 1 EL Butter,
6 Eisbergsalatblätter, in grobe Streifen geschnitten,
1 Hand voll Rucola, 1 Prise Puderzucker, Salz

1 EL glatte, gehackte Petersilie

Die Kabeljaufilets im Olivenöl mit Thymian, Rosmarin, Knoblauch, Salz und Pfeffer eine Stunde marinieren.
Für den Risotto: Die Butter in einem Topf mit dickem Boden erhitzen. Knoblauch anschwitzen, den Reis unterrühren, 2 Minuten unter Rühren anbraten, ohne Farbe nehmen zu lassen. Mit Weißwein und Brühe aufgießen, unter Rühren 15 Minuten bei kleiner Hitze köcheln, bei Bedarf etwas Wasser nachgießen. Die Tomatenhälften und Olivenstreifen zugeben, weitere 5 Minuten köcheln, zum Schluss die Sahne unterrühren. Mit Salz und Pfeffer abschmecken. Warmhalten.
Für die Sauce: Rosmarin und Knoblauch in einem kleinen Topf im Sonnenblumenöl anbraten. Mit dem Weißwein ablöschen, auf die Hälfte einkochen, dann die Sahne zugeben und erneut auf die Hälfte einkochen. Mit einem Schneebesen die kalte Butter stückchenweise unterrühren. Die Sauce durch ein feines Sieb passieren, mit Salz und Pfeffer abschmecken.
Die Schalotte in einer Pfanne in der Butter glasig dünsten. Die Salatblätter zugeben, mit Puderzucker überstäuben und braten, bis die Blätter zusammenfallen. Mit Salz leicht würzen.
Fertigstellung: Den Ofen auf 180° C vorheizen. Die marinierten Fischfilets in der heißen Pfanne von beiden Seiten kräftig anbraten. In einen Bräter legen, im Ofen 10 Minuten fertig braten. Risotto auf vorgewärmte Teller anrichten, mit gedünstetem Salat bedecken und mit je einem Kabeljaufilet belegen. Die Sauce rund um den Reis gießen, mit Petersilie überstreuen.

STEAMED SEA BASS ON A WASABI POTATO-PURÉE WITH HEART OF PALM SALAD

WOLFSBARSCH GEDÄMPFT AUF WASABI-KARTOFFELPÜREE MIT PALMHERZ-SALAT

Serves 4

600 g/1¹/₃ lb sea bass filets, skin on

For the wasabi-potato purée:
4 large potatoes,
100 ml/¹/₃ cup cream,
1 tbsp wasabi powder,
50 g/¹/₄ cup butter, 1 tsp salt

10 black peppercorns, crushed,
1 kaffir lime leaf, finely minced,
1 tbsp olive oil,
100 ml/¹/₃ cup white wine,
4 tbsp cream,
150 g/5 oz butter, cut into small chunks,
1 tbsp soy sauce,
1 tbsp oyster sauce

For the salad:
60 g/2 oz palm hearts (can), cut into julienne strips,
60 g/2 oz snow peas, halved lengthwise,
60 g/2 oz red and yellow pepper, cut into julienne strips,
1 tbsp fresh coriander,
1 tbsp olive oil,
juice of half a lemon,
salt, freshly ground white pepper

Für 4 Personen:

600 g Wolfsbarschfilet, mit Haut

Für das Wasabi-Kartoffelpüree:
4 große Kartoffeln,
100 ml Sahne,
1 EL Wasabipulver,
50 g Butter, 1 TL Salz

10 schwarze Pfefferkörner, zerdrückt,
1 Kaffir-Limettenblatt, fein geschnitten,
1 EL Olivenöl,
100 ml Weißwein,
4 EL Sahne,
150 g Butter, in kleine Stücke geschnitten,
1 EL Sojasauce,
1 EL Austernsauce

Für den Salat:
60 g Palmherzen (Dose), in Streifen geschnitten,
60 g Zuckerschoten, der Länge nach halbiert,
60 g rote und gelbe Paprika, in lange dünne Streifen geschnitten,
1 EL Koriandergrün,
1 EL Olivenöl,
Saft einer halben Zitrone,
Salz, weißer Pfeffer aus der Mühle

Cut the sea bass filets into four longish pieces of equal size. Spread them out on a working surface, skin-side up. Score the skin diagonally every 2 cm/³/₄ inch. Do not cut all the way through to the edge of the skin but leave a 1 cm/¹/₃ inch edge uncut at the top and the bottom of the filet. Roll up the filet pieces with the skin-side out and fasten the rolls with sharp wooden toothpicks. Steam the rolls for about five minutes until just done.

For the wasabi-potato purée: Peel the potatoes and cut them into chunks. Boil them in salted water until tender. Drain and allow the steam to escape. In a small bowl, mash the potatoes vigorously with a firm wire whip. Heat cream and wasabi powder in a small pan, stir in butter and fold this mixture into the mashed potatoes. Check for salt.

For the sauce: Sauté black pepper and lime leaf strips in olive oil. Douse with white wine and reduce by half. Add the cream and allow to reduce again. Season with soy and oyster sauce. Finally whisk in the butter with a wire whip, one piece at a time. Check the seasonings and pass the sauce through a fine sieve. Keep warm.

For the salad: Toss all ingredients together. Allow to marinate for a few minutes.

Serving: Arrange the wasabi-potato purée on pre-warmed plates. Remove toothpicks from sea bass filets and place the rolls onto the purée. Garnish with salad and drizzle some sauce around and on top. Serve immediately.

Das Wolfsbarschfilet in vier gleichmäßige, längliche Stücke schneiden. Mit der Haut nach oben flach auslegen, alle 2 cm die Haut quer einschneiden, so dass jedoch der obere und untere Rand mindestens 1 cm intakt bleibt. Die Filets der mit Hautseite nach aussen zusammenrollen und mit spitzen hölzernen Zahnstochern feststecken. Über Dampf ca. 5 Minuten garen, bis sie durch sind.

Für das Wasabi-Kartoffelpüree: Kartoffeln schälen, in grobe Stücke schneiden und in Salzwasser gar kochen. Abschütten, gut abdampfen lassen, mit einem festen Schneebesen in einer kleinen Schüssel zerdrücken. Die Sahne mit dem Wasabipulver verrühren, in einem Topf erhitzen, die Butter unterrühren und diese Mischung unter die Kartoffeln ziehen. Mit Salz abschmecken.

Für die Sauce: Den schwarzen Pfeffer und die Limettenblattstreifen im Olivenöl anbraten. Mit Weißwein ablöschen, auf die Hälfte einkochen, dann die Sahne zugeben, erneut einkochen, mit Soja- und Austernsauce würzen. Zum Schluss die Butter stückchenweise mit einem Schneebesen unterziehen. Die Sauce abschmecken, durch ein feines Sieb passieren, warm halten.

Für den Salat: Alle Zutaten in einer kleinen Schüssel vermischen und ein paar Minuten ziehen lassen.

Zum Servieren: Das Wasabipüree auf vorgewärmte Teller verteilen. Die Zahnstocher aus den Wolfsbarschfilets entfernen, die Rollen auf das Püree setzen. Mit Salat garnieren, mit der Sauce um- und übergießen und sofort servieren.

CRISPY-FRIED TUNA FISH WITH A MUSTARD SOY SAUCE

THUNFISCH IN DER KNUSPRIGEN HÜLLE MIT SENF-SOJA-SAUCE

Serves 4

350 g/12¹/₂ oz tuna fish filet,
1 tsp wasabi powder,
12 large basil leaves,
4 sheets of nori (seaweed),
20 g/³/₄ oz cornstarch,
2 egg whites, beaten into stiff peaks,
150 g/5 oz breadcrumbs (original recipe: Japanese
breadcrumbs),
oil for deep-frying

For the relish:
100 g/3¹/₂ oz pineapple, finely chopped,
¹/₂ red pepper, seeded and finely diced,
1 tsp minced shallot,
1 tbsp chopped basil,
1 tbsp rice vinegar,
a pinch of ground red chili, salt

For the Soy Cream:
1 tbsp yellow mustard powder,
2 tbsp light soy sauce,
1 tbsp sesame oil,
4 tbsp olive oil,
mixed lettuce leaves

Cut the tuna fish into four slender, longish pieces of a uniform shape. Mix the wasabi powder with a little water until you have a fine paste. Rub the fish pieces with paste and stick the large basil leaves directly onto the paste. Wrap each piece in a sheet of nori. Turn the packages in cornstarch, shake off any excess starch, then dip them in egg white and finally turn them in breadcrumbs.

For the spicy relish: In a small bowl, combine pineapple and red pepper cubes with shallot, basil, rice vinegar, red chili powder and salt. Mix until blended. Set aside to marinate.

For the soy cream: Combine mustard powder and soy sauce in a small dish and stir until dissolved. Add sesame oil and, beating continually with an electric mixer, slowly drizzle in olive oil until you have a creamy consistency. Add a little lukewarm water if necessary.

Finish: Deep-fry tuna fish pieces in hot oil (175° C/ 350° F) until golden brown. Remove them from the oil and allow to drain on paper towels. Cut the pieces on the bias and arrange them on plates with the lettuce leaves. Garnish with pineapple relish and soy cream. Serve.

Für 4 Personen:

350 g Thunfischfilet,
1 TL Wasabipulver,
12 große Basilikumblätter,
4 Blätter Nori (getrockneter Laver-Seetang),
20 g Maisstärke,
2 Eiweiß, zu Schnee geschlagen,
150 g Semmelbrösel (Originalrezept: japanische
Brotbrösel),
Öl zum Frittieren

Für das Relish:
100 g Ananas, fein gewürfelt,
¹/₂ rote Paprika, entkernt und fein gewürfelt,
1 TL fein gehackte Schalotte,
1 EL gehacktes Basilikum,
1 EL Reisessig,
1 Prise rotes Chilipulver, Salz

Für die Sojacreme:
1 EL gelbes Senfpulver,
2 EL helle Sojasauce,
1 EL Sesamöl,
4 EL Olivenöl,
gemischte Blattsalate

Den Thunfisch in 4 gleichmäßig schlanke, längliche Stücke zuschneiden. Das Wasabipulver mit wenig Wasser zu einer Paste anrühren und die Fischstücke damit einstreichen. Mit den großen Basilikumblättern belegen und einzeln in Noriblätter wickeln. In Maisstärke wenden, gut abklopfen, dann in den Eischnee tunken und zum Schluss mit Semmelbröseln panieren.

Für das würzige Relish: Ananas- und rote Paprika-Würfel mit Schalotte, Basilikum, Reisessig, Chilipulver und Salz in einem kleinen Schüsselchen vermischen; beiseite stellen.

Für die Sojacreme: In einem kleinen Gefäß das Senfpulver mit der Sojasauce anrühren. Das Sesamöl unterrühren, mit einem Handrührgerät nach und nach das Olivenöl einarbeiten und zu einer luftigen Creme rühren. Bei Bedarf mit etwas lauwarmem Wasser verdünnen.

Fertigstellung: Die Thunfischstücke im 175° C heißen Öl goldbraun frittieren. Herausnehmen und auf Küchenpapier abtropfen lassen. Jede Fischrolle quer aufschneiden und mit den Blattsalaten auf Teller anrichten. Mit Ananas-Relish und Soja-Creme garnieren und servieren.

GRILLED LAMB CHOPS IN A CORIANDER-SOY MARINADE
WITH A MEDITERRANEAN LENTIL SALAD

GEGRILLTE LAMMKOTELETTS MIT KORIANDER-SOJAMARINADE
UND MEDITERRANEM LINSENSALAT

Serves 4	*Für 4 Personen:*
8 lamb chops	*8 Lammkoteletts*
For the marinade:	*Für die Marinade:*
100 ml/¹/₃ cup sweet soy sauce, 2 tbsp water,	*100 ml süße Sojasauce, 2 EL Wasser,*
2 kaffir lime leaves,	*2 Kaffir-Limettenblätter,*
1 stalk lemongrass, diced,	*1 Zitronengrasstängel, gehackt,*
3 garlic cloves, minced,	*3 Knoblauchzehen, fein gehackt,*
2 tbsp coriander seeds, 1 red chili pepper, cut into rings	*2 EL Koriandersamen, 1 rote Chili, in Ringe geschnitten*
2 tbsp olive oil,	*2 EL Olivenöl,*
2 garlic cloves, minced,	*2 Knoblauchzehen, fein gehackt,*
¹/₄ fennel bulb, finely diced,	*¹/₄ Fenchelknolle, in kleine Würfel geschnitten,*
¹/₂ carrot, finely diced,	*¹/₂ Karotte, in kleine Würfel geschnitten,*
1 tsp ground cumin,	*1 TL Kreuzkümmelpulver,*
¹/₂ tsp coarsely crushed black peppercorns,	*¹/₂ TL grob zerstoßene schwarze Pfefferkörner,*
1 tbsp lemon juice,	*1 EL Zitronensaft,*
2 tbsp chopped parsley, salt,	*2 EL gehackte Petersilie, Salz,*
250 g/¹/₂ lb cooked green lentils	*250 g gekochte grüne Linsen*
80 g/3 oz feta,	*80 g Fetakäse,*
80 ml/¹/₄ cup cream,	*80 ml Sahne,*
1 small garlic clove, minced,	*1 kleine Knoblauchzehe, fein gehackt*
1 tsp flat-leaf parsley, chopped	*1 TL glatte gehackte Petersilie*
12 romaine lettuce leaves, chili pepper, cut into rings	*12 Romanasalatblätter, Chili, in Ringe geschnitten*

For the marinade: One day ahead, combine the soy sauce, water, lime leaves, lemon grass, garlic, coriander seeds and red chili rings in a low dish. Refrigerate the marinade overnight, covered, so that the flavors can meld.

When you are ready to cook, place chops into the marinade. Turn them after half an hour and allow them to marinate on the other side for thirty minutes more.

Heat the olive oil in a small pan. Add garlic, fennel and carrot and sauté over low heat until tender. Add ground cumin, pepper, lemon juice and parsley. Check for salt. Incorporate lentils into the vegetable mixture and allow them to heat through. Keep warm.

For the feta sauce: Crumble the cheese with a fork, work in the cream and process the mixture into a smooth paste. (You may also use a blender if you prefer.) Fold in garlic and parsley at the end.

Finish: Remove lamb chops from the marinade and roast them under the grill on both sides according to taste.

Cut the romaine lettuce leaves into even rectangles. Place one leaf on each plate, top each leaf with warm lentil mixture and repeat the procedure until lettuce leaves and lentil mixture are used up. Spoon the feta cream over the salad and garnish the plate with chili pepper rings. Place two lamb chops each next to the salad stacks and serve immediately.

Für die Marinade: Am Vortag die Sojasauce mit Wasser, Limettenblättern, Zitronengras, Knoblauch, Koriandersamen und den roten Chiliringen in einem flachen Gefäß vermischen, über Nacht zugedeckt stehen lassen.

Die Koteletts in die Marinade legen, nach einer halben Stunde umdrehen und weitere 30 Minuten marinieren.

In einem Topf das Olivenöl erhitzen. Knoblauch, Fenchel und Karotte zugeben, bei kleiner Hitze weich dünsten. Kreuzkümmel, Pfeffer, Zitronensaft und Petersilie zugeben, mit Salz würzen. Mit abgetropften Linsen vermischen, leicht erhitzen und warm halten.

Für die Feta-Sauce: Den Käse mit einer Gabel zerdrücken, die Sahne zugeben und zu einer glatten Creme verarbeiten (nach Belieben mit dem Handmixer pürieren). Zum Schluss den Knoblauch und die Petersilie unterrühren.

Fertigstellung: Die Lammkoteletts aus der Marinade nehmen und auf dem Grill von beiden Seiten beliebig lang rösten.

Aus den Salatblättern gleichmäßig große Vierecke schneiden. Teller mit je einem Salatblatt belegen, einen Löffel warme Linsen darüber geben, dann abwechselnd weiter schichten, bis alle Salatblätter und die Linsen aufgebraucht sind. Die Fetasauce über den Salat gießen, mit Chilischeiben garnieren. Die Lammkoteletts neben den Salat legen, sofort servieren.

TAMARIND GLAZED DUCK BREAST ON GARLIC-BACON POTATOES WITH ARUGULA

ENTENBRUST MIT TAMARINDENGLASUR AUF SPECK-KNOBLAUCHKARTOFFELN UND RUCOLA

Serves 4

4 duck breast halves, about 150 g/5 oz each,
$^1/_2$ tsp Chinese five-spice-powder,
2 tbsp sunflower oil

For the glaze:
50 g/1$^1/_2$ oz tamarind paste,
1 tsp grated ginger,
1 small garlic clove, minced,
$^1/_2$ tsp red chili pepper, finely diced,
2 tsp sugar, 2 tbsp rice vinegar,
4 tsp Thai sweet chili sauce,
120 ml/$^1/_2$ cup brown chicken stock,
120 ml/$^1/_2$ cup water,
2 tsp cornstarch, dissolved in 2 tbsp water

4 potatoes,
2 tbsp bacon, diced, 1 tbsp sunflower oil,
$^1/_2$ small white onion, finely diced,
1 garlic clove, minced,
4 tbsp cream,
1 tbsp flat-leaf parsley, chopped,
salt, freshly ground black pepper,
100 g/3$^1/_2$ oz arugula,
1 tbsp sunflower oil,
16 stalks wild asparagus, cooked al dente

Mix five-spice-powder and sunflower oil and brush the duck breast halves. Place duck breasts on a baking sheet and set them aside.
For the glaze: Combine tamarind paste, ginger, garlic, diced chili pepper, sugar, rice vinegar, chili sauce, chicken stock and water in a pot and bring the mixture to a boil. Simmer, uncovered, on very low heat for one hour. Add a little more water if necessary. Thicken lightly with dissolved cornstarch and check for salt.
Peel the potatoes and cut them into pieces. Boil them in salted water until tender. Drain well and allow the steam to escape. In a small pan, render the bacon in the oil. Add onion and garlic and sauté until translucent. Add cooked potatoes, cream and parsley. Mix well. Check for salt and pepper. Fill the mixture into metal rings and allow to cool.
Finish: Preheat the oven to 180° C/350° F. Sear the duck breast halves on both sides in a hot pan and return them to the baking sheet, skin-side up. Brush the meat with the tamarind glaze and bake in a hot oven for about fifteen minutes. Press potato mixture from the rings into the hot pan and fry them on both sides until lightly brown. Place potato cakes onto pre-warmed plates. In another pan, sauté arugula in oil until the leaves are wilted. Scatter arugula over the potato cakes. Cut the duck breast halves on the bias and place the pieces on top of the arugula. Garnish the plates with the wild asparagus spears and surround the arrangement with remaining tamarind glaze. Serve.

Für 4 Personen:

4 halbe Entenbrüste à ca. 150 g,
$^1/_2$ TL chinesisches Fünf-Gewürzepulver,
2 EL Sonnenblumenöl

Für die Glasur:
50 g Tamarindenpaste,
1 TL geriebener Ingwer,
1 kleine Knoblauchzehe, fein gehackt,
$^1/_2$ TL fein gehackte rote Chili,
2 TL Zucker, 2 EL Reisessig,
4 TL süße thailändische Chilisauce,
120 ml brauner Hühnerfond,
120 ml Wasser,
2 TL Maisstärke, mit 2 EL Wasser angerührt

4 Kartoffeln,
2 EL Speckwürfel, 1 EL Sonnenblumenöl,
$^1/_2$ kleine Gemüsezwiebel, fein gewürfelt,
1 Knoblauchzehe, gehackt,
4 EL Sahne,
1 EL gehackte glatte Petersilie,
Salz, schwarzer Pfeffer aus der Mühle,
100 g Rucola,
1 EL Sonnenblumenöl,
16 Stangen wilder Spargel, knapp gar gekocht

Das Fünf-Gewürzepulver mit Sonnenblumenöl anrühren, die Entenbrüste damit einpinseln. Auf ein Backblech legen, beiseite stellen.
Für die Glasur: Die Tamarindenpaste mit Ingwer, Knoblauch, Chili, Zucker, Reisessig, Chilisauce, Hühnerfond und Wasser in einem Topf erhitzen. Eine Stunde ohne Deckel bei kleinster Hitze köcheln, bei Bedarf etwas Wasser hinzufügen. Mit der angerührten Maisstärke leicht binden, mit Salz abschmecken.
Die Kartoffeln schälen, in grobe Stücke schneiden, in Salzwasser weichkochen. Anschließend gut abtropfen und abdampfen lassen. In einem Topf den Speck mit dem Öl auslassen. Die Zwiebel und den Knoblauch glasig dünsten, die gekochten Kartoffeln, die Sahne und die Petersilie zugeben, mit Salz und Pfeffer abschmecken und gut vermischen. In Metallringe füllen, erkalten lassen.
Fertigstellung: Den Ofen auf 180° C vorheizen. Die Entenbrüste in einer Pfanne von beiden Seiten kurz anbraten. Mit der Hautseite nach oben auf das Backblech zurücklegen, mit der Tamarindenglasur bestreichen, im heißen Ofen 15 Minuten backen.
Die Kartoffeln aus der Form in die heiße Pfanne drücken und von beiden Seiten hellbraun anbraten. Auf vorgewärmte Teller anrichten. Rucola in der Pfanne im Öl unter Rühren braten, bis die Blättchen zusammenfallen. Über die Kartoffeln verteilen. Die Entenbrüste quer aufschneiden und über das Rucolagemüse legen. Mit wildem Spargel garnieren, die Köstlichkeit mit der restlichen Tamarindenglasur umgießen.

SESAME CRUNCH WITH MANGO AND MASCARPONE ICE CREAM

SESAM-KNUSPERBLÄTTER MIT MANGO UND MASCARPONE-EIS

Serves 4

For the sesame tuiles:
30 g/1 oz flour, 100 g/3¹/₂ oz sugar,
30 g/1 oz sesame seeds, 30 g/1 oz orange juice, 30 g/1 oz butter

For the butterscotch sauce:
100 g/3¹/₂ oz sugar, 50 g/1¹/₂ oz butter, 150 ml/²/₃ cup cream

For the vanilla sauce:
200 ml/³/₄ cup milk, 50 ml/¹/₄ cup cream,
50 g/1¹/₂ oz oz sugar, 4 egg yolks, ¹/₂ vanilla bean

For the mascarpone ice cream:
300 ml/1¹/₄ cup milk, 60 g/2 oz sugar,
1 heaping tbsp glucose, 1 heaping tbsp powdered milk,
150 g/5 oz mascarpone, at room temperature, 1 tbsp Amaretto liqueur

4 ripe mangoes,
200 g/7 oz double cream mixed with the zest
and juice of one ripe lime, a little confectioners' sugar for dusting

Für 4 Personen:

Für die Sesam-Tuiles:
30 g Mehl, 100 g Zucker,
30 g weiße Sesamsamen, 30 g Orangensaft, 30 g Butter

Buttersauce:
100 g Zucker, 50 g Butter, 150 ml Sahne

Vanillesauce:
200 ml Milch, 50 ml Sahne,
50 g Zucker, 4 Eigelb, ¹/₂ Vanillestange

Für das Mascarpone-Eis:
300 ml Milch, 60 g Zucker,
1 gehäufter EL Traubenzucker (Glukose), 1 gehäufter EL Milchpulver,
150 g Mascarpone (Raumtemperatur), 1 EL Amaretto-Likör

4 reife Mangos,
200 g Doppelrahm, mit dünn abgeriebener Schale und Saft einer
reifen Limette vermischt, etwas Puderzucker zum Bestäuben

For the sesame shingles: Preheat oven to 200° C/390° F. Quickly combine all ingredients. With the help of a teaspoon, place twelve small heaps onto a baking sheet lined with baking paper. Bake until you have twelve flat, more or less perfect circles which are golden brown and crispy. Allow to cool on the baking sheet.

For the butterscotch sauce: Slowly heat sugar in a small stainless steel pan until you have a light brown caramel. Stir in butter and keep on the burner until well blend. Remove from heat and gradually incorporate cream. Keep at room temperature.

For the vanilla sauce: Split open vanilla bean lengthwise. Scald the milk with vanilla bean and remove pot from heat before the milk comes to a boil. In a bowl, whisk egg yolks and sugar with a wire whip until light and airy. Gradually fold in hot milk mixture, return to the pot and heat to just below the boiling point, stirring constantly. Place in a bath of ice water and stir until cool. Refrigerate.

For the mascarpone ice cream: Scald milk, sugar, glucose and powdered milk in a stainless steel pot. Place the mascarpone into a large bowl and gradually work in the milk mixture. Stir in the amaretto liqueur. Freeze the ice cream base in an ice cream maker according to the manufacturer's directions.

Cut the mangoes in half, remove the cores and scoop out as many balls of flesh as possible with a melon baller. The scoops should be slightly flattened on one side.

Finish: Spoon the butterscotch and vanilla sauce onto four plates to make an attractive pattern. Place one shingle onto the plate, place a dollop of double cream into the center and surround the cream with mango balls. Cover with a second shingle and repeat the procedure. Finish with a third shingle and dust everything with a little confectioners' sugar. Carefully balance a scoop of mascarpone ice cream on top and serve immediately. (Decoration photograph: "angel hair" made from caramelized sugar).

Sesam-Tuiles: Den Ofen auf 200° C vorheizen. Alle Zutaten rasch verrühren. Mit einem Teelöffel 12 kleine Häufchen auf ein mit Backtrennpapier ausgelegtes Blech setzen. Im Ofen zu möglichst runden Scheiben zerlaufen lassen und goldbraun und knusprig backen. Auf dem Blech erkalten lassen.

Buttersauce: Zucker in einem kleinen Edelstahltopf langsam erhitzen, bis er hellbraun karamellisiert. Butter unterrühren, weiter erhitzen, bis alles gut vermischt ist. Vom Herd nehmen, nach und nach die Sahne einrühren. Bei Raumtemperatur aufbewahren.

Vanillesauce: Die Sahne mit der Milch und der längs aufgeschnittenen Vanillestange zum Kochen bringen. Den Topf vom Herd ziehen. Eigelb und Zucker in einer Schüssel mit dem Schneebesen zu hellem Schaum rühren. Die heiße Sahnemilch nach und nach unterziehen, die Masse in den Topf gießen und unter ständigem Rühren bis kurz vor den Siedepunkt erhitzen. Im Eisbad die Sauce kaltrühren. Im Kühlschrank aufbewahren.

Mascarpone-Eis: Milch mit Zucker, Traubenzucker und Milchpulver in einem Edelstahltopf verrührt bis zum Siedepunkt erhitzen. Unter Rühren in einer Schüssel mit Mascarpone vermischen, Amaretto-Likör unterziehen, die Masse in der Eismaschine gefrieren.

Die Mangos halbieren, Kerne entfernen und mit einem Melonenausstecher möglichst viele Kugeln ausstechen. Die Kugeln sollten auf einer Seite leicht abgeflacht sein.

Fertigstellung: Auf vier Teller mit Butter- und Vanillesauce ein schönes Muster gießen. Jeweils ein Tuilegebäck auf die Teller legen, einen Löffel voll Doppelrahm in die Mitte geben und rundherum mit Mangokugeln belegen. Mit einem zweiten Tuile bedecken und dieses ebenso mit Doppelrahm und Mangokugeln garnieren. Die dritte Tuilescheibe darüberlegen, mit etwas Puderzucker bestäuben. Vorsichtig mit je einer Kugel Mascarponeeis abschließen, sofort servieren. (Dekoration Foto: „Fäden" aus karamellisiertem Zucker).

MOUSSE OF MILK CHOCOLATE WITH FRUIT STEWED IN RED WINE

MILCHSCHOKOLADENMOUSSE MIT ROTWEIN-KOMPOTTFRÜCHTEN

Serves 4

For the mousse:
50 ml/¼ cup milk, 50 ml/¼ cup cream,
2 egg yolks, 10 g/1 tsp sugar,
140 g/5 oz light couverture chocolate,
40 g/1½ oz dark couverture chocolate,
180 g/6½ oz cream, whipped into stiff peaks

For the pastry shells:
85 g/3 oz flour,
100 g/3½ oz melted butter, 100 g/3½ oz sugar,
15 g/1 tbsp cocoa powder, 100 g/3½ oz egg white

For the stewed fruit:
300 ml/1¼ cups red wine, 200 ml/¾ cup water,
12 prunes, pitted,
12 apricot halves

Caramelized nuts:
100 g/3½ oz sugar, 100 ml/⅓ cup water,
50 g/1½ oz macadamia nuts

Für 4 Personen:

Für die Mousse:
50 ml Milch, 50 ml Sahne,
2 Eigelb, 10 g Zucker,
140 g Milchschokoladenkuvertüre,
40 g dunkle Kuvertüre,
180 g Sahne, steif geschlagen

Für die Gebäckschalen:
85 g Mehl,
100 g geschmolzene Butter,
100 g Zucker 15 g Kakao, 100 g Eiweiß

Für das Kompott:
300 ml Rotwein, 200 ml Wasser,
12 Dörrpflaumen, entkernt,
12 Aprikosenhälften

Für die karamellisierten Nüsse:
100 g Zucker, 100 ml Wasser,
50 g Macadamianüsse

For the mousse: Heat the milk and cream in a small pot. Whip egg yolks and sugar in a large bowl with a wire whip until foamy. Gradually whisk in hot milk-cream mixture. Heat the mixture in a double boiler to 85° C/180° F, stirring constantly. Meanwhile, melt both kinds of chocolate in a second double boiler. Incorporate chocolate mixture into the egg-cream mixture and allow to cool to about 40° C/100° F. Fold in whipped cream and refrigerate for about four hours, until set.

For the pastry shells: Preheat the oven to 200° C/400° F. In a bowl, combine flour and melted butter, add sugar and dust with cocoa powder. Mix well, then slowly incorporate egg white without increasing the volume. Spread the batter thinly on a non-stick baking sheet or a baking sheet coated with non-stick spray. Bake in the oven until golden brown, remove from oven and cut and shape the batter into the desired form while still warm. Allow the shells to cool on a rack.

For the stewed fruit: In a saucepan, bring wine, water and fruit to a boil. Simmer, uncovered, on low heat until the liquid is syrupy and thick and the fruits are tender.

For the caramelized nuts: Heat the sugar and water in a pot, stirring constantly, until all sugar crystals are dissolved. Add the nuts and keep stirring until the sugar has turned a medium brown. Pour the caramel mixture onto a baking sheet lined with baking paper. Allow to cool. Crush the brittle into uneven pieces with a rolling pin.

Finish: Place pastry shells onto plates with the opening pointing upwards. Fill the chocolate mousse into a pastry bag with a round tip and pipe the mousse into the shells. Spoon the stewed fruit including the syrup around the shells and finish by sprinkling nut brittle over everything. Serve.

Für die Mousse: Die Milch mit der Sahne in einem Topf erhitzen. Eigelb und Zucker mit dem Schneebesen in einer Schüssel schaumig schlagen. Langsam die heiße Milch-Sahnemischung einrühren. Die Mischung über einem Wasserbad unter ständigem Rühren auf ca. 85° C erhitzen. Die beiden Schokoladensorten in einem zweiten Wasserbad schmelzen, unter die Eiercreme rühren und auf ca. 40° C abkühlen. Die steif geschlagene Sahne unterziehen, dann die Creme im Kühlschrank ca. 4 Stunden fest werden lassen.

Für die Gebäckschalen: Den Ofen auf 200° C vorheizen. Mehl und geschmolzene Butter verrühren, Zucker zugeben, dann das Kakaopulver dazusieben. Gut vermischen, langsam das Eiweiß unterrühren, ohne dass es an Volumen zunimmt. Den Teig auf ein beschichtetes Backblech oder mit Antihaftspray besprühtes Blech dünn ausstreichen. Im Ofen goldbraun backen, anschließend in noch warmem Zustand in die gewünschte Form schneiden und biegen. Erkalten lassen.

Für das Kompott: Wein, Wasser und Früchte in einem Topf zum Kochen bringen. Bei kleiner Hitze ohne Deckel köcheln, bis die Flüssigkeit zu Sirup eingedickt ist und die Früchte weich sind.

Für die karamellisierten Nüsse: Zucker und Wasser in einem Topf unter Rühren erhitzen, bis alle Kristalle aufgelöst sind. Die Nüsse zugeben und weiterhin rühren, bis der Zucker mittelbraun karamellisiert. Die Masse auf eine mit Backtrennpapier ausgelegte Arbeitsfläche gießen, erkalten lassen, dann mit einem Wellholz zu groben Splittern zerschlagen.

Fertigstellung: Die Gebäckschalen aufrecht auf Teller stellen. Die Schokoladenmousse in einen Spritzsack mit runder Tülle füllen und in die Gebäckformen spritzen. Das Kompott mit dem Saft auf die Teller verteilen, zuletzt die Desserts mit karamellisierten Nusssplittern überstreuen.

MALAYSIA

MALAY CUISINE

Like in almost all Asian kitchens, Malay cuisine is based on the interplay of spices and herbs. The art lies in the finding of a balance of "dry" spices (coriander seeds, cumin, anise, cloves, cinnamon and cardamom seeds) and "moist" ones (shallots, ginger, garlic, chili pepper and fresh turmeric). The respective mixture is ground in a mortar and then used to season fish, meat or chicken. Saté skewers, for instance, are brushed with the paste, grilled on charcoal and dipped in peanut sauce. Curries – stews that is – are refined with herbs such as lemongrass, fresh coriander, lime and curry leaves. The mixtures vary from region to region, but the dishes are always accompanied by plenty of white rice. In general, Malays don´t eat pork, something that is true for all thirteen states. With a predominantly Muslim population, the food must be "halal" and, like under kosher food laws, the consumption of pork is prohibited. Usually, Malay dishes are not eaten with chopsticks but with normal cutlery, often without a knife. If the left hand – which is considered impure – has nothing to do, it is placed on the thigh under the table. While the roots for this type of cuisine are to be found mostly in the surrounding countries, a certain influence from Indians and Arabs, who imported pepper, ginger and cardamom, also makes itself felt.

Wie in fast allen asiatischen Küchen ist das Spiel mit Gewürzen und Kräutern in der malaiischen Küche die Hauptsache. Die Kunst liegt in der Abstimmung und Mischung von „trockenen" Gewürzen (Koriandersamen, Kreuzkümmel, Anis, Gewürznelken, Zimt und Kardamomsamen) mit „feuchten" (Schalotten, Ingwer, Knoblauch, Chilis und frische Kurkumawurzel). Der jeweilige Mix kommt in den Mörser und wird als Würze für Fisch, Fleisch oder Geflügel verwendet. So werden auch die Saté-Spießchen damit mariniert, über Holzkohle gegrillt und anschließend in Erdnusssauce gestippt. Curries – das sind Eintopfschmorgerichte – erfahren ihre geschmackliche Veredelung durch Kräuter wie Zitronengras, frischen Koriander, Limetten- und Curryblätter. In keinem der dreizehn Bundesstaaten ist die Rezeptur dieselbe, doch immer wird viel weißer Reis dazu gereicht. Schweinefleisch dagegen ist tabu. Malaien sind Moslems, und ihre Kost ist „Halal", was, wie in der koscheren Küche, den Verzehr von Schweinefleisch verbietet. Gegessen wird nicht mit Stäbchen, sondern mit normalem Besteck – oft ohne Messer. Hat die linke Hand nichts zu tun, kommt sie auf den Schenkel unterm Tisch, denn sie gilt als unrein. Auch Inder und Araber steuerten mit dem Import von Pfeffer, Ingwer und Kardamom ihren Teil zur Würze bei, obwohl die Quelle dieser Küche hauptsächlich in den umliegenden Ländern zu finden sind.

HILTON KUALA LUMPUR
FIC'S RESTAURANT & WINE BAR

A dark face is glowing brightly under a crisp white chef's hat: "You want some more?" Generously ignoring my hesitant gesture, another slice of delicately pink roast beef finds its way onto my plate where it joins other items that have landed there by virtue of an unbridled collector's mania. Professional eyes rest approvingly on my plate whose contents soon find the hoped-for approval given my obviously ravenous appetite. Among the choice of Asian delicacies filling my plate, this piece of meat is something of a stranger and out of place – but for me it means a small bit of culinary home: Everything else is from the other end of the earth. We are in Kuala Lumpur, Malaysia's upstarting capital and business metropolis. The place is the Planters' Inn Restaurant at the Hilton, which is surrounded by scores of hotels, bank palaces and office highrises – always within sight of the modern landmark of the city, the sleek Petronas Twin Towers rising high up into the sky. People are diminished to ant-size, reflecting glass façades govern the cityscape with their faceless power. Downstairs, the city's traffic roars by, its constant din accompanied by the gigantic air-hungry humming of air conditioner ventilators which keep hotels and office towers inhabitable. And every now and then, you can hear the singsong of a muezzin's voice ringing out from tape.

The reality of this country must be elsewhere, far away on the countryside, in small villages whose activities have little to do with the big money of the international transactions happening here. Some of it may be found in other parts of the city, where the houses are lower, the streets less clean and the shops have the compact dimensions meant for ordinary citizens. Where the ingredients for pots and woks are bought in the dense crowds of local markets, between freshly butchered chickens, dark, crispy-fried pieces of pig and mountains of vegetables and fruits. Malaysia's cuisine mirrors that of the different countries in this hemisphere. Here, China blends with Thailand, Malaysia with Straits Chinese, East with West. Thus, I am trying to find my way through the alluring selection of food at the Hilton Planters' Inn: a cross-section of Asian cooking with an emphasis on Malay cuisine. The delicacies are arranged on counters, islands and flower-decorated tables and require a high degree of systematics and discipline – something I presently just do not have. With big eyes and an expectant palate, I keep looking at pots and pans containing bubbling curries and simmering soups. Stand-by chefs place skewered shrimp on the grill or are busy stir-frying vegetable strips in the wok. Japan sends its greetings with a selection of finely cut sashimi and sushi, and rice is resting white or curry-yellow under silvery domes. The smell of soy noodles, fried or in a herby alliance with small shrimp, invades my nostrils. What else is there to be desired? Such buffets have the tendency to turn off my brain, leaving only hands, mouth and palate to function. At the end of such delectation, all the body needs is a place to rest and digest. All fellow sufferers similarly inclined are advised to stay away from this place of delights, or, better, to cancel all other eating plans for the day to be able to give up all resistance and succumb entirely to gluttony. In general, visitors to Kuala Lumpur are here on business. They hardly have the time and opportunity to look at what happens outside of air-conditioned conference rooms and hotel restaurants. It is a nice surprise that guests of the Hilton at least do not have to forego culinary adventures. After having been lucky enough to survive the above-mentioned cross-national buffet, new discoveries are just around the corner: The Chinese restaurant "Tsui Yuen", governed by master chef Tang Lai, resides on the fifth floor. Exquisite Chinese cuisine may be enjoyed in a Chinese gardenscape with paintings, huge vases and figurines. Aside from the unavoidable Peking duck, noodles of all kinds are served – braised, stir-fried, deep-fried or immersed in a rich soup – along with a broad range of dim sum wrapped in tender flaky dough stuffs.

And yet, one of the culinary hot spots of the city is one floor down. Competition is fierce, and it has to be something extraordinary to draw attention. In the background of the reception area, the generous sweep of a broad stainless steel staircase leads down to "FIC's Restaurant & Wine Bar". Stuffy hotel air is replaced by a fresh breeze. Even the greatest culinary ignoramus cannot help but notice which way the wind blows here. It's food that counts – nothing else (well, almost). White banners spelling the alphabet of culinary terms in large letters are suspended from the ceiling. Beneath your feet, there is black granite featuring excerpts from the menu in large stainless steel letters. The room is framed by three massive monoliths of green marble, which are dedicated to wine: Shiraz, Chablis and Napa Valley. They function as service stations for the waiters and are equipped with ultra-modern computer terminals placed next to a line-up of salt and pepper shakers. Marble walls spout water gathering in a small stone-framed stream that runs across the culinary space, passing tables set with white linen, all the way back to the glass wall which encloses the realm of master chef Thornton and his crew of fourteen. Everything is geared towards the unmitigated experience of food here, even the decoration, which is not merely a playful end in itself. A high class place, modern and in the best tradition of state-of-the-art cuisine, without being in any way trendy. Strands of jazzy music float in the high room, underlining the noiseless kitchen activities behind the glass wall, which serves to satisfy the occasional voyeuristic curiosity of many a guest. Food in action.

Rhys Thornton, a 27-year-old top chef with long years of experience in the best houses of his homeland, has come from down under, the green island of New Zealand that is, to his first job overseas. Quite new in the country, he first brought despair to the Hilton's kitchen personnel with his down-under accent, so that at the beginning, things had to be written down for a while when communication failed. His next project was to rewrite the menu of FIC's, aligning it with his Pacific rim style, the more or less elaborate blend of Asian cooking with Western cuisine. His style favors light dishes, lighter than most local cooking, and he prefers vegetarian food. Sauce bases made from chicken or veal are more often than not replaced with vegetable stocks, something for which mother nature has given him the raw ingredients in abundance. His menu (which changes only every four months) features whatever the world has to offer – of which he picks only the very freshest and, if available, also seasonal products. Gourmets appreciate it. Thus, his cheese comes from France, asparagus from Holland, lamb from New Zealand, game and duck breast from the U.S. Every three weeks, beef and lamb is sampled at a blind test at his suppliers'. Strawberries from the U.S., however, are likely to be replaced by Malaysian ones if the quality is right. A great selection of vegetables and fruit, herbs and spices is, after all, grown in the near surroundings. And on Friday evening, the chef buys fresh sea perch at the wholesale market.

Rhys Thornton

The native of New Zealand was no greenhorn at combining Eastern and Western cuisines when he packed his suitcase in Auckland for his new job. Much of his sophistication, however, entered the stage at Kuala Lumpur, in the kitchen of the Hilton, in the creative co-operation of a crew from Malaysia, Indonesia and China. Thornton raves: "In New Zealand we also used Asian ingredients. But now I am working with people who have handled them all their lives and who are in a position of explaining to me for what such and such a spice or a herb has been used traditionally. That and the very fact that every ingredient has yet a different taste and smell here. It's a great exchange, for the benefit of everyone. I teach them Western cuisine, they teach me how they cook." Utterly relaxed, he clip-clops through his realm in his wooden clogs, drawing rave reviews from his guests.

Ein dunkles Gesicht strahlt mich unter weißer Kochmütze an. „You want some more?" Mein Zaudern wird großzügig übergangen, und ungefragt findet sich eine Scheibe zartrosa gebratenen Roastbeefs in gedrängter Nachbarschaft zum Ergebnis ungezügelter Sammelwut auf meinem Teller. Wohlgefällig wird dieser von professionellen Augen einer Prüfung unterzogen und erfährt die erhoffte Anerkennung angesichts meines offensichtlich großen Appetits. Inmitten der asiatischen Genüsse auf meinem Teller ist das Stück Fleisch eigentlich fremd und schlicht fehl am Platz – doch für mich ist es ein kleines Zipfelchen geschmacklicher Heimat. Alles andere stammt vom anderen Ende des Erdballs. Wir befinden uns in Kuala Lumpur, der aufstrebenden Hauptstadt und Business-Metropole Malaysias. Ort des Geschehens ist das „Planters' Inn Restaurant" im Hilton, in dessen Nachbarschaft sich weitere Hotels, Bankpaläste und Bürohochhäuser drängeln – immer in Sichtweite zum neuzeitlichen Wahrzeichen der Stadt, den sich grazil zum Himmel reckenden Petronas Twin Towers. Menschen sind zu Ameisen verkleinert, spiegelnde Glasfassaden regieren mit gesichtsloser Macht über das Stadtbild. Unten braust und flutet der städtische Automobilverkehr, ständig untermalt vom lufthungrigen Atem der gigantischen Ventilatoren der Klimaanlagen, die Hotels und Bürotürme am Leben erhalten. Und hin und wieder zwängt sich gellend die melodische Singsangstimme eines Muezzins vom Band dazwischen.

Die Realität dieses Landes spielt sich sicherlich anderswo ab, weit draußen auf dem Land, in den kleinen Dörfern, deren Geschäfte wenig zu tun haben mit dem Big Money internationaler Transaktionen, die hier getätigt werden. Doch einiges davon findet man auch in den Stadtteilen, wo die Häuser niedriger, die Straßen weniger sauber sind und die Läden handliche Dimension für den Normalbürger besitzen. Wo die Zutaten für Topf und Wok im dichten Gedränge des Stadtteil-Marktes erstanden werden, zwischen frisch geschlachteten Hühnern, dunkelbraun knusprig gebratenen Ententeilen und Bergen von Gemüsen und Früchten. Die Küche Malaysias ist ein Spiegel der verschiedenen Länder dieser Hemisphäre. Hier mischt sich China mit Thailand, Malaysia mit Straits Chinese, Osten mit Westen. Und so taste ich mich durch die verlockenden Angebote in Hiltons „Planters' Inn": asiatische Küche im Querschnitt, malaiisch der Schwerpunkt. Deren Kostbarkeiten liegen auf Tresen, Inseln und blumendekorierten Tischen ausgebreitet und verlangen nach Disziplin und Systematik – deren ich einfach nicht fähig bin. Augen groß, Gaumen in Wartestellung, beäuge ich Töpfe und Tiegel, in denen Curries schmurgeln und Suppen köcheln. Standby-Köche werfen Garnelenspieße auf den Grill oder schwenken Gemüsestreifen im Wok. Japan grüßt mit einer Auswahl artig geschnittener Sashimis und Sushis, und unter silbrigen Glocken lauert Reis in currygelb und weiß. Sojanudeln gebraten oder in kräuterwürziger Alliance mit kleinen Shrimps duften mir entgegen. Was will man noch mehr? Solche Büffets sind für mich ein kleiner Tod, schalten die Gehirntätigkeit ab und lassen nur Hände, Mund und Magen am Leben.

Am Ende einer solcher Sättigung braucht der Körper dann nur Ruhe und ein Plätzchen, wo er sich erholen kann. Allen ähnlich veranlagten Leidensgenossen sei daher angeraten, einen großen Bogen um diese gastliche Stätte zu schlagen oder alle weiteren Ess-Termine des Tages zu streichen und sich widerstandslos der Völlerei zu ergeben.

Der Normal-Besucher Kuala Lumpurs ist in Geschäften hier. Er hat kaum die Zeit und Gelegenheit, mehr von dem, was außerhalb klimatisierter Konferenzräume und Hotelrestaurants vor sich geht, zu erfahren. Welch angenehmer Umstand, dass der Gast im Hilton wenigstens auf kulinarische Erlebnisse nicht verzichten muss. Hat er das oben erwähnte Quer-durch-die-Länder-Büffet glücklich überstanden, harren weitere Entdeckungen auf ihn: Im fünften Stock residiert das China-Restaurant „Tsui Yuen" unter der Herrschaft von Meisterkoch Tang Lai. Eine chinesische Gartenlandschaft, Gemälde, riesige Vasen und Figurinen sind der Rahmen feiner China-Küche. Neben der unvermeidlichen Peking Ente locken „Noodles" in allen Spielarten – geschmort, Wok-gerührt, frittiert oder großzügig in Suppe getränkt –, nebst einer ergiebigen Auswahl Dim Sums, die in wächsern-zarten Nudelteig gehüllt sind.

Einer der kulinarischen Hotspots der Stadt liegt jedoch wenige Stockwerke tiefer. Die Konkurrenz ist hart, und da muss es schon etwas Besonderes sein, was Aufmerksamkeit erregen kann. Im Hintergrund der Empfangsebene schwingt sich in ausladendem Bogen eine breite edelstahlbewangte Treppe hinunter zu „FIC'S Restaurant & Wine Bar". Hotelluft wechselt zu frischer Atmosphäre. Hier wird auch dem größten Banausen unmissverständlich klar, worauf es ankommt.

Es geht um Essen und sonst (fast) gar nichts. Von der Decke hängen weiße Banner, die in großer Schrift das Alphabet kochtechnischer Begriffe deklinieren. Unter den Füßen liegt schwarzer Granit, in den Auszüge der Speisekarte mit großen Edelstahl-Lettern eingelassen sind. Massive Monolithe aus grünem Marmor erheben sich dreimal an der Peripherie des Raumes und sind Weinen gewidmet: Shiraz, Chablis und Napa Valley. Sie fungieren als Kellner-Servicestationen, hochmodern mit Computerterminal ausgerüstet, Salz- und Pfefferstreuer stehen in Reih und Glied. Aus marmorner Wand plätschert Wasser, um sich als steingefasstes Bächlein quer durch die kulinarische Halle, an weiß gedeckten Tischen vorbei, zur gläsernen Wand vorzuschlängeln, hinter der die 14-köpfige Küchenmannschaft Chefkoch Thornton zur Hand geht. Hier ist alles aufs Essen konzentriert, selbst die Dekoration spielt mit und ist nicht zum verspielten Selbstzweck verkommen. High Class, modern und in der jungen Tradition heutiger Küche, ohne nur kurzläufig trendy zu sein.

JAZZIGES FLUTET DURCH DEN HOHEN RAUM UND UNTERMALT DAS LAUTLOSE KÜCHENGESCHEHEN HINTER GLAS, DEM DER GAST MIT VOYEURISTISCHER NEUGIER HIN UND WIEDER SEINE AUFMERKSAMKEIT SCHENKT. FOOD IN ACTION.

RHYS THORNTON, EIN 27 JAHRE JUNGER TOPKOCH MIT LANG-JÄHRIGER KOCHERFAHRUNG IN

den besten Häusern seines Landes, kam vom unteren Ende der Welt, der grünen Insel Neuseeland zu seinem ersten Übersee-Job. Kaum wenige Wochen im Land, brachte er zuallererst Hiltons Küchenpersonal mit seinem Down-under-Akzent zur Verzweiflung, sodass man anfangs Zettel tauschte, wenn die Sprache versagte. Dann ging er daran, die Karte des FIC'S neu zu schreiben und auf seinen Pacific-Rim-Stil auszurichten – die mehr oder weniger kunstvolle Verquickung von asiatischer Küche mit westlicher. Doch seine Küche ist leicht, leichter als die hier

gebräuchliche, und er favorisiert Vegetarisches. Eine Saucenbasis aus Huhn oder Kalb ersetzt er gerne und häufig durch Gemüse-fonds, für welche ihm Mutter Natur die Rohprodukte in äu-ßerst reichhaltiger Form zur Ver-fügung stellt. Was immer die Welt zu bieten hat, setzt er auf die Speisekarte (die alle vier Mo-nate wechselt) und sucht sich da-für – wir wissen es zu schätzen – nur das Allerfrischeste, Allerbeste und, wenn erhältlich, die jahres-zeitlich stimmigen Produkte her-aus. So kommt Käse aus Frank-reich, der Spargel aus Holland, Lamm ist neuseeländisch, Wild und Entenbrust stammen aus den USA. Alle drei Wochen gibt es eine Blindverkostung von Rind- und Lammfleisch bei den Liefe-ranten. Doch Erdbeeren aus Kali-fornien ersetzt er, wenn die Qua-lität stimmt, durch malaiische.

Denn ein beträchtlicher Reich-tum an Gemüse und Früchten, Kräutern und Gewürzen wächst in allernächster Umgebung. Und Freitag Nacht kauft er frischen

Seebarsch auf dem Großmarkt ein. In der Kombination von östlicher Küche mit westlicher war der Neuseeländer bereits ein Profi, als er in Auckland die Koffer für seinen neuen Arbeitsplatz packte. Aber der Prozess der Verfeinerung fand erst in Kuala Lumpur statt, in der Küche des Hilton, im Zusammenspiel mit einer kooperativen Crew, zusammengesetzt aus Malaien, Indonesiern und Chinesen. Thornton ist begeistert: „In Neuseeland haben wir schon immer auch asiatische Zutaten verwendet. Nun aber arbeite ich mit den Leuten zusammen, die ihr ganzes Leben damit gekocht haben und mir endlich erklären können, wofür und wie sie dieses Gewürz, dieses Kraut verwenden, und wann welche Kochtechnik die richtige ist. Mal davon abgesehen, dass jede Zutat hier noch mal anders schmeckt oder riecht. Es ist ein guter Austausch, und jeder gewinnt dabei. Ich lehre sie westliches Kochen, sie lehren mich ihre Küche."

Seither schlappt er auf seinen Holzpantinen sichtlich entspannter durch die Welt und genießt die allseitige Zustimmung der Gäste.

DIM SUM MENU

Serves 4 - 6

For the noodle dough: 250 g/¹/₂ lb flour,
200 ml/³/₄ cup boiling water (colored green or yellow with spinach
or saffron, according to taste), a pinch of salt added

For the four-part dumpling:
160 g/6 oz shrimp, shelled and diced, 1 tsp cornstarch, 1 tbsp water,
salt, white pepper, 1 tbsp sugar, 1 tbsp each finely diced red ground
chili pepper (or paprika, according to taste),
orange sago (or trout caviar),
chopped egg, chopped blanched green beans

For the shrimp and prawn dumplings:
100 g/3¹/₂ oz chicken breast, diced, 40 g/1¹/₂ oz shrimp, shelled,
1 tbsp cornstarch, salt, white pepper, 1 tbsp sugar,
1 tsp sesame oil, 1 tbsp red sago for garnish

For the yeast dough:
300 g/11 oz flour, 30 g/1 oz sugar, 180 ml/³/₄ cup warm water,
1 heaping tsp dry yeast, 1 tbsp rendered lard

For the BBQ chicken filling:
120 g/4 oz chicken breast, finely diced, 1 tbsp sugar,
a pinch white pepper, 2 tsp oyster sauce, 2 tsp hoisin sauce,
1 tsp soy sauce, 100 ml/¹/₃ cup chicken stock, 1 tsp cornstarch

Für 4 - 6 Personen:

Für den Nudelteig: 250 g Mehl,
200 g kochendes Wasser (nach Belieben mit Spinat grün oder mit
Safran gelb gefärbt), mit einer Prise Salz gewürzt

Viergeteilte Nudeltasche:
160 g Garnelen, geschält, 1 TL Maisstärke, 1 EL Wasser,
Salz, weißer Pfeffer, 1 EL Zucker,
je ein EL fein gehackte rote Chili (oder Paprika, nach Belieben),
orange gefärbter Sago (oder Forellenkaviar),
gehacktes Eigelb, gehackte grüne blanchierte Bohnen

Für die Garnelen-Hühnchentaschen:
100 g Hühnerbrust, gewürfelt, 40 g Garnelen, geschält,
1 EL Maisstärke, Salz, weißer Pfeffer, 1 EL Zucker,
1 TL Sesamöl, 1 EL rot gefärbter Sago zum Garnieren

Für den Hefeteig:
300 g Mehl, 30 g Zucker, 180 ml warmes Wasser,
1 gehäufter TL Trockenhefe, 1 EL ausgelassenes Schweineschmalz

Für die BBQ-Hühnchenfüllung:
120 g Hühnerbrust, in kleine Würfel geschnitten, 1 EL Zucker,
1 Prise weißer Pfeffer, 2 TL Austernsauce, 2 TL Hoisin-Sauce,
1 TL Sojasauce, 100 ml Hühnerbrühe, 1 TL Maisstärke

For the noodle dough: Sieve flour into a large bowl. Bring water to a rolling boil and pour it onto the flour. Using a wooden spoon, quickly beat the mixture into a firm dough. Cover and allow to rest for half an hour. Knead until smooth. Roll out thinly, then cut out a number of squares, rounds or triangles, according to taste.
Four-part noodle dumpling: Combine shrimp, cornstarch and water. Finely purée in a blender and season to taste with salt, pepper and sugar. Place a teaspoon of filling each on square noodle dough pieces and pinch the four ends together at the top, leaving four openings on the sides. Steam for about ten minutes. Fill each opening with a differently colored garnish before serving.
Shrimp and prawn dumplings: Purée chicken meat, shrimp, cornstarch, salt, pepper, sugar and sesame oil in a blender, allow to rest and blend again. Spread on round dough pieces and close them at the top. Steam for ten minutes. Decorate with red sago before serving. For the yeast dough: Sieve the flour into a bowl. Combine warm water, sugar and dry yeast. Mix well. Cover and allow to rise for ten minutes. Add mixture and lard to the flour and knead for three minutes. Shape the dough into a long roll and cut the roll into twelve pieces. Flatten the dough pieces with your hand and place a piece of baking paper under each round. Cover with a moist cloth and allow to rest and rise while you prepare the filling.
For the filling: Combine the diced chicken meat, sugar, pepper, oyster sauce and hoisin sauce in an oven-proof pan, mix well and marinate for an hour. Preheat the oven to 160° C/325° F. Bake the marinated meat for about 40 minutes. Combine stock, cornstarch and baked chicken dice in a saucepan and reduce until thickened. Allow to cool. Place a teaspoon of filling onto each yeast dough round and pinch the top closed like a change purse. Steam in a bamboo steamer or in a steamer oven for 12 to 15 minutes.

Nudelteig: Mehl in eine Schüssel sieben. mit sprudelnd kochendem Wasser übergießen, mit einem Holzlöffel rasch zu einem festen Teig verarbeiten. Zugedeckt 30 Minuten ruhen lassen, dann zu einem glatten Teig kneten. Dünn ausrollen, nach Belieben Vierecke, Dreiecke oder Rondellen ausschneiden.
Viergeteilte Nudeltasche: Garnelenfleisch mit Stärke und Wasser vermischen, im Mixer kurz pürieren, mit Salz, Pfeffer und Zucker würzen. Die Füllung auf viereckige Nudelteigstücke geben, an den Längsseiten fassend in der Mitte zusammendrücken, so dass vier Öffnungen entstehen. Über Dampf 10 Minuten garen. Zum Servieren jede Öffnung mit verschiedenfarbigen Garnituren füllen.
Garnelen-Hühnchentaschen: Hühnerfleisch und Garnelen mit Stärke, Salz, Pfeffer, Zucker und Sesamöl im Mixer kurz pürieren, etwas stehen lassen, dann nochmals kurz pürieren. Runde Teigblätter damit bestreichen, oben zusammenschlagen. Über Dampf 10 Minuten garen, mit rot gefärbtem Sago dekorieren.
Für den Hefeteig: Mehl in eine Schüssel sieben. Das warme Wasser mit Zucker und Hefe verrühren, zugedeckt 10 Minuten gehen lassen. Mit dem Schmalz zum Mehl geben, zu einem glatten Teig kneten. Zu einer langen Rolle formen, in 12 Stücke teilen. Plattdrücken, unter jedes Teigstück ein Stück Backtrennpapier legen, ein feuchtes Tuch darüberlegen, 30 Minuten gehen lassen.
Für die Füllung: Hühnerfleisch mit Zucker, Pfeffer, Austern-, Hoisin- und Sojasauce in einer feuerfesten Schale eine Stunde marinieren. Im 160° C heißen Ofen ca. 40 Minuten backen. Die Brühe mit der Stärke verrühren, mit der gebackenen Hühnerbrust in einen Topf geben und dick einkochen. Erkalten lassen. Die Hefeteigstücke mit je einem Löffel Füllung belegen, den Teig rundum hochziehen und oben verschließen. Im Bambuskörbchen über Dampf oder im Dampfofen 12 - 15 Minuten garen.

FIC´S OYSTER VARIATIONS

FIC'S AUSTERNVARIATIONEN

Serves 4

36 oysters

For the grilled oysters:
120 g/4 oz butter,
1 tbsp shallots, finely diced,
1 tsp chopped tarragon and chervil each,
4 peppercorns,
40 ml/¹/₈ cup white wine vinegar,
2 egg yolks,
1 tbsp tarragon and chervil, chopped,
1 tbsp fresh coriander, leaves only,
1 tbsp pastrami (marinated smoked beef,
alternatively dry-cured beef),
cut into fine strips

60 g/2 oz smoked salmon,
2 tbsp oil for frying,
2 tbsp balsamic vinegar,
2 tbsp lemon juice

Garnish:
green lettuce leaves, herbs, lemon wedges,
4 small Bloody Mary shots

For the grilled oysters: Melt butter in a small pot, skim off foam and keep warm. Combine shallots, tarragon, chervil, pepper and vinegar in a saucepan and simmer until reduced by half. Strain through a fine sieve and allow to cool.

Combine egg yolks and herb reduction and whisk until foamy. Incorporate warm butter, one piece at a time, beating vigorously all the time. Correct the seasonings and add chopped herbs. Set aside.

Shuck twelve oysters, wash and dry them and place them back onto the half shell. Top with Béarnaise sauce and sprinkle with coriander leaves and pastrami strips. Grill until golden brown.

Thinly slice the smoked salmon and fry it in hot oil until crispy and brown. Combine balsamic vinegar and lemon juice and mix well.

Serving: Divide grilled and raw oysters equally between serving platters. Garnish with lettuce leaves, herbs and lemon wedges. Sprinkle three of the raw oysters on each plate with the lemon-and-balsamic vinegar mixture, the remaining three with fried salmon strips. Place shot glasses with Bloody Mary in the middle and serve immediately.

Für 4 Personen:

36 Austern

Für die grillierten Austern:
120 g Butter,
1 EL fein gehackte Schalotten,
je 1 TL gehacktes Estragon und Kerbel,
4 Pfefferkörner,
40 ml Weißweinessig,
2 Eigelb,
1 EL gehacktes Estragon und Kerbel,
1 EL Korianderblättchen,
1 EL in feine Streifen geschnittenes Pastrami
(mariniertes geräuchertes Rindfleisch, ersatzweise
geräucherten Rinderschinken verwenden)

60 g Räucherlachs,
2 EL Öl zum Braten,
2 EL Balsamessig,
2 EL Zitronensaft

Garnitur:
grüne Salatblätter, Kräuter, Zitronenschnitze,
4 kleine Gläser mit Bloody Mary

Für die grillierten Austern: Butter in einem Topf schmelzen, abschäumen und warm halten. Schalotten mit Estragon, Kerbel, Pfeffer und Essig in einem kleinen Topf köcheln, bis die Hälfte der Flüssigkeit verdampft ist. Durch ein Sieb passieren. Die Eigelb mit der Reduktion schaumig schlagen. Nach und nach die warme Butter unterrühren, abschmecken, zum Schluss mit gehackten Kräutern vermischen.

Zwölf Austern aus der Schale lösen, waschen, trocknen und zurück in die Schale legen. Mit Béarnaise füllen, mit Korianderblättchen und Pastramistreifen bestreuen, unter dem Grill goldbraun backen.

Den Räucherlachs in dünne Streifen schneiden, in einer Pfanne mit Öl knusprig braten.

Den Balsamessig mit Zitronensaft verrühren.

Zum Servieren: Die gegrillten und die rohen Austern auf vier Servierplatten verteilen, mit Salatblättern, Kräutern und Zitronenschnitzen garnieren. Je drei der rohen Austern mit Zitronensaft-Balsamessig beträufeln, die restlichen drei rohen Austern mit dem gebratenen Lachs bestreuen. Die Gläser mit Bloody Mary in die Mitte der Teller stellen, sofort servieren.

TERRINE OF PEPPERED TUNA WITH A SPICY TOMATO COULIS

TERRINE VON GEPFEFFERTEM THUNFISCH AN WÜRZIGEM TOMATENCOULIS

Serves 8

3 red peppers, 2 tbsp olive oil, 1 eggplant, 4 zucchini,
salt, freshly ground black pepper,
300 g/11 oz fresh tuna fish, 1 tsp crushed black peppercorns,
300 g/11 oz smoked eel (alternatively smoked salmon), cut into slices

For the tomato coulis:
1 onion, finely diced, 1 tbsp garlic, minced, 2 tbsp olive oil,
1 ripe tomato, chopped, 4 tbsp brown sugar,
200 ml/³/₄ cup Worcestershire sauce,
1 tsp tabasco, salt and pepper, 2 tbsp tomato juice

For the saffron oil:
1 tsp saffron threads, 5 tbsp water,
120 ml/¹/₂ cup olive oil, 2 tbsp grapeseed oil

For the herbed oil:
1 bunch parsley, 100 ml/¹/₃ cup ice water,
100 ml/¹/₃ cup grapeseed oil, salt, pepper

Für 8 Personen:

3 rote Paprika, 2 EL Olivenöl, 1 Aubergine, 4 Zucchini,
Salz, schwarzer Pfeffer aus der Mühle,
300 g frischer Thunfisch, 1 TL zerstoßene schwarze Pfefferkörner,
300 g geräucherter Aal (Ersatz: Räucherlachs), in Scheiben geschnitten

Für den Tomaten-Coulis:
1 Zwiebel, in kleine Würfel geschnitten, 1 EL gehackter Knoblauch,
2 EL Olivenöl, 1 reife Tomate, gehackt, 4 EL brauner Zucker,
200 ml Worcestershire-Sauce,
1 TL Tabasco, Salz und Pfeffer, 2 EL Tomatensaft

Für das Safranöl:
1 TL Safranfäden, 5 EL Wasser,
120 ml Olivenöl, 2 EL Traubenkernöl

Für das Kräuteröl:
1 Bund Petersilie, 100 ml Eiswasser,
100 ml Traubenkernöl, Salz, Pfeffer

Halve the red pepper and remove the seeds. Brush the halves with olive oil and roast them in a 200° C/390° F oven until cooked. Cut the eggplant and zucchini lengthwise into ¹/₂ cm/¹/₅ inch slices. Brush the slices with olive oil, sprinkle them with salt and pepper and roast them under the broiler until cooked through. Drain well on paper towels.
Cut the tuna fish into thin slices and sprinkle them with coarsely crushed black pepper. Line a terrine mold with plastic wrap. Place a flat layer of red pepper on the bottom and top with alternate layers of zucchini, tuna fish, eggplant and eel. Repeat until terrine is full. Cover tightly with foil. Weight down with a heavy object and place the mold into the refrigerator overnight.
For the tomato coulis: Sauté onion and garlic in olive oil until translucent. Add tomato and sauté for a minute, then season with sugar, Worcestershire sauce and tabasco and simmer for ten minutes, uncovered. Purée the sauce in a blender and strain it through a fine sieve. Return it to the rinsed pot and reduce to the desired consistency. Check for salt and pepper and thin it with a little tomato juice if necessary.
For the saffron oil: In a small pan, toast the saffron threads over low heat for about twenty seconds. Add water and allow to reduce by half, stirring constantly. Pour saffron essence into a blender jar and gradually drizzle in the two oils. Continue blending for another thirty seconds. Refrigerate oil for a few hours.
For the parsley oil: Blanch parsley in salted water, drain in a sieve and refresh in cold water. Allow excess water to drip off, then purée with the ice water in a blender. Add grapeseed oil, a little at a time, and season with salt and pepper. Strain through a cloth.
Serving: Unmold the terrine and remove foil. Dip a sharp knife into hot water and carefully cut the terrine into 1 cm/¹/₃ inch slices. Arrange the slices on plates and decorate plates with alternating dribbles of differently colored oil. Serve.

Paprika halbieren, entkernen, mit Olivenöl bepinselt im 200° C heißen Ofen rösten, bis sie gar sind. Aubergine und Zucchini der Länge nach in ¹/₂ cm dicke Scheiben schneiden. Mit Olivenöl bepinseln, mit Salz und Pfeffer bestreuen, auf dem Grill von beiden Seiten rösten, bis sie gar sind. Auf Küchenpapier abtropfen lassen. Den Thunfisch in dünne Scheiben schneiden, mit dem zerstoßenen Pfeffer bestreuen. Eine Terrinenform mit Frischhaltefolie ausschlagen. Den Boden flach mit Paprika bedecken, dann abwechselnd eine Lage Zucchini, Thunfisch, Aubergine und Aal einschichten. Den Vorgang wiederholen, bis die Terrine voll ist. Die Folie oben dicht verschließen. Die Terrine mit einem Gewicht beschwert über Nacht in den Kühlschrank stellen.
Für den Tomaten-Coulis: Zwiebel und Knoblauch im Olivenöl glasig dünsten. Tomate kurz mitbraten, Zucker, Worcestershire-Sauce und Tabasco zugeben, 10 Minuten ohne Deckel köcheln. Im Mixer pürieren und die Sauce durch ein Sieb passieren. In einen sauberen Topf geben und auf die gewünschte Konsistenz einkochen. Abschmecken, nach Belieben mit Tomatensaft verdünnen.
Für das Safranöl: Die Safranfäden in einer Pfanne bei kleiner Hitze 20 Sekunden rösten. Das Wasser zugeben, unter Rühren zur Hälfte verdampfen lassen. Das Safranwasser in einen Mixer geben, nach und nach die beiden Öle zugeben und dann während ca. 30 Sekunden den Mixer weiterlaufen lassen. Das Öl im Kühlschrank einige Stunden ruhen lassen.
Für das Kräuteröl: Petersilie in Salzwasser blanchieren, anschließend in kaltem Wasser abschrecken. Abtropfen lassen, im Mixer mit Eiswasser fein pürieren. Nach und nach das Traubenkernöl zugeben, mit Salz und Pfeffer würzen. Durch ein Tuch passieren.
Zum Servieren: Die Terrine aus der Form stürzen, Folie entfernen. Mit einem scharfen Messer, die Klinge in kochendem Wasser erhitzt, in ca. 1 cm dicke Scheiben schneiden und auf Teller verteilen. Mit verschiedenfarbigen Saucen rundum beträufeln.

WARM AND COLD VENISON TAPAS VARIATIONS

WARME UND KALTE TAPAS-VARIATIONEN VOM HIRSCH

Serves 4

For the smoked venison:
200 g/7 oz loin of venison, 1 tbsp onion, finely diced,
1 tsp garlic, minced, 1 tbsp grainy mustard,
120 ml/¹/₂ cup grapeseed oil,
2 tbsp whiskey, 2 tbsp maple syrup, salt, black pepper
For the paté:
60 g/2 oz roasted pepper,
100 g/3¹/₂ oz quark (alternatively cottage cheese, pressed through a fine
sieve), 2 tsp sesame seeds, ¹/₂ tsp tahin (sesame paste),
1 tbsp chervil, minced, 1 tsp olive oil, 30 g/1 oz hazelnuts,
1 garlic clove, squeezed through a garlic press,
black pepper, 1 roasted pepper, peeled
For the carpaccio:
160 g/6 oz loin of venison, 2 tbsp olive oil, 50 g/2 oz pickled ginger,
50 g/2 oz cucumber, peeled, seeds removed and thinly sliced
For the coffee marinade:
160 g/6 oz loin of venison, 100 ml/¹/₃ cup espresso,
¹/₂ tsp cumin seeds, ¹/₂ tsp caraway seeds, ¹/₂ tsp mustard seeds,
¹/₂ tsp ground chili, ¹/₂ garlic clove, minced, ¹/₂ tsp ginger, minced,
4 black peppercorns, crushed, 1 tsp fresh thyme leaves
For the potato salad:
200 g/7 oz sweet potato, 3 tbsp maple syrup, 1 tbsp bourbon, salt,
¹/₂ handful watercress leaves, chopped, 2 tsp lemon juice,
2 tbsp yoghurt, 1 tsp dried tomatoes, chopped,
1 tsp liquid honey, 1 tbsp onion, finely diced, salt, pepper
Garnish: pepper purée (puréed pepper stewed at low heat), herb oil

Place loin of venison into a small dish. Finely purée onion, garlic, mustard, grapeseed oil, whisky, syrup and spices in a blender. Spoon the mixture onto the venison, cover with foil and allow to marinate, tightly covered, for 2 - 3 days in the refrigerator. Scrape off marinade and smoke venison loin in a smoker for ten minutes.
For the paté: Toast sesame seeds and hazelnuts in the oven until medium brown. Purée hazelnuts, sesame seeds, pepper, quark, tahin, chervil, oil and garlic in a blender, season with pepper. Line a small terrine mold with plastic wrap. Line bottom with roast peppers. Top with filling and smooth out the top. Cover with foil and weight down slightly. Place in the refrigerator for two hours.
For the carpaccio: Wrap loin of venison in plastic wrap and place into the freezer for 30 minutes. Unwrap and cut it into paper-thin slices. Arrange 4 rosette forms of alternating meat and cucumber slices and pickled ginger. Drizzle with oil and place in the refrigerator. Finely purée all ingredients of coffee marinade except meat in a blender. Brush meat and place in the refrigerator for 12 hours.
Potato salad: Peel sweet potatoes, cut into cubes and simmer with maple syrup, bourbon, salt and water for 15 minutes. Drain and allow to cool. Toss with remaining ingredients and set aside.
Finish: Cut terrine into slices and place serving plates and next to it a portion of potato salad. Sear coffee-marinated venison in hot oil and slice it thinly. Put one slice onto each plate. Cut smoked venison into similar slices and arrange it on top of the terrine. Add a meat-cucumber-ginger rosette to each plate and spoon a little pepper purée next to it. Drizzle rosette with herb oil and serve.

Für 4 Personen:

Für den geräucherten Hirsch:
200 g Hirschlende, 1 EL fein gewürfelte Zwiebel,
1 TL gehackter Knoblauch, 1 EL grobkörniger Senf,
120 ml Traubenkernöl,
2 EL Whisky, 2 EL Ahornsirup, Salz, schwarzer Pfeffer
Für die Paté:
60 g geröstete Paprika, 100 g Quark,
2 TL Sesamsamen, ¹/₂ TL Tahini (Sesampaste),
1 EL gehackter Kerbel,
1 TL Olivenöl, 30 g Haselnüsse,
1 Knoblauchzehe, durchgedrückt,
schwarzer Pfeffer 1 geröstete Paprika, enthäutet
Für das Carpaccio:
160 g Hirschlende, 2 EL Olivenöl, 50 g eingelegter Ingwer,
50 g Gurke, geschält, entkernt, in dünne Scheiben geschnitten
Für die Kaffee-Marinade:
160 g Hirschlende, 100 ml Espresso-Kaffee,
¹/₂ TL Kreuzkümmel, ¹/₂ TL Kümmel, ¹/₂ TL Senfsamen,
¹/₂ TL Chilipulver, ¹/₂ Knoblauchzehe, gehackt, ¹/₂ TL gehackter Ingwer,
4 schwarze Pfefferkörner, zerdrückt, 1 TL frische Thymianblättchen
Für den Kartoffelsalat:
200 g Süßkartoffel, 3 EL Ahornsirup, 1 EL Bourbon, Salz,
¹/₂ Hand voll Wasserkresseblättchen, gehackt, 2 TL Zitronensaft,
2 EL Joghurt, 1 TL gehackte getrocknete Tomaten,
1 TL flüssiger Honig, 1 EL fein gehackte Zwiebel, Salz, Pfeffer
Garnitur: Paprikapüree (gekocht), Kräuteröl

Hirschlende in ein flaches Gefäß legen. Zwiebel, Knoblauch, Senf, Traubenkernöl, Whisky, Sirup und Gewürze im Mixer fein pürieren. Das Fleisch damit übergießen, im Kühlschrank mit Folie bedeckt 2 - 3 Tage marinieren. Marinade abstreifen, die Hirschlende im Räucherofen 10 Minuten räuchern.
Für die Paté: Sesamsamen und Haselnüsse im Ofen mittelbraun rösten, im Mixer mit Paprika, Quark, Tahini, Kerbel, Öl und Knoblauch fein pürieren. Mit Pfeffer würzen. Eine kleine Terrinenform mit Folie ausschlagen, geröstete Paprika hineinlegen, andrücken, die Füllmasse zugeben und glattstreichen. Mit Folie dicht verschlossen und leicht beschwert im Kühlschrank 2 Stunden kühlen.
Für das Carpaccio: Die Hirschlende in Plastikfolie wickeln und im Gefrierschrank 30 Minuten anfrieren lassen. Auswickeln, in hauchdünne Scheiben schneiden. Mit Ingwer und Gurkenscheiben zu Rosetten formen. Mit Öl beträufeln, kühl stellen. Alle Zutaten für die Kaffee-Marinade im Mixer fein pürieren. Die Hirschlende damit bestreichen, im Kühlschrank 12 Stunden marinieren.
Kartoffelsalat: Süßkartoffel schälen, würfeln, mit Ahornsirup, Bourbon, Salz und Wasser bedeckt 15 Minuten kochen. Abgießen, erkalten lassen, mit den restlichen Zutaten vermischen, beiseite stellen.
Fertigstellung: Terrine aufschneiden und auf Teller legen. Kartoffelsalat verteilen. Die marinierte Lende im heißen Öl von allen Seiten gut anbraten, in Scheiben schneiden, auf dem Kartoffelsalat anrichten. Den geräucherten Hirsch in Scheiben schneiden und über die Terrine anrichten, die Fleisch-Ingwer-Rosetten daneben legen. Mit Paprikapüree und Kräuteröl beträufeln und servieren.

RED PEPPER AND BASIL SOUP

SUPPE VON DER ROTEN PAPRIKA MIT BASILIKUM

Serves 4

2 red peppers,
500 g/1 lb ripe tomatoes,
1 head garlic, olive oil

1 onion, chopped,
2 tbsp olive oil,
2 tbsp tomato paste,
4 sprigs basil, leaves only
(lemon basil, if available),
1 tsp fresh oregano, chopped,
1/2 tsp coarsely crushed black pepper,
1 tbsp brown sugar, 1 tsp salt,
180 ml/3/4 cup red wine,
1 liter /4 cups vegetable broth

Garnish;
100 g/3 1/2 oz green olives, pitted,
30 g/1 oz black olives, pitted,
2 tsp capers, 1 tbsp olive oil

4 slices baguette,
1 garlic clove, halved, olive oil,
30 g/1 oz feta, cut into 8 cubes,
1 sprig basil

Für 4 Personen:

2 rote Paprika,
500 g reife Tomaten,
1 Knolle Knoblauch, Olivenöl

1 Zwiebel, gehackt,
2 EL Olivenöl,
2 EL Tomatenmark,
4 Zweige Basilikum, nur die Blätter
(wenn erhältlich: Zitronenbasilikum),
1 TL frisches Oregano, gehackt,
1/2 TL grob zerstoßene schwarze Pfefferkörner,
1 EL brauner Zucker, 1 TL Salz,
180 ml Rotwein,
1 Liter Gemüsebrühe

Garnitur:
100 g grüne Oliven, entkernt,
30 g schwarze Oliven, entkernt,
2 TL Kapern, 1 EL Olivenöl

4 Scheiben Baguette,
1 Knoblauchzehe, halbiert, Olivenöl,
30 g Feta Käse, in 8 Würfel geschnitten,
1 Basilikumzweig

Halve pepper and remove seeds. Place pepper halves, tomatoes and garlic head onto a roasting pan. Brush with olive oil and bake them in a 200° C/390° F oven until the skin of the pepper is dark and blistery and the tomatoes are soft. Cut the head of the garlic in half horizontally and squeeze out the cloves.
In a medium pot, sauté the onion in olive oil until translucent. Add the roasted vegetables and mix in tomato paste, herbs and seasonings. Douse with wine and stock. Bring to a boil and allow the soup to simmer, uncovered, on low heat. Skim of any foam that rises to the surface. Finely purée soup with a hand-held mixer and check for salt and pepper.
For the garnish: Finely dice olives and capers and toss them with olive oil.
Rub the bread slices with the halved garlic clove and brush with olive oil. Toast the slices in a hot oven until golden brown.
Serving: Ladle the hot soup into small soup bowls. Spread a generous amount of olive mixture on the toasted bread slices and place them on top of the soup. Garnish with two feta cubes and a basil leaf each. Serve immediately.

Paprika halbieren und entkernen. Paprikahälften, Tomaten und Knoblauchknolle auf ein Backblech legen. Mit Olivenöl einpinseln, im 200° C heißen Ofen backen, bis die Paprikahaut dunkelbraune Blasen wirft und die Tomaten weich sind. Beide Gemüse häuten, das Fruchtfleisch fein hacken. Die Knoblauchknolle quer halbieren, die Zehen ausquetschen. In einem Topf die gehackte Zwiebel im Olivenöl anschwitzen. Geröstete Gemüse zugeben. Tomatenmark, Kräuter und Gewürze unterrühren, mit Wein und Brühe ablöschen. Zum Kochen bringen, eine Stunde ohne Deckel bei kleiner Hitze köcheln, den Schaum abschöpfen. Mit dem Stabmixer nicht zu fein pürieren, abschmecken.
Für die Garnitur: Oliven und Kapern fein hacken, mit dem Olivenöl vermischen. Brotscheiben mit der halbierten Knoblauchzehe abreiben, mit Olivenöl bepinseln. Im vorgeheizten Ofen goldbraun rösten.
Zum Servieren: Die Suppe in Suppenschüsselchen schöpfen. Die gerösteten Brotscheiben mit gehackten Oliven bestreichen und auf die Suppen legen. Mit je zwei Feta-Würfeln und einem Basilikumblatt garniert servieren.

MARINATED SALMON IN A WASABI BEURRE BLANC

MARINIERTER LACHS MIT WASABI-BUTTERSAUCE

Serves 4

600 g/1 1/3 lb salmon,
4 tbsp sake,
4 tbsp rice wine vinegar, 2 tsp salt,
2 tbsp brown sugar,
3 tbsp dill,
2 tbsp grated ginger,
1 tbsp ground black pepper

4 rice paper skins

For the wasabi beurre blanc:
1 small onion, finely diced, 1 tbsp butter,
120 ml/1/2 cup white wine,
2 tbsp white wine vinegar,
1 bay leaf, 4 peppercorns,
120 ml/1/2 cup cream,
250 g/1/2 lb cold butter,
1 tsp wasabi paste, salt, pepper

1 head bok choy, leaves only,
1 tbsp pickled ginger

Für 4 Personen:

600 g Lachs,
4 EL Sake,
4 EL Reisweinessig, 2 TL Salz,
2 EL brauner Zucker,
3 EL Dill,
2 EL geriebener Ingwer,
1 EL gemahlener schwarzer Pfeffer

4 Reispapierblätter

Für die Wasabi-Buttersauce:
1 kleine Zwiebel, fein gewürfelt, 1 EL Butter,
120 ml Weißwein,
2 EL Weißweinessig,
1 Lorbeerblatt, 4 Pfefferkörner,
120 ml Sahne,
250 g kalte Butter,
1 TL Wasabipaste, Salz, Pfeffer

1 Staude Pak-Choi, nur die Blätter,
1 EL eingelegter Ingwer

Combine sake, rice wine vinegar, salt, sugar, ginger and dill. Mix well. Rub salmon with pepper, place it into a flat dish and brush it all over with marinade. Cover with foil and allow to marinate in the refrigerator for three days. Turn once a day and make sure that the fish is well covered with marinade.
Cut the rice paper skins into thirds. Heat oil in a pan and fry the rice paper thirds until crisp. Allow to drain on paper towels.
For the wasabi beurre blanc: Sauté onions in butter until translucent. Add the wine and vinegar, bay leaf and pepper. Reduce liquid by half. Stir in cream and allow to reduce again. Work in cold butter, a piece at a time, stirring constantly. Strain sauce through a sieve, then season it with wasabi paste, salt and pepper. Keep warm.
Steam the bok choy leaves until tender.
Finish: Thinly slice the marinated salmon. Fry the slices in a little oil on both sides, until they start browning.
Flood pre-warmed plates with some beurre blanc. Arrange stacks of alternating layers of salmon slices, bok choy leaves and rice paper skins. Garnish the stacks with pickled ginger. Serve.

Sake, Reisweinessig, Salz, Zucker, Ingwer und Dill gut verrühren. Den Lachs mit Pfeffer einreiben, in einem flachen Gefäß mit der Marinade bestrichen und mit Folie bedeckt im Kühlschrank 3 Tage marinieren. Jeden Tag wenden, darauf achten, dass der Fisch mit Marinade gut bedeckt ist.
Die Reispapierblätter in Drittel schneiden. Im heißen Öl in einer Pfanne knusprig braten, auf Küchenpapier abtropfen lassen.
Für die Wasabibuttersauce: Zwiebelwürfel in der Butter anschwitzen. Mit Wein und Essig aufgießen, Lorbeer und Pfeffer zugeben, die Flüssigkeit um die Hälfte einkochen. Dann die Sahne einrühren, erneut einkochen. Unter Rühren kalte Butter stückweise einarbeiten. Sauce durch ein Sieb passieren, mit Wasabi, Salz und Pfeffer würzen. Warm halten.
Die Pak-Choi-Blätter über Dampf weich garen.
Fertigstellung: Den marinierten Lachs in Scheiben schneiden. In einer Pfanne mit wenig Fett von beiden Seiten anbraten, bis er beginnt zu bräunen.
Vorgewärmte Teller mit der Buttersauce ausgießen. Den Lachs abwechselnd mit den Gemüseblättern und den Reisblättern aufschichten, zum Schluss mit eingelegtem Ingwer garnieren.

SEARED SCALLOPS WITH CAPER BLINIS AND A RED PEPPER BEURRE BLANC

GEBRATENE JAKOBSMUSCHELN MIT KAPERN-BLINIS UND PAPRIKA-BUTTERSAUCE

Serves 4

20 scallops, white part only,
2 tbsp clarified butter,
smoked salmon, cut into strips,
¹/₂ red pepper, cut into thin strips, brushed with a little olive oil and
baked in a 90° C/200° F oven until soft and dry

For the blinis:
80 ml/¹/₄ milk, 10 g/1 tsp fresh yeast, a pinch of sugar,
80 g/3 oz flour, 1 egg yolk,
2 tbsp capers, chopped,
2 tbsp parsley, chopped,
2 tbsp dill, chopped,
1 egg white, whipped into soft peaks,
2 tbsp sunflower oil

For the red pepper beurre blanc:
1 red pepper, ¹/₂ small onion, chopped,
100 ml/¹/₃ cup white wine,
50 ml/¹/₄ cup white wine vinegar, 1 bay leaf,
4 black peppercorns, coarsely crushed,
125 ml/¹/₂ cup cream,
200 g/7 oz cold butter

Garnish: sprigs of dill

In a small pot, heat milk until tepid. Add yeast and sugar and whisk until dissolved. Cover and allow to rise for half an hour. Stir in half of the flour and the egg yolk and allow to rise for another half hour. Mix in chopped capers and herbs, add a little salt and fold in egg whites.

Heat the oil in a non-stick pan and place a ladleful of batter into the hot oil. Bake until bubbly and golden brown. Turn the blini over and allow it to brown on the other side. Repeat the procedure until you have four blinis. Allow blinis to cool on a wire rack.

For the red pepper beurre blanc: Halve the pepper, remove core and place halves onto a baking pan, cut side down. Roast them in a 200° C/390° F oven until the skin turns dark brown and blistery. Peel off the skin under running water. Purée flesh in a blender. Sauté the chopped onion in butter until translucent. Add white wine, vinegar, bay leaf and pepper and allow the liquid to reduce by half. Add cream and allow to reduce again. Whisk in the cold butter with a wire whip, a piece at a time. Do not let the sauce come to a boil again. Strain the sauce through a fine sieve and incorporate pepper purée.

Finish: Reheat the blinis in the oven. In a very hot pan, sear the scallops in clarified butter on both sides. Remove from the pan and sauté the salmon and pepper strips in the same pan until heated through.

Flood the plates with red pepper beurre blanc. Place five scallops onto each plate to form a circle. Cover the circles with blinis. Top blinis with sautéed salmon and pepper strips and garnish with sprigs of dill. Serve.

Für 4 Personen:

20 Jakobsmuscheln, nur das weiße Nüsschen,
2 EL geklärte Butter,
Räucherlachs, in dünne Streifen geschnitten,
¹/₂ rote Paprika, in dünne Streifen geschnitten, im Ofen
bei 90° C mit wenig Olivenöl backen, bis sie gar und trocken sind

Für die Blinis:
80 ml Milch, 10 g frische Hefe, 1 Prise Zucker,
80 g Mehl, 1 Eigelb,
2 EL gehackte Kapern,
2 TL gehackte Petersilie,
2 TL gehackter Dill,
1 Eiweiß, zu Schnee geschlagen,
2 EL Sonnenblumenöl

Für die Paprika-Buttersauce:
1 rote Paprika, ¹/₂ kleine Zwiebel, gehackt,
100 ml Weißwein,
50 ml Weißweinessig, 1 Lorbeerblatt,
4 schwarze Pfefferkörner, grob zerdrückt,
125 ml Sahne,
200 g eiskalte Butter

Garnitur: Dill

Milch in einem Topf lauwarm erhitzen. Die Hefe und den Zucker zugeben und rühren, bis sich alles gut aufgelöst hat. Eine halbe Stunde zugedeckt gehen lassen. Die Hälfte des Mehls und das Eigelb unterrühren, erneut eine halbe Stunde gehen lassen. Das restliche Mehl einarbeiten und nochmals eine halbe Stunde gehen lassen. Nun die gehackten Kapern und Kräuter untermischen, leicht salzen und den Eischnee unterziehen.

In einer beschichteten Pfanne das Öl erhitzen. Mit einer Kelle nacheinander vier Portionen Teig in das heiße Öl schöpfen und backen, bis der Teig Blasen wirft. Umdrehen, die zweite Seite goldgelb backen. Die Blinis auf einem Gitter auskühlen lassen.

Für die Paprika-Buttersauce: Paprika halbieren, entkernen und mit Schnittfläche nach unten im auf 200° C vorgeheizten Ofen rösten, bis sich die Haut dunkelbraun verfärbt und Blasen wirft. Unter fließendem Wasser häuten. Das Paprikafleisch im Mixer pürieren. Die gehackte Zwiebel in der Butter anschwitzen. Weißwein, Essig, Lorbeerblatt und Pfeffer zugeben, um die Hälfte einkochen. Sahne zufügen und erneut einkochen. Mit dem Schneebesen nach und nach die kalte Butter einrühren, nicht mehr kochen. Die Sauce durch ein Sieb passieren und mit dem Paprikapüree verrühren.

Fertigstellung: Die Blinis im Ofen erwärmen. Die Jakobsmuscheln in der geklärten Butter von beiden Seiten sehr heiß anbraten. Aus der Pfanne nehmen, die Lachs- und Paprikastreifen im gleichen Fett unter Rühren braten, bis sie beginnen, Farbe anzunehmen.

Von der Paprika-Buttersauce einen Spiegel auf Teller gießen. Je fünf Jakobsmuscheln kreisförmig darauf auslegen, mit einem Blini bedecken. Mit Lachs- und Paprikastreifen belegen, mit Dill garnieren.

THYME-RUBBED CHICKEN BREASTS SERVED WITH A CHEESE SALAD

HÜHNERBRUST MIT THYMIAN UND KÄSESALAT

Serves 4

4 chicken breasts, about 160 g/6 oz each, skin removed,
4 tbsp thyme, leaves only, 1 sprig basil,
1 tbsp marjoram,
100 ml/¹/₃ cup olive oil,
salt, freshly ground black pepper

For the cheese salad:
200 g/7 oz smoked havarti cheese (Danish tilsiter),
2 tbsp finely diced red onion,
1 tbsp balsamic vinegar, 1 tbsp olive oil,
2 dried tomatoes, finely diced (brushed with a little oil
and dried in a 120° C/250° F oven for about 6 hours)

For the chicken jus:
200 ml/³/₄ cup white wine,
200 ml/³/₄ cup chicken stock,
200 ml/³/₄ cup veal stock, 1 tsp cornstarch,
salt, freshly grated black pepper

For the vegetable garnish:
200 g/7 oz leeks, cut into julienne strips,
200 g/7 oz green onions, cut into julienne strips,
oil for deep-frying

Place the chicken breasts into a shallow dish. Purée the herbs and oil in blender and season the purée with salt and pepper. Brush the chicken breasts with the mixture. Cover with foil and allow to marinate in the refrigerator overnight.

Cut the havarti into 1 cm/¹/₃ inch cubes, place them into a bowl and toss with onion, balsamic vinegar, olive oil and dried tomatoes. Set aside.

For the chicken jus: Combine the wine with chicken and veal stock in a small saucepan and reduce the liquid by half. Mix the cornstarch with a little water and thicken the jus with it. Reduce the jus to the desired consistency. Strain through a sieve and check for salt and pepper.

For the vegetable garnish: Deep-fry the green onion and leek strips in oil until golden brown. Drain well on paper towels.

Finish: Preheat the oven to 200° C/390° F. Broil the marinated chicken breasts on both sides until brown. Finish by baking them in the oven for ten minutes and allow to rest for five minutes.

Arrange cheese salad on plates. Cut chicken breasts into three pieces each and place the pieces onto the salad. Drizzle with a little chicken jus and top with crispy fried vegetable julienne. Serve.

Für 4 Personen:

4 Hühnerbrüste à ca. 160 g, ohne Haut,
4 EL Thymianblättchen, 1 Zweig Basilikum,
1 EL Majoranblättchen,
100 ml Olivenöl,
Salz, schwarzer Pfeffer aus der Mühle

Für den Käsesalat:
200 g geräucherter Havarti (dänischer Tilsiter),
2 EL fein gewürfelte rote Zwiebel,
1 EL Balsamessig, 1 EL Olivenöl,
2 getrocknete Tomaten, fein gehackt (im Ofen
bei 120° C mit etwas Öl ca. 6 Stunden trocknen)

Für den Hühnerjus:
200 ml Weißwein,
200 ml Hühnerbrühe,
200 ml Kalbsfond, 1 TL Maisstärke,
Salz, schwarzer Pfeffer aus der Mühle

Für die Gemüsegarnitur:
200 g Lauch, in dünne Streifen geschnitten,
200 g Frühlingszwiebel, in dünne Streifen geschnitten,
Öl zum Frittieren

Die Hühnerbrüste in ein flaches Gefäß legen. Die Kräuter mit dem Öl im Mixer pürieren, mit Salz und Pfeffer würzen, das Hühnerfleisch mit dieser Mischung bestreichen. Mit Folie zudecken und im Kühlschrank 12 Stunden marinieren.

Den Havartikäse in 1 cm große Würfel schneiden, in einer Schüssel mit Zwiebel, Balsamessig, Olivenöl und Tomaten vermischen, beiseite stellen.

Für den Hühnerjus: Den Wein mit der Hühnerbrühe und dem Kalbsfond in einem Topf um die Hälfte einkochen. Die Maisstärke mit etwas Wasser anrühren, den Jus damit binden und auf die gewünschte Konsistenz reduzieren. Durch ein Sieb passieren, mit Salz und Pfeffer würzen.

Für die Gemüsegarnitur: Die Frühlingszwiebel- und Lauchstreifen in Öl goldgelb frittieren, auf Küchenpapier abtropfen lassen.

Fertigstellung: Den Ofen auf 200° C vorheizen. Die marinierte Hühnerbrust auf dem Grill von beiden Seiten bräunen. Im Ofen 10 Minuten durchgaren, anschließend zugedeckt 5 Minuten ruhen lassen.

Den Käsesalat auf Teller anrichten. Hühnerbrust in je drei Stücke schneiden und über den Salat legen. Mit Hühnerjus begießen, zum Schluss die knusprig ausgebackenen Gemüsestreifen darüber häufen.

WILD MUSHROOM RISOTTO
SERVED WITH A HERB SALAD
IN BROWN BUTTER VINAIGRETTE

WALDPILZ-RISOTTO
MIT KRÄUTERSALAT
UND BRAUNER BUTTER-VINAIGRETTE

Serves 4

For the risotto:
170 g/6 oz arborio rice,
200 g/7 oz mixed mushrooms: shiitake, oyster mushrooms,
champignons and chanterelles,
1 onion, chopped, 2 tbsp butter,
200 ml/³/₄ cup mushroom stock,
400 - 500 ml/1 ¹/₂ - 2 cups vegetable stock

150 g/5 oz mixed herbs: basil, chervil, chives, tarragon and arugula

For the vinaigrette:
100 g/3 ¹/₂ oz butter, 2 tbsp chopped pecans,
4 tbsp balsamic vinegar, 2 tbsp olive oil,
salt, black pepper

Clean and trim the mushrooms and cut them into slices. In a large pan, sauté onions in butter until translucent. Add mushrooms and keep stirring until they start giving off juice. Add rice and douse with mushroom stock. After the liquid is evaporated, keep adding mushroom stock, a little at a time, as the rice absorbs it. The rice should be done, but still firm to the bite, after about fifteen minutes.
For the vinaigrette: In a small pan, toast the nuts in butter on medium heat until they turn a hazelnut brown. Remove pan from heat and add balsamic vinegar and olive oil. Check for salt and pepper.
Serving: Press the risotto into ring molds and unmold them onto four plates. Toss the herbs with a little vinaigrette and arrange them on top of the risotto. Serve at once.

Für 4 Personen:

Für den Risotto:
170 g Arborio Reis,
200 g gemischte Pilze: Shiitake, Austernpilze, Champignons und Pfifferlinge,
1 Zwiebel, gehackt,
2 EL Butter,
200 ml Pilzfond,
400 - 500 ml Gemüsebrühe

150 g gemischte Kräuter: Basilikum, Kerbel, Schnittlauch, Estragon und Rucola

Für die Vinaigrette:
100 g Butter, 2 EL gehackte Pekannüsse,
4 EL Balsamico, 2 EL Olivenöl,
Salz, schwarzer Pfeffer

Pilze putzen, in Scheiben schneiden. Zwiebel in einem Topf mit schwerem Boden in der Butter anschwitzen. Pilze zugeben, unter Rühren dünsten, bis sie Wasser ziehen. Den Reis unterrühren, dann mit dem Pilzfond ablöschen. Wenn die Flüssigkeit verdampft ist, nach und nach den Gemüsefond zugeben und einkochen lassen. Nach ca. 15 Minuten Kochzeit soll der Reis gar sein aber noch "Biss" haben.
Für die Vinaigrette: Die Butter mit den Nüssen in einer Pfanne bei mittlerer Hitze erhitzen, bis sie haselnussbraun ist. Die Pfanne vom Herd nehmen, mit dem Balsamico sowie Olivenöl verrühren, mit Salz und Pfeffer würzen.
Zum Servieren: Den heißen Risotto in eine runde Form drücken und auf Teller stürzen. Die Kräuter mit der Vinaigrette vermischen und über den Risotto anrichten. Sofort servieren.

Serves 4

4 beef medallions, about 250 g/¹/₂ lb each, salt, black pepper

For the chervil pesto:
120 g/4 oz chervil, chopped, 50 g/1 ¹/₂ oz pine nuts,
80 ml/¹/₄ cup olive oil, 1 tbsp soy sauce,
1 tbsp balsamic vinegar, 1 tbsp lemon juice, ¹/₂ garlic clove, minced, salt

For the vinaigrette:
2 tbsp honey, 2 tbsp grainy mustard,
3 tbsp red wine vinegar, 8 tbsp olive oil, salt, pepper

For the vegetable confit:
200 g/7 oz white turnips, 200 g/7 oz spinach, 3 small zucchini, 2 small carrots

BEEF MEDALLIONS WITH PEPPER AND CHERVIL PESTO

TOURNEDOS VOM RIND MIT PFEFFER UND KERBELPESTO

Tie the medallions into cylindrical round shapes with kitchen string. Rub with salt and pepper and set aside. For the chervil pesto: Purée all ingredients in a blender and check for salt and pepper.
For the vinaigrette: Combine all ingredients and mix well. Set aside.
For the vegetable confit: Cut all vegetables into thin strips. Heat olive oil in a heavy-bottomed casserole and saute vegetables until wilted. Add half of the vinaigrette and stew until tender on low heat. Check for salt and pepper.
Finish: Broil the medallions on all sides until brown, then bake them in a hot oven for five to ten minutes until the desired degree of doneness. Remove from oven and allow to rest for five minutes. Reserve pan juices. Arrange vegetable confit on plates. Remove string from medallions and place them upright onto the bed of vegetables. Spoon some pesto on top of the meat and over the vegetables and surround with dribbles of pan juice. Serve.

Für 4 Personen:

4 Filetstücke à ca. 250 g, Salz, schwarzer Pfeffer

Für das Kerbelpesto:
120 g Kerbel, gehackt, 50 g Pinienkerne, 80 ml Olivenöl,
1 EL Sojasauce, 1 EL Balsamessig, 1 EL Zitronensaft,
¹/₂ Knoblauchzehe, fein gehackt, Salz

Für die Vinaigrette.
2 EL Honig, 2 EL grobkörniger Senf,
3 EL Rotweinessig, 8 EL Olivenöl, Salz, Pfeffer

Für das Schmorgemüse:
200 g Navetten (Mairübchen), 200 g Spinat, 3 kleine Zucchini, 2 kleine Karotten

Die Filetstücke mit Küchengarn in eine zylindrische Form binden, mit Salz und Pfeffer würzen, beiseite stellen.
Für das Kerbelpesto: Alle Zutaten im Mixer pürieren, mit Salz würzen.
Für die Vinaigrette: Alle Zutaten gut verrühren, beiseite stellen.
Für das Schmorgemüse: Gemüse in kleine Streifen schneiden. In einem Topf mit schwerem Boden im Öl unter Rühren anschwitzen. Mit der Hälfte der Vinaigrette vermischen, bei kleiner Hitze weich garen. Abschmecken.
Fertigstellung: Die Filetstücke auf dem Grill von allen Seiten bräunen, im Ofen bis zum gewünschten Gargrad 5 - 10 Minuten fertig braten. Herausnehmen, 5 Minuten ruhen lassen, den Bratsaft aufheben. Schmorgemüse auf Teller anrichten. Den Bindfaden von den Tournedos entfernen, die Fleischstücke aufrecht auf die Gemüse stellen. Das Pesto auf und um das Fleisch geben, den Bratsaft rundherum verteilen.

RACK OF LAMB WITH MACADAMIA NUTS AND LAVENDER JAM

LAMMRÜCKEN MIT MACADAMIANÜSSEN UND LAVENDEL-MARMELADE

Serves 4

700 g/1¹/₂ lbs rack of lamb, hacked into four equal pieces,
100 g/3¹/₂ oz macadamia nuts, toasted, coarsely chopped,
3 tbsp orange juice,
4 tbsp grainy mustard, 2 tbsp honey

1 large carrot,
1 sweet potato,
1 piece of pumpkin,
60 ml/¹/₄ cup olive oil,
salt, black pepper

For the lavender jam:
a handful of fresh lavender blossoms (stemmed),
60 g/2 oz sugar,
60 ml/2 oz sherry,
60 ml/2 oz port,
250 ml/1 cup water,
2 tbsp honey

For the jus:
2 tbsp rosemary,
1 tbsp mint, chopped,
120 ml/¹/₂ cup red wine,
200 ml/³/₄ cup beef stock,
1 tbsp red currant jelly,
1 tbsp tomato paste

Für 4 Personen:

700 g Lammrücken mit Knochen, in vier Portionen geteilt,
100 g Macadamianüsse, geröstet, grob gehackt,
3 EL Orangensaft,
4 EL grobkörniger Senf, 2 EL Honig

1 große Karotte,
1 Süßkartoffel,
1 Stück Kürbis,
60 ml Olivenöl,
Salz, schwarzer Pfeffer

Für die Lavendelmarmelade:
1 Hand voll frische Lavendelblüten (vom Halm gestreift),
60 g Zucker,
60 ml Sherry,
60 ml Portwein,
250 ml Wasser,
2 EL Honig

Für den Jus:
2 EL Rosmarinnadeln,
1 EL gehackte Minze,
120 ml Rotwein,
200 ml Rinderbrühe,
1 EL roter Johannisbeergelee,
1 EL Tomatenmark

Trim rack of lamb of all fat and silvery skin. With a sharp knife, make a longish incision into the meat part and carefully insert nuts. Combine orange juice, mustard and honey and mix well. Rub the meat with the mixture all over. Cover and allow to rest in the refrigerator.

Preheat the oven to 200° C/390° F. Peel carrot, potato and pumpkin and chop them coarsely. Boil vegetables in salted water for three minutes, then drain. Place vegetables in an oven-proof dish, drizzle with olive oil and sprinkle with salt and pepper. Bake in the oven for 20 - 30 minutes. Turn vegetable pieces from time to time.

For the lavender jam: Combine all ingredients in a small saucepan and bring to a boil. Reduce on low heat for about half an hour. Allow to cool.

For the jus: Combine all ingredients in a saucepan and reduce to the desired consistency. Season with salt and pepper and strain through a fine sieve. Set aside.

Finish: Roast the pieces of lamb rack under the grill from all sides. Place them into the dish with the vegetables and bake them for another 10-15 minutes, until the desired degree of doneness has been reached. Allow the meat to rest for five minutes, then cut each piece in half. Arrange two pieces of lamb rack on each plate and garnish the plate with vegetables. Brush the meat with a little lavender jam and surround it with jus. Enjoy. The side dish on the photograph is a puff pastry stuffed with mushrooms.

Die Rippenknochen sauber putzen, das Fleisch vollständig von allen Silberhäutchen und Fett befreien. In den Fleischteil jeweils einen langen Einschnitt machen und mit den Nüssen füllen. Den Orangensaft mit dem Senf und dem Honig verrühren, das Fleisch rundum damit bepinseln. Zugedeckt in den Kühlschrank legen und marinieren.

Den Ofen auf 200° C vorheizen. Karotte, Kartoffel und Kürbis schälen und in grobe Würfel schneiden. In Salzwasser 3 Minuten kochen, abgießen. Das Gemüse in eine feuerfeste Schale füllen, mit Olivenöl beträufeln, mit Salz und Pfeffer würzen und im Ofen 20 - 30 Minuten backen. Von Zeit zu Zeit das Gemüse wenden.

Für die Lavendelmarmelade: Alle Zutaten in einem kleinen Topf zum Kochen bringen. Bei kleiner Hitze ca. eine halbe Stunde einkochen, erkalten lassen.

Für den Jus: Alle Zutaten für den Jus in einem Topf zur gewünschten Konsistenz einkochen. Mit Salz und Pfeffer würzen, durch ein Sieb passieren.

Fertigstellung: Die Lammrückenstücke unter dem Grill von allen Seiten rösten, dann mit dem Gemüse in einen Bräter geben, im Ofen 10 - 15 Minuten bis zum gewünschten Gargrad fertig braten. Das Fleisch fünf Minuten ruhen lassen, dann jeweils einmal durchschneiden. Auf Teller anrichten, mit Gemüse garnieren, das Fleisch mit Marmelade bepinseln, zum Schluss mit Jus umgießen. Beilage Foto: Mit Champignons gefülltes Blätterteiggebäck.

BEEF WITH AVOCADO AND ONION CONFIT IN A RED WINE SAUCE

RINDFLEISCH MIT AVOCADO, ZWIEBELMARMELADE UND ROTWEINSAUCE

<table>
<tr><td>

Serves 4

400 g/14 oz filet of beef, trimmed

For the avocado spread:
1 avocado, 1 tbsp finely diced onion,
1 tbsp lemon juice, 1 tsp sweet chili sauce,
1 small tomato, peeled, cored, chopped,
freshly ground black pepper

For the tomato sauce:
1 onion, chopped, 2 garlic cloves, minced,
2 tbsp olive oil,
3 tbsp Worcestershire sauce, 1 tsp tabasco, 1 tbsp soy sauce,
1 kg/2 lbs tomatoes, peeled, seeded, chopped,
1 tbsp each chopped thyme, marjoram,
parsley, chives and chervil,
salt, freshly ground black pepper

For the onion confit:
2 large red onions, 2 tbsp butter,
2 tbsp maple syrup, 2 tbsp sherry,
salt, freshly ground black pepper

For the red wine sauce:
100 ml/¹⁄₃ cup red wine,
400 ml/1 ¹⁄₃ cups beef stock,
1 tbsp red currant jelly, 1 ¹⁄₂ tbsp tomato paste,
salt, freshly ground black pepper

</td><td>

Für 4 Personen:

400 g Rinderfilet, sauber pariert

Für den Avocado-Aufstrich:
1 Avocado, 1 EL fein gewürfelte Zwiebel,
1 EL Zitronensaft, 1 TL süße Chilisauce,
1 kleine Tomate, enthäutet, entkernt, gehackt,
schwarzer Pfeffer aus der Mühle

Für die Tomatensauce:
1 Zwiebel, gehackt, 2 Knoblauchzehen, gehackt,
2 EL Olivenöl,
3 EL Worcestershire-Sauce, 1 TL Tabasco, 1 EL Sojasauce,
1 kg Tomaten, gehäutet, entkernt und gehackt,
Je ein EL gehackter Thymian, Majoran, Petersilie,
Schnittlauch und Kerbel,
Salz, schwarzer Pfeffer aus der Mühle

Für die Zwiebelmarmelade:
2 große rote Zwiebeln, 2 EL Butter,
2 EL Ahornsirup, 2 EL Sherry,
Salz, schwarzer Pfeffer aus der Mühle

Für die Rotweinsauce:
100 ml Rotwein,
400 ml Rindfleischbrühe,
1 EL Johannisbeergelee, 1 ¹⁄₂ EL Tomatenmark,
Salz, schwarzer Pfeffer aus der Mühle

</td></tr>
</table>

Cut the beef into twelve even slices. Brush the slices with oil and refrigerate.

For the avocado spread: Purée all ingredients in a blender. Place the spread in a small porcelain dish and cover tightly with plastic wrap. Refrigerate.

For the tomato sauce: Sauté onion and garlic in olive oil until translucent. Add tomatoes, Worcestershire sauce, tabasco and soy sauce and simmer for about five minutes. Stir in herbs and check for salt and pepper. Set aside.

For the onion confit: Halve the onions and slice them thinly. In a small pan, sauté the slices in butter, add maple syrup and allow to caramelize slightly. Add the sherry and simmer until liquid is evaporated. Season with salt and pepper and keep warm.

For the red wine sauce: Combine all ingredients for the sacue and simmer, uncovered, until the sauce has thickened slightly. Check for salt and pepper. Strain the red wine sauce through a cloth and keep warm.

Finish: Broil the meat slices under the broiler for about two minutes a side. Place a slice of beef each onto four pre-warmed plates. Spread avocado mixture and tomato sauce on top and cover with another slice of meat. Spread the second slice with onion confit and top with another slice of beef. Surround the stacks with red wine sauce and garnish the plates with herbs according to taste. Serve at once.

Das Filet in 12 gleichmäßige Scheiben schneiden. Mit Öl bepinseln, im Kühlschrank aufbewahren.

Für den Avocado-Aufstrich: Alle Zutaten im Mixer kurz pürieren. In ein Porzellanschüsselchen füllen, mit Frischhaltefolie gut zugedeckt in den Kühlschrank stellen.

Für die Tomatensauce: Zwiebel und Knoblauch im Olivenöl anschwitzen. Tomaten, Worcestershire-Sauce, Tabasco und Sojasauce zugeben und 5 Minuten köcheln. Zum Schluss die Kräuter unterrühren, mit Salz und Pfeffer würzen.

Für die Zwiebelmarmelade: Die Zwiebeln halbieren und in dünne Scheiben schneiden. In einem Topf in der Butter anschwitzen, mit dem Ahornsirup leicht karamellisieren, dann den Sherry zugeben und köcheln, bis die Flüssigkeit verdampft ist. Mit Salz und Pfeffer würzen, warm halten.

Für die Rotweinsauce: Alle Zutaten ohne Deckel köcheln, bis die Sauce leicht eindickt. Mit Salz und Pfeffer würzen. Durch ein Tuch passieren, warm halten.

Fertigstellung: Das Fleisch auf dem Grill von jeder Seite ca. zwei Minuten rösten. Je eine Scheibe Fleisch auf vorgewärmte Teller legen. Mit Avocado bestreichen, etwas Tomatensauce darüber geben, mit einer zweiten Fleischscheibe bedecken. Diese mit Zwiebelmarmelade bestreichen, dann die dritte Fleischscheibe darüber legen. Mit etwas Rotweinsauce umgießen, nach Belieben die Teller mit Kräutern garnieren.

JASMINE AND ROSE PETAL ICE CREAM WITH ICED FRUITS IN A "CHAMPAGNE" ICE CUP

JASMIN-ROSENBLÜTEN-EIS UND GEEISTE FRÜCHTE IM „CHAMPAGNER"-EISBECHER

Serves 4

For the champagne ice cups:
250 ml/1 cup light sparkling grape juice,
25 g/1 oz sugar, 350 ml/1 1/2 cups water

For the jasmine and rose petal ice cream:
220 ml/1 cup milk, 220 ml/1 cup cream,
1 vanilla bean, 1 tbsp dried jasmine petals,
45 g/1 1/2 oz sugar, 3 egg yolks,
a handful of rose petals,
1 tbsp rose water, 2 tbsp sugar, 4 tbsp water

For the syrup:
120 ml/1/2 cup red grape juice, 80 ml/1/4 cup grapefruit juice,
20 g/3/4 oz sugar, 1 tsp cornstarch

For the iced fruit:
100 g/3 1/2 oz water melon, 100 g/3 1/2 oz honeydew melon,
100 g/3 1/2 oz ripe papaya, 8 grapes, 4 strawberries

Decoration: banana leaves, cut into rounds (according to taste),
jasmine and rose petals, mint leaves

Für 4 Personen:

Für die Champagner-Eisbecherformen:
250 ml heller Traubensaft, mit Kohlensäure,
25 g Zucker, 350 ml Wasser

Für das Jasmin-Rosenblüten-Eis:
220 ml Milch, 220 ml Sahne,
1 Vanillestange, 1 EL getrocknete Jasminblütenblättchen,
45 g Zucker, 3 Eigelb,
1 Hand voll rote Rosenblütenblätter,
1 EL Rosenwasser, 2 EL Zucker, 4 EL Wasser

Für den Sirup:
120 ml roter Traubensaft, 80 ml Grapefruitsaft,
20 g Zucker, 1 TL Maisstärke

Geeiste Früchte:
100 g Wassermelone, 100 g Honigmelone,
100 g reife Papaya, 8 Traubenbeeren, 4 Erdbeeren

Dekoration: Bananenblätter, rund ausgeschnitten (nach Belieben),
Jasmin- und Rosenblütenblätter, Minzeblättchen

Combine all ingredients for the ice cups in a pot and bring mixture to a boil. Allow to cool. Place into molds or cups, according to taste. The liquid should come about half way up. Place another, smaller mold in the middle and weight down slightly from the top, so that the liquid rises up to the rim of the outer mold. Be careful that the inner mold does not quite touch the bottom of the outer one. Deep-freeze overnight. Carefully remove both inner and outer molds. (Dip outer mold in hot water for a few seconds, then fill inner mold with hot water.) Store ice cups in the deep freezer.
For the ice cream: Combine the milk, cream, slit vanilla bean and jasmine in a pot and bring to a boil. Whisk egg yolks and sugar until light and fluffy. Remove vanilla bean, then pour the hot milk mixture into the egg yolk mixture, beating constantly with a wire whisk. Return the mixture to the pot and heat, stirring constantly, until the custard begins to thicken. Place the pot into a basin with ice water and stir until cold, then strain it through a sieve. Combine rose petals, rose water, sugar and water in a small pot. Bring to a boil and simmer, uncovered, until liquid is reduced by half. Stir it into ice cream mixture, mix well and freeze in an ice cream maker.
For the syrup: In a small pot, combine grape and grapefruit juices with the sugar and bring to a boil. Mix the cornstarch with a little water, add to the liquid and allow to simmer until the syrup has thickened slightly. Allow to cool.
For the iced fruit: Cut the fruits into bite-sized pieces, lay them out flat on a tray and place them in the deep freezer for about an hour.
Serving: Line plates with banana leaf circles and place a champagne ice cup onto each circle. Fill cup with iced fruit and top each cup with a scoop of jasmine and rose petal ice cream. Drizzle syrup over the plate and garnish with blossoms and mint leaves. Serve at once.

Die Zutaten für die Eisbecherformen zum Kochen bringen, anschließend abkühlen lassen. In Becher- oder Glasformen nach Wunsch halb hoch einfüllen. Jeweils eine zweite, kleinere Form in die Mitte platzieren und von oben beschweren, so dass die Flüssigkeit am äusseren Rand bis nach oben steigt. Aufpassen, dass die innere Form unten nicht an die äussere Form stößt. Im Tiefkühlgerät über Nacht gefrieren lassen. Die inneren und äusseren Formen entfernen (kurz in heißes Wasser tauchen, heißes Wasser in die innere Form gießen. Die Eisbecher im Tiefkühler aufbewahren.
Für das Eis: Milch mit Sahne, aufgeschnittener Vanillestange und Jasmin in einem Topf zum Kochen bringen. Zucker mit Eigelb in einer Schüssel schaumig rühren. Die Vanillestange aus der Milch entfernen, dann unter kräftigem Rühren mit dem Schneebesen die heiße Milch zu den Eigelb gießen. Die Masse zurück in den Topf geben und unter Rühren erhitzen, bis die Flüssigkeit beginnt, zu binden. Topf in Eiswasser stellen, die Creme kalt rühren, durch ein Sieb passieren. Die Rosenblütenblätter mit Rosenwasser, Zucker und Wasser in einem kleinen Topf erhitzen. Ohne Deckel köcheln, bis die Häfte der Flüssigkeit verdampft ist. Mit der Eiscrememasse verrühren und in der Eismaschine gefrieren.
Sirup: Trauben- und Grapefruitsaft mit Zucker in einem Topf zum Kochen bringen. Maisstärke mit etwas Wasser anrühren, unterrühren und köcheln, bis der Sirup leicht eindickt. Erkalten lassen.
Für die geeisten Früchte: Früchte in fingergroße Stücke schneiden, flach ausgebreitet im Tiefkühler ca. eine Stunde anfrieren lassen.
Zum Servieren: Je ein Bananenblatt auf Teller legen, in die Mitte einen Champagner-Eisbecher stellen. Mit geeisten Früchten füllen, darauf eine Kugel Jasmin-Roseneis geben. Mit Sirup über- und umgießen, mit Blüten- und Minzeblättern garniert sofort servieren.

JALAN PASAR PUDU MARKET KUALA LUMPUR

Comparisons to a European food market must necessarily be doomed to failure in describing the fascinating hustle and bustle of the „Pasar Pudu". Yet, the seeming chaos does have system, and on its winding paths through rows of sellers of exotic fruit, boiled meats and glittering fish bellies, a vast mass of people has been pushing and shoving its way through since early morning in order to procure its daily kitchen needs. Hundreds of market stands and eateries below colorful umbrellas fill every square meter of space in between houses and walls of corrugated metal. Anything is to be had, anything that might be needed by local households: fish, chicken, pork, eels, snakes or frogs alike. Steaming, frying and boiling noises are in the air, slaughtering, plucking and scaling is going on live. The market at the Jalan Pasar Pudu is the shopping mall for the little people, and the place for all bon vivants who turn up their noses at vacuum-packed vegetables or proscribed menus. Fast food is available here, too, quite literally, since it is being prepared with incredible speed fresh in front of the customer´s eyes, in vats or woks respectively.

Wer einen europäischen Wochenmarkt zum Vergleich heranziehen will, wird kläglich scheitern, das faszinierende Gewimmel des „Pasar Pudu" auch nur annähernd adäquat zu beschreiben. Doch das scheinbare Chaos hat System, und auf dessen verschlungenen Wegen durchs bunte Spektrum von Gemüse-Exoten, gesottenem Fleisch und glänzenden Fischleibern schiebt sich seit dem Morgen eine unübersehbare Menge an Menschen, die sich mit Vorräten für die heimische Küche eindecken will. Hunderte von Marktständen und Garküchen unter bunten Schirmen und Zeitungspapier füllen bis auf den letzten Quadratmeter den Platz zwischen Häusern und Wellblechwänden. Es wird jeglicher Bedarf gedeckt, hier gibt es alles, was der einheimische Haushalt an Lebensmitteln zu benötigen scheint. Fische, Hühner, Schweinefleisch, aber auch Aale, Schlangen oder Frösche kann man hier erstehen. Da wird gebraten, gebacken und gekocht, es wird geschlachtet, gerupft und geschuppt. Der Markt an der Jalan Pasar Pudu ist der Supermarkt der kleinen Leute und die Einkaufsquelle für all jene Kostverächter, die in Plastik eingeschweißtes Gemüse oder vorgestanzte Fertigmenüs nicht schätzen zu wissen. Fast Food kann man auch hier erwerben, doch wird dies mit unglaublicher Geschwindigkeit frisch und vor den Augen der Kundschaft im Kessel, im Wok zubereitet.

JW MARRIOTT KUALA LUMPUR

Stefan Stumke

AT THE CRACK OF DAWN, THE NIGHT IS STILL DARK AND HUMID OVER KUALA LUMPUR, STEFAN STUMKE AND HIS MASTER CHEF ONG FROM THE JW MARRIOTT HOTEL ARE TRUDGING THROUGH PUDDLES AND POOLS OF THE SPACIOUS HALL OF THE SELAYANG WET MARKETS AT THE EDGE OF THE CITY.

All hell is loose here at three o´clock in the morning. Freshly caught sea fish is auctioned off to wholesalers and large buyers at incredible speeds: tuna fish, sea bass and tiger prawns, pomfret and squid – all that could be netted in Malaysia´s waters. The hotels in the Golden Triangle District usually require large quantities, even if they hardly ever buy directly but procure their goods mostly from retailers. Still, our two chefs would like to see for themselves this morning, to get an overview over the current selection, wandering around between high stacks of Styrofoam boxes with glittering fish bellies, checking the firmness of the meat, the state of the gills and eyes – all signs of freshness. Meanwhile, hundreds of small retailers have taken over. They offer the purchases they have made themselves, the huge quantities that have been left. Water is gushing out from everywhere as it is poured over the fish, or the fish is covered with ice – all to keep it fresh. Fish are slapped onto scales, weighed, packed in foil and made ready for transport. Orders are filled. The morning sky is taking on a bluish-grey color, and in the cold neonlight of the canteen, porters and fishmongers are having noodle soup for breakfast. For our two chefs from the Marriot, a mug of coffee must suffice before they return to the hotel.

Stefan Stumke, chef with a German passport, is the chief conductor of the culinary orchestra of all hotels in the YTL group, among them such exclusive places as the resort on the private island Pangkor Laut in the north, the Ritz-Carlton as well as the JW Marriot in Kuala Lumpur. The young native of Mönchengladbach obviously enjoys the highest respect of the owners, out-ranking even the general managers of the individual hotels in the position of an executive master chef – probably quite a unique arrangement in this sector. In exchange, he has not slept much in the last four months, working hard and taking care of every detail himself, establishing an exquisite culinary concept at the JW Marriott, which opened only in 1997. And indeed, it has already become a landmark in the culinary scene of Kuala Lumpur, with its fresh ideas, finest of cuisines, unmitigated quality and a team that knows what it is doing.

A large kitchen in the basement of the 514-room-palace provides the food for most of the restaurants in the house, for the room service, the food shops, a French-style café as well as the hundreds of guests at huge banquet events. Only the Chinese restaurant holds a special position, being logistically independent. The creations of one of the most exquisite cuisines of China are taking shape under the auspices of master chef Wong Sai Man. The beefy Chinaman learned his trade in his native Hong Kong. His father and mother were from Shanghai, however, immigrants who used to cling to the traditions of their ancestors. Thus, Wong learned to cook in a Shanghai fashion, and that's what he has been doing in his twenty years of professional life in Djakarta and Beijing. Today, at the JW Marriott, the master reigns over a crew of eighteen and 120 restaurant seats with an iron fist. The guests have the sole responsibility – not always easy – to choose among more than 70 specialties from the menu. The large glass table top may then feature stir-fried crayfish in a ginger sauce, deep-fried eel Wuxi Style, "Siew Loong Pau" (which roughly translates to "Shanghai-style steamed dumplings") or "Imperial Jewels" (stuffed halved duck eggs). Wong has customers from Europe, America, and China, of course – Malay guests, however, are quite rare. Why? There is a simple explanation: Pork, which plays quite an important role in Chinese cuisine, is taboo for Malays, who are for the most part Muslims keeping to the "halal" food regimen – and that means no pork. It also entails – not unlike kosher cooking – a special butchering technique for poultry. Not surprisingly, everything coming from a kitchen like Wong's is considered non-halal, making the Shanghai off limits for most Malay people and being the reason for the restaurant's separate status from the (halal) cuisine of the central hotel kitchen. The master chef himself is found on a plane to Shanghai at least once a month, whence he returns with a suitcase full of specialties.

Putting down our chopsticks and wiping our lips, we now ask for the bill, hesitantly leaving the place of fine dining to indulge in a lavish afternoon break. Hours later, we will begin to check out the nether parts of the hotel. Without warning, we find ourselves in the ranks of an adjacent shopping-temple, where designer fashions, electronics and cosmetics are arranged on several floors around a large and airy inner courtyard. The high glass roof admits the last rays of the sun falling onto the grey stone of the floors which we approach via gently moving escalators. We are submerged into the realm of a novel way of enjoying food (at least for locals). Welcome to the "Shook!" Here, everything is open. Semi-private at best, the restaurant lies directly at the feet of the visible and audible backdrop of shoppers and live jazz from the podium. Right there in the middle - no walls, no rooms, no roof. The materials are glass, wood and stone. The sweeping curve of a milk glass bar arrests the guest, making it clear that the first cocktail ought to be taken here and offering an opportunity for appreciating the juggling efforts of the barkeeper as well as the atmosphere of the restaurant. Who has not felt like trying a bit from the pots of different countries without having to cross borders for doing so? Well, let's start here. In four open kitchens, food is sizzling in front of the guests' eyes, with the tables placed in full view. You may choose to eat Italian – the pizza even comes from a wood-fired oven –, Chinese, Japanese or all sorts of grilled meats and fish. The latter still frolic around in huge tanks until you place your order, and the contents of more than three thousand wine bottles rests behind a wall-high glass front – in a controlled climate, of course. Among them, you may find an uninterrupted series of Château Mouton Rothschild since 1945. With the hustle and bustle around it, a seat at a table is nevertheless a small refuge whose intimacy allows for chatting and eating in a small group. In the background, two, three restaurant overseers are busy supervising the choreography of the agile young service team, all high-tech with the support of head microphones and buttons in the ear.

IT'S CASUAL, EASY-GOING, RE-LAXED CULINARY ENJOYMENT.

Back to the food, however, the salt in the soup – where could be the hair? Cross-over again, the confusion of blends, many a fusion sceptic will sigh. Not at all. The selection is diverse but there is a clear, precise focus on the authentic. The mix is limited to the "Grill", for everything else the motto is "straight food". This means that the China island serves Chinese food (albeit pork-free – halal that is) and the Italian counter features home-made pasta as well as Italian classics. And Abd Aziz, a native from Malaysia with salt-and-pepper hair who learned his trade with Japanese masters, and his team concentrate on turning out Japanese delicacies behind the sushi counter. Even the raw ingredients are imported directly from Japan. Hamachi (tuna fish), for instance, is of an altogether different quality if it acquires more fat on the bones in a colder ocean. Ong Beng Yew, whom we accompanied to the fish market above, first cooked on the private yacht of the owner before he came to the Marriot. Here at the "Shook!", he is the boss and responsible for smooth sailing. He explains the concept: "For me, fusion is confusion. Here we have four in one, four open kitchens in one restaurant. So why confusing everything? Guests can take something from everywhere, but at every counter they get the original." This keeps connoisseurs of Asian cuisine happy, and the culinary beginner does not end up with some hodgepodge but with real samples of individual cuisines. And, most importantly, the overall pleasure of the culinary experience stays in the foreground. As master chef Stefan Stumke says: „Fine dining is dying out, jackets and ties are out – entertainment and enjoying things to the full is what's hot. That's fun and it is cool, "syok" in Malay – "Shook!", that is. And outside, life continues to vibrate with a Parisian flair in the heat of the evening. All seats around the hotel are taken, sidewalk cafés and bistros are full of people. Broad sidewalks, more than a hundred palms and huge terracotta planters lush with plants – the Marriott owners spared neither pains nor considerable expense to infuse the formerly rather drab surroundings with life. Behind palm leaves swaying in the wind, the light circles of the Petronas Twin Towers rise up high into the night sky, and our Tiger beers are sweating in their glasses. Shook!

IN ALLER HERRGOTTSFRÜHE, DIE NACHT HÄNGT NOCH DUNKEL ABER SCHWÜLWARM ÜBER KUALA LUMPUR, STAPFEN STEFAN STUMKE UND CHEFKOCH ONG VOM JW MARRIOTT HOTEL DURCH PFÜTZEN UND LACHEN IN DER WEITLÄUFIGEN HALLE DES SELAYANG WET MARKETS AM RANDE DER STADT. UM DREI UHR MORGENS IST HIER SCHON DER TEUFEL LOS. AUS DEM MEER FRISCH ANGELANDETER FISCH WIRD AN GROSSHÄNDLER UND GROSSAB-NEHMER VERSTEIGERT. SCHNELLER GEHT'S NICHT.

Thunfisch, Seabass und Tiger Prawns, Pomfrets und Tintenfische sind den Schiffen in den Fanggründen rund um Malaysia ins Netz gegangen. Vor allem die Hotels des Golden Triangle Districts sind Abnehmer in großem Stil, kaufen aber selten direkt, sondern erhalten normalerweise ihre Ware durch Händler. Die beiden Männer wollen sich heute Morgen einmal selbst ein Bild vom aktuellen Marktangebot machen und wandern zwischen hoch-gestapelten Styroporboxen mit glitzernden Fischleibern umher, prüfen Festigkeit des Fleisches, Zustand von Kiemen und Augen

– Zeichen der Frische des Materials. Mittlerweile haben Hunderte von Kleinhändlern das Geschehen übernommen. Sie handeln mit dem, was sie selbst ergattert haben, mit dem immensen Rest, der übrig geblieben ist. Überall spritzt es, Wasser wird über Fischkör-per geschwappt, Eis darüber geschippt, das hält ihn frisch. Auf die Waagschale klatscht Fisch, wird abgewogen, in Folie verpackt und transportfertig gemacht. Orders werden ausgefüllt. Blaugrau däm-mert der Morgen, und im kalten Neonlicht der Kantine geneh-migen sich Träger und Fischhändler eine Nudelsuppe zum Früh-stück. Für die beiden vom Marriott reicht ein Becher Kaffee, be-vor sie ins Hotel zurückfahren.

Stefan Stumke, Koch mit deutschem Pass, ist Chefdirigent des kulinarischen Orchesters aller Hotels der YTL Gruppe. Zu ihnen zählen auch so feine Plätze wie ein Resort auf der Privatinsel Pangkor Laut im Norden, das Ritz-Carlton sowie das JW Marriott in Kuala Lumpur. Der junge Mönchengladbacher genießt offen-sichtlich größte Wertschätzung der Eigner, da er als Executive Chefkoch – wohl einzigartig in dieser Branche – selbst den Gene-ral Managern der einzelnen Hotels übergeordnet ist. Dafür hat er sich auch in den letzten Monaten fast jede Nacht um die Ohren geschlagen, geschuftet, sich um jedes Detail gekümmert und im erst 1997 eröffneten JW Marriott ein erlesenes gastronomisches

Konzept aufgebaut, das neue Eckpfeiler in die Gastroszene Kuala Lumpurs errichtet hat. Sprich: Neue Ideen, Küche vom Feinsten, Qualität ohne Kompromisse und eine Mannschaft, die auch versteht, was sie tut. Eine Großküche im Untergeschoss des 514-Zimmer-Palastes versorgt die meisten Restaurants des Hauses, den Zimmerservice, Food Shops, ein französisch angehauchtes Café und und und, sowie viele Hunderte von Gästen riesiger Bankett-Veranstaltungen. Einzig das China-Restaurant besitzt eine Sonderstellung und ist logistisch völlig autark. Die Schöpfungen einer der exquisitesten Küchen Chinas werden im „Shanghai Restaurant" unter Chefkoch Wong Sai Man produziert. Der bullige Chinese hatte seine Profession in seiner Heimatstadt Hongkong erlernt. Vater und Mutter stammen jedoch aus Shanghai, und solche Einwanderer pflegen die Tradition ihrer Vorfahren zu konservieren. Wong lernte folglich Shanghai-Küche und hat selbige in den zwanzig Jahren seines bisherigen Berufslebens in Djakarta und Peking exerziert. Heute regiert der Meister im JW Marriott mit strenger Hand eine achtzehn-köpfige Crew und 120 Restaurantplätze. Den Gästen obliegt die nicht immer leichte Aufgabe, aus

einer Karte von über siebzig Spezialitäten ihr Menü zu wählen. Auf der großen Glasplatte des Esstischs drehen sich dann Wok-gebratene Flusskrebse in Ingwersauce, frittierter Aal nach Wuxi Style, „Siew Loong Pau" (auf gut deutsch „Shanghai-Dampfknödel") oder „Imperial Jewels" (in Sojasauce gekochte Enteneierhälften). Zu Wongs Kunden zählen Europäer, Amerikaner und selbstredend Chinesen – Malaien werden jedoch selten gesichtet. Woran das liegt? Die Erklärung ist einleuchtend: Schweinefleisch, ein nicht ganz unwesentlicher Bestandteil chinesischer Küche, ist für die meisten Malaien tabu. Malaien sind größtenteils Moslems und dürfen eigentlich nur „Halal" essen, das bedeutet in erster Linie: kein Schwein. Dazu gehört, wie in der koscheren Küche, eine spezielle Schlachttechnik. Somit gilt alles, was in solcher Küche fabriziert wird als nicht-halal. Daher ist das Shanghai „off-limits" für Malaien und völlig losgelöst von den zentralen (halal-) Kücheneinrichtungen des Hotels. Der Küchenchef sitzt denn auch mindestens einmal monatlich im Flieger nach Shanghai und kehrt mit einem mit Spezialitäten gefüllten Koffer wieder zurück.

Doch nun Stäbchen beiseite gelegt, Mund abgeputzt und „die Rechnung, bitte". Wir verlassen die edle Stätte, genehmigen uns eine gehörige Nachmittagspause und erkunden Stunden später die rückwärtigen Bereiche des Hotels. Unvermittelt landen wir auf

WELCOME TO SHOOK!

den Rängen eines angegliederten Einkaufstempels, wo Designer-Fashion, Elektronik und Kosmetik etagenweise um einen luftig-weiten Innenhof kreiseln. Durchs hohe gläserne Dach schickt der Himmel letzte Sonnenstrahlen bis zum grausteinernen Boden, dem wir sanft per Rolltreppe entgegengleiten. Wir tauchen ein in die Gefilde einer (zumindest für hiesige Verhältnisse) neuen Art, Essen zu genießen. Welcome to „Shook!"
Alles ist offen hier. Das Restaurant liegt nur halbversteckt zu Füßen der sicht- und hörbaren Kulisse von Einkaufsbummlern und Live-Jazz vom Podium. Mittendrin und dicht dabei. Keine Wände, keine Zimmer, kein Dach. Die Materialien sind Glas, Holz und Stein. Das weite Rund eines milchgläsernen Bar-Tresens stoppt den Besucher, nötigt ihn unmissverständlich zum ersten Cocktail, der ihm Gelegenheit gibt, die Jonglierübungen des Barkeepers sowie die Atmosphäre des Restaurants erst einmal in Augenschein zu nehmen. Wer hat nicht schon die Lust verspürt, mal hier mal da aus den Töpfen verschiedener Länder und Küchen zu naschen, ohne dabei Lokal oder Land wechseln zu müssen. Der Spaß kann hier beginnen. Vier offene Küchen brutzeln vor den Augen der Gäste, die Tische in Sichtweite platziert. Man wählt von Italienischem, wo selbst die Pizza aus dem echten Steinbackofen kommt, von Chinesischem, Japanischem und von allerlei Gegrilltem aus Fleisch und Fisch. Die Letzteren schwimmen noch äußerst lebendig in großen Aquarien, und der Inhalt von über dreitausend Weinflaschen ruht klimageschützt hinter wandhohen Glasfronten. Château Mouton Rothschild lagert hier in lückenloser Serie ab Jahrgang 1945. Während drum herum das Leben flutet, ist der Platz am Tisch nichtsdestotrotz ein kleines Refugium, dessen Intimität das Plaudern und Gabeln in kleiner Runde ermöglicht. Zwei, drei Restaurantleiter dirigieren unauffällig und hightech-gestützt per Kopfmikro und Knopf im Ohr die Choreographie einer agilen jungen Service-Mannschaft. Das alles schafft unverkrampften Essgenuß, lässig und locker.
Doch zurück zum Food, zum Salz in der Suppe – wo schwimmt das Haar? Schon wieder Crossover, Verwirrung gemischter Genüsse, mag der Fusions-Skeptiker stöhnen. Gemach, gemach. So vielfältig auch das Angebot, so klar und präzise ist der Fokus aufs Authentische. Gemixt wird allenfalls am „Grill", ansonsten gilt die Devise „straight food". Will heißen, die China-Insel kocht chine-

sisch (allerdings schweinefrei – eben halal), und am Italien-Counter gibt es hausgemachte Pasta sowie italienische Klassiker. Der grau melierte Malaie Abd Aziz, der sein Handwerk bei japanischen Meistern erlernt hat, konzentriert sich mit seinen Leuten auf die Fertigung japanischer Köstlichkeiten hinter dem Sushi-Tresen. Selbst seine Rohware kommt überwiegend direkt aus Japan. Denn auch Hamachi (Thunfisch) ist von ganz anderer Qualität, wenn er im kälteren Meer mehr Fett auf die Gräten bekommen hat. Der junge Ong Beng Yew – wir haben ihn am Fischmarkt beobachtet (siehe oben) – hatte erst auf der Privatyacht der Eigner gekocht, ehe er zum Marriott kam. Hier im „Shook!" ist er nun der Boss und zuständig für den reibungslosen Ablauf. Er fasst das Konzept in Worte: „für mich bedeutet „fusion" Konfusion. Wir haben hier „four in one", vier offene Küchen in einem Restaurant. Warum also da mischen?".

DER GAST KANN VON ALLEN TÖPFEN KOSTEN – UND ER WIRD AN JEDEM HERD DAS ORIGINAL ERHALTEN.

Shanghai Restaurant

上海小籠飽
Shanghai Steamed Dumplings

生煎飽
Fried Fresh Meat Buns

素菜鍋貼
Pan Fried Vegetable Dumplings

玉佛素菜飽
Steamed Vegetable Buns

黃橋燒餅
Baked Chinese Pastry Topped with Sesame

菜肉鍋貼
Pan Fried Meat Dumplings

上海春卷
Deep Fried Shanghai Spring Rolls

蒸或炸銀絲卷
Steamed or Deep Fried Fortune Roll

三鮮湯飽
Steamed Three Treasures Buns

津白粉絲肉卷
Shredded Tien Tin Cabbage Spring Roll

羅卜絲酥餅
Baked Shredded Carrot Biscuit (by advance order)

Der Kenner asiatischer Kost ist somit zufrieden, und der Neuling erfährt kein Kauderwelsch sondern die korrekte Komposition dieser Küchen. Und der Spaß am Essen als Gesamterlebnis steht im Vordergrund. Chefkoch Stefan Stumke meint, „Fine Dining stirbt aus, Sakko und Krawatte sind out – Entertainment und lustvoll genießen sind jetzt angesagt. Das macht Spaß und ist cool, ist „syok", wie der Malaie sagt, – eben shook!" Und draußen vibriert in abendlicher Schwüle das Leben mit Pariser Flair. Alle Plätze rund ums Hotel sind besetzt, Sidewalk Cafés und Bistros sind proppevoll. Das Marriott hatte weder Mühe noch eine stattliche Summe Geldes gescheut und der ehedem leblosen Umgebung mit breiten Gehwegen, rund einhundert Palmen und riesigen Pflanzen bestückten Terrakottakübeln Leben eingehaucht. Hinter wiegenden Palmwedeln funkeln die Lichterringe der Petronas Twin Towers gegen den nächtlichen Himmel, und das Tiger Beer schwitzt im Glas. Shook!

Cheng Kong Home Style Ham – A Shanghai Classic

Serves 4

250 ml/1 cup soy sauce, 1 tbsp black pepper,
750 ml/3 cups water, 4 duck eggs

100 g/3 ¹/₂ oz cashews,
30 g/1 oz dried seaweed

2 tsp very finely diced Yunnan ham
(alternatively another raw ham),
pickled ginger

Combine soy sauce, water and pepper in a saucepan. Add seaweed, then carefully place the eggs in the pan. Allow to steep for one hour. Place the pot on a burner and bring to a boil. Poach the eggs for five minutes, then remove them with a skimmer and refresh them with cold water.

Place the seaweed and the cashew nuts into another pot, cover with water and bring to a boil. Simmer for ten minutes and drain in a sieve. Discard seaweed and allow excess water to drip off.

Peel and halve the eggs and arrange them on plates. Sprinkle with chopped ham and serve with pickled ginger and cashews on the side.

IMPERIAL JEWELS
Duck Eggs Cooked in Soy Sauce

KAISERLICHE JUWELEN
Enteneier in Soja gekocht

Für 4 Personen:

250 ml Sojasauce, 1 EL schwarzer Pfeffer,
750 ml Wasser, 4 Enteneier

100 g Cashewnüsse,
30 g getrocknete Meeralgen

2 TL sehr fein gehackter Yunnanschinken
(ersatzweise anderen Rohschinken
verwenden),
eingelegter Ingwer

Sojasauce mit Wasser und Pfeffer in einem Topf verrühren. Eier und Algen einlegen, eine Stunde ziehen lassen. Den Topf auf den Herd stellen und zum Kochen bringen. Vom Siedepunkt an gerechnet 5 Minuten pochieren, anschließend die Eier in kaltem Wasser abschrecken.

Die Cashewnüsse mit den Algen in einem Topf mit Wasser bedeckt zum Kochen bringen. Nach zehn Minuten Kochzeit durch ein Sieb abgießen, die Algen entfernen, die Nüsse gut abtropfen lassen.

Die Eier schälen, halbieren und auf Teller anrichten. Mit etwas gehacktem Schinken bestreuen, mit Cashewnüssen und eingelegtem Ingwer als Beilage servieren.

FRIED PICKLED CARP

GEBRATENER UND EINGELEGTER KARPFEN

Serves 4

600 g/1¹/₃ lb carp filets, skin on,
120 ml/¹/₂ cup soy sauce,
oil for deep-frying

For the marinade:
120 ml/¹/₂ cup sweet, mild vinegar,
80 ml/¹/₄ cup rice wine,
2 tbsp ginger, finely diced,
2 shallots, finely minced

Working from the bottom side, make finger-deep scores into the carp filet, taking care to leave the skin intact. Marinate the filets in the soy sauce and allow them to rest for one hour. Remove them from the marinade, shake off of excess liquid and fry them on both sides until crisp.
Combine the rice wine vinegar, ginger and shallots in a shallow pan and mix well. Place fried carp into the marinade and allow to rest in the refrigerator overnight.
Serving: Cut the marinated filets into four equal pieces and place the pieces on plates. Garnish with herbs according to taste and serve cold.

Für 4 Personen:

600 g Karpfenfilet mit Haut,
120 ml Sojasauce,
Öl zum Frittieren

Für die Marinade:
120 ml süßer, milder Reisweinessig,
80 ml Reiswein,
2 EL fein gehackter Ingwer,
2 fein gehackte Schalotten

Das Karpfenfilet einige Male fingerdick einschneiden, ohne die Haut zu beschädigen. In die Sojasauce einlegen, eine Stunde ziehen lassen. Herausnehmen, abtropfen lassen, im heißen Öl von beiden Seiten knusprig braten.
In einer flachen Form den Reisweinessig mit dem Wein, dem Ingwer und den Schalotten verrühren. Den frittierten Karpfen in die Marinade legen, im Kühlschrank über Nacht marinieren.
Zum Servieren: Das marinierte Filet in vier Stücke schneiden und auf Teller anrichten. Nach Belieben mit Kräutern garniert kalt servieren.

DRUNKEN CHICKEN

BETRUNKENES HÜHNCHEN

Serves 4

1 farm-raised chicken, ready-to-cook,
2 liters/8 cups chicken stock

1 bottle shao shin wine (Chinese yellow rice wine),
1 tsp white pepper,
1 tsp sugar,
1 tsp salt,
1 tbsp instant chicken stock

Simmer the chicken in the stock for half an hour. Stir instant chicken stock into a little wine and heat to dissolve. Mix wine, spices and chicken stock in a bowl. Allow boiled chicken to drain well and cut it into serving size pieces, bone and skin on. Place chicken pieces into the wine. Take care that the pieces are completely submerged. Cover and refrigerate for two to three hours.
Serving: Place individual pieces of chicken onto plates and drizzle with a little marinade. Garnish with a little radish or cucumber, according to taste.

Für 4 Personen:

1 Huhn aus Freilandhaltung, küchenfertig,
2 Liter Hühnerbrühe

1 Flasche Shao Shin (chinesischer gelber Reiswein),
1 TL weißer Pfeffer,
1 TL Zucker,
1 TL Salz,
1 EL gekörnte Hühnerbrühe

Das Huhn in der Brühe eine halbe Stunde köcheln. Den Wein mit den Gewürzen in einer Schüssel verrühren, vorher die gekörnte Brühe mit wenig Wein erhitzen, bis sie aufgelöst ist. Das gekochte Huhn abtropfen lassen, in Portionen teilen, das Fleisch am Knochen in Stücke schneiden. In den Wein einlegen, so dass das Fleisch überall bedeckt ist. Im Kühlschrank zwei bis drei Stunden marinieren.
Zum Servieren: Die Hühnerstücke mit Marinade auf Teller anrichten, nach Belieben mit Gurken oder Rettich garnieren.

FRIED DUMPLINGS
WITH CABBAGE AND PORK

GEBRATENE TEIGTASCHEN
MIT KOHL UND
SCHWEINEFLEISCH

Serves 4

For the dough:
315 g/11 ½ oz flour,
200 ml/¾ cup water

For the filling:
300 g/11 oz ground pork,
150 g/5 ½ oz curly kale, boiled in salted
water, finely chopped,
50 g/1 ½ oz green onions, finely diced,
1 tbsp Chinese rice wine,
1 tsp ginger, finely diced,
½ tsp sugar, salt

1 egg, beaten, for brushing,
oil for frying

40 g/1 ½ oz ginger, cut into thin strips,
120 ml/½ cup black Chinese rice vinegar

For the dough: Sieve flour into a large bowl and add water, a little at a time. Work into a smooth dough. Knead the dough for three to four minutes, then wrap it in foil and allow to rest for half an hour.
For the filling: Knead all ingredients for the filling into a smooth paste.
Roll out the dough very thinly and cut it into square or round pieces. Place heaping teaspoons of filling in the middle of each piece and brush the edges with beaten egg. Fold them over into crescent shapes and press down firmly to close.
Heat oil in a wok and fry the dumplings on both sides on medium heat until golden brown. Arrange the dumplings on plates, garnish with ginger strips and serve black rice vinegar on the side for dipping.

Für 4 Personen:

Für den Teig:
315 g Mehl,
200 ml Wasser

Für die Füllung:
300 g gehacktes Schweinefleisch,
150 g Grünkohl (oder Wirsing),
in Salzwasser gekocht, fein gehackt,
50 g Frühlingszwiebel, fein gehackt,
1 EL chinesischer Reiswein,
1 TL fein gehackter Ingwer,
½ TL Zucker, Salz

1 Ei, verquirlt, zum Bepinseln,
Öl zum Braten

50 g Ingwer, in dünne Streifen geschnitten,
120 ml schwarzer chinesischer Reisessig

Für den Teig: Das Mehl in eine Schüssel sieben, nach und nach das Wasser zugießen und zu einem Teig verarbeiten. Den Teig aus der Schüssel nehmen, drei bis vier Minuten kneten. In Folie einwickeln, eine halbe Stunde ruhen lassen.
Für die Füllung: Alle Zutaten zu einer geschmeidigen Masse verkneten.
Den Teig sehr dünn ausrollen und in quadratische oder runde Stücke schneiden. Mit je einem Löffel Füllung belegen, die Ränder mit verquirltem Ei bepinseln und die Teigtaschen fest verschließen.
Das Öl in einem Wok erhitzen. Die Teigtaschen bei nicht zu starker Hitze von beiden Seiten langsam goldbraun ausbacken. Auf Teller verteilen, mit Ingwerstreifen und schwarzem Reisessig zum Tunken servieren.

Serves 4

400 g/14 oz pumpkin pulp,
250 ml/1 cup coconut milk,
250 ml/1 cup water,
100 g/3 1/2 oz sugar,
2 tbsp black rice,
2 tbsp sago

60 ml/1/4 cup cream

Steam the pumpkin pulp until very soft. Combine coconut milk, water, sugar, rice and sago in a large saucepan and simmer on low heat until rice is done. Add the cooked pumpkin and whisk with a wire whip until you have a soupy consistency. Add cream and allow soup to cool. Serve the soup well chilled in individual bowls.

SWEET PUMPKIN SOUP
WITH RICE

SÜSSE KÜRBISSUPPE
MIT REIS

Für 4 Personen:

400 g Kürbisfleisch,
250 g Kokosmilch,
250 ml Wasser,
100 g Zucker,
2 EL schwarzer Reis,
2 EL Sago

60 ml Sahne

Das Kürbisfleisch über Dampf garen, bis es butterweich ist. Die Kokosmilch, Wasser, Zucker, Reis und Sago in einen Topf geben und bei kleiner Hitze köcheln, bis der Reis weich ist. Den gegarten Kürbis zugeben, alles mit dem Schneebesen zu einer dicken Suppe verrühren. Zum Schluss die Sahne unterziehen, die Suppe erkalten lassen, gut gekühlt servieren.

SHOOK!

SHOOK! ANTIPASTI

<table>
<tr><td>

Serves 4

120 g/4 oz cooked sushi rice (glutinous rice),
1 tbsp sushi vinegar (Japanese sweet vinegar),
sugar, salt,
160 g/6 oz salmon, very fresh,
sliced thinly,
2 tbsp mayonnaise, seasoned with wasabi
(Japanese horseradish),
2 tsp salmon caviar

4 softshell crabs
(newly molted blue crabs),
4 nori sheets (Japanese seaweed),
4 tbsp flour,
4 tbsp chickpea flour, salt,
rice flour for dusting,
oil for deep-frying

150 g/5 oz crabmeat,
2 tbsp mayonnaise,
1 tbsp chopped coriander leaves, salt, pepper,
50 g/1 1/2 oz wonton skins (Chinese supermarket),
cut into very thin strips

Garnish:
a handful of mesclun lettuce mixture,
tossed with a little vinegar, oil, salt and pepper,
herbs, sprouts, pickled ginger

</td><td>

Für 4 Personen:

120 g gekochter Sushireis (Klebreis),
1 EL Sushi Essig (japanischer süßlicher Essig),
Zucker, Salz,
160 g Lachs, sehr frisch,
in dünne Scheiben geschnitten,
2 EL Mayonnaise, mit Wasabi
(japanischer Meerrettich) gewürzt,
2 TL Lachsrogen

4 Softshell Crabs, (frisch gehäutete,
weiche Blaukrabben),
4 Nori-Blätter (japanischer Seetang),
4 EL Mehl,
4 EL Kichererbsenmehl, Salz,
Reismehl zum Bestäuben,
Öl zum Frittieren

150 g Krebsfleisch,
2 EL Mayonnaise,
1 EL gehacktes Koriandergrün, Salz, Pfeffer,
50 g Wonton-Teigblätter (chin. Feinkostgeschäft),
in möglichst dünne Streifen geschnitten

Garnitur:
1 Hand voll Mesclun Salat (junger aromatischer
gemischter Wildsalat), mit etwas Essig, Öl, Salz und
Pfeffer angemacht, Kräuter, Sprossen, eingelegter Ingwer

</td></tr>
</table>

Season the cooked sushi rice with vinegar, sugar and salt and allow to cool to room temperature. Shape the rice into four balls and place them on serving platters. Arrange the salmon slices in the shape of four rosettes and place the rosettes over the rice. Top with a little wasabi mayonnaise and garnish with salmon caviar. Refrigerate.

Wash the softshell crabs and wrap them in nori sheets. Mix flour and chickpea flour with salt and as much water as it takes to make a thick batter. Dust the crabs with rice flour, dip them in batter and deep-fry in hot oil until golden brown on all sides. Allow to drain on paper towels and keep warm.

Combine the crabmeat, mayonnaise and coriander leaves and season with salt and pepper. Divide the mixture into four equal portions and wrap them in wonton skin strips. Deep-fry the crabmeat balls in hot oil until golden brown and allow them to drain on paper towels.

Serving: Place the deep-fried softshell crabs on plates next to the salmon rosettes, and the other end of the plate a little nest made from mesclun lettuce mixture. Place a crabmeat ball each into the lettuce nest. Garnish according to taste with herbs, sprouts and pickled ginger. Serve at once.

Den frisch gekochten Sushireis mit Essig, Zucker und Salz würzen und erkalten lassen. Vier Bällchen daraus formen und auf Servierplatten legen. Aus den Lachsscheiben vier Rosetten formen und auf den Sushireis legen. Jeweils etwas mit Wasabi gewürzte Mayonnaise darüber geben, mit Lachsrogen garnieren. Kühl stellen.

Die Softshell Crabs säubern, nicht essbare Teile entfernen und die Krebse mit Noriblättern umwickeln. Mehl und Kichererbsenmehl mit Salz und soviel Wasser anrühren, dass ein dickflüssiger Teig entsteht. Die Krebse mit Reismehl bestäuben, in den Teig tauchen, im heißen Frittieröl goldbraun ausbacken. Auf Küchenpapier abtropfen lassen, warm stellen.

Das Krebsfleisch mit Mayonnaise und Koriandergrün vermischen, mit Salz und Pfeffer würzen. In vier Portionen teilen und mit den Wonton-Streifen umhüllen. Im heißen Öl goldgelb ausbacken, auf Küchenpapier abtropfen lassen.

Zum Servieren: Auf eine Seite der auf Servierplatten angerichteten Lachsrosetten die frittierten Softshell Crabs legen, auf die andere Seite etwas Mesclun Salat anrichten. Die ausgebackenen Krebsfleischbällchen darauflegen. Nach Belieben mit den Kräutern, Sprossen und eingelegtem Ingwer garnieren.

CHICKEN SATAY SKEWERS

SATAY-SPIESSCHEN VOM HUHN

Serves 4

600 g/1¹/₃ lb chicken meat, cut into cubes,
1 tbsp cumin,
1 tbsp fennel seed,
1 stalk lemongrass, the tender core only, chopped,
1 tsp sugar,
1 tbsp vegetable oil

For the satay sauce:
1 tsp galangal root, minced (alternatively
ground galangal),
1 tbsp diced ginger,
1 shallot, diced,
2 garlic cloves, minced,
2 tbsp vegetable oil,
2 tbsp minced red chili pepper (according to taste),
200 g/7 oz peanuts, toasted and crushed,
2 tbsp tamarind juice,
150 g/5 oz sugar,
250 ml/1 cup water,
1 tsp salt

1 cucumber, cubed,
1 onion, halved and cut into thick slices

Crush cumin, fennel seeds, lemongrass, sugar and oil in a mortar until you have a fine paste. Coat the chicken pieces evenly with paste. Mix well and allow to marinate overnight.

For the satay sauce: Crush galangal, ginger, shallot and garlic in a mortar. Heat the oil in a small pot and fry the mixture on low heat until the spices release their fragrances. Also grind the chili pepper into a paste and stir it into the spice mixture. Sauté for a few minutes, then add peanuts, tamarind liquid and sugar. Douse with water and check for salt. Simmer on low heat until the sauce has taken on a syrupy consistency. Allow to cool.

Finish: Skewer meat pieces with bamboo skewers (or ordinary wood skewers) and grill them on both sides until done. Arrange skewers on plates with diced cucumber. Spoon satay sauce into four individual small dishes and serve it as a dipping sauce with the finished skewers.

Für 4 Personen:

600 g Hühnerfleisch, in Würfel geschnitten,
1 EL Kreuzkümmel,
1 EL Fenchelsamen,
1 Stängel Zitronengras, nur den inneren
weichen Teil, gehackt,
1 TL Zucker, 1 EL Pflanzenöl

Für die Satay-Sauce:
1 TL Galangawurzel, gehackt (ersatzweise
Pulver verwenden),
1 EL gehackter Ingwer,
1 Schalotte, gehackt,
2 Knoblauchzehen, gehackt,
2 EL Pflanzenöl,
2 EL gehackte rote Chili (oder nach Belieben),
200 g geröstete, zerstoßene Erdnüsse,
2 EL Tamarindensaft,
150 g Zucker,
250 ml Wasser,
1 TL Salz

1 Gurke, in Würfel geschnitten,
1 Zwiebel, halbiert und in dicke Scheiben geschnitten

Kreuzkümmel, Fenchelsamen und Zitronengras mit dem Zucker und dem Öl im Mörser fein zerstoßen. Die Hühnerfleischstücke mit dieser Paste gut vermischen und über Nacht marinieren.

Für die Satay-Sauce: Galanga, Ingwer, Schalotte und Knoblauch im Mörser zerstampfen. Das Öl in einem kleinen Topf erhitzen, die Mischung bei kleiner Hitze anbraten, bis die Aromen frei werden. Die gehackten Chili ebenfalls zur Paste verstampfen, kurz mitbraten, dann die Erdnüsse, Tamarindensaft und Zucker zugeben, mit Wasser auffüllen und mit Salz würzen. Bei kleiner Hitze köcheln, bis die Sauce dick eingekocht ist. Erkalten lassen.

Fertigstellung: Das Fleisch auf Bambusspieße (oder normale Holzspieße) stecken, von beiden Seiten auf dem Grill rösten. Mit den Gurkenwürfeln und den Zwiebeln auf Teller anrichten. Die Satay-Sauce in Portionsschälchen füllen und zum Dippen zu den Spießchen servieren.

SASHIMI OF RED SNAPPER

SASHIMI VOM ROTEN SCHNAPPER

Serves 4

*400 g/14 oz very fresh red snapper filet, skin
removed,*
1 fresh pineapple,
*4 tbsp wasabi powder, mixed
with water into a thick paste,*
120 ml/¹/₂ cup soy sauce

Cut the red snapper filet into thin strips
with a sharp knife. Cut the pineapple horizontally into four slices and place them
onto four plates. Top each pineapple slice
with red snapper strips. Put the soy sauce
and wasabi paste separately into four small
dishes each and place them next to the
plates with the fish. At dinner, each guest
may mix as much wasabi paste as desired
into the soy sauce, dipping the fish into his
own wasabi-soy sauce mixture.

Für 4 Personen:

*400 g sehr frisches Red Snapper Filet, ohne
Haut,*
1 frische Ananas,
*4 EL Wasabipulver, mit Wasser zu einer
dicken Paste angerührt,*
120 ml Sojasauce

Das Red Snapper Filet mit einem scharfen
Messer in dünne Streifen schneiden.
Die Ananas quer in vier Scheiben schnei-
den und auf Teller legen. Die Schnittfläche
der Ananas mit den Fischscheiben belegen.
Wasabipaste und Sojasauce getrennt in je
vier kleine Schälchen füllen. Jeder Gast
mischt sich am Tisch soviel Wasabi in seine
Sojasauce, wie er mag. Zum Essen nach
Belieben die Red Snapper-Scheiben in die
Wasabi-Sojasauce tunken.

Serves 4

300 g/11 oz sushi rice (glutinous rice), cooked,
1 tbsp wasabi paste mixed with 2 tbsp light
soy sauce and 1 tbsp Japanese sweet vinegar

500 g/1 lb fresh salmon filet, skin on,
6 nori sheets (seaweed),
1 egg, 300 g/1¹/₄ cups flour, salt,
oil for deep-frying

Mix hot sushi rice with the soy sauce mixture. Allow to cool to room temperature.
Place the salmon filet skin-side down on a working surface and cut into 2 cm/³/₄ inch strips. Cut the nori sheets into pieces to fit the fish strips. Place some sushi rice on top, then roll the salmon strips up tightly. Refrigerate.
In a large bowl, combine egg, flour and as much water as it takes to make a firm batter. Whisk the batter with a wire whip until smooth. Lightly salt the batter and allow it to rest for half an hour.
Finish: Dip the rolled up salmon pieces into the batter, shake off any excess batter and deep-fry the rolls in hot oil until golden brown. Arrange rolls on plates and decorate with blossoms and herbs. Serve.

TEMPURA SUSHI
WITH SALMON

TEMPURA SUSHI
MIT LACHS

Für 4 Personen:

300 g Sushireis (Klebreis) fertig zubereitet,
1 EL Wasabipaste, mit 2 EL heller Sojasauce
und 1 EL japanischem süßem Essig angerührt

500 g frisches Lachsfilet mit Haut,
6 Noriblätter (Seetang),
300 g Mehl, 1 Ei, Salz,
Öl zum Frittieren

Den Sushireis noch heiß mit der Sojasaucenmischung vermischen. Erkalten lassen.
Den Lachs mit der Hautseite nach unten flach hinlegen und in ca. 2 cm breite Streifen schneiden. Die Noriblätter zuschneiden und die Fischstücke damit belegen. Den Sushireis darauf verteilen, dann die Lachsstreifen zusammenrollen. Kaltstellen.
Das Mehl mit Ei und soviel Wasser, daß ein nicht zu flüssiger Teig entsteht, mit einem Schneebesen in einer Schüssel verrühren. Leicht salzen, den Teig eine halbe Stunde stehen lassen.
Fertigstellung: Die Lachsrollen in den Teig tauchen, abtropfen lassen, dann im heißen Öl goldgelb frittieren. Auf Teller anrichten, mit Blüten und Kräutern garnieren.

ASIAN BOUILLABAISSE

ASIATISCHE BOUILLABAISSE

Serves 4

4 rock lobsters,
8 tiger prawns,
200 g/7 oz shrimp,
400 g/14 oz mussels,
200 g/7 oz carpet shells,
200 g/7 oz octopus, ready-to-cook

1 onion, chopped,
1 tomato, chopped,
1 stalk lemongrass, chopped,
3 kaffir lime leaves,
1 tbsp coriander leaves,
1 tsp green curry paste,
2 star anise,
1 tsp ground coriander,
1 tsp turmeric,
1 tsp ground cumin,
2 tbsp butter,
200 ml/³/₄ cup white wine,
500 ml/2 cups fish stock,
salt, white pepper

4 tbsp cream,
2 tbsp cold butter,
1 small carrot, cut into julienne strips,
50 g/2 oz white radish, cut into julienne strips,
1 tbsp diced tomato,
chives, finely chopped

Für 4 Personen:

4 Kaisergranaten,
8 Riesengarnelen (Tiger Prawns),
200 g Garnelen,
400 g Miesmuscheln,
200 g Teppichmuscheln,
200 g Oktopus, küchenfertig

1 Zwiebel, gehackt,
1 Tomate, gehackt,
1 Zitronengrasstängel, gehackt,
3 Kaffir-Limetten-Blätter,
1 EL Koriandergrün,
1 TL grüne Currypaste,
2 Sternanis,
1 TL Korianderpulver,
1 TL Kurkuma,
1 TL Kreuzkümmelpulver,
2 EL Butter,
200 ml Weißwein,
500 ml Fischfond,
Salz, weißer Pfeffer

4 EL Sahne,
2 EL kalte Butter,
1 kleine Karotte, in dünne Streifen geschnitten,
50 g weißer Rettich, in dünne Streifen geschnitten,
1 EL kleine Tomatenwürfel,
Schnittlauch, fein geschnitten

In a large pot, sauté onions, tomato, spices and herbs in butter. Douse with white wine, add fish stock and simmer on low heat, uncovered, for thirty minutes. Check for salt and pepper and strain the seasoned stock through a sieve into another clean pot. Bring the stock to a boil again. Add the seafood and poach for about ten minutes.
Serving: Remove the seafood from the broth with a skimmer, dividing it equally between four soup plates. Using a wire whip, whisk cream and butter into the soup base and allow to heat through. Pour the soup over the seafood in the bowls, sprinkle the plates with vegetable julienne, cubed tomato and chopped chives.

In einem großen Topf die Zwiebel, Tomate, Gewürze und Kräuter in der Butter anschwitzen. Mit Weißwein ablöschen, den Fischfond zugießen, die Suppe ohne Deckel 30 Minuten bei kleiner Hitze köcheln. Mit Salz und Pfeffer abschmecken, durch ein Sieb in einen sauberen Topf passieren. Erneut zum Kochen bringen. Die Meeresfrüchte zugeben und bei kleiner Hitze 10 Minuten pochieren.
Zum Servieren: Die Meeresfrüchte aus der Suppe nehmen und in vier Suppenschalen verteilen. Mit einem Schneebesen die Sahne und die Butter unter die Suppe rühren. In die Schalen über die Meeresfrüchte verteilen, mit Gemüsestreifen, Tomatenwürfeln und Schnittlauch bestreuen und servieren.

SKEWERED PRAWNS WITH A STARFRUIT SAUCE

GARNELENSPIESSE AN STERNFRUCHTSAUCE

Serves 4

24 tiger prawns,
8 stalks lemongrass

For the marinade:
1 onion,
2 garlic cloves,
1 tbsp ginger,
1 tsp tomato paste,
a dash of tabasco,
2 tsp paprika,
2 tsp ground chili pepper,
1 tsp turmeric,
salt,
1 tbsp vegetable oil

For the starfruit-chili sauce:
2 starfruits (carambolas),
2 shallots,
1 small onion,
1 garlic clove,
30 g/1 oz red pepper,
10 g/1 tsp red chili pepper,
2 tbsp vegetable oil,
100 ml/¹/₃ cup hearty chicken stock, salt

Shell tiger prawns as you please, then wash and dry them thoroughly.
Finely dice onion, garlic and ginger and mix with the remaining ingredients for the marinade. Rub the prawns with the spice mixture and allow them to marinate overnight in the refrigerator.
For the starfruit-chili sauce: Peel the skin of starfruits and finely dice the pulp. Finely mince shallot, onion, garlic, red pepper and chili pepper and sauté the dice in oil over low heat. Add the starfruit and chicken stock and simmer for about twenty minutes until reduced to the desired consistency. Whisk vigorously with a wire whip and check for salt.
Finish: Skewer three prawns each with a lemongrass stalk and broil or grill the skewers on both sides to the desired degree of doneness. Place the skewers on plates and serve the sauce in small bowls on the side for dipping. Fragrant rice would make a good accompaniment.

Für 4 Personen:

24 Riesengarnelen, (Tiger Prawns),
8 Stängel Zitronengras

Für die Marinade:
1 Zwiebel,
2 Knoblauchzehen,
20 g Ingwer,
1 TL Tomatenmark,
ein Spritzer Tabasco,
2 TL Paprikapulver,
2 TL Chilipulver,
1 TL Kurkuma,
Salz,
1 EL pflanzliches Öl

Für die Sternfrucht-Chilisauce:
2 Sternfrüchte (Karambolen),
2 Schalotten,
1 kleine Zwiebel,
1 Knoblauchzehe,
30 g rote Paprika,
10 g rote Chili,
2 EL pflanzliches Öl,
100 ml kräftige Hühnerbrühe, Salz

Riesengarnelen nach Belieben schälen, gut waschen und abtrocknen.
Zwiebel, Knoblauch und Ingwer fein hacken, mit den restlichen Zutaten für die Marinade gut vermischen. Die Garnelen mit dieser Mischung einreiben, über Nacht im Kühlschrank marinieren.
Für die Sternfrucht-Chilisauce: Die Haut der Karambolen abziehen, die Früchte fein hacken. Schalotten, Zwiebel, Knoblauch, Paprika und Chili in kleine Würfel schneiden und in einem Topf im Öl anschwitzen. Sternfrüchte und Hühnerbrühe zugeben, ohne Deckel ca. 20 Minuten zur gewünschten Konsistenz köcheln. Mit einem Schneebesen kräftig umrühren, die Sauce mit Salz abschmecken.
Fertigstellung: Je drei Garnelen auf einen Zitronengrasstängel spießen, auf dem Grill zum gewünschten Garpunkt von beiden Seiten rösten. Auf Teller anrichten, die Sauce zum Dippen in kleinen Schälchen daneben servieren. Als Beilage passt Duftreis.

MARINATED SPRING CHICKEN IN AN AROMATIC COCONUT SAUCE

MARINIERTE STUBENKÜKEN AN AROMATISCHER KOKOSSAUCE

Serves 4

2 large spring chickens, ready-to-cook

For the spice mixture:
2 shallots, minced,
1 garlic clove, minced,
1 tsp turmeric root, minced (alternatively
ground turmeric),
80 g/3 oz red chili pepper ground in a mortar
(according to taste),
2 tsp fennel seeds,
2 tsp cumin seeds,
1 tbsp sugar,
1 tsp minced galangal root (alternatively
ground galangal),
2 macadamia nuts, chopped
(original recipe: candlenuts),
1 tbsp ginger, diced,
1 tsp salt

2 tbsp vegetable oil,
250 ml/1 cup coconut milk,
50 g/1 1/2 oz toasted grated coconut,
1 tbsp tamarind juice

Für 4 Personen:

2 große Stubenkücken, küchenfertig

Für die Würzmischung:
2 Schalotten, gehackt,
1 Knoblauchzehe, gehackt,
1 TL gehackte Kurkumawurzel (ersatzweise
Pulver verwenden),
80 g im Mörser verstampfte rote Chili
(oder nach Belieben),
2 TL Fenchelsamen,
2 TL Kreuzkümmelsamen,
1 EL Zucker,
1 TL gehackte Galangawurzel
(ersatzweise Pulver verwenden),
2 gehackte Macadamianüsse
(Originalrezept: Candlenut),
1 EL gehackter Ingwer,
1 TL Salz

2 EL pflanzliches Öl,
250 ml Kokosmilch,
50 g geröstete Kokosraspel,
1 EL Tamarindensaft

Cut the spring chickens in half and press down the halves with the blade of a broad knife until flat.
For the spice mixture: Grind all ingredients in a mortar until you have a fine paste. Alternatively, grind them in a blender. Brush the chicken halves with the spice mixture, inside and outside, and allow to marinate overnight in the refrigerator.
On the next day, scrape marinade off the chicken halves and fry the paste in a heavy-bottomed casserole in hot oil. Wenn the paste begins to take on color, stir in coconut milk. Add grated coconut and tamarind juice. Simmer the sauce for about ten minutes to the desired consistency. Thin with a little water if necessary. Correct seasonings.
Finish: Tie the spring chicken halves securely between two bamboo sticks with kitchen string. Grill or fry them in a large pan on both sides, until done. Place halves on plates and drizzle with sauce. Serve with brown or white rice on the side.

Die Stubenküken in jeweils zwei Hälften teilen und flachdrücken.
Für die Würzmischung: Alle Zutaten im Mörser zu einer Paste verstampfen oder im Mixer fein pürieren. Die Hühnerhälften innen und außen gleichmäßig damit bestreichen, über Nacht zugedeckt im Kühlschrank marinieren. Am nächsten Tag die Marinade vom Huhn abstreifen und im Öl in einer Kasserolle anbraten. Wenn die Paste beginnt, Farbe anzunehmen, mit Kokosmilch ablöschen. Kokosraspel und Tamarindensaft zugeben, die Sauce ca. zehn Minuten zur gewünschten Konsistenz köcheln, wenn nötig etwas Wasser zugeben. Abschmecken.
Fertigstellung: Die Stubenkükenhälften zwischen je zwei Bambusstäbchen klemmen und festbinden. Auf dem Grill oder in der Pfanne von beiden Seiten braten, bis das Fleisch gar ist. Auf Teller anrichten, mit Sauce übergießen, servieren. Als Beilage passt weißer oder brauner Reis.

ASIAN „KACANG" ICE

ASIATISCHES EIS „KACANG"

Mixed fruit such as kiwi,
strawberries, banana, papaya and mango,
cut into bite-size pieces,
palm seeds (can),
toasted cashews,
differently colored fruit jellies,
kidney beans cooked in syrup,
sweet corn kernels cooked in syrup (can),
palm sugar syrup,
rose water,
sweetened condensed milk,
sweetened coconut milk (cooked),
crushed or scraped ice

Arrange the kidney beans, corn kernels and cubed fruit jellies in dessert bowls. Top with a mound of crushed ice, heaping it as high as you can. Garnish mound with nuts and fruit and drizzle with syrup and milk. Serve.
Note: Ice Kacang is very popular in South East Asia, an ever-present after-dinner treat.

Gemischte Früchte (z.B. Kiwi,
Erdbeeren, Banane, Papaya und Mango,
in Stücke geschnitten),
Palmensamen (Dose),
geröstete Cashewnüsse,
verschiedenfarbige Fruchtgelee-Speisen,
in Sirup gekochte Kidney-Bohnen,
in Sirup gekochte Maiskörner (Dose),
Palmzuckersirup,
Rosenwassersirup,
süße Kondensmilch,
gesüßte Kokosmilch (gekocht),
geschabtes oder zerstoßenes Eis

Kidney-Bohnen, Maiskörner und in Würfel geschnittene Fruchtgelees in Dessertschalen anrichten. Mit dem geschabten Eis auffüllen und zu einem Berg anhäufen. Mit den Früchten und Nüssen belegen, zum Schluss mit Sirup und Milch übergießen.
Anmerkung: Ice Kacang ist in ganz Südostasien eine sehr beliebte Nachspeise und fehlt bei keinem größeren Essen.

TIRAMISU WITH CAPPUCCINO CREAM

TIRAMISU MIT CAPPUCCINOCREME

Serves 6

8 egg yolks,
200 g/7 oz sugar,
60 ml/¹⁄₄ cup water,
40 ml/¹⁄₈ cup coffee liqueur,
2 sheets of gelatin, soaked in water,
600 g/1 ¹⁄₃ lb mascarpone,
500 g/1 lb whipped cream,
24 ladyfingers,
1 cup hot, strong coffee

For the garnish:
cocoa powder for dusting,
fruit or berries

In a double boiler, whisk egg yolks with a wire whip until light and fluffy. Remove the bowl from the double boiler.

Mix water and sugar and cook until syrupy. Allow to cool and mix the syrup into the egg yolks. Heat the coffee liqueur and the soaked gelatin until gelatin is dissolved and whisk the mixture into the egg yolks.

In a large bowl, fold the whipped cream into the mascarpone, then carefully fold mascarpone cream into the egg yolk mixture.

Dip ladyfingers into hot coffee and line four shallow dessert bowls with six ladyfingers each. Top the ladyfingers with cream mixture and allow to set in the refrigerator.

Right before serving, dust the bowls with a generous amount of cocoa and garnish with fruit.

Für 6 Personen:

8 Eigelb,
200 g Zucker,
60 ml Wasser,
40 ml Kaffee-Likör,
2 Gelatineblätter, in Wasser eingeweicht,
600 g Mascarpone,
500 g steif geschlagene Sahne,
24 Löffelbiskuits,
1 Tasse starker, heißer Kaffee

Zum Garnieren:
Kakaopulver zum Bestäuben,
Früchte oder Beeren

Eigelb in einer Schüssel über dem Wasserbad mit dem Schneebesen schaumig rühren. Die Schüssel aus dem Wasserbad nehmen.

Den Zucker mit Wasser zu Sirup kochen, abkühlen lassen, unter das Eigelb rühren. Den Kaffee-Likör erhitzen, die eingeweichte Gelatine darin auflösen, unter Rühren zum Eigelb geben.

Den Mascarpone in einer Schüssel mit der steif geschlagenen Sahne verrühren, mit einem Löffel unter die Eigelbmischung ziehen.

Die Löffelbiskuits kurz in heißen Kaffee tauchen und vier Dessertschalen damit auslegen. Die Creme in die Schalen verteilen, im Kühlschrank fest werden lassen.

Vor dem Servieren die Cremes mit Kakaopulver bestäuben und mit Früchten garnieren.

ORANGE CHOCOLATE MOUSSE

ORANGEN-SCHOKOLADENMOUSSE

Serves 4

For the tear drop form:
150 g/5 oz dark chocolate

For the mousse:
450 g/1 lb dark chocolate,
180 g/6¹/₂ oz egg yolk,
75 g/2¹/₂ oz egg white,
2 tbsp sugar syrup (equal amounts of sugar and water boiled until syrupy),
100 ml/¹/₃ cup cream,
6 sheets gelatin, soaked,
thinly grated zest of one untreated orange

Garnish:
differently colored berry sauces such as raspberry and blackberry, simmered with confectioners' sugar, puréed in a blender and strained through a sieve, fruits according to taste

For the tear drop form: Cut four 5 x 25 cm/2 x 10 inch strips from heavy plastic (such as freezer bags). Melt the chocolate in a double boiler and brush it thinly onto the plastic strips. Allow to set in the refrigerator until the chocolate has hardened but has not yet become brittle. Fold the strips over to make a tear drop shape and press both ends together firmly. Return to the refrigerator to chill.

For the mousse: Melt the dark chocolate in a double boiler, being careful not to let it overheat.

In a separate boil, mix the egg white and egg yolks and whisk with a wire whip until fluffy. Add the syrup and continue beating for one minute. Incorporate the egg mixture into the chocolate. Whip the cream into stiff peaks and fold it into the chocolate mixture. Heat the soaked gelatin in a small pot until dissolved and carefully stir it into the chocolate mixture together with the orange zest.

Spoon the mousse into a pastry bag and pipe it into the prepared chocolate tears. Allow to cool in the refrigerator for eight hours.

Remove the plastic strips just before serving. Arrange the mousse and chocolate tear drops on plates, surround with berry purées and garnish the plates with fruit. Serve.

Für 4 Personen:

Für die Tränenform:
150 g dunkle Schokolade

Für die Mousse:
450 g dunkle Schokolade,
180 g Eigelb,
75 g Eiweiß,
2 EL Zuckersirup (Zucker mit Wasser 50:50 gekocht),
100 ml Sahne,
6 Blätter Gelatine, eingeweicht,
die dünn abgeriebene Schale einer unbehandelten Orange

Garnitur:
verschiedenfarbige Beerensaucen (z. B. Himbeeren und Brombeeren, mit Puderzucker gekocht, im Mixer püriert, durch ein Sieb passiert), Früchte nach Belieben

Für die Tränenform: Aus einer starken Plastikfolie (z.B. Gefrierbeutel) vier 5 x 25 cm große Streifen schneiden. Schokolade im Wasserbad schmelzen, die Plastikbänder dünn damit bestreichen. Im Kühlschrank abkühlen lassen, bis die Schokolade fest geworden aber noch nicht brüchig ist. Die Schokoladenbänder in Tränenform zusammenklappen, beide Enden fest zusammendrücken. Im Kühlschrank durchkühlen lassen.

Für die Mousse: Die dunkle Schokolade in einer Schüssel über dem Wasserbad schmelzen, ohne stark zu erhitzen. In einer separaten Schüssel Eigelb und Eiweiß mit einem Schneebesen schaumig schlagen. Den Sirup zugeben und eine Minute weiter schlagen. Die Eiermasse unter die Schokolade rühren. Die Sahne steif schlagen, ebenfalls unter die Schokolade ziehen. Die eingeweichte Gelatine in einem kleinen Topf auflösen, zusammen mit der abgeriebenen Orangenschale unter die Schokoladenmousse rühren. Die Mousse in einen Spritzsack füllen und in die vorbereiteten Schokoladenformen spritzen. Im Kühlschrank acht Stunden durchkühlen lassen. Vor dem Servieren die Plastikbänder entfernen. Die Mousse auf Teller anrichten, mit Beerensaucen umgießen, mit Früchten garnieren.

EXOTIC FRUIT SALAD WITH A GINGER SAUCE

EXOTISCHER FRUCHTSALAT MIT INGWERSAUCE

Serves 4

exotic and local fruit and berries
according to season and taste

For the ginger sauce:
60 g/2 oz butter,
40 g/1 1/2 oz brown sugar,
60 g/2 oz ginger, peeled,
cut into julienne strips,
160 ml/6 oz freshly squeezed orange juice,
30 ml/1/8 cup freshly squeezed lime juice,
2 star anise

For the pastry shells:
50 g/1 1/2 oz egg white,
50 ml/1/4 cup water,
150 g/5 oz flour,
150 g/5 oz confectioners' sugar,
100 g/3 1/2 oz dark chocolate

Garnish: vanilla and fruit ice cream

Peel the fruit and cut them into bite-size pieces if necessary. Place them in a bowl and refrigerate.
For the ginger sauce: Melt the butter and sugar in a heavy-bottomed saucepan and caramelize the sugar until medium brown. Add ginger strips and stir to coat. Douse with orange and lime juice (be careful of splattering). Add star anise and simmer until the caramel is dissolved and the liquid has reduced somewhat. Strain the sauce through a fine sieve, allow to cool and toss with the fruit pieces. Place in the refrigerator and allow to marinate for half an hour.
For the pastry shells: In a large bowl, whisk the egg white and the water with a wire whip until foamy. Incorporate flour and confectioners' sugar, a little at a time. Preheat the oven to 180° C/350° F. Make a circle stencil with a diameter of 15 - 20 cm/6-8 inches from cardboard, cut out the middle and place the stencil onto a baking sheet lined with baking paper. Brush the inner opening with a little butter and spoon a fourth of the dough into the stencil. Smooth out the top of the dough and bake it in the oven until golden brown. Place the pastry onto an inversed cup or bowl while still warm, letting it cool in the cup or bowl shape. Repeat procedure three times until you have four pastry shells. Melt the chocolate in a double boiler and brush the insides of cooled pastry shells with a thin layer of chocolate.
Serving: Place the pastry shells onto dessert plates and fill them with fruit salad. Serve with a scoop of vanilla or fruit ice cream on the side.

Für 4 Personen:

Exotische und heimische Früchte und Beeren nach
Saison und Belieben

Für die Ingwersauce:
60 g Butter,
40 g brauner Zucker,
60 g Ingwer, geschält, in sehr dünne Streifen
geschnitten,
160 ml frisch gepresster Orangensaft,
30 ml frisch gepresster Limettensaft,
2 Sternanis

Für die Gebäckschale:
50 g Eiweiß,
50 ml Wasser,
150 g Mehl,
150 g Puderzucker,
100 g dunkle Schokolade

Garnitur: Vanille- oder Obsteis

Die Früchte wenn nötig schälen, in nicht zu kleine Stücke schneiden. In einer Schüssel kalt stellen.
Für die Ingwersauce: Die Butter mit dem Zucker in einem Topf mittelbraun karamellisieren. Ingwerstreifen zugeben und gut vermischen, mit Orangen- und Limettensaft ablöschen (Vorsicht, kann spritzen.) Sternanis zugeben und köcheln, bis sich der Karamell gut aufgelöst hat und die Flüssigkeit etwas eingekocht ist. Die Sauce durch ein Sieb passieren, erkalten lassen und die vorbereiteten Früchte damit eine halbe Stunde im Kühlschrank marinieren.
Für die Gebäckschale: Das Eiweiß und Wasser mit dem Schneebesen in einer Schüssel schaumig rühren, nach und nach das Mehl und den Puderzucker zugeben und einarbeiten. Den Ofen auf 180° C vorheizen. Aus Karton eine Schablone in Kreisform von 15 - 20 cm Durchmesser ausschneiden und auf ein mit Backtrennpapier ausgelegtes Blech legen. Die runde Öffnung leicht mit Butter bepinseln, dann ein Viertel des Teigs in die Schablone füllen. Den Teig glatt ausstreichen, im Ofen goldbraun backen. Das Gebäck noch warm über eine umgedrehte Tasse oder Schale legen, so dass es sich zu einer Schale wölbt. Aus dem restlichen Teig auf die gleiche Weise weitere drei Gebäckschalen herstellen. Die Schokolade im Wasserbad schmelzen, die Innenseite der erkalteten Gebäckschalen damit auspinseln.
Zum Servieren: Die Gebäckschalen auf Dessertteller legen und mit dem Fruchtsalat füllen. Mit je einer Kugel Vanille- oder Obsteis als Beilage servieren.

BAKED SPRING ROLLS WITH A MANGO-GINGER FILLING

OFENGEBACKENE FRÜHLINGSROLLEN MIT MANGO-INGWERFÜLLUNG

Serves 4

For the pastry cream:
100 ml/¹/₃ cup milk,
1 egg yolk,
20 g/³/₄ oz sugar,
a pinch of salt,
1 heaping tsp flour

1 ripe mango,
2 tbsp butter,
2 tbsp brown sugar,
1 tbsp ginger, cut into thin strips

4 large phyllo sheets,
2 tbsp clarified butter, warmed,
confectioners' sugar

200 ml/³/₄ cup vanilla ice cream

Für 4 Personen:

Für die Patisserie-Creme:
100 ml Milch,
1 Eigelb,
20 g Zucker,
1 Msp Salz,
1 gehäufter TL Mehl

1 reife Mango,
2 EL Butter,
2 EL brauner Zucker,
1 EL in dünne Streifen geschnittener Ingwer

4 große Philoteigblätter,
2 EL geklärte Butter, erwärmt,
Puderzucker

200 ml Vanilleeis

For the pastry cream: Scald the milk in a small saucepan. In a large bowl, whisk egg yolks, sugar and salt until light and fluffy. Add the flour, a little at a time. Slowly drizzle in milk, beating vigorously all the time. Return mixture to the pot and bring it to a boil, stirring constantly. When the cream has thickened, place it into a bowl of ice water and allow it to cool. Stir frequently in order to prevent a skin from forming.

Peel the mango and cut the pulp into 1 cm/¹/₃ inch cubes. Melt butter in a heavy saucepan, sprinkle in sugar and allow to caramelize to medium brown. Add mango and ginger and toss for a few minutes until well coated, stirring constantly with a wooden spoon. Remove the saucepan from the burner, allow the fruit to cool and mix into the pastry cream.

Preheat the oven to 200° C/390° F. Cut the phyllo sheets into four squares or rectangles. Brush each piece with clarified butter and stack four pieces each on top of each other. Spoon mango cream into the center of the stacks, then fold over the corners to make a package. Place packages on a baking sheet and bake them in the preheated oven for twenty minutes. Dust the mango spring rolls with confectioners' sugar and serve while still warm with a scoop of vanilla ice cream.

Für die Patisserie-Creme: Die Milch zum Kochen bringen. Eigelb mit Zucker und Salz in einer Schüssel schaumig schlagen, dabei nach und nach das Mehl unterrühren. Die heiße Milch unter kräftigem Rühren zugießen. Die Masse zurück in den Topf geben, unter Rühren zum Kochen bringen. Wenn die Creme dick ist, den Topf zum Abkühlen in Eiswasser stellen. Die Creme immer wieder umrühren, damit sich keine Haut bildet.

Die Mango schälen und das Fleisch in 1 cm große Würfel schneiden. Butter in einem Topf schmelzen, Zucker zustreuen und mittelbraun karamellisieren. Die Mangowürfel und Ingwerstreifen zugeben und unter Rühren mit einem Holzlöffel 1 - 2 Minuten köcheln. Den Topf vom Herd nehmen, die Mangomasse vollständig abkühlen lassen, dann mit der Patisserie-Creme vermischen.

Den Ofen auf 200° C vorheizen. Philoteigblätter in vier Rechtecke oder Quadrate teilen. Jedes Blatt mit flüssiger geklärter Butter bepinseln, jeweils vier Blätter übereinander legen. Die Mangocreme auf dem Teig verteilen und zu Päckchen zusammenschlagen. Auf einem Backblech im vorgeheizten Ofen während ca. 20 Minuten goldgelb backen. Die Mango-Frühlingsrollen mit Puderzucker bestäuben, lauwarm mit je einer Kugel Vanilleeis servieren.

SPICE MOUSSE ON A SPONGE CAKE

GEWÜRZMOUSSE AUF KUCHENBODEN

Serves 4

For the sponge cakes:
4 egg yolks,
120 g/4 oz sugar,
100 g/3 1/2 oz flour,
60 g/2 oz melted butter,
4 egg whites, whipped into stiff peaks

For the mousse:
300 g/11 oz dark chocolate,
125 ml/1/2 cup glucose syrup (equal amounts
of glucose and water boiled until syrupy),
130 g/4 1/2 oz butter,
375 g/14 oz cream, whipped into stiff peaks,
5 sheets gelatin,
2 tsp five-spice-powder (equal amounts of allspice,
cinnamon, cloves, fennel seeds and anise
ground in a mortar)

Garnish:
fruits of the season, fruit purées

Preheat the oven to 180° C/350° F. Beat egg yolks and sugar in a double boiler until light and airy. Remove the bowl from the double boiler. Sieve the flour onto the egg mixture, incorporate the melted butter and fold in a third of the whipped egg whites. Carefully fold in the remaining egg whites with a palette knife, taking care not to overmix. Spread the dough thinly onto a baking sheet lined with baking paper. Bake in a hot oven for about ten minutes. While the dough is still hot, use four large cookie cutters to cut the dough repeatedly (thickness allow-ing) until you have several layers of dough in each cookie cutter. Press down slightly on the top and allow the stacked layers to cool in the cookie cutters. For the mousse: Melt chocolate and glucose syrup in a double boiler and mix. Dissolve gelatin in a small pot. Fold whipped cream into the chocolate mixture and incorporate dissolved gelatin and spices.
Spread the mousse into the cookie cutters on top of the cake layers. Smooth out the top and refrigerate for eight hours until well chilled. Right before ser-ving, carefully press the mousse out of cookie cutters from the bottom, and place stacks onto plates. Gar-nish with fruit and fruit purées according to taste.

Für 4 Personen:

Für den Kuchenboden:
4 Eigelb,
120 g Zucker,
100 g Mehl,
60 g flüssige Butter,
4 Eiweiß, zu Eischnee geschlagen

Für die Mousse:
300 g dunkle Schokolade,
125 ml Glukosesirup (Glukose und Wasser
50:50 gekocht),
130 g Butter,
375 g Sahne, steif geschlagen,
5 Gelatineblätter,
2 TL Fünf-Gewürze-Mischung (Piment, Zimt,
Gewürznelken, Fenchelsamen und Anis zu gleichen
Teilen, im Mörser zu Pulver zermahlen)

Garnitur:
Früchte der Saison, Fruchtsaucen

Ofen auf 180° C vorheizen. Eigelb und Zucker in einer Schüssel über dem Wasserbad schaumig schla-gen. Die Schüssel aus dem Wasserbad nehmen. Das Mehl über die Eiermasse sieben, die flüssige Butter zugeben und alles zusammen mit einem Drittel des Eischnees vermischen. Restlichen Eischnee mit einer Palette locker unterziehen, dann den Teig dünn auf ein mit Backtrennpapier ausgelegtes Blech streichen. Im Ofen ca. 10 Minuten goldbraun backen. Den Teig noch heiß mit Ausstechformen mehrmals (je nach Dicke) ausstechen, so dass jede Form mit meh-reren Schichten Teig gefüllt ist. Den Teig von oben etwas hinunterdrücken, erkalten lassen.
Für die Mousse: Schokolade mit Glukosesirup und Butter in einer Schüssel im Wasserbad schmelzen und verrühren. Steif geschlagene Sahne unterziehen, zum Schluss die in einem kleinen Topf geschmol-zene Gelatine und das Gewürz untermischen. Die Mousse in die Ausstechformen füllen, Oberfläche glatt streichen, zugedeckt im Kühlschrank 8 Stun-den durchkühlen. Zum Servieren die Mousse vor-sichtig von unten aus den Formen drücken und auf Teller legen. Nach Belieben mit Früchten der Saison und Fruchtsaucen garnieren.

PANGKOR LAUT RESORT

Uncle Lim takes small, nimble steps on his way from market stand to market stand, where every morning vegetables, fish and spices are offered up for sale. He is here everyday and well-known, buying whatever he needs for his kitchen. Dry fish of all sorts are dangling in their plastic bags from sun blinds, with the next batch already drying on mats in the sun on the sidewalk. In the back of the shop front, the same takes place on a much larger scale. Not far from tied-up fishing boats, the catch of day is laid out for drying in the burning hot afternoon sun on hundreds of square meters of squeaking wooden planks: the smallest of anchovies, for instance, the dried version of which often substitutes for salt in local cuisine. Noodles are to be gotten at another corner, where a small shed functions as the manufacturing place for all shapes and sizes. A dough mixer, a noodle machine – that's all. Strands of rolled dough are resting on sieves for drying before they are parboiled and sold in bags. Two generations are working together in the dark rooms, covering the noodle demand of the entire neighborhood. For better lighting, the door is open, admitting the rays of the sun. Egg noodles, soy noodles and the broad Kway Teow noodles made from rice flour, which are so popular in Chinese cooking, are on sale. Lim, too, has ordered his quantity.

WE ARE IN THE LIVELY CENTER OF A SMALL, UNSPECTACULAR LITTLE VILLAGE ON PANGKOR ISLAND, AN ISLAND IN FRONT OF MALAYSIA'S SOUTH COAST. RIGHT IN FRONT OF IT, AT THE EDGE OF THE STRAITS OF MALAK-KA, THERE IS THE SMALL PRIVATE ISLAND PANGKOR LAUT FLOATING IN THE EMERALD GREEN OCEAN – A SMALL PIECE OF PARADISE.

The white yacht is plowing the waters with its bow high up in the glistening sun. New guests from the mainland are aboard. Captain and crew are dressed casually in black pants and white polo shirts, caps tight on their forehead. In a sweeping curve around Pangkor Island out towards the sea, we approach the holiday paradise, which is densely covered with rain forest. Coming closer, the wooden pavilions of seaside villas resting on stilts above the water appear, with long piers and banisters connecting the fragile structures. The boat finally comes to a halt at the jetty of the „Pangkor Laut Resort", rocking gently, and ropes are fastened to the bollards while the luggage of the newcomers is unloaded. After a much needed, very refreshing welcoming cocktail, the upper stories of dense green are reached with a kind of lift, passing further cozy-looking villas (Royal Hill Villas) jutting out from the mountain forest. The day starts early up here. The squeaking, chirping and squealing of birds and cicadas will even wake the soundest sleeper out his restful beauty sleep. Yet, this morning spectacle should by no means be missed, it is not to be repeated at one's home balcony

at Stuttgart or Castrop-Rauxel. The view is breathtaking. From the balcony, the eye can roam freely past the green of the trees and further across the inlet between the islands, where a small fleet of local fishing boats is moving seaward. Their wakes draw long lines in the otherwise undisturbed mirror-like water. The sky takes its time to lighten up while everything is awash in a pink glow, and the dark silhouette of the buildings on stilts appears as a filigree pattern against the light.

In the very back, towards the end of the village on stilts, two large round roofs seem to rest right on the rocks, the home of "Uncle Lim's Kitchen" and the sphere of activity of the sixty-seven year old Chinaman for the last sixteen years. Since the beginning of the resort owned by the YTL group, that is, one of the largest building firms and energy suppliers in Malaysia. Kuala Lumpur's "Ritz-Carlton" and the "JW Marriot" are other pearls in their string of hotel activities. Uncle Lim is living inventory, so-to-speak, and enjoys the friendly protection of the owner family Yeoh. "At that time, there were still tuna fish and dolphins frolicking here in the shallows" he recalls. "And in the woods, there were wild boar and pygmy deer." He owes his popularity equally to his charming personality and to his expertise as a chef. His cooking is not spectacular, it is his personal interpretation of island cuisine, full of variety and never boring. His repertoire draws from the rich resources of Nyonya cuisine (a mixture of Chinese and Malay cooking), and his ingredients are always fresh from the market (where we first spotted him). He opens only in the evening and can take his time for a morning shopping trip on the main island, while his chefs are already busy with preparing the curries. His shopping list includes both daily staples and ingredients for the dishes requested by guests, since there is no menu. Uncle Lim likes to cook according to his guests' wishes and orders, which makes a visit on the previous day advisable. He is also willing to leave out one or the other spice, too, should it prove a burden to a Westerner's sensitive stomach. "You would like it without ginger, just garlic? No problem, we'll make it", Uncle Lim says with a laugh. "We do need our guests."

The most beautiful spot on the island for the sun and water-hungry alike is the "Emerald Bay". Here, in the shade of palm trees, the travel-weary may stretch out their bodies on upholstered sun beds, while the ocean gently and unhurriedly laps up on the white sand beach. In the background, "Mummy" is busy below the roof of an open wooden pavilion structure. Her small kitchen gleams brightly. Handling the large ladle with the routine of many years, she puts oil in the wok which rests on a gas burner. Her hand seizes a red bowl from which she extracts small pieces of meat to be thrown in the sizzling fat. Vegetables, herbs and, last but not least, noodles are added until everything is scraped onto a white plate and proudly placed on the counter. This portion will have no problem satisfying even the biggest appetite. Fifty-seven years old, the dark-skinned woman is an attractive beauty, with white teeth shimmering behind bright red lipstick if you catch one of her shy smiles. Mummy is a legend like Uncle Lim and also belongs to the living inventory of Pangkor Laut Resort. Her task is to keep the palates of beach-goers happy. She does this all by herself, serving ham sandwiches as well as Malay noodle specialties, small snacks or substantial dishes – something suitable for every beach hunger. Only when there is a lot of demand, when a hundred people are waiting to be fed at once, will she request help from the resort. While Uncle Lim and Mummy are largely taking care of their own operations, most other culinary activities on the island are under the supervision of master chef Mano. Only the exclusive, separate "Marina Bay", reserved for special guests of the family, operates independently. The equipment of those splendid villas not only includes an own pool but, naturally, also a chef and a butler. Such luxuries are reserved for international VIPs like Luciano Pavarotti or formula one star Jacques Villeneuve. But the Malay chef of Indian origin has enough to do anyway. He is most often found at the "Samudra", which features mostly Malay and Malay-Chinese specialties. The focus here is on curries, too, there is just no getting around them. At the "Samudra", they are offered in a variety that is almost bewildering for the guest. Happy he who can make up his mind and knows a little bit about this kind of food. Basic knowledge in Malay cuisine as well as Malay pronunciation of English, in which "r" generally mutates to "l" (as in "welli good" for "very good") are also helpful. Doubts with respect to menu composition are usually cleared up by the waitress in a friendly but not always comprehensible manner (what on earth is "kulli"?). A little time must pass before the guest gets used to things and can identify "kulli" as "curry". Things become easier after that, and you now have the choice between combining different spice combinations or ways of preparation with beef, chicken, shrimp and fish as well as vegetables. Nevertheless, the first try is by necessity a blind one, at the next visit, personal preferences have already taken on shape. And the young chef is full of energy and ideas, endeavoring to give the island's rather conservative gastronomical curve an upward tilt. Crew and kitchen technology still have to be updated. Modern and foreign influences are to make the local cuisine lighter, more dazzling, the optics more creative. Many years at the kitchen of the Raffles in Singapur, where the whole world's cooking elite likes to put in a guest appearance, provided the necessary routine and experience. And his art shines forth brightly at an evening „Dinner on the Rocks" at the "Emerald Bay". For this luxury version of a picnic, the kitchen crew has arrived in vans carrying numerous devices to keep things warm at the culinary event on the platform above the rock. Both the ocean and Mano's cooking send a fresh breeze across the festive dinner table: his kind of "fusion cooking", which excludes all too alien Western influences, rather tapping local Asiatic traditions in its attempt to infuse classical regional dishes with a bit of pizzazz. Every dish is a pleasure, the cappuccino of mushrooms or the crêpes stuffed with crabmeat, for instance. Inspired combinations feature ingredients that have rarely been seen together: king prawns coupled with lamb chops done to perfection and seasoned with lemon pepper, and as an accompaniment a fluffy potato purée that impresses even a practiced potato cook. Hoisin sauce is the culinary ribbon that holds the trio together. Banana strudel in a flaky, crispy dough and cardamom ice cream make for a fitting culinary coda.

Dreamily, one continues to nibble on the contents of the fruit basket, riveted by the view of the sinking sun, enjoying small, slow sips of French red wine.

Manogaran Balakrishnan

"Mummy"

MIT KLEINEN ABER RASCHEN SCHRITTEN TRIPPELT UNCLE LIM VON STAND ZU STAND, WO JEDEN

Vormittag Gemüse, Fisch und Gewürze feilgeboten werden. Hier kennt ihn jeder, er ist ja täglich da und kauft frisch ein, was er für die Küche benötigt. Trockenfische jeglicher Art hängen in Plastikbeuteln von der Markise herab, und auf dem Gehweg liegt schon die nächste Lage zum Trocknen auf Matten in der Sonne. Doch im Rücken der Ladenzeile findet dasselbe in weit größerem Maßstab statt. Unweit der festgemachten Fischerboote breitet sich unter dem Grill der grellen Mittagssonne, auf Hunderten Quadratmetern knarzender Holzplanken, der Fang des täglichen Fischzugs zum Trocknen aus. Kleinste Sardellen, die als Trockenwürze in der heimischen Küche häufig das Salz ersetzen. Eine Ecke weiter gibt es Nudeln. In der kleinen Hütte werden Teigwaren jeden Formats fabriziert. Ein Teigrührgerät, eine Nudelmaschine – mehr ist nicht nötig. Auf Sieben liegt die stranggewalzte Ware zum Trocknen und wird anschließend im großen Kessel kurz vorgekocht, ehe sie zum Verkauf in Beutel abgepackt wird. Zwei Generationen arbeiten in den kleinen dunklen Räumen zusammen und decken den Nudelbedarf der Umgebung. Zur besseren Beleuchtung steht die Tür weit offen und lässt Sonnenlicht herein. Im Angebot sind Eiernudeln, Sojanudeln und die in der chinesischen Küche äußerst beliebten Bandnudeln Kway Teow aus Reismehl. Auch Lim hat schon seinen Vorrat bestellt. Das kleine unscheinbare Dorf mit seiner quirlig bunten Ortsmitte liegt auf Pangkor Island, einer Insel vor der Küste Malaysias.

IHR VORGELAGERT, AM RANDE DER STRASSE VON MALAKKA, SCHWIMMT IM SMARAGDGRÜNEN MEER DAS KLEINE PRIVATINSELCHEN PANGKOR LAUT – EIN KLEINES STÜCK VOM PARADIES.

Unter gleißender Sonne pflügt die weiße Yacht mit erhobenem Bug durchs Wasser. Neue Gäste vom Festland sind an Bord. Captain und Crew salopp in schwarzer Hose und weißem Polo-Shirt, das Käppi tief in die Stirn gezogen. Im großen Bogen wird Pangkor Island umrundet und man steuert hinauf aufs Meer, auf die mit dichtem Regenwald bewachsene Urlaubsinsel zu. Im Näherkommen wachsen die Holzpavillons der See-Villen auf Pfählen über den Wasserspiegel, lange Stege und Geländer klammern die fragile Struktur aneinander. Leicht wippend kommt das Boot schließlich am Anleger vom „Pangkor Laut Resort" zum Halt, die Leinen werden an Pollern festgezurrt und das Gepäck der Ankömmlinge an Land gehievt. Nach einem dringend erforderlichen und erfrischenden Begrüßungs-Cocktail geht´s per Fahrstuhl hinauf in die Oberetage dichten Grüns, wo am Hang weitere komfortable Villen (Royal Hill Villas) hochaufgerichtet aus dem Bergwald ragen. Am frühen Morgen ist hier die Hölle los. Das Kreischen, Zirpen und Schrillen von Vögeln und Grillen weckt auch den mit gesundem Tiefschlaf gesegneten Schläfer zur rechten Zeit. Denn dieses morgendliche Schauspiel darf er sich nicht entgehen lassen, desgleichen bietet der heimische Balkon in Stuttgart oder Castrop-Rauxel nicht. Der Blick ist einfach bombastisch. Vom Balkon schweift das Auge durchs Grün der Bäume über die Meerenge zwischen den Inseln, wo die Flotte der einheimischen Fischerboote zum offenen Meer strebt. Ihr Kielwasser zieht lange Linien in den Spiegel kaum gekräuselten Wassers. Ein zögerlich heller werdender Himmel haucht rosafarbenen Schimmer darüber, und die dunkle Silhouette der Pfahlbauten zeichnet ihr filigranes Muster ins Gegenlicht. Ganz hinten, am Ende des Pfahldorfes sitzen zwei große runde Dächer auf den Felsen. Darunter verbirgt sich „Uncle Lim's Kitchen", die Wirkungsstätte des siebenundsechzigjährigen Chinesen seit gut sechzehn Jahren. Das heißt, seit den ersten Anfängen der Resorts im Besitz der YTL Firmengruppe, die zu den größten Baufirmen und Energielieferanten Malaysias zählt. Kuala Lumpurs „Ritz-Carlton" und das „JW Marriott" sind weitere Perlen in der Kette ihrer Hotelaktivitäten. Uncle Lim ist quasi lebendes Inventar und genießt freundlichen Bestandschutz bei der Besitzerfamilie Yeoh. „Damals schwammen hier am Strand noch Thunfische und Delfine", erinnert er sich. „Und im Wald gab es noch Wildschweine und Zwerghirsche." Seine Popularität ist wohl gleichermaßen seiner charmanten Person wie auch seiner Kochkunst zuzuschreiben. Er kocht nicht spektakulär, sondern seine Art von Inselküche, die aber immer abwechslungsreich und selten langweilig ist. Sein Brevier ist der reichhaltige Schatz der Nyonya-Küche (eine chinesisch-malaiische Mischversion), und seine Zutaten holt er sich fast immer frisch vom Markt (wir haben ihn eingangs dort erlebt). Da er nur abends geöffnet hat, kann er sich auch die Zeit nehmen, morgens auf der Hauptinsel einzukaufen, während seine Köche schon die Curries ansetzen. Der Einkaufszettel listet den täglichen Grundbedarf der Küche sowie all das, was die Gäste an Wünschen geäußert haben. Denn eine Speisekarte gibt es nicht. Er kocht vorzugsweise nach Wunsch und auf Bestellung, was eine Visite am Vortage zwecks Bestellung ratsam erscheinen lässt. Und er lässt auch bereitwillig dieses oder jenes Gewürz weg, sollte es einem seiner westlichen Kunden auf den empfindlichen Magen schlagen. „Sie wollen es ohne Ingwer, nur mit Knoblauch? Kein Problem, we make it," lacht Uncle Lim. „Wir brauchen schließlich unsere Gäste." Des Eilands schönste Nische für Sonnenhungrige wie Badelustige ist „Emerald Bay". Unter Palmenschatten streckt man an der Smaragdbucht seine Glieder auf gepolsterten Liegen Richtung Meer, das unaufgeregt seine Wellen über den weißen Sandstrand schwappen lässt. Im Hintergrund werkelt „Mummy" unterm Dach eines offenen Holzpavillons. Alles ist blitzsauber in ihrer kleinen Küche. Mit routinierten Bewegungen packt sie eine große Schöpfkelle und schwappt Öl in den Wok über der Gasflamme. Ihre Hand greift in eine rote Schüssel und wirft kleine Stücke Fleisch ins zischende Fett. Nach und nach kommen Gemüse, Kräuter und – nicht zu vergessen – die Nudeln hinzu bis sie alles zusammen auf einen weißen Teller befördert und stolz auf den Tresen stellt. Diese Portion wird problemlos auch den größten Hunger stillen. Mit ihren siebenundfünfzig Jahren ist die dunkelhäutige Frau eine attraktive Schönheit, deren weiße Zähne zwischen knallrot geschminkten Lippen blitzen, wenn sie scheu ein Lächeln wagt. Mummy ist wie Uncle Lim schon Legende und gehört zum Inventar vom Pangkor Laut Resort. Ihr obliegt es, die Strandbevölkerung kulinarisch bei Laune zu halten. Und das schultert sie ganz allein und serviert vom Schinken-Sandwich bis zum malaiischen Nudelgericht kleine, leichte Snacks oder nahrhafte Gerichte – eben passend für jeden Strandhunger. Nur wenn es richtig Druck gibt, wenn doch mal hundert Personen nach Nahrung verlangen, lässt sie sich vom Resort Hilfe schicken.

Während Uncle Lim und Mummy weitgehendst autark ihr Revier bestellen, unterliegen die meisten anderen kulinarischen Aktivitäten der Insel der Oberaufsicht von Chefkoch Mano. Nur das exklusive und leicht abgesonderte, den Spezialgästen der Familie vorbehaltene Refugium „Marina Bay", versorgt sich selbst. Schließlich gehört zur Ausstattung jeder der prachtvollen Villen nicht nur der eigene Pool, sondern selbstredend auch Koch und Butler. Derlei Annehmlichkeiten sind internationalen VIPs

wie Luciano Pavarotti oder Formel-1-Star Jacques Villeneuve vorbehalten. Doch der erst vor kurzem hier gestrandete Malaie indischer Herkunft hat genug am Hals. Am häufigsten ist er im „Samudra" zu finden, dessen Küche vorzugsweise malaiische und malai-chinesische Speisen serviert. Auch hier stehen im Mittelpunkt Curries, an denen kommt man zwangsläufig nicht vorbei. Sie werden im Samudra jedoch in einer für den Gast fast schon verwirrenden Variationsfülle angeboten. Wohl dem, der Entscheidungsfreudigkeit und gewisse Grundkenntnisse vorweisen kann. Grundkenntnisse sowohl in malaiischer Küche als auch in der malaiischen Aussprache des Englischen, dessen „r" grundsätzlich zu „l" mutiert und aus einem „very good" ein „welli good" macht. Unsicherheiten in der Speisewahl werden sehr freundlich, doch nicht immer ganz verständlich (was bedeutet denn verflixt noch mal „Kölli"?) von der Kellnerin behoben. Es braucht schon einige Zeit, bis man sich in die Eigenart der Sprache hineingehört hat und das „Kölli" als „Curry" entdeckt. Von da an wird's deutlich einfacher, und man steht nun vor der Wahl, die verschiedenen Würz- oder Zubereitungsarten mit Rindfleisch, Huhn, Shrimps und Fisch sowie Gemüse zu kombinieren. Beim

ersten Mal ist es immer ein Blindversuch, aber beim nächsten Besuch weiß man schon, wo die eigenen Vorlieben liegen. Doch der junge Koch Mano steckt voller Tatendrang und neuer Ideen, um der bisher eher konservativen gastronomischen Kurve des Inselreichs zu einem Kick nach oben zu verhelfen. Beides, Küchentechnik und Mannschaft haben noch gewissen Nachholbedarf. Moderne und auch fremde Einflüsse sollen die lokalen Gerichte leichter, frecher und optisch kreativer gestalten. Viele Jahre in den Küchen des Raffles in Singapur, wo allenthalben die kochende Weltelite ihren Auftritt hatte, haben ihm dafür die notwendige Erfahrung und Routine vermittelt. Seine Kunst blitzt auf, als eines Abends „Dinner on the Rocks" in der „Emerald Bay" angesagt ist. Fürs Luxus-Picknick ist die halbe Küchenmannschaft mit Lieferwagen und zahllosen Wärmecontainern ausgerückt, um auf der Plattform überm Felsen das kulinarische Event vorzubereiten. Und nicht nur das Meer, sondern auch Mano schickt eine frische Brise über die festlich gedeckte Tafel: seine Art der „Fusion-Küche", die Westliches, allzu Fremdes außen vor lässt und viel mehr im Umfeld des asiatischen Raums jene Kontrapunkte sucht, die klassischen und traditionellen Regionalspeisen zu neuem Schwung verhelfen können. Jeder Gang wird zum Genuss, so beispielsweise das Cappuccino von Pilzen oder die mit Garnelenfleisch gefüllten, gebratenen Pfannkuchen. Und frech wird kombiniert, was vorher noch selten in dieser Form zusammengefunden hat. King Prawns gepaart mit auf den Punkt gegarten und mit Zitronenpfeffer gewürzten Lamb chops. In der Begleitung: ein duftiges Kartoffelpüree, das selbst der geübten Kartoffel-Köchin Bewunderung abnötigt. Hoisin-Sauce schlingt ihr geschmackliches Band ums Trio. Bananenstrudelstücke im blättrigknusprigen Teigmantel setzen den kulinarischen Schlusspunkt mit Kardamom-Eiskrem.

Verträumt knabbert man schließlich, in den Anblick der im Meer untergehenden Sonne versunken, am Früchtekorb und genießt in langsamen Schlucken etwas vom französischen Rotwein.

NYONYA

Nyonya is a very popular South East Asian cuisine. Its roots go all the way back to the fifteenth century, when Malakka blossomed into one of the world´s biggest trading centers. At the time, the city attracted many Chinese people, and something similar happened again centuries later in the times of the Malaysian tin boom. Chinese workers, in search of prosperity and work, emigrated, settled down and brought their eating and cooking traditions along. In lack of Chinese, they married Malay women. The melding of both cultures made for an independent ethnic group, the so-called Straits Chinese (named after the Straits of Malakka), also called „Perana-kans". Their cuisine was unique, combining both Malay and Chinese elements and named after the person who had developed it, the „nyonya", which simply means woman or mother. (Italians would call it „cucina della mamma".) Typical ingredients include lemon-grass (serai), galangal (lengkuas) - a type of ginger, coconut milk (santan), chili and limes, palm sugar and rice flour.

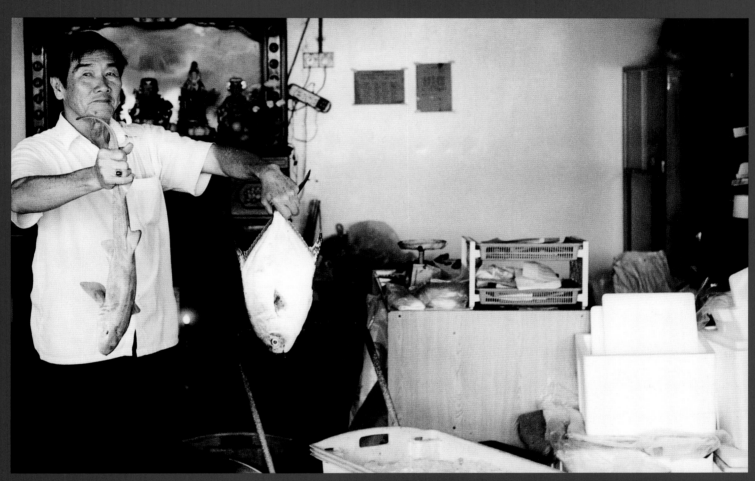

"Uncle Lim"

Hand Made Noodles
625g hand made noodles
90 g lean pork, shredded
185g Tientsin cabbage,
      coarsely shredded
1/2 tsd ginger, minced
1/2 tsd scallion, miniced
4 tbsp cooked oil

NYONYA ist eine in Südostasien äußerst beliebte Küche. Ihre Wurzeln reichen bis ins fünfzehnte Jahrhundert zurück, als Malakka sich zu einem der großen Handelszentren der Welt entwickelte. Viele Chinesen strömten seinerzeit in die Stadt, und Jahrhunderte später wiederholte sich Ähnliches zu Zeiten des Zinn-Booms in Malaysia. Chinesische Arbeiter, auf der Suche nach Reichtum und Arbeit, wanderten aus, ließen sich hier nieder und brachten natürlich ihre Essgewohnheiten und Speisen mit ins Land. In Ermangelung chinesischer Frauen heirateten sie malaiische. Die Kombination beider Kulturen führte zu einer eigenen, sich selbständig entwickelnden ethnischen Bevölkerungsgruppe, den Straits Chinesen (Meerenge, Straße von Malakka) oder auch „Peranakans". Und gleichfalls eigenständig ging daraus eine Küche hervor, die sich sowohl malaiischer wie chinesischer Elemente bediente und der man einfach den Namen jener verehrte, die sie entwickelt hatten, nämlich „Nyonya", was Frau oder Mutter heißt. Der Italiener würde dazu „Cucina della mamma" sagen. Typische Zutaten sind Zitronengrass (serai), Galanga (lengkuas), Kokosmilch (santan), Chili und Limetten, Palmzucker und Reismehl.

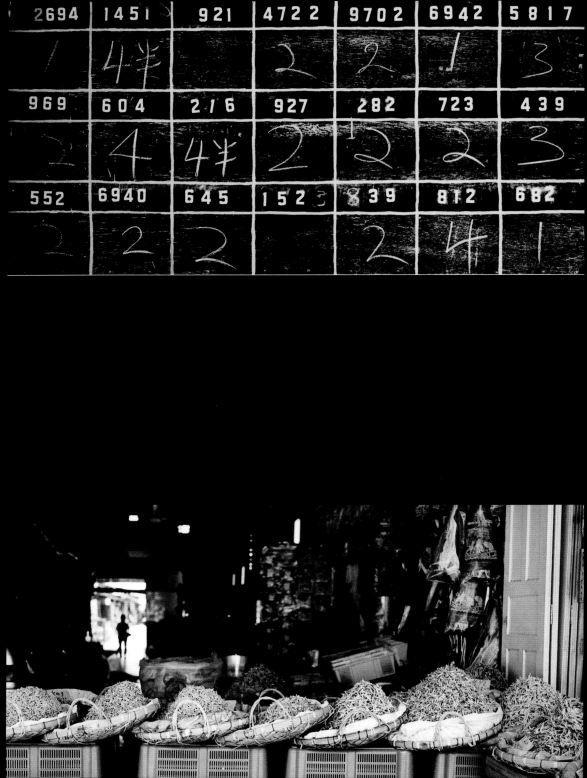

MALAY SAMPLER MENU

Serves 4 - 6

FRIED VEGETABLES
IN A COCONUT-TURMERIC SAUCE
(Sayur Lodeh, 1st dish from the left)

100 g/3 ¹/₂ oz green beans,
100 g/3 ¹/₂ oz cauliflower,
100 g/3 ¹/₂ oz broccoli,
100 g/3 ¹/₂ oz white cabbage,
100 g/3 ¹/₂ oz carrot,
2 tbsp vegetable oil,
¹/₂ onion, finely diced,
1 tbsp dried shrimp,
1 tbsp red chili pepper, finely minced,
2 tsp ground turmeric,
100 ml/¹/₃ cup coconut milk, salt

Cut all vegetables in not too small strips and blanch them separately in salted water. Allow to drain in a colander.
Heat the oil in a wok. Sauté onion until translucent, add dried shrimp and sauté without letting them take on color. Add vegetable strips, chili pepper, turmeric and mix well. Pour in the coconut milk and simmer, covered, for 6 - 8 minutes. Check for salt.

PRAWNS IN A SPICY SAUCE
(Sambal Prawn, 2nd dish from the left)

400 g/14 oz prawns, shells on,
2 red chili peppers (according to taste), 2 shallots, 1 garlic clove,
a small piece of ginger, 1 tbsp lemongrass, the tender core, diced,
2 tbsp vegetable oil,
1 tbsp shrimp paste,
100 ml/¹/₃ cup coconut milk,
1 tbsp tamarind juice, 1 tsp sugar, salt

Leave the prawn shells on or partially remove them, according to taste. Set aside. Coarsely chop chili peppers, shallots, garlic, ginger and lemongrass, then purée it in a blender with the oil. Heat in a dry pan until fragrances are released. Stir in shrimp paste and sauté for another minute. Add coconut milk and season with tamarind juice, sugar and salt. Place prawns into the paste and simmer on low heat for five minutes.

CHICKEN
IN A TOMATO-COCONUT CREAM
(Chicken Masak Merah, 3rd dish from the left)

400 g/14 oz chicken breast, boned, skin removed,
1 red chili pepper (according to taste), 1 shallot,
1 garlic clove, 1 tsp ginger, minced,
4 macadamia nuts, ¹/₂ onion, sliced thinly,
¹/₂ stalk lemongrass, the tender core only, finely diced,
1 tbsp tomato paste, 1 small tomato, chopped, 2 tbsp vegetable oil,
100 ml/¹/₃ cup coconut milk,
salt, pepper, sugar

Cut chicken breast into slices. Finely purée chili pepper, shallot, garlic and ginger in a blender. Chop the nuts and crush them into a paste in the mortar. Sauté onion, lemongrass, tomato paste and fresh tomatoes in hot oil. Add puréed vegetables and fry on low heat until their fragrance is released. Add macadamia nuts and chicken breast slices and mix well. Stir in coconut milk, cover and simmer for ten minutes. Season to taste with salt, pepper and sugar.

TENDER BEEF
IN AN AROMATIC COCONUT SAUCE
(Beef Rendang, 4th dish from the left)

400 g/14 oz tenderloin, 120 ml/¹/₂ cup coconut milk, salt, pepper

For the rendang beef paste:
1 shallot, minced, 1 tbsp finely grated ginger,
1 tbsp finely grated galangal (alternatively ground galangal),
1 stalk lemongrass, finely diced, 1 tbsp diced chili pepper,
3 tbsp vegetable oil, 1 small piece of cinnamon stick,
1 tsp fennel and cumin seeds, mixed, toasted in a dry pan until they start popping, 1 tsp curry powder,
3 tbsp grated coconut, tasted until golden brown, 2 kaffir lime leaves,
¹/₄ tsp turmeric, 15 g/1 tbsp palm sugar (alternatively brown sugar)

Cut the meat into thin slices and refrigerate. For the rendang beef paste: Purée shallot, ginger, galangal, lemongrass and chili pepper in a blender. In a small saucepan, heat oil and drop in cinnamon to release its fragrance. Keeping the pan on the burner, add toasted seeds and all other ingredients and stir to mix well. Remove cinnamon and kaffir lime leaves. Allow the mixture to cool and grind it into a fine paste in a mortar. Discard excess oil. Heat the rendang paste in a wok and thin it with a little water until you have a thick, syrupy consistency. When the mixture comes to a boil, stir in beef and cook until the meat is tender. Add coconut milk and check for salt and pepper.

FISH FILETS
IN A SPICY COCONUT CURRY
(Ikan Masak Lemak, 5th dish from the left)

400 g/14 oz red snapper filet,
2 tbsp red curry paste (according to taste),
2 tbsp vegetable oil,
20 g/³/₄ oz finely diced ginger blossoms (purple blossoms of the ginger plant, alternatively 1 tsp finely minced ginger),
1 tbsp finely chopped peppermint leaves (original recipe: daun kesum, Vietnamese mint, rau bac ha),
200 g/7 oz okra, 1 small tomato, coarsely chopped,
120 ml/¹/₂ cup coconut milk, salt, sugar

Cut the fish filets into bite-size pieces. Fry the curry paste in hot oil, add ginger, peppermint leaves, okra and tomato. Saute for a few minutes. Douse with coconut milk, mix well and simmer for five more minutes. Add fish pieces and simmer for another ten minutes. Check for salt and pepper.

YELLOW RICE
(Nasi Kunyit)

250 g/1 lb Siamese rice (long grain rice),
1 tbsp clarified butter,
1 tbsp butter,
1 shallot, finely diced,
30 g/1 oz fresh turmeric, finely grated (alternatively 1 tbsp ground turmeric),
1 tsp finely grated ginger,
1 yellow cardamom pod,
1 star anise,
1 small piece of cinnamon stick,
2 pandan leaves (spicy leaves of the screwpine which impart a light green color),
100 ml/¹/₃ cup milk,
500 ml/2 cups water

Wash the rice in several changes of cold water. Heat both kinds of butter in a heavy pan. Add shallots and spices and sauté until they release their fragrance. Stir in rice and cover with water and milk. Cook on low heat for 15 - 20 minutes, until done. Stir occasionally and add a little water if necessary. The rice can also be prepared in a rice steamer, if available.

MALAIISCHES DEGUSTATIONSMENÜ

Für 4 - 6 Personen:

GEBRATENES GEMÜSE
MIT KOKOS-KURKUMA-SAUCE
(Sayur Lodeh, 1. Schälchen von links)

100 g grüne Bohnen, 100 g Blumenkohl,
100 g Broccoli, 100 g Weißkohl, 100 g Karotte,
2 EL Planzenöl, 1/2 Zwiebel, fein gehackt,
1 EL getrocknete Garnelen,
1 EL fein geschnittene rote Chili,
2 TL Kurkumapulver,
100 ml Kokosmilch, Salz

Alle Gemüsesorten in nicht zu kleine Stücke schneiden und in Salzwasser blanchieren. Durch ein Sieb abgießen.
Das Öl im Wok erhitzen. Die gehackte Zwiebel anschwitzen, dann die getrockneten Garnelen unterrühren und braten, ohne Farbe nehmen zu lassen. Gemüse, Chili und Kurkuma zugeben, gut vermischen. Kokosmilch zugießen, zugedeckt 6 - 8 Minuten köcheln. Mit Salz abschmecken.

GARNELEN IN SCHARFER SAUCE
(Sambal Prawn, 2. Schälchen von links)

400 g Garnelen, mit Schale

2 rote Chilischoten (oder Menge nach Belieben),
2 Schalotten, 1 Knoblauchzehe, 1 kleines Stück Ingwer,
1 EL gehacktes Zitronengras, vom inneren zarten Teil,
2 EL Pflanzenöl, 1 EL Garnelenpaste, 100 ml Kokosmilch,
1 EL Tamarindensaft, 1 TL Zucker, Salz

Die Garnelen nach Belieben ganz belassen oder schälen. Beiseite stellen. Chili, Schalotten, Knoblauch, Ingwer und Zitronengras zuerst grob hacken, dann mit dem Öl im Mixer pürieren. In einer Pfanne langsam erhitzen, bis die Aromen frei gesetzt werden. Garnelenpaste unterrühren, eine Minute weiter garen. Kokosmilch zugeben, mit Tamarindensaft, Zucker und Salz abschmecken. Die Garnelen in dieser Mischung bei kleiner Hitze während fünf Minuten köcheln.

HÜHNCHEN
AN TOMATEN-KOKOSCREME
(Chicken Masak Merah, 3. Schälchen von links)

400 g Hühnerbrust, ohne Knochen, ohne Haut,
1 rote Chilischote (oder Menge nach Belieben),
1 Schalotte, 1 Knoblauchzehe,
1 TL gehackter Ingwer, 4 Macadamianüsse

1/2 Zwiebel, in feine Scheiben geschnitten,
1/2 Stängel Zitronengras, nur den inneren zarten Teil, fein gehackt,
1 EL Tomatenmark, 1 kleine Tomate, gehackt, 2 EL Pflanzenöl,
100 ml Kokosmilch, Salz, Pfeffer, Zucker

Hühnerfleisch in Scheiben schneiden. Chili mit Schalotte, Knoblauch und Ingwer im Mixer fein pürieren. Die Nüsse hacken, anschließend im Mörser zu einer Paste zerstoßen.
Zwiebel, Zitronengras, Tomatenmark und frische Tomaten im heißen Öl anschwitzen. Die pürierten Gewürze unterrühren und bei kleiner Hitze braten, bis die Aromen aufsteigen. Macadamianüsse und Hühnerfleisch zugeben, gut vermischen. Die Kokosmilch zugießen, zugedeckt zehn Minuten garen. Mit Salz, Pfeffer und Zucker abschmecken.

ZARTES RINDFLEISCH
IN DUFTENDER KOKOS-SAUCE
(Beef Rendang, 4. Schälchen von links)

400 g Rinderlende, 120 ml Kokosmilch, Salz, Pfeffer

Für die Rendang Beef Paste:
1 Schalotte, gehackt, 1 EL fein geriebener Ingwer,
1 EL fein geriebene Galangawurzel (ersatzweise Galangapulver verwenden),
1 Zitronengrasstängel, fein gehackt, 1 EL gehackte Chili,
3 EL Pflanzenöl, 1 kleines Stück Zimtstange,
1 TL Fenchel- und Kreuzkümmelsamen gemischt, in der Pfanne geröstet, bis sie zu rauchen beginnen,
1 TL Currypulver, 3 EL goldgelb geröstete Kokosraspel,
2 Kaffir-Limetten-Blätter, 1/4 TL Kurkuma,
15 g Palmzucker (ersatzweise braunen Zucker verwenden)

Das Fleisch in dünne Scheiben schneiden, kühl stellen. Für die Rendang Beef Paste: Schalotte, Ingwer, Galanga, Zitronengras und Chili im Mixer pürieren. In einem Topf mit Öl und Zimt erhitzen, bis die Mischung stark zu duften beginnt. Geröstete Samen und alle restlichen Zutaten nach und nach zugeben und auf dem Herd gut vermischen. Zimt und Limettenblätter entfernen. Die Masse erkalten lassen, im Mörser zu einer Paste zerstoßen, überflüssiges Öl weggießen.
Die Rendang Paste im Wok erhitzen, mit etwas Wasser zu einer dickflüssigen Konsistenz verdünnen. Wenn die Sauce kocht, das Rindfleisch unterrühren und kochen, bis das Fleisch gar ist. Zum Schluss die Kokosmilch unterrühren, mit Salz und Pfeffer abschmecken.

FISCHFILETS IN WÜRZIGEM
KOKOSNUSS-CURRY GEKOCHT
(Ikan Masak Lemak, 5. Schälchen von links)

400 g Red Snapper-Filet,
2 EL rote Currypaste (oder Menge nach Belieben), 2 EL Pflanzenöl,
20 g fein geschnittene Ingwerblüte (rosa-lila Blüte der Ingwerstaude, ersatzweise 1 TL fein gehackten Ingwer verwenden),
1 EL fein geschnittene Pfefferminzblätter (Originalrezept: Daun Kesum, vietnamesische Minze/Rau bac ha),
200 g Okra, 1 kleine Tomate, grob gehackt,
120 ml Kokosmilch, Salz, Zucker

Fischfilet in nicht zu kleine Stücke schneiden. Die Currypaste im Öl anbraten. Ingwer, Pfefferminzblätter, Okra und Tomate zugeben und mitbraten. Mit der Kokosmilch ablöschen, gut verrühren, ca. fünf Minuten köcheln. Die Fischstücke zugeben, zehn Minuten mitköcheln, zum Schluss das Gericht mit Salz und Zucker abschmecken.

GELBER REIS
(Nasi Kunyit)

250 g Siamesischer Reis (Langkornreis),
1 EL geklärte Butter, 1 EL Butter,
1 Schalotte, fein geschnitten,
30 g frisches Kurkuma, fein gerieben (ersatzweise 1 EL Kurkumapulver),
1 TL fein geriebener Ingwer, 1 gelbe Kardamomkapsel,
1 Sternanis, 1 kleines Stück Zimtstange,
2 Pandanusblätter (würzige, leicht grün färbende Blätter vom Schraubenbaum „Screwpine")
100 ml Milch, 500 ml Wasser

Den Reis in kaltem Wasser waschen, bis das Wasser klar bleibt. Beide Buttersorten erhitzen. Schalotten und Gewürze zugeben und anschwitzen, bis die Aromen aufsteigen. Den Reis unterrühren, dann mit Milch und Wasser auffüllen. Bei kleiner Hitze 15 - 20 Minuten garkochen, von Zeit zu Zeit umrühren, wenn nötig, mehr Wasser zufügen. Wenn vorhanden, kann der Reis im Reiskocher zubereitet werden.

INDIAN BREAD WITH A LENTIL DAL

INDISCHES BROT MIT LINSENCURRY

Serves 4

For the dal:
250 g/¹/₂ lb brown lentils,
2 tbsp vegetable oil,
1 carrot, finely diced,
1 onion, sliced,
1 tomato, chopped,
2 garlic cloves, crushed,
1 piece of cinnamon stick, about 2 cm/³/₄ inch,
1 tbsp red chili pepper, diced,
a pinch of dried chili pepper flakes,
2 tsp halba campur (spice mixture made of equal amounts
of mustard seeds, cumin, fenugreek and fennel seeds,
ground in a mortar),
250 g/¹/₂ lb eggplant, sliced

For the bread:
400 g/14 oz flour,
160 ml/²/₃ cup water,
1 egg,
1 tbsp soft butter,
1 tsp sugar,
¹/₂ tsp salt,
3 tbsp clarified butter

For the lentil dal: Soak the lentils in cold water for an hour. Heat the oil in a large saucepan and sauté carrot, onion, tomato, garlic and cinnamon. Add chili and halba campur and keep stirring for a little while. Add eggplant slices and lentils, sauté for a few minutes, then add water to cover. Bring to a boil and simmer for half an hour, uncovered, until lentils are tender.

For the bread: Combine water, egg, butter, salt and sugar in a large bowl and mix well. Add flour, a little at a time, and knead the mixture into a smooth, elastic dough. Cover with a moist cloth and allow to rest for at least one hour. Shape the dough into small balls and place them on a tray. Brush them with clarified butter, cover and allow to rest for another half hour.

Pressing down with the palm of your hand, flatten out the balls, pulling the dough apart with your fingers as much as possible to make thin flatbreads. (Indian bakers whirl the dough sheets in the air with their outstretched arms until the flatbread is very thin.)

Heat a large pan until hot. Place a flatbread into the pan and keep shaking the pan to prevent it from sticking to the bottom. Fry until golden brown, turn and bake it on the other side. Repeat the procedure until the dough is used up and serve the flatbreads still warm with the lentil curry.

Für 4 Personen:

Für das Linsencurry:
250 g braune Linsen,
2 EL Pflanzenöl,
1 Karotte, in kleine Würfel geschnitten,
1 Zwiebel, in Scheiben geschnitten,
1 Tomate, gehackt,
2 Knoblauchzehen, zerdrückt,
1 Stück Zimtstange, ca. 2 cm,
1 EL gehackte rote Chili,
1 Prise getrocknete Chiliflocken,
2 TL Halba Campur (Gewürzmischung aus Senfsamen,
Kreuzkümmel, Bockshornklee und Fenchelsamen,
zu gleichen Teilen, im Mörser zerstampft),
250 g Aubergine, in Scheiben geschnitten

Für das Brot:
400 g Mehl,
160 ml Wasser,
1 Ei,
1 EL weiche Butter,
1 TL Zucker,
¹/₂ TL Salz,
3 EL geklärte Butter

Für das Linsencurry: Die Linsen eine Stunde in kaltem Wasser einweichen. In einem Topf das Öl erhitzen. Karotte, Zwiebel, Tomate, Knoblauch und Zimt anschwitzen. Chili und Halba Campur zugeben und unter Rühren anbraten. Auberginenscheiben und Linsen zugeben, kurz mitbraten, dann mit Wasser auffüllen, bis die Linsen bedeckt sind. Zum Kochen bringen, eine halbe Stunde ohne Deckel köcheln, bis die Linsen weich sind.

Für das Brot: Das Wasser mit dem Ei, Butter, Salz und Zucker in einer Schüssel verrühren. Das Mehl nach und nach zugeben und zu einem weichen, elastischen Teig kneten. Mit einem feuchten Tuch zugedeckt eine Stunde ruhen lassen. Aus dem Teig kleine Kugeln formen und auf eine Platte legen. Mit der geklärten Butter bepinseln und zugedeckt eine halbe Stunde ruhen lassen. Die Teigkugeln auf der Arbeitsfläche zu Fladen formen und flachdrücken. Mit den Fingern so dünn wie möglich auseinanderziehen (indische Brotbäcker wirbeln den Teig über der Faust in der Luft, bis der Teig hauchdünn ist).

Eine große Pfanne heiß werden lassen. Die Teigblätter hineinlegen, die Pfanne immer wieder schütteln, den Teig goldbraun backen, umdrehen und auf der zweiten Seite fertig backen. Sofort mit dem Linsencurry servieren.

Serves 8

Basic spice paste (needed for all dishes):
100 g/3 1/2 oz ginger, 100 g/3 1/2 oz garlic,
100 g/3 1/2 oz shallot, minced,
100 ml/1/3 cup vegetable oil, 2 tbsp halba campur (see page 471),
100 g/3 1/2 oz mango, finely diced,
100 g/3 1/2 oz tomato, finely diced,
zest of one lime, 1 tbsp fennel seeds, 1 tbsp ground cumin

For the lamb curry:
500 g/1 lb lamb, from the leg, well-trimmed, 2 tsp curry powder,
1 tsp dried chili pepper flakes (according to taste),
300 ml/1 1/3 cups water, 2 tbsp ketchup, salt, pepper

For the shrimp curry:
400 g/14 oz shrimp, 2 tsp curry powder,
4 finely chopped curry leaves (Indian supermarket, fresh or dried),
200 ml/3/4 cup water, 60 ml/1/4 cup yoghurt, salt, white pepper

For the chicken curry:
500 g/1 lb chicken breast, bone and skin removed, 2 tsp curry powder,
4 curry leaves, finely chopped (Indian supermarket, fresh or dried),
250 ml/1 cup water, 200 g/7 oz potatoes, cut into small cubes,
1 tomato, finely diced, 100 ml/1/3 cup coconut milk, salt, white pepper

For the vegetables:
300 g/11 oz green beans, 300 g/11 oz white cabbage,
300 g/11 oz okra, 1 tbsp halba campur (see page 471),
200 ml/3/4 cup water, salt, pepper, 100 ml/1/3 cup coconut milk

For the basic spice paste: Mince ginger and garlic and grind them into a fine paste in a mortar. In a small frying pan, sauté paste in oil, add shallot and halba campur and keep stirring until the spices have released their fragrance. Stir in mango and tomato cubes as well as lime zest and sauté a little longer. Add fennel seeds and ground cumin. When the spice mixture has become very fragrant, remove from heat and scrape it into a small bowl. Reserve.

Lamb curry: Cut the lamb into slices. Heat two spoonfuls of basic spice paste in a frying pan. Add curry powder and chili pepper, douse with water and stir in ketchup. Check for salt and pepper. Add lamb slices, cover and simmer for about one hour on low heat, until tender.

Shrimp curry: Heat two spoonfuls of basic spice paste. Add curry powder and finely chopped curry leaves, stir in yoghurt and check for salt and pepper. Add shrimp, cover and simmer on low heat for ten minutes. Set aside.

Chicken curry: Cut the chicken breast into slices. Heat two spoonfuls of basic spice paste. Add curry powder and finely chopped curry leaves, douse with water and mix in the chicken breast slices. Season with salt and pepper. Cover and simmer on low heat for five minutes. Add potato and tomato cubes, cover and simmer for another ten minutes. Uncover and stir in coconut milk. Allow the sauce to reduce a little. Check for salt and pepper.

Vegetables: Cut the beans, white cabbage and okra into small pieces. Heat two spoonfuls of basic spice paste in a large saucepan. Add vegetables and sauté for a few minutes. Sprinkle with halba campur, add water and check for salt and pepper. Cover and simmer for about five minutes. The vegetables should still be firm to the bite. Stir in coconut milk, bring to a boil once and set aside.

Für 8 Personen:

Grund-Gewürzpaste (wird für alle Gerichte benötigt):
100 g Ingwer, 100 g Knoblauch,
100 g Schalotte, fein gehackt,
100 ml Pflanzenöl, 2 EL Halba Campur (siehe Seite 471)
100 g Mango, fein gewürfelt, 100 g Tomate, fein gewürfelt,
dünn abgeriebene Schale einer Limette, 1 EL Fenchelsamen,
1 EL Kreuzkümmelpulver

Für das Lammcurry:
500 g Lammfleisch aus der Keule, sauber pariert, 2 TL Currypulver,
1 TL getrocknete Chiliflocken (oder nach Belieben),
300 ml Wasser, 2 EL Ketchup, Salz, Pfeffer

Für das Garnelencurry:
400 g Garnelen, 2 TL Currypulver,
4 fein geschnittene Curryblätter (indisches Feinkostgeschäft, frisch oder getrocknet), 200 ml Wasser, 60 ml Joghurt, Salz, weißer Pfeffer

Für das Hühnercurry:
500 g Hühnerbrust, ohne Knochen, ohne Haut, 2 TL Currypulver,
4 fein geschnittene Curryblätter (indisches Feinkostgeschäft, frisch oder getrocknet), 250 ml Wasser, 200 g Kartoffeln, in Würfel geschnitten,
1 Tomate, fein gewürfelt, 100 ml Kokosmilch, Salz, weißer Pfeffer

Für das Gemüse:
300 g grüne Bohnen, 300 g Weißkohl, 300 g Okra,
1 EL Halba Campur (siehe Seite 471),
200 ml Wasser, Salz, Pfeffer, 100 ml Kokosmilch

Für die Grund-Gewürzpaste: Ingwer und Knoblauch hacken, im Mörser zu einer Paste verstampfen. Diese Paste in einer Pfanne mit Öl bei kleiner Hitze anschwitzen, Schalotten und Halba Campur zugeben, unter Rühren braten, bis die Aromen aufsteigen. Mango- und Tomatenwürfel sowie geriebene Limettenschale unterrühren und mitkochen. Zum Schluss mit Fenchelsamen und Kreuzkümmelpulver vermischen. Wenn die Gewürzmischung kräftig duftet, in ein Schüsselchen umfüllen und erkalten lassen.

Für das Lammcurry: Fleisch in Scheiben schneiden. Zwei Löffel Grund-Gewürzpaste in einer Pfanne erhitzen. Currypulver und Chili zugeben, mit Wasser ablöschen, Ketchup unterrühren, mit Salz und Pfeffer abschmecken. Das Lammfleisch unterrühren und zugedeckt ca. 1 Stunde bei kleiner Hitze garen.

Für das Garnelencurry: Zwei Löffel Grund-Gewürzpaste in einer Pfanne erhitzen. Currypulver und fein geschnittene Curryblätter zugeben, mit Wasser ablöschen, Joghurt unterrühren, mit Salz und Pfeffer abschmecken. Garnelen zugeben, 10 Minuten köcheln.

Für das Hühnercurry: Fleisch in Scheiben schneiden. Zwei Löffel Grund-Gewürzpaste in einer Pfanne erhitzen. Currypulver, fein geschnittene Curryblätter und Hühnerfleisch zugeben, mit Wasser ablöschen, mit Salz und Pfeffer würzen. Zugedeckt 5 Minuten köcheln. Die Kartoffel- und Tomatenwürfel 10 Minuten mitgaren, dann die Kokosmilch unterrühren, die Sauce etwas einkochen.

Für das Gemüse: Zwei Löffel Grund-Gewürzpaste in einem Topf erhitzen. Das klein geschnittene Gemüse zugeben, unter Rühren etwas anschwitzen. Halba Campur und Wasser zufügen, mit Salz und Pfeffer würzen. Einige Minuten garen, das Gemüse soll noch Biss haben. Zum Schluss die Kokosmilch unterrühren und einmal aufkochen lassen.

BANANA LEAF CURRY

BANANENBLATT CURRY

Serving suggestion: Arrange curries and rice on large banana leaves instead of serving dishes and plates, and serve with papadums (lentil wafers), mango chutney and white rice (Basmati). In Malaysia, the curries are often eaten with one's fingers and the help of the papadums.

Serviervorschlag: Currygerichte statt in Schalen und Tellern auf großen Bananenblättern anrichten und mit Papadams (indisches Brot aus Linsenmehl), Mangochutney und Basmatireis servieren. In Malaysia wird dieses Gericht aus der Hand und mit Hilfe der Papadams gegessen.

Halba Campur:
Spice mixture made from equal parts of mustard seeds, cumin, fenugreek and fennel seeds, ground in a mortar.
Gewürzmischung aus Senfsamen, Kreuzkümmel, Bockshornklee und Fenchelsamen, zu gleichen Teilen, im Mörser zerstampft.

MALAYSIAN HIGH TEA

*In the afternoon, it's tea time in Malaysia
– not unlike in England.
Malaysian tea is strong and black and
mixed with sweetened condensed milk.
It is poured into the glasses from high above
to make it foam and often served with
small appetizers, sweet, savory or salty.*

*Nachmittags wird in Malaysien – wie in
England – gerne Tee getrunken. Es ist ein
starker Schwarztee, mit süßer Kondensmilch vermischt und mit einigem
Abstand ins Glas gegossen, so dass er
aufschäumt. Dazu werden kleine
Appetithäppchen, süß und salzig, gereicht.*

PASTRY SHELLS FILLED WITH SHRIMP

Serves 4

For the pastry shells:
1 egg, 220 ml/1 cup water, salt, 120 g/4 oz flour, oil for deep-frying

For the filling:
100 g/3 1/2 oz bamboo shoots (can), cut into julienne strips,
1 navet, cut into julienne strips, 2 tbsp vegetable oil,
140 g/5 oz small shrimp, shelled and deveined,
1 tsp bean paste, 1 tsp garlic, minced, 1/2 tsp sugar, salt,
1 tbsp chopped roasted onions

For the pastry shells: Mix egg, water and salt. Add flour and work the mixture into a thick batter. Heat the oil in a deep-fryer. Allow small metal molds with a crimped edge to get hot in the oil, about two minutes. Remove them with a pair of tongs. Coat the outside of the molds with batter and return them to the oil. Fry until the batter is golden brown and starts coming off the molds by itself. Remove the batter shells from the oil and drain on paper towels. For the filling: Sauté the vegetable julienne in the wok in hot oil. Add shrimp and spices and stir-fry until the vegetables are tender. Allow to cool. Serving: Arrange the filling in the pastry shells and sprinkle with roasted onions.

STUFFED STICKY RICE
WITH COCONUT IN A BANANA LEAF

Serves 4

250 g/1/2 lb freshly grated coconut, 250 g/1/2 lb glutinous rice

4 tbsp grated coconut, 2 tbsp corn oil,
2 tbsp dried shrimp, 1 tbsp minced shallot, 2 macadamia nuts,
1 stalk lemongrass, core only, minced,
2 tbsp corn oil, 1 tsp sugar,
1/2 tsp pepper, 1 tsp ground coriander,
1 tsp cornstarch, mixed with a little water and soy sauce,
12 boats made from banana leaves

Squeeze fresh coconut in a cloth until you have about 100 ml/ 1/3 cup of juice. Reserve virgin milk. Mix the coconut pulp with 100 ml/1/3 cup water and squeeze it out once more, reserving milk. Wash the rice and steam it for twenty minutes in a rice steamer. Mix with the second batch of coconut milk, allow to rest for a few minutes and steam for five minutes more. Mix with virgin coconut milk, allow to rest for a few minutes and steam for another five minutes. Turn off heat, cover the rice with a moist cloth.
For the filling: Heat corn oil in a wok and fry the dried coconut on low heat until it starts browning. Add shrimp and stir-fry for about ten minutes. Remove from wok and set aside. Stir-fry shallot, macadamia nuts and lemongrass in oil on low heat. Add sugar, pepper and coriander and stir-fry for a few minutes more. Add the fried coconut-shrimp mixture and thicken with cornstarch mixture. Correct seasonings and allow to cool to room temperature.
Serving: Arrange rice with your hands in the banana boats. Make a little well on the surface of each rice portion and place stuffing into the wells. Grill banana leaves under the broiler until golden brown.

GEBÄCKKÖRBCHEN MIT GARNELEN

Für 4 Personen:

Für die Gebäckkörbchen:
1 Ei, 220 ml Wasser, Salz, 120 g Mehl, Öl zum Frittieren

Für die Füllung:
100 g Bambussprossen (Dose), in dünne Streifen geschnitten,
1 Mairübchen, geschält, in dünne Streifen geschnitten,
2 EL Pflanzenöl, 150 g kleine Garnelen, geschält, Darm entfernt,
1 TL fermentierte Sojabohnenpaste, 1 TL fein gehackter Knoblauch,
1/2 TL Zucker, Salz, 1 EL geröstete Zwiebeln, gehackt

Für die Gebäckkörbchen: Ei mit Wasser und Salz verrühren. Das Mehl zugeben und zu einem dickflüssigen Teig verarbeiten. Öl in der Fritteuse erhitzen. Kleine Metallförmchen mit gewelltem Rand im heißen Öl zwei Minuten erhitzen. Mit einer Zange herausnehmen, die äußere Seite mit Teig überziehen und erneut ins Frittieröl tauchen. Goldbraun ausbacken, bis sich der Teig von alleine von den Förmchen trennt. Aus dem Öl nehmen, auf Küchenpapier gut abtropfen lassen. Für die Füllung: Gemüsestreifen im Öl im Wok anschwitzen. Garnelen und Gewürze zugeben, unter Rühren braten, bis alles gar ist. Erkalten lassen. Zum Servieren: Gebäckkörbchen mit der Füllung füllen, mit gerösteten Zwiebeln bestreuen.

GEFÜLLTER KLEBREIS
MIT KOKOS IM BANANENBLATT

Für 4 Personen:

250 g geriebene frische Kokosnuss, 250 g Klebreis

4 EL geriebene, getrocknete Kokosnuss, 2 EL Maiskeimöl,
2 EL getrocknete Garnelen, 1 EL sehr fein gewürfelte Schalotte,
2 im Mörser verstampfte Macadamianüsse,
1 Zitronengrasstängel, nur das Herz, sehr fein gehackt,
2 EL Maiskeimöl, 1 TL Zucker, 1/2 TL Pfeffer, 1 TL Korianderpulver,
1 TL Maisstärke, mit etwas Wasser und Sojasauce angerührt,
12 aus Bananenblättern zugeschnittene Schiffchen

Die geriebene Kokosnuss auspressen, bis ca. 100 ml Saft gewonnen wird. Diese erste (dicke) Milch aufheben. Den Brei mit 100 ml Wasser vermischen, erneut auspressen. Den Reis waschen, im Reiskocher 20 Minuten garen. Mit der zweiten (dünnen) Kokosmilch vermischen, 5 Minuten stehen lassen, dann weitere 5 Minuten dämpfen. Mit der ersten Kokosmilch vermischen, etwas stehen lassen, dann nochmals 5 Minuten dämpfen.
Für die Füllung: Getrocknete Kokosnuss bei kleiner Hitze im Wok im Maiskeimöl braten, bis sie beginnt, Farbe anzunehmen. Garnelen zugeben, unter Rühren ca. 10 Minuten braten. Aus dem Wok nehmen, erkalten lassen. Schalotte, Nüsse und Zitronengras im Öl bei kleiner Hitze anschwitzen. Zucker, Pfeffer und Koriander zugeben und kurz mitdünsten. Die gebratene Kokosraspel-Garnelenmischung unterrühren, mit der angerührten Maisstärke gut vermischen. Die Füllung abschmecken und erkalten lassen.
Zum Servieren: Reis von Hand in länglicher Form in die Bananenblätter füllen, mit dem Finger eine Vertiefung hineindrücken und mit der Füllung bedecken. Unter dem Grill goldgelb überbacken.

COCONUT-STUFFED RICE CUBES

REISWÜRFEL MIT KOKOSFÜLLUNG

Serves 4

200 g/7 oz grated fresh coconut, 200 g/7 oz glutinous rice, 2 tsp sugar, a pinch of salt

For the filling:
60 g /2 oz palm sugar (alternatively brown cane sugar),
100 g/3 ¹/² oz dried grated coconut, 2 pandan leaves (leaves of the screwpine)

Squeeze out the fresh coconut in a cloth until you have about 80 ml/¹/₄ cup of juice. Set virgin milk aside. Mix the pulp with 120 ml/¹/₂ cup water and squeeze it out again, reserving milk.
Soak the rice overnight. Drain well and steam in a rice steamer for twenty minutes. Mix with the second batch of coconut milk, allow to rest for five minutes and steam for another seven minutes. Mix virgin milk with sugar and salt, then fold it into the rice. Allow to rest for a little while, then steam the rice for another five minutes. Turn off heat, cover the rice with a moist cloth and allow to rest. If you do not have a rice steamer: Place washed rice in a heavy-bottomed saucepan and cover one finger deep with water. Bring to a boil, turn off the heat and allow the rice to rest, covered and undisturbed, for twenty minutes. Proceed as described above, bringing the rice to a boil each time and allowing it to rest again. Be careful not to burn it. When the rice is at room temperature, shape it into cubes with the help of baking paper cut into strips. Allow to cool.
For the filling: In a small saucepan, melt the palm sugar on low heat. Add pandan leaves and grated coconut and simmer, stirring constantly, until well mixed and fragrant. Remove from heat and allow to cool.
Serving: Unwrap rice cubes and arrange them on plates. Top with a small heap of filling. Note: The rice may be colored with a bit of blue food coloring if desired.

Für 4 Personen:

200 g frische, geriebene Kokosnuss, 200 g Klebreis, 2 TL Zucker, 1 Prise Salz

Für die Füllung:
60 g Palmzucker (Ersatz: brauner Rohr-Rohzucker), 100 g Kokosraspel, getrocknet,
2 Pandanusblätter, fein geschnitten (Blätter vom Schraubenbaum, Screwpine)

Die geriebene Kokosnuss in einem Tuch auspressen, bis ca. 80 ml Saft gewonnen wird. Diese „erste Milch" aufheben. Dann den Brei mit 120 ml Wasser vermischen und erneut auspressen. Den Reis über Nacht in Wasser quellen lassen. Abtropfen lassen, im Reiskocher 20 Minuten garen. Mit der zweiten Kokosmilch vermischen, 5 Minuten stehen lassen, dann weitere 7 Minuten dämpfen. Die erste Kokosmilch mit Zucker und Salz verrühren, unter den Reis mischen, etwas stehen lassen, dann nochmals 5 Minuten im Reiskocher dämpfen. Die Hitzezufuhr abstellen, den Reis mit einem feuchten Tuch bedeckt stehen lassen. Falls kein Reiskocher vorhanden ist: In einem Topf mit dickem Boden den gewaschenen Reis ein fingerbreit mit Wasser bedeckt, zum Kochen bringen. Den Deckel auf dem Topf lassen, die Hitzezufuhr abstellen, den Reis 20 Minuten, ohne den Deckel zu heben, garen. Anschließend wie beschrieben vorgehen, jeweils nur kurz erhitzen und stehen lassen. Aufpassen, dass der Reis nicht anbrennt. Den lauwarm abgekühlten Reis mit Hilfe von zugeschnittenem Backtrennpapier in Würfelform bringen und auskühlen lassen.
Für die Füllung: Den Palmzucker bei kleiner Hitze in einem Topf schmelzen. Pandanblätter und Kokosraspel zugeben und unter Rühren köcheln, bis das Ganze gut vermischt ist und stark duftet. Vom Herd nehmen, erkalten lassen.
Zum Servieren: Die Reiswürfel auspacken und auf Teller verteilen. Mit je einem kleinen Häufchen von der Füllung belegen. Anmerkung: Nach Belieben den Reis beim Kochen mit etwas blauer Lebensmittelfarbe einfärben.

SWEET COCONUT AND RICE PUDDING BALLS

SÜSSE KOKOS-REISPUDDING-KUGELN

Serves 4 - 6

20 g/³/₄ oz pandan leaves (leaves of screwpine),
green food coloring,
50 g/1 ¹/₂ oz cornstarch,
300 g/11 oz glutinous rice flour,
120 g/4 oz palm sugar,
1 tsp sugar,
200 g/7 oz dried grated coconut

Grind the pandan leaves in a mortar until you have a paste. Mix with 220 ml/ 1 cup of water and add a few drops of green food coloring. Strain the liquid through a sieve. Mix cornstarch and 90 ml/¹/₃ cup water in a small pot. Bring to a boil and simmer until the mixture has become transparent. Put the flour into a large bowl and mix with the green water and the cornstarch mixture. Work everything into a smooth dough. Cover with a moist cloth and allow to rest for half an hour.
Grate the palm sugar finely and mix it with the ordinary sugar. Set aside. In a large pot, bring water to a boil. Divide the glutinous rice flour dough into portions, shape them into walnut-sized balls and fill them with a little palm sugar. Simmer in batches in boiling water until they rise to the surface. Simmer for two more minutes, remove and place them on a cloth. Dry and turn them in grated coconut. Serve.

Für 4 - 6 Personen:

20 g Pandanusblätter (Blätter vom Schraubenbaum, Screwpine),
grüne Lebensmittelfarbe,
50 g Maisstärke,
300 g Klebreismehl,
120 g Palmzucker,
1 TL Zucker,
200 g getrocknete Kokosraspel

Die Pandanblätter im Mörser zu Brei zerstoßen. Mit 220 ml Wasser verrühren, ein paar Tropfen grüne Lebensmittelfarbe zugeben, die Flüssigkeit durch ein Sieb passieren. Die Maisstärke in einem kleinen Topf mit 90 ml Wasser verrühren. Zum Kochen bringen, bis die Masse transparent wird. Das Mehl in eine Schüssel geben, mit der Maisstärke und dem grünen Wasser vermischen und zu einem Teig kneten. Mit einem feuchten Tuch bedeckt eine halbe Stunde ruhen lassen. Den Palmzucker reiben und mit Zucker vermischen, beiseite legen.
In einem Topf Wasser zum Kochen bringen. Aus dem Klebreisteig Portionen teilen, mit etwas Palmzucker füllen und zu walnussgroßen Kugeln formen. Nach und nach im kochenden Wasser sieden, bis sie oben schwimmen. Nach weiteren zwei Minuten die Kugeln auf einem Tuch abtrocknen, anschließend in den Kokosraspel wälzen.

LENTIL CAKES

12 cakes

80 g/2 1/2 oz lentils,
200 g/7 oz lentil flour,
1 tbsp each green and red chili pepper, chopped (according to taste),
2 tbsp finely diced onion,
1 tbsp coriander leaves, chopped,
1 tsp halba campur (spice mixture made from equal parts of mustard
seeds, cumin, fenugreek and fennel seeds, ground in a mortar),
salt, pepper, oil for frying

Soak the lentils overnight in cold water. Drain them in a sieve and allow excess water to drip off. In a large bowl, coarsely mash the lentils with a potato ricer. Add the remaining ingredients and mix well. Add as much water as you need to make a firm dough. Season with salt and pepper. Divide the dough into twelve equal portions, shape them into balls and flatten the balls into cakes with your palm. Fry the cakes in hot oil until golden brown.

FRESH SPRING ROLLS

Serves 4

For the batter:
200 g/7 oz flour, 1/2 tsp salt,
3 tbsp cornstarch, 6 eggs,
400 ml/1 2/3 cup water,
1 tbsp corn oil, 2 tbsp oil for frying

For the filling:
2 garlic cloves, minced, 2 tbsp bean paste, 2 tbsp oil for frying,
2 tsp sugar, salt, 1 navet, peeled and cut into strips,
150 g/5 oz bamboo shoots, cut into thin strips,
50 g/1 1/2 oz tofu, chopped,
100 ml/1/3 cup chicken stock,
120 g/4 oz shrimp, shelled and deveined, coarsely chopped,
salt, white pepper,
60 g/2 oz red pepper, cut into julienne strips,
1 hard-boiled egg, chopped, 1 tbsp coriander leaves

For the batter: Sieve flour and starch into a bowl. Beat eggs, water and oil until well mixed. Add egg mixture to the flour and work everything into a smooth batter. Pass through a sieve and allow to rest for half an hour. Heat a small amount of oil in a non-stick pan, ladle a small portion of batter into the oil and tilt the pan to achieve a thin crêpe-like pancake. Turn and fry on both sides until golden brown. Repeat until batter is used up.
For the filling: Sauté garlic and bean paste in oil. Add salt and sugar, then tofu cubes and vegetable strips and sauté for a few minutes. Douse with chicken stock, add shrimp and simmer, uncovered, for about ten minutes. Correct seasonings.
Finish: Lay out pancakes on a working surface and spoon some filling on top. Sprinkle with the pepper strips, chopped egg and coriander leaves. Roll up pancakes into little rolls. Serve warm or cold, according to taste.

LINSENKÜCHLEIN

Für 12 Kuchen:

80 g Linsen,
200 g Linsenmehl,
je 1 EL gehackte grüne und rote Chili (oder Menge nach Belieben),
2 EL fein gehackte Zwiebel,
1 EL Koriandergrün, gehackt,
1 TL Halba Campur (Gewürzmischung aus Senfsamen,
Kreuzkümmel, Bockshornklee und Fenchelsamen, zu gleichen Teilen,
im Mörser zerstampft), Salz, Pfeffer, Öl zum Frittieren

Die Linsen über Nacht in kaltem Wasser einweichen. Durch ein Sieb abgießen, gut abtropfen lassen. Die Linsen mit einem Kartoffelstampfer in einer Schüssel grob verstampfen. Restliche Zutaten zugeben, gut vermischen und soviel Wasser zugeben, bis ein fester Teig entsteht. Mit Salz und Pfeffer würzen. Den Teig in zwölf Portionen teilen, daraus jeweils eine Kugel formen und flachdrücken. Die Kuchen im heißen Öl goldbraun ausbacken.

FRISCHE FRÜHLINGSROLLEN

Für 4 Personen:

Für den Teig:
200 g Mehl, 1/2 TL Salz,
3 EL Maisstärke, 6 Eier,
400 ml Wasser,
1 EL Maiskeimöl, 2 EL Öl zum Braten

Für die Füllung:
2 Knoblauchzehen, fein gehackt, 2 EL fermentierte Sojabohnenpaste,
2 EL Öl zum Braten, 2 TL Zucker, Salz,
1 Mairübchen, geschält, in Streifen geschnitten,
150 g Bambusschössling, in dünne Streifen geschnitten,
50 g Tofu, gehackt, 100 ml Hühnerbrühe,
120 g Garnelen, geschält, Darm entfernt, das Fleisch grob gehackt,
Salz, weißer Pfeffer,
60 g rote Paprika, in dünne Streifen geschnitten,
1 hart gekochtes Ei, gehackt, 1 EL Korianderblättchen

Für den Teig: Mehl und Stärke in eine Schüssel sieben. Eier mit dem Wasser und dem Öl gut verrühren. Zum Mehl gießen, nach und nach zu einem Teig verrühren. Durch ein Sieb passieren, eine halbe Stunde stehen lassen. Etwas Öl in einer beschichteten Pfanne erhitzen. Mit einer Kelle eine kleine Portion Teig zugeben, möglichst dünn schwenken und die Pfannkuchen von beiden Seiten goldbraun backen.
Für die Füllung: Knoblauch und Sojabohnenpaste im Öl anschwitzen. Gemüse, Tofu, Zucker und Salz untermischen und anbraten. Mit Hühnerbrühe ablöschen, Garnelen zugeben, ohne Deckel unter Rühren 10 Minuten garen. Abschmecken.
Fertigstellung: Die Pfannkuchen auf der Arbeitfläche flach auslegen. Die Füllung darüber verteilen, mit Paprikastreifen, gehacktem Ei und Korianderblättchen bestreuen. Die Pfannkuchen aufrollen. Nach Belieben kalt oder warm servieren.

SWEET SPRING ROLLS WITH MANGO

SÜSSE FRÜHLINGSROLLEN MIT MANGO

Serves 4

400 g/14 oz mango,
8 spring roll wrappers (Asian supermarket),
40 g/1 ¹/₂ oz flour,
oil for deep-frying,
200 g/11 oz vanilla ice cream

For the fruit sauces:
120 g/4 oz raspberries,
120 g/4 oz mango, peeled,
2 tbsp confectioners' sugar

Halve the mango, remove the seed and carefully peel the halves. Cut the pulp into eight longish pieces of equal size. Mix the flour with a little water into a thick paste. Wrap each mango piece into a wonton wrapper and seal the wrapper with flour paste.
For the fruit sauces: Purée the raspberries and the mango separately in a blender, adding a teaspoon of confectioners' sugar to each purée. Strain the purées through a fine sieve.
Finish: Heat the oil in a deep-fryer. Deep-fry the mango spring rolls until golden brown. Serve hot, garnish the plates with fruit sauces and a scoop of vanilla ice cream.

Für 4 Personen:

400 g Mango,
8 Frühlingsrollen-Teigblätter (fertig erhältlich),
40 g Mehl,
Öl zum Frittieren,
200 ml Vanilleeis

Für die Fruchtsaucen:
120 g Himbeeren,
120 g Mango, geschält,
2 EL Puderzucker

Mango halbieren, Kern entfernen und die Frucht vorsichtig schälen. Das Fleisch in acht gleichmäßige längliche Stücke schneiden. Mehl mit etwas Wasser zu einer dicken Paste anrühren. Die Mangostücke in je ein Frühlingsrollen-Teigblatt wickeln, dieses mit Mehlpaste verschließen.
Für die Fruchtsaucen: Himbeeren und Mango getrennt mit je einem Löffel Puderzucker im Mixer pürieren, anschließend durch ein Sieb passieren.
Fertigstellung: Das Öl in der Fritteuse erhitzen. Die Mangorollen schwimmend goldbraun ausbacken. Heiß servieren, mit den Fruchtsaucen garniert und je einer Kugel Vanilleeis als Beilage.

YOUNG COCONUT WITH SAGO AND EXOTIC FRUITS

JUNGE KOKOSNUSS MIT SAGO UND EXOTISCHEN FRÜCHTEN

Serves 4

For the coconut ice cream:
400 ml/1 ²⁄₃ cups coconut cream,
80 g/2 ¹⁄₂ oz sugar,
a pinch of salt

2 young coconuts (the shell is still thin
and the pulp very soft),
halved, reserve juice for other uses,
60 g/2 oz sago,
500 g/1 lb exotic fruit such as mango,
papaya, honeydew melon and palm seed (can)

For the coconut ice cream: Combine coconut cream, sugar and salt and bring to a boil, stirring constantly. Allow to cool and freeze in the deep freezer.
Cook the sago in water until translucent, drain it in a sieve and rinse it with cold water until cool. Allow excess water to drip off. Cut all fruits into bite-size pieces.
Serving: Half an hour before serving, remove the ice cream from the freezer. Place the fruit pieces and the sago into the coconut halves. Top with scoops of ice cream. Serve.

Für 4 Personen:

Kokos-Eis:
400 ml Kokoscreme,
80 g Zucker,
1 Prise Salz

2 junge Kokosnüsse (die Schale ist noch dünn,
das Fleisch ist noch weich), halbiert, das Kokoswasser
für eine andere Verwendung aufheben,
60 g Sago,
500 g exotische Früchte, z. B. Mango, Papaya,
Honigmelone und Palmensamen (in Dosen erhältlich)

Für das Kokos-Eis: Kokoscreme mit Zucker und der Prise Salz unter Rühren zum Kochen bringen. Erkalten lassen, im Gefrierfach gefrieren.
Die Sagoperlen in Wasser glasig kochen, durch ein Sieb abgießen und mit kaltem Wasser spülen, bis sie ganz kalt sind. Gut abtropfen lassen. Die exotischen Früchte in kleine Würfel schneiden.
Zum Servieren: Das Eis eine halbe Stunde vor dem Servieren leicht antauen lassen. Früchtewürfel und Sago in die Kokoshälften füllen. Von dem Kokos-Eis Portionen abstechen und über die Früchte geben.

Golden Club Class

We Fly The World

malaysia

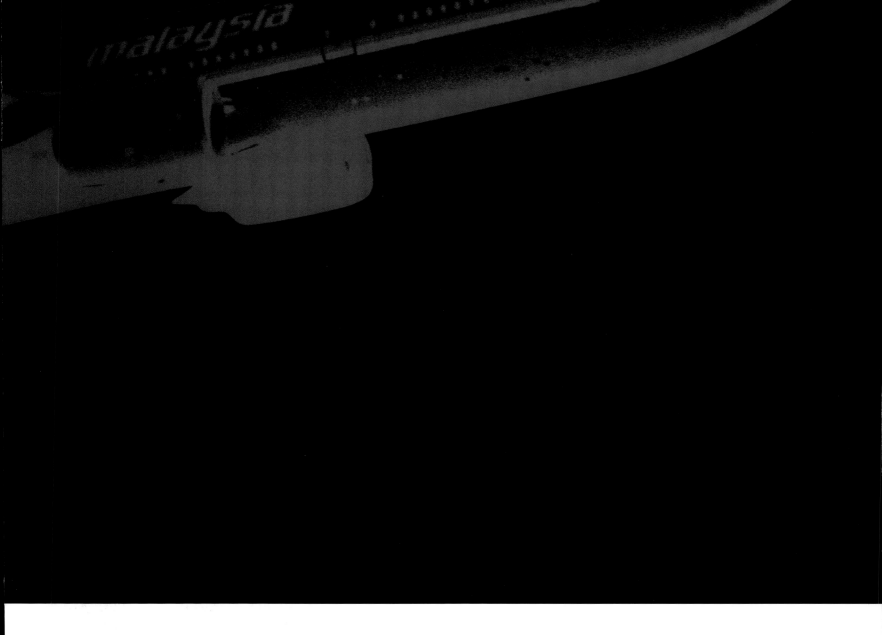

Addresses · Adressen

SPAIN

Akelare
Pedro Subijana
Paseo del Padre Orcolaga 56, Igueldo
20008 San Sebastián
Tel. (943) 21 20 52
Fax (943) 21 92 68
E-mail: restaurante@akelarre.net

Arzak
Juan-Mari Arzak
Alto de Miracruz 21
20015 San Sebastián
Tel. (943) 27 84 65
Fax (943) 27 27 53
E-mail: arzak@jet.es

El Bulli
Ferran Adrià
Cala Montjoi,
17480 Rosas
Tel. (972) 15 04 57
Fax (972) 15 07 17
E-mail: bulli@grn.es

El Racó de Can Fabes
Santi Santamaria
Sant Joan 6
08470 Sant Celoni
Tel. (93) 867 28 51
Fax (93) 867 38 61
E-mail: racoconfabes@troc.es

Martín Berasetegui
Loidi Kalea 4
20160 Lasarte
Tel. (943) 36 64 71
Fax (943) 36 15 99

Zuberoa
Hilario Arbelaitz
Iturriotz
20180 Oiartzun
Tel. (943) 49 12 28
Fax (943) 49 26 79

Hotel Maria Cristina
Calle Oquendo 1
2004 San Sebastián
Tel. (943) 42 49 00
Fax (943) 42 39 14
E-mail: hmc@sheraton.com

SOUTH EAST ASIA

Goodwood Park Hotel
22 Scotts Road
Singapore 228221
Tel. (65) 737 7411
Fax (65) 732 8558
E-mail: enquiries@goodwoodparkhotel.com.sg
www.goodwoodparkhotel.com.sg

Hilton Kuala Lumpur
Jalan Sultan Ismail
PO Box 10577
50718 Kuala Lumpur, Malaysia
Tel. (60-3) 248 2322
Fax (60-3) 244 2157
E-mail: info_kuala-lumpur@hilton.com
www.hilton.com

JW Marriott Hotel
183 Jalan Bukit Bintang
55100 Kuala Lumpur, Malaysia
Tel. (60-3) 925 9000
Fax (60-3) 925 7000
E-mail: info@ytlhotels.com
www.ytlhotels.com

Pangkor Laut Resort
Pangkor Laut Island
32200 Lumut, Perak, Malaysia
Tel (60-5) 699 1100
Fax (60-5) 699 1200
E-mail: plr@po.jaring.my
www.ytlhotels.com

The Peninsula Bangkok
333 Charoennakorn Road
Klongsan
Bangkok 10600, Thailand
Tel. (66-2) 861 2888
Fax (66-2) 861 1112
E-mail: pbk@peninsula.com
www.peninsula.com

Shangri-La Hotel Bangkok
89 Soi Wat Suan Plu,
New Road
Bangrak
Bangkok 10500, Thailand
Tel. (66-2) 236 7777
Fax (66-2) 236 8579
E-mail: slbk@shangri-la.com
www.shangri-la.com

Small Luxury Hotels of the World
800 525 4800 (North America)
00800 525 4800 (Deutschland, Great Britain, Schweiz/Suisse, France, The Netherlands, Italia, España)
http://www.slh.com

Preferred Hotels
800 323 7500 (North America)
00800 3237 5001 (Europe)
E-mail: info@preferredhotels.com
http://www.preferredhotels.com

Acknowledgements · Danksagung

In producing a book like THE CULINARY CHRONICLE,
innumerable people have been directly and indirectly involved.
We therefore wish to express our gratitude to all who have in any
way contributed to its completion. Our special thanks go to the
following persons and institutions for their cooperation and support:

An der Entstehung eines Buches wie THE CULINARY CHRONICLE
sind unzählige Menschen direkt und indirekt beteiligt. An dieser Stelle
möchten wir all jenen unseren Dank aussprechen, die in irgendeiner
Form dazu beigetragen haben, das Werk zu vollenden.
Bei den folgenden Personen und Institutionen möchten wir uns
besonders herzlich für ihre Mitarbeit und Unterstützung bedanken:

Monika Graff
Dieter Jacobs, djpr
Georg Kroemer
Chris Meier
Jutta Neu-Meier
Sabine van Ommen PR
Sabine Schramek, djpr
Claudia Spinner
Stefan Stumke

... and all the cooks and their staff, as well as the restaurants and hotels
that are presented in this volume.

... und allen Köchen und deren Mitarbeitern, den Restaurants und
Hotels, die im vorliegenden Band vorgestellt werden.

Illustration credits · Bildnachweis

SPAIN

COLD APPETIZERS

WARM APPETIZERS, LIGHT FIRST COURSES, SOUPS

FISH, SHELLFISH

POULTRY

MEAT

DESSERTS, PASTRIES

SOUTH EAST ASIA

In Asian cuisine, there are no fixed rules as to the order, the quantity or the combination of dishes to be served. Dishes listed as cold and warm appetizers work equally well as entrées if you slightly increase the quantities.

COLD APPETIZERS

WARM APPETIZERS, LIGHT FIRST COURSES, SOUPS

SPANIEN

SÜDOSTASIEN

In der asiatischen Küche gibt es keine festen Regeln, was, wieviel und in welcher Kombination serviert werden soll. So können Sie beispielsweise die unter Vorspeisen aufgeführten Rezepte durchaus als Hauptgericht servieren, wenn Sie einfach die angegebenen Mengen leicht erhöhen.

THE
CULINARY
CHRONICLE